The Digital Architect

The Digital Architect

A COMMON-SENSE GUIDE TO USING COMPUTER TECHNOLOGY IN DESIGN PRACTICE

Ken Sanders, AIA

John Wiley & Sons, Inc.
New York ▪ Chichester ▪ Brisbane ▪ Toronto ▪ Singapore

This text is printed on acid-free paper.

Library of Congress Cataloging in Publication Data:

Sanders, Ken, 1958–
The digital architect : a common-sense guide to using computer technology in design practice / Ken Sanders.
p. cm.
Includes index.
ISBN 0-471-12165-7 (pbk. : alk. paper)
1. Architectural practice—Data processing. I. Title.
NA1996.5.S26 1996
720′.285—dc20 95-17499

Printed in the United States of America

10 9 8 7 6 5 4 3 2 1

PREFACE

> *"Sometimes you have to look reality in the eye and deny it."*
>
> **Garrison Keillor**

As its title suggests, this book is directed toward architects, or more broadly, those participating in or learning about designing the built environment. As a target market, unfortunately, architects represent one of the most diverse collections of working professionals on the planet. Write a detailed job description for any individual within an architectural firm, even the sole practitioner, and it will apply to less than one percent of those in practice. More than half of all architects, for example, work in firms of five people or fewer. As Manager of Information Services for Zimmer Gunsul Frasca Partnership (ZGF), I am an architect working in a 150-person architecture, planning, and interior design firm with three offices in three states. How do my experiences relate to the smaller office?

Similarly, is this book for users of technology, managers of users of technology, or managers of technology itself? Each group faces different tactical and strategic problems. Would students who are studying architecture find this book useful? What about those in related professions: engineers, contractors, and facilities managers?

I will answer these questions in a moment. But another key question confronted me while deciding to write this book: do architects (presumably, you) really have room on their crowded shelves for yet another technology treatise? What information could possibly be discussed here that has not been addressed somewhere else already, either in print or on line?

I reflected on the various sources of information available today to architects. Professional journals such as *P/A, Architectural Record, Architecture,* and others regularly offer articles on computer technology in the practice and profiles of firms using such tools successfully. Indeed, these articles are an invaluable resource for learning about the uses of technology within the profession. Yet I often finish reading them with a yearning for more specifics, asking questions about how the issues presented relate back to my own situation. How did the profiled firm deal with training issue X? How do they organize their work to deal with limitation Y in software package Z? Are they *really* doing what they say they are doing with technology on a day-to-day basis, or is it still an experiment, or worse, simply marketing bravado?

At the same time, publications that do discuss specific computer hardware and software tools, such as *Byte, PC World, PC Week, InfoWorld,* and many others, rarely do so in a context that is meaningful to architects. They are excellent technology resources, but it is difficult to filter the tidal wave of information and retain what is relevant to one's practice.

Finally, numerous software-specific books and journals are available that focus on individual software applications and their features in an ostensibly user-friendly and thorough format, at least compared to the software's own documentation. Again, these resources often lack an architectural context. Publications that focus on a single software application rarely deal effectively with the critical issue of sharing information between different applications, nor do they describe how the application features overlap. Finally, such book and journals are rarely candid about the software's limitations. Like the software's own documentation, their presentation of information is not without bias and is too often self-serving.

For most of you, the benefit of this book will be information *context.* You will find information you may have seen or heard elsewhere, but assembled here in a way that makes it more meaningful and relevant. Chapter 1 introduces the idea of the "information pyramid" and the distinguishing attributes of data, information, knowledge, and wisdom. One of the key attributes of useful information is context: the more relevant the context, the higher the value and the longer the life span of the information. By providing an information context that is understandable to architects, this book aims not for volume but for value and life span.

But let's return to the first set of questions regarding the diverse audience for this book. Based on my professional experience in architectural offices ranging in size from 6 to 275 employees, I like to think I am sensitive to the technology issues faced by a wide range of architectural firms. My wife, Margie, in fact, is an architect and sole practitioner specializing in residential and retail design and does an excellent job keeping me honest. In fact, as desktop computers continue to become less expensive and more powerful, the sole practitioner and global corporation have more in common than you might think. Regardless of firm size, *the value of computer tools ultimately must be directed toward and realized by the individual.*

For what audience is this book written? Let's start by approaching the answer from the opposite direction. Although the book provides an overview of various hardware platforms, operating systems, and tools, it is not really directed at architects who are shopping for hardware or software. The book is not a training manual, and is not for architects who are searching for more specialized AutoCAD LISP routines. Although it includes a glossary, the book is not for those who need a dictionary of technology jargon; most of that (surprise!) is unimportant. And the book is not intended for those who seek, or have switched to, an alternative career involving technology, such as commercial rendering and animation, software development, or technology consulting.

People sometimes ask me, since I apparently inherited a recessive nerd gene from a long-lost ancestor, why I don't apply my technological aptitude in a business other than architecture, where the financial rewards are potentially greater. The simple fact is, as an architect, I am only interested in applying technology to the process of creating the built environment. The nature of my participation in that process—specializing in information technology—is unusual and certainly not for everybody. But if I had to choose between using technology or being involved in the design and construction of buildings, I would choose the latter hands down. The audience for this book is the people who would make the same choice. Indeed, understanding what that choice means is itself a key part of using technology effectively.

Technology is a tool, simply a means to some other end. The individual architect must still add value. You certainly can use technology to help add value and/or create new ways to do so. But technology will not relieve you of the burden of understanding the building design and construction market and how you and your firm deliver services within that market. To be successful, that understanding must still be the centerpiece of what you do.

Simply put, the intended audience for this book includes anyone who participates in creating the built environment, who wants to continue doing so, and who wants to understand and/or use computer technology to do so better. This includes students, interns, draftspersons, project managers, principals, and others. Admittedly, each faces a different set of issues in applying technology and may find different sections of this book more directly applicable to their work. At the same time, each individual has something to gain from understanding the issues that are important to the others.

I am an architect, of course, and this book is written from a practicing architect's perspective. As a result, students and practitioners of architecture should find the book more directly relevant than contractors or engineers will. In addition, despite my experience with a relatively wide range of firm sizes, I cannot possibly represent the experience of the diverse range of practitioners of which the architectural profession is comprised. So the book also contains a healthy dose of anecdotes, quotes, and shared experiences of other architects, engineers, and contractors successfully (and sometimes unsuccessfully) using technology.

In her book, *Uncommon Genius—How Great Ideas are Born,* author Denise Shekerjian quotes anthropological linguist and MacArthur award winner Shirley Brice Heath about her reaction to people seeking her out after she won the award: "There are no secrets, no inside easy steps that everybody hopes for. We all want to find the secrets, but they just don't exist."

A few people have asked me: will the book give away trade secrets? Am I divulging information that would be useful to ZGF's competitors? Not at all. Every architectural practice is unique, and appropriately demands a unique approach to technology implementation. This is not a magic book of technology tricks, nor a cookbook with easy recipes for achieving prosperity in the information age. At ZGF, we spend considerable time thinking about how to best leverage technology within the firm.

But the people who work here are the key to the firm's success. Even in a technological world, *talent and experience are still the primary determinants of value.*

What technology *can* do (but certainly is not guaranteed to do) is help you communicate and deliver to clients your talent and experience in new packages. This book is intended to help you generate ideas for doing so that are singularly appropriate for your practice. Sound advice is given by management consultant Tom Peters: "Find out what your competition is doing and do something different."

Part of ZGF's professional culture is the notion of the three-legged stool: design, management, and technology. If one leg is weak, the stool falls over. Over the years, the definition of technology has evolved, but the force of gravity has not.

In his book, *The Art of the Long View,* author Peter Schwarz discusses the challenges of information hunting and gathering and describes his five favorite research tactics for finding relevant information:

1. Remarkable people (socialized experiences)
2. Sources of surprise (research outside one's discipline)
3. Filters (books, magazines, and journals)
4. Immersion (in challenging environments)
5. Networks (in person or on line)

The Digital Architect is a collection of ideas, observations, experiences, anecdotes, and guidelines that I have found useful over the past fifteen years of using and managing technology in architectural firms. It is a record of my exposure to remarkable people, sources of surprise, filters, immersion in challenging environments, and networks—a portion of what has accumulated in my head over the last fifteen years hitchhiking on my own digital highway.

Most importantly, rather than simply describing digital tools in a theoretical framework, I have attempted to relate technology back to the practice issues that architects face every day in striving to deliver quality architectural services profitably. The material emphasizes the common sense practical application of computer technology, rather than its intellectual theory, and includes present-day, real-world examples. Since new software and hardware are constantly being introduced, this approach risks dating the book's contents prematurely, but the intended benefit is a more practical, useful resource for architects.

Architect Richard Saul Wurman describes "information anxiety" as the "black hole between data and knowledge, and it happens when information doesn't tell us what we want or need to know." Information anxiety is felt by those who are inundated with technology facts but starved for understanding. This book in intended to help fill the black hole, and *reduce* the information anxiety that some architects suffer relating to computer technology.

This book does not pretend to be an authoritative encyclopedia on computer technology for architects. It is yet another example of the classic 80/20 rule: I have attempted to include 20 percent of the information and knowledge about technology you are likely to need 80 percent of the time.

Architects must strive not to be seduced by technology evangelists nor spooked by technology doomsayers. Architects must regard such opposing points of view as border markers of a new digital terrain, within which each architect must find a place of appropriate, *common sense* technology. This book is my attempt to describe the features of that terrain, provide a few route-finding tools, means, and methods, and share the journeys and observations of fellow practitioners.

Within the new digital terrain, you and your firm must decide where you are, where your clients are, and where you want to go. This book is a map. You are the navigator.

Ken Sanders, AIA

TECHNICAL NOTES

This book was prepared using Microsoft Word 6.0 for Windows running on a 33 MHz 486 PC in the basement of my home in Portland, Oregon. I used a Toshiba T4400C laptop computer while on the road. Test proofs were printed on a Canon BJ-200e bubble jet printer and marked up using a red Flair marker. My four-year-old daughter, Hillary, occasionally contributed her own creative markups to the manuscript. Final copy and artwork were delivered digitally to John Wiley and Sons, Inc.

ACKNOWLEDGMENTS

This book includes the contributions of many people who have had a memorable impact on my professional life, including every partner and employee of Zimmer Gunsul Frasca Partnership, and particularly Cindy Cox, who introduced herself to me at an AEC Systems show in Dallas and connected me to ZGF.

Thank you Chuck Davis, of Esherick, Homsey, Dodge and Davis, who hired me to build a model (look, ma, no computer!) of the Monterey Bay Aquarium soon after I graduated from UC Berkeley in 1980. Thank you also Jim Hastings, my first professional mentor. I last saw Jim several years ago, and he still had an egg timer on his desk to remind his visitors about the value of communication brevity. I still haven't learned.

Many thanks to Jim Goring, with whom my unlikely encounter in 1982 in the lobby of Berkeley's Wurster Hall—where we discussed his impending departure from Skidmore, Owings, & Merrill to attend graduate school at Harvard—was the accidental event that got me into all this digital computer stuff in the first place. I ended up filling the position Jim left at SOM, although certainly not his shoes. Back then, the 275-person San Francisco office had one CAD terminal—a Tektronix 4014 connected to a 16-bit PDP 11/70 minicomputer—and one CAD user—me. I also want to thank the guy who was SOM's first choice for the job but turned it down.

Thanks also to David Jordani, Mike Schley, Mike Dingledein, Jerry Laiserin, Chris Clark, David Johnson, Doug Stoker,

Nick Weingarten, Steve Harrison, Barry Milliken, Terry and Pat Schilling, Tom Horan, Jim Kelly, Jim Wirick, Bob Kupper, Dan Heinfeld, Bob Coffee, Don Pender, Glenn Carels, Carlos Soria, John Hill, Brian Conner, Bruce Schulte, Day Tooley, Terry Beaubois, Creighton Nolte, and B.J. Novitski, each of whom planted seeds in my head over the last dozen years that have sprouted as words on these pages.

Special thanks are due Janet Feeney and Allison Morvay of John Wiley & Sons, Inc. for their hard work, patience, trust, and contagious enthusiasm for this project, and Ken Hall of Ketiv Technologies, whose many conversations with me over the past two years spawned several of the ideas in this book. The dumb ones are mine; the cool ones are his.

I also want to especially acknowledge the support of my immediate family: my wife, Margie, and children Ted and Hillary. Any spouse whose partner is an architect (or any child whose parent is one) knows all too well the impact of the professional practice on family life. Margie, whom I met when we both worked at SOM's Houston office in 1984, understands more than most. But I don't think it is reasonable for anyone to have a spouse or a parent who is an *architect writing a book*. Just reading that phrase gives me the creeps. Margie not only tolerated the intolerable but provided particularly valuable feedback and encouragement to me during the process. For her love and support, I am particularly grateful.

Ken Sanders, AIA

CONTENTS

The Digital Architect

CHAPTER

1

The Impact of Technology on the Practice

COMPUTER TECHNOLOGY: FRIEND OR FOE?

"Will we travel the information highway with ease, or are we destined to become technology roadkill, flattened by the same glut of information that was supposed to improve our minds?"

Neil Postman

Within the architectural profession, computer technology is positioned by its strongest advocates as a competitive white knight—a tool that empowers architects to fend off new competition, aggressively enter new markets, or secure new clients. As the perceived market value of some architectural services has declined over the past two decades, and as new competitors continue to emerge from both inside and outside the profession, many architects believe that technology will help level the playing field.

Some of the smartest practitioners and management consultants, in fact, have proclaimed a unique opportunity for architects to use computer technology to reestablish their roles as master builders by controlling the flow of digital information throughout the design, construction, and occupancy of a project. For those who wish to undertake such an ambitious journey, it is a real business opportunity, albeit one with substantial risks. Most architects have a more modest agenda, and simply hope that technology will allow them to more successfully compete against other firms who have enjoyed the inside track in key markets, or allow their small firm to win large commissions. Indeed, technology can and does play an important role in helping architects secure new work and appear brighter on the radar screens of clients, both old and new.

By itself, however, technology as a competitive differentiator is of short-term and limited value, and architects who expect

Commodity: ***1.*** **An economic good as** ***a:*** **a product of agriculture or mining;** ***b.*** **an article of commerce esp. when delivered for shipment.** ***2 a:*** **something useful or valuable;** ***b:*** **convenience, advantage.**

more from it are likely to be disappointed. Architects using computer technology as a way to distinguish themselves are forgetting that computers are slowly but surely becoming commodities. As the price of computer hardware continues to decline, and computers emerge as ubiquitous tools in both the office and the home, the task of grabbing client mind-share via technology will continue to be more difficult each year.

Think about it: when was the last time an architect landed a job because of her fax machine? Her cellular phone? Her voice-mail system? Any technology available to you is also available to construction managers, value engineers, design-build firms, and contractors, as well as other architects. (The economics of customized in-house software development also are not as rewarding today as they were in the 1980s, when off-the-shelf solutions were few, expensive, and of modest quality.) As a result, the competitive advantage gained through leading-edge implementation of technology is increasingly ephemeral.

The twenty-five-year-old Internet is a good case study of this phenomenon. The Internet will be discussed in more detail in Chapter 10, On-Line Resources, but I mention it briefly here to make a point about differentiation. The "Net" has been the focus of incredible media attention both within the profession and among the public. At ZGF (Zimmer Gunsul Frasca Partnership), as at many architectural firms, we began observing in early 1994 an increasing number of clients asking if we could communicate with them directly using E-mail systems, messaging services, and other tools of the so-called information superhighway, of which the Internet is the de facto backbone. At the same time, we needed better tools for ZGF's project teams in different offices to communicate and share information with each other and with their consultants. Today, as a direct response to these external market forces and our internal functional needs, every professional at ZGF has direct access to the Internet. Clearly, it is in the best interest of architects to be well prepared to communicate with clients, consultants, contractors, and each other in this manner.

Is it a competitive *requirement* for your firm's principals and employees to do so? Absolutely. Is it a competitive *advantage?* Absolutely not. They are two different things, and advocates and users of technology are well advised to understand the difference. It is the difference between true success and simply the avoidance of failure. The lack of technological expertise can certainly lose you clients and projects, but technological expertise on its own will rarely win them.

The point is that architects should not seek to level the playing field using technology (or any other tool, for that matter); they should seek to tilt it toward themselves. And technology simply does not do that by itself. Take a quick poll, and ask a random sample of your peers about the last five projects they landed, and the top five reasons for their success. Even when technology is on the top-five list, it is rarely number one. The most important value architects provide still lies elsewhere.

Computers are easy-to-use tools. It is just as easy to design and document lousy buildings with them as without them.

Clearly, technology has not given a secret weapon to anyone—it has simply raised the stakes for everyone. It has altered the landscape of practice, in sometimes radical and unexpected ways, and will continue to do so. To be sure, the risks to architects of falling behind by ignoring technology are real and substantial. But you should not believe that technology by itself will offer you a long-term significant advantage over your competition. It will not rescue you from bad planning, poor organizational skills, or lack of talent, and in most cases, technology will simply illuminate or further exacerbate those problems.

Technology: friend or foe? The answer is neither, and both. Technology is neither a life raft for the sinking architectural firm, nor an economic tsunami that will multiply their number. Technology is but one component of larger social, economic, and business revolutions that will continue to have a substantial impact on the markets in which architects deliver services. Each of these revolutions—the value-oriented consumer, the mobile work force, the global marketplace, the reengineered business, the virtual organization, and many others—presents new opportunities for architects, as well as new responsibilities, risks, and challenges. Remember that the technological changes that you confront are also confronted by your clients. Indeed, your clients (and your competitors' clients) are your best resource to help you visualize the future.

The client-driven future is discussed in more detail in Chapter 12, Future Trends.

> **"In America today, 'revolution' has become a marketing buzzword most often invoked by buttoned-down business executives at telephone companies and movie studios and computer companies. They blather on and on about the information revolution and the communications revolution, and say, in effect, if you thought sliced bread was something, wait'll we really transform people's lives and in the process makes lots and lots of money."**
> **EDMUND L. ANDREWS**
> ***The New York Times,* October 30, 1994**

REVOLUTION OR EVOLUTION?

Although its impact at times seems revolutionary, technological change has arrived within the architectural profession at a slower pace than many technology evangelists expected in the early 1980s. In those days, some experts predicted totally digital, "paperless" practices by the mid-1990s. Certainly, a few firms are close to realizing, if not the paperless practice, at least the digital practice. But most architects have implemented computer tools within their firms more cautiously. Architects are certainly using new computer tools and delivering new digital products to clients, but the process of architectural design and documentation still has not radically changed from twenty years ago.

As a result, architects are not infrequently characterized by both software developers and technology evangelists as "technophobic," "ignorant," or "cheap," at least when compared to their engineering counterparts. It is true that some architects believe (incorrectly) that computers and digital communications technology threaten the noble traditions and artistic foundations of the profession, and—consciously or not—tend to emphasize technology's weaknesses and downplay its strengths. However, the relatively slow pace of technology implementation among the profession over the past decade can be reasonably attributed to several factors other than the unenlightened attitudes of architects:

- Designing buildings is a more difficult, complex problem than engineering them. Architectural design is a gregarious endeavor, and involves both the invention and effective communication of ideas. Compared to lateral load calculations or duct flow analysis, the architectural design process is less easily translated to a computer's binary language of 0s and 1s. The functional requirements of architectural design tools are necessarily more demanding than those of engineers.
- Robust, easy-to-use tools, especially for high-end applications such as computer-aided-design (CAD), visualization, and image editing, have taken longer than once predicted to arrive in affordable, easy-to-use packages. To this day, the seamless integration of these programs with other desktop software remains an unfulfilled opportunity for software developers.

■ Just when desktop computing technology was maturing, the global recession of the late 1980s and early 1990s reduced the purchasing power of many architectural firms and slowed their capital investment in new hardware and software. In the United States, the excessive over-building that took place during the 1980s—the result of a potent mix of savings and loan deregulation and capital gains tax policy favorable to real estate investment—magnified the recession's impact on architects.

■ Unlike engineering schools, most architectural schools during the 1980s did not emphasize technology in their curricula, and those that did concentrated on high-end research and software development rather than present-day practical applications. For much of the 1980s and early 1990s, most architectural graduates entered firms with little practical computer experience or training. Only recently has this trend changed, but many top-tier universities still focus on research, not practice.

■ Hundreds of incompatible data formats invented by software developers, and thousands of organizational guidelines invented by architects, have created a digital Tower of Babel within the building design and construction industry. The lack of industry-wide information guidelines has constrained the flexibility and value of the computer tools used to manipulate such data, and is only recently being addressed jointly by organizations such as the National Institute of Building Sciences, the Construction Specifications Institute, and the American Institute of Architects.

Compared to engineers, architects must necessarily be more *selective* about the tools they purchase, and more *creative* in how they apply them.

During the 1980s, a familiar pattern of computer technology implementation emerged within architectural firms. The initial forays of most firms into computers involved word processing and financial management software. Larger firms also used CAD systems, but the use of those systems in many firms was primarily limited to production drafting. By the late 1980s and early 1990s, PC-based CAD systems had become commonplace in architectural firms of all sizes, although most were still limited to two-dimensional drafting functions. (Because many graduates entered the work force unprepared to use the new tools, the burden of training was largely carried by architectural firms.) Other office automation software, such as spreadsheets and databases, joined CAD on the desktop, although seamless

Rising proportionally to the quantity of new computer tools is the responsibility of the architect to continually evaluate their true value and, just as importantly, to evaluate the effectiveness of the tasks and processes in which they are used.

integration between different software applications was (and still is) largely unrealized.

Today, the quantity and types of software applications used by most architects have expanded dramatically, and continue to do so in sometimes bewildering fashion. Software programs used by architects today include not only word processing, spreadsheets, databases, and CAD, but also contact management, decision support, project scheduling, desktop publishing, multimedia presentation, digital image editing, electronic mail, on-line services, and other tools. PC-based CAD systems have extended their reach as well, and three-dimensional model-building, visualization, animation, and virtual reality tools are slowly becoming part of the architectural design and communication process for many firms. Fortunately, new architectural graduates are arriving in the work force increasingly well prepared technologically. Importantly, none of these tools are any longer the exclusive domain of the largest architectural firms. Today, sole practitioners use many of the same desktop software applications used by global corporations.

The good news for architects today is that most software applications are available for low to moderate cost, the integration and information-sharing capabilities of the applications are improving all the time, and the performance of personal computer hardware continues to increase year after year. The bad news is that the "expectation curve" of clients, which stayed relatively flat during the 1980s, is beginning to climb dramatically as a result. Technology's impact on the practice of architecture is sure to rise in parallel. Clearly, architects are well served by a clear understanding of technology's present and future impact on services, on the firm, and on the individual.

IMPACT ON SERVICES

Technology presents architectural firms with opportunities to enter new markets and/or provide new types of services, such as computer-aided facilities management (CAFM), as-built database capture, video animation, and others. With the architect as data coordinator, cradle-to-grave information services for buildings present intriguing long-term business opportunities, especially for architects working for large corporate, institutional, and government clients.

Facilities management services offered by architects may combine new services with some repackaging of traditional services, such as documentation of existing conditions and coordination of the architecture and engineering (A/E) disciplines. Services that architects experienced in digital drawing delivery might provide to facilities managers include:

Architects typically consider the digital drawings they deliver to a client as end products. On the other hand, the client's facilities managers view the drawings they receive as a beginning. The architect's drawings are the information baseline from which facilities managers create "living" digital documents that describe the changing state of a facility over its life span.

FACILITIES MANAGEMENT (FM) DATABASE CAPTURE

Document scanning and conversion
CAD input of existing drawings
Field verification of as-built conditions
Coordination of A/E disciplines
Coordination, review, and integration of third-party FM databases

INFORMATION SYSTEMS CONSULTING SERVICES

CAD, CAFM, GIS (geographic information systems)
Digital database design
Analysis of information flow
- Database scope and organization
- Exchange formats

Database reports and publications
Software competitive analysis
Training and personnel issues

FM DATABASE MAINTENANCE AND PUBLICATION

Fast turnaround services (fax or E-mail)
Document and change control
Update of renovation, remodeling, or leasehold changes
Database publication and reporting
- A- to E-size report formats
- Keymap indexes for large facilities
- Area calculations
- Tenant mix and lease expirations
- Department cost distributions

MODELBUILDING, VISUALIZATION, AND ANIMATION

Three-dimensional modelbuilding
CAD rendering
Video imaging and animation
  Walk-throughs and fly-arounds
  Vehicular motion paths
  Visual obstruction/sightline analysis

The decision of an architectural firm to provide new technology-based services requires a thoughtful analysis of the firm's market position and model of practice, existing business prospects, and in-house talent. Otherwise, technology can become simply a solution looking for a problem: a tactic without a strategy.

Accurately gauging the economic benefits of technology on individual architectural projects is extremely difficult, regardless of the measurement system. Technology is but one of dozens of issues that directly impact a project's bottom line, including client, fees, project type and location, regulatory environment, schedule, team experience, and many others. It is difficult to find two projects for comparison that differ only in their use of technology.

The practical technological objective of most architectural firms simply aims to improve the value and competitiveness of existing services. The biggest challenge for most firms is not deciding whether technology's impact is positive, but quantifying it, which means fully understanding technology's benefits and its costs. For individual hardware components or software applications, the exercise is a simple one—for example, "With a $500 upgrade, plots will arrive twice as fast." When evaluated as a total package, however, technology's net value is often harder to nail down. Today, this issue is still a subject of lively debate among many architects, and a few still believe that the payoff has not yet arrived.

It is somewhat easier to quantify technology's value if one recognizes that technology, like most new methods of practice, impacts service delivery in one of three ways: quality, productivity, and turnaround. The focus of an architectural firm's technology initiatives should be linked to the relative importance of these three benefits to the firm's clients.

For most firms, service quality is simultaneously the broadest, most important, and most difficult benefit to measure. Quality is not just a design issue, of course, but involves all aspects of service delivery, including client communications, proposals and presentations, construction documents, agreements, estimates, schedules, and many others.

Productivity (efficiency) and turnaround (speed) are two separate but related benefits. Productivity is the measure of the overall *effort* required to deliver a given service. Turnaround is the *time* required to deliver that service. Obviously, the less work required to do a task, the faster it *can* be accomplished. Productivity gains are sometimes realized without turnaround improvements, and sometimes the reverse is true. The fax machine, for example, has dramatically improved the turnaround time of architects' written communications. However, faxing often decreases productivity by adding new work to the process: walking to the fax machine, dialing a number, retransmitting, and so forth. E-mail, on the other hand, can improve both turnaround and productivity by providing the benefits of a fax without the added work. E-mail also improves productivity by delivering information in a reusable digital format, unlike "dead-end" fax copies.

QUALITY

Computer technology improves service quality through one of three basic channels: the knowledge base, communication, and design.

"Quality has been defined in the A/E/C industry as 'conformance to requirements' and is measured at the project stage of a facility. As competitiveness in the A/E/C industry grows, however, the definition of quality is evolving to be 'customer satisfaction' over the whole life cycle of a project."
Excerpt from Stanford University's Center of Integrated Facilities Engineering (CIFE) newsletter.

Knowledge Base

The knowledge base of an architectural firm is a filtered collection of its service products and the socialized experience of its employees: the firm's institutional memory. A good portion of design, after all, is derivative: most of the problems solved in every building have been solved before. It is the *recombination* of these solutions that makes each building unique, and where most architects appropriately spend their time. Computer tools are well suited to encapsulating in digital formats many (but not all) design ideas and technical solutions, organizing them, and providing appropriate access to them. The tools can provide an excellent resource to help architects "remember" problems already solved.

A firm's knowledge base includes three components: archives, resources, and guidelines. A firm's *archives*—both built and unbuilt work—is the detailed record of its portfolio of work and is one of the most valuable assets of any firm. External information *resources* include both on-line and CD-ROM databases and digitized work of interest produced by other firms. A firm's *guidelines* include organizational and procedural standards, as well as information standards such as reference details, component libraries, standard contracts, marketing boilerplate, and correspondence templates.

In firms of all sizes, bringing the knowledge base to the architect's desktop in a useful form is a complex problem, both in terms of the organization of the information, the media on which it is stored, and the tools used to search and filter it. The payoff in terms of quality, however, is substantial.

To underscore their importance, Chapter 9 is devoted exclusively to the subject of an architectural firm's in-house knowledge base, while Chapter 10 discusses on-line resources.

Communication

Perhaps more than any other piece of technology, digital communication tools in architectural firms have multiplied dramatically over the past decade. Noncomputer tools such as the fax machine and the cellular phone by themselves had a dramatic impact on communication turnaround, not all of it positive. Today they are joined by and often merged with digital communication tools such as E-mail, remote access to computer networks, video-teleconferencing, shared "whiteboards," and "groupware" software, such as Lotus Notes, on-line services, the Internet, and World Wide Web.

Architecture, after all, is a business of communicating ideas and managing information. To the extent that technology improves an architect's ability to communicate effectively, it certainly improves the quality of the work. This applies not only to the legibility and consistency of design and construction drawings, but also to the look and feel of correspondence, proposals, presentations, agreements, budgets, schedules, timesheets, and other documents.

"The entire economic model of telecommunications—based on charging per minute, per mile, or per bit—is about to fall apart. As human-to-human communications become increasingly asynchronous, time will become meaningless. Five hours of music will be delivered to you in less than five seconds. Distance is irrelevant: New York to London is only five miles further than New York to Newark via satellite."
NICHOLAS NEGROPONTE

At the same time, technology can occasionally hinder effective communication. A fax, for example, can be less meaningful than a hand-written note or personal phone call, and prettier documents do not necessarily make them more understandable. When image is tantamount to substance, the result is not always an improvement. Similarly, faster communication does not always mean better communication, like the fax or E-mail message that infers a sense of urgency which does not exist. A significant burden weighs on architects to use new digital communication tools appropriately, not arbitrarily.

Low-cost ink-jet and laser printing technologies, combined with illustration and desktop publishing software, are providing architects with more flexibility (but not necessarily subtlety) when compared to manually produced documents or typewritten correspondence. In many architectural firms, computer-generated illustrations, scanned images, and three-dimensional visualizations not only have been added to the vocabulary of presentation drawings, but are emerging in construction documents as well. The quality of computer visualization—both in terms of modelbuilding ease and image realism—is continually improving. Although certainly not a substitute for many traditional methods, such tools are providing increasingly powerful supplements.

If implemented and managed properly, digital tools clearly enhance the ability of architects to communicate more quickly and more effectively with clients, consultants, and peers.

Design

The design process at its core is an iterative one. Schemes are identified, explored, measured, revised, enhanced—and the loop repeats. As digital tools compress the loop and make it easier to iterate design alternatives and evaluate their effectiveness, they in theory can improve the quality of design. Some architects equate digital design tools with three-dimensional CAD, but powerful design tools can emerge from other desktop software programs as well, such as spreadsheets used to budget fees, or project scheduling software used to explore resource allocations or test critical paths.

Good digital design tools are hard to find. Their defining attributes, along with a few examples, can be found in Chapter 4, Tools of the Architect.

A contrarian view might hold that additional iterations do not ensure better design, which is true. Most design iteration, however, is desirable and adds value, and few architects are unappreciative of the opportunity for further study. Think about it: which design problem did you last solve on your first try? If the tools allow more iterations, the assumed result is a better product. (In design, of course, timing is everything. Revising a stair during construction so it actually conforms to building code requirements is not an effective design iteration. Digital design tools do not relieve the architect from decision-making discipline.)

"The success of a design practice is a function of its creativity as well as productivity. For many firms, creativity and innovation far outweigh productivity as factors that contribute to success. Rarely, if ever, you will find a firm promoting itself to potential clients on the merits of its productive and efficient drafting department. It is equally rare to find someone who says computers are being purchased for the purpose of improving creativity. . . . A commitment to a comprehensive integration of technology can promote a new work environment where innovation will thrive."
DAVID JOHNSON, AIA

PRODUCTIVITY

The first computer tools used in most architectural firms, such as word processing, financial systems, and spreadsheet programs, usually provided clear productivity gains, and those gains were the obvious reason why the tools were the first to be used. Real productivity gains from CAD, on the other hand, are more difficult to measure, and in most cases are smaller than those proclaimed by vendors or technology evangelists. As a

"Real productivity is the avoidance of work."
DOUG STOKER

The least efficient way to use a word processor is as a digital typewriter. Doing so ignores its advantages of information reuse. Similarly, the least efficient way to use a CAD system is as a digital pencil. Rather, it is a tool with which architects can develop full-size graphic descriptions of buildings (two- or three-dimensional), and share, reuse, and republish that information in a variety of formats, views, scale, and levels of detail.

The tools and techniques for reusing digital information in CAD systems are discussed in detail in Chapter 8.

result, specialized applications involving standardized components, such as furniture systems layout, reference details, or repetitive projects were the focus of early CAD usage, where the payoff was easier to identify. Today, if implemented properly, CAD and other digital tools can be used successfully and economically on projects of any scale and complexity. The overall rise in productivity, however, has as much to do with the mix of work within the firm and the training and experience of the staff as it has to do with the tools.

Achieving substantial productivity gains means not simply automating the individual tasks of traditional methods, but rethinking the service delivery process. Rethinking a process means redesigning or even eliminating tasks within the process, not just performing them faster.

Improvements in productivity will vary from firm to firm. A firm that already has well-organized libraries and standard procedures will find the path to automation relatively clear of major hurdles, but may also see smaller productivity gains from automation. Conversely, a disorganized firm that automates before being organized is usually headed for disaster. In this regard, technology is an amplifier.

Improvements to productivity should be a by-product of implementing technology effectively, not necessarily a goal. No one is successful in any professional endeavor by providing a bad service fast. Quality must come first and productivity second. Although client expectations are increasing pressure on many architects to produce work faster and for less money, productivity always must reinforce quality, not supplant it. Choosing technology that improves both is paramount.

TURNAROUND

Turnaround improvements are sometimes required where no more productivity improvements can be achieved within a task or process. Quite often, the redistribution of effort among additional staff is the only answer. Achieving faster turnaround in this context requires better communication and faster information delivery to the client, consultants, and members of the project team. Project financial information must be provided earlier and more often to managers, and data must be transmitted faster from the office to the field.

Market demands for faster turnaround reflect global business trends, of course, and extend far beyond the architectural profession. This point was made to me quite explicitly a couple of years ago in a conversation with Bruce Baxter, a CAD manager with Applied Materials, a company that makes the equipment used to manufacture silicon chips. (Two of its biggest customers are Intel and Motorola.) Needless to say, the company is quite successful and has grown dramatically over the past decade.

Bruce and I were members of the Autodesk Release 13 Steering Committee, providing solicited advice to Autodesk about new features our respective firms wished to see in Release 13. One of the features that architects miss dearly in AutoCAD is support for symbolic line weight, a feature found in virtually all other CAD software. Currently, architects using AutoCAD must control symbolic line weight by assigning colors to elements and mapping colors to pens using external plotter drivers: an unreasonably messy and tricky process. I was lobbying Autodesk to support symbolic line weights in R13 (the company subsequently decided not to), when Bruce weighed in with his opinion: "Hey, that issue just isn't important to us. We draw everything in one line weight. By the time you guys [architects] figure out what line weight to use, we've drawn it, faxed it to the fabricator, and it's getting built."

At Applied Materials, the issue of turnaround dominates their entire production effort, to a degree that most architects cannot (yet) imagine. Obviously, architects are in the business of communicating ideas to diverse audiences, which Applied Materials is not, and in doing so, we must demand more graphic robustness from the tools that we use. But Applied Materials is not alone—virtually all businesses today are operating in a far more competitive, fast-moving marketplace compared to five or ten years ago. The point is not to mimic their behavior, but to recognize that all of them, at one time or another, are clients of architects. A key benefit of technology is that it enables architects to not only survive, but thrive, in such a fast-moving market.

"Technological advances are reducing the cost of computer hardware by an order of magnitude every few years. The unreported bad news is that expectations are increasing at an even greater rate. This means that year by year, for a fixed sum of money, you will be able to purchase a significantly more powerful computer that will do somewhat less than you expected."
NICHOLAS WEINGARTEN, FAIA

Client interest in E-mail communication with architects has dramatically increased over the past several years. Unfortunately, such communication is sometimes established without a clear understanding of how the technology will be used, how information will be filtered and distributed appropriately between parties, and how the necessary paper trail will be maintained.

CLIENT EXPECTATIONS

As many architects successfully use computer technology to improve their service quality, productivity, and turnaround, as well as proactively seek new markets and services, client expectations change in response. Fast turnaround, on-line data exchange with consultants, consistent documents, and digital database delivery are services that many clients today reasonably expect from architects within their normal scope of services. Architects who meet or exceed these expectations will obviously be better positioned than those who do not. At the same time, the architect's interest is well served by aligning their clients' expectations with reality, and discussing with them up front and honestly not only technology's benefits, but also its costs and limitations.

Some clients, for example, may desire a technological solution without a clear justification or understanding. Clients may request digital drawings from architects without precisely specifying their content, organization, or purpose. The architect must take the initiative to discuss this issue before a fee is negotiated and an agreement is signed, long before it becomes a source of conflict down the road.

Clients may also require the use of specific systems or software, sometimes unnecessarily. Architects occasionally complain: "Hey, I would rather not use AutoCAD, but my client requires it!" Does the client really require the use of AutoCAD, or does she require well-organized, clean CAD deliverables in AutoCAD format? The two are not synonymous. More and more types of CAD software, such as CADVANCE, MicroStation, Visual CADD, and others, provide direct support of AutoCAD file formats without requiring the use of an intermediate translation format such as DXF. (Admittedly, most such support is still incomplete and not fully reliable, but eventually the software developers will get it right.)

Architects can find themselves responding to client requests that are at odds with their own knowledge or interests. "Why can't I get the revised drawings this afternoon. They're in the computer, aren't they?" "You provide remote dial-up access for your project managers; why can't I just log in and monitor the progress on your drawings?" "You've already drawn the plans and elevations; can't you just view the building in three dimensions and create an animation? Why is that an extra service?" Like architectural design itself, architects must walk a multithreaded tightrope between educating clients and disappointing them.

The widespread, almost annoying use of computer-generated graphics in TV commercials and motion pictures over the past decade has dramatically inflated the expectations of many clients when they hear the term "computer-generated" or "computer-aided." At ZGF, we call this the Jurassic Park Syndrome. After all, if computers can be used to realistically simulate stampeding herds of dinosaurs, what is so hard about rendering a building? Why, it is something else we call the Lucasfilm Fee Gap.

Today, new technology often arrives packaged within children's games before it arrives within business tools. Last year, one of ZGF's institutional clients requested a proposal for a computer animation of their project—a 100,000 square foot laboratory and classroom building. Striving to align the client's expectation with reality, we responded by sharing with them other animated videos we had produced recently. We explained the three-dimensional modelbuilding effort required, beyond what we normally would do during our design process, and submitted a fee proposal for the effort. The proposal specifically described the length of the video, the animation sequences, and the quality and detail of information the video would convey.

A recent issue of *Wired* defined the term "forelash" as "negative or indifferent reactions to nonexistent, but already over-hyped, technologies. Examples include video-on-demand, 500 channels, interactive TV, and anything promised in the AT&T "You Will" ads.

As it turned out, the institution's president, who was not at the meeting where these issues were discussed, had expected something completely different. Apparently, he had heard that architects could copy their design drawings to a diskette and allow him at his own desktop computer to interactively explore the proposed building—walking inside or outside, through the corridors, labs, classrooms, restrooms, on the roof, and so on. Although such "virtual reality" is certainly possible, given enough computer horsepower, no technology exists today that can place a fully developed 100,000 square foot three-dimensional lab and classroom building model on a 1.44 MB diskette. (The modelbuilding efforts required for virtual reality are necessarily more demanding than for choreographed animations, where one can control the animation views and sequences and limit the model-building to those views that will be seen in the animations.)

We assumed the president had seen a product such as Microsoft's Frank Lloyd Wright CD-ROM, which allows users to interactively explore (along limited, predefined paths) the interior spaces of the architect's classic works (Ill. 1.1). Although multiple animations can be assembled using multimedia authoring software to create similar interactive presentations, the effort involved is substantially greater than copying design drawings to a disk or creating a single video animation. At a minimum, a CD-ROM would be required to store the presentation.

Using multimedia authoring software to develop interactive presentations of building designs is discussed in Chapter 5, The Language of Digital Media.

Whether the president actually saw such a presentation, heard about it, or derived a conclusion based on faulty assumptions did not matter. The client's expectations, in terms of the cost of the service, had risen beyond what was reasonably possible. With technology, architects occasionally may find themselves in a position of saying "sorry, we cannot do that" to a client. To qualify the statement with "no one else can either" does not necessarily soften the disappointment.

The time span between leading-edge Hollywood technology and low-cost consumer products has dramatically shortened. When the film *Terminator 2* opened in 1991, it was the first commercial motion picture to use computer-generated "morphing" effects. Within twelve months, the first of many low-cost morphing programs appeared on retail shelves, allowing personal computer users to create similar, low-end effects on their own. Today, morphing is already passé.

The delivery of digital data to clients also requires diligent expectation management. Even though protected by copyright,

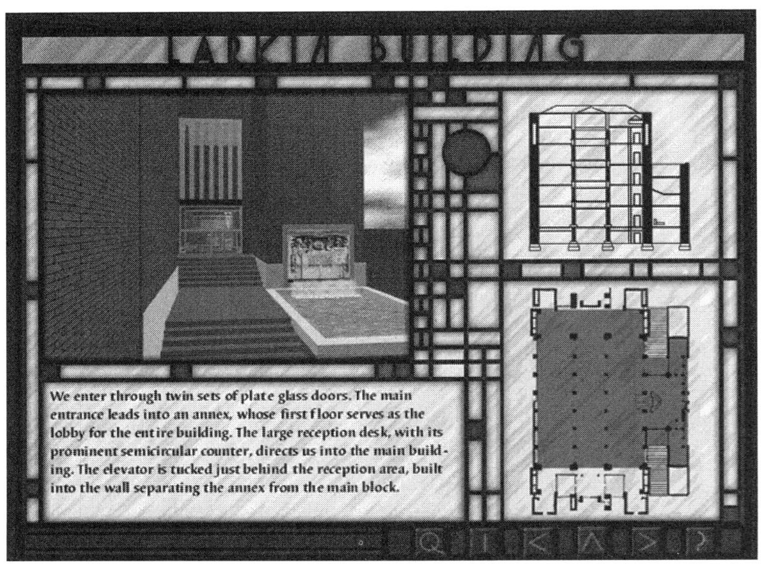

Illustration 1.1 Frank Lloyd Wright CD-ROM.

the architect is still at risk of digital data being misrepresented or misinterpreted. Ironically, the fact that information comes from a computer often lends it authenticity and credibility that is inappropriate. Area calculations derived from schematic design drawings, for example, even if extremely precise, are still preliminary and should not be represented otherwise. Many clients need reminders about the differences between progress drawings, record drawings, as-built drawings, and plug-and-play facilities databases.

What is the best response to rising client expectations? Meet or exceed them, of course, but use extremely clear language when doing so. Project managers already should be well versed in language clarity, especially in defining scopes of services and understanding client expectations. Technology introduces new vocabulary with which both managers and users must become familiar. The term "computer rendering," for example, may be interpreted differently by different people. The architect may intend to produce a massing model; the client may expect photo-realism.

Liability issues related to the delivery of digital data are discussed in more detail in Chapter 11, Managing the Digital Office.

Fine tune the technology feedback loop between you and your client, repeating to the client what you heard her say and what services you will be providing her. Negotiate, clarify, and document the understanding before the service is provided, instead of arguing about interpretations or confronting a client's disappointment after the fact.

INFORMATION VOLUME

Perhaps the best example of technology today where expectations have vaulted ahead of reality is the information superhighway. Many people, after being seduced by the hype and hooking up to bulletin boards, CompuServe, America On-Line, or the Internet, have been surprised at the sometimes awkward interfaces, difficult navigation, and vast amounts of "junk" information. The initial excitement of participating in anonymous forums or chat rooms quickly fades for most people. (Remem-

"Just the facts, sir."
SERGEANT JOE FRIDAY

ber CB radio in the late 1970s?) Public on-line services will achieve their ultimate usefulness when they are no longer cool.

Two visions of the information superhighway have emerged over the past two years. The first, widely publicized version is the highway as an extension of television: a high-volume distribution channel for information and interactive entertainment to the home. In this scenario, although services are more specialized, the one-to-many relationship between publisher and subscriber remains unchanged. This vision is where many entertainment and communications companies think the consumer dollars are, and they are probably right.

The less publicized but ultimately more powerful vision is the highway as an extension of the telephone: a tool whereby individuals and businesses can communicate and share resources directly with each other—providing one-to-one and many-to-many communication. This vision is not about climbing on board the superhighway to receive data and information from anybody, but to exchange knowledge and wisdom with clients, colleagues, and friends. This vision is where the business dollars are, and where architects should be focusing their attention. (Recall that in the 1800s, the telephone was first perceived as a paperless telegraph. For thirty years, Western Union ignored the technology, believing that no one would want to communicate with another over a wire without a written record.)

The results of a 1994 national survey: 67 percent of those polled think the information superhighway is a good idea—only 48 percent think they know what it is.

Although browsing the information superhighway is fine, and can be an enjoyable hobby at home, what architects really need at the office are knowledge country roads and wisdom bike paths. An important component of useful information is context; information is only understood by someone relative to what they already understand. What makes the scale of a building in an architectural rendering understandable? The presence of people, cars, and trees. The visual context provides a tangible measurement system with which the observer can comprehend the scale of the building. Appropriate context, not high-speed volume, adds value to information.

Many on-line forums, in which participants can exchange "public" E-mail that can be browsed by others, are enjoyable as a recreational activity for some people but not yet practical as a day-to-day business tool. A mid-1995 browse of the Internet's alt.architecture forum uncovered a bewildering array of messages, many by anonymous authors. The liveliest discussion thread revolved around the *Brady Bunch* house. One person started by asking for help finding a drawing of its floor plan, which evolved into a discussion of the social impact of the *Brady Bunch* television show on American culture and how the show affected the perceived image of the architect as represented by Mr. Brady. A few actual message titles are listed below in the same relative order in which they appeared on the forum:

Re: Cheap architecture at newest McD's—Tony Karp (21)
Parc Citroen—Here Your name (10)
  House Plans—Richard Stott (18)
  Cyberspace Architecture Thesis—Request for comments—Terence Chang (34)
  Brady Bunch house—Joseph Zupko (5)
    Dillon J Lin (19)
    TMichales (29)
    DJ Cheezy Whiz (17)
    Genius at Work (26)
  HELP! FIND POSTGRADUATE EARTHQUAKE MAT.STUDY—
  news@info.swan.ac.uk (11)
    D. Carlson (6)
  ARCHITECTURE BOOKS FOR SALE—kenneth starosciak (15)
  Is there any info about there about hospitals?—Benjamin Jay Nash (8)
  graphic design newsgroup?—Milena Gulia (8)
WTB: Sweets catalog on CD-Rom—Dj Michael (3)
  Re: Salary for Draftsman—davemann@ionet.net (44)
  UNDERGROUND HOUSING—doug beatty (2)
  programming a dance studio—Michael Todd Nichols (13)
  Is It Hopeless?—David P. Potosky (17)
    Dillon J Lin (37)
  job in europe—Anne Paul de Haan (13)
  Could someone please answer a few questions—V Blasius (56)
  HELP,PLEASE!!!!!!!—ELI (16)

"Modern corporations are faced with a profound dilemma. Increasingly, they are becoming information-based organizations, dependent on a continuous flow of data for virtually every aspect of their operations. Yet their ability to handle that data is breaking down because the volume of information is expanding faster than the capacity to process it. The result: corporations are drowning in their own data. Developing software to tap the potential of computers turns out to be a far greater challenge than building faster machines."
DAVID A. TAYLOR, PH.D.

Although occasionally useful for seeking the help of others in finding obscure information, the alt.architecture forum has a way to go before it is an efficient and useful communication tool for practicing architects.

It is useful to understand the relationships among the lifespan, availability, context, and cost of data (raw facts), information (summarized, organized data), knowledge (filtered, relevant information), wisdom (knowledge plus experience), and reality (truth), as shown below:

	HALF-LIFE	AVAILABILITY	CONTEXT	COST
Reality	Permanent	Singular	Absolute	Priceless
Wisdom	One decade	Endangered	Broad	Expensive
Knowledge	One year	Hard to find	Appropriate	Moderate
Information	One month	Easy to find	Narrow	Cheap
Data	One day	Everywhere	None	Free

The relative volume of each type of information can be visualized as a pyramid, with data at the base and reality at the apex. As shown in Illustrations 1.2 and 1.3, computer technology has dramatically increased the volume of data and information over the past decade, but not necessarily the volume of knowledge and wisdom.

Information value is a fixed-dividend game. The higher the overall quantity of information, the smaller the value of each individual piece of information.

INFORMATION OVERLOAD

One legitimate concern exists about the information superhighway and 500-channel TV: expanding the cultural effects of information overload. Neil Postman, chair of the Department of Culture and Communications at New York University, has eloquently described the narcissistic effect on people that results from information overload. Television, the virtual town square of McLuhan's global village, has not only connected us culturally, but exposed us to each other's tragedies. When we perceive that the outside world is largely beyond our control, according to Postman, we seek control elsewhere: the size of our belly or the shape of our nose. We also consume (today, without even getting up from one's couch) and, in doing so, we exercise con-

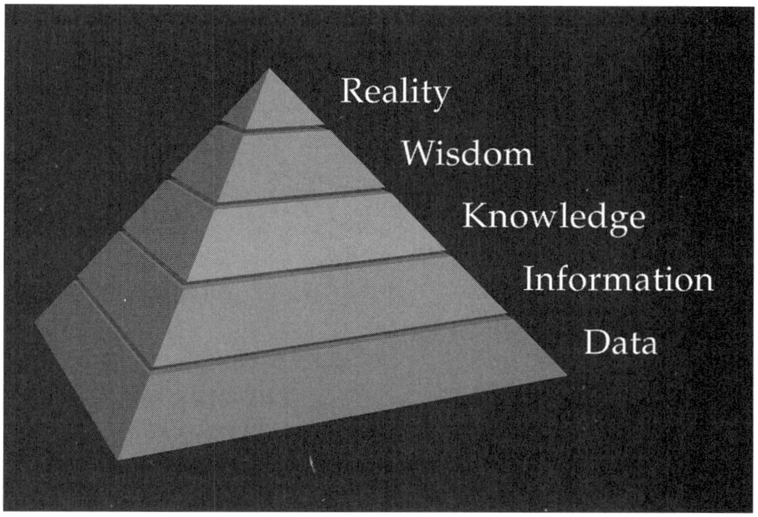

Illustration 1.2 *The information pyramid, circa 1985.*

trol by deciding what to buy and where to put it. For a moment, think about the effect on your own physiology and behavior the next time you channel surf between the Russian civil war on CNN, the Senate budget debate on C-SPAN, *This Old House* on PBS, *Monday Night Football* on ABC, and *Star Trek: Voyager* on UPN. When you turn the television off, observe how you decide to exercise control.

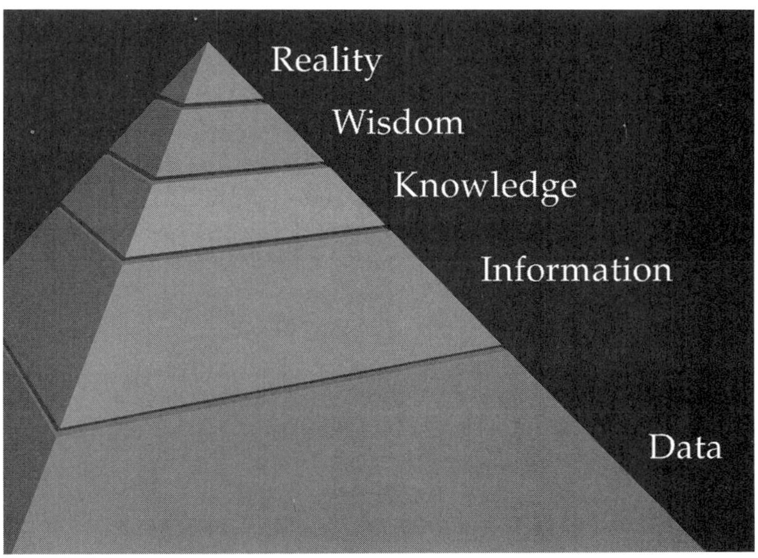

Illustration 1.3 *The information pyramid, circa 1995.*

Postman's thesis is evidenced by two consumer markets that have experienced explosive growth over the past two decades: personal fitness and do-it-yourself home improvement. What percentage of their growth is related to the desire of people to exercise control over the only personal, physical domains they have—their bodies and shelters—within a world they perceive to be beyond their control? For further evidence, look no further than the desktop computers in your office. How do most people spend time customizing their PCs? They choose wallpaper and configure screen savers: the body aesthetic of desktop computing. The need for individuals to assert control over their own personal environments with immediate, visible results is undeniable, and manifests itself quite directly on the computerized desktop.

The cost of digital information is falling even faster than the computer tools used to manipulate it. In 1994, personal computer manufacturer Gateway 2000 offered an eclectic multimedia starter pack. The contents (five *billion* bytes of data) included Mad Dog McCree, Microsoft Cinemania '94, *Better Homes and Gardens Cookbook,* Lawnmower Man, TuneLand (starring Howie Mandel), *Mayo Clinic Family Health Book,* Mavis Beacon Teaches Typing, Chess Master 3000, U.S. and world atlases, and finally, Sitting on the Farm. The price? $139. Low-cost, high-volume digital information is here to stay.

To what degree has information overload affected the professional behavior of architects? It's tough to control earthquakes, urban decay, asbestos, payroll taxes, adversarial contractors, litigious users or clients with high-end expectations and low-end pocketbooks, whose architects are their favorite bankers. But it's easy to reach for the yellow trace (or a laptop) and sketch a detail, lay out a floor plan, or write a paragraph. Is it only a coincidence that the art and intellect of architecture, as opposed to client service and problem solving, absorb such a large part of published architectural discourse today? On the control scale, art and intellect are easy—consciously or not, we often seek refuge there.

This is not, of course, to say that the information superhighway is without value. Its useful components, particularly the Internet's easy-to-use and rapidly growing World Wide Web, are the subject of Chapter 10, On-Line Resources. But its value must be judged by its present, useful incarnations, not by the wildly optimistic portraits painted by those with financial interests in promoting it.

IMPACT ON THE FIRM

Technology also impacts the management, operations, and culture of the architectural firm itself. Unfortunately, these changes are not often anticipated or well understood when a firm first computerizes. Depending on the firm's clients, employees, organization, and service delivery processes, the scope of these impacts can range from trivial to overwhelming.

For example, although technology is often described as a means to improve communications between individuals, it can actually widen communication gaps between an architectural firm's management and staff. In 1994, Fred Stitt, editor/publisher of *Guidelines,* measured an important discrepancy between how employees and managers perceive their time is spent. When Stitt asked employees how much time they spent each day actually doing productive work, the typical response ranged from 55 to 75 percent. When he asked employers and managers how much time the same employees spent actually doing productive work, the estimates were higher—75 to 85 percent of the day.

The introduction of new computer tools does not alleviate this problem, and can actually make it worse. For example, project managers may be faced with supervising a team of architects using CAD who possess skills they do not have and have access to information they lack. Certainly, an effective manager does not need to be an expert on all issues nor micromanage the day-to-day activities of every project team member. But technology changes the work equation, and without tightening communication between manager and the project team, communication breakdowns tend to occur more frequently. The key issue is trust, and trust takes time to develop.

According to management consultant O. Mark Marcussen, about 2.4 hours are wasted each day because of poor communication between employee and supervisor. In other words, employees waste time because they are not given appropriate direction and information. This includes unclear assignments, incomplete instruction, and unstated deadlines. Some managers do not have a good understanding of how long a particular task takes, which also contributes to wasted work time. Technology magnifies this problem.

Several tactics designed to help managers cope with computer technology are described in Chapter 11, Managing the Digital Office.

THE ARCHITECT'S PERCEIVED VALUE

Architects occasionally complain that they are not as well respected or well compensated as doctors and lawyers. Respect notwithstanding, the simple fact is that most people are willing to pay a premium to someone who helps them stay alive or out of jail, compared to someone who helps them stay warm or dry. In a free market, perceived value translates directly into revenue and profit.

"We have met the enemy, and they is us."
POGO

The key word is "perceived," because the value that really matters is the value perceived by the client. Perceived value can be found within an architectural firm's breadth of service, knowledge, responsiveness, talent and skills, and willingness to accept liability and risk. When architects narrow their scope of responsibility and abdicate services to others, including construction managers, value engineers, estimators, and others, they transfer some of their value and diminish their ability to command a premium for their efforts.

What does this have to do with technology? In efforts to use technology to distinguish themselves from their competition, too many architects are unintentionally transferring some of their perceived value to little boxes of software.

A good example of this phenomenon, and one company's response to it, can be found in the personal computer hardware industry. Several years ago, Intel commissioned a survey of computer buyers and asked them to name the manufacturer of the 80386 chip, which was Intel's highest-volume product at the time and the central processing unit (CPU) of most Windows personal computers. The number one answer? Compaq. Most buyers simply didn't know (or necessarily care) about who made the CPU in their computer, any more than car buyers know who actually manufactures their car engine.

The survey results alarmed Intel executives, who were well aware of the economics of perceived value. They responded by introducing the highly successful "Intel Inside" advertising campaign and encouraging PC manufacturers to put "Intel Inside" stickers on their computers. How did they encourage them? They offered cash. Many PC manufacturers took the bait, and in the process, transferred from themselves to Intel a key part of their products' perceived value. Today, that transfer is complete, and many computer buyers expect to see that sticker to reassure themselves that they are buying the "real thing."

Mind share includes blame share, of course. The displacement of value from computer maker to chip maker also explains why Intel felt virtually all of the heat when a mathematical flaw in their Pentium chip design was disclosed in late 1994. Although the bad press was painful for Intel to endure, the irony of the event is that it firmly cemented in customer's minds, once and for all, which company *really* was responsible for the hardware value in Windows personal computers.

Today, some architects are inadvertently putting "Intel Inside" stickers on their proposals and services. They are using technology to demonstrate to clients that they are using technology, but not much else. They are including detailed specifications in their brochures and proposals about the latest software and hardware they use, populated with technical jargon like 400 DPI and 90 Mhz, but little information about how the tools add value. Incredibly, some architects even participate in advertisements and marketing events for CAD software, essentially proclaiming: "Hey, it's not about me anymore, now my clients can hire anybody with this software to do their work!" Overpromoting computer tools in the minds of our clients—tools that are rapidly becoming commodities—only dilutes the value of our professional services.

Successful architects are not so generous in assigning their value. In 1983, for example, Skidmore, Owings, & Merrill purchased an Intergraph CAD system for their Houston office, although the firm's other offices were using SOM's home-grown CAD software. Under the terms of the purchase agreement, Intergraph was prohibited from using SOM in any of its advertisements or marketing literature, and was prohibited from publicly acknowledging that SOM was an Intergraph customer. At the time, a few people inside the firm believed the partners simply did not want to admit they actually bought someone else's CAD system. In fact, it was a smart business decision. SOM knew where the perceived value was, and where it should stay.

Software developers are also transforming the word "architect" itself into a commodity. At your local Egghead store, you can find a variety of software tools today for under $100 that help individuals with tasks normally requiring the help of a "professional." A few samples:

TITLE	COST	ADVERTISED USE
3D Home Architect	$59	Floor plan layout
Chief Architect	$49	3D architectural design
Willmaker	$40	Will preparation
Personal Law Firm	$20	Help with legal issues
PharmAssist	$40	Help with medications

In addition to "do-it-yourself" software, the booming "do-it-yourself" home improvement market is also diluting the perceived value of architects and others involved in the design and construction of small projects. Home Depot is one company aggressively extending its sales of home-improvement products into home-improvement *design services*. Walk into Home Depot, find the kitchen cabinet display, and an employee will sit down with you and walk you through a home kitchen layout and design software program. The software produces basic plan, elevation, and three-dimensional views, along with a customized materials and parts list. The service is offered "free." It is a simple example of collaborative design using technology, without an architect.

Obviously, Home Depot is not providing the same level of service that most architects would provide, and many of its customers probably would not hire an architect even if Home Depot's service were not available. The threat is not one of competition, but one of unchallenged perception. Many customers think they get an effective, computer-aided design service, without the overhead and expense of an architect.

3D Home Architect, developed by educational software developer Broderbund, is an excellent value. Developers of more expensive "professional" CAD software have much to learn from its friendly user interface and integrated tools.

Individually, consumer software programs such as 3D Home Architect (Ill. 1.4) and consumer design services such as those offered by Home Depot and others are relatively minor

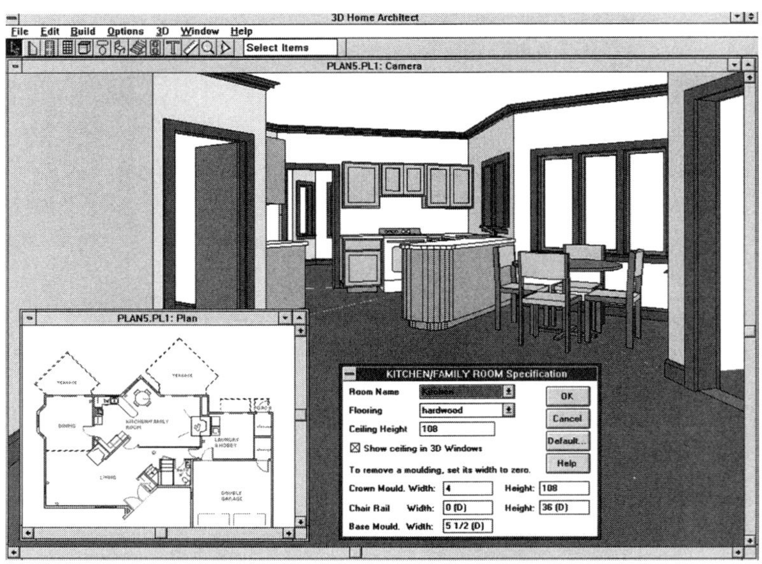

Illustration 1.4 3D Home Architect.

contributors to the erosion of the architect's value. Collectively, they should not be ignored, especially by sole practitioners and small firms. The bottom line is that the architect's perceived value is no longer a right that is inherited upon obtaining a professional license. Perceived value is something that must be earned, and should neither be taken for granted nor by accident assigned to technology.

A final note of caution: although you do not want to abdicate value to technology, neither should you overreact to the problem by making a design process that uses technology seem more complicated to your client than it is. One architect profiled in *Progressive Architecture* in 1994 described how he liked to sit down with clients and engage in interactive, one-on-one design sessions on a laptop computer. However, in order to keep the client from thinking that she could buy the software and design on her own, the architect "often generated complex drawings and perspectives views just to keep the process mysterious and a bit intimidating."

That approach, quite frankly, is a bad idea. Instead of trying to use the software in mysterious and intimidating ways, the architect should focus on communicating value. How? By demonstrating good listening skills, displaying effective graphic and verbal communication, providing thoughtful feedback, and creating original ideas. If you are confident about what you can do with the tools, you should not be afraid to demonstrate or explain how the tools work. In fact, by doing so you run a much smaller risk of the client assigning value to the technology instead of to you.

In a scene from the 1939 classic film *The Wizard of Oz,* Dorothy is accompanied by the Scarecrow, the Tin Man, the Cowardly Lion, and her dog Toto on a visit to the Wizard. Standing behind a curtain in his chamber, the Wizard operates a panel of knobs and levers to control a large image projector and various pyrotechnic devices. The result is a large, fiery, surreal image of himself that is at once authoritative and intimidating to his visitors (that is, until Toto the dog pulls back the curtain and exposes him as a balloonist from Kansas City). Some architects believe that they can stand behind a curtain of technology and impress their clients with their service wizardry. Unfortunately, technology is not the curtain. Technology is *Toto the dog*. Technology will continue to pull back the architect's curtain of magic until what is left to be seen by clients is plain old service value. Architects need to be prepared to provide just that.

Always strive to make the process in which technology is used simple and understandable to your clients. If your clients are interested, be honest about explaining the hardware and software you use, even if they are off-the-shelf, low-cost tools. Emphasize and clarify the service delivery process in which the tools are used, and how that process provides value. Do not advertise the technology itself, nor keep it shrouded in mystery. Instead, advertise what you can do with it.

IMPACT ON THE INDIVIDUAL

"As the architects in our office developed confidence with the computer, many of them found that executing their own correspondence and documentation was speedier and more satisfying than the traditional process of manuscript or dictation and repetitive cycles of editing the typed copy. We found that client correspondence, meeting reports, and field reports could be produced readily on laptop computers in flight, in airports, in hotels, at home, or on the job site while the information was fresh in the architect's mind and transferred by disk or modem to the clerical computer or made available on the office network for further critique."
NORMA DECAMP BURNS, FAIA

Finally, the most important but oft-forgotten impact of technology is on the individual architect, especially those who entered the profession before or during the 1980s. Many architects are simultaneously excited about the promise of computer technology and concerned about its potential threat to their livelihood. Rules are changing and, for most people, change induces fear and anxiety. Technology requires new skills and knowledge. The demand for specialized traditional skills, such as constructing perspectives, building physical models, or inking presentation drawings, may decline. In addition, the potential health impact on employees from regularly using computers (repetitive motion injury, eyestrain) is real, and not a matter to be ignored or treated lightly.

Anticipating and understanding technology's impact on the individual provides value to employees by reducing their technology-induced anxiety and encouraging them to take the initiative in planning for its impact. It also helps the firm respond appropriately to support, educate, and motivate employees. Implementing technology within a firm without responding to its impact on individuals is simply shortsighted.

NEW SKILLS

The ability to store and access information using computers demands improved organizational, analytical, and management skills of practitioners (not to mention knowing how to type). Most of these skills can be taught, but like practice itself, many are learned only through experience. The specific requirements will vary depending on the tools used and the operational characteristics of the firm.

The easiest skills are those that can be acquired through training: using software, printing, browsing databases, and so on. The more difficult skills—ones too often ignored—are those involving management practice: anticipating the pace at which digital information is developed and reproduced, controlling access to viewing and editing dynamically linked information, documenting the organizational structure of digital project data, and aligning expectations of quality and productivity improvements with the realities of the digital tools and the expertise of those who use them.

Project managers newly initiated to CAD, for example, are most often frustrated by their lack of access to information. An understanding of the project's status, previously gained by simply walking around the office, now requires access to a computer or waiting for time-consuming and often costly plots. As a result, it is vitally important to provide managers with easy access to digital information and the appropriate training to make sense of it.

The slow pace at which CAD information is developed in the early stages of design and documentation can also be a source of anxiety among managers. The productivity benefits of CAD are usually not realized early in a project, but only after the information has been shared and reused. Drawing a single floor plan in CAD may actually take longer than manually drafting it, for example, but creating the ceiling plans and enlarged plans can be done in a small fraction of the time.

Unlike manual drawings, plotted CAD drawings are themselves reproductions, separate and distinct from their digital originals. The additional step of plotting and/or printing drawings creates new bottlenecks that must be understood and anticipated. Similarly, embedding or linking nongraphic database attributes within drawings can also complicate the management of information access and update. In the past, the tasks of drawing doors on a floor plan and developing a door schedule required different levels of experience, and in larger firms

"By setting our sights on higher productivity, we are asking people to turn out more goods in less time. If possible, we'd like last year's forty hours of production to be turned out next year in thirty hours. Better still, we'd like every producer to think up ways of eliminating his work altogether—and we've had people gladly and ingeniously do just that. . . . But there's only one way we can ask people to strive toward that goal. They must be absolutely assured that by eliminating their work they are not eliminating themselves—or anyone else. They must know, without doubt, that elimination of work will bring not a penalty but a reward."
CLAIR F. VOUGH, MANAGEMENT CONSULTANT

"Another factor in successful computerization is discipline—and the A/E profession is notorious for its lack of discipline. Each of us is a free spirit who wants to do everything his way. With computers, you must dot your i's and cross your t's, or you are in big trouble."
CHARLES F. BOYD, FCSI, AIA

The issue of project manager training is discussed in more detail in Chapter 3, Technology Training and Education.

were often performed by two different people. In a CAD drawing, the graphic representation of the door and its nongraphic attributes are often in the same place. Moving a door to a new location, or deleting one and inserting another, has database implications beyond the graphics. Architects who perform those tasks must understand the nature of the drawings that contain such database intelligence and manipulate its information appropriately.

Architects who successfully leverage technology are usually generalists, not specialists. This is why many of the most effectively automated architectural firms are small ones. Because most architects in those firms are generalists who wear many hats, they are better prepared for dealing with new types of integrated digital information.

Along with new technical and management skills, administrative support skills are changing as well. Project support staff in automated firms are doing far more than typing correspondence; they are using spreadsheets, creating charts, graphs, and schedules, and preparing proposals and presentations. Firms that provide more stimulating, challenging job responsibilities and career paths, of course, will tend to attract and retain a higher quality staff. In many cases, computer technology and the new skills required to leverage it provide a means to do so.

Information float is the time span between the act of sending information and the subsequent receipt of the information by another party. It is derived from the use of the term "float" by financial institutions, which is the time span between sending checks or deposits to a bank, and the actual withdrawal or deposit of funds. E-mail effectively eliminates the luxury of information float.

NO EXCUSES, NO ESCAPE

In the old days, written correspondence demanded a certain investment of time and material. You had to write it, give it a typist, review and revise the drafts, and sign the final version. If the message had to be sent to multiple parties, it was copied, stapled, folded, and enclosed in addressed envelopes. The useful by-product of this investment was discipline—an awareness about who really needed to know what and when. Organizing and bundling related information together was a useful practice to minimize communication costs.

With on-line, desktop, digital communication tools such as E-mail, however, the time and material investment becomes trivial. Today, it is no more difficult nor expensive to send a message to one hundred people as it is to send a message to one. The result, when these tools are used by relatively disorganized people, is that volume goes up, way up. The most serious impact on the individual architect is the increase of in-bound communications from clients, consultants, and contractors. This effect has long been observed as a by-product of the fax machine and is only getting worse with E-mail.

Accompanying on-line, real-time message delivery systems can be an implied expectation of on-line, real-time responses from the architect. A decade ago, the contractor or client asked: "What do you mean you haven't reviewed it yet? I sent it to you five days ago!" Today, the contractor or client asks: "What do you mean you haven't reviewed it yet? I sent it to you *five minutes* ago!" In the on-line, digital world, there are few excuses for untimely response. The phrase "it's in the mail" is nothing if not obsolete.

At Xerox's Palo Alto Research Center (PARC), a team of researchers investigating future communication technologies is constantly connected to each other with portable devices (basically fancy pagers) that each team member carries at all times. Essentially, any person can locate and communicate with any other person at any time. Sounds powerful and flexible, right? What the researchers have observed is that most people eventually begin to seek sanctuaries—"quiet zones"—where they can go to be off line and inaccessible.

Instant communication between distributed work groups has been evangelized by software developers and technology consultants as a slam-dunk benefit with few liabilities. Indeed, in most creative endeavors, ad hoc, nonstructured communication is valuable and certainly has an appropriate place within the architectural firm. But architects do not just generate ideas, we document how the ideas will physically be constructed and necessarily create a sequential paper trail of the process. An undisciplined, real-time, free-for-all communication media is not necessarily the most appropriate way to do so. The question is: how does the individual architect exploit the creative aspects of on-line communication, while maintaining the information structure required of her business? Talented individuals who are also well organized and disciplined about how, when, and with whom they communicate typically are best prepared to leverage the new tools successfully.

CHAPTER

2

Planning and Implementing Technology in Your Firm

> *"Automate first what you don't want to do."*
> **Frank Mascia, AIA**

GUIDELINES FOR EFFECTIVE AUTOMATION

For any particular service delivery problem, there are literally hundreds of potential technology solutions. The specific solutions that others have found useful may not be appropriate for you or your firm, depending on your services, markets, clients, and the talents and experience of the people with whom you work. However, similar ideas reappear in almost all architectural firms—from the sole practitioner to the global corporation—that have a strong track record of effectively using computer technology.

The following "Top 10 List" is a summary of those ideas, and is intended to help you successfully plan and implement computer technology within your architectural firm. All are value-oriented, cost-effective, common sense guidelines, and should help you successfully implement technology with the least amount of capital investment and operational overhead. Combined with a keen understanding of your markets, your clients, and currently available software and hardware, you can generate most of the good ideas for bringing technology inside your firm and making it work by focusing on these ten guidelines:

1. Imagine the ordinary
2. Focus on demand, not supply
3. Focus on process, not task
4. Organize, then automate

> **"Technology goes through predictable stages of development in much the same way as people do. In the beginning, there is belittlement, snickering, and scoffing. Next comes the prophetic stage, where visionaries explore its capabilities. Then comes the cargo cult, people start to jump on the bandwagon, with more enthusiasm than understanding. This is followed by a period of euphoria, which is inevitably replaced by disillusionment and depression. The limits of technology loom. Only after this does the 'right-stuff' phase ensue, a time of renewal and resurgence."**
> **MIKE EDELHART**
> ***PC Week***

5. Emphasize information reuse
6. Simplify...simplify...simplify
7. Value knowledge over tools
8. Distribute expertise
9. Question your assumptions
10. *Always* test drive

Each guideline is more an attitude than a goal. Each lacks the two attributes of an effective goal: a specific timetable for achieving it, and a specific method for measuring success. Translating these ten guidelines into specific goals will vary widely depending on the firm and the individual. After reviewing other chapters, which deal more specifically with the tools, resources, management issues, and future trends of technology in the architectural practice, you may wish to merge these guidelines with the knowledge of your firm to develop specific goals and action plans.

A brief anecdote illustrates an important point about successfully implementing technology and demonstrates how the observations of technology cynics are sometimes more insightful and illuminating than those of technology evangelists. New York University's Neil Postman, whose views on information overload were introduced in Chapter 1, told me the story. Postman correctly asserts that individuals and society need to do a better job at anticipating technology's side effects and factoring their costs into technology's "value" equation.

A few years back, Postman visited a Honda dealership to buy a car and asked a salesperson about the standard features of the Accord. One of those cited by the salesperson was "cruise control." Postman politely asked the salesperson, "What is the problem to which cruise control is the solution?" The salesperson, somewhat taken aback that anyone would not want cruise control, finally mumbled: "Well, I guess it means you don't have to keep your foot on the gas pedal." Postman replied, "I have been driving for forty years, and I don't think I've ever had that problem."

> **Successful technology implementation means knowing your strategy, knowing your choices, and knowing your people. Two out of three isn't good enough.**

Postman ended up buying the Accord. It came with cruise control because you cannot buy an Accord without it. His experience reminds us that technology, usually advertised as expanding choices, often does the reverse. (The classic example:

the automobile, which effectively destroyed urban light rail transportation starting in the 1920s.) His query of the Honda salesperson is a valuable one that any person should ask about technology: "*What is the problem to which this is the solution?*" Don't even think about implementing new technology in your practice without thoughtfully considering the answer.

Within architectural firms and other service businesses, one example of a technological cart before the horse is voice mail. Most people who receive messages on voice-mail systems like them because they end the proliferation of desktop message slips and provide more information about a caller's intent. Voice-mail systems certainly are appropriate for after-hours access, or for sole proprietors or small firms without a dedicated receptionist or administrative staff to screen calls.

But few things are more frustrating to clients than being stuck in a voice-mail system, with one-way hierarchical menus and no escape hatches back to human contact. In addition, most voice-mail recipients end up writing their own message slips while listening to recorded messages, which defeats some of the "efficiency" of voice mail. The point is, when you look at new technology, ask Postman's question from the client's point of view. What is the added value? Faster turnaround time? Lower costs? Higher quality? If there is no clear answer, proceed cautiously.

There is an old saying: *if you are standing in front of the refrigerator asking yourself if you are hungry, you are probably not hungry.* If you do not have a clear, compelling reason to implement new technology, you may not need it. Keep an eye on future market trends, so you are not blindsided by new client expectations, but do not allow hype alone to convince you of the need.

---

1. Imagine the Ordinary

Like the weather, paradigm shifts are fun to observe, but hard to predict. Timing is everything. Most are like desert mirages—no matter how far you move toward them (building modeling, artificial intelligence, expert systems), they still seem the same dis-

"Any sufficiently advanced technology is indistinguishable from magic."
ARTHUR C. CLARKE

tance away. A few roar by like an express train—by the time you hear them coming (CD-ROM, the World Wide Web), they have already passed you by.

Many of the emerging technology-based paradigm shifts of architectural practice promoted today are actually not very new, and are ideas that have been tossed around for a decade or more. In fact, some of the frustration that architects have experienced with technology is because they were sold paradigm shifts by early proponents of technology, only to discover the tools far more ordinary. Space-age warriors prepared to do battle with phasers and photon torpedoes just do not know what to do with sticks, even perfectly good ones.

A paradigm shift is a by-product of technological success, not a goal; it happens after the good ideas are proven to really work, and never before. So do not worry too much about paradigm shifts—worry instead about distinguishing between practical tools that work today and those that do not.

At the same time, remember that the most conventional, ordinary pieces of technology in use today at one time were radical science fiction. Three examples did not exist fifteen years ago: fax machines, cellular phones, and digital compact disks. Today, a five-year-old child knows what these things are. To a child, in fact, they are not even technology—they are just part of how the world works. But to describe the present-day applications of these low-cost technologies fifteen years ago would have seemed outrageous to most people at the time. Correctly predicting their use and future impact on society and the profession would have meant visualizing their ubiquitous nature.

Prepare for the future not by visualizing how radical a new technology will be; visualize how conventional it will be. Imagine the ordinary. Imagine a place where technology, although it seems incredible today, is actually rather dull and uninspiring. In that place, truly useful technology—the stuff that will stick around—is far easier to identify.

At the same time, do not lose sight of your past success. Remember the basics of any architectural firm's core value: its reputation, experience, design talent, communication, management—the people skills. The key is to learn how to merge those skills, not replace them, with the demands of an information-age market. Do not advertise your firm's computer technology—advertise your skills in using it, integrating it, and

"Technology is anything invented after you were born."
ALAN KAY

customizing it to the process that is unique to your firm, and your client. Strive to make technology an ordinary, invisible part of your practice.

> **"Invisible computing describes information-based practices where computing technologies become so pervasive that they are no longer experienced as visibly separate from practice itself. This enables architects to redirect their attention to the basic client-centered values of traditional practice."**
> **JERRY ALBERT LAISERIN, AIA, CPA**

2. Focus on Demand, Not Supply

Firms that are excessively enthusiastic about computer technology, as well as firms that view technology only as a necessary evil of modern practice, often implement supply-side technology. In other words, the individual(s) responsible for technology within the firm determine needs, supply the technology, require project teams to use it, and thus artificially create the demand. (The term "technology manager" is used here to generically describe the position, although it is not necessarily filled by one person.)

A better alternative is the demand-side, free-market approach to technology implementation, where employees participate in the decision about when and how to use technology. The notion is that the technology manager first demonstrates the value of a new tool or process on a small scale, evangelizes it within the firm, and then provides the supply of technology as a response to genuine demand from architects within the firm. If the technology manager has done her homework, and the tools really do add value, the demand will be there. If the demand is not there, the technology manager must learn why, and respond to it. This is the essential cyclic behavior of a free market.

The demand-side approach recognizes that it is extremely difficult, if not impossible, to precisely predict how and how often a particular piece of new technology will end up being used on a day-to-day basis. The Heisenberg Uncertainty Principle, well known to physicists and political commentators, states that the very act of observing an event changes the event being observed. Similarly, implementing technology within a process changes the process itself, sometimes in trivial ways, sometimes in dramatic ways. Even the most experienced, well-read technology manager cannot always predict the scope or intensity of those changes.

Entrepreneurial managers and employees who focus on and are rewarded for providing practice value to the client (and business value to the firm) will seek out and use tools that do that. They will also avoid tools that do not. In the demand-side, free-market approach, the economic benefits of technology are inherently self-regulating. It places on the technology manager the burden of staying close to project teams and constantly monitoring how tools are being used. The technology manager effectively has a second in-house client: the project team. The approach places on managers and employees the burden of taking entrepreneurial risks, experimenting with new tools and methods, and socializing their experiences.

Shown below are the steps of a demand-driven technology cycle, compared to a supply-side technology cycle. Each cycle takes about six to twelve months, although the demand-driven cycle typically takes longer. Many staggered cycles can occur within a firm simultaneously.

THE SUPPLY-SIDE TECHNOLOGY CYCLE

1. Investigate practice or business problem and potential technology solutions
2. Select technology solution and determine how it will be used
3. Evangelize the proposed solution
4. Implement on a broad scale
5. Require employees to use it, creating demand
6. Repeat steps 1 through 5

THE DEMAND-DRIVEN TECHNOLOGY CYCLE

1. Investigate practice or business problem and potential technology solutions
2. Propose technology solution and estimate how it will be used
3. Test-drive the proposed solution thoroughly; evaluate the results
4. Implement the proposed solution on a small scale; evaluate the results
5. Acknowledge the failures; repeat steps 2 through 4 if necessary
6. Evangelize the success; clarify its boundaries; create demand within the firm
7. Supply technology to fill the demand
8. Repeat steps 1 through 7

Technology evangelists within architectural firms should not focus on convincing people *how* technology will work. Instead, they should focus on *making* technology work. Success stories are the best form of in-house evangelism. Build it well, and they will come.

3. Focus on Process, Not Task

Many computer tools provide value when applied to individual *tasks* in the same way as traditional tools: writing a memo, drawing a floor plan, or creating a budget. For many architects, this is an appropriate place to start. The highest value, however, arrives when the service delivery *process* within which the tools are applied is reengineered to take advantage of the tools.

The term "reengineering" has become somewhat overhyped and is frequently misunderstood as a code word for reducing the work force. It long ago achieved its fifteen minutes of fame from the title of Champy and Hammers' book *Reengineering the Corporation,* one of the standouts of a long parade of 1990s business management books. However, the central premise of reengineering is absolutely correct. Reengineering accompanies (or drives) many technology innovations within businesses around the world. While automating individual tasks may provide small improvements in quality, productivity, or turnaround, the real payoff arrives when the process of delivering a service is thoroughly reevaluated and, if necessary, reinvented from scratch.

Many traditional architectural service delivery processes are aggregate processes that have been revised and fine tuned over decades of practice. When confronted with entirely new tools and market demands, however, old techniques sometimes make less sense. Reengineering involves analyzing a process—regardless of its historical track record—and aggressively testing its old assumptions.

Some architects resist this idea because they feel it is the tail wagging the dog. After all, should not computers accommodate the way architects work, instead of requiring architects to change the way they work to accommodate computers? Sure. Reengineering is not an issue of us versus them, of architects versus computers, of tradition versus technology. It is an issue of synergy, and also a competitive reality. After all, the issue is not really how architects want to do work, but how our clients want us to do work. That is an important distinction that some architects fail to see through the foggy mist of practice nostalgia.

This is not to say that radically reinventing a process, instead of simply automating tasks within it, is always the best solution. In some cases, a much simpler implementation of technology, one that even mimics traditional methods or organization, is perfectly appropriate. Technology should supplement, not replace, traditional methods. The point is to be smart enough to recognize when it is appropriate to simply automate a task, when it is appropriate to reengineer a process, and when it is appropriate to do both. The goals are to first understand the flow of information within a process, use technology where appropriate, and continually evaluate the effectiveness of its use.

A few sample questions about typical processes within architectural firms are listed below:

- How is the flow of written and graphic information controlled and decision making documented from initial design sketches to construction drawings to record drawings? How is the information organized, indexed, and filed for future retrieval? What type of information is most commonly retrieved, and why?
- How are marketing proposals assembled? How are boilerplate materials retrieved and combined with project-specific information? How are old proposals stored for future reference?
- How are owner-architect and architect-consultant contracts written, reviewed, edited, and signed? How is their status tracked?
- How are fee budgets developed and revised during the course of a project?
- How are project costs—labor, consultant fees, and direct and reimbursable expenses—monitored and compared with the project fee budgets? What information do project managers require and when?
- How are insurance requirements for consultants monitored?
- How are photographic materials digitized, stored, and made accessible?
- How do project teams communicate with consultants, and keep them informed about new issues that affect their work? How is digital information shared with consultants? How often is it shared?
- How is cash flow managed? How are revenues projected? How are key financial indicators reported?

- How are the contractor's shop drawings, requests for information, product data, samples, and change orders logged and tracked during construction?
- How is digital data delivered to clients? What contents are required, and how is the information organized? How does the firm prepare itself to support client-specific organizational guidelines within their digital drawings?
- How are post-occupancy evaluations conducted? How are their results communicated to the project team and the rest of the firm?
- How are project archives organized, stored, and retrieved? What are the criteria for determining the inclusion of material in a project archive? At what milestones are archives created?

Most successful architectural firms have well-defined answers to these questions. The next (recursive) step is identifying problems or opportunities to improve the current process.

Instead of asking "how *does* the process work?" ask "how *should* the process work?" As simple as this sounds, this question is perhaps one of the most difficult for many architects to answer, particularly those within successful firms. The inertia of success is a remarkable and surprisingly powerful force that resists testing old assumptions.

The final aspect of successfully analyzing and refining service delivery processes using computer technology is understanding how those processes relate to each other. How your firm manages cash flow, for example, is directly related to how your firm monitors the financial performance of projects. Your choice of software tools must recognize these relationships and how information is shared or recycled between different processes. Understand each process, question it, refine it, clarify it, and only then start thinking about which software applications can provide value within it.

4. Organize, then Automate

A basic cause of inefficiency in architectural firms is disorganization. Unfortunately, computer technology does not automati-

"If your firm is a well-organized and well-managed manual production firm, computerization will give you a wonderful new management tool. You will be able to play all kinds of 'What if?' games to improve reporting and production control. However, you must not believe that computerizing will help you manage a disorganized firm. Nothing could be further from the truth. Do not expect a computer to organize your practice. Get organized, then get a computer."
CHARLES F. BOYD, FCSI, AIA

cally solve that problem. On the contrary, automating a disorganized practice will not only fail to improve the situation, but actually make it worse. In the absence of a clearly defined organizational structure for storing digital data, computers often make it easier to lose information than to find it.

A firm that already has organizational guidelines, well-structured libraries, and standardized procedures will find the path of automation relatively clear of major obstacles. Conversely, a disorganized firm that automates will experience a painful implementation, and leave productivity gains lying on the table.

Technology provides the highest return on investment in firms where committed management and well-defined guidelines and procedures are already in place. Improvements in revenue and profitability of successfully automated firms are often less attributable to the tools themselves, and more attributable to the operational characteristics of the firm and talents of its staff. Organization is a key prerequisite.

---

5. Emphasize Information Reuse

"Unless architects use information technology to win back the role of information gatekeeper, they risk slipping ever lower on the 'information food chain' until design itself is relegated to the status of just another subcontract specialty."
JERRY ALBERT LAISERIN, AIA, CPA

Information reuse is the foundation of the successful computerized architectural practice, and is also where technology pays off most dramatically. Although the benefits of information reuse certainly include improving productivity and turnaround, they have more to do with improving quality: maintaining consistency between documents, reducing errors and omissions, and recycling a firm's best work.

First, a brief acknowledgment of an opposing view is appropriate. Some architects consider information reuse a potential danger, and not necessarily a benefit, of automation. The popularly voiced argument is that computers encourage architects to create boring and repetitive buildings, or at the very least, make it easy to do so.

The logic to this argument is tantamount to saying that it rains because there are umbrellas. Such an argument devalues the decision-making roles of the architect, client, and contractor, and fails to recognize the social and economic forces that have long nourished mass production and mass distribution. These forces existed decades before the invention of the computer. They are, in part, simple by-products of a consumer society, one that today increasingly seeks low-cost products and services via high-volume distribution channels. Although one can argue persuasively that the computer is an enabler, and even an accelerator, of those forces, it is certainly not a catalyst.

A similar contrary argument might say that buildings are orthogonal because of the T-square or drafting machine. Indeed, most buildings are orthogonal, but primarily because of the laws of physics and manufacturing economy, not the tools of the draftsperson. Although drafting efficiency can and does have an impact on architectural design, it is trivial compared to the other economic and natural forces at work. In fact, it always has been, and always will be, easier to design boring and repetitive buildings than interesting and varied ones. (BSW International, for example, does not provide volume-building services to clients like Wal-Mart because computers make it possible; they are using computers to provide a service that the high-volume, low-margin business model of Wal-Mart demands. The computer has simply allowed them to do so more competitively and profitably.)

Avoiding computers, and the opportunities for information reuse, for fear of their negative influence on design is like avoiding one's kitchen for fear of food poisoning. Certainly, almost all lousy buildings built recently were designed or documented by individuals with computers. Similarly, most people who suffer from food poisoning were near a kitchen at the time. Like a well-stocked kitchen, a well-equipped computer requires talent and discipline on the part of the user (good recipes, purchasing from reputable suppliers, reading expiration labels, etc.). The risk of accident or abuse is always present but is no reason to avoid the tool.

Indeed, information reuse provides the opportunity to enhance, not constrain, creativity and quality, although no guarantee is implied. Today, the name of the game is mass producing

Inventing the wheel once is a deceptively simple idea. There are literally thousands of opportunities to apply it within an architectural practice using computer software, networks, and communications technologies.

customized services and products, and the tool that is a prerequisite to playing the game successfully is computer technology. Veteran mass producers are using it to learn how to customize; veteran customizers are using it to become more efficient and less error prone, and to raise the baseline of quality. The starting point for any architectural practice that strives to use computer technology successfully is learning how to effectively reuse information.

There are three distinct flavors of information reuse: information copying, information recycling, and information sharing. The three flavors are shown schematically in Illustration 2.1. Every successful application of information technology does one of these three things well; there are no exceptions.

Illustration 2.1 Information copying, recycling, and sharing.

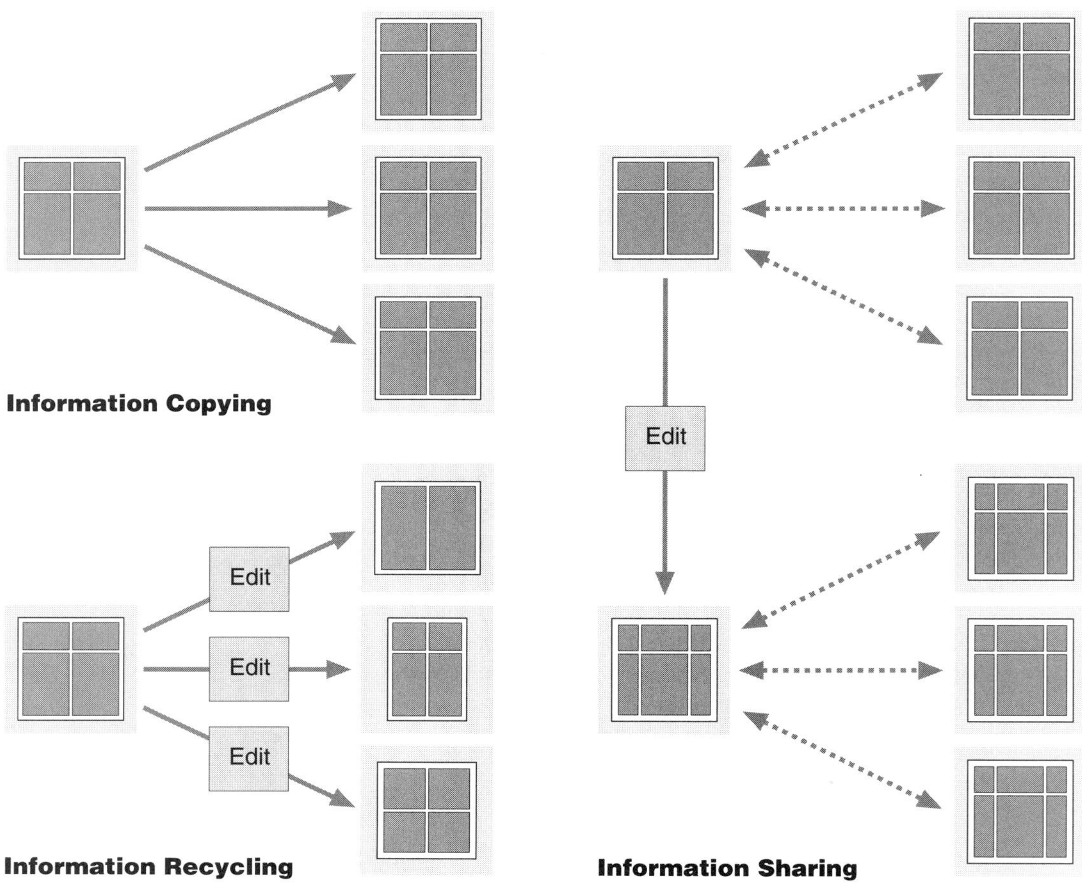

Although similar, the terms copying, sharing, and recycling describe distinctly different ideas. One of the challenges of information reuse is understanding which flavor should be applied to a particular information management problem.

Information copying means precisely duplicating information to another location. Examples include E-mail (both messaging and attachments), "copy and paste" within documents and drawings, and information libraries that are copied and distributed.

Information recycling means the adaptive reuse of information within new contexts. Examples include using an ADA-compliant toilet room layout as a starting point for a new toilet room design, updating a wall section to new reflect new building codes, or modifying a footing detail for a colder climate.

Information sharing means providing multiple parties access to a single information source. Examples include networked databases, CAD reference files, on-line resources, and object-oriented tools such as Microsoft's OLE and Apple's OpenDoc (discussed in Chapter 4).

When many architects think of information reuse, they think of information copying. Of the three types of information reuse, copying is the easiest and least important. Information *recycling* and information *sharing* create the highest value, and are where architects need to pay the most attention.

6. Simplify ... Simplify ... Simplify

An effective way to improve a tool or method is to simplify it. Unfortunately, technology evangelists sometimes forget that architects are still in the business of delivering architectural services, not managing computer technology. Simplification *must* be an ongoing theme of technology integration. This is not just about making tools easier to use and the methods simpler to comprehend, but also about simplifying the organizational structure of information and minimizing the types of hardware and software used within your firm.

Although some technology consultants advise against it, architects should standardize on a single computer platform (Mac, Windows, or UNIX) within their firm whenever possible. Although heterogeneous computing is a reality *outside of the office,* and you should prepare to work with clients and consultants who use different systems than you do, it is simply bad strategy *inside the office.* The burden of implementing, supporting, and providing training for multiple systems is not worth the shrinking differences between feature sets.

Like many architectural firms, ZGF started out using Macintoshes in the mid-1980s because of the Mac's intuitive interface and integrated graphics. As the firm's use of CAD transitioned from early VAX-based systems to PC-based systems in the early 1990s, the firm's use of DOS-based personal computers grew dramatically. Over time, these dedicated CAD systems evolved into more general-purpose computers, capable of running a wide variety of Windows software applications in addition to CAD. Eventually, as the functionality of Windows approached the Mac, it became clear that the dual-system environment would be harder and harder to justify.

Currently, ZGF is in the process of phasing out the firm's Macintoshes and standardizing on Windows, a process that will be complete in 1996. Is this because we believe Windows is technologically superior to the Macintosh? No. In fact, we do not. But the differences today are too small to justify the mixture of hardware and complexities of training, support, and information exchange. In addition, Windows is the only platform that runs all of the software we want to use. The benefit of simplicity of a single system for the entire firm outweighs the loss of individual features.

Let me make it clear that other firms may make the opposite decision for exactly the right reasons. Small or medium-sized firms that have Macintosh-based CAD software such as MiniCAD, ArchiCAD, or PowerDraw should consider standardizing on the Mac, if they haven't already. As more Mac-based CAD systems improve their ability to exchange AutoCAD .DWG files directly, the indirect pressure from clients to switch to DOS/Windows systems should subside.

Simplifying tools and processes makes it easier for computer users to become self-sufficient, and substantially reduces the operational overhead required to implement and maintain technological solutions. Many medium- to large-sized firms, in fact, incur substantial overhead costs to plan, implement, support, manage, repair, and train architects in the use of computers. Each of these support issues is important and should not be ignored. However, the cost of this overhead is usually in direct proportion to the complexity of the technology solutions. If the tools are well designed, reliable, and easy to use, and if users are encouraged and assisted to become self-sufficient, technology support should become a minimal overhead burden.

Software developers themselves have learned this lesson. Like many others in the early 1990s, for example, Microsoft faced a support crisis. Too many customers were calling for help, only to experience long waits on hold or not being able to get through at all. (Today, some software and hardware companies still have the same problem.) One of Microsoft's responses was, in Bill Gates's words, "to spend what it takes" to expand their support staff and provide a satisfactory level of customer support, and avoid the bad will that was generated every time someone who needed help couldn't get it.

Microsoft's other response was far more important to its success. It recognized that what people really wanted was not more support technicians, but simpler, more usable software. "Usability" became a mantra to the software teams at Microsoft, just as it was for Apple's Macintosh development team years before. (Some Microsoft programmers to this day lament the patrols of the "usability police" within the company.) More than any other software developer, Microsoft today invests aggressively in usability testing: observing how people use their software and evaluating the reactions of users to new and revised features.

The results of these efforts can be seen today in the relatively high degree of integration between Microsoft's applications (Word, Excel, PowerPoint et al.), measured by their consistent interfaces (menus, dialog buttons, icons) and their ability to share information with each other. The results also can be seen in Windows 95, which finally approaches the ease of use of the Macintosh. Apple, of course, never had to react to a support problem of the scale of Microsoft's, in part because ease of use was a religion of the Macintosh from the beginning.

All other issues being equal, choose a computer tool that delivers only 80 percent of the features you need if it is substantially less complicated or more reliable than a fully functional tool. Resist paying a complexity premium for leading-edge features.

However, even the Macintosh today has more complex hardware designs and software applications than its original incarnation as a portable computing appliance, and its support costs have drifted higher as a result.

Architects today need to create their own equivalent of Microsoft's usability police, by undertaking regular reviews of the procedures, tools, and information used in the service delivery process, automated or not, to determine how they add value to that process and how they can be simplified.

7. Value Knowledge over Tools

How does one assign value to a practice? For most firms, value includes two components. The first is the financial value of a firm derived from its balance sheet (a summary of its assets and liabilities), also known as its book value. The book value determines the value of a firm if its doors were closed—essentially, what would remain after debts were repaid and assets sold. The second component of value is known to accountants as goodwill. The goodwill of a firm is the value of its intangible assets, and the recognition that there is an intrinsic value associated with the firm's continuing existence and history of revenue and profitability, name recognition, and so on. As a result, the appraised value of a practice—used as a basis for justifying bank loans or determining the price of new ownership—is typically higher than the bottom line figure shown on a balance sheet.

The four primary intangible assets of an architectural firm are:

- The talents and experience of its principals and employees
- The firm's portfolio of built work
- The firm's client base and reputation
- The firm's knowledge base

For a moment, imagine your architectural practice after removing one of these four assets. For example, if you started a new firm using all the people from your present firm, it would be far more difficult to capture new commissions if you could not market your firm's portfolio of built work. Similarly, your firm may have the finest portfolio and client base of any, but if you replace your staff with untalented and inexperienced people, you will not likely succeed beyond the completion of your next several projects. And if you lose your firm's reputation, of course, you will likely lose the firm.

The knowledge base of an architectural firm is one of its key intangible assets. If your firm has a disorganized or inaccessible knowledge base, it will be increasingly difficult to profitably maintain and build on your past success. The size and importance of this asset have increased dramatically over the past twenty-five years, in direct proportion to the increase in regulatory requirements and the complexity and choice of building systems and components. More recent business trends, such as the mobile work force and the virtual organization, have also underscored the importance of maintaining a stable knowledge base within a practice.

Yet a firm's knowledge base is often inaccessible, stored in cardboard tubes or microfiche, or in off-site storage lockers. Other key information can only be found in the minds of specialists who may not be accessible or have time when the information is needed. Some information, such as a record of comparable construction costs of various projects, may be scattered in different places but never assembled to make the information useful.

Information and knowledge have zero value unless they are accessible.

Ask yourself a question: how much time each day do you spend looking for information, or how much time does someone else spend looking for information on your behalf? For many architects, the answer to this question can range from 5 to 25 percent of the day. Clearly, a key opportunity for improving productivity resides in improving the turnaround of information access and retrieval. You should spend as much time and resources on developing and organizing your firm's knowledge base and the tools to access it as on the tools to create and edit it. (Chapter 9 is devoted exclusively to this subject.)

8. Distribute Expertise

A good portion of popular advice on technology implementation deals with developing a formalized organizational structure to research, train, operate, manage, support, and implement technology. The assumption is that centralizing expertise, and dispensing it in a controlled, precise manner only to those who really need it, is somehow a good thing. In a typical architectural firm, and especially in smaller ones, this is a difficult and costly undertaking. Instead, the best approach to technology training and education today is a decentralized approach, one that emphasizes problem solving instead of button pushing and that emphasizes socializing of experience instead of classroom instruction.

Chapter 3 discusses approaches to technology training and education in more detail. New support roles and responsibilities are described in Chapter 11, Managing the Digital Office.

This philosophy applies not only to distributing expertise of technology users, but also distributing expertise of technology managers and educators. Although many larger firms require dedicated staff to support and manage computer systems, the system manager in many smaller and moderate-sized firms can be a virtual position shared by several people. When support is distributed, of course, specific responsibilities must be identified.

"In this period of intense competition, cost constraints, and scarce resources, every architectural practice is under intense pressure to do more with less. Firms are expected to produce more design alternatives, more quickly, with fewer mistakes than ever before, but receive lower fees than at any time in the last decade. To survive and prosper in the face of these demands, architects need tools and approaches that enable them to become more productive. Firms must get the most from the resources they have, especially from their primary one—people."
NORMAN KADERLAN

Cross-pollination of experience is important. When someone sees a drawing or image created with the help of a computer and asks you how it was done, do not answer with the name of the software. Instead, answer with the name of the person who produced the work. It is easier and more effective to learn new techniques by talking with an experienced individual than by navigating a software manual.

---

9. Question Your Assumptions

One of the first steps toward successfully applying technology is to acknowledge its limitations and not become swept away by the hype of its future promise. Technology has profoundly impacted the profession over the last decade but most of the change has been evolutionary. Much of what architects produce today—even in digital formats—is changing, but most is still not that far removed from what we did ten or even twenty years ago.

"I don't get too excited by my victories or too disappointed by my defeats, and in that way I come closer to peace of mind that creativity comes from."
MICHAEL LERNER,
Social Scientist, MacArthur Award Winner

Keeping a level head is an even greater challenge today, as new technology is often overpromoted to consumers before it is popularized within business. Obviously, software developers cannot be expected to emphasize the limitations of their tools, although they certainly should acknowledge them. But other resources for technology information also contribute to the hype, including magazines and journals, consultants, resellers, trainers, and even some architects, who defend their technology choice as the *one and only* solution.

Too many architects are defensive about their software or downright imperious about their hardware. They debate the trivial differences between the Mac and Windows as if they are actually important. My central premise: *it doesn't matter anymore.* You can succeed or fail with a wide variety of hardware and software tools. You should focus instead on what you are doing with the tools, how to integrate them into the service delivery process, and how they are adding value.

Simple advice for buying software: always assume you are making a mistake. Simple advice for buying hardware: visualize throwing it away in three years.

Don't be too enthusiastic, and therefore defensive, about what you buy—to your boss, to your employees, or to your peers. If your purchase decision included a thoughtful analysis based on information available at the time, be confident about the decision you made. Be equally confident that another tool may be a better choice for someone else, or that the decision you made today would not be the same one you would make six months from now. Every day the rules are changing. Vendor product plans change; markets and clients change; expectations change. Even after you buy, insist that the tool demonstrate its value. Always evaluate other options, and constantly take a fresh look at your assumptions. Planning for success includes preparing contingency plans.

To prepare ourselves for prospering in the information age, we must acknowledge both the opportunities and the limitations of new technology. The first step is to share our successes and failures with each other openly and honestly.

10. Always *Test Drive*

Ask most computer users what they want most from their computer and the answer (other than better performance) is reliabil-

"Question: How can you tell if someone is a technical pioneer? Answer: By the arrows in his or her back."
ALICE LAPLANTE

ity. Users reasonably expect computer hardware and software to do what the documentation says they do, without crashing, without bugs, and without inconsistent behavior. Although achieving 100 percent reliability is a virtual impossibility, striving for it is not.

In general, do not buy the first release of any software program, and always test drive before buying. Virtually all software developers and hardware manufacturers offer 30-day money-back guarantees on their products. If they don't provide the guarantee, don't buy the product.

Also, don't wait for your plotter to break down to figure out your backup plan. Talk to your reprographics service bureau, test E-mail connections, generate sample plots, and be sure that when your plotter fails, your firm can maintain uninterrupted plotting service. Similarly, do not wait for your computer's hard drive to crash to test your backup tape system.

Delivering architectural services today requires a dependence on computers more than ever before, and accepting the consequences when computers fail. And fail they will. It is not a question of if, but a question of when. The important issue is shielding the unreliability of software and hardware from clients.

CHAPTER

3

Technology Training and Education

TRAINING MYTHS AND REALITIES

> *"Ironically, training is one of the first items to be eliminated whenever organizations try to control costs. If top management lacks the strategic and long-term vision necessary to help their organizations achieve the potential of these new systems, they may have a difficult time justifying training costs, especially during slow economic periods. It's a dangerously short-sighted perspective."*
>
> **David Jordani, FAIA**

The desktop computer is a powerful and versatile tool, yet it provides little value without a talented, motivated, and well-prepared person at the keyboard. Some architectural firms invest more time and financial resources upgrading what is attached to the keyboard instead of who sits in front of it. Although new architectural graduates are better prepared than ever, and computer tools are easier to use than ever, technology education is still one of the most important components of implementing technology within the architectural firm. Technology education must extend beyond button pushing and training manuals, and encourage people to be curious, take initiative, solve problems, and adapt.

One of biggest myths about technology training is that individuals who receive formal classroom instruction in the use of a software program (often receiving an official certificate upon completion) can be officially labeled "trained." It is possible for those formally introduced to a software program via a training class not to be trained because they don't use the software regularly. Conversely, it is possible for those who have never taken a training class for a software application to learn it on their own. Complex software programs, especially CAD, can require hundreds of hours of project work before the learning curve flattens.

Most software training centers present certificates to people who successfully complete a class or pass a software exam. My advice? Discard them. A person's success in learning software tools cannot be measured by memorization or test scores. People usually value their certificates when their managers or supervisors don't understand the technology or don't appreciate their skill level. People must be evaluated by what they *produce* using technology, not by how well they *know* technology. A training certificate has little to do with that evaluation.

Indeed, the term training, as applied to technology, is somewhat of a misnomer. Training is the process of learning a finite, fixed set of knowledge or skills. Education is the process of learning how to learn and is a better term to describe the acquisition of new technology skills. Training is an event; education is a process. In fact, technology education and professional continuing education are similar in several ways:

1. An architect doesn't become proficient by attending classes on architecture, although that certainly provides an excellent starting point. An architect becomes proficient by practicing architecture. Similarly, an architect becomes proficient at using technology by using it. Training classes can provide a good jump start, but there are no other shortcuts.

2. Talent and aptitude matter a lot. No amount of training, coaching, economic incentives, motivational therapy, or other forms of education will completely overcome a lack of talent or aptitude. A few people will never use computer tools effectively, and that is okay, if they can provide value in other ways.

3. Technology education, like architectural education, is a lifelong process. The most effective teaching tool is not a classroom, but the socializing of experience between architects within the firm.

"Universal truths are impossible in a discipline as new and fresh as computer-aided design. There can be no replacement for experience. All else should be regarded as educated guessing."
NICHOLAS WEINGARTEN, FAIA

There are four basic ways of learning: learning by instruction, learning by example, learning by doing (preferably by immersion), and learning by failing. Failing is not the most efficient form of training, but if it is turned into a positive experience, it is certainly the most memorable and effective. Failing helps define boundaries—what can be termed "drawing the box." Often, you don't know where the boundaries are until you have bounced off them.

TRAINING RESOURCES

Should an architectural firm use internal or external training resources? The answer is yes. Mainstream business software, such as spreadsheets and word processing programs, are good candidates for outside training. More complex software programs or those that are more closely linked to professional service products, work processes, and information guidelines—such as CAD or specialized project management tools—are usually better taught in house. Off-the-shelf training programs introduce the features of a software program but do so outside of the context of your office's information work flow.

Many training and education resources are available to architects. They are listed below roughly in order of value:

1. Actual project experience using technology alongside experienced users
2. The socialized experiences of others inside and outside the firm
3. Help files, tutorials, and "wizards" provided within software programs
4. Formal classroom instruction
5. Self-paced video instruction
6. On-line services, software support, and technology user forums available on CompuServe, America On-Line, and others
7. Printed software documentation
8. Broadcast video education (Computer Chronicles, Microsoft TV, Oracle TV, et al.)

Some specialized on-line services can provide a useful resource to people learning about new software or hardware. CompuServe, America On-Line, and others offer product-specific forums sponsored by technology vendors, allowing people to dial in and share questions or answers with support staff and with each other. AIA Online, the private on-line service of the American Institute of Architects, also includes a technology forum, in which architects share their technology experiences with one another using a wide variety of hardware and software. The practical value of such on-line technology forums is difficult to measure, and depends on the type of software in question and the amount of on-line activity relating to it. Often, forums are simply a way to find other people with similar problems and interests, and with whom more traditional communications can take place (i.e., phone calls).

"It's simple. . . . We either get used to thinking about the subtle processes of learning and sharing knowledge in dispersed, transient networks. Or we perish."
TOM PETERS

Software developers such as Microsoft and Oracle are also producing digital video broadcasts as an education resource to cutomers. Via satellite, the companies broadcast training programs and new product introductions which can be picked up at no cost by anyone with an 18-inch digital satellite dish. Some larger firms find satellite training programs a good value, compared to outside training programs costing hundreds of dollars per individual. The major disadvantage of video training, in both broadcast and recorded formats, is that video is not yet a truly interactive medium.

DISCOVERABILITY

Over a decade has passed since the introduction of the Macintosh, the first high-volume personal computer to employ a graphical user interface, including icons, dialog boxes, pull-down menus, and overlapping windows. Based on research done at Xerox's Palo Alto Research Center in the late 1970s, the Macintosh dramatically improved the accessibility of computers for everyone, and has since influenced virtually every other personal computer, from Windows PCs to UNIX workstations to hand-held devices.

Over a decade has passed, but computers are still too hard to use. Some experts have predicted that computers will provide their ultimate value only when they are as easy to use as the telephone. The telephone, in fact, is occasionally cited as a good example of transparent user interface design. The user doesn't have to know how a phone call is routed from one destination to another, just that they need to push a few buttons, wait for a ring and an answer, and start talking. The key features: simplicity, speed, and reliability.

Unfortunately, the phone is a terrible example of user interface design when used for anything other than simple, direct phone calls. Most home phones are simple enough to use, but what about phones at the office? Have you set up a conference call recently? Do you know how to "call forward" your extension to another phone? If you are like many architects, you probably have difficulty remembering how to do these things. If your phone system tracks billable long-distance phone calls using project number prefixes, the key-in sequences can be slow and awkward. Speed dialing helps, but most people keep a list of speed-dial numbers taped to the phone or posted nearby, and often don't know how to set up new speed-dial numbers. Have you ever had to make a long-distance call from another phone system? Most likely, you had to ask for help.

The same ingredient is missing from both office telephone systems and many computer software programs: discoverability. Discoverability means that people should be able to figure out how to use a tool by themselves—not by watching training videos, or using help systems, or stepping through tutorials, or reading documentation—but simply by *using the tool*. Features should be self-evident.

The absence of discoverability is exactly why the digital clocks on many older VCRs still blink 12:00 to this day. A few years ago I visited the home of someone who actually *taped the instruction manual over the blinking VCR clock* instead of reading the manual. Although most people might think it was a symptom of technological phobia, this defiant act of protest was actually quite understandable. Who, after all, wants to peruse a 40-page manual in order to set a clock? For personal computers to become ordinary household and business appliances, they will have to exceed, not just match, the ease of use of telephones, televisions, audio systems, and VCRs.

Although still hobbled by the need for compatibility with older versions of Windows and DOS, Windows 95 is an important step forward in discoverability. Over the past decade, Microsoft's usability researchers learned what many architects who have trained other architects in the use of computers have known for quite some time: many features that have long been associated with ease of use, such as double clicking on an icon to launch a software program or start a procedure, are neither intuitive nor discoverable. Some nifty and productive features of Windows 3.1, such as using the Alt-Tab key sequence to quickly switch between different software applications, were rarely used by most people because they were not discoverable. The only way to learn about the features was to read the entire software manual or accidentally observe someone else use them.

Discoverability is an important attribute of good software programs. Discoverable software results in lower training costs and less distracted, more effective users. Indeed, one of the best ways to lower your firm's training costs is to evaluate software tools literally out of the box, without opening any documentation. If you cannot learn the software without referring to the documentation, the software has not been designed well or is too complex. Unfortunately, few software programs used by architects, and certainly no architectural CAD software program, satisfy this criterion.

In the not too distant future, we will remember the old days when a person actually had to read a manual in order to use a software program effectively. Eventually, the phrase "software documentation" will be an oxymoron.

WHO PAYS FOR EDUCATION?

One question that architectural firms must answer is how the responsibility for and cost of technology education is shared between the firm and the individual (assuming, of course, the firm is not a sole proprietorship).

The answer is different than it was ten years ago. In the early 1980s, for example, when most CAD software was available only on expensive, minicomputer-based turn-key systems, and before PC-based CAD software arrived in useful versions, the use of CAD was primarily restricted to large architectural firms. In those days, most firms underwrote virtually all of the training costs for their employees.

Today, the rules of the game have changed. As desktop computers have become a day-to-day part of the architectural practice, and more personal computers are being sold for home use than for business use, it is no longer appropriate for a firm to underwrite the entire cost of technology education for employees. As the average number of software applications used by architectural firms continues to rise, many smaller firms simply cannot afford to train everyone in the various software programs they may eventually use. Quite often, the missing resource is not money, but time.

While firm owners should understand the value of a well-educated staff and invest appropriately, employees also must take the initiative to prepare for the changing requirements of their jobs. Technology training and education should be a shared expense.

At ZGF, the time and expense burden of technology education is shared by the firm and the employee, and training resources provided by the firm are described clearly to everyone. These resources include:

1. Lunchtime technology seminars every week
2. Special in-house training classes as required
3. Software documentation in libraries available for checkout by individuals
4. On-line help systems for all ZGF software programs
5. Reimbursement for approved outside training classes
6. Reimbursement for home-PC modems
7. Twenty-four-hour-a-day access to all hardware and software programs

The key message: the firm provides the resources, but it is the individual's responsibility to take advantage of them to improve skills and provide value. The weekly lunchtime seminars are as much discussion as presentation and have proven quite popular. No one is required to attend; everyone is invited to attend. The presenters and agendas differ each week, and people choose to attend based on their interests and needs. Each individual takes ownership of upgrading his or her skills, and everyone is presented a level playing field in terms of access to technology and training resources.

EDUCATING THE MANAGERS

In a busy firm, training and education tend to be directed toward those with the most immediate need. As a result, project managers or principals who are not directly involved in the day-to-day use of computer technology, particularly CAD, are often left out of the training and education loop. This education gap between manager and employee is a common problem, particularly within larger firms. Educating managers is as important as educating users; indeed, managers must *become* users.

When managers are asked what they don't like about computer technology, particularly CAD, a common complaint is loss of control. Indeed, design and construction drawings that used to reside in a flat file, or were taped to a drafting board, available for walk-by review at any time, are now encapsulated in digital formats, accessible and understandable only to those who hold the key.

But the need for manager education extends far beyond their own anxiety and stress reduction. Attaining quality and productivity improvements demands that managers understand technology's new benchmarks, and that their expectations are aligned with reality. It is not uncommon for people, sometimes quite unconsciously, to use their one-sided knowledge of the computer as their best defense of inadequate work. A manager, for example, asking why a drawing looks lousy, might hear "It's the plotter" or "The CAD software can't do it any better."

"To err is human—and to blame it on a computer is even more so."
ORBEN'S CURRENT COMEDY

The uninformed manager, who is in no position to question the explanation or provide direction on how to solve the problem, silently accepts it. Not only does quality stagnate, but the manager is in a weakened position to judge the performance of the employee. Little incentive exists for people to invest their own time in learning the software more thoroughly if their supervisor may not appreciate the difference. In such a case, technology may be viewed as a disposable skill, and employees will focus their attention elsewhere. What occasionally happens to employees who use technology on a regular basis, but whose immediate supervisor is not well versed in the tools being used, is the third-party performance review. In such a review, the evaluation of an individual's performance is not made by a manager but by another individual who understands the technology issues and acts as an interpreter.

This is not a good situation, by any measure. Managers must know enough about technology to make an informed judgment about the performance of employees. Managers must strive to learn about the quality and productivity of work produced by others in the firm using the same tools, and determine appropriate benchmarks. For example, a manager who expects that CAD will provide an overall 10 percent productivity improvement, when most projects within the firm have experienced 20 to 30 percent, is not doing her job. Finally, managers should understand the value of their own technology education to the firm's overall performance and competitiveness.

Although they need not master every software application used by project teams, project managers should understand at least:

- The organization of the network file system, including heirarchy and file-naming conventions
- The organization of CAD documents, including layers, components, and reference files
- The scope of the firm's digital knowledge base and available on-line resources
- The pace at which digital information is developed and reproduced on a typical job
- The logistical issues and liabilities of sharing digital data with clients and third parties
- The availability of talent within the firm for a given task involving technology

At a minimum, a project manager should know how to:

- Locate a document in the computer file system
- Open a document, using the application used to create it
- Perform basic edits (margin notes or redmarks)
- Print or plot a document or drawing
- Comfortably use internal and external E-mail, messaging, and on-line services

These lists are minimum guidelines, intended for managers who are not involved in the day-to-day production of documents but instead spend the majority of their time as the primary client contact and/or financial manager of the project. Managers of smaller projects, or those who play a more active role in the day-to-day production of the work, should understand and use computer tools as well as the typical project team member.

Most people can only absorb so much technology so fast. Most college graduates today can absorb new tools quickly, but older, more experienced practitioners don't, and can't. Avoid upset stomachs by aligning the pace of training and education with the person's ability to swallow and digest new information.

"Think back to your best teachers. If you are a teacher, think of your best students. Or, consider your most admired engineer, scientist, or artist—living or dead. What do they all have in common? Passion . . . Certainly, some learning derives from telling a good story. We all remember our good teachers. But a major measure of learning results from exploration, from reinventing the wheel and finding out for yourself."
NICHOLAS NEGROPONTE

EDUCATING THE EDUCATORS

Firms that provide in-house education for their staff realize an additional benefit: improving the organizational and communication skills of those who teach. Such teaching takes place not only in training classes but, more importantly, in interactions between beginners and expert users. People who participate in in-house education should understand that the goal is not only to assist others in achieving high productivity, but also to encourage self-sufficiency, ingenuity, and creativity.

Although teachers should never discourage anyone from learning as much as they want to, they should recognize a point of diminishing returns when it comes to technology trivia and jargon. At ZGF, for example, understanding how computer hardware and software works is part of my job. I actually know what a write-back cache is, what an Ethernet collision is, and what linked lists and pointers in C programs are. There are probably a few of you reading this book who also know what those things are, and many more of you who don't.

I know obscure facts such as these for two reasons. Most are accidental fallout from my continuing effort to study and learn about new technology and how to integrate it into the firm. These facts sometimes (but not too often) provide context for new information and help me navigate through technology advertisements and marketing literature couched in jargon. In addition, I actually enjoy knowing trivial facts about how things work (that recessive nerd gene again) in the same way I enjoy remembering bits of old *Star Trek* dialog. These facts are fun to know but certainly not required to get work done. The average, typical, "normal" person has absolutely no need for this type of information.

Think about it for a moment: when you pick up the phone and make a call, do you know what really happens? Do you know how telephone circuits and switches work, allowing you to press a few buttons and cause one—and only one—of a *billion* phones on the planet to ring in response? Do you know if your voice signal is transmitted underground on fiber optic cables, or bounced off satellites, or both? Is it translated into digital bits, or does it remain an analog signal? It might be fun to know the answers. Do you need to know the answers to use a phone? Of course not.

In his book, *Information Anxiety,* Richard Saul Wurman describes symptoms of people who are overloaded with too much information. These symptoms are not unusual for people who are learning new computer tools and should be recognized and understood by those who teach. Note how you can substitute "new software feature" for "new story," or "computer" for "VCR" or "appliance," and the symptoms make just as much sense:

Symptoms of information anxiety:

- Nodding your head knowingly when someone mentions a book, artist, or story that you have never heard before
- Finding that you are unable to explain something that you thought you understood
- Refusing to buy a new appliance or piece of equipment because you are afraid you won't be able to operate it
- Feeling depressed because you don't know what all of the buttons on your VCR are for
- Buying high-tech electronics because you feel that, through osmosis, you'll become more technologically knowledgeable
- Thinking that the person next to you understands everything you don't
- Being too afraid or too embarrassed to say, "I don't know"

"Neophytes attempting to be creative in any field of endeavor frequently possess an advantage born of their very innocence. Rather than knowing and inherently accepting the established rules, newcomers are able to roam their new creative territory without feeling the hindrance of 'the way it's done'. . . . When people introduced to computing begin sentences with 'why can't you just . . .' you always know what will follow: 'What's that backslash for?' 'Why can't the computer just find the file you wrote last week?' 'What does *file already exists* mean?' We quickly label these people 'computer illiterate' as a defense against our subconscious acknowledgment that they are correct. Our arrogant egos, in accepting the way things are, mistakenly defend them as the way they should be."

STEVE GIBSON

While avoiding the discouraging answer "you don't need to know that," technology educators nevertheless should keep the focus of their presentations on that which will actually contribute to people getting their job done. Digital trivia and technology jargon do not qualify as useful knowledge.

WHEN TECHNOLOGY DOESN'T WORK

Even when architects do their homework before buying hardware and software, and invest appropriately in maintenance and upgrades, computers sometimes fail to do what is expected of them—it is not a question of if, but when and how often. In my job, I occasionally get to answer questions about computer hardware and software when they do not function as advertised or expected. One of my favorite questions is "Why?" One of my favorite answers is "I have no idea."

I really do not know why AutoCAD does not allow you to scale elements nonuniformly (i.e., enlarge or shrink elements in one direction more than the other). I know the mathematical algorithms are simple, but you will have to ask Autodesk's programmers or product managers why AutoCAD does not work that way. I do not know why the Hewlett-Packard DesignJet650C color plotter gives up when you try to plot a document containing PostScript fonts using HP's Windows driver. I do know that HP knows about the problem and is working on it. I do not know why "this Windows application has stopped responding to the system" at 4:30 PM, but not at 4:35 PM, when the same operation was performed on the same file using the same program on the same machine. And I am not inclined to spend much time figuring out why.

The real issue is whether, like deer in headlights, people freeze in the face of technology's infrequent failure. Technology does fail, and it will not always tell you exactly why. Backup and redundancy is one measure of protection; another is having confidence to get on with your work and, if necessary, seeking another route. This confidence is an attribute of people who are taught to not be intimidated by computers, but to demand more from them and learn how to distinguish between serious problems and infrequent (yet irritating) bugs. Instead of a blank stare, I would rather hear from someone: "What a dumb error message!" or "What a crummy piece of software!"

Everyone should understand that while frequent failures are not acceptable, no computer is 100 percent reliable. If a computer crashes once a year, ignore it. Once a month—take notes, but don't lose sleep. Once a day—keep a detailed record and seek in-house assistance in trying to isolate the problem before calling service or support. Once an hour—get on the phone.

Honestly acknowledging technology's current limitations, combined with anticipating (but not hyping) technology's future opportunities, is a far better way to motivate people than feigning enthusiasm about tools that do not quite work the way they should.

CAD TRAINING

CAD software remains one of the most complicated and difficult applications that architects learn to use, particularly 3D model building and visualization tools, and typically requires the largest investment in training and education. A few special issues are worth mentioning.

Typically, successful CAD training generally requires not only an introductory training class, but hands-on work on a regular basis for the next several months. It is impossible for people to learn all the capabilities of a CAD program in a one-day or one-week period. The transition from thinking about doing to doing and the development of planning and organizational skills takes time.

After the training class, each person should be assigned to work alongside a more experienced CAD user on his/her first project. This buddy system is useful both in helping the newly trained person acquire additional skills and in monitoring his/her progress.

There are two important points to keep in mind:

1. The ultimate skill level of a person depends highly on the amount of regular CAD use (i.e., 15 to 20 hours per week) following the initial training class. CAD training is a period that extends 300 to 500 hours or more after the formal introduction, and really never ends. Illustration 3.1 shows a typical CAD training time line.

2. Not everyone trained in CAD is ultimately successful using it. CAD is, and always will be, more complicated than manual drafting. Strong left-brains tend to do better. Disorga-

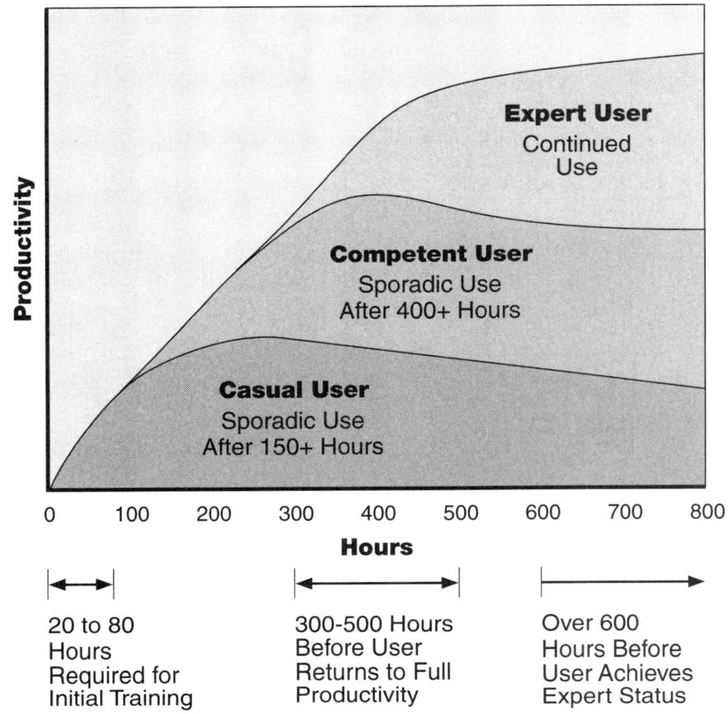

Illustration 3.1 CAD training time line.

nized people will fail. Do not expect everyone to be as good as your best user.

In general, try to distribute CAD work among your staff, even if it means short-term sacrifices in productivity. Although it is tempting to always put the best CAD users in front of the keyboard, especially during fire drills, it is a poor long-term strategy. Most full-time CAD users inevitably (and justifiably) feel shortchanged and burned out, and newer staff will not be motivated to use CAD well.

If you are a manager or firm owner, try to ensure that your staff does not view CAD as a disposable skill, to be learned and then discarded on the way to project management responsibilities. You can do this by not treating CAD as a black box or service bureau, by showing interest in the skills of your CAD users, and by reminding your staff that your firm expects everyone at all levels to be conversant with technology.

For firms who have not yet developed a formal CAD training program within their firm, David Jordani, FAIA, Executive Director of the CADD Management Institute, offers the following practical ten-step outline for implementation:

1. Justify and budget the training program
2. Identify the staff who should be trained
3. Identify training sources
    a. Vendor or authorized third party
    b. Alternate third party (consultants)
    c. In-house training
    d. Sources for system management training (more difficult)
    e. Sources for senior management training (most difficult)
4. Consider alternative training methods
    a. Hands-on, with instructor
    b. Self-directed training
5. Determine training scope
    a. Training for all tasks
    b. Training for specific tasks only
6. Assess schedule and workload before training
7. Identify projects to reinforce training
8. Schedule followup training
9. Plan for those who don't adapt
10. Evaluate the effectiveness of training programs

Five simple tips for new CAD users:

1. **Plan ahead**
2. **Document project organization**
3. **Share and recycle information whenever possible**
4. **No eyeballing allowed**
5. **If in doubt, ask**

GETTING STARTED

Technology literacy is absolutely crucial to effectively applying technology within the architectural firm. At least as much preparation and financial resources should be directed toward educating people as purchasing hardware and software. Nicholas Weingarten, FAIA, vice-president of Premisys Corporation, a software development firm in Chicago, observes that most architectural firms that effectively use technology devote about a third of their financial resources to hardware and software, a third to system management and support, and a third to training and education. This simple guideline is an excellent way for firms to measure their investment in technology training and education.

Fortunately, as computer technology continues to enter the educational mainstream, including architecture colleges and universities, the burden on the architectural firm to educate their employees in the use of computer tools should continue to decline. However, technology is a moving target. Every year new software and hardware is introduced that provides increased value to architects and clients. The training and education problem that faces most firms, in fact, is not the student intern, but the firm's 5- to 25-year employees. As technology continues to evolve, the burden on the firm of technology training and education will shrink but never disappear completely. Again, it is a process, not an event.

CHAPTER

4

Tools of the Architect

VISUALIZING DIGITAL TOOLS

"The art of design can associate itself with scientific skill, and do so without an inferiority complex."

Richard Neutra

When asked about how they use computers in their practices, most architects respond by ticking off the categories of software applications they use: CAD, word processing, desktop publishing, spreadsheets, databases, and so on. Specific software titles, such as Excel, WordPerfect, or FileMaker Pro, may or may not accompany the categories. (A few architects still confuse software titles with software categories, such as using the term "AutoCAD" to describe generic computer-aided design, like Kleenex, Velcro, and Xerox.)

Software category is often the most convenient organizational model for people to use when talking about computer tools because it reflects how desktop software is packaged and sold. During the 1980s, the functional dividing lines between software applications were clear: spreadsheets were for numerical and financial modeling, word processors were for creating and editing written documents, databases were for organizing, filtering, and reporting information in lists and tables, and CAD systems were for producing design and construction documents. It certainly makes practical sense to talk about software in the same way in which they are packaged for consumption, and provides a common ground for communication.

Some architects document how they use computer technology in a matrix comparing tools to tasks or departments, such as design, production, specifications, project management, estimating, accounting, marketing, and administrative support. (Ill. 4.1) In theory, a large, densely populated matrix indicates a more automated firm. In reality, such a matrix is usually evidence of unnecessary complexity. The goal is not to fill up the matrix, but to be smart about which tools make the most sense for a given task or process . In general, the fewer tools used, the better.

Yet another way to look at technology is outlined in *Digital Design Media*, an excellent conceptual guide to design-oriented computer tools coauthored by William Mitchell, dean of the School of Architecture and Planning at MIT, and Malcolm McCullough, associate professor of Architecture at the Harvard

	Design	Drafting	Specifications	Project management	Business	Estimating	Business development	Interiors	Administrative	Personnel	Contracts
Word processing			●	●	●	●	●		●	●	●
Spreadsheets	●				●					●	●
Flat file database	●	●						●		●	
Relational database		●		●	●	●					
Slide preparation	●						●				
Project scheduling		●	●	●	●	●		●			●
Contact management	●			●		●	●			●	
Calendar	●	●	●	●	●	●	●	●	●	●	●
Multimedia	●						●				
E-mail	●	●	●	●	●	●	●	●	●	●	●
Messaging				●						●	
Internet browsing			●			●				●	
Illustration software	●				●		●	●			
Two-dimensional CAD	●	●	●	●		●		●			
Three-dimensional CAD	●	●	●	●		●		●			
Visualization	●						●	●			
Animation	●						●	●			
Virtual reality	●						●	●			
Desktop publishing	●	●			●		●	●		●	

Illustration 4.1 *Software/task matrix.*

University School of Design. *Digitial Design Media* categorizes software tools by media "dimension." Excluding practical computation and numerical modeling tools such as databases and spreadsheets, Mitchell and McCullough organize their discussion of software not by category or task, but by the dimension of the media manipulated by the software as follows:

- One-dimensional media include words, text, and sounds
- Two-dimensional media include images, drafted lines, polygons, plans, and maps
- Three-dimensional media include lines in space, surfaces, renderings, and assemblies of solids
- Multidimensional media include motion models, animation, and hypermedia

A software program's media dimension is useful to understand because it often telegraphs its difficulty of use. In general, the higher the media dimension, the higher the investment required to learn and master the tool. The good news is that most architects are already well versed at visualizing three-dimensional space and movement through it, so the added investment is not as large as one might expect. The bad news is that many software tools no longer cleanly dovetail into the conceptual model of media dimension.

Today, the boundaries between software application types and their feature sets are increasingly blurred. Most popular word processors today include capabilities that only a few years ago were the exclusive domain of desktop publishing programs, such as merging or linking drawings and images within documents. Similarly, most popular spreadsheet programs today provide basic database tools, such as sorting, querying, and reporting, as well as graphics tools that make them useful for producing presentation-quality organization charts or project schedules. Many traditional business applications are acquiring multimedia features, such as inserting recorded sounds or animations within written documents, using new object-oriented tools such as OLE and OpenDoc (described later in this chapter). Finally, the boundaries between CAD software and illustration software are also dissolving, exemplified by new hybrid products such as Visio Technical.

Table 4.1 describes an organizational framework for digital tools and provides an information context that should be meaningful and understandable to most architects. The table is not

Table 4.1 is an organizational framework for discussing the *vocabulary* of digital tools, not a framework for their *implementation.* As discussed in Chapter 2, automating a process is more important than automating individual tasks.

intended to be a comprehensive list of the tasks architects perform or the tools we use. Every practicing architect knows that the service delivery process, even for the simplest projects, is nonlinear and rarely subdivides so cleanly.

Table 4.1 should not be interpreted as implying that each of the digital tools can or should be applied only to its corresponding task. A spreadsheet, for example, is used not only for information management in many architectural firms, but also for diagrams, presentations, and publications. Similarly, an easy-to-use, graphically robust CAD program (still a rare species) can alleviate the need for a separate illustration tool.

Note that the digital tools are not arranged in the traditional sequence of programming, schematic design, design develop-

Table 4.1 Tasks and Tools of the Architect

TASK	PHYSICAL TOOL	PHYSICAL MEDIA	DIGITAL TOOL	DIGITAL MEDIA
Sketches	Felt pen	Napkin, trace	Image editing	Bitmap
Diagrams	Magic Marker	Vellum, trace	Illustration	2D graphics
Model building	Exacto knife, saw, glue	Foamcore, wood, whiteboard	3D CAD	3D surfaces, solids
Visualization	Camera	Prints, slides	Rendering, animation	Bitmap, digital video
Graphic documentation	Pen, pencil	Vellum, mylar	2D/3D CAD	Model drawings, plot drawings
Written documentation	Pen, pencil, typewriter	8.5 × 11 paper	Word processing	Text streams
Information management	Pen, pencil, typewriter	8.5 × 11 paper	Spreadsheets, databases	Tables, lists
Publication	Pen, pencil, typewriter	8.5 × 11 paper	Desktop publishing	Composite documents
Presentation	All	All	Multimedia	All
Resource access	Bookshelf	Product catalogs, binders, brochures	On-line services, CD-ROM	All
Communication	Phone, mail, FedEx	All	FAX, E-mail, voice/data messaging	All, digital voice
Archive storage	Tubes, boxes, microfiche	All	Archiving software	Magnetic tape, optical disks

ment, construction documents, and so forth. Digital tools typically span each of these work phases. As a design is documented in CAD during the early schematic phase, for example, at what point does it become a construction document? From the moment of digital conception, when the first line is drawn? In the middle of design development? Or the start of the construction document phase? The answer is that the change never occurs. The digital document contains both representations. Indeed, the flow of digital information within the architectural design process, and the tools we use to manipulate it, often have little to do with how we bill for services. Phases will remain an important part of our work because they provide a sensible structure for defining our scope of services and negotiating fees. But the discussion here of digital tools and media will appropriately focus on what we do, instead of how we get paid for what we do.

HYBRIDS ARE OK

It is important to understand that digital tools are supplements to, not replacements for, physical tools. Despite the promise of the paperless office, digital media do not eliminate physical media, and probably never will. Models and paper drawings still provide an intimacy, spatial resolution, and portability that digital media are not yet equipped to compete with. Illustration 4.2 shows an example of a contour site model cut directly from a three-dimensional CAD drawing using a computer-controlled

Illustration 4.2 *Contour model cut from CAD geometry.*

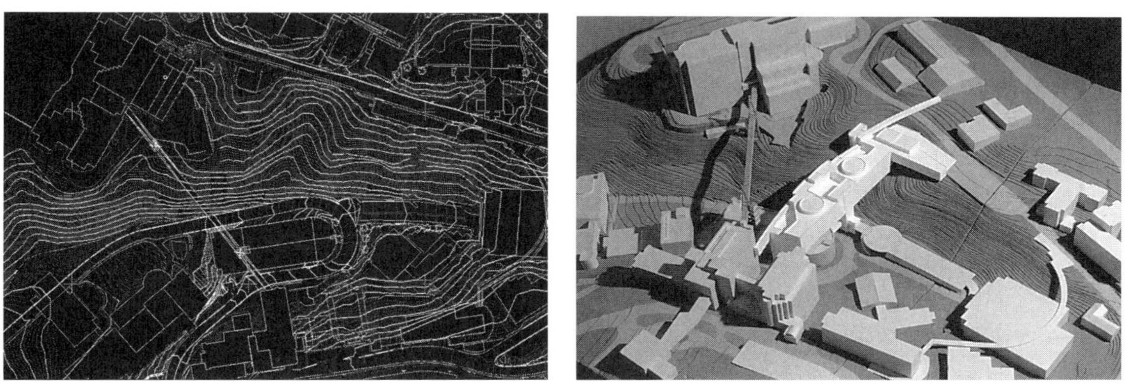

milling machine. Illustration 4.3 shows an example of a physical building model assembled usings "skins" from color CAD plots glued to foamcore.

Digital tools must not only manipulate information using digital media, but also report it on physical media. As a result, printing, plotting, and physical model prototyping will always remain important features of digital tools. In the future, physical media will not disappear, but will be exclusively used for *reporting* information instead of *storing* information.

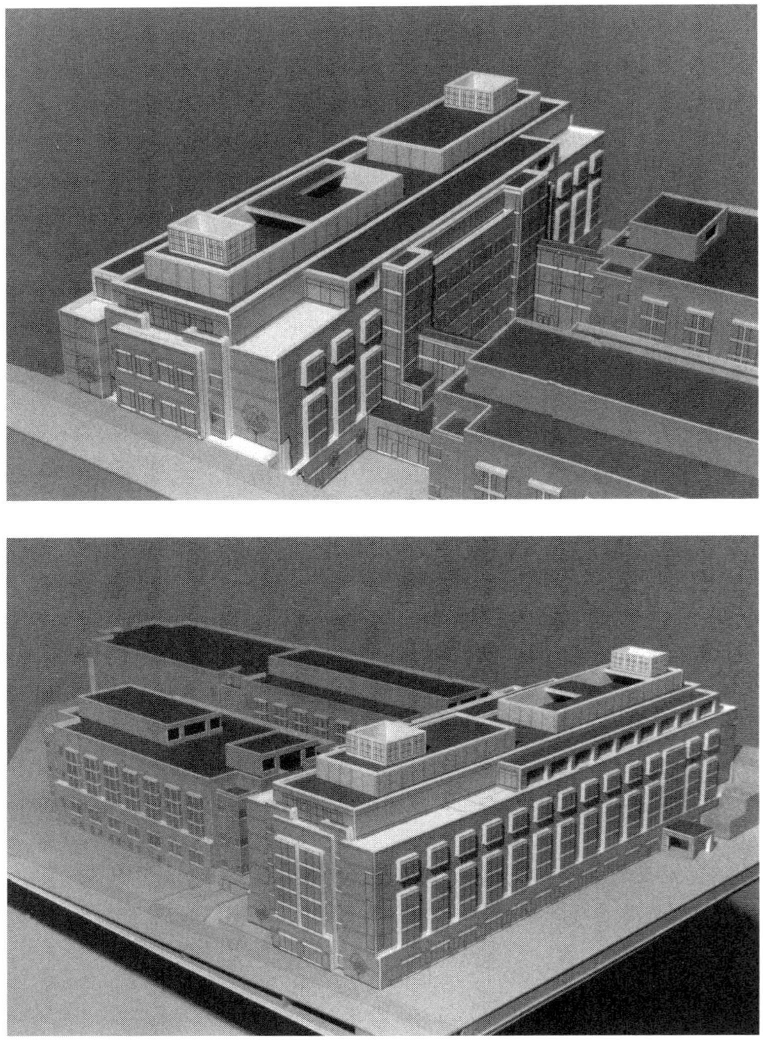

Illustration 4.3 *CAD plots used as "skins" for physical models.*

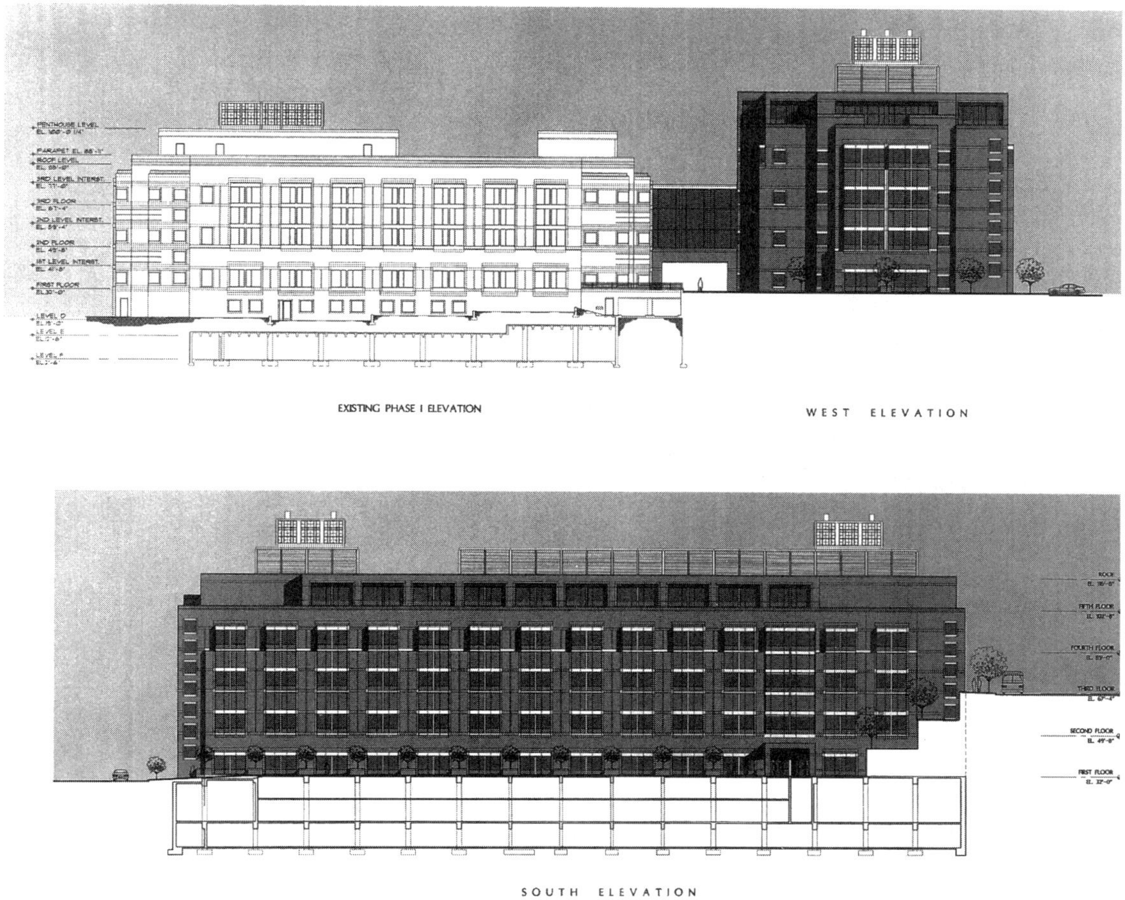

Illustration 4.3 *(Continued)*

Digital and physical media can happily coexist within a task or process, and architects need not exclusively choose between them. In fact, hybrid media are not only acceptable but often preferable. A hand-drawn sketch that is embellished digitally, or a digital drawing that is embellished by hand, is a perfectly ethical, legal, and honorable thing to do, as long as potentially reusable digital information does not become trapped in hybrid formats. Illustration 4.4 is an example.

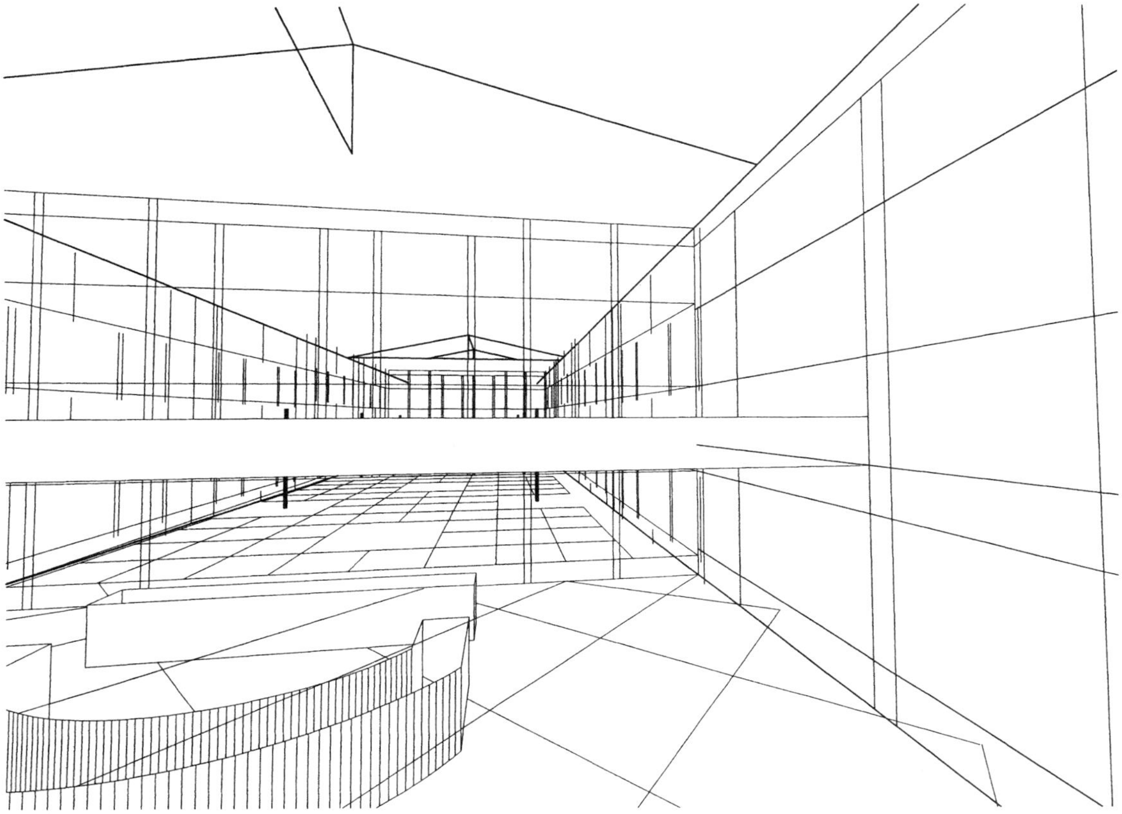

Illustration 4.4 Hybrid perspective sketch.

DIGITAL DESIGN TOOLS

Although most architects are quite willing to tolerate—and even enthusiastically embrace—the use of computers for producing written correspondence, organizing financial data and reporting, managing project schedules, or producing technical documents, some are less willing to allow computers to invade the sacred domain of design. (Part of this resistance is appropriate, since many of the software tools advertised as design tools by their inventors are not design tools at all—an issue which will be discussed shortly.)

Unfortunately, some of the most innovative design tools in use today by architects are not necessarily appropriate for mainstream architectural practice. For example, the use of computers and three-dimensional digitizers at Frank O. Gehry & Associates to model the nonorthogonal geometry of their projects,

such as the Barcelona "Fish" Pavilion, is a fascinating study of appropriately tailoring computer tools to a firm's unique design process and provides compelling evidence that computers do not constrain design. At the same time, the usefulness of Gehry's three-dimensional digitizers, used to capture the geometry of hand-built physical models into digital formats, is directly related to the complex geometry of the firm's buildings and the importance of physical models within the firm's design process.

Illustration 4.4 (Continued)

Significantly, Gehry's office has already delivered on the concept of the three-dimensional digital shop drawing. For the Disney Concert Hall in Los Angeles, the three-dimensional digital models of the curved stone panels were provided to the subcontractor responsible for coordinating the stonecutting and the fabrication of the steel supports. Mockup panels were manufactured directly from the digital model using computer-controlled milling machines. Using a digital model to describe the complex curved surfaces of the stone panels was a wholly sensible approach and far more efficient than attempting to describe the panels with two-dimensional drawings. In fact, the software Gehry's office uses—Catia from Dassault systems—was originally developed for the design of complex curved surfaces, such as aircraft fuselages or automobile bodies. (It should be pointed out that Gehry's use of three-dimensional models and digital shop drawings has not rescued the project from cost overruns nor delays. The low bid for the project came in $80 million over budget, and the project is stalled as of this writing. But the pricing for the curved stone panels was right on target.)

Gehry's innovative methods are sometimes characterized by technology evangelists as prototypes of future practice. For most architects, however, it is much easier to simply build digital models directly using modeling software, rather than build physical models first and digitize them into the computer. Using the architect's three-dimensional digital models as a basis for product manufacture—although perfectly appropriate for Gehry's Prague office building, where literally every piece of glass is a different size and shape—is not necessarily appropriate for simple projects, such as the orthogonal precast panels in a rectangular low-rise office building. The same payoff does not exist. The benefit to the client of sharing digital data between design and manufacture is directly proportional to the geometric complexity of the proposed building.

Architects can learn from the innovative use of digital models at Frank O. Gehry & Associates not by considering them as prototypes of fully descriptive, integrated three-dimensional building models, but in observing how digital media in his office peacefully and synergistically coexist with traditional clay and cardboard media.

To argue that all architects will eventually implement the kinds of tools that Gehry's office appropriately and effectively uses, as some academics and journalists have suggested, ignores the unique nature of the firm's design work and the commercial realities that most architects face in providing mainstream services to clients. The point is that the appropriate use of digital design tools in one practice, however unusual and innovative, does not necessarily mean the tools have widespread practical application.

An additional issue that contributes to the misunderstanding of digital design tools is that some architects associate the term *design* with *three-dimensional*. Many software developers consider the terms to be synonymous, as if adding three-dimensional features to drawing and illustration programs transforms them into design tools. In fact, design can and often should happen on two-dimensional surfaces. Many site concepts, floor plan layouts, and building assemblies are sketched and further refined in two dimensions quite appropriately.

Outstanding design is characterized not only by great concepts, but also by great execution, including the careful analysis of two-dimensional sections, profiles, and details. *The two-dimensional drawing surface is a powerful abstraction that should not be abandoned by architects in search of digital design tools.*

THE DESIGN TOOL DEFINED

Most software programs promoted as design tools are simply illustration, documentation, model building, and visualization tools. Certainly, they are used in the design process. However, parallel rules, triangles, electric erasers, Exacto knifes, and Magic Markers also satisfy that criterion. All are model-building tools and behave as design tools only when they are used interactively by the designer. The bar that defines true digital design tools must be set higher.

A digital design tool must satisfy the following basic criteria (note that the terms *graphics* and *three-dimensional* are nowhere to be seen):

1. A design tool must be used by the designer, not a surrogate
2. A design tool must allow the designer to define relationships between design components that affect the performance or appearance of the design, relative to explicit or implied criteria
3. A design tool must provide interactive (preferably dynamic) feedback concerning the performance or appearance of a design as the designer modifes its geometry

When does a physical model become a design tool, rather than just a visualization or presentation tool? When the designer herself manipulates it, adding a piece here, punching a hole there. With a physical model, the *criterion* of performance is the visual image sought by the designer, to which the physical model is compared. The *relationships* are defined by how the pieces are assembled and attached to each other. The relationships are stored in the physical model only in the sense that some of its pieces are attached to each other and move as a unit.

What are the characteristics of that design experience? They are dynamic feedback (holding the model in one's hand or walking around it); random access (the designer can change the design in arbitrary sequence); linked relationships (if the designer reduces the wall height, the roof drops in response); and iteration (the designer can try one idea after another). Although the language and media involved are different, the design process using computer tools shares similar characteristics.

A design component is defined by three things:

1. The component's static geometry
2. A procedure that generates or transforms the component's geometry based on parameter values provided by the user
3. A procedure that generates or transforms the component's geometry based on its relationships to other components

Optionally, a design component may contain a procedure that seeks "best-fit" solutions based on design criteria. However, for complex design problems, specifying the design criteria to the level of detail necessary to create the "best fit" sometimes can be a self-extinguishing effort. By the time you finish specifying the criteria, you've already solved the problem.

Human intuition and guesswork are often the source of inspired ideas and should not be targeted for extermination within the digital design process.

Where are examples of design components? You don't have to look far! In fact, some simple ones are probably on your desktop computer right now. An associative dimension in a CAD drawing, for example, is a simple design component, as shown in Illustration 4.5. Its graphic representation wholly depends on the location of the geometry that it references, as well as parameters defining its visual appearance, whose values are provided by the user.

The spreadsheet shown in Illustration 4.6, used to determine shared parking requirements based on program areas input by the user, is another example of a design component. The appearance of the chart wholly depends on parameter values provided by the user. The spreadsheet is fully interactive; when a program area is modified, the chart is immediately updated.

By itself, the spreadsheet is a powerful tool for mixed-use projects that must balance parking requirements with program requirements. How can it be extended further? First, with dynamic controls—movable scroll bars or dials could be used instead of fill-in-the-blank forms. As a control is manipulated by the user, the chart would dynamically respond. Second, goal-seeking tools could be included. The spreadsheet's major limitation is that the user must randomly explore solutions and search for patterns in the resulting chart to provide clues about what further adjustments should be made. A goal-seeking spreadsheet would allow the user to ask: "Given the annual amortized construction cost and revenue of each program component, and the limits on maximum area of program and parking, what is the optimum mix of program in terms of net revenue?" Third, the spreadsheet could be linked with the CAD program used to configure program boundaries, so the areas are extracted directly from a site plan drawing, rather than manually entered into the spreadsheet. Based on the shared parking requirements, the software would flag nonconforming site plan layouts.

Each extension to the spreadsheet, of course, increases its complexity and development costs. As a result, you need not wait for perfect digital design tools to start experimenting with them. Created in only a few hours, the spreadsheet shown in Illustration 4.6 allows a designer to explore options quickly with a small fraction of the development effort required to achieve a more refined, integrated tool. It is not only a true design tool, but also a good value.

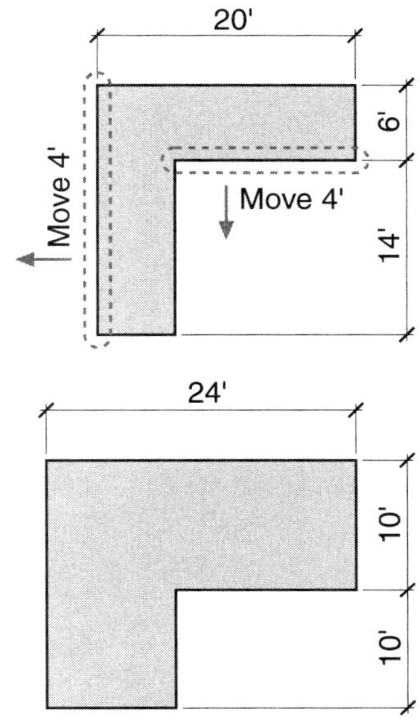

Illustration 4.5 Associative dimension.

THE VALUE OF USER CONTROL

The power of a spreadsheet as a design tool is not that its matrix of cells can contain numerical formulas, but that those formulas can be defined by the user. The grammar of mathematics is fairly straightforward, and devising spreadsheet formulas is an approachable task for most users. *As a general rule, the relation-*

Shared Parking Analysis - Weekday

	Area		Required Parking		Total Spaces
Office	**100,000**	Sq. Ft.	**5**	/1000 Sq. Ft.	500
Retail	**50,000**	Sq. Ft.	**5**	/1000 Sq. Ft.	250
Restaurant	**25,000**	Sq. Ft.	**22**	/1000 Sq. Ft.	550
Theatre	**1,500**	Seats	**0.33**	/Seat	495
Total					1795

Peak Demand Parking Spaces:	**1213**	Space Reduction:	**521**
Peak Demand Increased by 5%:	**1274**	Percent Reduction:	**29%**

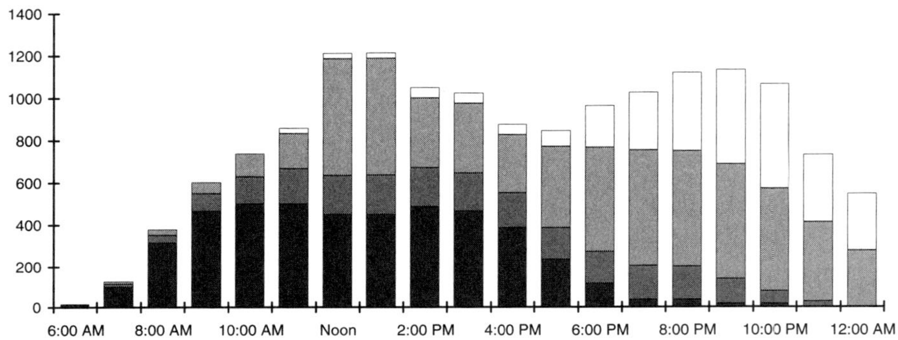

	Office Percent of Peak Demand	Office Parking Demand Spaces	Retail Percent of Peak Demand	Retail Parking Demand Spaces	Restaurant Percent of Peak Demand	Restaurant Parking Demand Spaces	Theatre Percent of Peak Demand	Theatre Parking Demand Spaces	Total Demand Spaces
6:00 AM	3%	15	0%	0	0%	0	0%	0	**15**
7:00 AM	20%	100	6%	15	2%	11	0%	0	**126**
8:00 AM	63%	315	14%	35	5%	27.5	0%	0	**377.5**
9:00 AM	93%	465	33%	82.5	10%	55	0%	0	**602.5**
10:00 AM	100%	500	51%	127.5	20%	110	0%	0	**737.5**
11:00 AM	100%	500	67%	167.5	30%	165	5%	24.75	**857.3**
Noon	90%	450	74%	185	100%	550	5%	24.75	**1210**
1:00 PM	90%	450	75%	187.5	100%	550	5%	24.75	**1212**
2:00 PM	97%	485	74%	185	60%	330	10%	49.5	**1050**
3:00 PM	93%	465	72%	180	60%	330	10%	49.5	**1025**
4:00 PM	77%	385	66%	165	50%	275	10%	49.5	**874.5**
5:00 PM	47%	235	60%	150	70%	385	15%	74.25	**844.3**
6:00 PM	23%	115	62%	155	90%	495	40%	198	**963**
7:00 PM	7%	35	67%	167.5	100%	550	55%	272.25	**1025**
8:00 PM	7%	35	65%	162.5	100%	550	75%	371.25	**1119**
9:00 PM	3%	15	48%	120	100%	550	90%	445.5	**1131**
10:00 PM	3%	15	24%	60	90%	495	100%	495	**1065**
11:00 PM	0%	0	10%	25	70%	385	65%	321.75	**731.8**
12:00 AM	0%	0	0%	0	50%	275	55%	272.25	**547.3**

Illustration 4.6
Shared parking spreadsheet.

Source: Urban Land Institute; "Shared Parking"; Washington D.C., 1983. City of Costa Mesa; "Planning, Zoning and Development Regulations"; Chapter V: Off-Street Parking; Section 13-554: Parking requirements for mixed-use developments; P13-55.1; July, 1985; Linscott, Law & Greensp various published and unpublished studies of theatre parking demand: 1976 through 1986, All Suites parking demand: 1984 through present. Office building type includes medical office. Residential requirements applicable to unassigned spaces only.

ships between design components must be accessible and easy to describe by the designer.

Unfortunately, the customized software development tools of many CAD programs, even macro languages such as AutoCAD's AutoLISP and Dialog Control Language (DCL), are beyond the reasonable comprehension of most people (Ills. 4.7 and 4.8). As a result, most CAD programs do not allow the designer to easily create custom components nor define their relationships. Such development is typically left to in-house programmers or software consultants, and the designer must use parametric macros created for her by someone else.

The major limitation of such predefined components is that they are parametric, not procedural. Most parametric macros in CAD are excellent drafting aids but not true design tools, and suffer from one or more of the following limitations:

1. Parametric macros are not iterative. Components created by parametric macros are simply collections of geometry. They do not remember the procedure or the parameter values that created them.
2. Parametric macros are sequential. Design is not a sequential, prompt-and-answer process. (In some applications,

```
;       Change Entity(ies) Layer
;       Copy from ACAD, change an entity
;       to a specific layer by
;       picking.
(DEFUN CL (/ A1 A2 N INDEX B1 B2 D1 D2 B3)
  (GRAPHSCR)
  (PROMPT "SELECT ENTITIES TO BE CHANGED ")
  (TERPRI)
  (SETQ A1 (SSGET))
  (PROMPT "POINT TO ENTITY ON TARGET LAYER ")
  (TERPRI)
  (SETQ A2 (ENTSEL))
  (SETQ N (SSLENGTH A1))
  (SETQ INDEX 0)
  (SETQ B2 (ENTGET (CAR A2)))
  (SETQ D2 (ASSOC 8 B2))
  (REPEAT N
    (SETQ B1 (ENTGET (SSNAME A1 INDEX)))
    (SETQ D1 (ASSOC 8 B1))
    (SETQ B3 (SUBST D2 D1 B1))
    (ENTMOD B3)
    (SETQ INDEX (+ INDEX 1))
  )
)

(defun c:cl () (cl))
```

Illustration 4.7 *AutoLISP program to change an element's layer to match another element's layer.*

```
scales : dialog {
  label = "ZGF Scale Dialog";
  : row {
    : boxed_radio_column {
      label = "DRAWING SCALE";
      : radio_button { label = "Full Size";            key = "S1";     }
      : radio_button { label = "Half Size";            key = "S2";     }
      : radio_button { label = "3\"     = 1'-0\"";     key = "S4";     }
      : radio_button { label = "1 1/2\" = 1'-0\"";     key = "S8";     }
      : radio_button { label = "1\"     = 1'-0\"";     key = "S12";    }
      : radio_button { label = "3/4\"   = 1'-0\"";     key = "S16";    }
      : radio_button { label = "1/2\"   = 1'-0\"";     key = "S24";    }
      : radio_button { label = "1/4\"   = 1'-0\"";     key = "S48";    }
      : radio_button { label = "1/8\"   = 1'-0\"";     key = "S96";    }
      : radio_button { label = "1/16\"  = 1'-0\"";     key = "S192";   }
      : radio_button { label = "PaperSpace";           key = "PLOT";   }
      : text { label = " "; }
      : toggle { label = "Use Detail Viewports";      key = "DVP";    }
      }
    : column {
    : boxed_radio_column {
      label = "TEXT HEIGHT";
      : radio_button { label =  "8  pt.";               key = "T8";  }
      : radio_button { lab
      : radio_button { lab
      : radio_button { lab
      : radio_button { lab
      : radio_button { lab
      : radio_button { lab
      }
    : boxed_radio_column
      label = "TEXT STYLE
      : radio_button { lab
      : radio_button { lab
      : radio_button { lab
      : radio_button { lab
      }
    }
  }
ok_only;
}
```

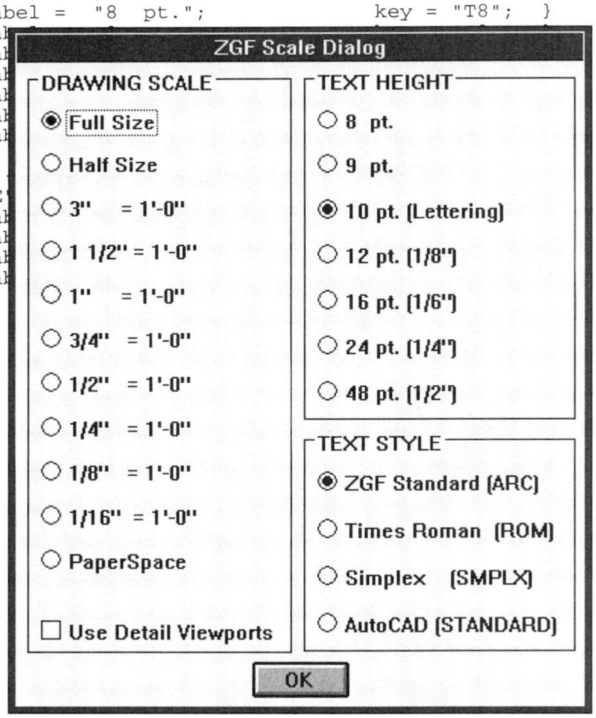

Illustration 4.8 AutoCAD dialog control language and dialog box.

the use of dialog boxes and forms has alleviated this problem.)

3. Parametric macros are not dynamic. As a design parameter is adjusted, little visual or performance feedback is provided. All parameters must be specified before geometry is constructed.
4. Parametric macros usually create "stand-alone" components that are not linked to each other. They use local parameter values, instead of global values, and cannot reference each other.

Components that remember the procedure and parameter values which created them are sometimes called procedural components. For example, each stair generated by Ketiv Technologies' three-dimensional stair layout program (Ills. 4.9 and 4.10) retains its parameter values and can be modified later utilizing the same dialog boxes used to create it.

GENERATIVE DESIGN

Parametric macros and procedural components are simple forms of generative design tools, which can create different design solutions based on parameter values provided by the user. Generative design tools that have built-in constraints are sometimes known as "rule-based" tools and are appropriate in one of two situations.

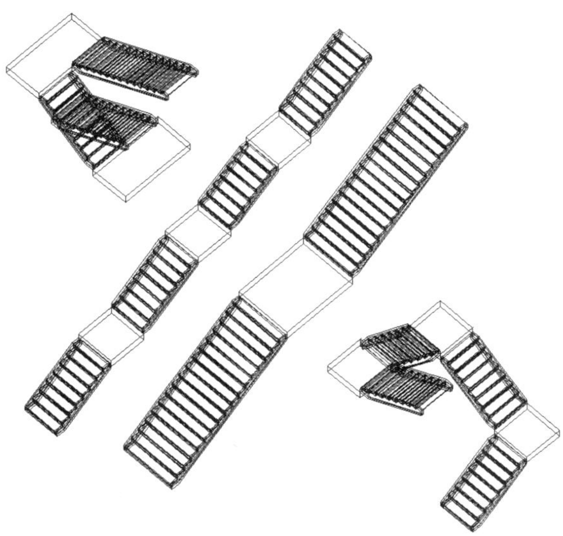

Illustration 4.9 Procedural stairs.

The first involves small-scale, localized design problems with a finite, understandable set of design variables. Examples include designing a wood deck, laying out a kitchen, configuring an exit stair, designing an ADA-compliant bathroom, or selecting a building product. Well-designed generative systems also can be useful in developing solutions for large-scale, highly specialized design

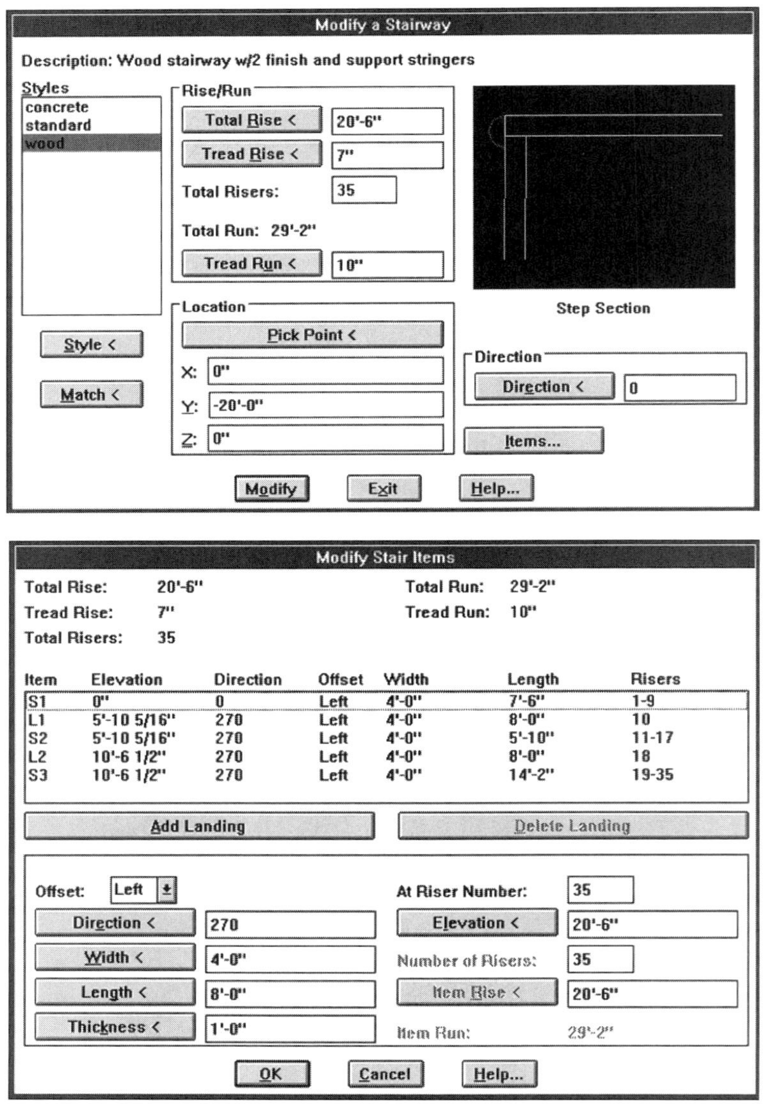

Illustration 4.10 *Procedural stair dialog boxes.*

problems, such as construction scheduling of projects with complex phasing and logistical requirements, where the sheer magnitude of design variables and systems complexity makes the traditional planning process inherently costly and inefficient. Unfortunately, most architectural design problems fall between these two ends of the spectrum, as shown in Illustration 4.11.

Home Depot, for example, provides simple, rule-based wood deck design software for use by customers in their stores. Based on design parameters provided by the customer, the program constructs a deck design and prints a plan, elevation,

Illustration 4.11 Iterative versus generative design.

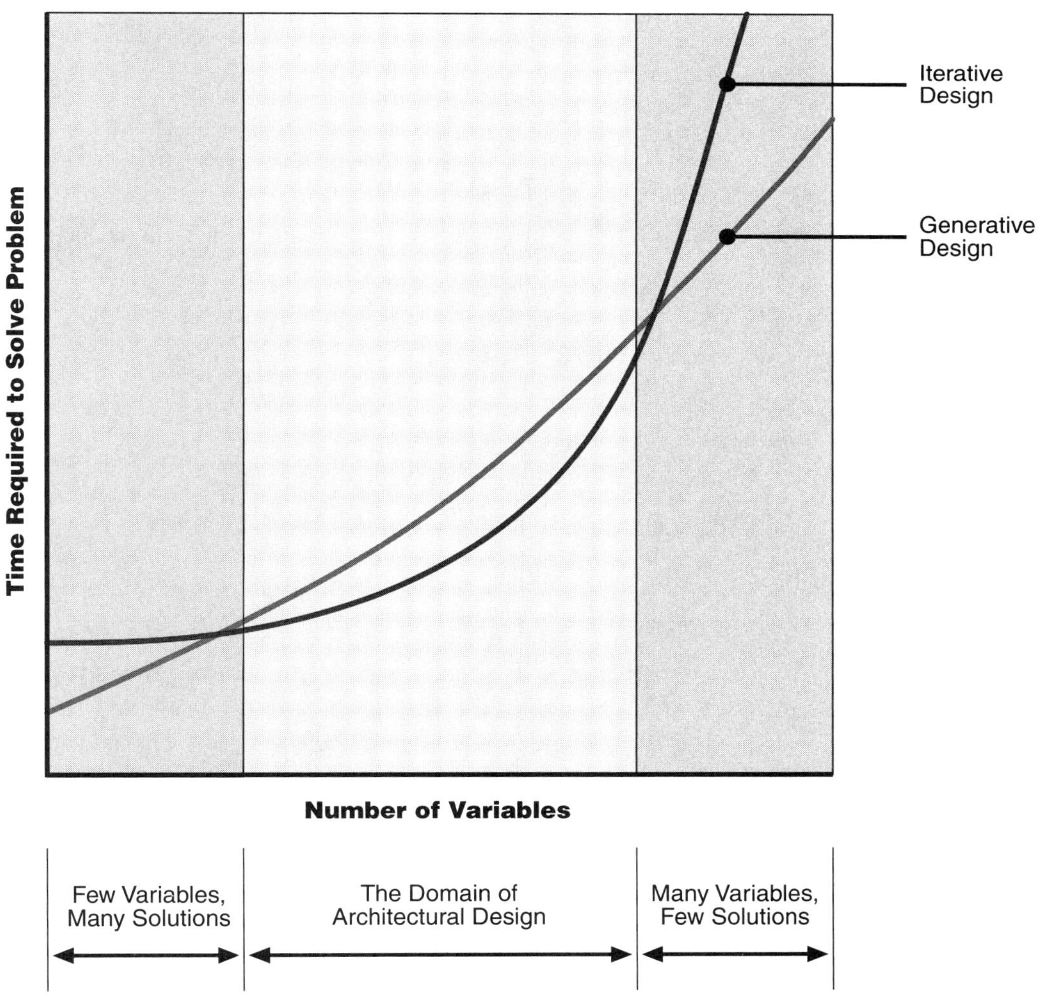

three-dimensional view, and material and parts list. Home Depot's software highlights the limitation of parametric, generative design software: reducing the number of design variables, in order to make the design software easy to use, unreasonably constrains the solution set to a design problem. The options available in Home Depot's deck design software are presented to the customer, who then selects the variables acceptable to him/her. An example is given in the following table:

VARIABLES	ACCEPTABLE VALUES
Wood	Cedar or outdoor
Decking	2 × 4 or 2 × 6
Load	40 or 60 psf
Footing	Precast or poured in place
Maximum height	Up to 12 feet
Railing style	One of three choices
Shape	Rectangle or L configuration
Number of sides touching house	Up to six
Orientation to house	One of six choices
Overall X dimension	No limit
Overall Y dimension	No limit
Partial X dimension (L configuration only)	No limit
Partial Y dimension (L configuration only)	No limit
Number of stairs (one or two) and height of stair	(36 permutations)
Stair style	Two choices

For purposes of illustration, let us assume that for an L configuration deck, only ten values could be selected for the height, and X and Y dimensions of the deck. The software's decision tree would still be able to produce *25 billion* different deck designs, each very similar but slightly different. Are 25 billion similar designs really better than several dozen varied ones?

This is not to say that such design tools are not helpful to consumers. Certainly, Home Depot would not provide them if they were not. But the useful aspect of Home Depot's software is not its rule-based paradigm, but the generation of the materials and parts lists. Again, that task is easier when the construction vocabulary is purposely minimized.

Unless your firm provides high-volume design services based on standard prototypes (e.g., Wal-Marts, log cabins, or mobile homes), do not focus on using rule-based architectural design software. Instead, look for design tools that provide a more practical and visible payoff. Look for tools that help you quickly document, measure, and visualize design iterations, but that do not necessarily generate them for you.

Ordinary design certainly can be derived from a set of rules, but extraordinary design derives from bending them—from intuition, insight, and leaps of faith. Leaps of faith are relatively difficult to encapsulate in digital formats. Most rule-based software programs are most useful as information resources, not as design tools.

GRAPHICAL SPREADSHEETS

Some low-cost software is emerging that provides dynamic, spreadsheet-like functionality within a drawing program. One example is VISIO Technical, which allows a user to create procedural components that are reevaluated each time they are displayed (Ill. 4.12). Using a mouse, a user can grab a procedural component by a handle, drag the handle, and immediately see the result.

VISIO's approach is an interesting one, but it suffers from two limitations. First, the graphics vocabulary provided for creating components is extremely limited: lines, arcs, and elliptical arcs. Second, although the procedure and variables are retained by each component, the variables cannot be shared between multiple documents and are limited to the location, rotation, and scale of the component. VISIO provides a hint of how future digital design tools may work, but so far is best used for designing simple diagrams, not architecture.

VISIO implements an object-oriented approach to illustration, by making the procedure that draws the component part of the component itself. Combining data and procedures is a key part of object-oriented software and is discussed later in this chapter.

DIGITAL CONVERGENCE

Digital convergence is the notion that the computer, television, and telephone are converging into a single communication medium. Indeed, computers (slowly) are gaining the ability to play digital video and sound, and televisions (more slowly) are becoming interactive. Computer software companies, phone companies, cable TV companies, financial institutions, and television and motion picture entertainment companies are viewing

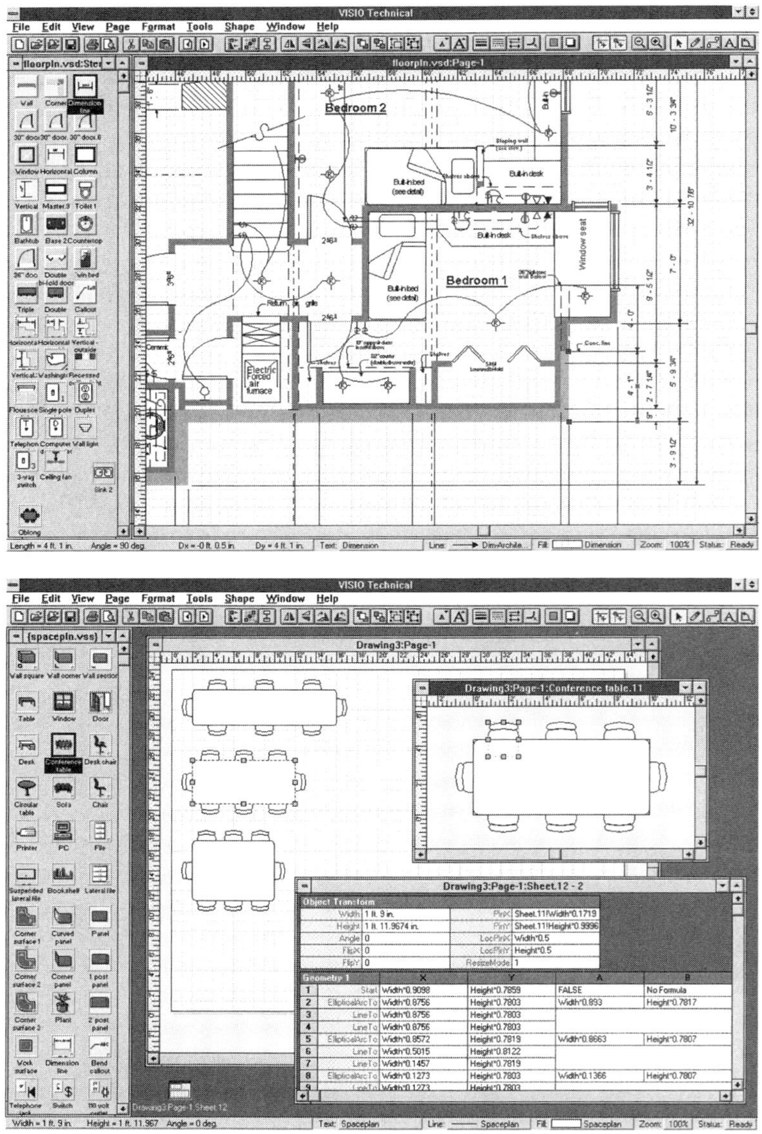

Illustration 4.12 *VISIO Technical.*

each other as potential competitors as never before. New corporate mergers, alliances, and strategic partnerships are announced each day.

In the United States, every one of the seven "Baby Bell" phone companies has received permission from the federal government to offer television services over their phone lines (not the one currently running to your home, but newer, faster lines yet to be installed). At the same time, cable TV companies are exploring ways to provide both TV and phone services over their cable network, which can easily handle both audio and video.

Ironically, the complex corporate maneuvering is the natural by-product of an incredibly simple, supremely elegant fact. At its lowest level, the vocabulary of digital data consists of only two values: 0 and 1. This binary vocabulary is universal, absolute, and will *never* change. In theory, if video signals and telephone signals are stored in digital formats, as strings of 0s and 1s, then given appropriate horsepower, a computer should be able to process them just like word-processing documents and CAD drawings. All bits are created equal.

Each bit can store a single logical value: yes/no or on/off. How are 0s and 1s combined to represent useful information? ASCII, the American Standard Code for Information Interchange, is one of the few universally standard formats in which to store digital data. ASCII defines a method for storing individual characters and numbers as a string of eight bits each. ASCII is really a code that represents alphanumeric characters as decimal values between 0 and 255, which in turn can be represented as a string of eight bits, or one byte. A few examples in ASCII are shown below:

"Bits are the DNA of information."
NICHOLAS NEGROPONTE

CHARACTER(S)	DECIMAL VALUE(S)	BINARY VALUE(S)
The letter *A*	65	01000001
The number *4*	52	00110110
A tab space	9	00001001
The word *HELLO*	72 69 76 76 79	01001000 01000101 01001100 01001100 01001111

ASCII text files can be displayed and printed by almost any computer on the planet, so ASCII is a wonderfully portable way to encapsulate information in digital formats. It is used for PostScript, a popular printing language, as well as the hypermedia documents of the Internet's World Wide Web (discussed in Chapter 10). Text files that are delivered with software programs (such as README.TXT) are ASCII files. ASCII files are also commonly used to exchange information between different CAD programs and database programs. DXF files, for example, are ASCII files that can be viewed from word processor programs. (Instead of a drawing, only the characters of the DXF file are displayed.) Database records, such as names, addresses, and phone numbers, can be exported to an intermediate ASCII file for subsequent import into another database program.

Although ASCII files are portable, they are not very compact. ASCII is an efficient way to store unformatted text, but not an efficient way to store numbers, images, or sounds. A nine-digit integer, for example, requires nine bytes of data in ASCII format. In binary format, most integers (up to 4 billion or so) can be stored in four bytes or fewer by representing them as base two numbers instead of decimal numbers. For example:

			BINARY	**DECIMAL**
			00000000	0
			00000001	1
			00000010	2
			00000011	3
			00000100	4
			00001000	8
			00010000	16
			11111111	255
		11111111	11111111	65,535
	11111111	11111111	11111111	16,777,215
11111111	11111111	11111111	11111111	4,294,967,295

CONVERGENCE OF TOOLS VERSUS DATA

If all digital information is stored as 0s and 1s, why can't Mini-CAD read a PowerDraw file? Why can't AutoCAD read a Microstation file? Although there is general agreement about how to store logical, text, and numerical values in digital formats, different software programs use different *sequences* and *patterns* of these values to store their information. The specific sequence and pattern used by a software program to store information in external files is commonly known as its file format. Although at its basic level, digital data is pure and elegant, software developers have over time invented complicated ways to store information digitally.

The large number of incompatible digital file formats invented by software developers is one reason why software applications do not share information with each other more easily. The problem is made worse because most software developers protect their file formats as intellectual property. Strategically, it is both unfortunate and risky that the digital knowledge bases of architects are encapsulated in proprietary file formats. Architects may own the information and knowledge, but they are locked inside proprietary file formats, to which only the software developer holds the key.

Using reverse engineering techniques, software programmers can figure out most nonencrypted file formats. Reverse engineering file formats is accomplished by iteratively performing operations on a drawing and inspecting the changes in the file as a result of the operation. For example, if you open an AutoCAD drawing, change the color of a line from blue to red, and save the file under a different file name, the location of bits used to store line color can be determined by comparing the original file with the modified file. If this process is repeated for all elements, attributes, and variables, eventually the format of all data inside the file can be decoded.

Reverse engineering is allowed by law, if a company documents the process by which they deduced the file format. Some CAD vendors have already reverse engineered AutoCAD's R12 file format (or enlisted the services of others to do it for them) and as of this writing are working on R13. As a result, many CAD programs today have the capability to read and write AutoCAD drawings from other software programs.

Why do software developers protect their file formats and force others to reverse engineer them? The ostensible but disingenuous answer is that they want to reserve the right to change the file formats in order to improve their software. If they had to coordinate such changes with other software developers, it would inhibit their ability to create a better product in a timely manner. But no one is asking for coordination, just publication. The burden of conformance would rest with other developers. In the long run, software developers must stand behind their tools, not the keys to their customer's digital information. Software developers who are confident about the value of their tools should have no problem with publishing their file formats.

Clearly, digital convergence of the tools used to create, edit, and display information—the merging of computer, television, and telephone—is less important than digital convergence of the information itself. The real payoff for architects must await the day when information is not locked within incompatible, proprietary formats kept secret by software developers. The architect's best interest is served by having digital information archives and resources stored in open, published file formats, ensuring their portability and longevity.

THE ELUSIVE GOAL OF SEAMLESS INTEGRATION

Incompatible software combined with inadequate long-term planning have resulted in the growth of islands of automation within some architectural firms, where information is trapped on different systems or in different software file formats. Unfortunately, the major constraint to bridging these islands is often not the architect's lack of will, but the failure of different computer hardware and software programs to work with each other in a truly integrated fashion. Finding easy-to-use tools that fit well within new service delivery processes and perform as seamless conduits of information can be a difficult and frustrating task.

The early efforts of many CAD vendors focused on so-called integrated software with drawing/database links and parametric macros. These packages provided tools to automate simple tasks such as drawing stairs, producing area calculations, counting furniture, and creating three-dimensional models from two-dimensional plans, but were limited by their task orientation and often placed inflexible constraints on the user. As such, most integrated architectural software programs never lived up to their advance billing. Many architects today are using such tools successfully, but certainly not to the extent that was originally promoted by developers. The ultimate extension of this all-in-one, integrated approach to tools is three-dimensional building modeling, where architects construct a centralized database describing a project from which

Illustration 4.13 *Area calculations using AutoCAD and Excel.*

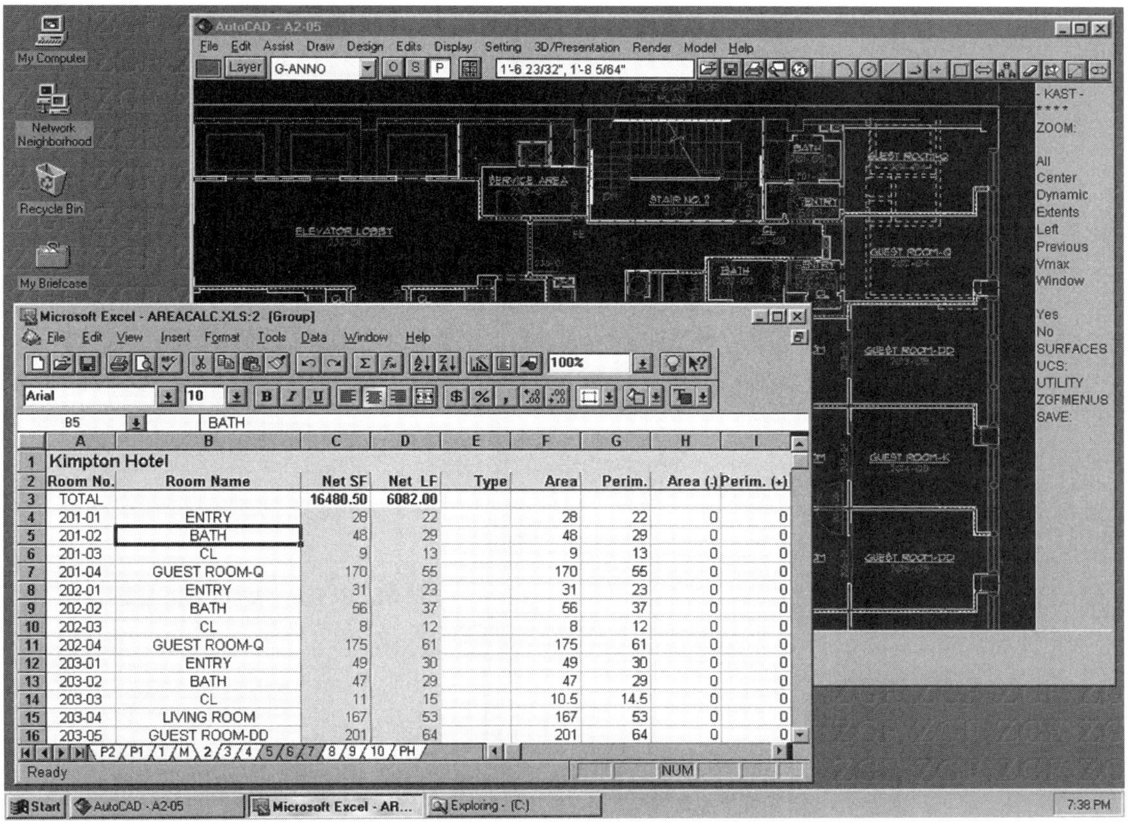

all drawings are automatically extracted. This idea will be discussed shortly.

More recently, the tools for software and data integration have been migrating from specialized, third-party applications to general-purpose operating systems of desktop computers. Window's OLE and Visual Basic and the Macintosh's Publish & Subscribe and OpenDoc are early efforts by Microsoft and Apple to put the power of integrated information and customization closer to the end user via general-purpose software tools. As a result, many software tools are (slowly) improving in their ability to communicate with each other and to create compound documents containing information from more than one source.

An important criterion of software applications is their ability to communicate and share information with other applications and their ability to read and write multiple file formats.

In the future, integrated architectural software will likely be assembled from sets of general-purpose software programs that work well with each other, rather than built from scratch as large, complex, special-purpose software programs. Illustration 4.13 shows a custom program developed at ZGF using Microsoft Windows' Dynamic Data Exchange (DDE). The program transfers building area and perimeter calculations from AutoCAD drawings to Excel spreadsheets for use by ZGF's cost estimators.

Providing architects with access to shared information using general-purpose software tools benefits small firms by leveraging the architect's role as generalist, and benefits large firms by bridging departmental islands of automation. In addition to their high cost and underlying complexity, many all-in-one integrated programs are often too inflexible for such diverse demands.

THE THREE-DIMENSIONAL BUILDING MODEL

Users of contemporary mechanical engineering CAD software have long enjoyed the ability to design simple three-dimensional models and generate two-dimensional drawings as views of the models. Since the 1970s many architects, researchers, and software developers have somewhat romantically clung to this idea as the ultimate architectural CAD system, providing the ability to generate two-dimensional working drawings, building code analyses, cost estimates, bills of materials, and shop drawings directly from three-dimensional models. "If only we didn't have to do working drawings," dreams the hypothetical architect, "we would just design a building in three dimensions, and the system would do the rest *automatically*."

As far back as the 1970s—before the personal computer was invented—much research in architectural CAD was directed toward several goals:

■ to allow architects to design directly in three dimensions, using solid modeling tools. The solid model, created in schematic design, would be embellished with additional detail and refinements through the completion of construction documents. Ultimately, the three-dimensional building model would itself become the contract document, instead of the drawings.

■ to allow architects to derive plans, sections, and elevations automatically as sectional orthographic projections of the three-dimensional model.

■ to allow architects to produce energy, lighting, structural, estimating, and other analyses from the model by assigning descriptive properties to each component in the three-dimensional model (material, weight, unit cost, etc.).

Many of the researchers believed that the only way to guarantee that all the drawings of a project were geometrically consistent was to derive them directly from a literal three-dimensional model. In addition, the researchers thought, since architects are in the business of designing and visualizing three-dimensional environments, the three-dimensional model was a more appropriate design medium than two-dimensional drawings. Indeed, the three-dimensional model would eventually *become* the construction drawings. An early article on this concept appeared in the March 1975 issue of the *Journal of the American Institute of Architects* (now *Architecture*).

Some academic researchers and software developers, although educated in architecture and experienced in observing the design and production process, have not really participated in it personally. This has contributed to a serious credibility gap separating those who tell architects they are doing it all wrong from the architects who must make a living using currently available technology.

Twenty years later, the idea is still a pipe dream. Why? Although the process involved in producing construction documents is often filled with inefficiencies, good documents are an incredibly efficient form of graphic communication for most buildings. Just think for a moment about the compression involved: a 70-story building can be documented on a set of drawings (including those produced during construction) whose volume is smaller than the average four-drawer file cabinet. A minimum set of construction documents describing a single-family, wood frame residence can be drawn on six 11- by 17-inch sheets of paper, small enough to fold up and put in one's coat pocket. The efficiency of the *product* should not be confused with the efficiency of the *process* used to create it. Today's technology should be focused on the latter, not the former.

"Architecture has itself to blame for the lack of proper design tools. If other disciplines are more successful at utilizing the potential of CAD, it is because they have devoted much more time and energy understanding that which they design and how they design it. They have prioritized their goals and have built tools to realize them."
NICK WEINGARTEN, FAIA

Those who have watched this discussion over the years may have observed that the literal three-dimensional building model always has been a moving target, and software developers are never armed with exactly the right ammunition. Initially, computers lacked the necessary horsepower. Then, the paradigm awaited the development of artificial intelligence, expert systems, or rule-based knowledge systems. Later still, better object-oriented software development tools were required. To some evangelists, the growing popularity of simpler, lower-cost, PC-based software tools among architects represented only a temporary detour on their eventual road to CAD nirvana. Today, only the maturing of the architectural market ostensibly is required to embrace the holy idea of unified building models. The point is that for 20 years, the advocates of literal three-dimensional building models have claimed to be just one step away from making them real, always lacking either the necessary development tools, CPU horsepower, or enlightened market.

In fact, other far more practical issues have prevented the promise from being realized. The idea remains an elusive goal for architects, and will probably never happen. The reason it has not happened has little to do with computer horsepower or software development tools, and much to do with the appropriately decentralized nature of the decision-making process of building design and construction, as well as the institutional, professional, and legal environments in which architects practice. For example:

1. Construction drawings produced by architects are intentionally schematic. Buildings are built from a combination of architectural drawings, shop drawings, manufacturer's data, and field decisions. Architects do not precisely locate every stud, anchor bolt, or sprinkler line in a building. We provide quantitative and prescriptive standards, such as 2 × 4 @ 16″ o.c., or

½″ × 6″ A.B. @ 6′-0″ o.c., or the location of sprinkler heads. A substantial portion of decision making about how a building is assembled—far more than academic researchers apparently realize—happens on the site. Although this distribution of decision making seems like an inefficiency, it is in fact quite efficient and appropriate.

2. The responsibilities for (and risks of) designing and constructing buildings are purposely distributed among several parties. Architecture is a multidisciplinary effort that reflects the economic realities of building construction. The subdivision of labor and decision making is an institutional reality that will not vanish overnight. Integration of the *process* must precede integration of the *information*.

3. Most buildings are prototypes—customized, crafted products. The economies of scale that exist in mechanical design don't exist in architecture, nor should they. Unlike integrated three-dimensional models created in the automotive or aircraft industries, the cost of creating a fully detailed three-dimensional building model cannot, and should not, be distributed over hundreds or thousands of buildings.

4. The assertion that the process of producing construction documents is simply the process of documenting something already designed—a process that architects, as designers, should be rescued from—is not true. An enormous amount of design happens during documentation, and CAD systems have blurred the distinction between the two more than ever.

5. The assertion that designing in three dimensions is always better than working in two dimensions, since it more accurately reflects what is being designed, also is not true. As discussed earlier, two-dimensional drawings are often the most appropriate medium for conceptualizing and studying a design problem and remain useful abstractions that isolate the specific design problem at hand, and exclude others that are unimportant or irrelevant. Design will always rely on various representations of information to resolve issues; they allow design to be broken down into smaller components. Three-dimensional models should be one of several abstractions available to the designer, but not the only one. For most buildings, two-dimensional drawings will always provide a simpler, faster, more direct interface.

6. Buildings have millions of components. Many are messy and do not snap together in a clean, prefabricated fashion. Examples include poured-in-place concrete, sheetrock, and insulation. Computers are not well prepared to handle messy things. (Even object-oriented systems, which will be discussed shortly, demand finite and well-defined behavior for the objects described within the computer.)

Today, some academic research is still exploring the unified building model paradigm, most notably the work of graduate students at the Center for Integrated Facilities Environments (CIFE) under the direction of Dr. Eric Teicholz at Stanford University. As demonstrated at CIFE, the three-dimensional building model approach is most useful in one of two situations—first, when it is applied to engineering structures such as process piping plants, where two-dimensional visualization is extremely difficult and the interfaces between discrete, premanufactured components (pipes, valves) are well defined; second, when the models are representational, rather than literal, such as simple massing models that describe construction sequencing of buildings. However, when technology evangelists promote the idea that architects should start doing *all* their projects in three dimensions, from beginning to end, they simply have the cart before the horse.

Paradoxically, although its implied benefit is better coordination between architect and contractor, the literal three-dimensional building model paradigm seeks to reduce, if not eliminate, the decision-making involvement of those in the field who actually assemble the building. Perhaps this is why the paradigm seems so attractive to some architects. Clearly, it is aligned with the interests of those who strive to take away control from the parties most directly connected to the construction of a building: the contractor, subcontractors, and material suppliers. Understandably, this desire is the result of declining craftsmanship, but it is also the institutional fallout of the traditional contractual separation between those who design and construct a building. The worker in the field is not considered by many architects to be a member of the team, but at best, someone who cannot be trusted, or at worst, an adversary. This attitude is an unfortunate by-product of the industrial age.

While businesses around the globe are creatively inventing ways to empower the individual most directly connected with the manufacture of a product or the delivery of a service, the literal three-dimensional building model does exactly the opposite. It centralizes, instead of decentralizes, knowledge and decision making.

One academic researcher described a typical problem in many buildings: architects draw typical cross sections—a flashing condition, for example—but sometimes fail to fully document transitions or corners. These are the places where the waterproofing design usually fails. The researcher described a future scenario where the waterproofing installer could watch an animated presentation, prepared by the architect, that would describe exactly how the flashing should be installed at a special condition.

In fact, that may be the case in the future (and we have all seen the AT&T "You Will" commercials which promote similar visions), but such a video will likely be prepared by the material supplier or subcontractor, not the architect. The scenario represents a radical departure from the responsibility (and liability) of the architect, and would have us not only producing shop drawings, but producing training videos for subcontractors as well. Today, it would be difficult, if not impossible, to find an insurance company who would provide an architect with coverage for this type of service. In fact, such "means and methods" are specifically excluded from virtually all architects' professional liability policies.

The fundamental issue is whether the institutional separation between design and construction, in place since the Renaissance, will eventually dissolve. Certainly, in the mid-1990s, design/build service delivery is an increasingly attractive option to many clients, in markets small and large. The long-term viability of design/build, however, will be driven less by the availability of technology than by its success in eliminating the inefficiency and cost of adversarial service providers and simplifying the interface to the client. This does *not* mean the extinction of the architect. Most design/build services of the future, in

A more detailed discussion of the differences between the architect's liability and the contractor's liability, and how digital tools are blurring the line between the two, can be found in Chapter 11, Managing the Digital Office.

fact, will likely be performed by architects, engineers, and contractors who present themselves to the client as a team—virtual design/build firms—but maintain their independence as business entities. In a design/build firm, the unified three-dimensional building model makes more sense, although it will still likely be as schematic and representational in nature as construction documents are today.

One can visualize the range of digital tools used within the spectrum shown in Illustration 4.14. On the left is the architect's pipe dream: a literal, unified three-dimensional building model in which all design knowledge resides and from which all documentation is extracted. At the other end of the spectrum is the limited approach of simply automating individual traditional tasks and methods using incompatible tools, creating orphaned information and islands of automation. Like most spectrums, somewhere in the middle lies common-sense reality.

OBJECT-ORIENTED SOFTWARE

Most software programs today, regardless of the programming languages in which they are written or the computers on which they are run, are organized in a very similar way. Most programs are organized into small modules (procedures or subroutines),

Illustration 4.14 *The spectrum of digital tools.*

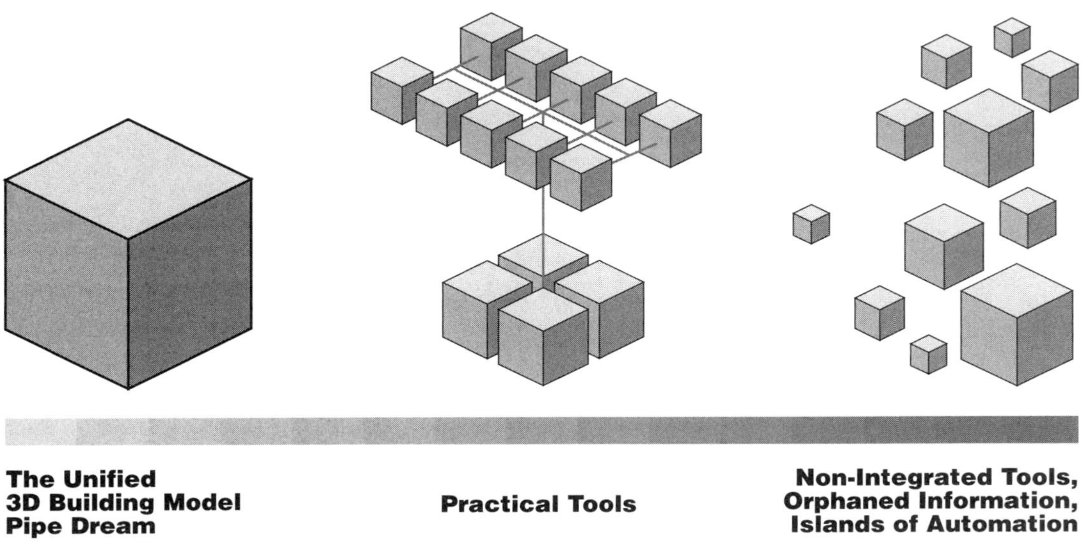

each of which performs a specialized function on a set of data. Some of the data is temporary—stored inside the program and shared by the different subroutines—but most of the data is stored outside the program in files. This program structure is exemplified by virtually all of the programs currently in use on the architect's desktop—CAD, desktop publishing, image editing, and word processing. Each is a fairly large, complex software program that provides hundreds of commands or operations the user can perform on a set of external data—a CAD drawing, a publication, an image, or a written document.

The disadvantage to the approach is that most software programs arrange data in a very specialized way. As discussed earlier, although all computer data files are simply long sequences of 0s and 1s, the proprietary methods in which they are arranged has long made it difficult not only to clone and recycle, but also to share information between different programs. Although bitmaps and image files are fairly simple internally (just a stream of pixels and their colors), the internal structure of other types of files can be very complicated, and new ones are invented every day.

Until recently, only two methods were used to allow programs to exchange information with each other, only two approaches were possible. The first, using a clipboard or other temporary storage buffer between programs, or an intermediate translation format such as DXF, involved a lowest common denominator, and never reliably preserved the graphic representation of information. This approach also only supported information copying, but not dynamic sharing of the same set of information between two different programs. The second approach was to burden programmers to keep up with the ever-changing inventory of file types. For example, to allow the user to insert images and drawings into documents with text, the programmers of desktop publishing programs had to support a wide variety of other file formats within the desktop publishing program.

There are other disadvantages to separating data and software. When the data formats change, the subroutines in the software that access that data must also change. When AutoCAD Release 11 was introduced, for example, and the line element was upgraded to a truly three-dimensional element, literally hundreds of different subroutines had to be located, changed, and tested to support the new type of line. This type of programming complexity is one reason why it takes software vendors a long time to develop new software versions, and why they are so difficult to debug.

When data and programs are separated, data can easily be operated on by more than one program only when data structures are relatively simple (such as ASCII text files or digital image files). For example, a digital image file might be created by a rendering program, edited using a paint program, and inserted into a document using a desktop publishing program. Each of these programs knows how information is stored within that file, and knows how to read and write the file. Image files such as TARGA, TIF, BMP, and others are supported by a large number of different programs. The use of objects is intended to provide this similar type of functionality to a wider variety of data types, including word processing, desktop publishing, database programs, and even CAD.

OBJECTS: COMBINING SOFTWARE AND DATA

The basic idea of object-oriented software is to combine software and data into the same object. Objects originated in the 1960s in the Simula programming language, developed in Norway. Simula is an acronym for "simulation language," and as the name implies, the language was designed to help create computer simulation of real-world processes in which independent systems interacted, such as assembly lines, automated vehicle systems, or conveying systems.

The major difference in the Simula language, compared to other languages such as Fortran or BASIC, was that its modules were not procedures that performed operations on external data. Instead, the modules were self-contained and based on real-world objects being modeled in simulation. In Simula, for the first time, the program's data and the program's procedures were contained inside the same object (Ill. 4.15).

Today, "objects" have become almost a religion among many software developers. Like the information superhighway, unfortunately, objects have received substantial hype far in advance of their useful packaging. Both are characterized by basic technology concepts that are over two decades old, but are only now finding their place in mainstream software applications.

While the ostensible future benefits of the superhighway are being advertised daily to consumers by those who are building its infrastructure, the ostensible future benefits of objects are harder to describe. In fact, most of the benefits of objects are explained by its advocates from a software programmer's point of view, not a user's point of view. Because more programs will be built from small, reusable software components instead of large, custom-built programs, the user is presumed to gain trickle-down benefits in the form of lower costs, better customization, and more frequent upgrades (!). As a result, the term "object-oriented" has generated a fair share of confusion, especially since it has become a favorite marketing buzzword of software developers and resellers. (The issue is made even more complicated because the term "object" is used within many software programs to generically describe an element or component of a drawing or document.)

" 'Object-oriented' has become a buzzword. As such, it has enjoyed the fate of most buzzwords in the software industry: it has been preempted and corrupted by many products claiming to be object-oriented only so they could sell more copies."
EXCERPT FROM TALIGENT CORPORATION WHITE PAPER

Illustration 4.15 Structured programming versus objects.

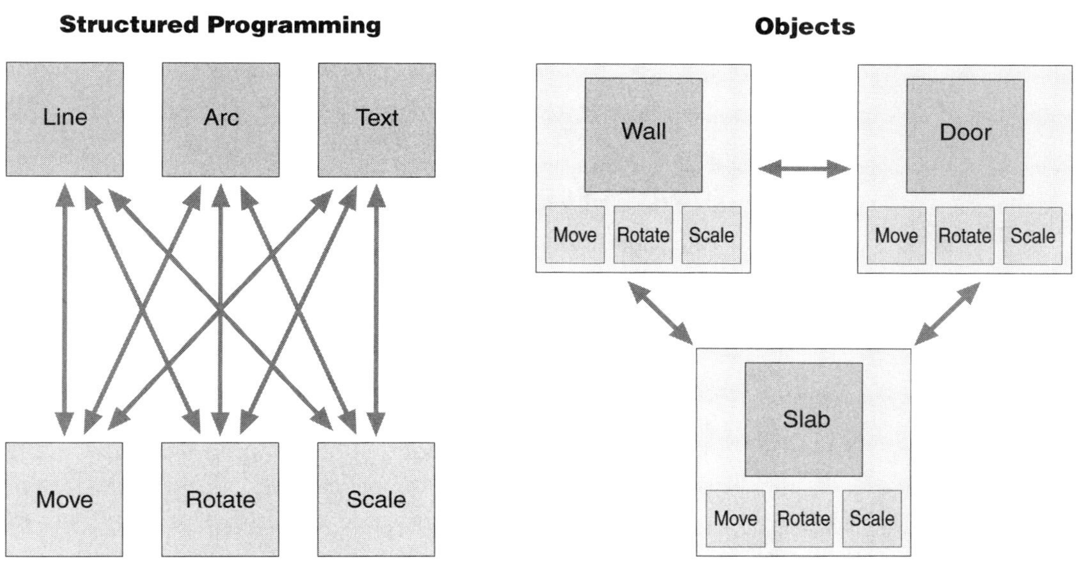

THE ATTRIBUTES OF OBJECTS

A detailed discussion of the theory of objects and object-oriented software is beyond the scope of this book, but there are four basic attributes of objects and object-oriented software, each of which has a fancy name. (If you really want to appear cool among nerds, sprinkle these terms liberally in your conversation.) The four concepts are:

1. *Encapsulation.* Software objects combine data with the operations to be performed on that data, an idea known as encapsulation. The benefit is that an object can only be changed using simple, well-defined methods associated with it. The modular objects are highly reusable and reliable.
2. *Data abstraction.* Abstraction is the process by which complex data structures are made simpler and more understandable by removing their detail and generalizing their behavior.
3. *Inheritance.* This is the mechanism by which specialized objects inherit the attributes and behavior of simpler, generalized objects and add their own unique attributes and behavior to them.
4. *Polymorphism.* Polymorphism is the idea that the same command, or message, can be interpreted differently by different objects. The command "draw," for example, is interpreted differently by a rectangle object (which displays a four-sided shape) and a triangle object (which displays a three-sided one).

TODAY'S PARADIGM: OLE AND OPENDOC

Object-oriented concepts are applied today in software applications that support Microsoft's OLE (Object Linking and Embedding). Using OLE, developers build applications that allow information from other applications to be combined into compound documents. Both Microsoft's OLE, built into Windows, and Apple's new OpenDoc technology are based on the idea of encapsulation: a piece of digital data should also carry instructions within it about how it is displayed and where it came from. Illustration 4.16 shows a schematic diagram of how OLE works by maintaining links between source documents and a compound document within which they are displayed. OLE and OpenDoc are intended to lift from the programmer's shoulders the burden of knowing how to support hundreds of different file formats and to provide tools with which users can assemble compound documents containing objects from a variety of different software applications.

OLE is implemented on both Windows personal computers and Apple Macintoshes. Using OLE-compliant applications, users can drag and drop objects from one document to another and create a link between the two. For example, a user might insert a digital image into a spreadsheet. If the digital image is modified, the spreadsheet will reflect the change the next time it is opened. In this way, OLE objects behave just like external reference files in a CAD drawing.

Reference files in CAD software are discussed in more detail in Chapter 8.

Users can edit OLE objects from within compound documents by double-clicking on them. This action launches the application the object originally came from, allowing the user to modify the object and save it. OLE 2.0 supports the notion of in-place editing, which means the object stays put and the

Illustration 4.16 *How OLE works.*

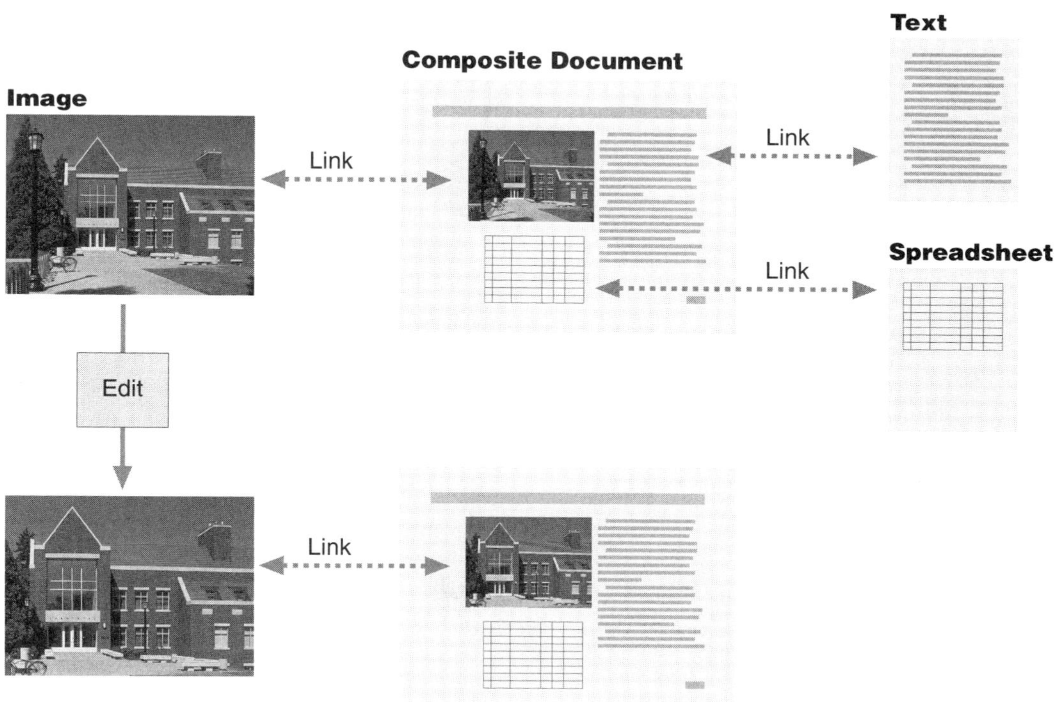

menus simply change to its source program. (This can be a blessing but is usually a curse, because the user is limited to an editing window the size of the object as displayed in the compound document.)

OLE's major limitations to date have been lack of reliability and speed. Object-oriented theories do not matter very much if the tools do not work reliably, and OLE objects are still too easy to break, even within Microsoft's own applications. Also, the use of OLE places substantial demands on a computer's memory, and unless your personal computer is equipped with 32 MB of RAM, using OLE with several applications at once can be a painful experience. (Windows 95 has improved this somewhat.)

OpenDoc is an alternative to OLE proposed by Apple, Novell, and IBM which provides similar functionality, but is not as closely tied to the Windows operating system. OpenDoc supports the industry-standard CORBA (Common Object Request Broker Architecture) technology, which is designed to work across a wide range of distributed computer systems and networks, including the Internet and World Wide Web.

One limitation of OpenDoc is that it depends on "parts viewers" to display objects within compound documents, thus limiting the portability of the documents. For example, if a user inserts a digital image into a spreadsheet using OpenDoc and sends the spreadsheet to a client, the image will not be displayed on the client's computer unless the corresponding parts viewer for the image is also present. OLE objects, on the other hand, include an image of each object within the compound document, so that the documents are correctly displayed even if all the associated applications that created the objects are not present.

Unfortunately, OpenDoc has yet to be shipped as a real product while OLE continues to gather momentum and support from software developers. Ultimately, Microsoft, Apple, IBM, and others will likely bury the hatchet and agree upon a single method of sharing objects between different software applications, which is what everyone really needs.

TOMORROW'S PARADIGM: OBJECT-ORIENTED ARCHITECTURE

Object-oriented design, when you think about it, is what architecture is all about. An electrical appliance is an object. Its interface is a 110-volt plug. Since the interface to the building is so well defined, the building designer need not worry about the details of what will be plugged into that outlet—just that it is requires 110 volts. Cannot architects use object-oriented software to describe the attributes and behavior of a broad range of architectural objects, most of which are characterized by well-defined interfaces?

Some have compellingly argued that many architectural "styles" can be encapsulated into explicitly defined objects with simple interfaces. Thoman Seebohn of the University of Ontario has shown examples of student work which resemble (at least to the untrained eye) the work of Palladio, Frank Lloyd Wright, and Alvar Aalto, by defining the "interfaces" of the architects' styles inside a computer—proportion, rhythm, vocabulary, and so forth. If one is to accept these types of limits—aesthetic or otherwise—there is potential value in the approach if the interfaces are user definable.

Beyond aesthetics, the ability of people to construct cutomized buildings quickly in an economical manner has long depended on using prefabricated components that have defined, predictable interfaces. A few examples of such interfaces are:

Nails, screws, mechanical fasteners
110-, 220-volt electrical supply
Simpson framing connectors
Plumbing fixtures
Standard bolt diameters and thread sizes
Standard reinforcing bar diameters
Concrete masonry units
4 × 8 and 4 × 12 sheets of plywood
2 × 2 ceiling grid and fixtures
Wood and metal stud dimensions
FFE (furnishings, fixtures, and equipment)

As discussed earlier, not all building materials are well-defined, discrete components with simple interfaces. Poured-in-place concrete, earth, and sheetrock, for example, are simple materials with flexible, complex interfaces. Indeed, their flexibility is one of their basic virtues. At the same time, well-defined interfaces and methods are commonplace in the built environment, and play a key role in making buildings economically constructable.

At various points in history, people stopped debating whether 110 volts was better than 105 or 115, or whether a 2 × 5 stud was better than a 2 × 4, and decided that if everyone used similar methods and interfaces, electricity could flow a lot easier and wood-framed structures could get nailed together faster. The standards themselves are less important than the fact that they exist. They establish well-defined interfaces between building components and the methods for assembling them.

Architecture is all about building complex, prototype environments from a set of parts—some off the shelf and some custom built. So, in a very real sense, although objects are not the best way to model certain complex phenomena, such as weather patterns or ecosystems (the domain of chaos theory), in most cases objects are a reasonable way to simulate parts of the built environment, which is full of objects with articulated interfaces and well-defined methods.

CAD INTEROPERABILITY

Most major CAD software developers, including Autodesk and Bentley Systems, are working on new object-oriented versions of their software. Bentley's Microstation V6, also known as Objective Microstation, is due to be released in 1996. The new version is expected to allow users to expand the element vocabulary of Microstation with their own custom objects. With AutoCAD Release 13, Autodesk began implementing a new object-oriented AutoCAD database that allows programmers to implement new AutoCAD data structures more easily. Release 13 introduced ARX, a tool kit (in addition to AutoLISP and ADE) for software developers to build specialized applications running on AutoCAD. Some of Release 13's new element types, such as multilines, ellipses, and multiline text, were implemented with ARX instead of modifying AutoCAD's core code. However, since the new database structure has provided few tangible benefits to the end user other than the new element types, Release 13 is best characterized as an object-oriented work in progress.

In June 1995, Autodesk announced the creation of the A/E/C Interoperability Association, whose founding members include AT&T, Carrier, Lawrence Berkeley Laboratory, Honeywell, Softdesk, Timberline, Tishman, HOK, and others. The association's mission is to create a common object-oriented language for building projects by defining a set of "industry foundation classes" (IFC), allowing information to be shared easily between different CAD software. At that time, the association had described only a theoretical framework for the foundation classes.

Alas, an excerpt from a June 1, 1995 management overview published by Autodesk introducing the foundation classes contains healthy portions of ambiguity and hype:

> Consider an office building where, due to changes in requirements, two private offices need to be converted to a PC training lab. Say that this happens after construction for the project has begun.
>
> Today, this change would require extensive rework by all members of the building team. After the architect had redesigned the space, several other team members must complete significant work to modify their subsystems. The HVAC engineer would need to manually take off the new room dimensions, computers, wall types, and exposures to recalculate heating and cooling loads for the room; redesign the air distribution for the new space use; and ensure that the HVAC equipment for that part of the building will satisfy the increased load generated by the PCs. In addition, the new PCs would have power and communications requirements that would entail extensive new cabling.
>
> With IFC, this change process is simplified and less error prone. For the architect, redefining the spaces is easier, and schedules stay consistent throughout the project model. The HVAC engineer would be notified of changes in thermal zone boundaries, could extract new room loads automatically from the project model, and would stretch ducting automatically as he repositions air outlets in the new space. The cabling engineer could query the project model for devices and equipment needing service, and automate the process of designing the cabling to these devices and equip-

> ment. Finally, the builder is able to update estimates and schedules automatically, providing accurate cost management and better knowledge of how this design change would effect the project construction timetable. Throughout this process, future intelligent applications will be able to use IFC to verify code requirements and dependencies.

At first glance, the hypothetical scenario is compelling, but it fails to address a basic question: what is the cost of developing and maintaining such a comprehensive set of data, and when the design is *not* changed, what is the payback? Today, a distributed design team equipped with two-dimensional CAD and FAX machines could turn around this type of design change in less than a day. After all, how difficult is it really to determine the heating and cooling loads for a new training lab? A good engineer can do that on the back of an envelope. How does IFC make redefining the spaces easier? A good architect could sketch and hardline the training lab in a couple of hours. Exactly what project model is the cabling engineer querying if the computer equipment has not yet been purchased by the building owner? Finally, who controls the objects and defines their relationships in the project model, which makes the updating of schedules and estimates for the builder "automatic"? Whose estimate is it? Who is held accountable for it? Does the project model contain an updated price list of every building material or component that *might* be used in its construction?

Unfortunately, parts of Autodesk's white paper vision for its object-oriented Industry Foundation Classes sound suspiciously like the literal three-dimensional building model pipe dream. As long as the A/E/C Interoperability Association focuses on simple and practical object-oriented languages and tools, the standards defined by the Association may significantly help architects, engineers, contractors, and clients to easily share information with each other in formats supported by multiple software developers. Otherwise, the Association's efforts will likely experience the same fate as dozens of other literal three-dimensional building model software prototypes over the past two decades, and fail to materialize within useful tools.

CHAPTER

5

The Language of Digital Media

ALGORITHMS AND DATA STRUCTURES

"Can you be more . . . specific?"

Computer Psychiatrist, THX1138

Software applications, even object-oriented ones, consist of two basic components: data structures and algorithms. Data structures are the organizational templates for information that a software application is designed to manipulate. They contain placeholders for values (text, numbers, color, etc.) provided by the user. The data structure of a line in a CAD drawing, for example, might be defined by two coordinate points, a layer, a color, a line type, and a line weight.

An algorithm is a sequence of instructions designed to manipulate the data structures to generate a desired, reproducible result. Algorithms are usually outlined by a programmer before the software is actually written and debugged. Typically, algorithms and data structure definitions are contained in the software program, while the data structure values are contained in data files.

Some algorithms of a program are hidden from the user and used only to perform internal housekeeping, such as memory management. Others are exposed to the user in the form of menu items and commands. Simple algorithms for editing two-dimensional graphics include move, copy, rotate, mirror, stretch, and trim. More complex algorithms include maintaining links (associativity) between a dimension and its referenced geometry or between crosshatching and the shape that encloses it. Image-editing programs support simple algorithms, such as changing the lightness or contrast of an image, and complex algorithms, such as watercolor or dry-brush image filters.

Similarly, some data structures of a program are hidden from the user, such as internal system variables, and others are exposed to the user in the form of elements the user can place and edit within a drawing or document. The data structures of a CAD program include lines, arcs, circle, text, and dimensions. The data structures of a database program include fields, records, tables, and links; those of a desktop publishing program include text blocks, borders, images, and imported graphics.

Together, data structures and algorithms are the nouns and verbs of a new digital vocabulary: *the language of digital media.* This chapter presents an introduction to the language used in desktop software applications useful to architects, with a special focus on the new vocabulary of three-dimensional modelbuilding, visualization, and animation.

DIGITAL TEXT

The simplest desktop software applications are generally those that deal with text: characters, words, sentences, and paragraphs. The data structures and algorithms in word processors and other text editing programs designed to create written documents are relatively small in number. A simple and effective word processor really needs only eight or ten basic commands, although the most sophisticated programs typically have hundreds. Today, virtually all desktop software applications, including CAD, spreadsheets, databases, and image editing, provide basic tools for creating and editing digital text.

See Chapter 4, Tools of the Architect, for more information about the ASCII format.

The simplest form of digital text is ASCII, which contains only a stream of characters without any special formatting. Word-processing documents, such as those created by Microsoft Word, WordPerfect, or WordPro, also include formatting information that describes the placement and appearance of text within them. Although no single standard has yet emerged that defines how formatted text is stored in binary files (as strings of 0s and 1s), the features of most programs that manipulate words are quite similar.

Text formatting features supported within most desktop word-processing programs today include:

Multiple fonts, styles (bold, italic), and sizes (Ill. 5.1)
Special formatting, such as strikethrough, superscript, subscript, small caps (Ill. 5.2)
Paragraph control, including justification, indents, tabs, line spacing
Page headers and footers
Automatic indexing and table of contents
Multiple column layout
Support for tables

Since there are only so many ways to graphically tweak the printed word, developers of text editing software today are focusing as much on usability as on feature expansion, such as the ability to drag and drop text selections between different parts of a document instead of using pull-down menus. Developers have also learned the value of providing users with easy access to the

Illustration 5.1 Font examples.

Times Roman
Times Roman Italic
Times Roman Bold
Times Roman Bold Italic
underline
~~strikethrough~~
Shaded
E x p a n d e d
Condensed
$\text{Superscript}^{\text{superscript}}$
$\text{Subscript}_{\text{subscript}}$

Illustration 5.2 Formatting examples.

10 percent of the features they use 90 percent of the time via customizable buttons and icons displayed on the screen (Ill. 5.3).

In-line spell checkers, which correct small but common typographical errors as they are being typed (such as "teh" instead of "the"), also help assure quality. Most word-processing programs today provide both built-in spelling and grammar checkers, but neither tool is foolproof. Spell checkers will generally not detect a word spelled incorrectly that itself is a legitimate word (such as a missing "r" in "through"). Also, grammar checkers often fail to understand language context and meaning as well as one would hope. The important point is to use spelling and grammar checkers as supplemental aids, but not rely exclusively upon them (Ill. 5.4).

FONTS AND STYLES

Most desktop software that is used to create and edit digital text supports one or more of three flavors of fonts (Ill. 5.5). Bitmap fonts are fixed-size fonts typically used for screen display, and are represented by a small matrix of dots. (The dots are actually called pixels, a term that will be defined shortly.) Vector fonts are described by linework and are usually found in CAD systems. Filled fonts are described by closed, filled shapes. Unlike

Illustration 5.3 Buttons and icons.

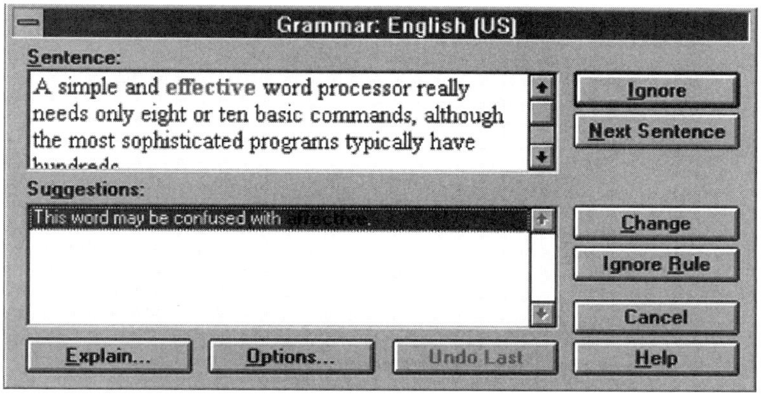

Illustration 5.4 *Microsoft Word grammar checking.*

bitmap fonts, both vector and filled fonts are scalable, meaning they can be enlarged or reduced in size without a noticeable loss of display quality.

In most word-processing programs, a *style* is a user-defined collection of formatting attributes that is given a name (Ill. 5.6). Instead of explicitly specifying formatting attributes to control the visual appearance of text, the user can select from style lists. Styles can also inherit the attributes of other styles. If a body of text defined by a style also contains specially formatted words or phrases, such as bold, *italicized*, or underlined text, the style defining the body text can be changed without affecting the specially formatted words or phrases.

Illustration 5.5 *Bitmap, vector, and filled fonts.*

FLEXIBILITY VERSUS COMPLEXITY

Some text editing programs have grown in complexity, often rivaling CAD software in their size and breadth. How many features for editing text do you really need? The following table compares four text editing programs developed by Microsoft:

APPLICATION	MENU ITEMS	SIZE
Notepad (Win 3.1)	22	32,736 bytes
Write (Win 3.1)	50	244,976 bytes
WordPad (Win95)	50 + 20 icons	179,200 bytes
Word for Windows	108 + 200 icons	3,483,136 bytes (plus 20,000,000 bytes of accessory files)

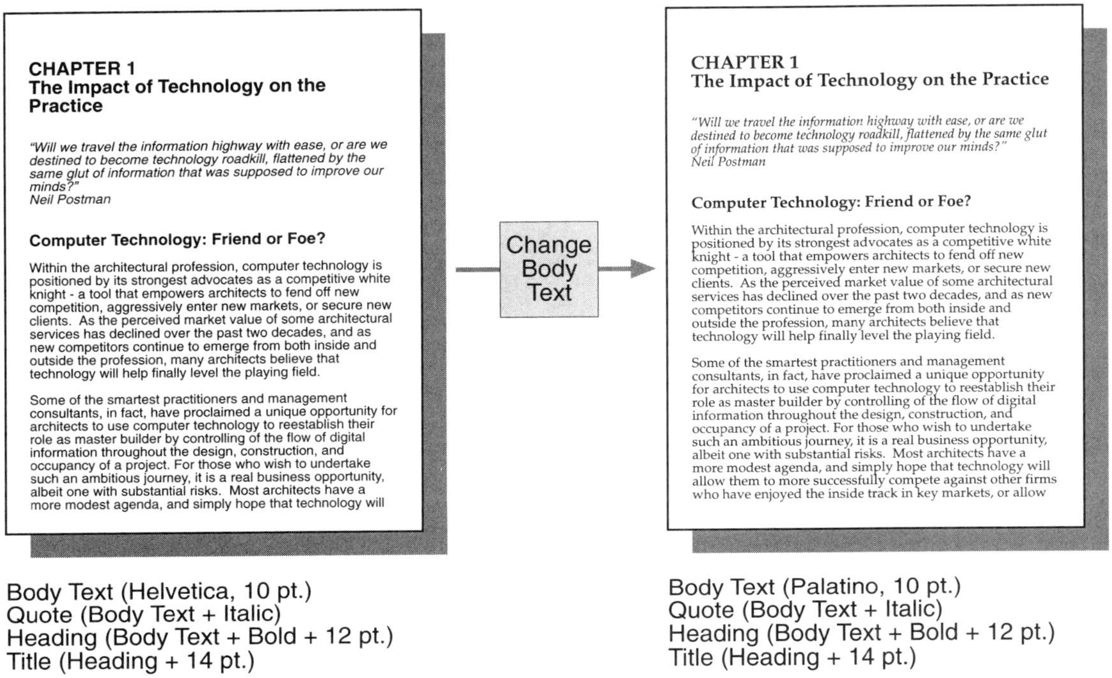

Illustration 5.6 Styles.

Notepad really isn't usable other than for editing plain ASCII text files, and provides no text formatting features at all. Word, on the other hand, is a software behemoth of dizzying depth and complexity. Write and WordPad, simple word processors shipped with every version of Windows 3.1 and Windows 95 respectively, are nice, fast, easy-to-learn tools that each occupy less than 1 percent of the disk space of Word.

If you are a person who uses a word processor on a regular basis, such as a specification writer or an administrative support person, the features of a heavyweight word-processing program such as WordPerfect, Microsoft Word, or IBM/Lotus WordPro are definitely worth the time and expense. But if you only occasionally prepare meeting minutes or internal memos, or if you prepare rough drafts for final preparation by an assistant, you probably do not need the bells and whistles. A simple program such as Write or WordPad provides a good balance of features, ease of use, and cost.

OPTICAL CHARACTER RECOGNITION

Two methods can be used for inputting words and sentences into a text editing program. The first, obviously, is to type. The second is to use optical character recognition (OCR) software designed to interpret scanned images of printed documents and convert the images into text characters. Although early versions of OCR software were both expensive and unreliable, most desktop OCR software programs today do a good job of capturing printed text from clean, crisp originals. The reliability of most OCR programs still drops off dramatically when fuzzy copies, such as faxes, are used as source material (Ill. 5.7). For architects who have access to a desktop scanner and need to input large amounts of text from high-quality originals, an OCR program can be a substantial time-saver.

Original Image

After performing an analysis of four sites to accommodate the expansion of OMSI, ZGF developed a site master plan, programming and design for the 200,000 SF museum, which includes an OMNI-Max theatre. The museum incorporates both permanent and changing exhibit areas, classroom/laboratory facilities, design and production facilities for exhibits, plus public areas and administrative space. Primary users of the museum are children and families. The selected Station L site, 18 acres along the Willamette River, lends itself to a museum park concept. OMSI has become a regional landmark and has been instrumental in connecting the east and west sides of the river.

After performing an analysis of four sites to accommodate the expansion of OMSI, ZGF developed a site master plan, programming and design for the 200,000 SF museum, which includes an OMNI-Max theatre. The museum incorporates both permanent and changing exhibit areas, classroom/laboratory facilities, design and production facilitie for exhibits, plus public areas and administrative space. Primary users of the museum are children and families. The selected Station L site, 18 acres along the Willamette River, lends itself to a museum park concept. OMSI has become a regional landmark and has been instrumental in connecting the east and west sides of the river.

First Generation FAX

After performing an analysis of four sites to accommodate the expansion of OMSI, ZGF developed a site master plan, programming and design for the 200,000 SF museum, which includes an OMNI-Max theatre. The museum incorporates both permanent and changing exhibit areas, classroom/laboratory facilities, design and production facilities for exhibits, plus public areas and administrative space. Primary users of the museum are children and families. The selected Station L site, 18 acres along the Willamette River, lends itself to a museum park concept. OMSI has become a regional landmark and has been instrumental in connecting the east and west sides of the river.

After performing an mwysis of four sites to accommodate the expansion of OMSI, ZC;F developed a site master plan, progra ng and design for the 200," SF museum, which includ an OMM-Max theatre. The museum bxorporaws both pe t and changing exhibit areas, dassroom/laboratc)ry facilities, design and production facilities for exhibits, plus public areas and administrative space, Primary users of the museum are children and families. The selected Station L site, 18 acres along the Willan-tette River, lends itself to a museum park concept. OMSI has become a re&nal landnmrk and has been instrumental in connecting the east and west sides of the river.

Second Generation FAX

After performing an analysis of four sites to accommodate the expansion of OMSI, ZGF developed a site master plan, programming and design for the 200,000 SF museum, which includes an OMNI-Max theatre. The museum incorporates both permanent and changing exhibit areas, classroom/laboratory facilities, design and production facilities for exhibits, plus public areas and administrative space. Primary users of the museum are children and families. The selected Station L site, 18 acres along the Willamette River, lends itself to a museum park concept. OMSI has become a regional landmark and has been instrumental in connecting the east and west sides of the river.

Ahm tog... a an analysir. Of kkar SINS tD be the
expamwn of OMS, Zr.F dev a site awler p PM . g and dmign
for " 2--M-.OW SF m which includes
an OMNI-Max tm. Dv m
incorporates
F=Bl and awbit areas,
mroom/ twy tin, design and

pmduction fm fcc ewnbits, plus public areas
nd mnm tive space. Frimury users of dw
m are ren faimi@. Tlhe wiecftd
Siaticm L sim 18 along Ow Willamette River,

Illustration 5.7 *OCR examples.*

Most OCR programs today:

- understand complex page layouts, such as magazine or newspaper formats
- match text formatting attributes (such as bold and italic)
- ignore illustrations and images while converting text
- scan documents at speeds above 10,000 characters per minute
- scan clean documents at 99 percent accuracy and above

The accuracy figure is somewhat misleading. Even at 99 percent accuracy, OCR documents still require substantial correction by the user, although usually less work than retyping the original document. A double-spaced typewritten page, for example, contains approximately 2000 text characters, so a five-page document converted at a 99 percent accuracy rate may have up to 100 errors. In terms of error correction, there is a big difference between 99 percent accuracy and 100 percent accuracy. Most OCR programs can attain 100 percent accuracy when a clean original is used, but fail miserably when poor quality copies are used as source material.

Illustration 5.8 *Spreadsheet formulas.*

Spreadsheet Display

	A	B	C	D	E	F	G
1	**Project Summary**					**Project Costs**	
2						Labor	$4,725
3	**Staff**	**Hours**	**Rate**	**Total**		Consult.	$2,500
4	JAK	180	$10.00	$1,800		Direct	$248
5	XLD	24	$12.50	$300		Reimb.	$1,000
6	QAJ	72.5	$22.50	$1,631		**Total**	**$8,473**
7	LLK	20	$13.00	$260			
8	ZPS	3	$15.00	$45		**Project Performance**	
9	JTK	20	$28.50	$570		**Fee**	**$10,000**
10	JLP	12.5	$9.50	$119		**Profit**	**$1,527**
11	**Total/Ave.**	**332**	**$14.23**	**$4,725**		**% Profit**	**15%**

Spreadsheet Formulas

	A	B	C	D	E	F	G
1	**Project Summary**					**Project Costs**	
2						Labor	=D11
3	**Staff**	**Hours**	**Rate**	**Total**		Consult.	$2,500
4	JAK	180	$10.00	=B4*C4		Direct	$248
5	XLD	24	$12.50	=B5*C5		Reimb.	$1,000
6	QAJ	72.5	$22.50	=B6*C6		**Total**	**=SUM(G2:G5)**
7	LLK	20	$13.00	=B7*C7			
8	ZPS	3	$15.00	=B8*C8		**Project Performance**	
9	JTK	20	$28.50	=B9*C9		**Fee**	**$10,000**
10	JLP	12.5	$9.50	=B10*C10		**Profit**	**=G9-G6**
11	**Total/Ave.**	**=SUM(B4:B10)**	**=D11/B11**	**=SUM(D4:D10)**		**% Profit**	**=G10/G9**

DIGITAL NUMBERS

The most popular tool that architects use to manipulate numerical information is the spreadsheet. A spreadsheet is a matrix of cells (information placeholders), each of which can contain a text or numerical value, or—most importantly—a formula. The power of a spreadsheet as a design and analysis tool is directly related to its use of formulas, which dynamically reflect changes to the values of other cells (Ill. 5.8).

As discussed in the previous chapter, formulas are the source of a spreadsheet's power and flexibility, but because they are typically hidden from the user's view, they are also a source of potentially costly mistakes. A user may unintentionally change a formula to a fixed value simply by typing a new value into the cell. One common problem, as shown in Illustration 5.9, is inserting a new row at the end of a list of values that is not reflected in the total. To alleviate this problem, most programs allow spreadsheet authors to protect individual cells within a spreadsheet or protect the format of the spreadsheet itself.

Illustration 5.9 The danger of formulas.

Before

		SD	DD	CD	
01	Project Management	100	100	200	
03	Contract Negotiations	10			
08	Client Meetings/Presentations	20	20	20	
15	Document Coordination	10		120	◄— New row inserted here
16	Agency Liaison	30		40	
17	Program Development				
18	Conceptuals				
	TOTAL	**170**	**120**	**380**	◄— New row inserted here

After

		SD	DD	CD	
01	Project Management	100	100	200	
03	Contract Negotiations	10			
08	Client Meetings/Presentations	20	20	20	
09	In-House Reviews	20	20	20	◄— New values are reflected in column totals
15	Document Coordination	10		120	
16	Agency Liaison	30		40	
17	Program Development				
18	Conceptuals				
19	Field Investigation & Research	25	10	5	◄— New values are not reflected in column totals
	TOTAL	**190**	**140**	**400**	

Over the past several years, spreadsheets have gained a wide variety of features that allow architects to convey information graphically. Fonts, styles, borders, linework, and basic illustration tools are provided in most spreadsheet programs. Special-character fonts can also be used to indicate special types of information, such as yes/no values in a checklist. Most spreadsheets provide tools to create charts or graphs quickly that visually represent numerical data and respond dynamically when that data is changed. As a result, spreadsheets have evolved far beyond their original incarnation as financial analysis tools and are today used in many architectural firms not only for number crunching, but also for scheduling, database management, and graphics presentations. Several examples are shown in Illustration 5.10.

Illustration 5.10 *Spreadsheet examples.*

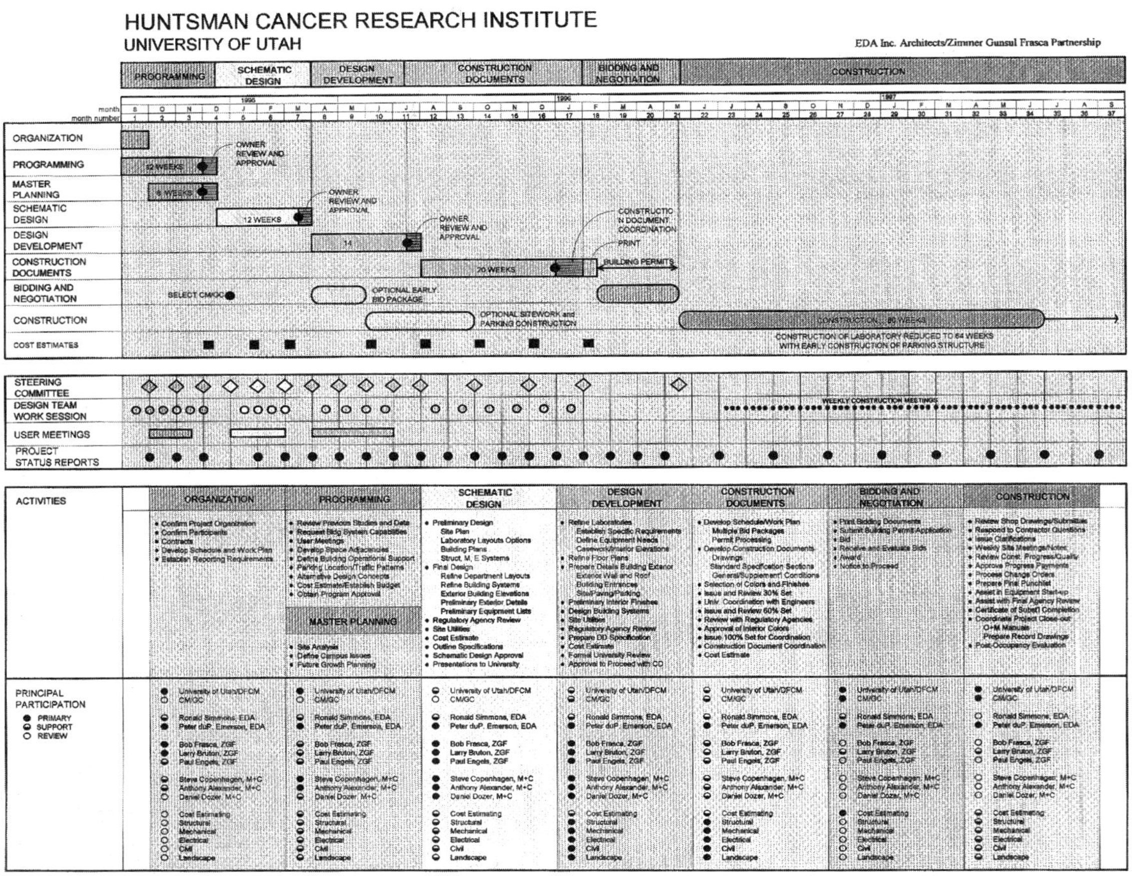

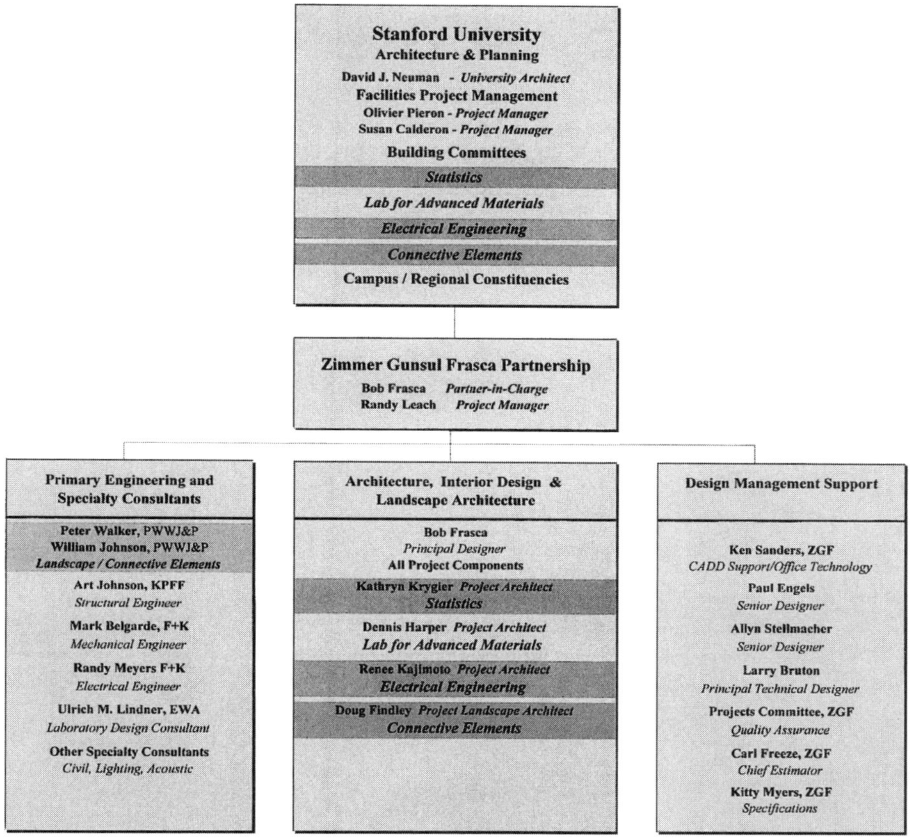

Organization Chart

Illustration 5.10 (Continued)

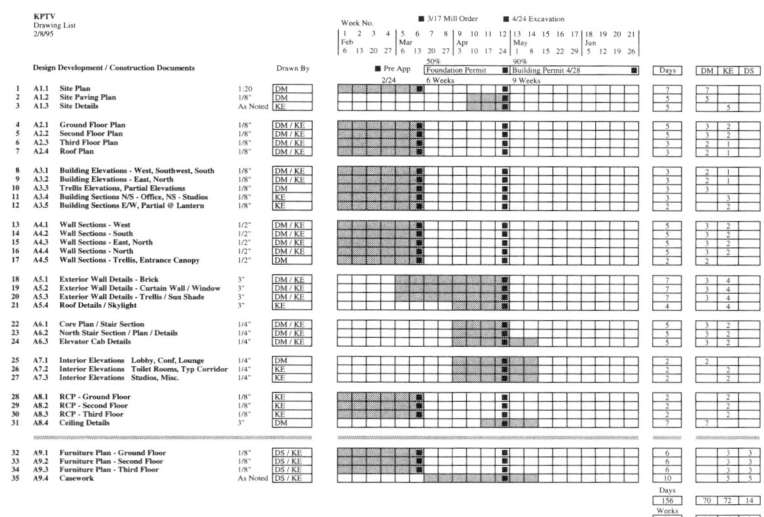

VISUALIZING TIME AND RESOURCES

A variety of computer tools are available to assist architects schedule, budget, and staff projects. Specialized project scheduling software packages allow users to define tasks, start dates, and durations, establish dependencies between tasks, assign resources, analyze critical paths, and output a variety of reports, including Pert and Gantt charts (Ill. 5.11). For small projects, project scheduling software often is not necessary; a spreadsheet does just fine to help an architect monitor the project schedule and/or staffing requirements (Ill. 5.12). The main limitation of a spreadsheet used for those purposes is the lack of task dependencies or critical path analysis. Spreadsheets generally provide better graphics flexibility, but less intelligence.

Illustration 5.11 *Project scheduling software.*

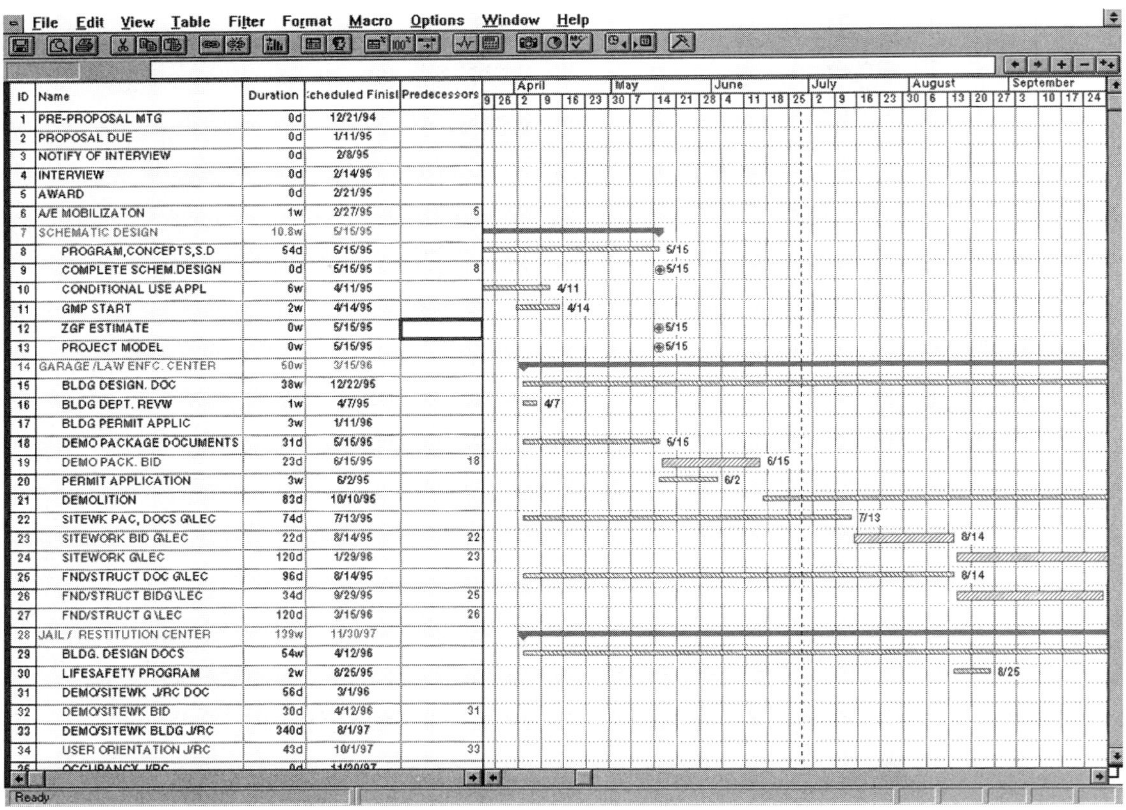

ID	Name	Duration	Scheduled Finish	Predecessors
1	PRE-PROPOSAL MTG	0d	12/21/94	
2	PROPOSAL DUE	0d	1/11/95	
3	NOTIFY OF INTERVIEW	0d	2/8/95	
4	INTERVIEW	0d	2/14/95	
5	AWARD	0d	2/21/95	
6	A/E MOBILIZATON	1w	2/27/95	5
7	SCHEMATIC DESIGN	10.8w	5/15/95	
8	PROGRAM,CONCEPTS,S.D	54d	5/15/95	
9	COMPLETE SCHEM.DESIGN	0d	5/15/95	8
10	CONDITIONAL USE APPL	6w	4/11/95	
11	GMP START	2w	4/14/95	
12	ZGF ESTIMATE	0w	5/15/95	
13	PROJECT MODEL	0w	5/15/95	
14	GARAGE /LAW ENFC. CENTER	50w	3/15/96	
15	BLDG DESIGN. DOC	38w	12/22/95	
16	BLDG DEPT. REVW	1w	4/7/95	
17	BLDG PERMIT APPLIC	3w	1/11/96	
18	DEMO PACKAGE DOCUMENTS	31d	5/15/95	
19	DEMO PACK. BID	23d	6/15/95	18
20	PERMIT APPLICATION	3w	6/2/95	
21	DEMOLITION	83d	10/10/95	
22	SITEWK PAC, DOCS G\LEC	74d	7/13/95	
23	SITEWORK BID G\LEC	22d	8/14/95	22
24	SITEWORK G\LEC	120d	1/29/96	23
25	FND/STRUCT DOC G\LEC	96d	8/14/95	
26	FND/STRUCT BIDG \LEC	34d	9/29/95	25
27	FND/STRUCT G \LEC	120d	3/15/96	26
28	JAIL / RESTITUTION CENTER	139w	11/30/97	
29	BLDG. DESIGN DOCS	54w	4/12/96	
30	LIFESAFETY PROGRAM	2w	8/25/95	
31	DEMO/SITEWK J/RC DOC	56d	3/1/96	
32	DEMO/SITEWK BID	30d	4/12/96	31
33	DEMO/SITEWK BLDG J/RC	340d	8/1/97	
34	USER ORIENTATION J/RC	43d	10/1/97	33
35	OCCUPANCY J/RC	0d	11/30/97	

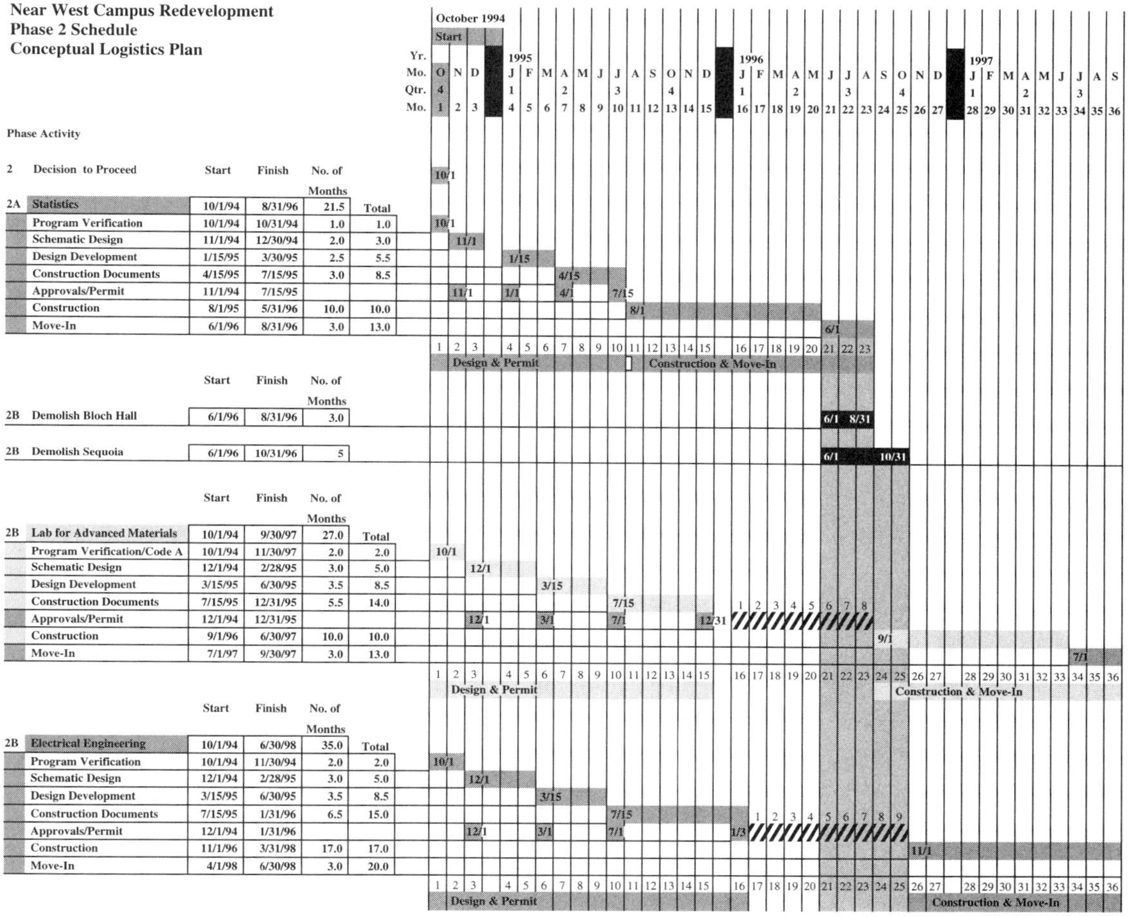

Integrating the resource planning of individual projects into a summary of the firm's manpower and revenue forecasts, although usually easy in small firms, is often a thorny problem in larger firms. Most desktop project management software programs, for example, handle only one project at a time, although more sophisticated (i.e., more expensive) project management software programs provide support for multiple-project consolidation. One spreadsheet-based solution is to create an office-wide summary that contains links to project-specific spreadsheets maintained individually by project managers.

Illustration 5.12 Spreadsheet as schedule.

Management issues related to using computer tools for project reporting are discussed in more detail in Chapter 11, Managing the Digital Office.

DATABASES

Database programs are software applications designed to manipulate lists, or tables, of digital information. The simplest and most familiar physical example is a Rolodex containing the names, addresses, and phone numbers of individuals. In a database, the information on each card in the Rolodex is stored in a *record*. Each piece of information on each card—first name, last name, address, city, state, zip, phone, fax—is stored in a *field* within each record. A database table can be visualized as a matrix, where each row is a record, and each column is a field (Ill. 5.13). Database programs provide a variety of tools to sort, filter, query, and report information, as well as create customized forms for data entry.

For many uses in architectural firms, spreadsheets can perform the functions of a simple database program. A spreadsheet, after all, is a matrix of cells containing text or numerical information, and most spreadsheets provide basic sorting capabilities. For simple applications involving individual lists of data, such as shop drawing and submittal logs, a spreadsheet is generally easier and simpler to use and sometimes just as effective as a database program. What spreadsheets lack that database programs provide are flexible querying and reporting tools. For example, it is difficult to ask a spreadsheet: "What are the submittals from plumbing subcontractors older than five days that have not been reviewed?" Most database programs can handle that query easily.

Illustration 5.13 Records and fields.

Fields

Records

Name	Address	City	State	Zip
Joe Smith	123 Main St.	Saratoga	CA	95070
Karen Jones	555 Front Ave.	Santa Ana	CA	92706
Ted Franks	900 2nd St.	Portland	OR	97219
Will Stewart	1515 Pioneer St.	Seattle	WA	98133
John Adams	23 Cabbage Court	San Antonio	TX	78208
Bill Daly	5698 Rose Lane	Yonkers	NY	10705
Joe Reynolds	714 Hilltop Dr.	Orlando	FL	32808
Sally Baker	900 32nd Ave.	Berkeley	CA	94705
Sue Fisher	512 Eagle Crest Dr.	New Orleans	LA	70127
Ryan Kelly	2020 Twin Peaks Rd.	San Diego	CA	92117

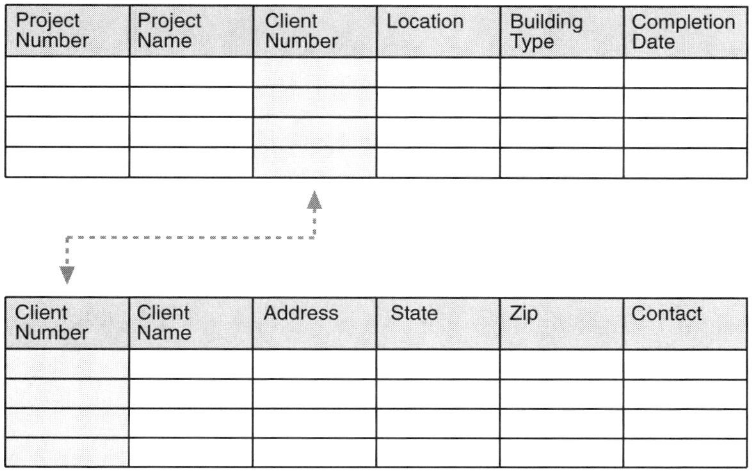

Illustration 5.14 Linked tables in relational databases.

Relational databases are those designed to handle the "one-to-many" relationships between different sets of information. A project database, for example, might include a job number, name, description, project type, site, fee, manager, budget data, and client. Storing detailed client information in each project record means that redundant information about a client (name, address, contact, etc.) will be stored in different projects that share the same client. In a relational database, each project record contains a client number that references another database list containing detailed client information, including a unique number assigned to each client (Ill. 5.14). The unique client number is an example of a database *key*. As a result, the project database does not need to store client information redundantly for multiple projects with the same client.

The power of relational databases is derived from their ability to search for, find, assemble, and report information contained in separate but related tables of information. Organizing information into tables, and defining the one-to-many relationships between them, is an important prerequisite of efficiently storing, updating, and sharing information in relational databases.

THE LANGUAGE OF TWO-DIMENSIONAL GRAPHICS

Both technical CAD and nontechnical illustration software programs share a common vocabulary of two-dimensional graphical elements and operations that can be performed on them. Compared to illustration software, CAD generally provides better precision, tools for information reuse, fast display algorithms that effectively deal with large sets of data, three-dimensional modelbuilding tools, links to nongraphic databases, and various customization tools. The following section describes the basic data structures and algorithms of two-dimensional graphics that are common to both CAD programs and illustration software. (The technical and organizational issues unique to CAD are discussed exclusively in Chapter 8.)

Basic two-dimensional elements include points, lines, multilines, enclosed shapes, arcs, circles, ellipses, curves, and text. The graphic attributes of these elements vary between different software programs, but most programs support color, thickness, line type (dotted, dashed, etc.), line terminator (arrow, dot, slash), and uniform, graduated, or bitmap color fill for enclosed shapes. Basic text formatting tools include font, size, and justification. Illustration 5.15 shows examples of two-dimensional elements and graphic attributes.

Illustration 5.15 Two-dimensional elements and graphic attributes.

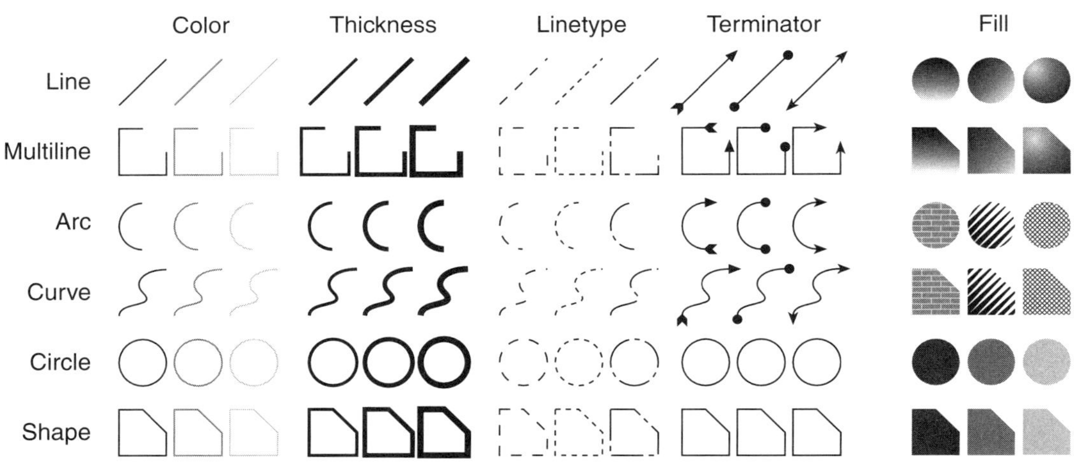

One important attribute of two-dimensional graphic elements is their display order. A software program typically maintains a drawing in its memory as a sequential list of elements. By default, the order of this display list is the same order in which the elements were originally drawn. Virtually all illustration programs and a few CAD programs allow the user to change the order of the display list, by moving an element to the front or back of the list, or in front of or behind other elements (Ill. 5.16).

Elements with color fill are either opaque or partially transparent. Opaque elements completely obscure elements beneath them. The color of partially transparent elements, on the other hand, is mixed with the color of elements beneath them. The mixing of color can be additive, the same way that light is mixed, or subtractive, the same way that inks or pigments are mixed. A shadow can be portrayed in a two-dimensional illustration by copying an element, assigning it a darker shade, turning off its border, and placing it behind and slightly offset from the original opaque element. Opaque shadows, unfortunately, will not reveal elements beneath them. As a result, partially transparent shadows with subtractive color mixing are generally more effective. Illustrations 5.17–5.20 are examples of using color fill in architectural illustrations.

Most CAD and illustration programs support either opaque fill or partially transparent color fill, but not both. A notable exception is IBM's AES CAD software.

Illustration 5.16 Display order.

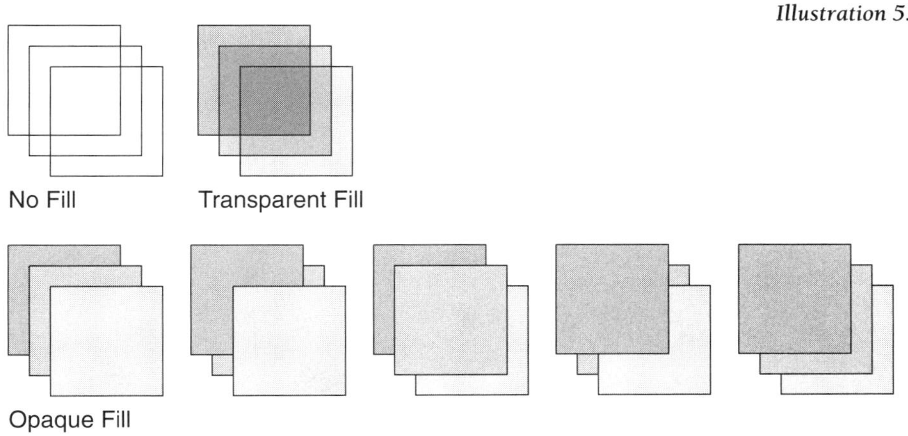

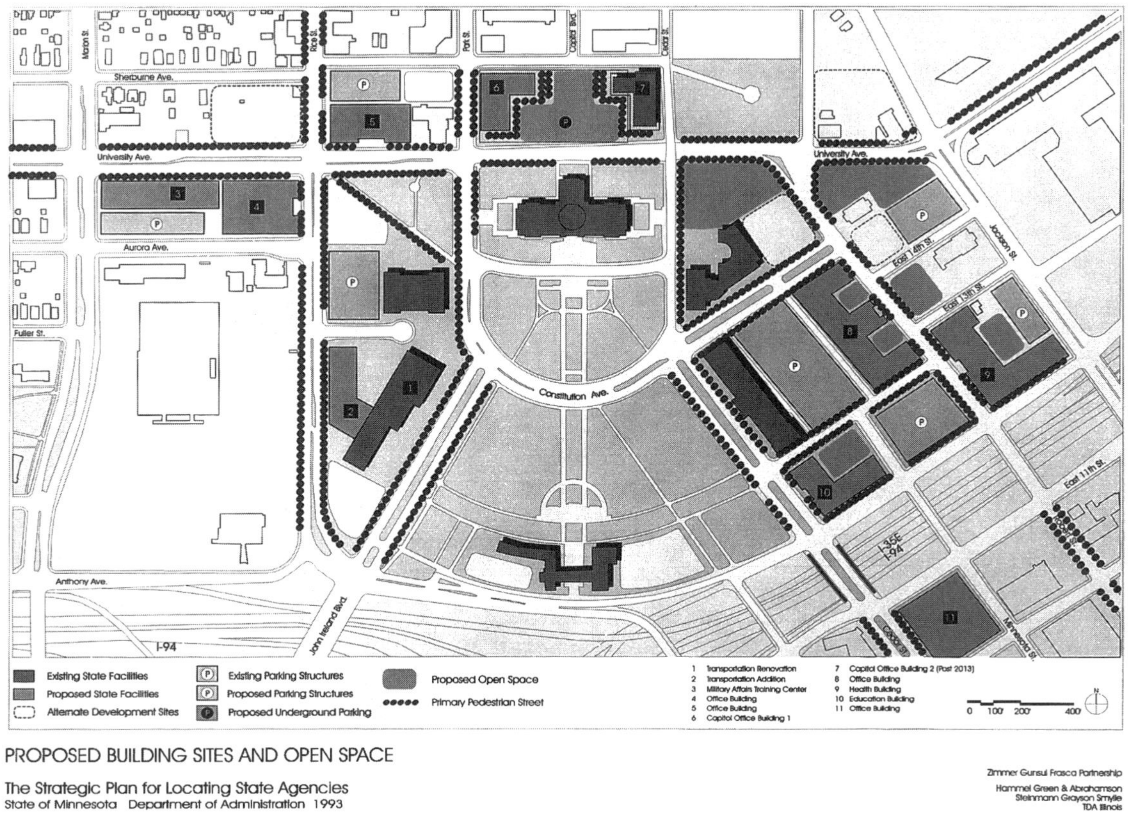

Illustration 5.17 *Site plan.*

Illustration 5.18 *Elevation.*

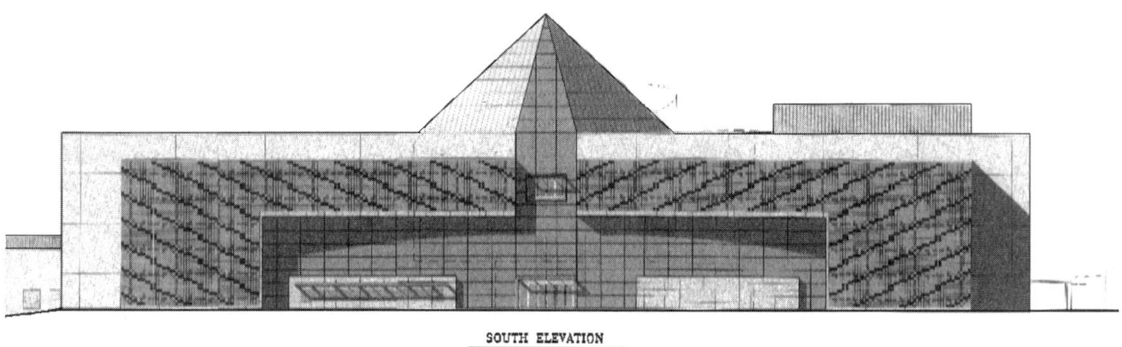

Illustration 5.19 Elevation.

Illustration 5.20 Composite illustration.

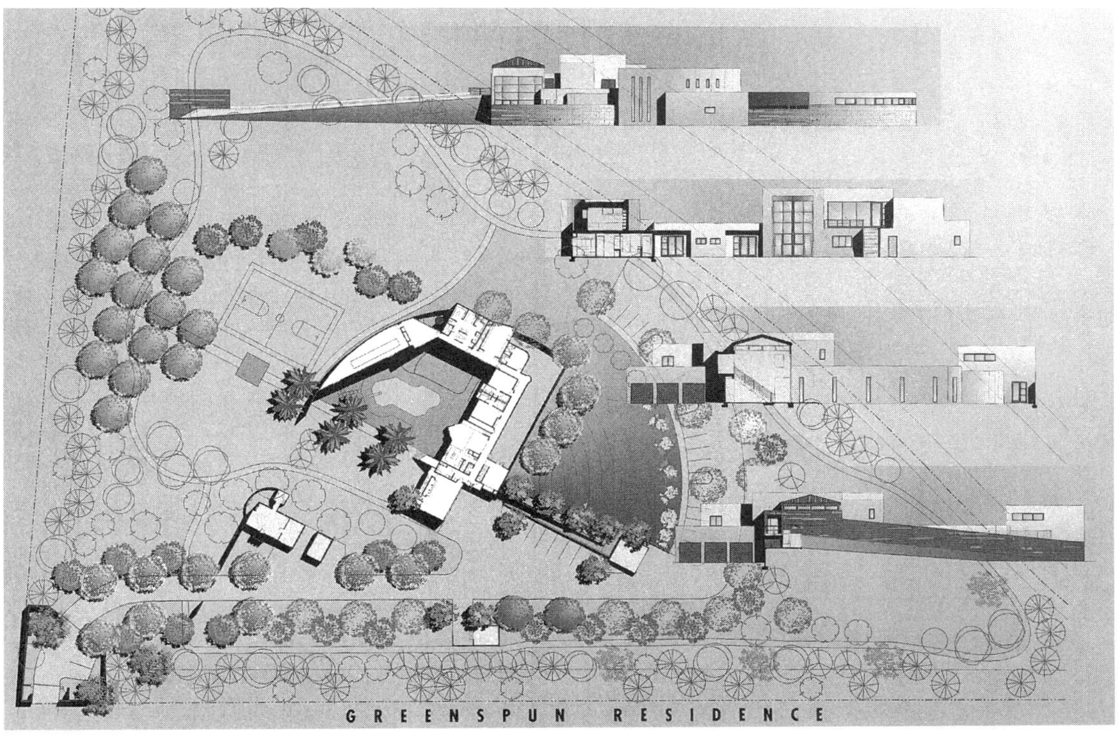

As shown in Illustration 5.21, the basic transformations applied to two-dimensional graphic elements include move, copy, rotate, scale, mirror, and skew. Additional editing operations include drag, stretch, extend, trim, fillet, chamfer, and break. Some programs provide additional tools for creating new geometry, including tracing interior or exterior paths of existing elements or merging, subtracting, or intersecting elements with each other. Most programs also provide the ability to group or join individual elements into a single composite element.

Virtually all CAD and illustration programs also provide tools for precisely locating geometry, by using a predefined grid or by snapping new elements to points on existing elements. Most illustration programs support basic grid and element endpoint snapping and alignment. CAD systems generally provide more advanced support for snapping, including midpoint, endpoint, intersection, and arc or circle center (Ill. 5.22). Some systems provide visual cues about the selection or placement of a point by changing the visual appearance of the cursor or highlighting the location of interest.

DIGITAL IMAGES

The digital image is perhaps the most elegant and portable form of digital data. Unlike word processing, spreadsheet, database, or CAD documents, whose file formats vary widely between different software programs and present nontrivial translation problems to the user, most digital images share similar file formats and translate cleanly and reliably. Digital images can be used to store photographs, output from CAD and visualization programs, diagrams, logos, material samples, and snapshots of computer screen displays. Digital images are also emerging as a cost-effective alternative to microfiche as a storage medium for paper archives. Basically, anything that can be photographed or displayed on a computer screen can be stored as a digital image.

Unfortunately, digital images are also one of the least intelligent forms of digital data. The digital image is a visual picture of graphic information only and cannot be edited using the familiar tools found in CAD, illustration, and other programs. A digital image of a printed document, for example, cannot be edited using word processing tools unless it is converted to text

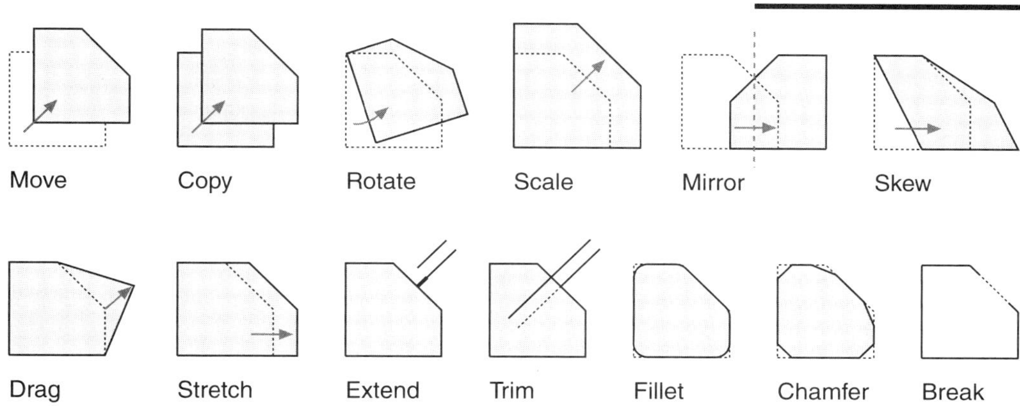

Illustration 5.21 *Two-dimensional transformations and editing.*

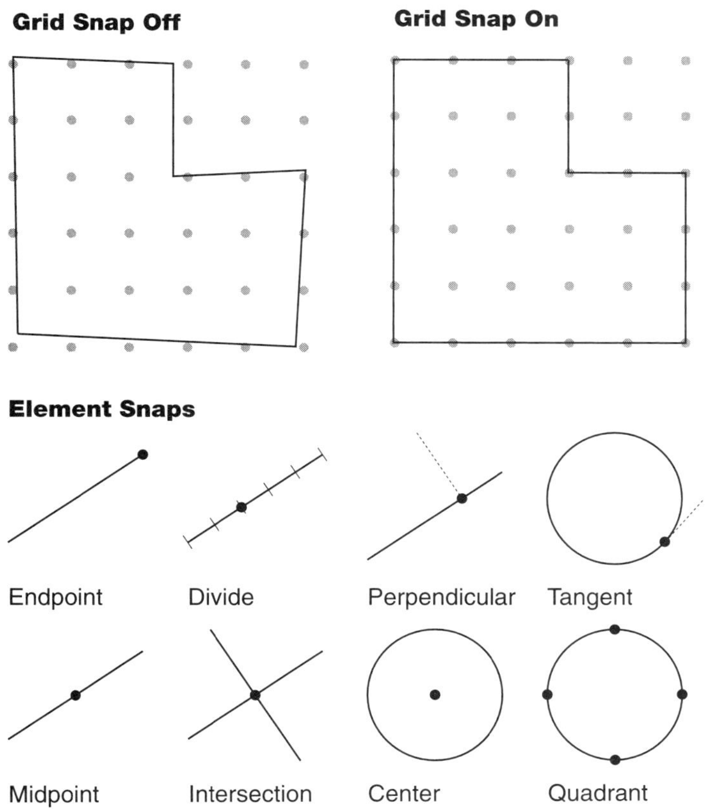

Illustration 5.22 *Grid and element snaps.*

first using OCR software. Although manipulating the information in archives is often not as important as keeping a legal record, digital images are a poor storage format if the information needs to be retrieved and reused. Converting text, spreadsheets, or drawings to images means losing the flexibility of those data structures.

A digital image consists of a mosaic of pixels ("pixel" is a creative truncation of "picture element"). The number of pixels in an image determines its resolution. The greater the number of pixels, the higher the resolution, and the higher the level of detail discernible within the image. Over the years, different software developers and hardware manufacturers have invented a surprisingly large array of digital image file formats, some of which are listed below:

BMP	Generic Windows bitmap format
GIF	Graphics Interchange Format, commonly used on CompuServe
JPEG	JPEG, a public-domain format developed by the Joint Photographic Experts Group and commonly used on the Internet
PCX	ZSoft PC Paintbrush proprietary format
PSD	Adobe PhotoShop proprietary format
PhotoCD	Kodak Photo-CD format that stores multiple resolutions of images on CD-ROM
Targa	Targa format, developed to support early 24-bit Truevision expansion cards for PCs
TIFF	Tagged Image File Format, supported by most Mac and Windows image-editing software

Which file format is better, and why? With the exception of JPEG and Kodak's PhotoCD formats, both of which are described later, these file formats are 99 percent identical and vary only in their inclusion of descriptive information within the file, such as author, description, and copyright. In general, TIFF is supported by the largest number of digital image-editing programs, and is a good candidate for a standard, portable file format within the architectural office. JPEG, because of its outstanding file compression, is also an increasingly popular choice. (Adobe's PSD format, like those of most high-end digital image editing programs, also supports multiple layers within digital images, a concept that is discussed later in this chapter.)

BITMAPS

The simplest digital image is a bitmap. Each pixel contains a single bit, the value of 0 or 1. Typically, a pixel containing the value 0 represents black, and the value 1 represents white. Bitmaps are generally used to store black-and-white linework, although high-resolution bitmaps can also be used to store gray-scale images or photographs. Intermediate gray tones are approximated in high-resolution bitmaps by using patterns of black and white pixels.

The number of bytes required to store a bitmap is the number of pixels divided by eight, plus a few dozen more for descriptive information. An uncompressed 512 × 512 bitmap image, like the one shown in Illustration 5.23, requires about 33,000 bytes, about the same as a sixteen-page ASCII text document. Over forty such images can be stored on a single 3.5-inch diskette. Illustration 5.24 shows a 50 × 50 detail of the bitmap; Illustration 5.25 shows the same detail as a mosaic of bits.

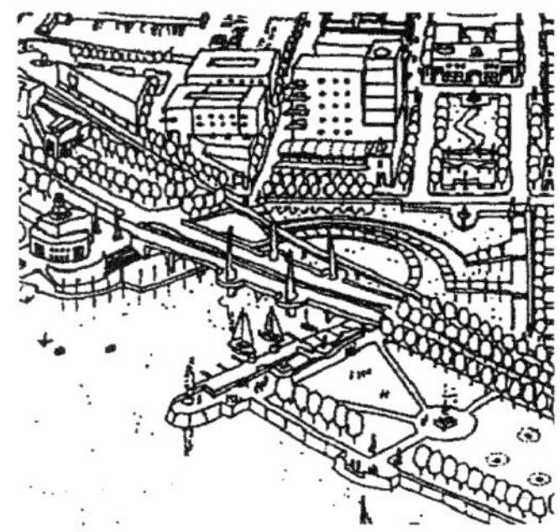

Illustration 5.23 *A 512 × 512 bitmap.*

Illustration 5.24 *A 50 × 50 detail.*

```
00001111111111110100000011111111111111111111111111
00001111111111111110000011111111111111111111111111
00000011111111111111100011111111111111111111111111
11000000111111111111100011111111111111111111110000
11100000111111111111110011111111111111110100000000
11100000000111111111110011111111111100000000000000
11111110000011111111100011111111010000000000000000
11111111000000111111100011110000000000001111111110
11111111100000000001110000000000000000011111111110
01111111111100000001000000000000011111111111111110
00011111111111000000000000001111111111111111111100
00001111111111111000000011111111111111111111110000
10000011111111111110100011111111111111111111000000
11100000111111111111111111111111111111110000000010
11110000000111111111111111111111111111000000001110
11111100000000111111111001000000000000000000111110
10011111000000000000000000000000000000001111111110
00001111111000000000000000000000000001111111111110
00000011111111100010001001111111111111111111111110
10000000011111111111111111111111111111110000001110
10000000011111111111111111111111111110000000001110
10000000011111100011111111001111011100000000000110
10000000001111000010000100001000011000000000001110
10000000011111000010000100001000011000000001001110
10000000011111000010000100001000011100000001001110
10000000011111110010000100001100011110000001001110
10000000001111111111111111111111111110000001001110
00000000001111111111111111111111111110000000001110
00000000011111000111111111111110011110000000001100
00000000001111000010000100001000011110000000001100
10000000001111000010000100001000011110000000000000
11100000000111000010000100001000011110000000000000
11111100000001000010000100001000011111001000000001
11111111000000000010000100001000011100000000001111
11111111111000000000000000001000000000000000111111
11111111111110000000000000000000000000000011111111
11111111111111100000000000000000011101011111111111
11111111111111111111111111001111111111111111111111
11111111111000111111111111111111111111111111111111
11111111111000011111111111111111111111111111111000
11111111111000000011111111111111111111111110000000
11111111111000000000111111111111111111110000000000
11111111110000000000000111111111111111000000000001
10000011110001111000000000000000000000000000111111
00000001110001111100000000000000000000000111111111
00000000111000111111100000000000000000011111111111
00000000111000111111111111111100100011111111111111
01111000011000011111111111111111111111111111111111
11111100001100001111111111111111111111111111111111
11111110000110001111111111111111111111111111111111
```

Illustration 5.25 *A 50 × 50 detail as a mosaic of bits.*

GRAY-SCALE IMAGES

Bitmaps containing one bit per pixel are most suitable for representing black-and-white linework. Ranges of gray in such bitmaps must be approximated using halftone patterns or other forms of dithering. Alternatively, a digital image can contain more than one bit of information per pixel. A gray-scale image, for example, contains eight bits (one byte) of data per pixel (Ill. 5.26). One byte can store a positive integer from 0 to 255, so each pixel can range in value from 255 (white) to 0 (black) or 254 levels of gray in between. A pixel value of 127, for example, indicates a 50 percent gray value. Gray-scale images which contain fewer than 8 bits per pixel usually have a posterized appearance, as shown in Illustrations 5.27 and 5.28, since there are fewer discrete values of gray available to display the image.

Illustration 5.26 *A 512 × 512 gray-scale image.*

Depending on the resolution of the image, the visual differences between a gray-scale and a bitmap image can vary widely. At extremely high resolutions, the eye cannot discern the differences between individual black and white pixels, and will combine the values of adjacent pixels into shades of gray. At low resolutions, however, the differences are substantial (Ill. 5.29).

Illustration 5.27 *Posterized image containing two bits per pixel (four gray levels).*

Since digital images are mosaics of square pixels, they can be useful tools for mapping artwork or photographs onto large areas of brick or tile. Illustration 5.30 is a photograph of the entrance to the DeFremery public pool in Oakland, California. Artists Larry Sultan and Mike Mandel digitized two photographs into eight shades of gray (including black and white), and used the resulting bitmaps as templates to lay out over 20,000 tiles in two 5- by 18-foot murals.

8-BIT COLOR IMAGES

In a gray-scale image, the value of each pixel represents an intensity of gray, ranging from 0 (black) to 255 (white). Alternatively, each value between 0 and 255 can represent a unique color. An 8-bit color image, therefore, can contain up to 256 unique colors. Most digital image-editing programs provide color editing tools with which users can define the colors; the color models used to do so are described later in this chapter.

Because each 8-bit color value is really an index into a palette of 256 colors, 8-bit color images are also known as indexed color images. Useful 8-bit images include the color palette in the file along with the pixel values of the image itself. The images shown in Illustration 5.31 were hand-drawn, scanned, and converted to 8-bit color images. Spot color was added using a digital image-editing program.

24-BIT COLOR IMAGES

Although 256 colors work well for diagrams and representational illustrations, additional color depth is required for most photographic images. Using only 256 colors to portray color photographs, like using black and white pixel values to portray gray-scale images, requires dithering of adjacent pixels to approximate intermediate color values. The dithering can add a grainy appearance to the image. Most digital photography, therefore, is stored in images with three bytes (24 bits) per pixel, providing a total of 16.7 million possible colors (Ill. 5.32). Each byte contains an intensity value between 0 and 255 for red, green, and blue, corresponding to the electron guns of a television set or a computer monitor. The color value of each pixel in the image is a composite of the red, green, and blue (RGB) values contained within it.

Illustration 5.28 Posterized image containing four bits per pixel (sixteen gray levels).

Illustration 5.29 Gray-scale image converted into a dithered bitmap image.

Illustration 5.30 DeFremery public pool entrance.

Illustration 5.31 Scanned images with spot color.

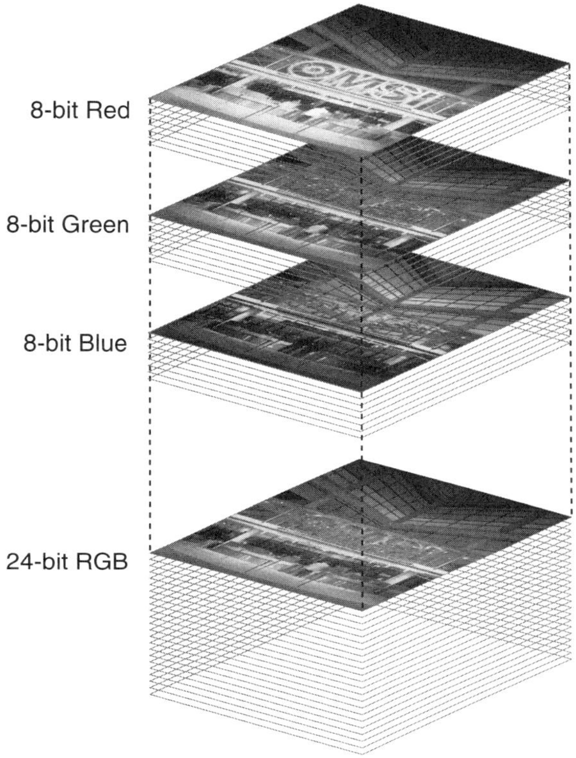

Illustration 5.32 RGB image.

IMAGE EDITING

Image-editing programs support a wide variety of tools to manipulate the appearance of digital images. Simple tools include cropping and resizing images, and adjusting contrast, brightness, clarity, fuzziness, or color balance of an image. Filters also can be used to apply special effects to images, such as stippling, charcoal or watercolor effects, or even simulated photographic lens flares. Illustration 5.33 shows some of these image-editing operations.

Many programs support the concept of image layering, which allows a person to assemble a composite image consisting of individual images layered on top of each other. Each layer can be edited independently of the other. This technique is extremely useful in merging text or other graphic annotation into digital images (Ill. 5.34, 5.35) or compositing computer visualizations with photographic backgrounds (Ill. 5.36). With single-

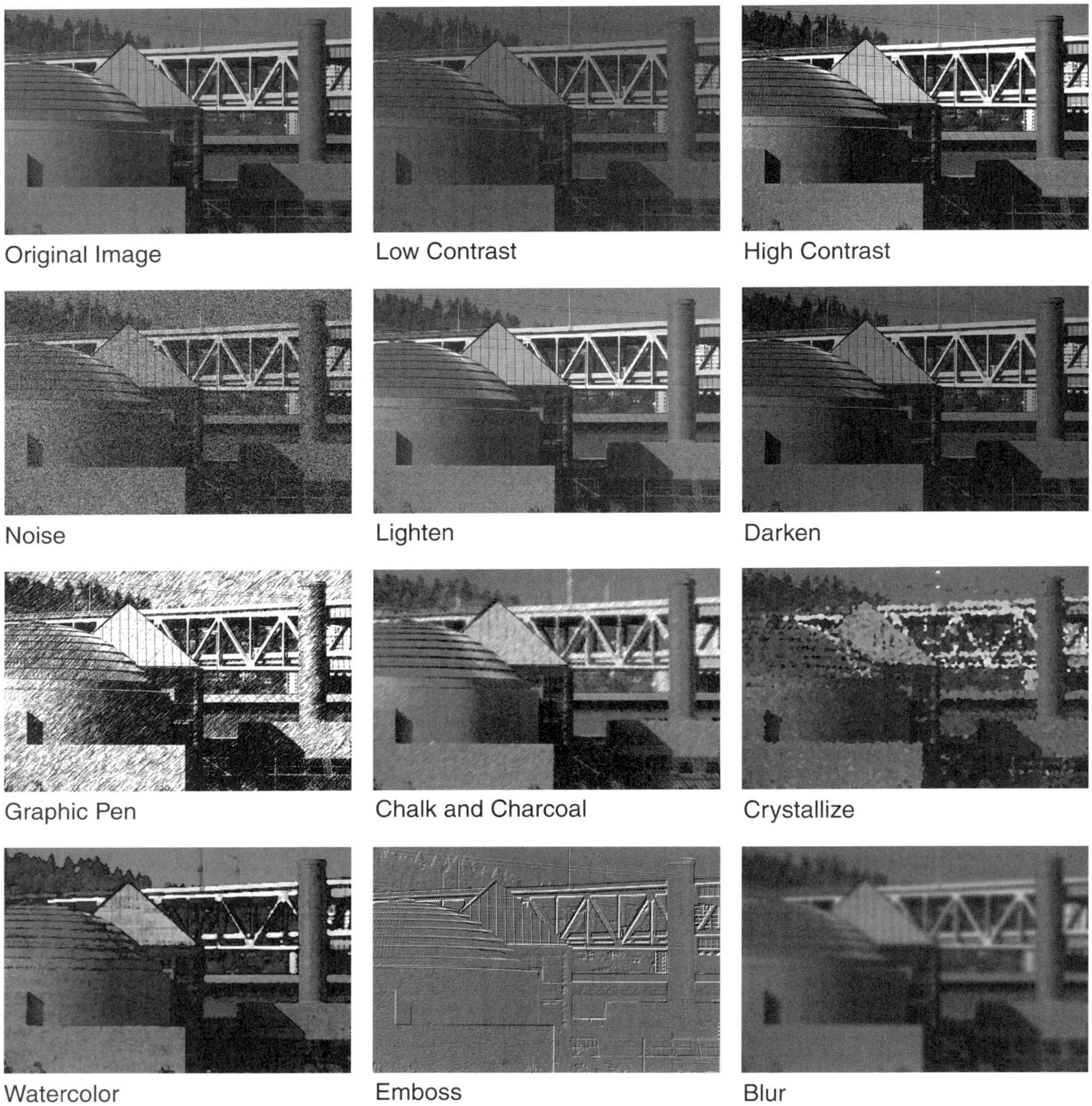

Illustration 5.33 *Image-editing operations.*

Illustration 5.34 Multilayer image.

Composite Image

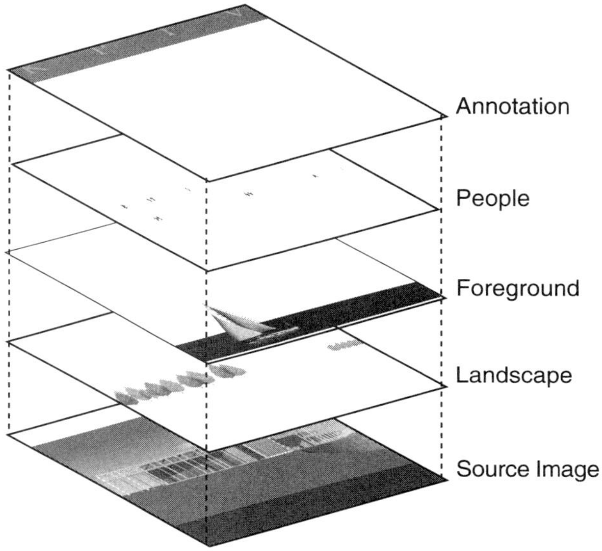

Image Layers

Detail

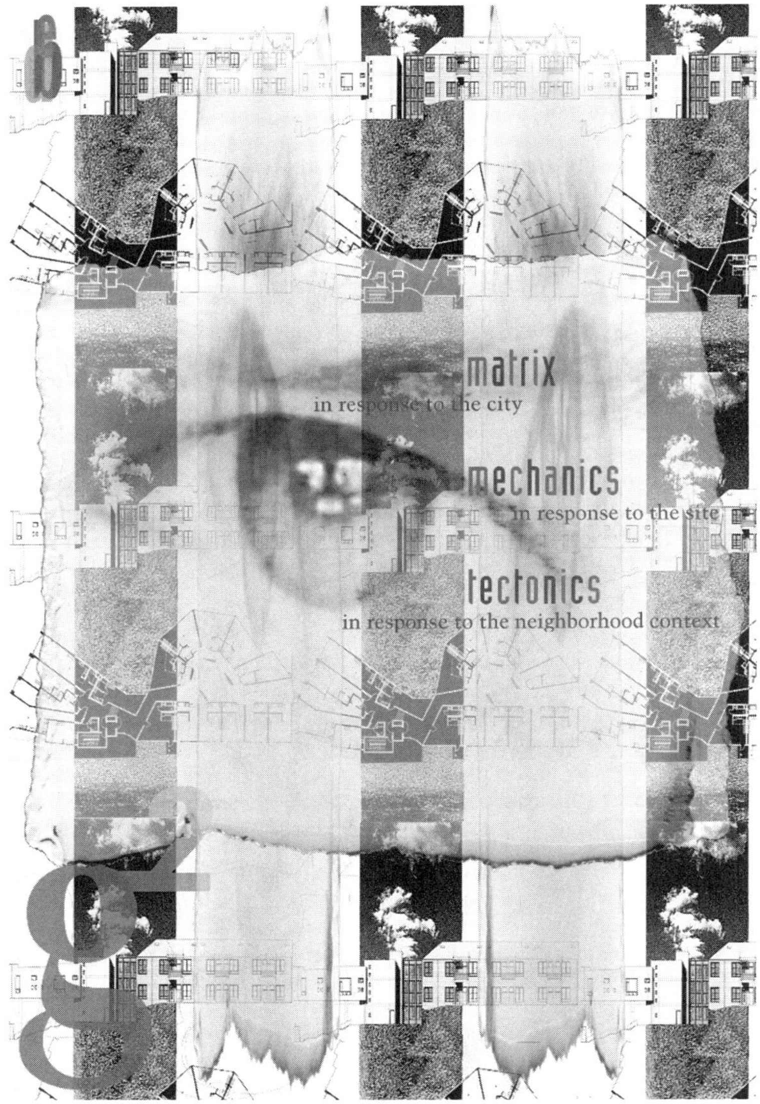

Illustration 5.35 Multilayer poster artwork.

layer image editing, for example, placing text on an image destroys the original information in the pixels occluded by the text. With multiple-layer image editing, the original image is preserved below on a separate layer, allowing the text to be moved, resized, or otherwise modified independently.

Illustration 5.36 Composite rendering.

COMPRESSION ALGORITHMS

Various compression algorithms can be used to reduce the amount of space required to store high-resolution color images, which are notorious for devouring disk space. Compressed Targa, TIF, and BMP files faithfully reproduce a digital image, with no loss of information, and can provide substantial savings in storage requirements. The amount of compression will depend on the amount of detail in the image. A simple diagram can often be compressed to just 5 to 10 percent of its original size, while a highly detailed and textured photograph may only compress to 90 percent of its original size. Four examples are shown in Illustration 5.37. Most compression algorithms search for horizontal sequences of pixels of the same color or adjacent areas of pixels of the same color. For example, in an 8-bit color image, 75 consecutive pixels of color 19 can be saved as two bytes (75 and 19), instead of 75 bytes each containing the value 19.

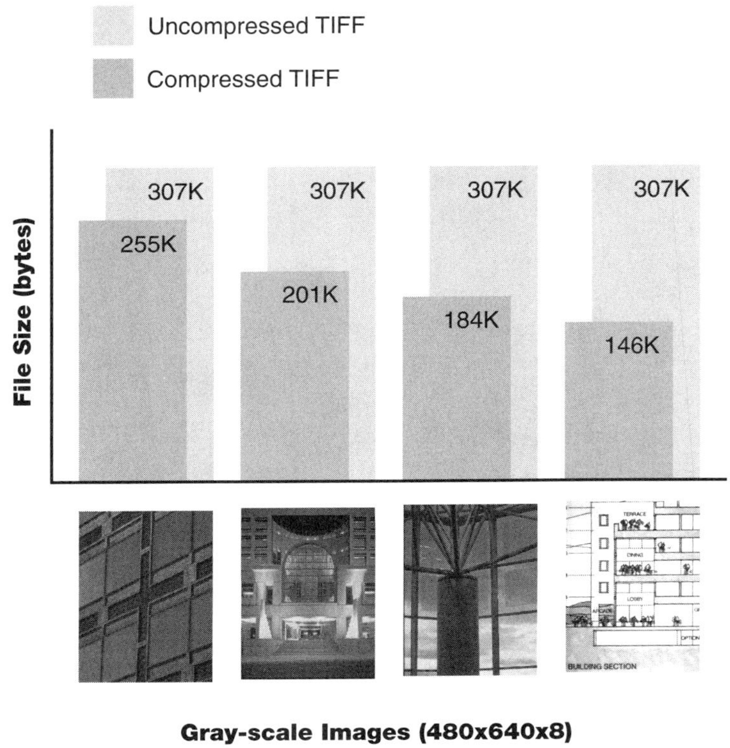

Illustration 5.37 Image compression.

JPEG is a compression algorithm that provides a variable tradeoff between image quality and storage requirements. JPEG can be an extremely efficient way to store digital images, and is the compression algorithm of choice on the Internet, where images transmitted over slow phone line connections require long periods of time to display. The JPEG algorithm will remove detail from an image if there is an opportunity to significantly reduce the amount of space required to store the image. Because the algorithm discards data, the JPEG algorithm is referred to as "lossy." This means that an image that has been compressed into JPEG format, and later decompressed, will not be identical to the original image.

In most digital image-editing programs that can save images in JPEG format, this tradeoff can be controlled by the user. JPEG images that preserve a high degree of detail are often indistinguishable from their originals, and yet can achieve compression ratios between 3:1 and 5:1, depending on the com-

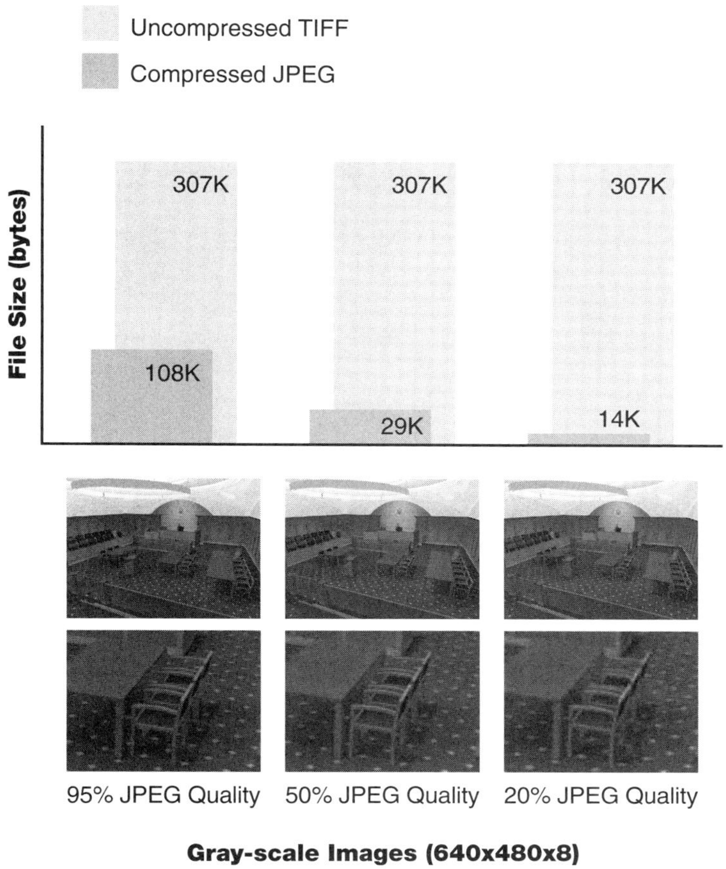

Illustration 5.38 JPEG compression.

plexity of the image (Ill. 5.38). The visual quality of a highly compressed JPEG image, on the other hand, can decline considerably, so it is appropriate to check the quality of compressed images before permanently saving them.

IMAGE CAPTURE

As recently as five years ago, the capture of high-resolution color images into digital format was a relatively expensive process. Today, photographic service bureaus around the world provide Kodak PhotoCD scanning services for slides or film negatives, at a cost of $1 to $2 per image (Ill. 5.39). Combined with the low-cost CD-ROM drives that are now shipped with

Illustration 5.39 Kodak PhotoCD.

Over the past several years, several key hardware technologies have become available (i.e., affordable) to architects, including color scanners, digital cameras, color printers, and video capture hardware. Collectively, they provide firms of all sizes—even the sole practitioner—access to publication and presentation techniques that only a few years ago were the exclusive domain of the largest architectural firms. Each is discussed in more detail in Chapter 7, Desktop Hardware.

virtually every desktop PC system, Kodak PhotoCD provides a cost-effective way for architects to convert their existing slide libraries into digital images. Kodak's low-cost viewing software, PhotoEdge, can be used to browse CD-ROMs containing PhotoCD images (Ill. 5.40).

One unique aspect of the Kodak PhotoCD format, compared to other digital image formats, is that multiple resolutions of each image are stored within a single file. The user selects one of the following resolutions when opening the file:

192 × 128	Thumbnail
384 × 256	Low resolution
768 × 512	Medium resolution
1536 × 1024	High resolution
3072 × 2048	Very high resolution
6144 × 4096	Professional version only

Excluding the professional version, each PhotoCD can store up to 100 images at five different resolutions. The images can be recorded on the CD at one time or in multiple sessions. Like all recordable CDs, each image can be written to the CD only once, and never erased. For a permanent digital slide library, the write-once read-many format is perfectly appropriate.

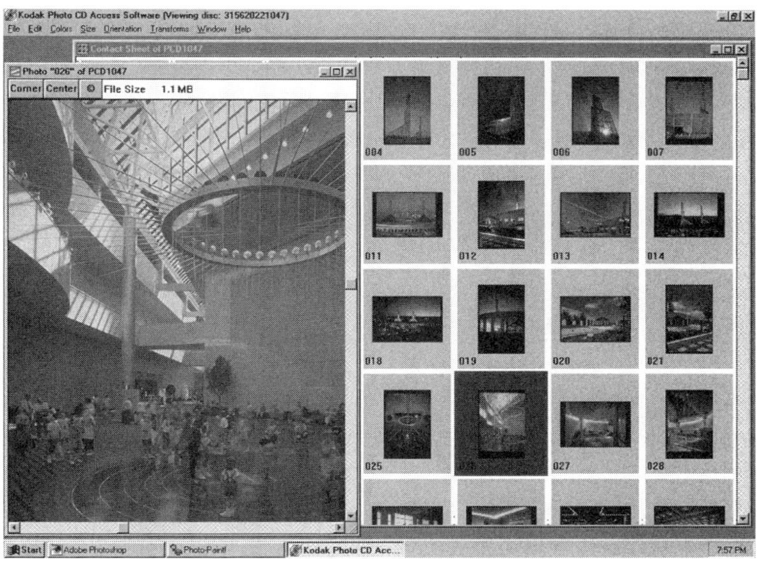

Illustration 5.40 PhotoEdge software.

Like film processing and printing, the quality of PhotoCD scanning services can vary widely. Sample the quality, cost, and turnaround of several service bureaus before you begin large-scale scanning of slide libraries.

DIGITAL COLOR

How are colors defined and adjusted in digital images and illustrations? The three most common techniques for defining colors within a color palette are the RGB (red, green, blue), CMY (cyan, magenta, yellow), and HLS (hue, lightness, saturation) color models.

RGB

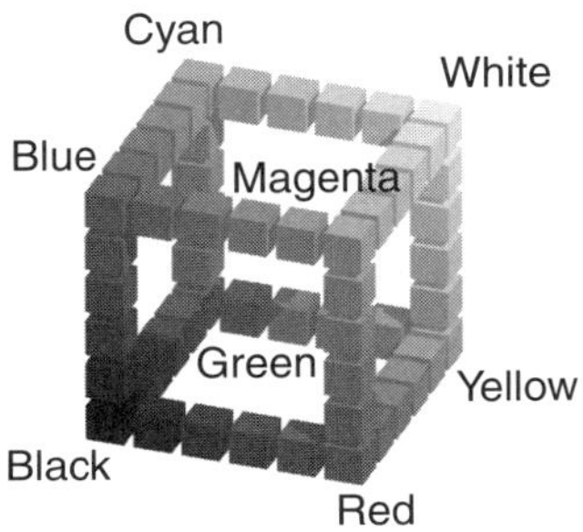

Illustration 5.41 RGB color model.

The RGB color model defines colors as mixtures of red, green, and blue (Ill. 5.41). The RGB model is additive; that is, the more color added, the lighter the color becomes. The three colors combine to create white. Because the three electron guns of most color TVs and computer displays illuminate red, green, and blue phosphor coatings on the screen surface, defining colors in this way makes practical sense, at least from the point of view of a TV or computer. It doesn't make a whole lot of sense from an architect's point of view, however, and is not particularly intuitive. Most people, unless they recall their college physics, will fail to predict that adding green to red turns it yellow. On the other hand, the RGB model does allow a designer to easily warm a color by increasing its red component, or cool a color by increasing its blue component.

CMY

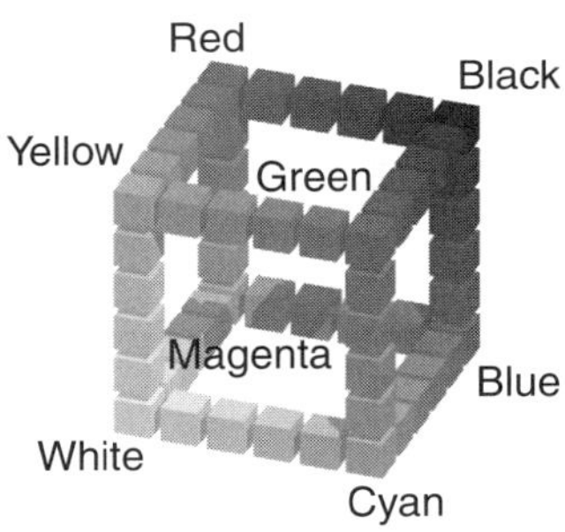

Illustration 5.42 CMY color model.

The CMY color model is exactly the opposite of the RGB model, and defines colors as mixtures of cyan, magenta, and yellow pigments (Ill. 5.42). The CMY color model is subtractive; the more color added, the darker the color becomes. The CMY model simulates the way in which pigments or paints are mixed together (in this case, there are only three paints to work with). In theory, cyan, magenta, and yellow inks mixed together create black. Because of impurities, however, they actually create a muddy brown, so in most printers black ink is also used to achieve true black. You may have noticed that cyan, magenta, and yellow are the color wheel opposites of red, green, and blue. Like the RGB model, the CMY model is not particularly intuitive, but it does come in handy when a color is too yellow, or not yellow enough.

HLS

The HLS color model (Ill. 5.43) defines colors in terms of hue, lightness (also known as value or brightness), and saturation (also known as chroma). The hue is the color of the spectrum, the lightness is just what it says, and the saturation is the color's purity. A low saturation results in a grayish, washed-out color, while a high saturation results in a brilliant, pure color. The HLS color model is based on the human perception of color, and usually is the easiest for people to use. Even the uninitiated in color theory understand the notion of too dark, too light, or too gray.

Illustration 5.44 shows a sample color definition dialog box from Adobe Photoshop 3.0. The hue rainbow is displayed as a vertical bar in the center of the dialog box. The ranges of lightness and saturation values for a given hue are displayed in the box to the left of the rainbow. The dialog box allows the user to pick a color visually, or by specifying RGB, CMY, or HLS values.

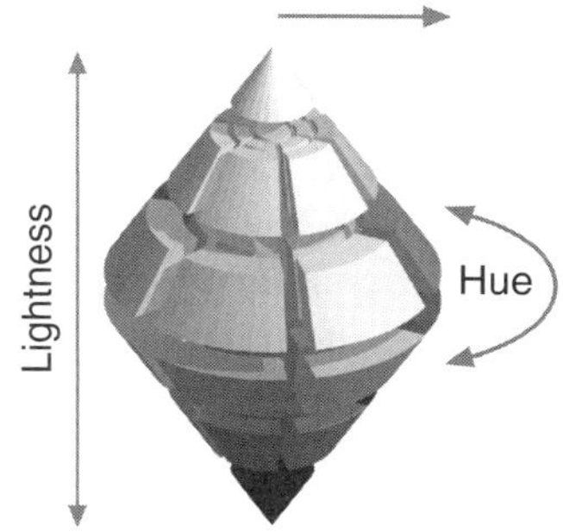

Illustration 5.43 HLS color model.

COLOR CONSISTENCY

Although CMY and RGB equivalents are available for many standard colors, including the Pantone system, it is often difficult and occasionally impossible to exactly duplicate known colors on a computer display. Fluorescent colors, for example, simply cannot be reproduced on a computer display (nor on your television set). Metals such as gold, brass, copper, chrome, or stainless steel depend on reflectance characteristics to be perceived

Adding spot color to spreadsheets, diagrams, organization charts, or other board or proposal material can bring clarity and punch to otherwise visually bland presentations. Color is a universally understood language and a powerful communication tool.

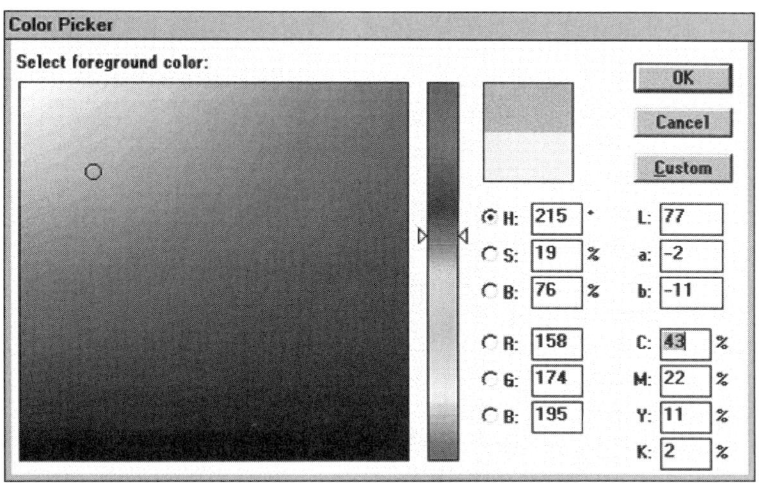

Illustration 5.44 Adobe PhotoShop color dialog box.

Professional artists often use custom inks to reproduce finished artwork, and are not limited to the predefined cyan, magenta, yellow, and black (CMYK) inks of most color printers. CMYK printing inks, like the RGB computer and video display, have limitations of color representation.

Color approximations are acceptable as long as they are consistent and therefore predictable. Architectural illustrators know that the mixture of Prismacolor Blush pencil with speckles of Warm Gray and Black does not exactly duplicate the color of Spanish Rose granite, but is close enough to make it recognizable.

correctly. Most three-dimensional visualization programs can render such materials in a recognizable fashion, but the materials are difficult to portray in two-dimensional illustrations.

Many illustration programs allow the user to specify Pantone equivalents within the software, rather than RGB, CMY, or HLS values. For diagrams, illustrations, or black-and-white drawings with spot color, it is far easier to select a known Pantone color number than iteratively experiment with mixtures of light or ink to approximate it. Many graphics card manufacturers also provide color calibration tools, allowing the user to tell the computer about how color is perceived as displayed on the screen. These settings depend on the location of the monitor within the workspace and the ambient light around it, and must be recalibrated when a monitor is moved.

Perhaps the most vexing problem of all is achieving color consistency between display and printer, or between different printers. Unlike business graphics, where it doesn't really matter if the color indicating "weekly volume" turns a paler red when plotted, most architectural renderings and illustrations require more control and consistency. It can be frustrating to define a perfect beige on the screen, only to have it plot as a muddy brown. (Color copiers introduce similar problems, and many architects find that their favorite pale lemon Magic Marker turns traffic-signal yellow when reproduced on a color copier.) Some printer and plotter manufacturers publish tables of CMY equivalent values necessary to achieve standard Pantone colors. For example, Yellow 650 on an HP Designet 650C requires using the CMY values of 242, 201, and 23 respectively. Even then, printed colors can vary slightly due to variances in paper stock, ink, and humidity.

The cyan, magenta, yellow, and black inks of most color printers can produce a wide range of colors and are designed to be compatible with the red, green, and blue optics of computer displays. However, digital color reproduction is not an exact science and requires human intervention to achieve consistent, desirable results. Try to limit the number of different color printers your firm uses and always test drive.

COLOR PLOTTING IN AUTOCAD

Although it is a fine drafting package, AutoCAD is not particularly friendly to architects who wish to produce presentation-quality color drawings using the software. At ZGF, we use Principium's OWL plotter drivers and PenPal color palette editing tools.

ZGF's standard color palettes reserve roughly half of AutoCAD's 256 predefined colors for assignment to layers and for controlling line weights when plotting. These reserved colors, in the top half of the AutoCAD color selection dialog box (Ill. 5.45), will always plot in various black line weights using standard palettes, even on a color plotter. The rest of the colors, in the lower half of the AutoCAD color selection dialog box, are used for color fill and linework. Most architectural illustrations include a mix of black linework and color fill; this approach allows us to keep the technical linework and presentation color fill inside the same AutoCAD drawing. The user does not need any special script files, pen settings, or conversion programs in order to add color fill to an existing technical drawing.

Three nontrivial problems with this approach involve limitations of AutoCAD. First, because AutoCAD does not permit adjusting the color palette within the software, the plotted colors never match the screen colors. (Screen colors sometimes can be adjusted outside of AutoCAD using various graphics card drivers, but this forces users to use a different technique depending on the machine they are using—an unreasonable practice.) When selecting colors, ZGF's architects refer to plotted palette drawings that show the available colors as plotted (Ill. 5.46). Second, although the Principium drivers can *plot*

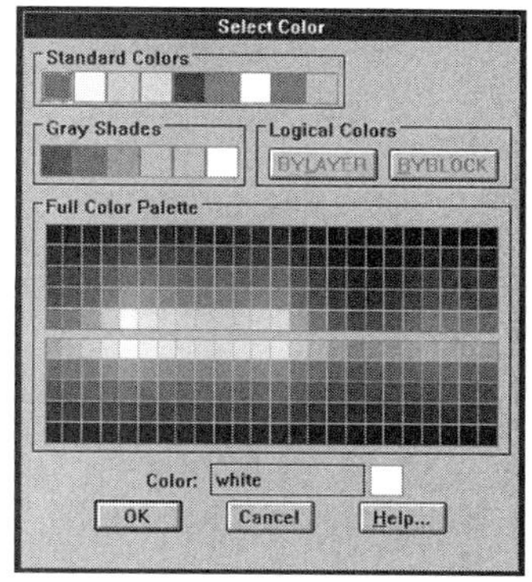

Illustration 5.45 AutoCAD color selection dialog box.

Like most third-party workarounds, Principium's color plotter drivers are not as well integrated as a native solution inside AutoCAD should be and cannot overcome all of AutoCAD's color plotting weaknesses.

Illustration 5.46 Palette drawing.

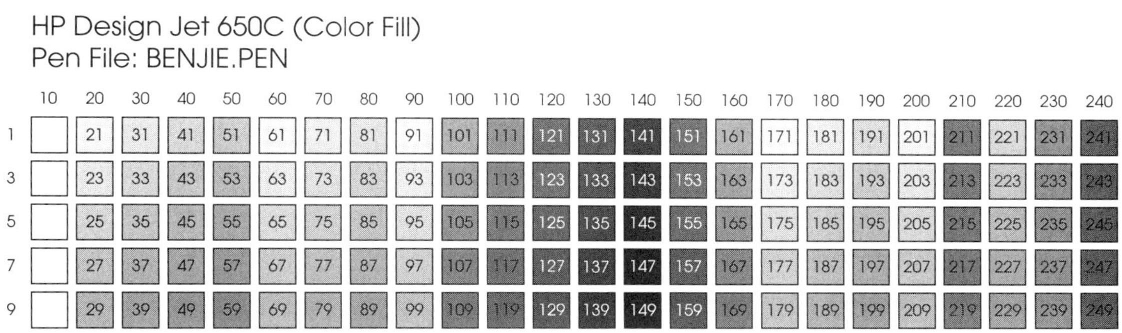

closed polylines (multisided shapes with arc segments) with color fill, AutoCAD cannot *display* closed polylines with color fill. Many shapes that include curved surfaces are more easily constructed using polylines than building regions or using four-sided faces or shapes. Again, the user must plot the drawing to see what it is going to look like. Third, when plotting a partial region of a drawing, AutoCAD clips faces and shapes into lines, circles into arcs, and closed polylines into open polylines. Therefore, filled areas that are cropped in either a plot view or PaperSpace viewport will not plot correctly (Ill. 5.47).

Instead of using AutoCAD for color presentation drawings, another approach is to use illustration programs such as Adobe Illustrator, MicroGrafx Designer, CorelDraw, or Macromedia Freehand to import CAD drawings via DXF and embellish them. However, if a well-defined process is established, most architects find it easier to suffer AutoCAD's limitations (as unreasonable as they are) than learn an additional software program. In addition, the presentation drawing and the technical drawing are kept inside the same document, which is important in an iterative design process. (Sample drawings from a ZGF competition entry for Stanford University prepared by the design team using AutoCAD and Principium's plotting drivers are shown in Ill. 5.48.) Another alternative, of course, is to use a

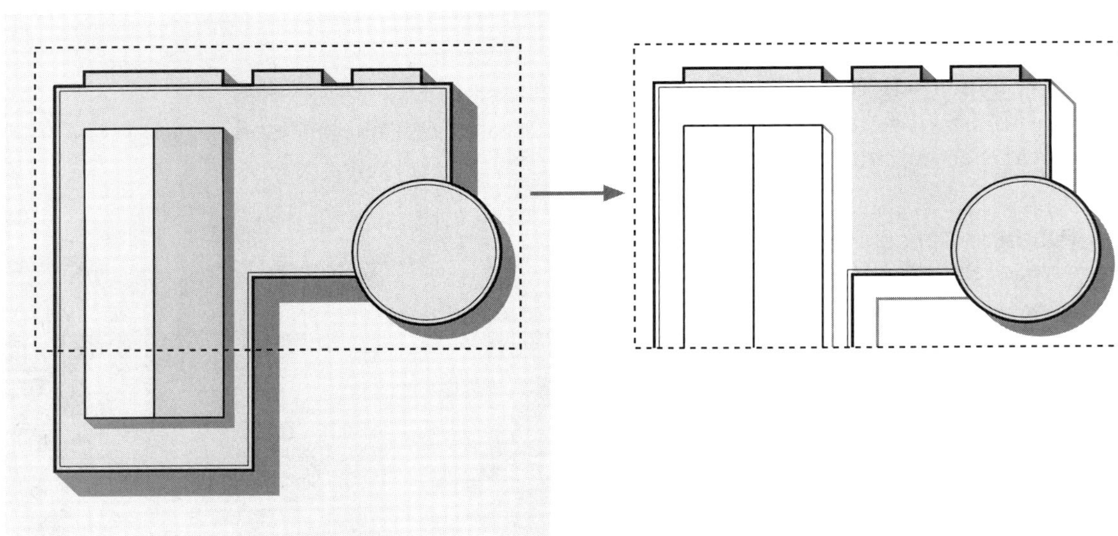

Illustration 5.47 Plot cropping.

CAD program which is better suited for both design and technical drawings. Most Macintosh-based CAD programs, for example, are far better suited for color illustrations than AutoCAD.

Illustration 5.48 *Color drawings using AutoCAD and Principium plotter drivers.*

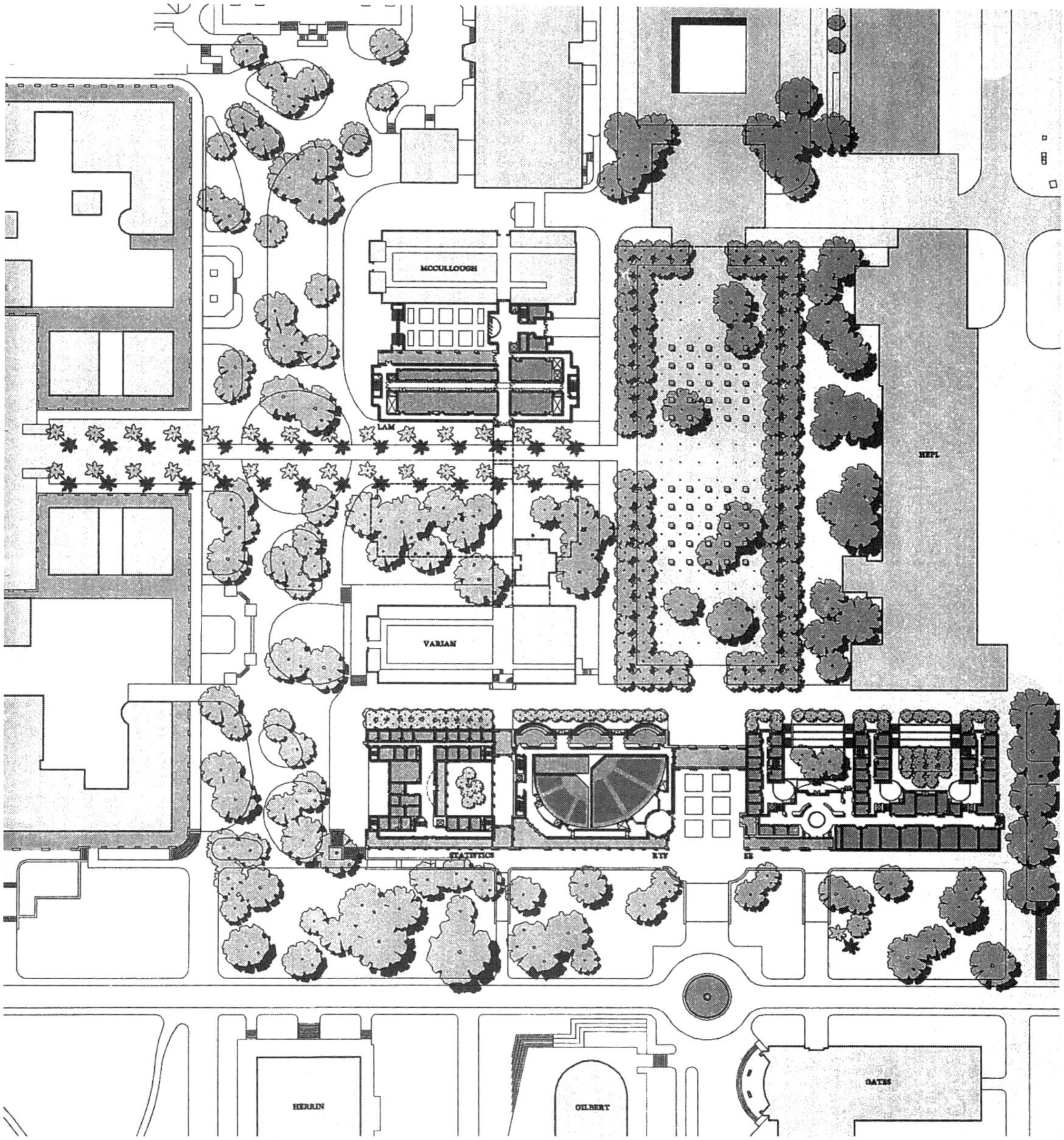

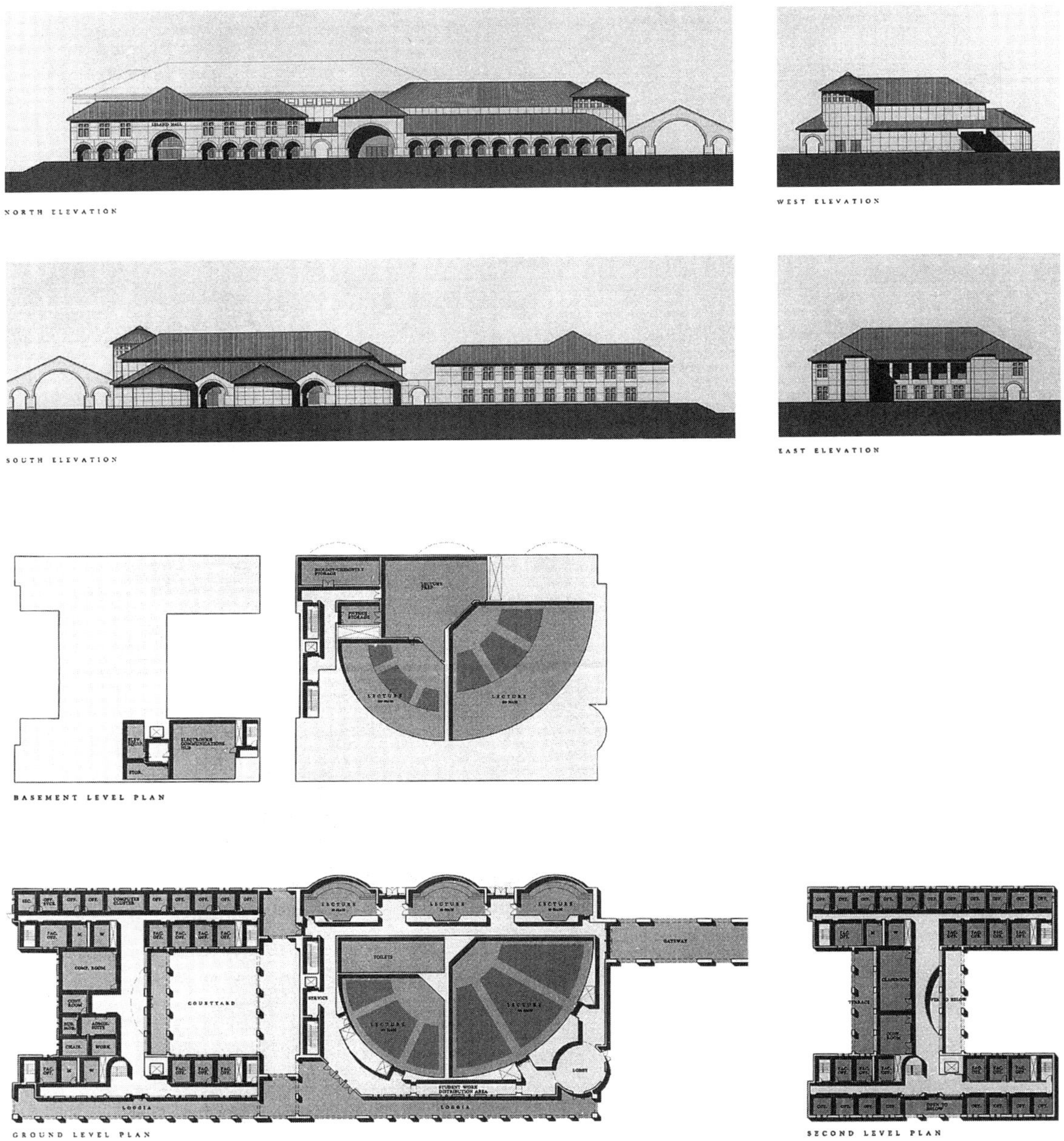

STATISTICS AND REGIONAL TEACHING FACILITY

Illustration 5.48 (*Continued*)

Illustration 5.48 (Continued)

The palm and sycamore trees shown in Illustration 5.49 were sketched by hand, scanned using an HP ScanJet, converted to a DXF file using CorelTrace, imported into AutoCAD, and placed as blocks into the building elevations.

Illustration 5.49 Tree detail.

THREE-DIMENSIONAL MODELS

Architects typically build three types of three-dimensional models:

1. *Massing models* are simple models of a single building or collection of buildings, without windows, doors, or other detail (Ill. 5.50). These models are relatively easy to build, usually taking only a few hours.

2. *Building models* are more complex models that include walls, doors, windows, parapets, eaves, mullions, and major architectural features (Ill. 5.51). Joints, reveals, and other small but important architectural details are typically not included. Building models can take several days or longer to construct and require good organizational planning.

3. *Detail models* are studies of a small portion of a building—an interior space, a window/precast mockup, a cornice detail, or a light fixture (Ill. 5.52). These models are intended to be fully literal, and include all the detail of the actual construction: joints, reveals, material patterns, and so forth. Normally, it is not possible to develop this amount of detail for large projects, but it may be possible for a small area of study. Depending on their complexity, detail models can take as long to construct as a building model.

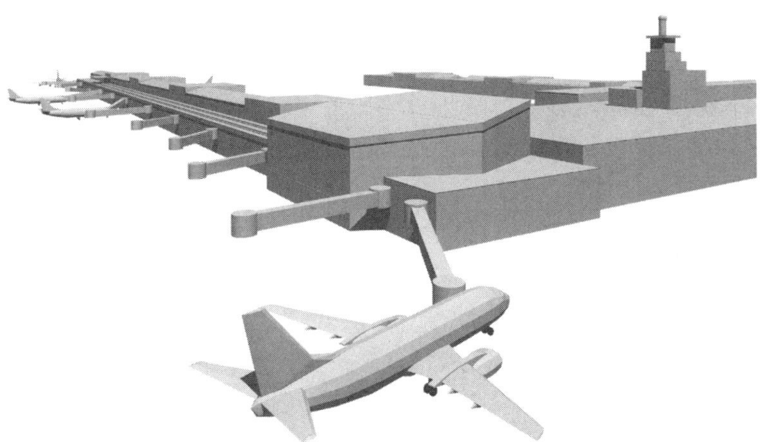

Illustration 5.50 Massing model.

THREE-DIMENSIONAL PRIMITIVES

Architectural models typically include two distinct flavors of three-dimensional elements: surfaces, which are analogous to paper or cardboard physical models, and solids, which are analogous to solid foam, wood, or clay physical models. In either case, most modelbuilding programs provide a basic set of three-dimensional primitives—cubes, cones, cylinders, gables, pyramids, wedges—with which a wide variety of architectural models can be constructed by scaling the primitives in different directions (Ill. 5.53). New three-dimensional elements can also be constructed by rotating, sweeping, and rulesurfing two-dimensional elements (Ill. 5.54). Solid modeling tools

Illustration 5.51 Building model.

Illustration 5.52 Detail model.

If your modeling software does not provide a library of three-dimensional primitives, build your own.

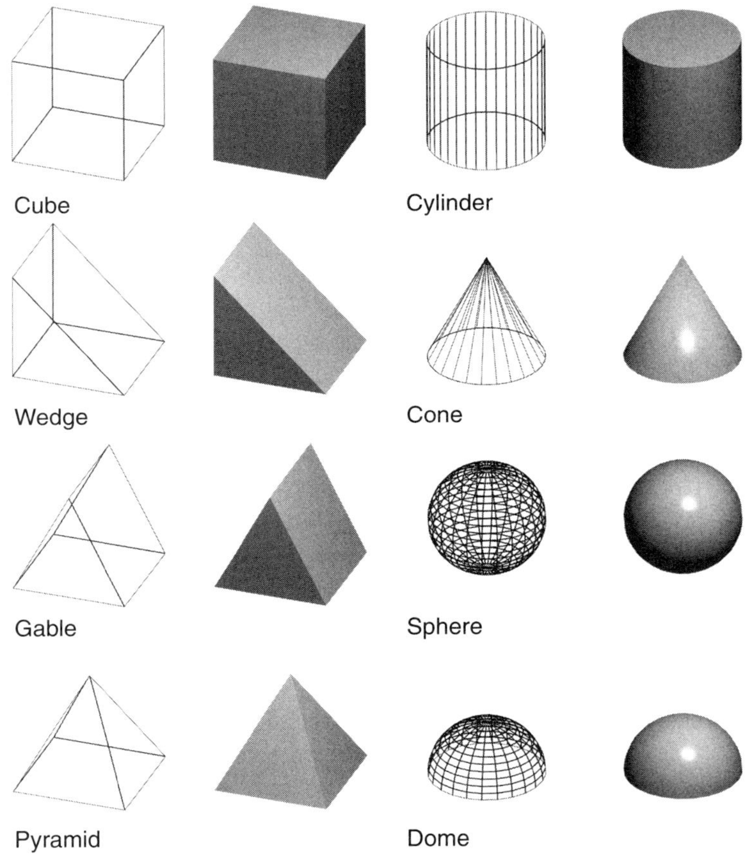

Illustration 5.53 Three-dimensional primitives.

Illustration 5.54 Three-dimensional element construction.

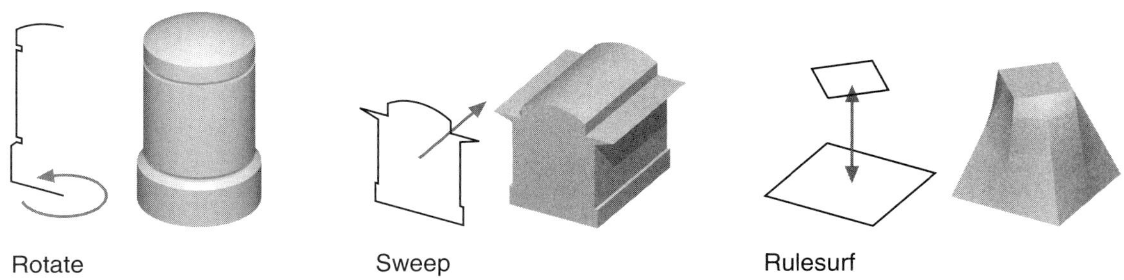

understand the notion of volume and provide additional editing tools to merge, subtract, and intersect solids with each other (Ill. 5.55).

Most contemporary CAD programs include basic three-dimensional modelbuilding features. Most support surface models; a few, including AutoCAD Release 13, also support solid models. Specialized non-CAD three-dimensional modelbuilding software programs have also emerged. One of the most popular among architects is Form-Z (Ill. 5.56), which provides an intuitive (if somewhat icon-heavy) user interface appreciated by most designers and is available for both Macintosh and Windows.

THREE-DIMENSIONAL COORDINATE SYSTEMS

Placing elements in three-dimensional space requires a frame of reference, or coordinate system. The three-dimensional Cartesian coordinate system is defined by an origin point (0,0,0) and three coordinates axes (*X, Y, Z*). Typically, the positive *X* axis is to the east, the positive *Y* axis is to the north, and the positive *Z* axis points up in the air. Each point in three-dimensional space is defined by an *X, Y,* and *Z* value. Some systems also provide support for cylindrical or spherical coordinate systems (Ill. 5.57).

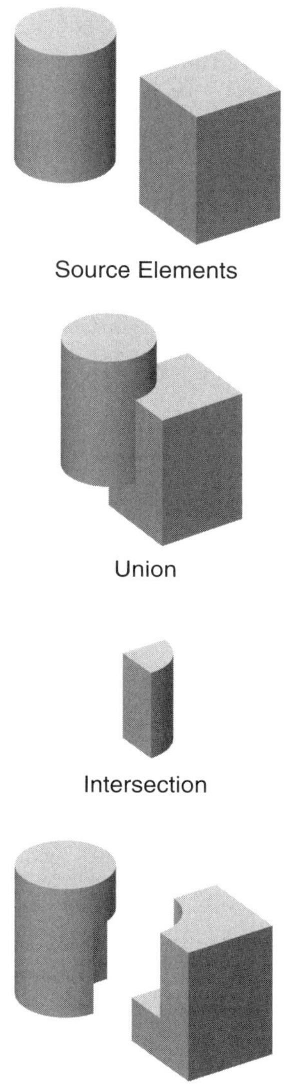

Illustration 5.55 Solid modeling operations.

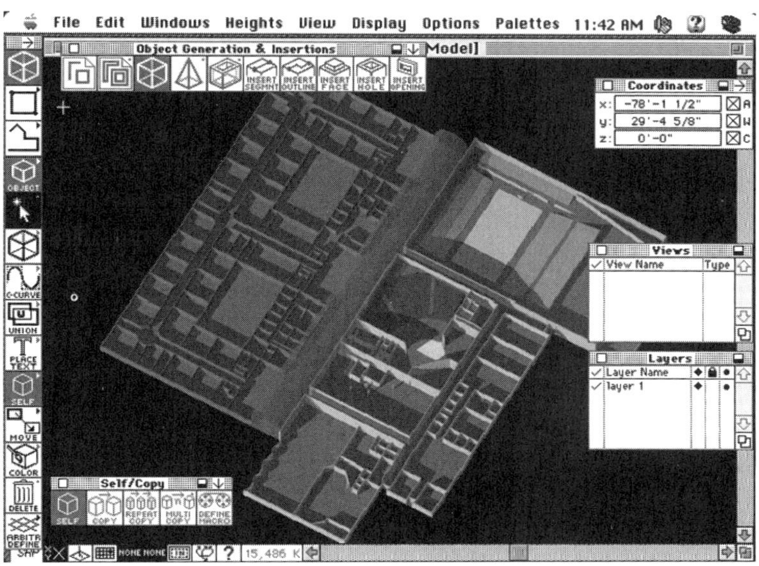

Illustration 5.56 Form-Z.

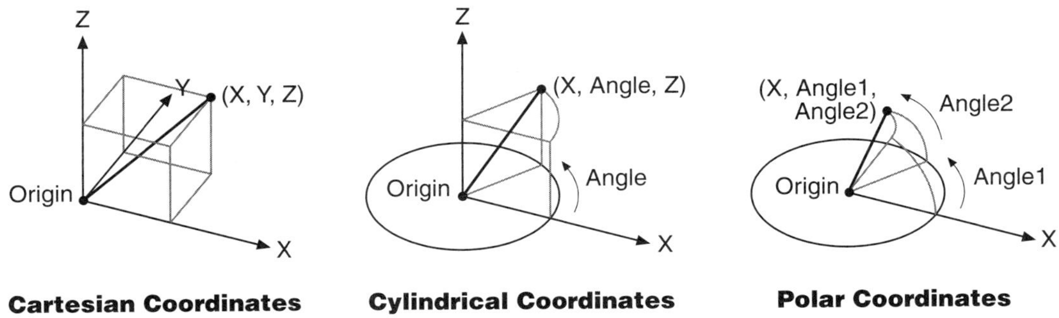

Illustration 5.57 Coordinate systems.

COORDINATE SYSTEM	COORDINATE VALUES
Cartesian	*X, Y, Z*
Cylindrical	Distance, angle, height
Spherical	Distance, angle, angle

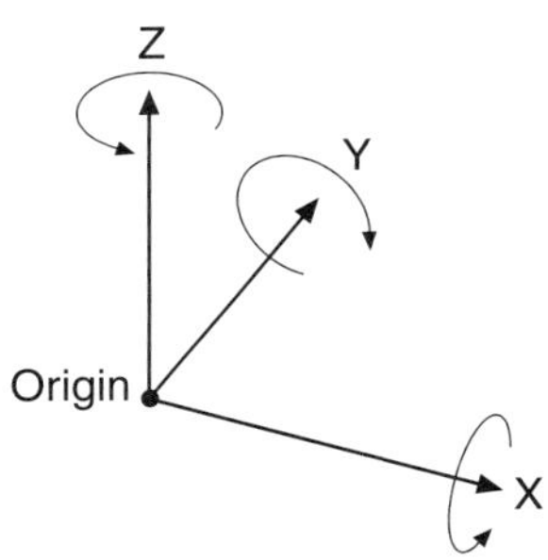

Illustration 5.58 Axis rotation.

In two-dimensional space, elements are rotated about points. In three-dimensional space, elements are rotated about axes. How does one know the direction of positive rotation? Most systems follow the right-hand rule, which you may recall from high-school physics. The right-hand rule identifies the direction of positive rotation about an axis (Ill. 5.58). Align your right thumb with the positive direction of an axis, and the curl of your fingers indicates positive rotation about that axis. In plan view, positive rotation is counterclockwise. As you build three-dimensional models, the right-hand rule can help you visualize the direction of rotation when you rotate elements around an axis of revolution.

Most three-dimensional modeling tools allow you to define local coordinate systems that relate to elements within the three-dimensional scene. A local coordinate system can be described by three points: an origin, a point defining the positive direction of the local *X* axis, and a third point defining the *XY* plane. When a local coordinate system is active, all coordinates are placed relative to it, not to the global coordinate system (Ill. 5.59). In most modeling software, users can save and recall local coordinate systems.

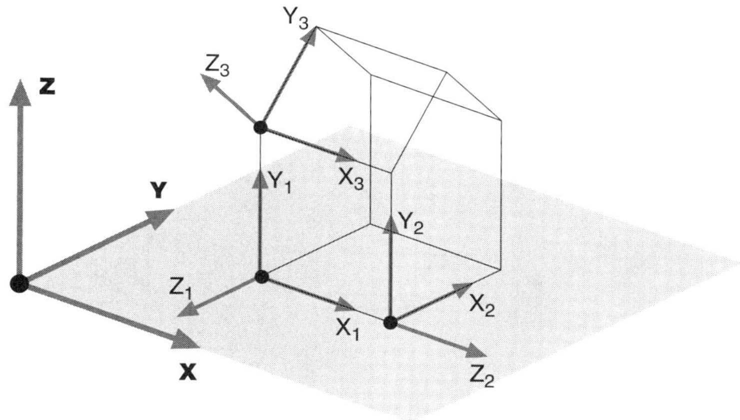

Illustration 5.59 *Local versus global coordinate systems.*

STILL FRAMES

As computer hardware continues to decline in price and increase in performance, and as more sophisticated rendering algorithms are built into desktop software, computer visualization is becoming an ordinary, day-to-day tool in many architectural practices. Less than a decade ago, a high-resolution rendering of a complex architectural model required several hours of computer time, and was often reserved for overnight computation. Today, it can be produced over lunch. Hidden-line drawings or low-resolution renderings, even with smooth shading and shadows, can be produced in minutes or even seconds on fast personal computers. Creating digital animations by calculating hundreds of individual still frames and displaying them in rapid sequence can now be done by even the smallest practitioner.

The oldest form of three-dimensional visualization available to architects is the hidden-line drawing (Ill. 5.60). Hidden-line algorithms remove from a model the edges that are not seen from a particular point of view. Most hidden-line programs simply remove lines from view and do not create new edges implied by the model, such as interior corners of intersecting geometry (Ill. 5.61). In most hidden-line programs that do attempt to display implied edges as lines, the process is both time-consuming and not 100 percent reliable, requiring tedious cleanup of hidden-line drawings to make them graphically acceptable.

Also, the shared edge between two adjacent coplanar surfaces may appear as a line in a hidden-line drawing. For expressing reveals and joints, of course, this is a benefit. However, most

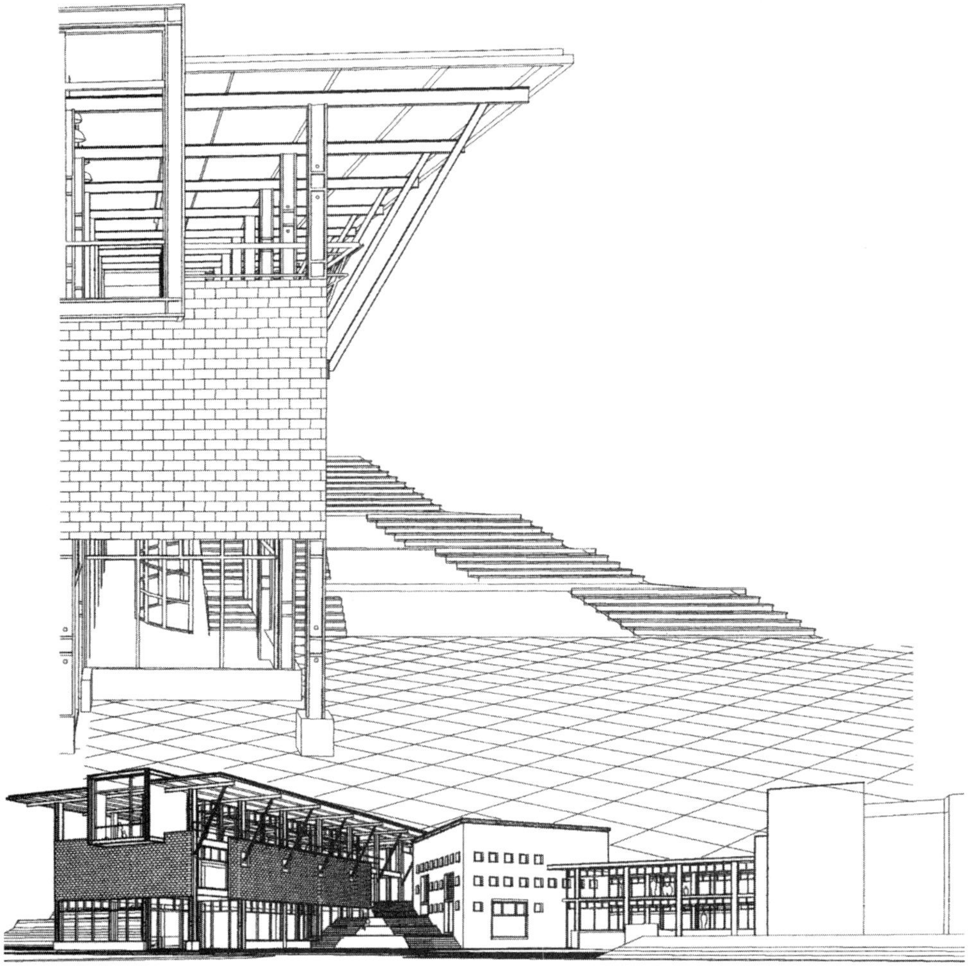

Illustration 5.60 Hidden line drawing.

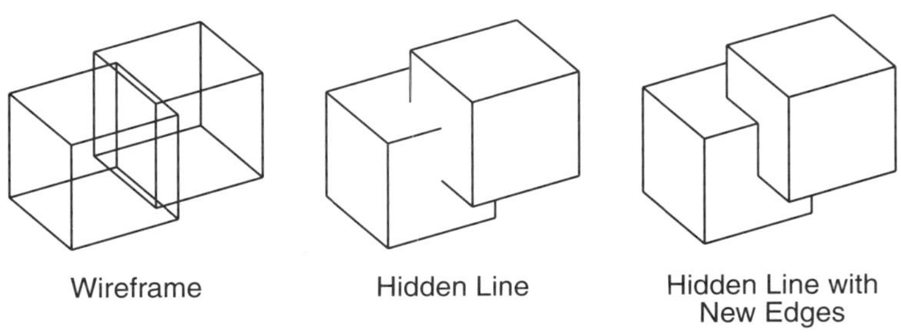

Illustration 5.61 Intersections.

architectural models also contain other edges that are artifacts of model construction but are not intended to be seen. Such edges may not be objectionable in mechanical engineering models, but in architectural models they are often distracting and undesirable. Some programs allow the user to make shared edges invisible before rendering, but such an approach places the burden of doing so on the modelbuilder instead of on the software.

In addition to creating hidden-line drawings that portray the visible edges of a model, most three-dimensional visualization software programs use various algorithms to create digital images that portray the visible surfaces of a model. Most provide the same basic features:

- Ambient, point, and spotlight sources
- Shadows (shadow maps and/or cast shadows)
- Shading algorithms—Flat, Gouraud, Phong (Ill. 5.62)
- Material surface maps—texture, bumpiness, opacity, reflectance, shininess

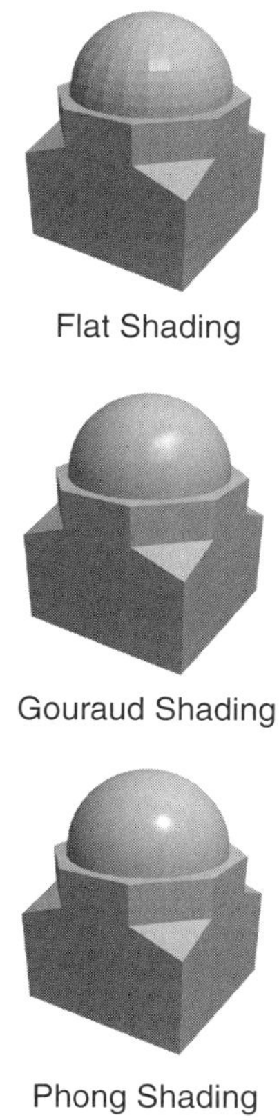

Illustration 5.62 Shading algorithms.

Computer visualization tools, contrary to popular belief, are not great equalizers. The claim that anyone equipped with computer visualization tools can create professional-quality renderings is simply not true. In the absence of talent, such tools do nothing more than help a person create mediocre renderings more quickly. When you use such tools, seek advice not only from those who are experienced in using the software, but also from those who are experts in the crafts of sketching, drawing, and painting.

VIEWING THE SCENE

Software applications view digital models in a remarkably similar way to the traditional perspective projection that many architects learned in college. A virtual camera and target is placed by the user at a location in three-dimensional space, which defines the point and direction of view. The line between camera and target is the view vector. The picture plane, perpendicular to the view vector, is the two-dimensional surface on which an image is projected. For each pixel in the two-

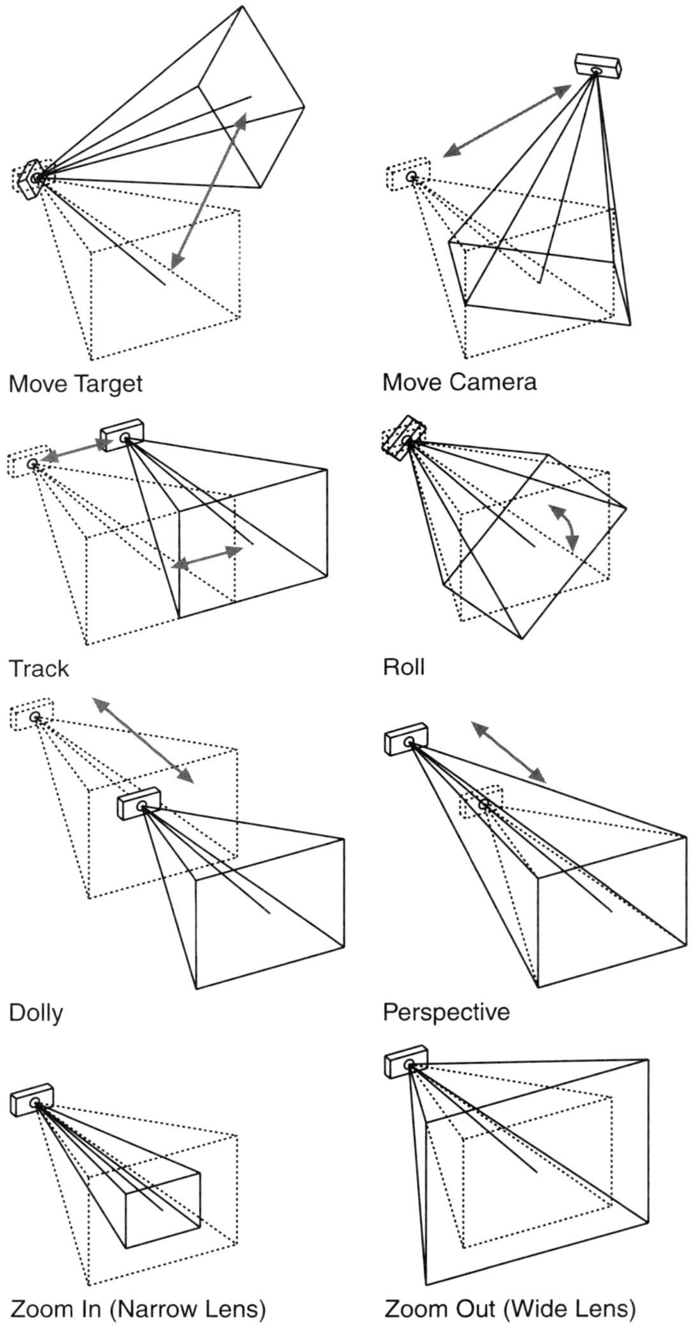

Illustration 5.63   Camera control.

dimensional picture plane, the software determines where a line between the camera and the pixel intersects the scene. The color of the element at that point of intersection is assigned to the pixel. The result is a mosaic of pixel colors that portrays the scene as seen by the camera.

Most visualization programs provide several camera controls (Ill. 5.63), including a lens value which defines the angle of view of the camera. A camera's view can also be modified by specifying a new XYZ location for the camera or the target, by tracking (moving parallel to the picture plane), or by dollying (moving the camera perpendicular to the picture plane). Some programs also allow the camera to roll or bank.

To create two-point perspectives with no vertical foreshortening, simply place the camera and target at the same height—for example, five feet above the ground plane.

In a three-dimensional coordinate system aligned with the overall geometry of the model, a one-point perspective is created when two of the three (*XYZ*) coordinate values defining the location of camera and target are the same. A two-point perspective is created when one of the coordinate values is the same. A three-point perspective is created when none of the coordinate values are the same. Illustration 5.64 compares the three perspectives.

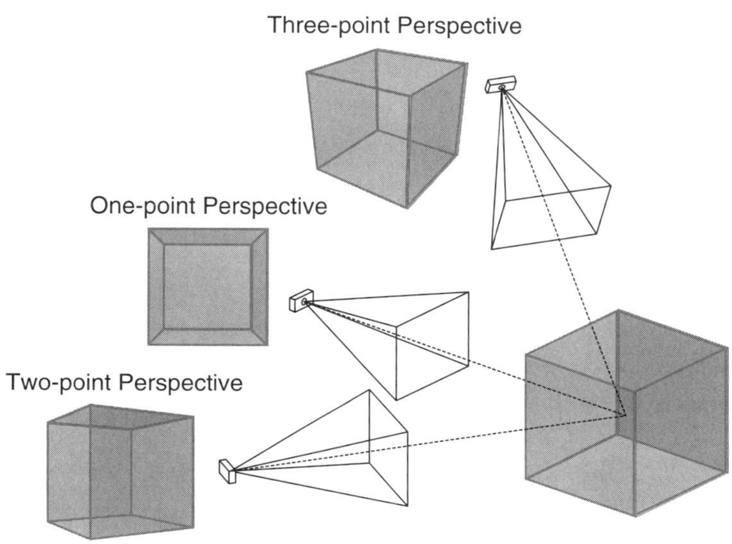

Illustration 5.64 *One-, two-, and three-point perspectives.*

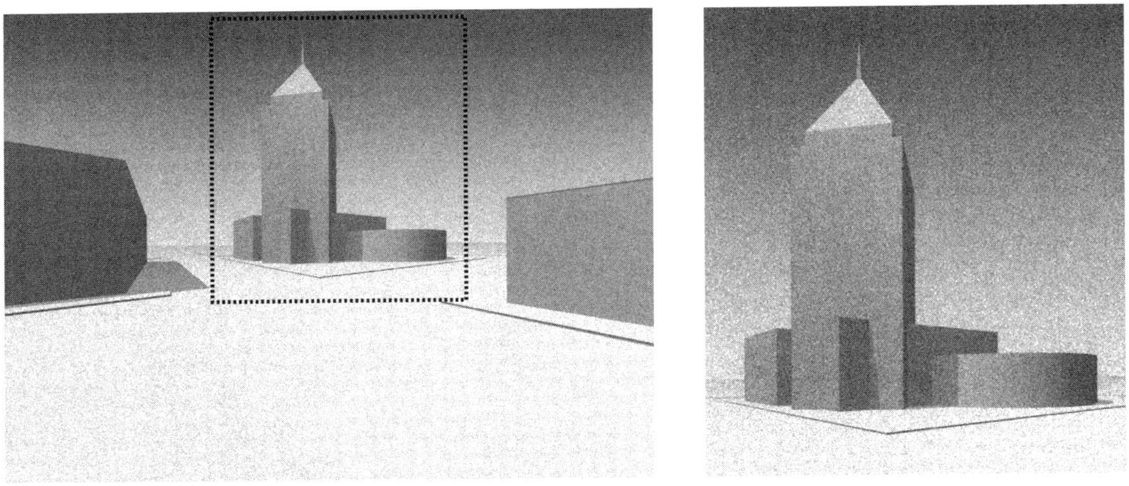

Illustration 5.65 *Cropping.*

The camera's angle of view defines a virtual pyramid, with the camera located at the apex and the sides of the pyramid defining the edges of the image where they intersect the picture plane. In most software programs, unfortunately, the viewing pyramid is wholly symmetrical about the viewing vector. The visual effect is that an image with no vertical foreshortening will result in a poor composition with the horizon line centered in the image. Some software programs allow you to define the sides of the viewing pyramid (also known as clipping planes) by specifying a distance offset from the view vector. Otherwise, you must render the scene with a larger than necessary viewing angle, and crop the resulting image in an image-editing program (Ill. 5.65).

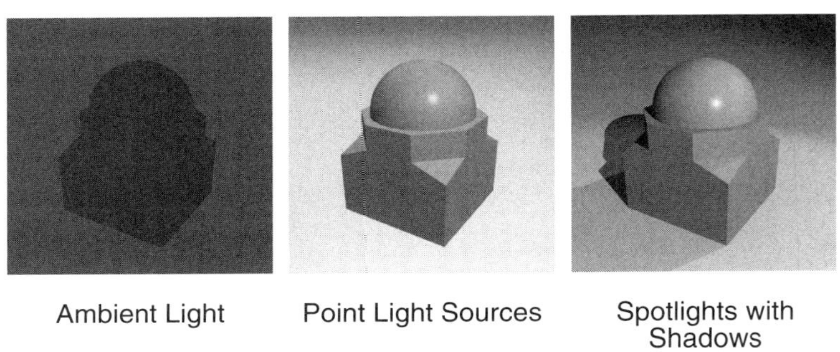

Illustration 5.66 *Types of lights.*

LIGHTING, SHADOWS, AND MATERIALS

Most visualization programs support three basic types of lights, as shown in Illustration 5.66:

1. *Ambient light* describes the general light level of a scene. It has equal intensity everywhere and does not produce highlights or shadows.
2. *Point lights* are omnidirectional lights—like light bulbs without fixtures. They are point light sources that emit light in all directions.
3. *Spotlights* are like Luxo lamps. They have a specific direction, hotspot, and falloff. In most rendering programs, only spotlights can cast shadows.

Shadows help provide clarity and depth to computer-generated images, and two algorithms are typically used to portray them within a scene: shadow maps and cast shadows (Ill. 5.67). Shadow maps essentially render the scene from the point of view of the light source, and use that information to determine what is in light and what is in shadow. The resolution of the shadow map image affects the clarity of the shadows, and low-resolution shadow maps often result in jagged shadows, which are the same type of aliasing artifact as jaggies on a computer display screen. Cast shadows (or ray-traced shadows) are more compute-intensive, but accurately portray sharp-edged shadows. For each point in the scene visible at a pixel, the software constructs a vector back to the light source and determines

Illustration 5.67 *Types of shadows.*

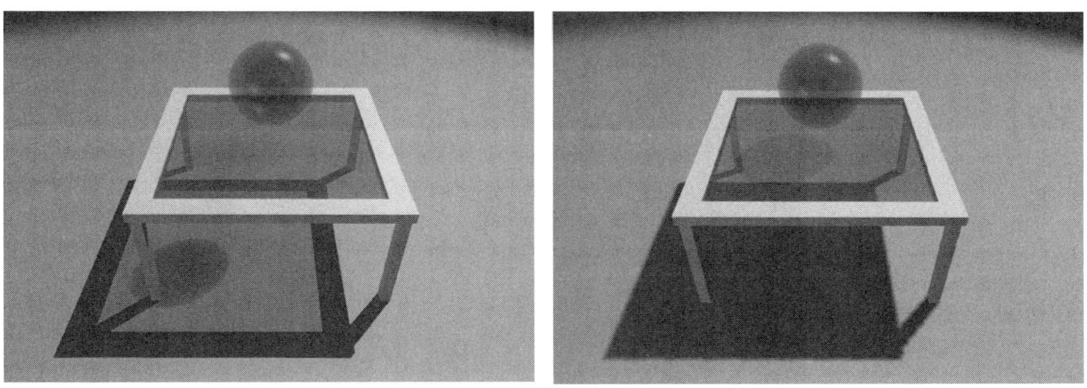
Cast Shadows Shadow Maps

if other geometry in the scene intersects it. If so, the point is in shadow; if not, the point is illuminated.

A wide variety of material attributes are also available in most visualization programs, including color, shininess, transparency, texture, bumpiness, and reflectance (Ill. 5.68). Most massing and study models, however, are best rendered using fairly simple, matte finishes. In addition to using custom materials unique to each project, most firms develop libraries of standard materials, such as glass, concrete, brick, stainless steel, brass, and standard paint colors.

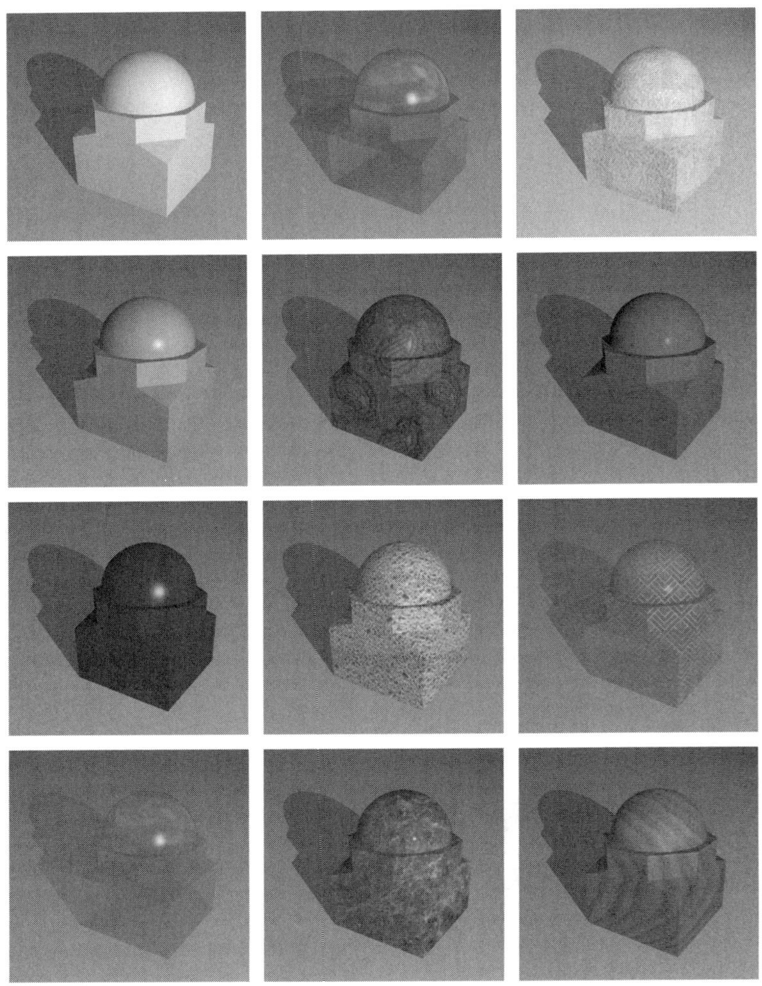

Illustration 5.68 Materials.

THE CULT OF PHOTOREALISM

A common misconception regarding images of computer models is that the more realistic the visualization, the better. In fact, the most useful computer visualizations in architectural firms are sometimes simple images of study models, including basic massing only, without materials.

Building owners and users, in fact, may react inappropriately to realistic images presented too early in the design process. At worst, they can feel cut out, threatened that the design has developed so far without their participation. Such feelings can easily harm a collaborative design process. At best, clients can become distracted. One urban planner described how he spent a good portion of a schematic design presentation explaining that the lampposts in the computer image really weren't the *actual* lampposts that were going to be specified, just an *example* of a lamppost that would be selected later, one with similar style, proportion, and spacing. Designers themselves can become distracted by too much detail in a conceptual or schematic design image, and need to maintain their focus on the design issues relevant to those phases.

When seen in a computer rendering, an idea or concept can appear inappropriately literal. This is not an issue of technological comfort level, but an issue of communication clarity and focus.

The photorealistic images that are displayed in software journals and advertisements are technically impressive, but are usually one-shot end products, and rarely reflect the iterative process of design, and how visualization tools can be applied within that process. They are finished *products* but not necessarily part of the *process*.

Many of the computer models built today at ZGF are purposely diagrammatic or schematic, without too much detail or color. They are representational, not literal. Monochrome models simply lit, in fact, are as effective as physical whiteboard models for the same reasons. Quite often, they are not only more effective in communicating ideas to clients, but also more effective as study models. They allow designers to focus on a smaller set of design issues, such as proportion, scale, and massing, without the visual noise and distraction of a finished prod-

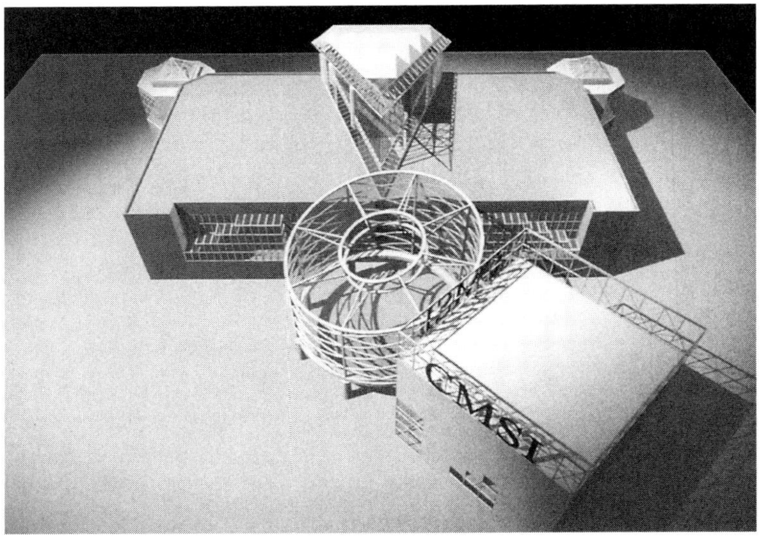

Illustration 5.69 *California Museum of Science and Industry —schematic design phase.*

uct. Illustrations 5.69–5.71 are images of digital study models built for a new exhibit hall for the California Museum of Science and Industry in Los Angeles, California. Illustration 5.72 is an example of simple massing model images integrated with color CAD plans on conceptual design presentation boards for a laboratory project for the National Institutes of Health in India. Illustration 5.73 shows a design development rendering for the same project.

When presenting a computer-generated image during conceptual or schematic design, take care to communicate to the client that the image represents *a* solution, not *the* solution.

Illustration 5.74 shows two detailed conceptual design images prepared for the Portland International Airport's enplaning roadway and parking expansion project. In this case, one of three conceptual design alternatives was to link the airport terminal and new parking garage with an overhead structure and twin pedestrian bridges. Two other alternatives did not involve the structure and bridges. The client was interested in realistic computer-generated images to help them visualize each conceptual alternative. The result: each was resolved to a higher degree of detail than usual for conceptual design, and a larger amount of dead-end design effort was expended. However, the images were very helpful in communicating each alternative to the client and helping them understand the scale and design issues involved.

Illustration 5.70 California Museum of Science and Industry —design development phase.

The best approach to computer visualization is not to mimic the style of traditional renderings or to emulate the realism of photographs, but to communicate design concepts in ways that physical models or renderings cannot. This usually does not involve realism, but instead abstraction, disassembly, and motion.

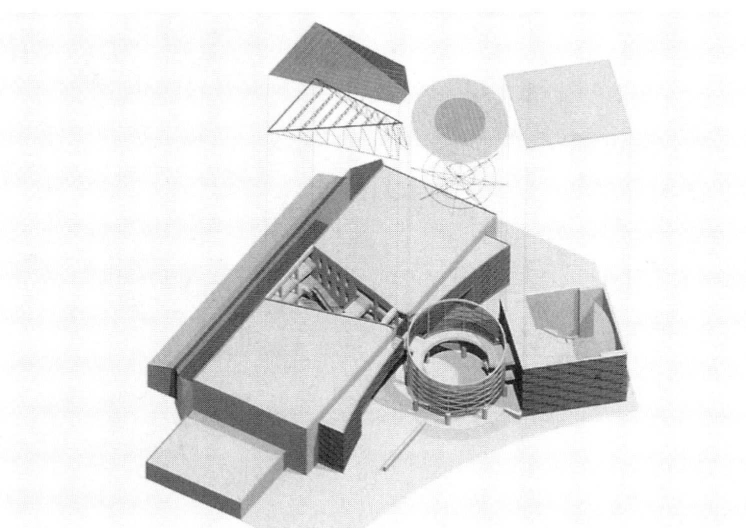

Illustration 5.71 California Museum of Science and Industry —construction documents phase.

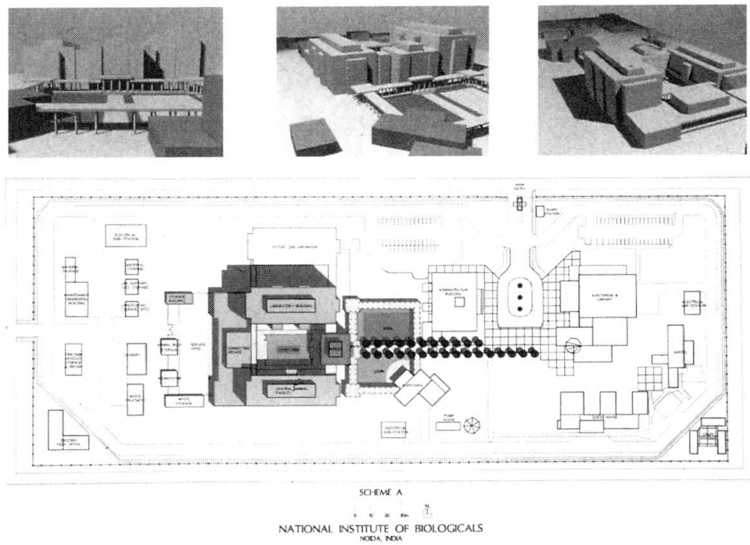

Illustration 5.72 *National Institutes of Health—conceptual design alternatives.*

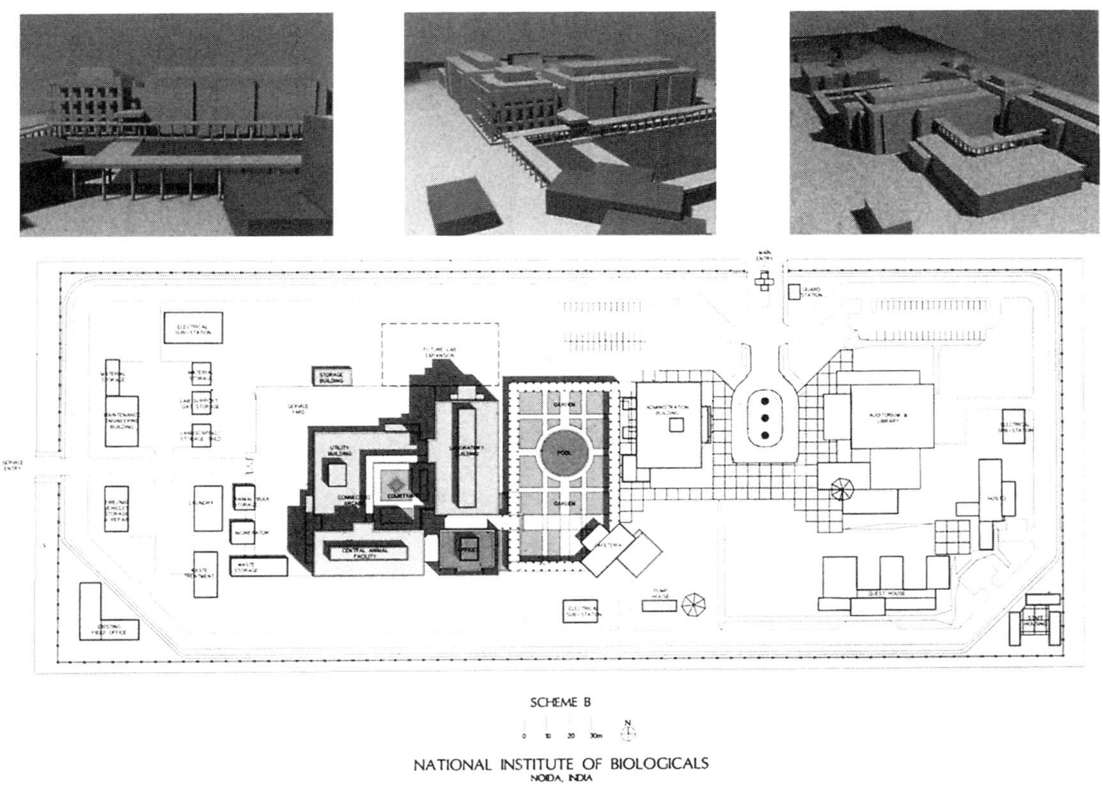

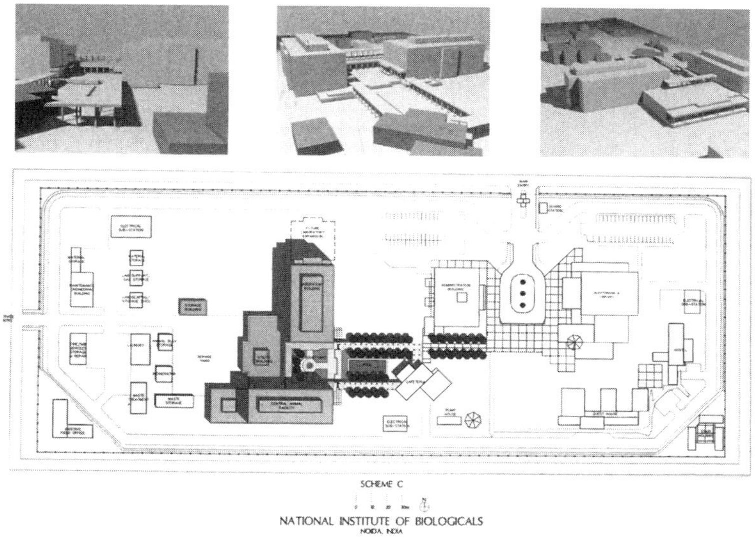

Illustration 5.72 *(Continued)*

Illustration 5.73 *National Institutes of Health—design development.*

Illustration 5.74 Portland International Airport Enplaning Roadway Expansion—conceptual design studies.

ANIMATION

One of the best ways to help someone visualize a computer model is to make the model move. Well-choreographed animations, in fact, are one of the most compelling forms of digital media available to the architect. The illusion of motion of a computer-generated animation is the same one used in film: when a sequence of still frames is displayed quickly enough to the eye, the mind perceives motion.

The fluidity of the motion depends on how fast the individual frames are displayed and the amount of motion. In film, the camera samples the scene 24 times a second. In video, the camera samples the scene 30 times a second. Most desktop computers display digital animations at a slower rate, from 10 to 20 frames per second, although their performance is increasing each year.

Illustration 5.74 (Continued)

Interestingly, the human eye can detect the flicker from movie projectors operating at 24 frames per second. As a result, each frame is actually illuminated twice: the movie projector moves a frame into position, the shutter is raised, the image is illuminated, the shutter is lowered, the shutter is raised a second time, the *same frame* is illuminated, the shutter is lowered, and the cycle repeats. If you look closely, the leading profile of a fast-moving object in a movie sometimes appears to have a double edge. This illusion is created because your eyes track the motion of the object. When an identical frame is projected twice, a double image is created—a combination of what your eyes *expect* to see in the next frame and what is actually there. The next time you watch *Star Wars,* look for the double edges on the Millenium Falcon.

The Showscan system, developed in the 1980s by Hollywood special effects whiz Douglas Trumbull, is a camera and projector system that records and displays film at 60 frames per second. The increased realism provided by the higher sampling rate is substantial. Although Trumbull originally hoped that Showscan would replace the 24-frames-per-second camera and projector system in the film industry, its relatively high cost has prevented that from occurring. It has found a home, however, in entertainment venues such as the Luxor Hotel in Las Vegas.

Video, in fact, employs a similar technique to increase the apparent sampling rate and smooth out motion. A video image consists of a series of 512 horizontal scan lines. Although a video frame is displayed 30 times a second, the odd scan lines are displayed in 1/60th of a second, and then the even scan lines are displayed in the next 1/60th of a second. This interlacing of the video image reduces the amount of flicker in the video display. (A computer-generated animation can take advantage of this interlacing to produce a smoother animation, a technique that is discussed later.)

KEYFRAMES

In most animation software, the user choreographs motion by changing the location of the camera or elements in the three-dimensional scene at different points in time, usually every few seconds. Each frame of the animation in which the user changes camera or element location is known as a keyframe (Ill. 5.75). The software interpolates between the keyframes and creates the intermediate views. Similarly, elements can be moved, rotated, or otherwise transformed within the scene at different points in time. The computer software will also interpolate the movement of the elements for each frame of the animation to provide the appearance of motion when the frames are rendered and displayed successively.

Defining the motion of the camera as well as elements within the scene is critical to the success of an animation. Camera or element motion that occurs too quickly will be difficult for the observer to interpret. Similarly, motion that is too slow is uninteresting.

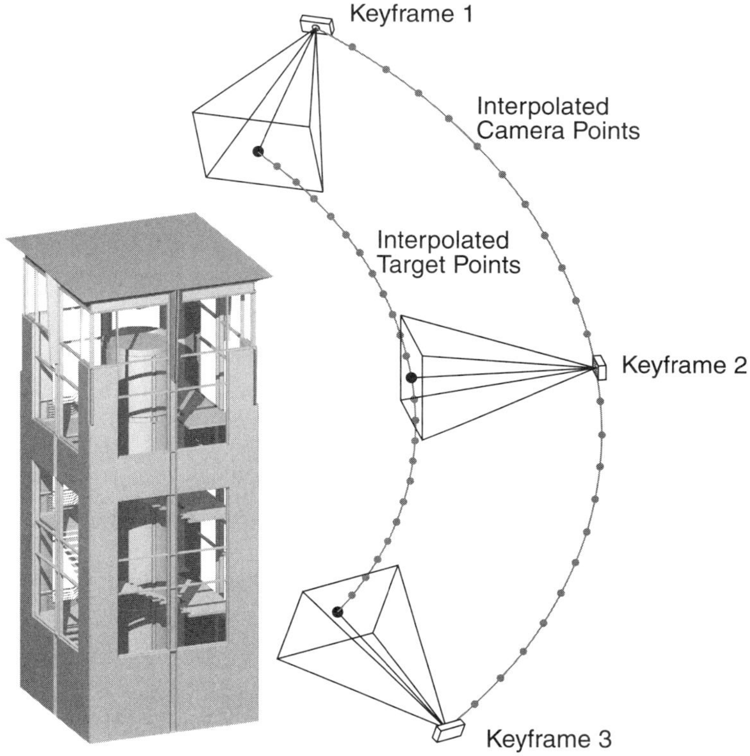

Illustration 5.75 Animation keyframes.

THREE-DIMENSIONAL MORPHING

Morphing is the popular name given to the special effect of combining two still-frame digital images to create a digital animation of one still image transforming into another. In three-dimensional animations, the effect is even more dramatic, because it takes place while the observer is moving through an environment.

Three-dimensional morphing in computer animations is really a "moving dissolve" between two animation sequences and requires rendering two different models with the same camera motion. Once the animation sequences are rendered into individual frames, they can be dissolved into each other to create a composite animation. As shown in Illustration 5.76, given two source animations, A and B, the first frame of the composite animation would be the first frame of A and the last frame of the composite animation would be the last frame of B. The middle

Illustration 5.76 *Three-dimensional morphing sequence.*

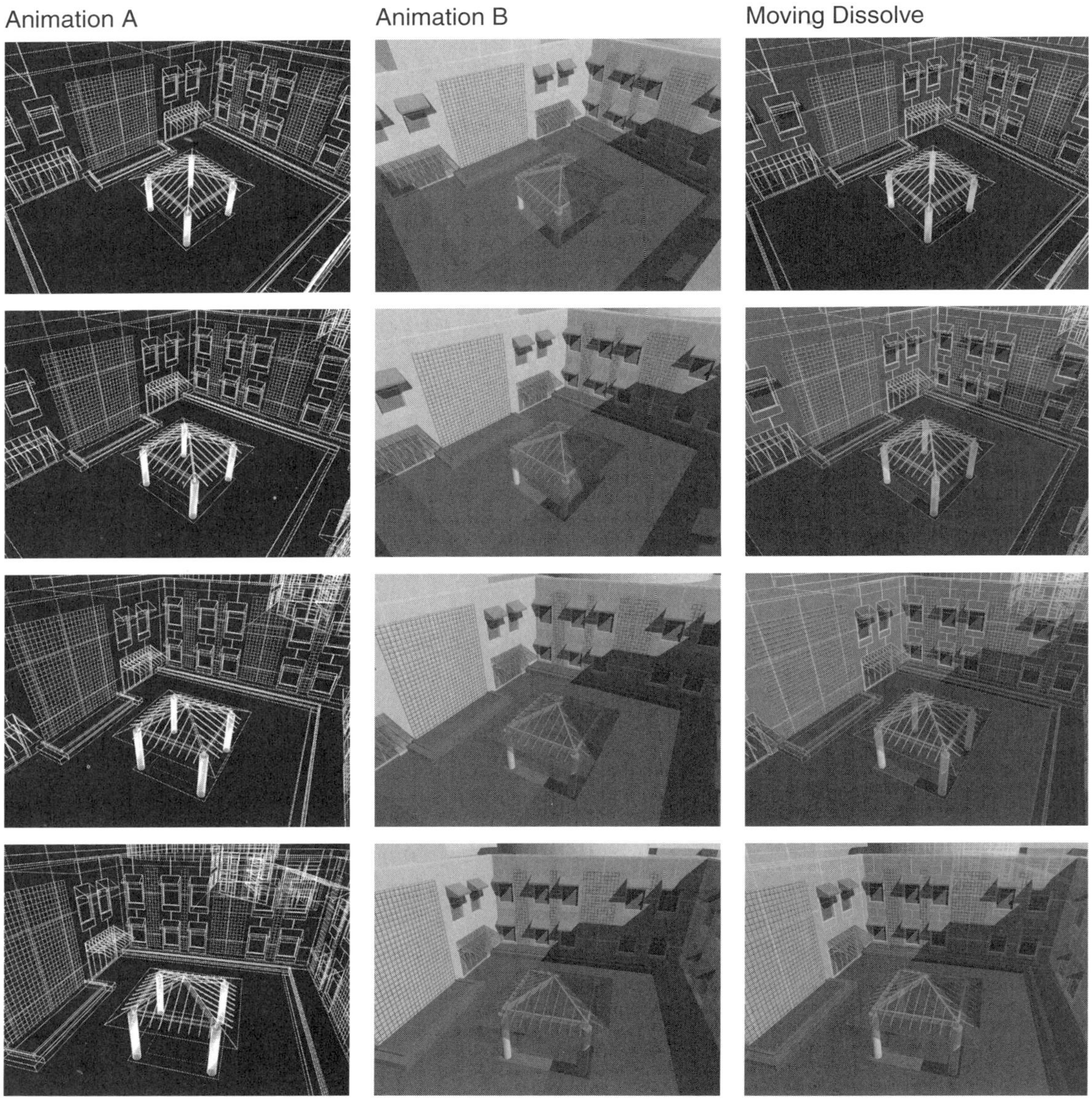

frame of the composite animation would be 50 percent A, 50 percent B. Since each composite frame is simply the result of mixing the pixel values of each source frame in a ratio based on their relative position in the dissolve, the process is fast and easy, and usually requires only a few seconds of compute time per frame.

The three-dimensional morphing technique can be used to dissolve between "before" and "after" images of a building renovation, between a three-dimensional stacking and blocking diagram and the completed exterior building shell, between a wireframe and shaded image, or between a schematic massing model and a finished, detail model. Since the dissolve occurs while the camera is in motion, the effect is better integrated into the overall flow of the animation.

RECORDING TO VIDEOTAPE

Producing computer animations involves the same process as film or video: a series of single frames is recorded to film or video media. With movie cameras and video recorders, this recording happens in real time and captures live action scenes. With computer-generated animations, each frame is rendered individually, in the same way that a still image is rendered (there are a few differences, which are discussed later). The frames can be stored on disk for subsequent recording to videotape or recorded to tape as they are rendered.

The conversion of 24-bit digital images to the analog NTSC or PAL signal stored on videotape can be accomplished by using inexpensive video expansion cards or external RGB-to-video signal converters. Since desktop computers are not (yet) fast enough to display full 24-bit video frames at 30 frames per second, each frame must be displayed and recorded to tape one at a time. Unfortunately, consumer VCRs are not capable of recording individual frames of video, and owning and maintaining specialized video equipment that supports single-frame recording is beyond the means of most architectural firms.

ZGF, for example, builds models and produces frame images in-house and hires a consultant to record the frames to videotape. The cost of recording frames to videotape can vary, but most service bureaus charge between 25 and 50 cents per frame. To reduce the cost and time required to compute individual frames, animations are often recorded at 15 frames per second, resulting in motion that is less fluid but animations that are twice as long. Despite the relatively high cost of single-frame recording, analog videotape is still an attractive format because of its portability.

DIGITAL VIDEO

Instead of rendering individual frames for recording to videotape, a more cost-effective approach is to create digital animations for playback on a computer. However, there is still a substantial difference in quality between video and current desktop animation formats, such as Autodesk Animator FLIC files, Apple's Quicktime, and Microsoft's AVI (Audio-Video Interleave). Most display 8-bit color, 320 × 240 images at 10 to 20 frames per second, compared to single-frame recording to videotape, which effectively displays 24-bit color, 640 × 480 images at 30 frames per second. However, for many applications, such as simple study models, the quality is acceptable. Illustration 5.77 shows frames from four examples of digital video presentations produced at ZGF.

In 1995, desktop computers do not yet provide the horsepower to display digital videos that rival the quality of analog broadcast television signals or videotape recordings. By the end of the decade, however, high-quality digital video playback will be an integral part of all desktop computers. The quality of digital videos displayed on computers will match or exceed that of analog video, virtually eliminating the need to record animations to videotape.

Instead of recording individual digital frames to a single-frame video recorder, low-resolution digital videos displayed on the computer screen can be recorded to a consumer VCR by using a video converter expansion card. This is an attractive option for budget-conscious firms, but at present the quality is inferior to single-frame recording.

The most compelling advantage of keeping animations in digital format is that the sequential nature of videotape is no longer a limitation. Low-cost interactive walkthroughs can be produced without special hardware by using a series of precomputed digital animations with multimedia authoring software. Although a user is not provided with real-time, interactive control over movement through a simulated environment provided by a true virtual reality system (described later in this chapter), she can control the viewing sequence of precomputed animations—for example, walking through the front door and turning

Illustration 5.77 Animation examples.

left into the living room or right into the dining room. Most desktop multimedia authoring programs provide tools to combine digital video clips with interactive buttons, allowing the user to decide how to move through a simulated environment. Indeed, this technique has been used in best-selling CD-ROM computer games such as Myst, Doom, and Seventh Guest, as well as interactive resources such as Microsoft's Frank Lloyd Wright CD-ROM.

ALIASING ISSUES

A software program creates a digital image by determining what is visible at each pixel and assigning a color to it. In essence, it spatially samples the three-dimensional model, or looks at the model through a tiny monoscope defined by the square boundary of each pixel. What the computer sees through each tiny monoscope is a single color, which it assigns to the pixel. More pixels in the image means higher sampling and a sharper image.

Compared to photographs or slides, video is an extremely low-resolution, fuzzy medium. Digital video images (approximately 640 × 480 pixels) contain only about one-tenth the number of pixels of the average digitized 35-mm slide or photograph (approximately 2000 × 1500 pixels). The low resolution of each frame of a video limits how often, and therefore how precisely, the computer software samples the model.

The visual artifacts that appear in digital images as a result of sampling are known as *aliasing*. There are two types of aliasing in digital film and video: spatial and temporal. Spatial aliasing is better known as the "jaggies," and refers to the stair-stepping that appears on diagonal lines or edges of computer-generated images. In rendered images, spatial aliasing also appears as moire patterns in surfaces with geometric textures such as brick or tile rendered at low resolution. Most rendering programs include antialiasing algorithms (usually by oversampling each pixel or jittering the samples to reduce moire patterns), but the artifacts rarely disappear completely. The emerging high-definition video standard (HDTV) will reduce aliasing problems in digital video because it provides approximately twice the image resolution in each dimension, although still less than half that of a 35-mm slide.

Temporal aliasing is a fancy phrase to describe the visual artifacts resulting from displaying still frames in quick succession. The classic example of temporal aliasing is the curious behavior of spoked wagon wheels in old movie westerns. When a wagon is filmed speeding up or slowing down, its wheels appear to go forward, then backward, then forward again. This is a visual artifact of the interaction between the frequency of the turning wheel and the sampling of its motion by the camera.

Other temporal aliasing artifacts can appear in computer-generated animations. The aliasing of edges can get even worse, because the jaggies that may not be that noticeable in a still image can begin to crawl. Very small elements may appear and disappear between different frames of the animation (such as the pickets in a small picket fence). Moire patterns that are subtle in still images can also move in dramatic and distracting fashion in animations. (Temporal aliasing is why TV personalities never wear clothing with small, horizontal stripes; if they did, their clothing would jitter when they moved.) The lesson: if you want to avoid annoying temporal aliasing in your animations, keep your models simple.

Another form of temporal aliasing is the apparent jerkiness of animations involving substantial motion, where there are large differences between consecutive frames. There are two solutions that most animation software programs provide: motion blur and frame interlacing. Motion blur is a computationally expensive algorithm that simulates the effect of a moving object in a photograph when the camera aperture is held open. Frame interlacing is a less expensive algorithm that takes advantage of the interlacing of video signals, where an image is rendered to every other scan line of the frame. Then, a second image—the result of interpolating the current frame with the next frame—is written to the alternative scan lines.

Although the resulting individual frames actually look worse, as shown in Illustration 5.78, the result is smoother animation when the frames are recorded. Frame interlacing is only appropriate when the animation will be recorded to videotape. Digital videos do not benefit from frame interlacing, because the images are not displayed in the same interlaced fashion.

DIGITAL VIDEO COMPRESSION

Ignoring current quality limitations for the moment, the biggest problem with digital video is the enormous amount of disk space required to store it. Without compression, a single second of digital video requires about 27 megabytes of storage. No desktop computer or network in any architectural firm in the mid-1990s can deliver information that fast. A two-hour movie

Non-interlaced Frame

Interlaced Frame

Illustration 5.78 Interlaced frame versus noninterlaced

would require over 100 gigabytes (100 billion bytes) of disk storage, or about two orders of magnitude larger than the hard disks provided on midrange personal computers in 1995. The challenge is to compress digital video to not only reduce its storage requirements, but also to allow it to be transmitted over computer networks.

New high-density CD-ROM formats (also known as digital video disks or DVDs) can store up to two hours of compressed video. These formats are described in Chapter 7, Desktop Hardware.

Clearly, this has already been accomplished with desktop video-teleconferencing products. However, such products are well suited for talking heads without much motion, but not for full-color, 30-frames-per-second video. Desktop video-teleconferencing products, like most desktop digital video, does not yet approach the quality of analog TV.

The MPEG (Motion Picture Expert Group) video compression algorithm is emerging as a unified standard for desktop video hardware and software vendors. MPEG is designed to efficiently compress a digital video with negligible impact on quality. How much does the MPEG algorithm compress a video? It depends on the complexity of the images in the frames, the complexity of motion between frames, and like JPEG, the loss of quality that is acceptable in the compressed version. MPEG, like most video compression algorithms, contains only a small percentage of complete video frames, and mostly contains the differences between consecutive frames. It is very efficient at compressing the evening news, because the differences between each video frame is small. MPEG is not so efficient at compressing *Raiders of the Lost Ark*. MPEG generally requires special hardware to handle its compression and decompression in real time.

Intel has built hardware logic in its forthcoming P6 chip (the Pentium's successor) to handle MPEG video compression and decompression. Do not be surprised if P6 chips eventually show up in television sets or cable boxes.

VIRTUAL REALITY

Virtual reality describes computer tools that allow people to interactively control their movement through and around three-dimensional models, instead of viewing prescripted and prerecorded animations of them. Most virtual reality systems require specialized hardware to display three-dimensional models in real time, generally achieved when frames are displayed at least 10 times per second. Immersive virtual reality systems are those that provide special viewing and interaction hardware, such as stereoscopic display goggles or headsets for viewing the scene, and a glove that can track the motion of the user's hand. Nonimmersive virtual reality describes systems that display environments interactively on a typical computer display screen, without any special hardware.

Immersive virtual reality systems that can display large, complex architectural models in real time are still beyond the financial reach of most architects, costing well over $50,000. At the same time, fast desktop personal computers today provide adequate horsepower for displaying small, simple three-dimensional models in real time. Low-end virtual reality software programs for personal computers, such as Eagle Point's Virtual Simulator (Ill. 5.79), generally provide simple shading algorithms (flat surface shading, no shadows) and low image resolutions (320 × 240).

QUICKTIME VR

Apple's QuickTime VR is a unique hybrid technology that combines the best of low-cost digital video and interactive virtual reality. QuickTime VR allows users to interactively look around an environment from a fixed location, or interactively examine a three-dimensional element by rotating it in different orientations. The technology supports both real-world environments as well as computer-generated ones.

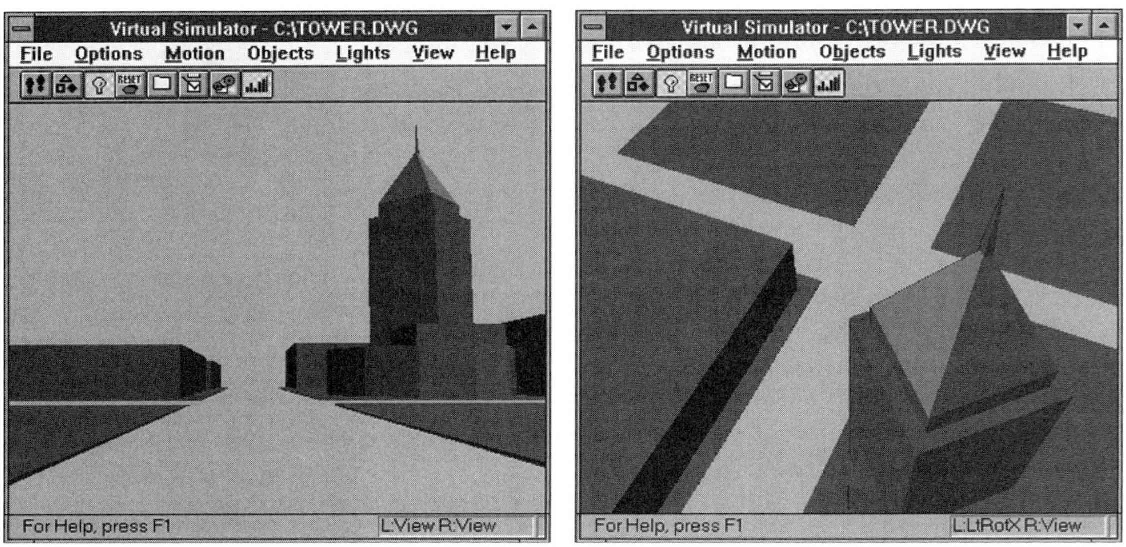

Illustration 5.79 Virtual simulator.

QuickTime VR movies are created by merging still-frame images that visually describe a 360-degree panoramic view of an environment. Each image represents the view seen at predetermined orientations from a single point in space. The number of images required can vary, but typically a minimum of 12 are required (360 degrees at 30-degree increments). The images can be scanned photographs taken from a tripod-mounted camera or digital images created using a three-dimensional visualization program. Special software is used to stitch together the twelve images into a seamless composite image, which the QuickTime VR software navigates and plays back in real time under the control of the user.

The visual effect is similar to standing at a single location within a space and looking around, changing the orientation of one's view—up, down, left, right—at will. A QuickTime VR can

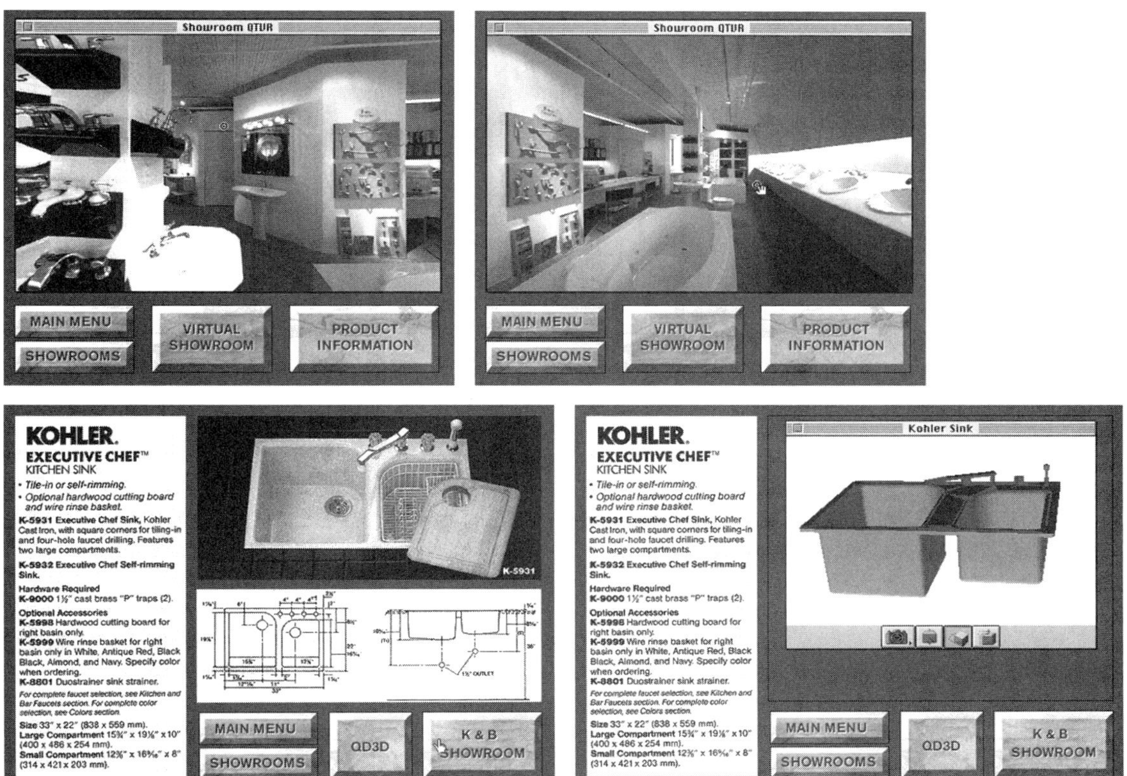

Illustration 5.80 *Demonstration of QuickTime VR software application.*

Illustration 5.81 Hybrid virtual reality.

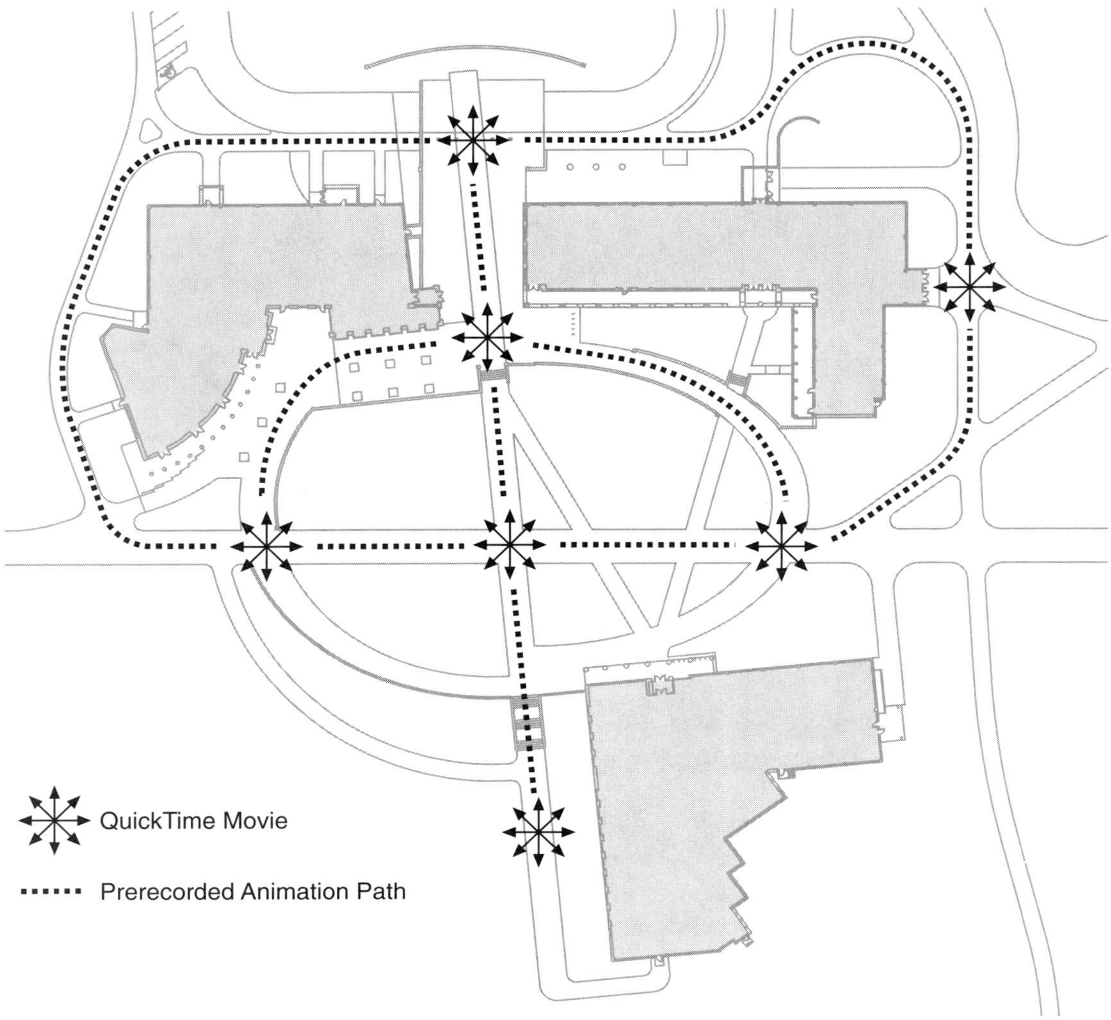

store the completed navigable movie, for display at 320 × 240 resolution, in less than one megabyte of storage. QuickTime VR is appropriate for visualizing architectural environments because, unlike real-time virtual reality systems, it has no practical limit on model complexity. QuickTime VR also provides tools for software developers to make elements within the scene interactive—for example, clicking on a book on a shelf would display the book's contents on the screen.

So far, QuickTime VR has been used primarily in entertainment software, such as Paramount's *Star Trek* Interactive CD-ROM. Illustration 5.80 shows examples of screen images of demonstration software developed by Apple Computer of a kitchen and bathroom fixture showroom displayed as a QuickTime VR movie. The user can navigate around the showroom and click on fixtures for more information.

Simple virtual tours of proposed built environments can be constructed by combining QuickTime VR scenes and prerecorded animations (Ill. 5.81). Such a hybrid approach is not true virtual reality, because a person cannot freely navigate the three-dimensional environment, but a person is able to travel using predetermined routes and 'look around' from predetermined locations.

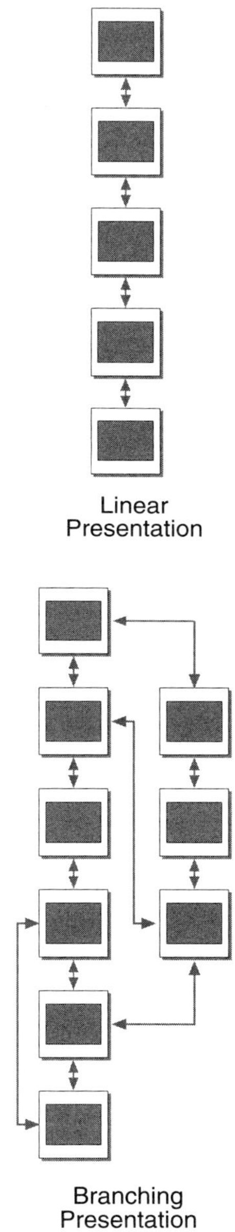

Illustration 5.82 Linear versus branching presentation.

DIGITAL MULTIMEDIA

A variety of software programs can be used to assemble different types of digital media together. These tools include:

TOOL	OUTPUT	EXAMPLES
Desktop publishing	Printed documents	Aldus PageMaker, Quark Express
Slide presentation	Linear presentations, slide shows	Microsoft PowerPoint
Multimedia authoring	Interactive presentations	MacroMind Act, Director

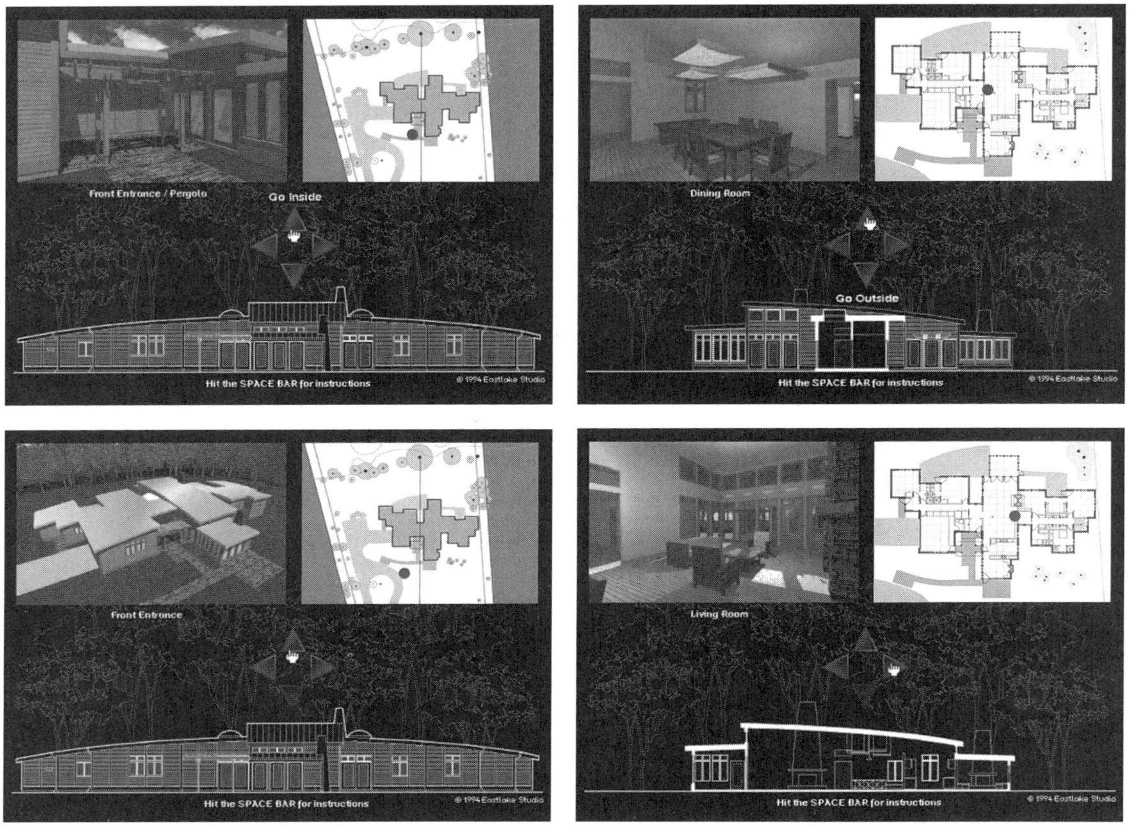

Illustration 5.83 *Interactive presentation of single-family residence.*

Desktop publishing software is commonly used in many architectural firms to prepare printed marketing proposals, presentation boards, and/or small format design documents. Slide presentation software is used to create linear sequences of digital images for playback on a computer, or for recording to 35-mm transparencies using in-house film recorders or the services of a film-processing center. Multimedia authoring software is used to create interactive presentations (Ill. 5.82) which branch in response to actions by the person viewing the presentation, such as clicking on a button or graphic element. Authoring software provides simple tools to script and choreograph the motion of elements—grow, shrink, fade in, fade out—within a presentation based on a timeline.

Each of these software programs can assemble a variety of digital source material into the same document or presentation, including words, numbers, charts, graphs, illustrations, images, animations, and sound clips. Illustrations 5.83–5.87 are examples of digital presentations and documents using a variety of source material.

The unique aspect of computer-based presentations is not their support for different types of digital media, but their interactive nature. To many architects who have spent years pressing only the forward and backward buttons on a slide projector remote control, interactive computer-based presentation tools appear difficult to learn and master. But they support more responsive, contextual presentations by providing the ability to drill down to more detail in response to a question about an issue discussed only in general terms during a formal presentation.

General-purpose software programs are gaining the ability to assemble compound documents containing mixed-media objects by using tools such as OLE and OpenDoc. OLE and OpenDoc are described in more detail in Chapter 4, Tools of the Architect.

Illustration 5.84 Digital slide show images.

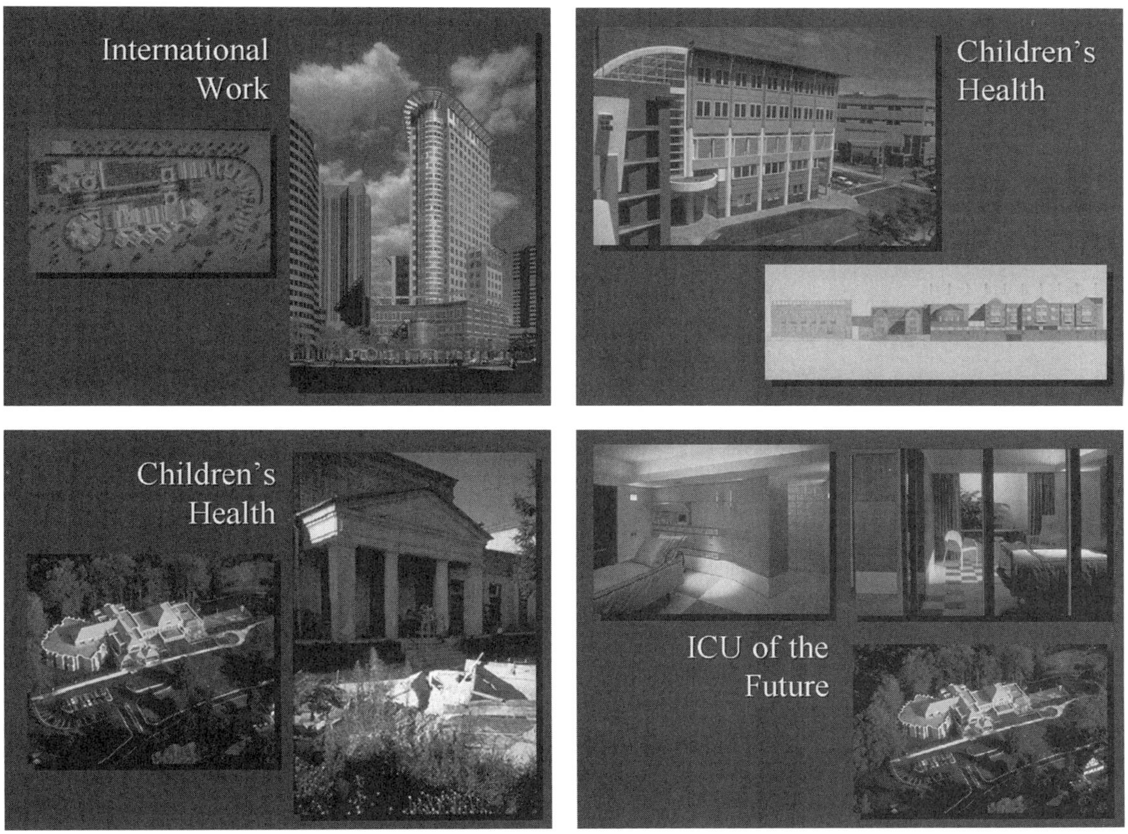

Like all forms of information, of course, more media is not always better media. Too much visual baggage in a presentation or document can easily distract from the message or idea that is being conveyed. Although all of these programs provide tools to rearrange and modify documents and presentations, this does not eliminate the requirement to properly plan and organize them.

The biggest threat to quality communication in many architectural firms is not the lack of time, but the lack of planning. Before a presentation is prepared, it is vital that the person understand what is to be explained, to whom, in what format, and with what supporting material.

Illustration 5.85 Multimedia presentation based on a time line.

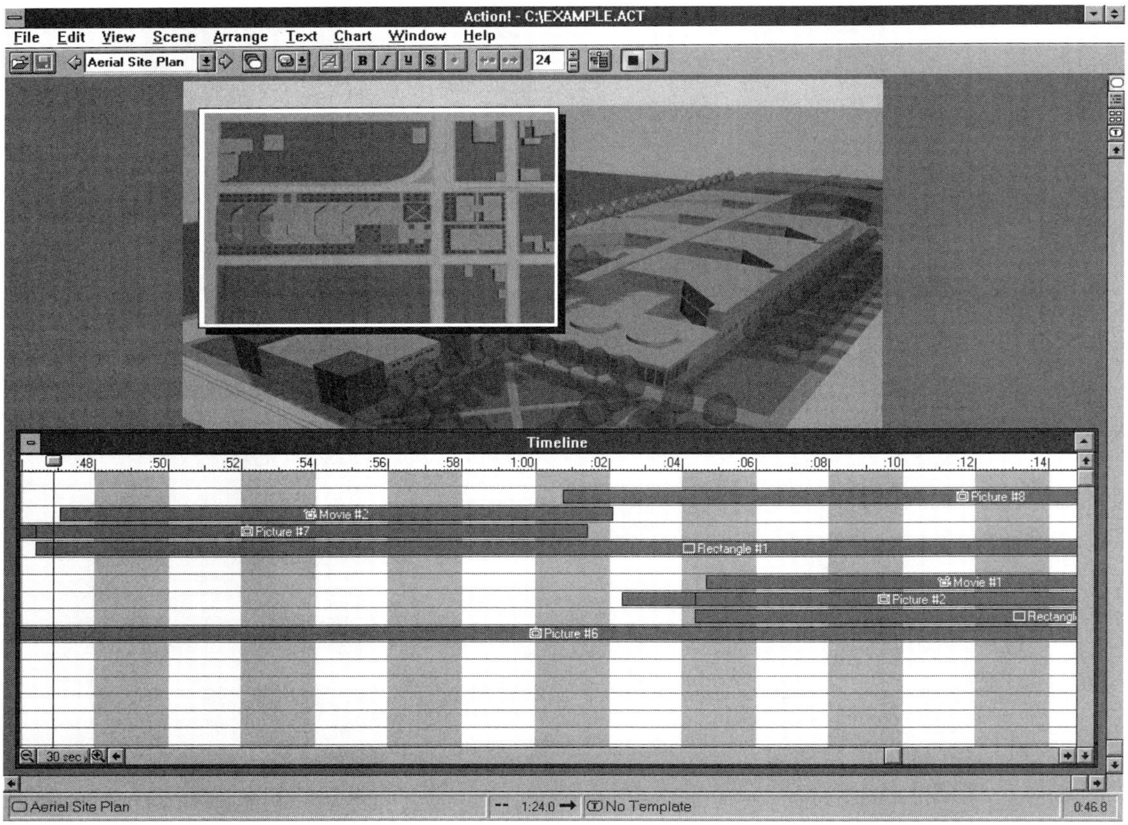

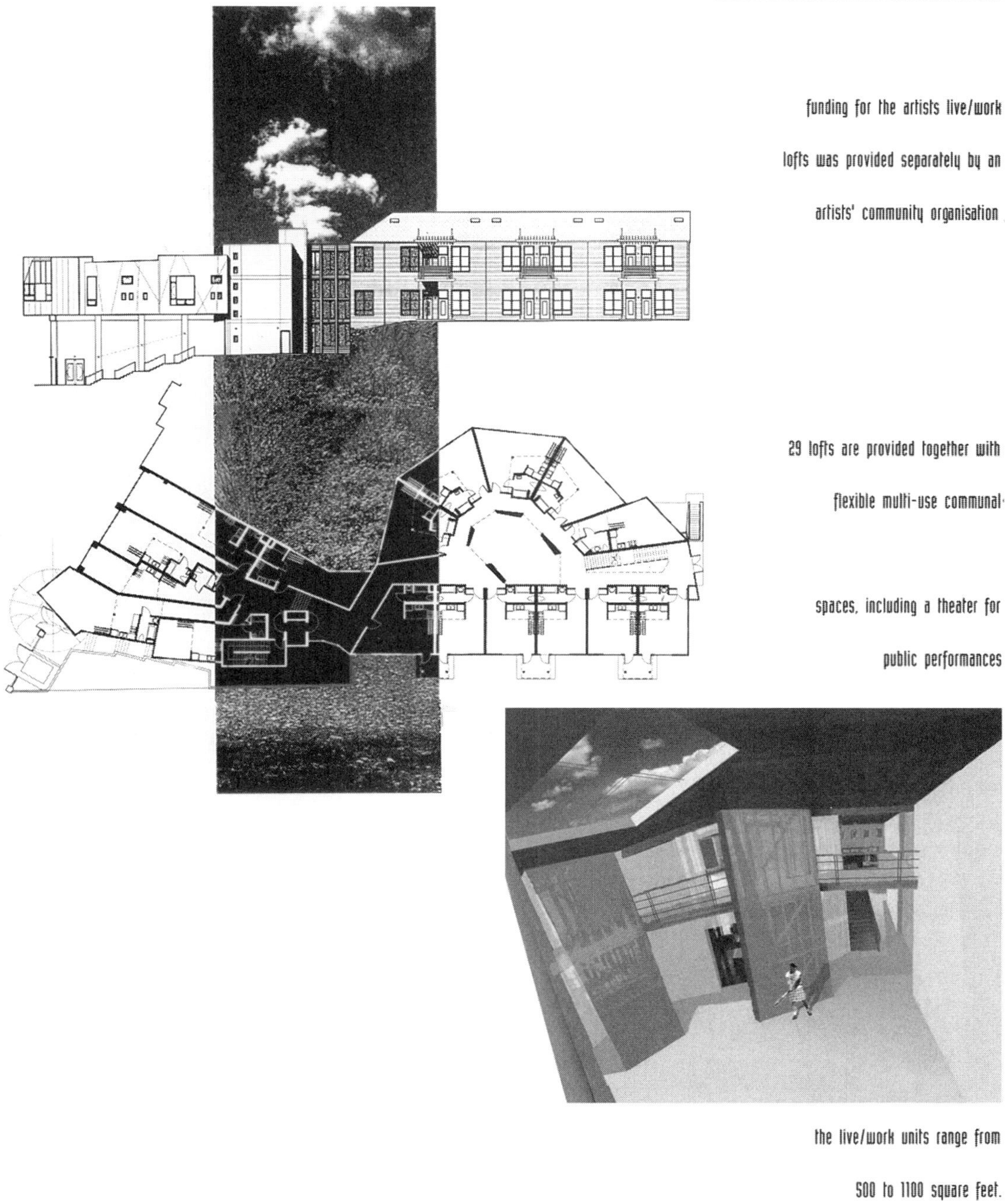

Illustration 5.86 *Composite design award submittal.*

THE PLAN

The Boise Art Museum is a regional attraction within the plan area.

2. Build on existing attributes within the areas

- Extend the character of the Greenbelt an Julia Davis Park into adjacent subdistricts;
- Expand the range and strength of cultural uses in the 8th Street area. Incorpoate public art to identity, define and enhance streetscapes, public spaces and neighborhoods;
- Reinforce established uses that contribute to the diversity of activities in Downtown Boise;
- Preserve and reinforce areas of existing urban character.

3. Foster an urban character in redevelopent:

- Respect existing urban neighborhood development patterns: blocks, grid streets, mid-block parking, street-oriented buildings and detached sidewalks with street trees;
- Encourage a pedestrian orientation of new development in the design and location of buildings, streets, parking and open space;
- Provide flexibility in the design of buildings for the changing nature of uses, anticipating the influences of information technology, live-work, etc.;
- Provide a continuity of pedestrian connections such as sidewalks, entry paths and signalized crossings;

Urban housing can be developed to improve the quality of the pedestrian environment in streets and neighborhoods....

.....as can office buildings.

The Boise River Greenbelt is an important destination for recreation in downtown Boise.

RIVER STREET-MYRTLE STREET
URBAN DESIGN PLAN

THE PLAN

- Develop an overall parking strategy for the greater Downtown area that includes the following:
  - maximum as well as minimum parking requirements for various uses (the initial phase of a metropolitan area plan);
  - neighborhood protection ordinances for spill-over parking;
  - a transportation management plan for larger projects with incentives for shared parking, car pooling, transit use, bike use, shuttle service and pedestrian orientation of development;
  - incentives for below grade and structured parking as well as air rights development over surface parking and/or structured parking.

Main Street in Old Boise typifies the street level character that would be encouraged on mixed use streets in the plan area.

4. Create memorable and dignified streets that complement the activity and design of adjacent work

- Reinforce a hiearchy of streets in Downtown Boise not only by traffic capacity but also by design treatment of sidewalks, crosswalks, street trees, lighting and furnishings:
  - The five distinct design treatments are Urban Street, Parkway, special Parkway at Capitol Boulevard, Neighborhood Street and Visual/Circulation Access Corridor (see Street Character Framework for detail description);
  - Ensure coordination between the pedestrian and bicycle route system and the public open space system;
- Incorporate public art to identify, define and enhance streetscapes, public spaces and neighborhoods;

Front and Myrtle currently lack any distinguishing characteristics.

Harrison Boulevard is an example of complementary street character and adjacent land use.

Capital Boulevard should develop with the character of a ceremonial parkway.

RIVER STREET-MYRTLE STREET
URBAN DESIGN PLAN

Illustration 5.87 Urban planning document.

The Internet's World Wide Web allows users to publish and access mixed-media documents that contain hyperlinks to other documents on the Web. Documents on the World Wide Web are written in HTML (HyperText Markup Language) and can be assembled using a variety of HTML editing tools. The World Wide Web and HTML are described in more detail in Chapter 10, On-Line Resources.

In fact, before you jump on the interactive multimedia bandwagon, try this experiment at home: watch the news portion of the MacNeil-Lehrer News Hour one evening, and then watch Entertainment Tonight the following evening. After each program, write down the major stories and issues which were presented. Then, compare your notes. From which program did you retain more information? The one with zoomy graphics, three-dimensional animations, and fast-paced editing? Or the one with people presenting information in a straightforward, understandable way? Certainly, the graphics can play a pivotal role in capturing a person's attention and explaining ideas visually, but too much visual imagery can distract from important content.

Similarly, it makes little sense to hide a simple, linear story within a complex, interactive presentation. The major themes of an interactive presentation should be easily discoverable, and important information should not be buried within branches of a complex hierarchical tree.

As your firm begins to apply the language of digital media to your presentations and service products, be sure that the medium does not obscure the message. An excellent measure of effective communication, after all, is the amount of information retained by those to whom you are communicating: *your* impact on *their* memory. The digital media you use, and the methods and tools you use to mix the media, should be aligned with that basic idea.

If the act of telling a story distracts from the story itself, you should rethink how you are telling it.

CHAPTER

6

Operating Systems and Networks

"If you need efficiency in your life, you should get a computer. I recommend the kind I have, which is a DOS computer. The other major kind of computer is the Apple, which I do not recommend, because it is a wuss-o-rama New-Age computer that you basically just plug in and use. This means you don't get to participate in the most entertaining aspect of computer-owning, which is trying to get the computer to work. This is where DOS really shines. It is way beyond normal human comprehension."

Dave Barry

An operating system (OS) is the layer of software between the software applications that a person uses and a computer's hardware, such as memory, disk drives, file systems, and input/output devices, such as displays, keyboards, mice, modems, and printers. The operating system manages resources for software applications. At first glance, operating systems appear to be just part of the internal plumbing of computers, seemingly far removed from people actually doing useful work with them. However, a computer's operating system is the software foundation upon which all other programs are built. The performance and usability of software applications are directly linked to the performance and usability of the operating system that sits beneath them.

The operating system debate in the 1980s (DOS vs. Macintosh vs. UNIX) was fairly straightforward and driven largely by software availability, ease of use, and cost. As the power, complexity, and choice of desktop operating systems have increased in the 1990s, so has the difficulty of comparing them. Useful architectural software tools run on a variety of operating systems, including Windows 95, Windows NT, OS/2 Warp, Solaris, and others. New operating systems for hand-held computers are emerging, such as Magic Cap, NewtonOS, and Microsoft's forthcoming WinPad OS. Unreleased object-oriented operating systems such as Microsoft's Cairo should also gain support for leading-edge architectural software applications.

A note of caution for casual computer users: the discussion of operating systems and networks in this chapter is fairly technical in nature. It provides a general discussion of operating system features and a brief comparison of OSs currently used within architectural firms, including Windows 95. The information may be most useful to those responsible for planning and implementing technology within the architectural firm.

(Table 6.1 lists the various operating systems and their developers.) For those using high-end CAD, database, visualization, and multimedia applications, the new object-oriented operating systems promise a new era of integrated tools and information sharing. Clearly, gauging the merits of different operating systems in the 1990s has become more complicated.

Table 6.1 Desktop Operating Systems

	OPERATING SYSTEM	DEVELOPER
Operating systems of the 1980s	DOS	Microsoft and others
	MacOS	Apple
	SunOS	Sun Microsystems
	XENIX	Santa Cruz Operation (SCO)
Operating systems of the 1990s	MS/DOS	Microsoft
	IBM/DOS	IBM
	DR/DOS	Novell
	MacOS	Apple
	OS/2 Warp	IBM
	Windows 3.1	Microsoft
	Windows for Workgroups 3.11	Microsoft
	Windows 95	Microsoft
	Windows NT	Microsoft
	Solaris	SunSoft
	Interactive UNIX	SunSoft
	UnixSVR4	Novell
	UnixWare	Novell
	AIX	IBM
	MagicCap (for handhelds)	General Magic
	NewtonOS (for handhelds)	Apple
Vapor of the 1990s	MacOS System 8	Apple
	"Cairo"	Microsoft
	WinPad OS (for handhelds)	Microsoft

Today, most architects use Macintoshes, DOS/Windows computers, or a combination of both. A smaller percentage of firms use UNIX workstations as well, primarily as network servers or high-end CAD machines. With good reason, many firms—especially smaller ones—may not place a high priority on changing operating systems or upgrading ones they already have. More than application software upgrades, operating system upgrades should be evaluated carefully. In general, those who want software applications that:

- are easier to use
- are more robust and reliable
- easily share data
- take advantage of higher-performance hardware
- lower system management costs
- provide better networking and security

may wish to change or upgrade their operating systems.

The downside of upgrades is discussed in more detail in Chapter 11, Managing the Digital Office.

1980S OPERATING SYSTEM FEATURES

In the 1980s, most desktop operating systems were distinguished by only a few major features: a file system, a basic user interface, and program development tools.

The File System

The file system is the organizational structure of digital information stored on disk, tape, or other storage media. A file system segregates information into files, each of which has a name, creation date, modification date, and various bits to control file access (read-only vs. read-write) and backup. The Macintosh file system supports additional file attributes, such as the icon used to represent a file graphically on the screen and the name of the application used to create the file. Network file systems usually track file ownership and determine which users can gain access to the file. Some file systems maintain both a creation date and modification date for each file, while others only keep track of a modification date.

Most file systems are hierarchical, allowing the creation of special types of files (directories or folders) which contain other files (Ill. 6.1). Most desktop operating systems support only one kind of file system, although more advanced operating systems (UNIX, Windows NT) support multiple, installable file systems.

The characteristics of a file system can impact the usability and security of the operating system. Windows 95, for example, supports password-based file protection only for shared directories, not for individual files. This is a limitation of the MS-DOS file system. The Macintosh does not suffer from this limitation, nor does Windows NT, which uses the newer NTFS file system with built-in network file attributes.

The User Interface

The user interface is the primary means of communication between the user and the computer. The legacy command line interfaces of MS-DOS and UNIX, although flexible and powerful, are intimidating to casual users and difficult for most people to master. The Macintosh set the standard of user interface design upon its introduction in 1984, borrowing heavily from

Illustration 6.1 *Hierarchical file system.*

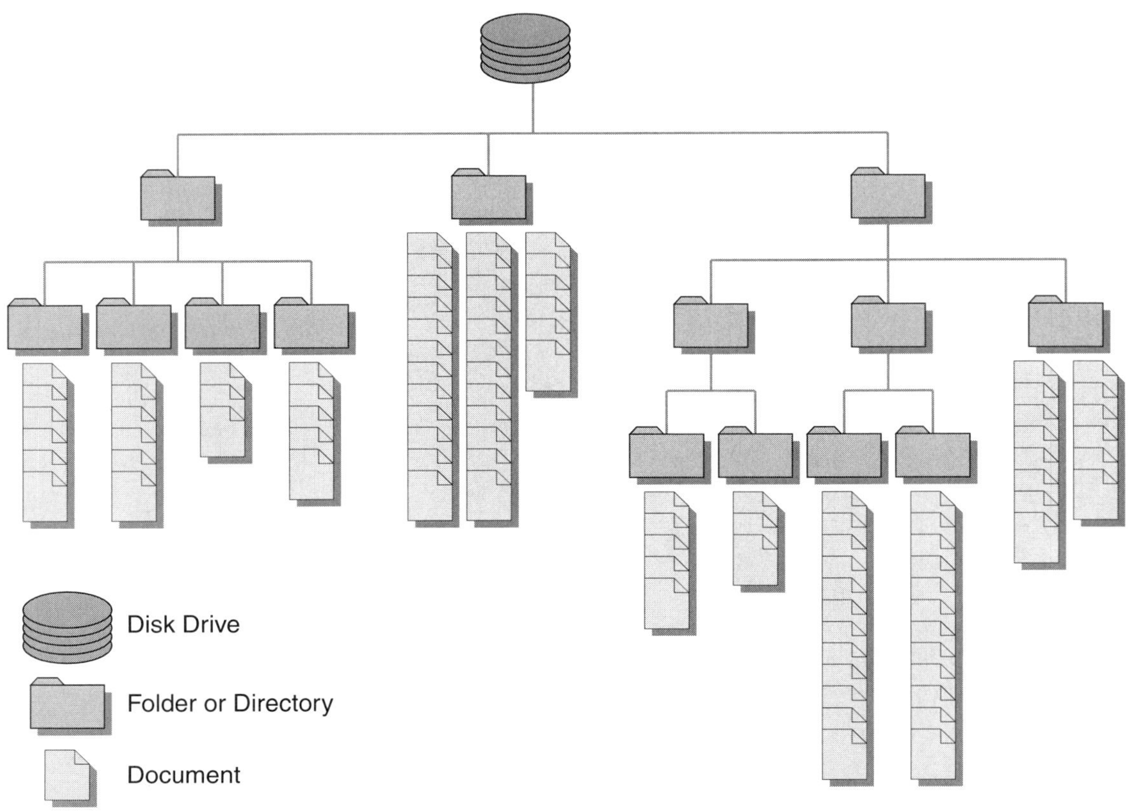

pioneering work done at Xerox's Palo Alto Research Labs (PARC) in the 1970s. Since then, Windows has borrowed heavily from the Mac, and UNIX's Motif interface has borrowed heavily from Windows. Today, most operating systems have the same basic user interface characteristics: overlapping windows, slider bars, pull-down menus, dialog boxes, a mouse-driven screen pointer, and icons that graphically represent files, directories, and software applications. Although debate about user interface design can sometimes take on religious overtones, the user interface differences today between Windows 95, MacOS, and UNIX are no longer substantial. Most users still have clear preferences, but the differences are as much aesthetic as they are functional and should not be assigned a high priority.

Program Development Tools

Program development tools are the prefab construction kits used by software developers. In the 1980s, these tools mostly included compilers and application programming interfaces (APIs). Compilers are software programs that translate the human-readable source code of a program into a binary program that is read and executed by the computer (Ill. 6.2). Popular compiler languages include BASIC, Fortran, Pascal, COBOL, C, and its object-oriented extension, C++. Users rarely see the source code of programs nor should they want to. APIs are libraries of predefined functions and subroutines which programmers can use in their software. Although not technically part of the operating system itself, compilers and APIs provide support for operating system functions, such as opening files, reading and writing files, and displaying menus and dialog boxes. Without compilers and APIs, an operating system is of little value. The degree to which a software application can take advantage of an operating system's features depends entirely on the compilers and APIs that support those features.

1990S OPERATING SYSTEM FEATURES

In the 1990s, the list of important operating system features has become lengthy and complex. The features include multitasking, multiprocessing, 32-bit memory addressing, integrated networking, interprocess communication, security, portability, scalability, multimedia support, and objects.

Multitasking refers to the ability (as perceived by the user) of a computer to run more than one program at the same time. The term is misleading, since the ability is illusory. The central processing unit (CPU) of every personal computer is designed around the original Von Nuemann computer architecture of the 1950s, in which a computer's CPU basically executes only one instruction at a time. However, a multitasking operating system is able to switch back and forth quickly between different programs to give the illusion that two or more things are happening at once. Preemptive multitasking refers to the ability of software programs to grab the CPU time they need on demand, rather than waiting in line, and tend to provide higher performance and faster response. Preemptive multitasking is a feature that Windows 95 and Windows NT provide, but that the Macintosh will not support until the release of System 8, which is due in 1996.

Multiprocessing means that the operating system can run on computers that have more than one CPU and can distribute its computing load between them. For example, a multiprocessing computer may run a rendering program on one CPU and a CAD program on another. Although multiprocessing systems are still rare and relatively expensive, and are used primarily for network or database servers, they will become more popular over the next decade, even on the desktop. Ultimately, as more operating systems and software applications support multiprocess-

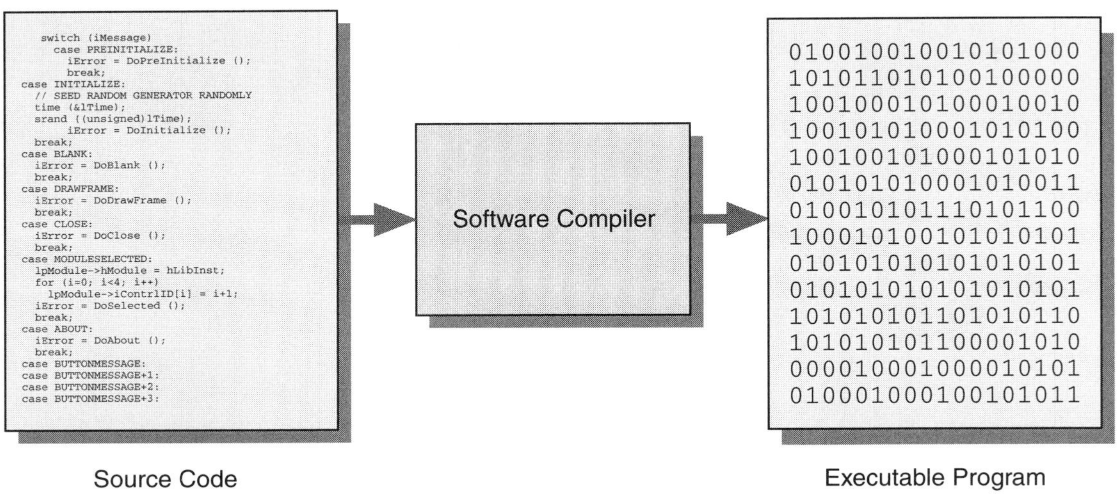

Illustration 6.2 Source code conversion to machine code via a compiler. Most compilers translate one kind of source code language (C, Fortran, Pascal, BASIC) into instructions for one kind of CPU (Intel, Motorola, PowerPC).

ing, and as the limits of silicon density are approached (ultimately there is only so much logic and circuitry that can be stuffed into one CPU chip), multiprocessing computers will become a flexible, cost-effective way to incrementally add computing power to desktop computers without waiting for new, more complex generations of CPUs. Today, only Windows NT and special flavors of UNIX support multiprocessing.

32-Bit memory addressing means that the operating system knows how to access up to four gigabytes (four billion bytes) of memory at any given time. (The highest value that a binary 32-bit number can store is somewhere around four billion.) This is quite a stretch from DOS's 640K memory limitation. Ironically, the Intel 80386, first introduced in 1987 and already obsolete, was a true 32-bit central processing unit. For eight years, it supported 32-bit memory addressing, but DOS and Windows did not. This, in turn, severely affected the performance and robustness of DOS and Windows applications. Windows 95 finally supports 32-bit memory addressing, a feature offered in UNIX and other operating systems for years.

There are other distinguishing features of contemporary operating systems which are worth mentioning:

Integrated networking	Includes built-in networking, E-mail, and access to on-line services.
Interprocess communication	Allows programs to direct the actions of other programs. Examples include AppleEvents and Windows Dynamic Data Exchange (DDE).
Multiuser security	Provides access to secure resources only to selected users.
Portability	The ability of the operating systems to run one more than one type of CPU (PowerPC, Intel, Motorola, etc.).
Scalability	The ability of the operating system to run on a range of computer hardware, from handhelds to supercomputers.

Multimedia support	Integrated support for digital sound and digital video.
Objects	Composite documents with persistent links to networked objects.

The relative importance of an operating system's features and benefits depends on who is evaluating them. From an individual architect's point of view, the benefits are better performance, more consistent user interfaces and, most importantly, application software quality, choice, and interoperability. From a firm or project team's point of view, the benefits are fully integrated networking, built-in workgroup tools such as messaging and E-mail, and scalability. From a software developer's point of view, the benefits are 32-bit object-oriented development tools, and support for multiprocessing hardware. The success or failure of operating systems of the 1990s will depend largely on how well—and how soon—they provide those benefits and software applications take advantage of them.

THE LOST OPPORTUNITY OF UNIX

Developed in the 1970s at AT&T's Bell Labs, UNIX was the first portable mainstream operating system, purposely designed to run on different types of computer hardware. Compared to proprietary operating systems linked to a single hardware architecture (such as DOS/Windows running on Intel-based computers), software applications written for UNIX could more easily be "ported" to different types of computers. This feature was attractive to institutions and in-house corporate software developers, who wanted an operating system independent of any particular hardware. In addition, UNIX was freely licensed to universities, producing a generation of computer science graduates well-versed in its theory, use, and enhancement. Many of today's computer technologies (e.g., Ethernet, the Internet, Mosaic, object-oriented software) were first developed on UNIX platforms, and the operating system remains fertile ground for computer science research around the world.

By the mid-1980s, UNIX vendors saw an enormous market opportunity for selling faster, more powerful UNIX computers to personal computer buyers, many of whom were (and still are) starving for true 32-bit systems, better memory management, robust networked file systems, and true multitasking. Emerging RISC processors promised (and delivered) high-performance workstations under $5000 by the end of the 1980s. As a result, many experts predicted that UNIX would emerge as the predominant operating system in the 1990s.

RISC is an acronym for reduced instruction set computing and is discussed in Chapter 7, Desktop Hardware.

Unfortunately, several things got in UNIX's way. First, the exploding DOS/Windows PC marketplace redefined portability. With UNIX, programs needed to be recompiled by the programmer for each different type of computer. This is known as *source code compatibility,* because only the program's original source code, not the compiled program, was portable between different UNIX computers. With DOS/Windows, the same compiled program, shrink-wrapped on a diskette, would run on any Intel-based personal computer out of the box without modification. This is known as *binary compatibility,* which turned out to be far more powerful and necessary in the high-volume personal computer software market.

In addition, while the personal computer market consolidated around two standards during the 1980s—DOS/Windows PCs and Apple's Macintosh—dozens of UNIX vendors continued to add value to distinguish themselves from (and become incompatible with) their competition. This approach served only to confuse, not unify, the UNIX market for years. In fact, a clear parallel exists between today's UNIX market—fractured, incompatible, and lacking economies of scale—and Japan's PC market, where there are still a dozen incompatible PC standards, where PC software development lags far behind the United States, and where PC prices are considerably higher.

Does this mean that architectural firms should ignore UNIX? Almost. Beyond network file servers or Internet hosts, it is increasingly difficult to justify UNIX computers as a strategic platform for architectural firms. The largest A/E/C CAD vendor, Intergraph, long a champion of UNIX, is now moving all of its applications to computers running Windows NT. UNIX is likely to remain a high-end, specialty operating system, tailored for research institutions and large in-house corporate software developers, but will never achieve the mainstream success once predicted for it.

Ironically, the UNIX vendors who bitterly fought each other during the 1980s realize today that their true enemy is not each other, but a software company they virtually ignored until the 1990s: Microsoft.

WINDOWS 95

Much to the chagrin of Macintosh enthusiasts, the juggernaut of Microsoft Windows continues and appears unstoppable. Windows is installed on nine out of ten computers sold today, despite having suffered from 12-year-old limitations of DOS during its rise to prominence. Only in 1993, for example, did Microsoft include built-in networking and E-mail messaging tools in Windows for Workgroups, features found in Mac and UNIX operating systems years before. Windows 95 has finally discarded most, but not all, of the DOS baggage that prevented Windows for so many years from supporting advanced operating system features.

Windows 95 is actually a replacement for three operating systems: MS-DOS, Windows 3.1, and Windows for Workgroups 3.11. Although DOS is no longer required in order to run Windows, Windows 95 still supports DOS applications, since there are still a few useful ones out there. Microsoft also performed a major overhaul on the Windows 95 user interface, the result of which approaches the Macintosh's ease of use and ease of maintenance.

"As a Macintosh user, I find it depressing to see Apple mess up this great idea (integrated E-mail) and let Microsoft walk away with the prize. It's one more item in the grab bag that will probably get me to switch eventually, along with the promise of hot docking that comes with Plug and Play."
STEWARD ALSOP,
Editor-in-Chief, *InfoWorld*

Windows 95 supports plug-and-play hardware, an integrated information manager called Explorer, built-in access to the Microsoft Network on-line service, and a universal E-mail and messaging client. Windows 95 provides desktop usability features long appreciated by Macintosh users, such as desktop folders, animated window outlines that shrink to and expand from icons, and direct editing of file names by simply clicking on them. In some areas, such as the integration of mail and on-line services within the operating system, Windows 95 has actually surpassed the ease of use of the Macintosh.

The most visible improvement of Windows 95 can be found in its user interface. The program manager, file manager, task manager, and print manager of Windows 3.1 are gone, and in their place there is a more consistent set of tools. The Windows 95 file system supports shortcuts, which allow users to create a reference to a file without having to make a copy of the file. A shortcut icon is distinguished from the original by the appearance of a small arrow in its lower left hand corner. Shortcuts provide a way for users to group documents and resources together in a convenient way, independent of a hierarchical file system. Although a hierarchical file system is a useful model for organizing information resources, most people don't work hierarchically and are not comfortable with its constraints.

The Network Neighborhood of Windows 95 allows users to see in one place all of the available network resources available, including both file servers and printers. Windows 95 also includes built-in network drivers for a wide variety of networks, including Netware, Windows network, and TCP/IP (the Internet protocol), making Windows a cooperative desktop client with virtually any type of high-performance network operating system. The silly DOS convention of alphabetically named disk drives, A: to Z:, is also gone in Windows 95, although it is still an optional feature.

Windows 95 also provides new support for traveling computer users. Before unplugging their notebook computers from the office network, Windows 95 users can download files from the network into a software "briefcase" (Ill. 6.3). When the notebook is reconnected to the office network later, the modified files in the "briefcase" are automatically synchronized and updated with those on the network. This feature is particularly valuable for architects involved in construction observation or architects who are away from the office on a regular basis.

The shortcuts of Windows 95 provide a powerful tool to develop alternative nonhierarchical structures of information resources, an issue which is discussed in more detail in Chapter 9, Organizing the Knowledge Base.

Microsoft has finally provided a robust, easy-to-use, easy-to-install, and easy-to-support version of Windows, twelve years after the company first announced Windows, and five years after its first usable release, Windows 3.0.

WINDOWS NT

Two years before Windows 95, Microsoft introduced Windows NT, its operating system alternative to the performance and sophistication of UNIX. At the time, Windows NT was probably

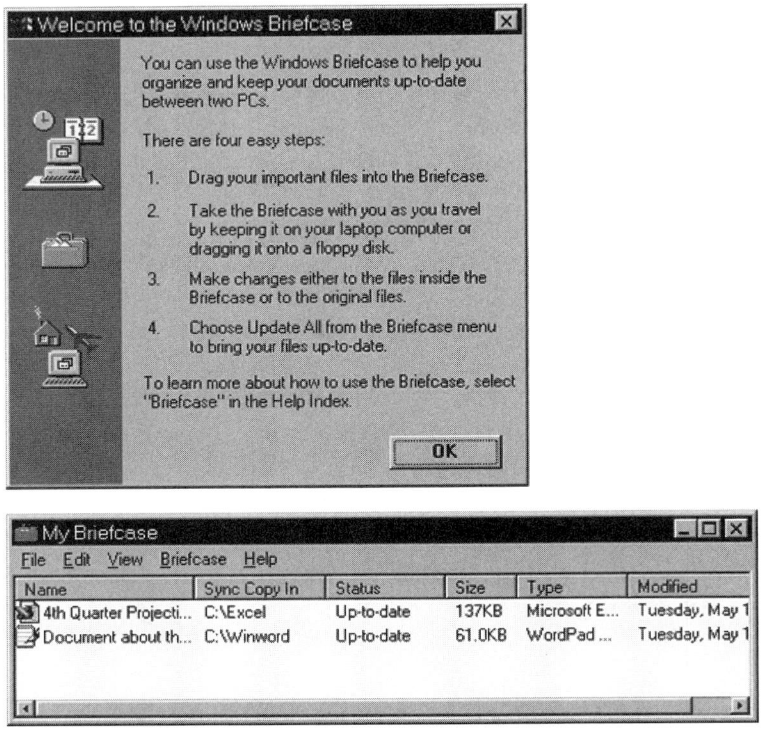

Illustration 6.3 Windows 95 briefcase.

the most eagerly awaited desktop operating system since the original Macintosh. NT provides true multitasking, security, multiprocessing, installable file systems, and 32-bit software development tools. And Windows NT, unlike Windows 95, is portable, has no DOS baggage at all, and currently runs on five different kinds of microprocessors: Intel (386, 486, Pentium), MIPS, DEC's Alpha, HP's PA-RISC, and IBM/Apple's PowerPC. (PC-style binary compatibility between each processor family is not provided.)

Although NT's hardware requirements are not for the timid (16 to 32 MB of memory are recommended), some software developers are betting that Windows NT will be the high-end, high-volume operating system that UNIX never was, providing them with robust development tools and an enormous user base. Hundreds of PC and UNIX software developers, including major architectural software vendors such as Autodesk and Intergraph, have committed to porting their products to Windows NT.

So far, however, that bet has not paid off. Although Microsoft projected over a million copies of Windows NT during its first year, only about half that many were shipped. The preintroduction excitement over Windows NT quickly subsided once it began shipping, and people discovered that 16-bit Windows programs actually ran slower on Windows NT than Windows 3.1. This essentially killed Windows NT as a desktop operating system, although many companies purchased it as a network file server or database server, for which it is well suited. Autodesk originally announced Windows NT as the first supported platform for AutoCAD R13, but backed off as Windows NT failed to generate the sales volume that was predicted for it. Other firms decided to wait until the second release of Windows NT, Version 3.5, was shipped, which made substantial performance improvements and provided new network administrative support tools.

Some architects are justifiably confused about the differences between Windows NT and Windows 95. The two operating systems can best be understood by considering the competitive forces that influenced their development. Windows NT was built from scratch and was designed to provide many of the high-performance capabilities of UNIX systems, such as preemptive multitasking, multiprocessing, a secure file system, and advanced networking. Windows 95, although it also supports preemptive multitasking, borrows more heavily from the Macintosh and still carries some DOS baggage to achieve broader compatibility with older applications than Windows NT.

"The simplest summary is to repeat our strategy in its simplest form: 'Windows—one evolving architecture, a couple of implementations and an immense number of great applications from Microsoft and others.' The 'a couple of implementations' is a somewhat humorous reference to the fact that our NT-based versions and our non-NT versions have different code in a number of areas to allow us to have both the advanced features we want and be fairly small on the Intel architecture. Eventually we will get back to one implementation but it will take four years before we use NT for everything."
From Internal Microsoft Memo "Challenges and Strategy," May 16, 1991
BILL GATES,
CHAIRMAN AND CEO OF MICROSOFT CORPORATION

Although it appears that Windows 95 is the low-end version of Windows and Windows NT the high end, Windows 95 is *not* a subset of NT. Instead, the two operating systems have overlapping feature sets. Differentiating the two operating systems and clarifying their appropriate use continues to be a difficult problem for Microsoft. In general, Windows NT is the better network server, while Windows 95 is the better desktop client.

Ultimately, Microsoft will need to merge the two operating systems into the same product, but this will likely not happen for several more years. For example, Microsoft is planning to introduce the object-oriented features of Cairo, such as reliable persistence of linked objects on a network, to Windows NT before Windows 95. Until they are merged, Microsoft's strategy of two versions of Windows is the least attractive feature of the operating system. Indeed, some architectural firms are beginning to lean toward Windows NT, which is a cleaner, less compromised operating system than Windows 95, to run their high-end 32-bit software applications.

MacOS

What about the Macintosh? Popular among architects, some technology experts have predicted its ultimate demise. The historical example most commonly cited is Sony's Beta video format which, although technologically superior, ultimately lost out to Matsushita's VHS format. It didn't really matter that Beta was better when consumers couldn't buy or rent videotape to play on the machines.

Although generally recognized as more thoughtfully designed than Windows (at least until Windows 95), the Macintosh continues to represent only about 10 percent of all desktop computer sales. Distracted by the disappointing Newton personal digital assistant and focusing on the transition from Motorola CPUs to the new PowerPC CPUs, Apple has abdicated over the last decade much of the Macintosh's technological edge in terms of desktop graphics and ease of use to Microsoft Windows. Indeed, one can persuasively argue that the gap has been closed to the point where it really doesn't matter anymore. The key questions: will most software developers continue to move to Windows, where the market volume is? As a result, will the Macintosh suffer the same fate as Sony's Beta?

My personal feeling is that Apple will not only survive, but thrive. Apple's market share numbers will probably never exceed 15 to 20%, but as the computer hardware and software market continues to grow each year, Apple can grow with it. The Macintosh continues to enjoy a high degree of loyalty among many of its users, although many are noticing the variety of Windows applications that are not available for the Macintosh. Apple will have to focus on software markets that are not high volume but that leverage its strength: desktop publishing, digital image editing, digital music editing, rendering, visualization, multimedia authoring tools, and others. Significantly, most of these applications are the ones of interest to many architects.

In addition, the Macintosh continues to provide a fertile development ground for many unique architectural software tools, including three-dimensional modeling software such as Form-Z, desktop animation, and digital image editing. Apple's new QuickTime VR is a wonderful tool for capturing three-dimensional environments (real or simulated) and allowing users to navigate interactively through them. Given its market share, the number of Mac software applications will continue to be substantially less than Windows, but the Macintosh will continue to represent an attractive development environment for small and innovative software developers, where the costs to enter the market are smaller. As a result, the Macintosh will continue to be a viable platform for many architects, who require graphically rich tools and media.

See Chapter 5 for more information on Apple's QuickTime VR.

SHADES OF PINK

To be sure, Microsoft's interest in building high-end features into its desktop operating systems is not a solitary one. In 1990, IBM and Apple announced their intention to form two joint-venture companies to develop new leading-edge desktop technologies. The first, Kalieda, whose mission was to focus on multimedia application, has been a disappointment. While the multimedia software market has grown exponentially over the last several years, especially as CD-ROM drives become standard equipment on desktop PCs, Kalieda has not, and has struggled with defining its mission and creating presence in the market. The second company, far more important from a strategic perspective, is Taligent, whose flagship product was originally a brand new operating system code-named Pink.

Over the last five years software companies have discovered how incredibly difficult it is to build new operating systems, perhaps the most horrifically complicated pieces of software. Microsoft discovered this with Windows NT and Windows 95, both of which shipped more than a year after originally predicted, and Taligent is no exception. In 1995, Taligent finally introduced its first product, CommonPoint, a set of tools for software developers to build object-oriented applications. CommonPoint is not an operating system itself, but provides an application development environment that runs on existing operating systems and will ostensibly create new kinds of object-oriented software applications. It includes over 100 "frameworks," or predefined collections of objects, which software developers can use in their programs. CommonPoint for AIX was first shipped for IBM's AIX operating system, and will be supported on the Macintosh, Windows, and other UNIX platforms.

The Taligent joint venture was in part a response to the launch of Microsoft's Windows 3.0 in 1990, the first usable version of Windows. At the time, it was a signal that Apple intended to stay well ahead of Microsoft, this time with the help of IBM. In hindsight, Apple probably should have remained focused on enhancing the Macintosh OS.

The Pink operating system originally promised to provide many of the features of Windows NT, while preserving and extending the Macintosh's edge in simplicity, elegance, and object-oriented ease of use. Instead of files, networks, disk drives, and other computer terminology, users would have moved through a desktop world populated by People, Places, and Things. Unfortunately, Taligent cancelled the Pink development project in mid-1995.

OS/2 WARP

Long after development partner Microsoft abandoned OS/2 after promoting it for years as the operating system of the future (and eventually introduced its version of OS/2 3.0 as Windows NT), IBM and its stubborn commitment to OS/2 has won it respect from many of its corporate customers. OS/2 is largely being used for PC network servers and as clients for custom applications developed within large corporations.

OS/2 Warp simultaneously runs OS/2, DOS, and Windows 3.x applications, but not Windows 95 applications. It is a multitasking operating system, and provides an excellent, object-oriented user interface, the WorkPlace shell. Unfortunately, in September 1993, IBM's rights to use Microsoft's Windows source code within its products ended. Windows compatibility must be reverse-engineered by IBM, a costly and time-consuming process. And Windows compatibility is crucial for OS/2's success in the small-business market, where architects can be found in great numbers.

Following Microsoft's NT lead, IBM has announced that OS/2 will be ported to other platforms, including IBM/Apple's PowerPC chip, HP's PA-RISC, and Sun's SPARC. As part of this program, OS/2 will be rebuilt around a new portable core, the Mach microkernel developed at Carnegie-Mellon University.

IBM will support two versions of OS/2—one for Intel-based PCs, the other based on Mach. What type of compatibility will exist between the two versions remains to be seen.

Although through 1994 over four million copies of OS/2 were shipped worldwide, the operating system is almost invisible in architectural firms. More recently, IBM has attempted, through major TV advertising campaigns, to extend OS/2's reach out of large corporations and into the consumer mass market with OS/2 Warp. Unfortunately, the attempt to position OS/2 Warp as a desktop operating system is doomed to fail, primarily owing to the lack of software applications. IBM's recent acquisition of Lotus may help, since 1-2-3, WordPro, and other Lotus applications will likely become available for OS/2, but this will be not be enough to convince large numbers of Windows users to switch.

How does OS/2 fit into IBM's vision for the desktop, and its long-term strategy? That's a tough question to answer. While it promotes OS/2 as a strategic operating system, it is also actively involved in Taligent, and the relationship between the two has never been made clear. All of these issues have cost OS/2 support by software developers. Although the Macintosh will likely not face the same fate as Sony's Beta video format, OS/2 will. I have two words of advice for architects: ignore it. OS/2 is already an obsolete desktop operating system.

THE FUTURE OF DOS

With the rollout of Windows 95, is DOS effectively dead? Probably not. Like W.C. Fields, rumors of the death of DOS have been greatly exaggerated. DOS 7.0 is due to enter beta testing in 1996, providing the 32-bit engine of Windows 95 without the graphical user interface. A surprising number of DOS computers are still at work in many architectural firms, as archive/backup systems, plotter controllers, or E-mail gateways, or performing other miscellaneous background tasks. Despite the attention surrounding Windows 95, don't be surprised if DOS continues to be enhanced and sold separately by Microsoft until the end of this century.

For many architectural firms, especially those committed to high-end CAD, database, and visualization applications, the new generation of desktop operating systems that will be available

Operating system emulators and computers that run more than one operating system in native mode can be used to provide compatibility for those transitioning between systems. But they should not be part of a long-term strategy. OS/2, Windows NT, and UNIX will ultimately have to stand on their own as operating systems without DOS/Windows/Mac compatibility.

before the end of the 1990s could potentially usher in a new era of integrated automation. The key word is potential, because the value to architectural firms will be provided not only by the presence of improved information-sharing tools in operating systems, but also by the availability of key software applications that leverage them and architects who understand how to use them well. The real payoff is likely to occur one to two years after the introduction of the operating systems themselves. Like any new technology, those who understand the new tools and anticipate their arrival will be better prepared to evaluate, choose, and apply the most appropriate ones for their firms.

Operating system rules of thumb:

1. An operating system is only as good as the applications that support it.
2. One operating system is better than two, which is better than three, and so on.
3. Networks, utilities, E-mail, and on-line services should be thoroughly integrated.
4. ALWAYS test drive.

NETWORKS

The concept of computer networking is simple: providing shared access to files, printers, and other resources from multiple computers (Ill. 6.4). Architecture is a collaborative and gregarious endeavor, and networking is absolutely essential to the effective use of computer technology within the architectural firm. Here are a few reasons why:

■ *Shared information.* Computer networks allow project teams to access a single set of up-to-date project information. There is no need to manage and reconcile multiple copies on different computers.

■ *Quality guidelines.* The firm's knowledge base must be a shared resource. Guidelines are easier to implement and enforce if the information they describe is conveniently accessible to everyone in the firm. Guidelines are also easier to update, because a single copy can be used by architects throughout the firm.

■ *Staffing flexibility.* People and the computers they use can be located independently of data, allowing firms to more easily assign project staff and resources where they are needed.

■ *Centralized archive/backup.* Compared to backing up individual computers one at a time, creating digital archives and backups is a much simpler procedure on a network.

These benefits are not provided free, of course. Unfortunately, the implementation and management of computer networks can potentially be one of the most frustrating technology issues faced by architectural firms. The problems are as plentiful as their solutions are evasive. Many PC-based software applications, for example, still do not provide reliable, robust support of networked environments. In addition, some firms who use multiple vendor hardware and operating systems (Windows,

Question: What is the maximum number of computers an architectural firm should use before installing a network? Answer: One.

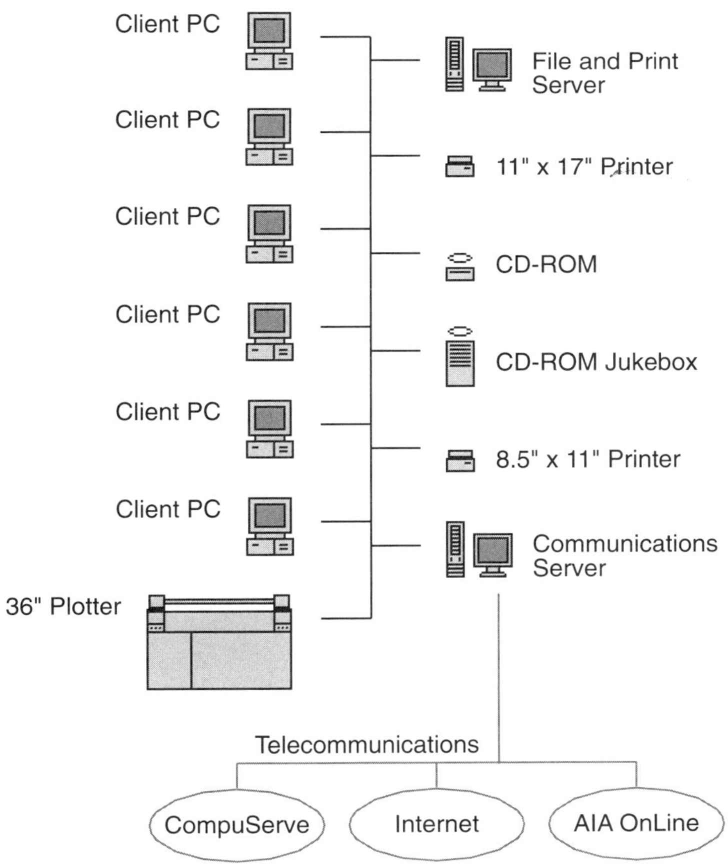

Illustration 6.4 Network schematic.

Macintosh, UNIX, etc.) are burdened with incompatibilities—some relatively minor, but irritating nonetheless. Other firms succeed in implementing networking technology but suffer from disorganized file systems or high costs of day-to-day network management and maintenance.

The definition of networking is changing and includes not only file and printer sharing, but also integrated E-mail, messaging, fax, and access to on-line services and public and private networks outside the firm.

Eventually, adding any computer to a high-performance network will be as easy as plugging a phone into a wall jack. Until then, here are four recommendations about how architecture firm principals, managers, and employees can network their computers successfully and economically:

1. Demand robust networking support, not just network coexistence, from all software applications in use by the firm (CAD, office automation, marketing, decision support, etc.) Networking support includes use of the network's file protection and locking services, as well as enabling support for built-in E-mail and messaging when those services are provided by the network. Users should be able to send E-mail and fax messages directly from within their software applications, without using a special program.
2. Design and implement a single firm-wide file system with published organizational guidelines for distributed digital data. (Refer to Chapter 9, Organizing the Knowledge Base, for more information.)
3. Migrate toward single-vendor, homogenous computing within the firm, and away from multiple-vendor, heterogeneous computing whenever possible.
4. Migrate toward client-server networks, and away from peer-to-peer networks, even for small networks of four to five machines.

APPLICATIONS SUPPORT

Some architectural firms implement networking solutions only to discover that their software applications interact poorly with them and provide little, if any, support for distributed file sharing. Most are DOS or Windows programs originally designed as stand-alone, single-user applications. Like operating systems, the degree to which a network is supported by the applications running on it is the network's weakest link.

Most operating systems and network software provide file-locking tools, which allow applications to reserve access to a file for itself and prevent other users from reading from and/or writing to the file. Most applications fall into one of five categories, in terms of their support for network file locking. The first type ignores file locking completely. In such an environment, one user can open a file to edit it, another user can open the same file and edit it, and whoever saves the file last "wins." This problem is rare today, since almost all mainstream applications have implemented file locking, but some low-end and shareware programs still assume there is only one user in the universe.

The second type of file locking is to reserve both read and write access to a file when it is being edited, thereby locking out all access by anyone else, even read-only access. This method of network file locking is unacceptable in architectural firms, where simultaneous sharing of information by project teams is a fact of life. The analogy in traditional practice would be a policy prohibiting anyone from even glancing at a manual drawing currently being worked on at someone's desk.

Unfortunately, more applications than you would expect suffer from this problem. AutoCAD, for example, will not allow one user read-only access to a file if it is being edited by another user. It will allow other users to attach that drawing as a reference file, but it will *not* allow someone to open the drawing in AutoCAD to review it.

AutoCAD uses a proprietary file-locking scheme instead of that provided by the operating system or network. When a user opens a file, AutoCAD creates a temporary lock file (with a file extension .DWK). When a user closes a file, AutoCAD deletes the lock file. AutoCAD will not allow anyone to open the file if the lock file is present. Unfortunately, when AutoCAD crashes, the lock file remains. Another user has no way of knowing whether someone else actually has the file open, or whether the .DWK was not properly deleted. The burden is on the user to track down the person who last accessed the file and determine whether that person is actually editing the drawing. On the other hand, if a .DWK file is deleted accidentally while someone is working on a file, then file-locking protection is lost. AutoCAD's "roll-your-own" file locking is inherently unreliable compared to other CAD programs, such as CADVANCE or MicroStation, which use file-locking tools provided by the network and operating system.

The third method of file locking is to allow multiple users read-only access while one user has read-write access. Fortunately, all mainstream operating systems (Windows, Macintosh, UNIX) and/or network software (Netware, Lantastic, etc.) provide tools for software developers to implement such file locking in their programs. Unfortunately, too many software programs don't take full advantage of them.

The fourth method extends file locking beyond the file itself to records within the file. This allows multiple users to read and write to the same database file simultaneously. Architectural firms who intend to use distributed database applications should make sure that their database software supports this.

A fifth method is that employed in AutoCAD's ADE (Advance Data Exchange) application. Using ADE, a user can assemble a collection of data from several different sources and edit it, and then the data is saved back to its original sources. The method is similar to an imaginary library, where you could rip out pages from several books, edit them, and return them to their original location. While other users could not get access to the pages you ripped out, they could rip out other pages for the same purpose. It is similar to the fourth method because the locking is handled inside the file.

NETWORK LICENSING

Software developers sometimes support network licensing for their programs. Instead of buying individual licenses for every machine, users can install the software on all of their machines and are limited only by how many are simultaneously running the software. Like proprietary file locking, some implementations don't recognize when a machine hangs or is prematurely turned off or rebooted, and don't properly release the license in use. (One of the best PC-CAD network licensing implementations can be found in IsiCad's Cadvance, which is tightly integrated with Novell's Netware and Lantastic networks.) Other vendors use network messaging to determine whether another user is using the application with the same serial number (Ill. 6.5). This method allows a firm legally to install the same software on a number of machines if only one person will be using it at any one time.

Some third-party network license programs provide tools to manage access of software applications in a network to ensure that licensing agreements are not violated. We don't use them at ZGF, and I don't recommend that you do either. Our philosophy is that if the software vendor builds in network licensing protection, that's great, because we don't have to worry about violating the terms of the licensing agreement. If they don't, then we will make a good faith effort not to exceed the number of users accessing a product at any one time. Every vendor we have spoken to finds this policy acceptable. (Make sure you check with yours as well before following our example.) At ZGF, we purposely avoid third-party licensing products; they are just one more software program to pay for, maintain, and upgrade.

Although progress has been made during the past several years in making software applications better behaved on networks, much work remains to be done. If you evaluate software applications, you must ascertain more than whether the applications run on a network. Specifically, you should ask:

- What if a machine hangs when a user is editing a file? Will the user be able to reopen the file later?
- Can other users reference or open as a read-only file a file on which you are working?

Illustration 6.5 *PageMaker 5.0 copyright violation notice.*

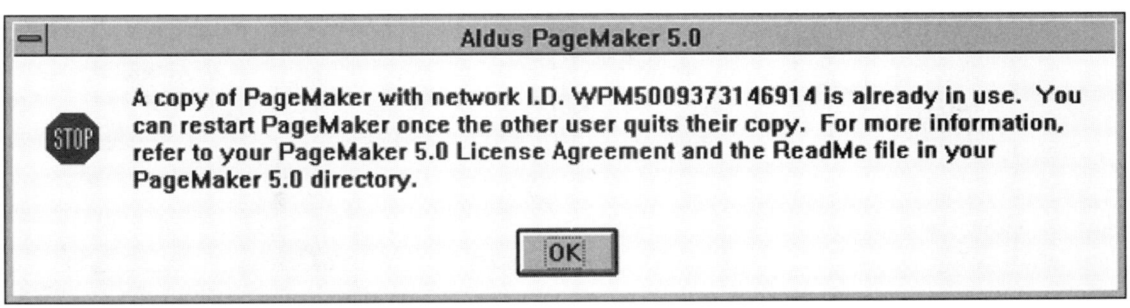

■ Will the software notify you when a read-only file is available for editing?

■ Does the software provide information about why a file is unavailable, such as who is working on it?

■ Is the file-locking and notification scheme used by the software compatible with other software?

Clarity of error messages is an important issue. If a user's attempt to open a file fails because of file locking, one would expect to be informed of the problem in a rather specific way, such as "Cannot open file A2-2.DWG because it is in use by user XYZ on station P12." Instead, you might get a message such as "Cannot open file" or "file not available." (An example of appropriate file locking and messaging in Microsoft Excel is shown in Ill. 6.6.) You cannot learn this from marketing literature (or even documentation); it can only be determined by test driving the software on your network. How well a system supports network file locking, and how well a program informs a user of potential problems, will affect the amount of support you will have to provide for users of those tools.

TRANSPARENT FILE SYSTEMS

Although some architectural firms (including ZGF) occasionally use their networks to distribute processing tasks among multiple computers, such as using several computers controlled by a rendering program to compute individual frames of an animation, the key benefit of a network for most architectural firms is in creating a distributed, transparent file system. *Distributed* means a file system which all users can access, regardless of the machine at which they are sitting. *Transparent* means that the look and feel of the network file system is identical to the com-

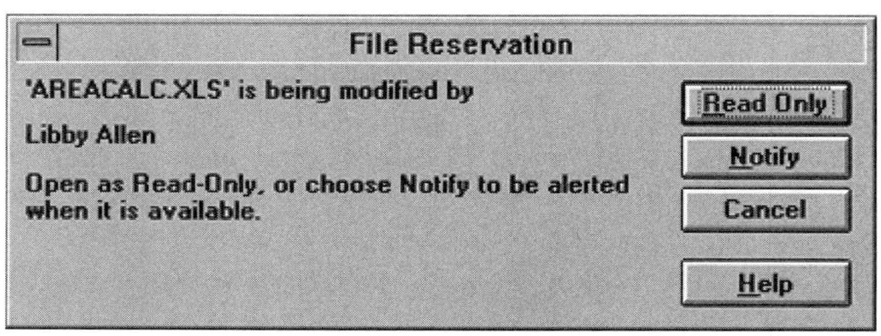

Illustration 6.6 *File locking in Microsoft Excel.*

puter's local file system, whether it is DOS, Windows, Macintosh, or UNIX. An architect should not need to learn any additional skills to access files on a network nor be concerned about the physical location of the files themselves. In that sense, the distributed file system is transparent to the user.

Ideas for organizing networked files systems are described in Chapter 9, Organizing the Knowledge Base.

Useful distributed file systems must include well-designed organizational structures, well-defined support and backup procedures, and well-educated users. A disorganized file system inevitably makes information only easier to lose, not easier to use. Although each application area within the architectural firm—design, documentation, specifications, marketing, decision support, and so on—has special organizational requirements, each should be part of a single, firm-wide file system and should be documented as such. Users should never be in doubt as to where to find information.

HOMOGENEOUS VERSUS HETEROGENEOUS NETWORKING

Architectural firms implementing networks must sometimes connect several types of computers with different operating systems. A typical example is a mix of DOS/Windows personal computers for CAD and accounting, and Macintoshes for desktop publishing, word processing, and/or marketing.

Heterogeneous networking—using different types of computers for specialized tasks and connecting them together—is something that many computer vendors openly acknowledge and even encourage. It is true that many different types of computers, operating systems, and networks are available to solve different types of problems, some better than others. Windows, Macintosh, and UNIX computers peacefully coexist at many architectural firms, but they are not (and probably never will be) integrated into a totally transparent, seamless system. The simplest path to cost-effective network implementation and management is to limit the types of computers that your firm uses and supports.

What users want and what architectural firms need is one kind of computer, one operating system, one user interface, and one network in the office which reasonably supports their work. The long-term advantages of firm-wide standardization far outweigh the short-term individual benefits of each computer or operating system. Architectural firms with heterogeneous systems invariably have higher support and training costs, more complicated networks, and harder-to-use systems than single-platform firms. To actively pursue a strategy of heterogeneous networking, other than a temporary one to ease a transition, is a roadblock to effective information sharing within the architectural firm.

PEER-TO-PEER VERSUS CLIENT-SERVER

Two basic types of networks can be used to provide information and resource sharing within the architectural firm: peer-to-peer and client-server. Client-server networks distinguish between dedicated *servers,* which control file access, printer queues, network security, and so on, and individual *clients.* Examples include Novell's Netware, Sun Microsystems' Network File System (NFS), and Microsoft's Windows NT Advanced Server. Peer-to-peer networks essentially allow any computer to act as both client and server: Bob can read a file from Jane's machine or print on Walt's printer. Some examples are Artisoft's Lantastic, AppleTalk, and Windows 95. Many firms begin with peer-to-peer networks because of their lower initial cost (a dedicated server is not required).

Although at first glance, peer-to-peer networks appear more flexible than client-server networks, they suffer from several problems. First, they often encourage the practice of file copying and file borrowing (from her machine to my machine) rather than transparent file sharing. Second, peer-to-peer file systems are usually more complicated than they should be, because information is distributed among many workstations rather than just a few file servers. This often places on users the burden of knowing or having to find out which computer contains the files they need. Third, although they work fine for low-speed applications such as word processing or electronic mail, peer-to-peer networks are usually not well-suited to high-end applications, such as CAD, which create and modify large files and require high throughput. The lack of dedicated servers means a user's computer may unexpectedly slow down to respond to an external file or printer request from another computer.

In general, client-server networks ultimately provide flexibility, easier growth paths, simplified system management, and better backup and network security. The concept of a distributed, transparent file system on a client-server network is well known to UNIX users, but relatively new territory for many Macintosh and Windows users. Yet the concept is as powerful as it is elegant, and it provides an excellent organizational framework for the distributed information need of architectural firms.

CHAPTER

7

Desktop Hardware

> *"Damn it, Jim, I'm a doctor, not a bricklayer."*
>
> **Dr. Leonard McCoy, Chief Medical Officer**

This chapter briefly outlines the basic hardware components of desktop computers (circa 1995), and is intended as a quick reference to help you avoid experiencing information anxiety about computer hardware. Since many architects I talk to want to know more about computer hardware, I have included this information for general background only. The chapter contains information that is probably least directly relevant to the practice of architecture than any other, but may be of interest to those considering purchasing computers for office or personal use.

A key point: understanding the hardware components inside a desktop computer does not matter as much as knowing what software will run on the computer, how fast the software runs, and how easy and comfortable the computer is to use, support, and service. Test-driving different desktop computers using key software applications, not comparing hardware specifications, will always be the best way to evaluate their price and performance.

CPUS AND MOTHERBOARDS

The CPU (central processing unit) is the microprocessor brain of the computer. Intel is the dominant CPU manufacturer for desktop computers with its 486, Pentium, and P6 CPUs. Other CPU manufacturers include Motorola (68030, 68040), Motorola/IBM/Apple (PowerPC), Sun Microsystems (SPARC), Silicon Graphics (MIPS), and DEC (Alpha). The latter three

CPUs are used primarily in high-end UNIX workstations and are not well known to most personal computer users.

Some desktop computer buyers estimate the performance of a computer by the clock speed of the CPU, usually measured in megahertz (MHz). However, a computer's clock speed is only one measure of its performance and can often be misleading. A 75-MHz 486, for example, is roughly 50 percent faster than a 50-MHz 486. However, a 60-MHz Pentium is faster than both. The clock speed of a CPU is roughly equivalent to the RPM (revolutions per minute) of a car engine—the faster the RPM of an engine in a given gear, the faster the speed of the car. Upshifting or downshifting the gears, however, also affects speed, and is comparable to shifting between different brands of CPU: 386, 486, Pentium, and so on.

The motherboard of a desktop computer is the printed circuit board that contains the CPU, memory, input/output chips, slots for expansion cards, and other specialized circuitry for video, sound, or networking. In addition to CPU type and clock speed, overall computer performance will also depend on the performance of these motherboard components. Brand-name PC manufacturers such as Apple, IBM, Compaq, and Hewlett Packard engineer and manufacture their own motherboards. Gateway 2000 and other mail-order vendors purchase motherboards from suppliers like Micronics or Intel. The motherboards of most powerful desktop computers today are less than 8.5 by 11 inches in size.

Some components of a computer's motherboard may operate at a lower clock speed than the CPU itself, usually one-half or one-third the speed. The motherboard in Apple's 8100/80 Power Mac, for example, runs at 40 MHz, while the CPU runs at 80 MHz. An Intel 100-MHz 486DX4 performs instructions at 100 MHz but fetches memory at only 33 MHz. This imbalance can cause "wait states" in the CPU, where the CPU pauses to allow the motherboard to catch up. Again, the clock speed of a CPU is only one small indicator of system performance.

One debate still raging in the microprocessor industry that architects may hear about is "CISC versus RISC." CISC is an acronym for "complex instruction set computing" and is based on the philosophy that faster performance can be attained if complex operations are hard coded into the chip's silicon and executed as a single instruction instead of a series of individual instructions. RISC is an acronym for "reduced instruction set computing" and is based on the philosophy that CPUs should contain a smaller set of instructions most often used by software programs. The theory of RISC is that a chip tuned to perform, say, 20 percent of the instructions used 80 percent of the time will perform better than a CISC chip. In theory, the RISC design philosophy is correct, and RISC chips run most software programs faster. Unfortunately, the price/performance advantage of RISC chips has historically been erased by CISC vendors via manufacturing economics of scale. Intel, for example, ships more CISC chips (486, Pentium) in a month than Sun, Silicon Graphics, and DEC have shipped since the invention of the computer. The PowerPC, which powers Apple's latest Macintoshes and IBM's high-end workstations, is the first RISC chip to alter this equation significantly, but is still outnumbered ten to one in sales volume by Intel.

The effective performance of a RISC chip in real-world applications, such as the PowerPC CPUs inside Apple's Power Macs, depends on the availability of native software specifically written for it. Power Macs can run older software written for Motorola's 680x0 CPUs, but the CISC instructions of those programs must be emulated in software on the Power Mac's RISC CPU. As a result, older software programs can actually run substantially slower on faster PowerPC CPUs than on Motorola 680x0 CPUs. Again, test drive the software applications important to you to determine a system's performance.

At last count, there were over 50 desktop computer manufacturers in the United States, not including the resellers who assemble personal computers using off-the-shelf components. The types of desktop CPUs have proliferated since the 1980s, as shown in Table 7.1.

Because software programs developed for RISC chips have to do more work in software, instead of using the chip's hardware, the size of the programs written for RISC chips are typically between 10 and 20 percent larger than programs written for CISC hardware. This, in turn, impacts software loading speeds and disk space requirements.

MEMORY

RAM (random access memory) is the fast, silicon memory accessed by the CPU, and is used to store programs and data for fast access. In general, the more memory, the faster the performance of the computer, depending on the software application. Most RAM is packaged in what are known as SIMMs (standard in-line memory modules), which are small cards with memory

Table 7.1 Desktop CPUs

	CPU	MANUFACTURER	OPERATING SYSTEMS
1980s CPUs	8088, 80286, 80386	Intel	DOS, Windows, UNIX[a]
	68000, 68010, 68020	Motorola	MacOS, UNIX
1990s CPUs	80486/ Pentium/P6	Intel	DOS, Windows, UNIX, Windows NT
	68030, 68040	Motorola	MacOS, UNIX
	SPARC	Sun Microsystems	UNIX
	Alpha	DEC	VMS, UNIX, Windows NT
	PowerPC	IBM/Motorola	MacOS, UNIX, Windows NT
	PA-RISC	Hewlett-Packard	UNIX, Windows NT
	R3000, R4000	Silicon Graphics	UNIX, Windows NT

[a]UNIX is used here generically to describe multiple variants of UNIX, including A/UX, AIX, SunOS, ULTRIX, XENIX, UNIX SVR4, OpenDesktop, UNIXWare, and others.

chips that snap into memory slots on the motherboard. Memory capacity, like disk storage, is generally measured in megabytes (MB, about one million bytes of data). RAM is a volatile storage medium, which means it does not retain information when turned off.

The typical memory requirements of both operating systems and software applications continue to climb every year. When not enough memory is available, a computer will do one of two things: refuse to work properly and complain about not enough memory, or begin to "page" to disk, which means moving data and programs out of memory temporarily onto disk and back again when needed later. Paging slows down computer performance dramatically. If your computer is accessing your disk constantly and suffers from sluggish performance, adding more memory is usually the best prescription.

A special, high-speed type of memory, cache memory, is also provided on most desktop computers. A cache is a temporary holding area for data and programs retrieved by the CPU. Information stored in cache can be accessed much faster than in ordinary RAM. Since cache memory is more expensive, most desktop computers provide only a small amount—128 K or 256 K.

EXPANSION CARDS

Expansion cards provide additional functionality not found on the motherboard of a desktop computer, and typically provide support for graphics display, networking, modems, sound cards, disk controllers, video capture, and the like.

Most motherboards provide slots for additional memory and expansion cards. Different manufacturers provide different types of slots, most of which are incompatible with each other. Older Macintosh models have NuBus slots; some IBM PCs have Micro-Channel slots. Virtually all Windows PCs support the 16-bit ISA cards; some also support 32-bit EISA, Local Bus, or PCI cards. PCI is emerging as a standard 32-bit bus design supported by both Apple and Windows PC-compatible manufacturers.

Personal computer manufacturers are finally learning the value of purging unnecessary and obscure jargon from hardware products. The standard format for portable computer expansion cards—PCMCIA—is now known simply as the PC Card format. PC Cards are credit-card size expansion cards that typically provide fax/modem or network support for portable computers.

One of the worst aspects of Windows personal computers, compared to Macintoshes, is their excessive reliance on expansion cards to provide functions (sound, networking, graphics display) that should be an integrated part of the basic system and supported on the motherboard. The result is unbalanced systems, especially in computers where individual components have been upgraded or replaced over time. For example, it is not unusual to find architectural firms with 90-MHz 32-bit Pentiums running 32-bit Windows 95 equipped with 16-bit ISA networking cards. Configuring the expansion cards, installing drivers for them, and avoiding conflicts between their input/output memory addresses and interrupts has always been a major headache for people who customize their PCs.

Intel is one CPU manufacturer aggressively pushing desktop video-teleconferencing. In fact, video compression and decompression algorithms are built into the company's new P6 processor. Eventually, standard desktop computers of the future will include built-in digital video cameras and microphones.

The "plug and play" capabilities of Windows 95 finally brings Macintosh-like ease of configuration to Windows PCs, but only for newer expansion cards. Many older expansion cards must still be configured manually, even with Windows 95. In the future, more functionality will be built into motherboards, and as CPUs become faster, they will handle specialized processing such as video image processing.

MAGNETIC DISK DRIVES

Most desktop computers are equipped with one or two diskette drives, either 3.5 or 5.25 inches, as well as an internal hard disk drive that stores between 200 MB and 1 GB (gigabyte, or 1000 megabytes) of data. Unlike faster volatile RAM, software and data stored on magnetic disks are retained even when the computer is turned off. Within a hard disk drive, digital data is written to and read from specially coated platters. The data is arranged in concentric circles on the platters known as tracks. Seek time, an oft-quoted statistic for disk drive speed, measures how fast the disk drive can access a track—9- to 13-millisecond seek time is about average.

The issue of software bloat is discussed in more detail in Chapter 11, Managing the Digital Office.

The continued expansion of the size of software applications has also increased the capacity requirements for disk drives. Fortunately, the price/performance improvements of disk drives has always prevented this from adding to the average unit cost of desktop computers.

OPTICAL DISKS

Optical disks are an excellent medium for information publishing and distribution, and for archiving large volumes of digital data within the architectural firm. Types of optical disk technology include:

■ Low-end, CD-ROM (read-only) disk drives. Each 5.25-inch CD can hold about 600 MB of data, or the contents of about 500 5.25-inch diskettes. CD-ROM drives are inexpensive (around $100 to $200), can read Kodak PhotoCDs as well as music CDs, and today are standard equipment on Windows PCs and Macintoshes. Early single-speed CD-ROM disk drives suffered from low data-transfer rates, about 300 KB per second, and even today's quad-speed and six-speed drives are still substantially slower than hard disk drives. CD-ROMs compensate for their performance limitations, however, with their low cost. CD-ROM is emerging as the ubiquitous high-capacity portable medium for storing and delivering software and information libraries.

Examples of CD-ROM information resources useful to architects can be found in Chapter 10, On-Line Resources.

■ Mid-range, read/write optical disk drives. Small 3.5-inch optical disks, the same size as a magnetic diskette, can hold between 128 and 256 KB of data. The 5.25-inch optical disk can hold between 500 MB and 4 GB of data, depending on the manufacturer.

■ High-end, read/write optical disk "jukeboxes." A jukebox contains a single drive mechanism with a lift arm that automatically switches between multiple read/write optical disks to retrieve data. Up to 20 GB of "near-line" storage can be provided for about $10,000. Jukeboxes containing multiple CD-ROM disks also can be used for networked read-only information resources.

Recordable CD-ROMs are an excellent storage medium for digital stick sets: portable digital archives containing project information, including CAD drawings, specifications, and correspondence files.

■ Recordable CD drives. These optical disk drives, available in 1995 for less than $2000, can record CDs that can be read subsequently by inexpensive CD-ROM drives. The optical disks used in recordable CD drives are "write-once, read-many" (WORM) disks. In other words, the disks can only be written to one time, but read (or copied) from over and over again. As such, recordable CDs are appropriate for archiving project information and for delivering digital data to third parties. Because they are WORM media, their contents cannot be tampered with once written and provide a digital paper trail admissible in court. The media cost of recordable CDs is generally less than read/write optical disks.

New high-density CD-ROM formats (also known as Digital Video Disks, or DVDs) are arriving that can store two hours or more of compressed video. Unless they reach agreement on a unified format, Sony/Phillips and Toshiba/Time-Warner are each set to introduce their own incompatible high-density CD-ROM formats in 1996. Sony's Super Density CD-ROM format stores data on both sides of the disk, and holds up to 8 GB. Toshiba's Multi-Media Compact Disc stores 3.7 GB on only one side. It remains to be seen which competing standard survives, and which will join the eight-track tape cassette of the

1970s and the Beta video cassette of the 1980s as the white-elephant media format of the 1990s.

DISPLAY MONITORS AND GRAPHICS CARDS

The display monitor is the place where the user and the computer meet eye to eye, and is not where architects should pinch pennies. For CAD, rendering, image editing, desktop publishing, or word-processing applications that require high graphics resolution, a 17-inch monitor is a must. A 19- to 21-inch monitor is a nice option, but demands a high price premium and is often the costliest component of the system. "Dot pitch" refers to the resolution of the screen and is an important criterion for determining screen sharpness. A .28-mm dot pitch is a typical value for most desktop computer displays.

Most display monitors are analog devices, so special circuitry on a computer's graphics card is required to translate the image stored in digital display memory (usually on the card) into an analog video signal understandable by the monitor. The quality of a digital image on your computer display depends not only on the dimensional size of the monitor and the resolution and color depth of the image, but also on the amount of display memory.

If your graphics card can display only 256 colors, for example, a full-color 24-bit image will not be displayed in its true representation and will have dithering or banding artifacts. Architects who intend to use image editing tools for full color photographic images should equip their desktop computers with the appropriate graphics hardware. This does not necessarily mean 24-bit graphics hardware; 16-bit color does just fine and is usually less expensive and faster. The slight loss in quality for most applications is not substantial.

The number of colors available and the maximum resolution of the screen depends on the display memory available and how many bits are used to store the color value of each pixel of the image. Table 7.2 summarizes how many colors (or shades of gray) a computer can store based on the number of bits per pixel: The original Macintosh display screen, for example, was a one-bit display. The screen consisted of a grid of pixels (picture

Table 7.2 Color Depth

BITS PER PIXEL	POSSIBLE COLORS/SHADES OF GRAY
1	2 (usually black/white)
2	4
4	16
8	256
16	65,536
24	16.7 million

elements) measuring 512 × 384. Each pixel was either on (white) or off (black). Storing a display image in memory required 512 × 384 bits (24,576 bytes).

As shown in the comparison in Illustration 7.1, the CGA display standard of early IBM-compatible PCs was a 4-bit color display (16 colors), with a resolution of 320 × 200. Storing a CGA image in memory required 320 × 200 × 4 bits (32,000 bytes). Later, PCs equipped with standard VGA displays (640 × 480 × 8 bits) required 307,200 bytes of display memory.

Today, the memory requirements of 24-bit, high-resolution graphics displays are an order of magnitude higher. The average Windows PC today, for example, includes a graphics card with

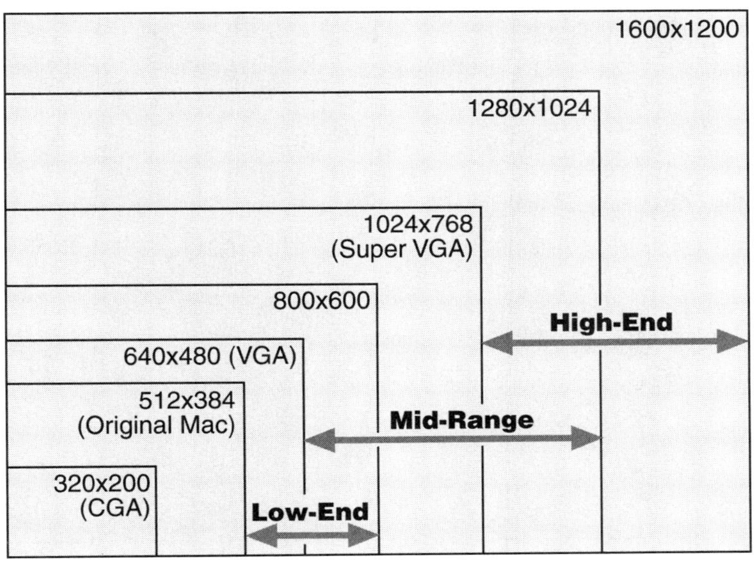

Illustration 7.1 Display resolutions.

two megabytes of display memory, and many high-end systems are equipped with graphics cards with four megabytes of display memory. Table 7.3 lists display memory requirements for typical image resolution and color depth combinations.

The display memory required in megabytes is simply the product of the display resolution and color depth divided by eight million. (One megabyte equals approximately eight million bits.) Considering the display memory of the graphics card, you can determine what image size and what color resolution a graphics card will support (Ill. 7.2). For example, a one-megabyte

Table 7.3 Display Memory Requirements

RESOLUTION	COLOR DEPTH	MEMORY (MB)
640 × 480	4-bit (16 colors)	0.15
	8-bit (256 colors)	0.31
	16-bit (65,536 colors)	0.62
	24-bit (16.7 million colors)	0.93
800 × 600	4-bit	0.24
	8-bit	0.48
	16-bit	0.96
	24-bit	1.44
1024 × 768	4-bit	0.39
	8-bit	0.79
	16-bit	1.58
	24-bit	2.36
1280 × 1024	4-bit	0.66
	8-bit	1.31
	16-bit	2.62
	24-bit	3.93
1600 × 1200	4-bit	0.96
	8-bit	1.92
	16-bit	3.84
	24-bit	5.76

graphics card can support 24-bit color only up to 640 × 480 display resolution. A two-megabyte graphics card can support 24-bit color up to 800 × 600 display resolution, and 16-bit color up to 1024 × 768 resolution.

A two-megabyte graphics card is the minimum requirement if you intend to use high-resolution color image editing tools. A four-megabyte graphics card is better, especially with 19-inch monitors or larger, because you can display true-color, 24-bit images at 1280 × 1024 resolution.

Some multisync monitors, which can support a wide variety of display resolutions and frequencies, will not support high resolutions at a high enough frequency—60 to 72 MHz—to avoid annoying flickering and eye fatigue. Be sure to check the specifications of the monitor before you buy.

Note that the display resolution (measured in pixels) is different from the display size (measured in inches). Displaying high-resolution (1024 × 768 or 1280 × 1024) graphics on a small 14- or 15-inch monitor is not recommended, because the dot pitch is not fine enough to resolve the individual pixels. Images and linework will appear fuzzy and will contribute to user eyestrain. Make sure you use a large enough monitor, with a small enough dot pitch, to accommodate high-resolution graphics.

IMAGE CAPTURE HARDWARE

Over the past two years, color scanning technology has reached a price/performance threshold affordable for most architects, and color desktop scanners are now the rule, rather than the exception, on the architectural desktop. Most support resolu-

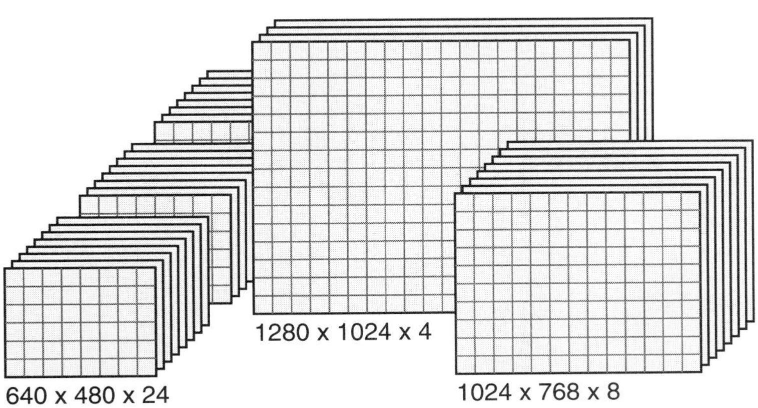

Illustration 7.2 Display memory configurations.

tions up to 600 DPI for under $800. Color desktop scanners are excellent for scanning small-format sketches or photographic prints, as well as company logos, or other printed literature.

Color scanners are an important tool for building more realism into computer-generated images. The use of scanning is most appropriate for capturing elements or scenes that do not lend themselves to the rigid geometric modeling of CAD systems. These include cloud formations, trees, people, or other landscape elements that can be composited into a rendered scene. Scanning is also appropriate for realistically representing an existing site without the overhead of modeling it in three dimensions. Material samples, such as tile, carpet, stone, and grout, can also be captured with a scanner for use in visualization.

Photorealism is not always the goal of computer-aided visualization, an issue that is discussed in more detail in Chapter 5, The Language of Digital Media.

Digital cameras can also be used to capture images, without the intermediate step of storing images on film. Affordable cameras such as Apple's QuickTake Camera and Kodak's Digital Camera essentially combine a scanner with the optics of a traditional camera. The major limitation of these cameras is the resolution of the images they capture—approximately 640 × 480, similar to the resolution of video. For some applications, such as documenting construction activity or quickly capturing site photographs for design studies, the low resolution is fine. For other more demanding applications, however, such as large-format presentations or visualizations, video resolution images do not hold up well. (Kodak's professional digital cameras provide resolutions matching those of 35-mm film but are still very expensive.) Until affordable digital cameras provide better resolution, using a film intermediate still assures the best image quality.

In addition, video-capture expansion cards are widely available for both Macintosh and Windows PCs, allowing individual frames or sequences of frames of video to be captured into digital formats. Again, video capture cards suffer from the same limitation as digital cameras: the resulting images are low resolution and do not hold up well when compared to higher-resolution photographic images.

KEYBOARDS

The keyboard, not the mouse, is still the primary user interface component of most desktop computers used by architects.

Compare mouse clicks to keystrokes on a typical day, and you will understand why. Apple, Microsoft, and others now offer ergonomic keyboards (which look like they have been sawn in half and twisted) to minimize the amount of wrist rotation by users (Ill. 7.3). The ergonomic keyboards take some getting used to, but are well worth it for regular computer users. In addition, configure your workstation so the keyboard is slightly below the work surface to minimize bending of the wrists.

Some computer vendors offer programmable keyboards, which allow users to associate command sequences with individual keys or key sequences (control-A, for example). For CAD and other software programs that have complex command sets, keyboard shortcuts provide an efficient way to access commonly used commands, and can save substantial time compared to pull-down menus or dialog box navigation.

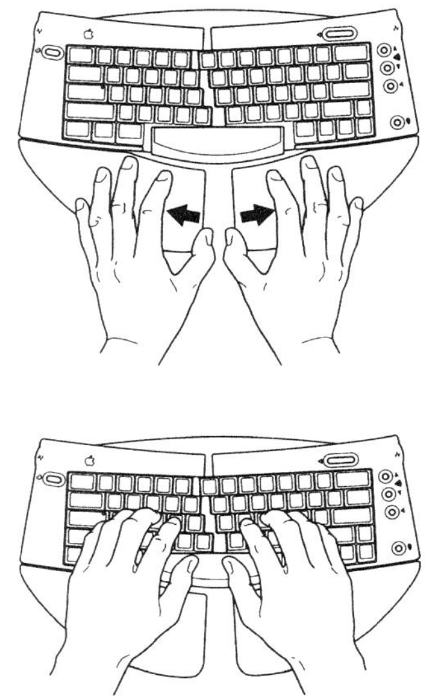

Illustration 7.3 *An ergonomic keyboard.*

POINTING DEVICES

The most popular pointing device on desktop computers today is the mouse. A mouse is a *relative* pointing device, because its cursor movement depends on the relative movement of the mouse, not its absolute location on the desktop. If you pick up a mouse, move it, and place it down on the desk in a new location, the cursor displayed on the screen will not move.

Although the mouse has become the standard pointing device on computers that have a point-and-click graphical user interface, and is a recognized symbol for ease of use, the mouse is actually an awkward and inefficient pointing device. Consider the amount of time required to move your hand from the keyboard to grab the mouse, multiplied by the number of times each day you must do so. Trackballs and pressure pads built into keyboards, popular for years in portable and laptop computers, are only now emerging in desktop computer keyboards. In a few years, such pointing devices should become standard equipment on most desktop computers.

Digitizing tablets typically used in CAD and image editing applications are *absolute* pointing devices. Most tablets contain a grid of wires just below the tablet's surface, which detect the location of a puck moved over it. Typically, a region of the tablet is mapped to the screen. Unlike a mouse, if you pick up a digitizing tablet puck, move it, and place it down on the tablet in a new location, the cursor displayed on the screen will move. Because digitizing tablets are absolute pointing devices, they can be used to digitize drawings by tracing locations on the drawing with the puck.

Some digitizing tablets are equipped with pressure-sensitive pens, rather than pucks. Pressure sensitivity is useful in many digital image editing and painting programs, allowing the user to achieve a fatter line or brush stroke by applying more pressure to the pen.

The ultimate pointing device will be an interactive display surface. What architects really need are desk-mounted E-size flat-panel display devices with pressure-sensitive pens: not WYSIWYG (what you see is what you get) but WYDIWYG (what you draw is what you get). When that happens within the next decade, sketching on a computer will actually be a plausible concept. Until then, using a mouse to do so is an inefficient, painstaking endeavor that few architects have attempted to master.

MODEMS

Modem is an acronym for modulator–demodulator, the hardware component responsible for converting a computer's digital signal into an analog signal suitable for transmission over telephone lines. A modem is required for your computer to communicate with other computers over a telephone line or for you to access on-line services, such as AIA OnLine, CompuServe, or the Internet. Most modems today also support fax transmission protocols which, when used with the appropriate software, allow you to send and retrieve faxes from your computer.

Ten years from now, modems will be largely obsolete because most telephone lines will be capable of handling digital signals directly. ISDN, an acronym for Integrated Services Digital Network, is the de facto digital telephone standard that provides support for voice and data on a telephone line at 56 K bits/second, substantially faster than most modems. Providing

ISDN to a desktop computer eliminates the need for a modem, since the telephone line itself supports digital signals.

Modems support different speeds; in general, the faster, the better. If you are planning to use software to access the Internet, be sure to get a 28.8-K modem, which is the minimum speed for reasonable response time for browsing graphically rich World Wide Web documents.

See Chapter 10, On-Line Resources, for more information about using modems to access the Internet and the World Wide Web.

TAPE DRIVES

In the early 1980s, when desktop computers were sold with 10- or 20-MB hard drives, backing up data using diskettes was not impractical. Today, with 500-MB and 1-GB disk drives standard equipment on most personal computers, it is unreasonable to do so. Stand-alone PCs that cannot be backed up from a network should always be equipped with a backup tape drive.

Most tape backup systems use 4-mm tapes of varying length. Two types are available: low-capacity, low-cost 120- to 250-MB tape drives, and high-capacity, high-cost 2- to 8-GB tape drives. The major limitation of backup tape drives is their sequential, linear storage formats. Accessing a file that is stored at the end of a tape can take time, as the tape is forwarded and rewound. As discussed earlier, optical media are an emerging alternative to magnetic tape and generally provide longer shelf life, but recordable CD-ROM drives are still more costly than most tape drives.

PRINTERS AND PLOTTERS

In the 1990s, the terms *printing* and *plotting* are virtually synonymous. In the past, *printing* was used to describe small formats (8.5 by 11 or 11 by 17 inches), while *plotting* was used to describe larger formats. Today, the definitions have blurred. Printer technologies such as laser and inkjet are now offered in large format plotters. Most large-format plotters also include Windows and Macintosh printer drivers, and most small-format printers also include CAD plotter drivers.

Laser and inkjet printers are the most popular small-format devices. Both types of printers produce a printed image by depositing small dots of ink or toner on the page. During printing, the text, graphics, and images within documents are scaled and converted into a matrix of dots. Sometimes, the conversion is performed by the printer; sometimes it is performed by the software application. At smaller sizes, the appearance of the fonts may vary depending on the printer resolution and the printer language.

The two most popular printer languages that are used to convert text, linework, and images into the dots of the printer are Hewlett Packard's Printer Control Language (PCL) and Adobe's PostScript. PostScript was the printing language in Apple's original LaserWriter introduced in 1985 and is today supported by a wide variety of graphics printers and plotters. PostScript is a more robust, flexible printing language, but is also more memory intensive and generally adds more cost to printers.

The resolution of most printers and plotters (except for older pen plotters) is typically measured in dots per inch (DPI). The preferred resolution for desktop, small-format printers is 600 DPI; 300 DPI is a minimum (Ill. 7.4). Be sure to evaluate not only the plotter cost and speed, but also media cost and quality. Thermal plotters, for example, are often less expensive than electrostatic or laser plotters, but must use special, expensive thermal paper (which doesn't take kindly to hot electric erasers and sepia-printing machines). Electrostatic plotters have fallen out of favor, in part because of the toxic nature of the chemicals involved, and the fact that most specially coated electrostatic paper cannot be recycled. Laser and inkjet technologies are ecologically friendlier.

Illustration 7.4 *Printer resolutions.*

Popular desktop color printing technologies include inkjet, thermal wax, and dye sublimation. Small-format thermal-wax color printers melt colored wax onto paper to produce sharp color output, but thermal-wax prints are easily scratched and therefore inappropriate for marketing proposals or other small-format publications that may be handled by many people. Dye-sublimation printers, which actually inject dye into specially coated (and very expensive) paper, provide outstanding color output, but are notoriously slow. Inkjet printers are emerging as the most flexible, general purpose printing devices, and inkjet quality is improving all the time. Watch out for color fading, however, especially with water-soluble inks.

Perhaps the most important recent printing technology for architects is the affordable, 600 DPI, 11- by 17-inch black-and-white laser printer. Hewlett Packard's 4MV printer, for example, can plug directly into a network, supports both PostScript and PCL (and can switch dynamically between them), is fast (up to 16 pages per minute), and is an excellent printer for CAD check plotting. Some small architectural firms produce 11- by 17-inch CAD construction documents sets by printing them directly on the laser printer, and avoid blueprinting altogether. At 600 DPI, the 11- by 17-inch format is suitable for a wide range of small projects and excellent for reduced-size printing of larger projects.

NOTEBOOK COMPUTERS

Some architects are replacing their desktop computers with portable notebook computers. In the past, notebook computers were useful for traveling but inappropriate for full-time use at the office because of dim monochrome displays, no CD-ROM, and small hard disks. Today, those limitations are close to disappearing, and project managers, construction administrators, and others who are out of the office frequently may want to consider using notebooks or laptop computers exclusively.

For architects who still need large display screens at the office, for CAD or other graphics-intensive applications, most portable computers today are sold with optional port replicators, which connect the monitor, keyboard, modem, mouse, and network through a single adapter. Connecting a portable computer to any of these resources simply requires plugging the notebook into the port replicator. Eventually, redundant monitors may not be necessary, since notebook displays are starting to rival the resolution and color depth of desktop computers, including 1024 × 768 resolution and true 24-bit color at 640 × 480 resolution.

Useful criteria for evaluating notebook computers include:

- Comfort and usability, particularly built-in pointing devices, such as track balls or pressure pads

- Display screen size, brightness, resolution, and color depth
- Battery life, typically two to five hours
- Durability (notebook computers tend to be knocked around)
- Performance, rarely as fast as high-end desktop machines, but not by much
- Weight

DESKTOP MULTIPROCESSING

New hardware designs are emerging to complement and leverage new high-end operating systems on the desktop. One of the most intriguing is multiprocessing desktop computers, based on hardware designs previously found only in high-end workstation, minicomputer, and mainframe systems. Multiprocessor computers are based on the simple idea that many CPUs working side by side are better than one working alone.

The basic performance limitation of all personal computers is their single central processing unit. (As discussed in Chapter 6, the term *multitasking* on a single-chip PC is actually a misnomer, since the CPU can physically execute only one process at a time, but is able to switch back and forth between tasks fast enough to appear to be doing several things at once.) In multiprocessing computers, each processor can be assigned to a different software application, or even a different procedure, or "thread," within a single software application.

In architectural firms, multiprocessing computers have several potential uses. CAD, database, and spreadsheet applications exchanging data in real time, each with its own dedicated processor, will make many of today's advanced architectural applications run dramatically faster. Although it remains to be seen exactly when the power of multiprocessing machines will be leveraged enough in day-to-day use to justify their added cost, the opportunities for increased productivity in advanced applications are certainly worth investigating.

As network servers, multiprocessing computers are also poised to provide much better performance. Again, however, that advantage will not be automatic—the developer of the network software will be required to build threads into her program to be distributed among multiple processors. But in the simplest scenario, one can imagine a network server with one processor dedicated to network printing, one for file dispensing, and one performing as a remote-access or database engine.

Computer-aided visualization also lends itself beautifully to multiprocessing hardware because most contemporary imaging algorithms process each pixel or scan-line independently of the rest. Quite easily, each processor could be assigned to render a separate portion of the image. The concept applies equally well to animation, with each processor able to work on a different frame or sequence of the animation.

Pixar's Ed Catmull once described the ultimate multiprocessing rendering computer as having a processor per pixel.

HARDWARE RECOMMENDATIONS

One of the most popular but vexing questions asked of people with a decent grasp of computer hardware knowledge is: "What kind of computer should I buy?" (This question is inevitably followed by another one 18 to 30 months later, "My computer at home has stopped working. What should I do?") The first question is always difficult to answer and depends on a variety of factors, including budget, the software applications to be used, and office compatibility. One of the best ways to decide is by talking to other people who have purchased hardware recently and learning from their successes and failures.

Below are a few basic recommendations designed to ensure that the hardware you buy is not obsolete after 12 to 18 months. Take them all with a grain of salt, because hardware changes on a daily basis, but they may help you narrow down your menu of choices to a more digestible selection. When you discuss computer hardware with other people, take care to avoid all "religious" debates, including PowerPC versus Intel and RISC versus CISC. These issues are not that important relative to getting your work done.

1. Buy only Pentium, P6, or PowerPC systems. Do not purchase computers with Motorola 680x0 or Intel 486 chips, which will have a relatively short useful life span (less than two years).
2. Buy PCs equipped with a minimum of 8 MB for Mac or Windows, 16 MB minimum for CAD or heavy-duty office automation, or 32 MB minimum for three-dimensional visualization or digital image editing and

file servers. The general rule: whatever the software developer recommends as the minimum memory requirement, double it.

3. Buy systems with expansion card slots that can accept 32-bit PCI cards.
4. Do not buy any more 5.25-inch diskette drives, even if they are cheap.
5. Do not buy a hard drive smaller than 500 MB, and look for seek times under 13 ms.
6. Buy a CD-ROM drive. A quad-speed drive is the minimum.
7. If your computer is not networked, buy a tape backup unit or recordable CD-ROM.
8. Purchase a fax/modem that supports a minimum 14.4 K baud (bits/second) rate, preferably 28.8 K or 38.4 K.
9. In monitors, look for .28 mm dot pitch, 17-inch screen minimum for CAD, rendering, image editing, or desktop publishing, and 15-inch minimum for all other applications; 19-inch monitors are a nice option; 21-inch and larger monitors are overkill and usually don't provide good value.
10. Standardize keyboards as much as possible. Windows users should purchase keyboards that include the special function keys of Windows 95. Programmable keyboards are a great option.
11. Do not buy digitizing tablets unless you need to digitize, even if your CAD program supports tablet menus: they clutter up the desktop, are more expensive than mice, and discourage "heads-up" computer use.
12. In general, the smaller the desktop footprint, the better, but make sure the power supply can handle expansion cards you plan to buy. Large, tower cases look impressive but are mostly empty, and reaching under the desk to insert a diskette or CD-ROM is backbreaking.
13. Listen carefully to the computer before you buy it—fans and disk drives vary dramatically in decibel output. A computer's noise may not be noticeable in a retail environment but can be annoying in your office or at home.

14. Look for large-format plotters that can plot on inexpensive plain bond paper and reproducible vellum. Look for small-format printers that have straight-through sheet feeds, to allow for printing on heavy stock. Large-format color inkjet plotters are a terrific value for bringing large-format color output to architectural firms of all sizes. Use 600-DPI 11- by 17-inch desktop laser printers for check plots, and save substantial time and money on plotting costs.

How much should a desktop computer cost? A high-end CAD personal computer generally costs around \$3000 to \$4000, and perhaps as high as \$5000 for a souped-up machine with a large (19- to 21-inch) monitor. Low-end computers, suitable for word processing, spreadsheets, and other office automation tasks (but not high-performance CAD), generally cost around \$2000 to \$2500. For DOS/Windows PCs, those figures have been fairly stable for several years, and more recently have been matched by more aggressive Macintosh pricing by Apple. Use them with confidence for budgeting purposes. What changes dramatically year to year, of course, is the average performance and storage capacity provided by desktop computers at those price points.

CHAPTER

8

CAD—The Keystone of an Automated Practice

> *"We are hired in the first place because no owner or contractor in his right mind would try to build without plans. Yet some architects and engineers think they can improvise their way through something as complex as a set of working drawings by the seat of their pants. Good plans require their own planning."*
>
> **Fred Stitt, AIA**

For over a decade, CAD has been the primary technology focus of architects seeking to automate their firms. During the 1980s, successful CAD implementation required substantial investments in specialized hardware, training, support, and management. Today, CAD software remains one of the most complex and difficult software applications for architects to learn, use, and manage.

The complexity of today's CAD software partially results from the focus of software developers on continually adding features, often at the expense of usability, that expand the scope of CAD toward an all-in-one modeling and documentation tool (and create a stream of upgrade revenue for themselves). Because it is used to produce the architect's primary service product—technical drawings—CAD likely will remain a keystone of the automated architectural practice. However, its relative importance within the spectrum of digital tools available to the architect is equally likely to decline over the next decade.

In many architectural firms, the digital documents that describe architectural projects are being developed using a variety of smaller general-purpose software applications that share information with each other, not a single monolithic CAD program. Clearly, CAD can no longer be treated as a specialized, stand-alone application, but must be well integrated as a general-purpose tool with other software applications within the architectural firm.

Most importantly, as discussed in Chapter 4, architects (and software developers) should discard the idea that CAD software will eventually allow architects to develop literal three-dimensional building models from which technical drawings are push-button by-products. The 20-year-old three-dimensional building model paradigm must be preceded by radical institutional and economic shifts in the delivery of architectural services, and even then will be appropriate only for a small percentage of architectural projects. Most useful three-dimensional models of architecture will always be *representational,* not *literal.* And two-dimensional abstractions will always be extremely efficient forms of communication.

At the same time, the notion of distinguishing between *models* and *drawings* is a powerful one, even within a two-dimensional domain, and is an idea that can be applied successfully using many of today's CAD software programs. The practical payoff of CAD, in fact, is provided by its tools of information reuse. This chapter describes those basic tools, most of which are supported by CAD software today and a few that should be.

TOOLS OF INFORMATION REUSE

During the 1980s, CAD was widely perceived as appropriate only for repetitive, large-scale projects. Today, well-trained and well-managed staff should be able to use CAD successfully and economically on virtually any project of any size. Efficient and high-quality results require not only properly trained users, of course, but enlightened, informed, and committed management.

The least efficient way to use CAD is as a digital pencil or digital typewriter, simply emulating traditional methods of drawing and annotation. In fact, CAD is best understood as a design information management system. It is a tool with which architects can develop full-size graphic descriptions of buildings (in two or three dimensions), and share, reuse, and republish that information in a variety of formats, views, scales, and levels of detail. The following are examples of information reuse:

BETWEEN PROJECTS

Standard details, assemblies, systems
Schedules

Specifications
Title blocks, cover sheets
General notes, legends, abbreviations
Conformance statements, disclaimers

BETWEEN PROJECT PHASES
Capturing design intent
Accurate site plan geometry, constraints
Overlays of design intent—ADA, parking, etc.
Hard-line floor plans, sections, elevations
Area calculations

BETWEEN DISCIPLINES
Architecture; interiors; planning
Structural; MEP
Landscape; civil

BETWEEN DRAWINGS
Building grids
Site plans; floor plans; ceiling plans; enlarged plans; TI plans
Elevations; enlarged elevations
Building sections; wall sections
Perspective and isometric drawings

BETWEEN PARTS OF A DRAWING
Cloned components: doors, windows, columns, fixtures, etc.
Typical annotation: keynotes, section cuts, targets, etc.

BETWEEN ARCHITECT AND CLIENT
Financing support documents
Marketing materials; leasing documents
Three-dimensional presentation; video
Facilities management databases

CAD drawings are no longer static collections of information, but dynamic documents that share information with other drawings. In addition, their usefulness extends beyond documentation. CAD documents may contain supplemental annotation that is not meant to be included in the finished model or plotted drawing but is useful to store internally, such as marginalia (digital "post-it" notes) about design intent. Most architects don't do this naturally, because a technical drawing is viewed as a finished product, not a scratch pad. In fact, the plotted CAD drawing is just a filtered snapshot of a design process at a specific point in time.

ELEMENT TYPES

A brief review of the different types of graphic elements within CAD systems is worthwhile. As shown in Illustration 8.1, most architectural models and drawings contain three kinds of graphic elements:

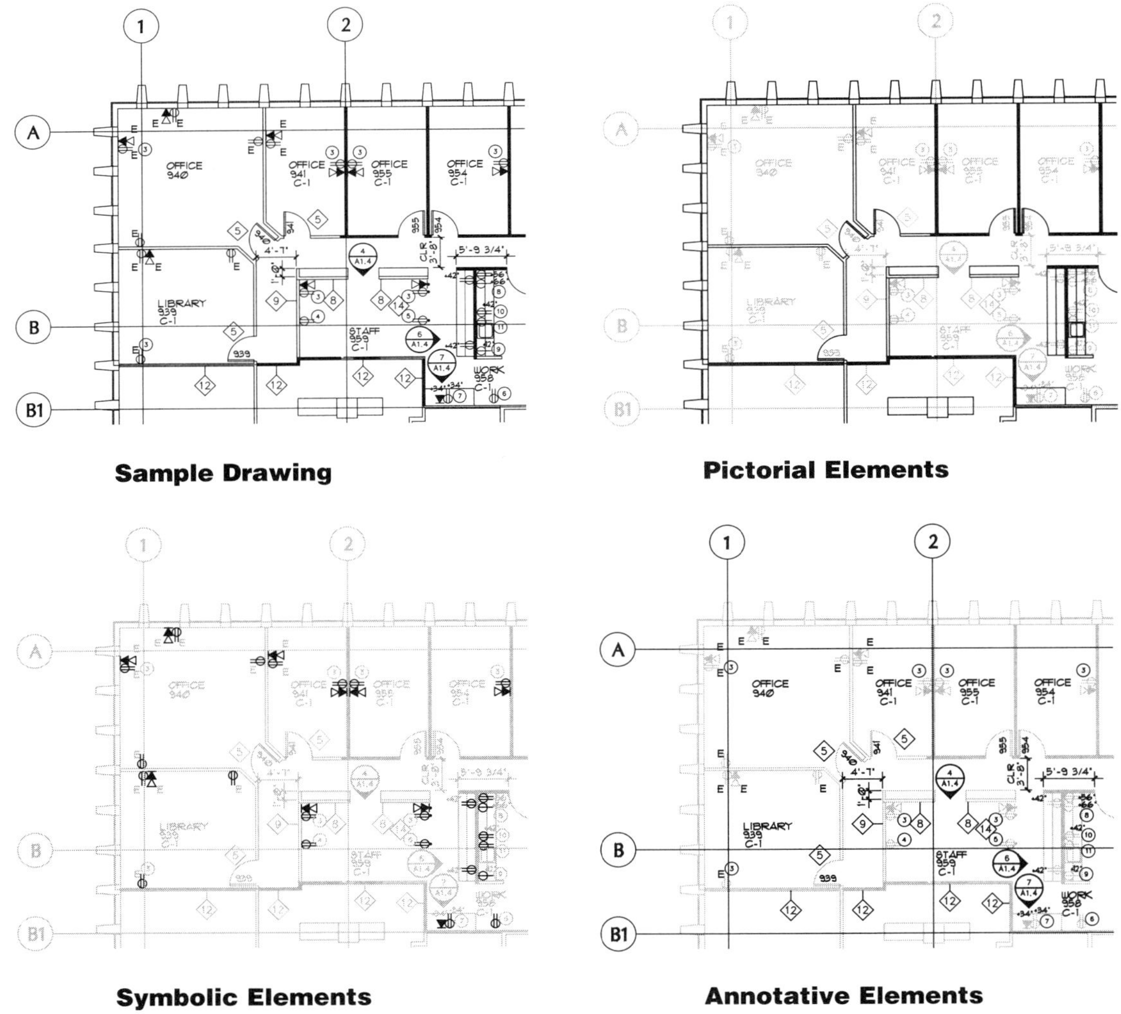

Illustration 8.1 *Pictorial, symbolic, and annotative elements.*

1. *Pictorial Elements.* These elements represent the physical components of a building model, and are drawn pictorially. The pictorial representation may not be literal or fully detailed but is dimensionally accurate. The size of pictorial elements on a plotted drawing depends on the scale of the drawing—the smaller the scale, the smaller they appear. Examples include walls, doors, windows, stairs, furniture, and fixtures.

2. *Symbolic Elements.* These elements also represent the physical components of a building model, but are drawn symbolically. Symbolic elements describe location, not appearance—in other words, "put one of these here." The size of symbolic elements on a plotted drawing is constant and does not depend on the scale of the drawing. Examples include electrical outlets, telephone jacks, exit signs, sprinkler heads, and speakers.

3. *Annotative Elements.* These elements provide supplemental information for reference only and do not represent physical components of the building model. Like symbolic elements, the size of annotative elements on a plotted drawing is constant, and does not depend on the scale of the drawing. Examples include dimensions, targets, and notes.

An element is a drawing primitive: a line, arc, circle, or piece of text. The term *element* is used here instead of *object*, to avoid confusion with the reusable components of object-oriented software, which are discussed in Chapter 4.

The following is a summary of the characteristics of graphic elements:

ELEMENT TYPE	PART OF THE MODEL?	SCALED WHEN PLOTTED?
Pictorial	Yes	Yes
Symbolic	Yes	No
Annotative	No	No

Unfortunately, many CAD systems do not easily distinguish between these three types of elements. In AutoCAD, for example, the uniform appearance of symbolic and annotative elements on plots of different scales is left to the user, by assigning values to variables such as LTSCALE and DIMSCALE to control the display of line types and dimensions, or by assigning a scale value to symbolic or annotative components (AutoCAD blocks) when they are inserted into drawings. Some CAD systems, such as Powerdraw and ArchiCAD, do distinguish between pictorial elements and some types of annotative elements, such as dimensions, targets, and notes, and provide dynamic scaling of those elements when the plotted scale of the drawing is changed.

An important point: dynamic scaling of symbolic and annotative elements should be an option, not automatic. In half-size sets of drawings, everything on a drawing is plotted at 50 percent size, including symbolic and annotative elements. The CAD software should distinguish between intended scale, used to size the symbolic and annotative elements, and the actual scale used when plotting.

Line weight is also a symbolic graphic attribute of all three types of elements in a drawing. Symbolic line weight is not intended to represent dimensional thickness of an element, but only to illustrate the relative importance of graphical information. Many people confuse symbolic line *weight* and pictorial line *thickness*. AutoCAD, for example, does not support symbolic line weight for any of its elements, but does support, for polylines only, a literal thickness. AutoCAD's polylines are not useful for symbolic linework between drawings of different scales, but are appropriate for pictorial linework, such as pochéed walls.

VIEW, SCALE, AND DOCUMENT FILTERS

The same elements in an architectural model are often displayed or plotted differently:

1. At different scales (Ill. 8.2). Examples include single-line versus double-line wall furring, representational material indicators, and symbolic or annotative elements.
2. In different views (Ill. 8.3). An example is a door shown open in plan and closed in elevation.
3. On different types of documents (Ill. 8.4). An example is wall linework shown solid on floor plans and screened on reflected ceiling plans.

Since most CAD systems do not readily distinguish between pictorial, symbolic, and annotative elements, nor provide view and scale filtering, users must create organizational guidelines to

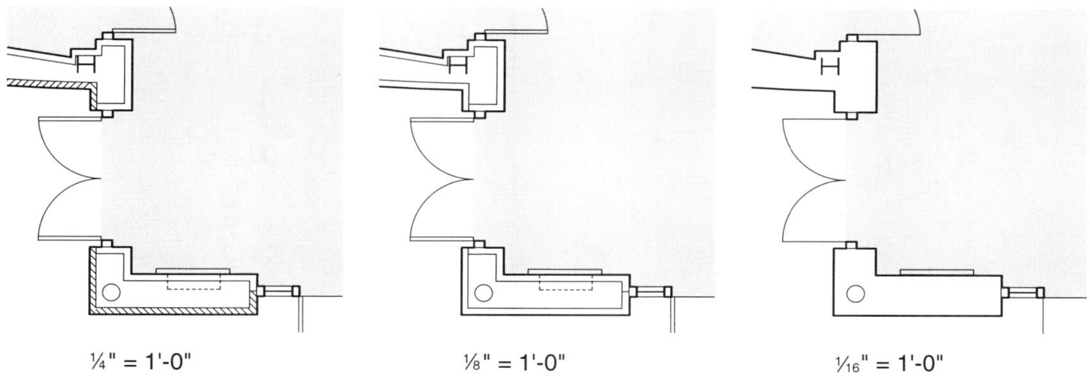

Illustration 8.2 *Scale filtering.*

implement these features. Expanded layer conventions and/or specialized plotting routines can help. (Be careful, however, not to make the operation of your system too complex, extinguishing the efficiencies you gain by using these features.) In some systems, filtering can be handled by storing multiple representa-

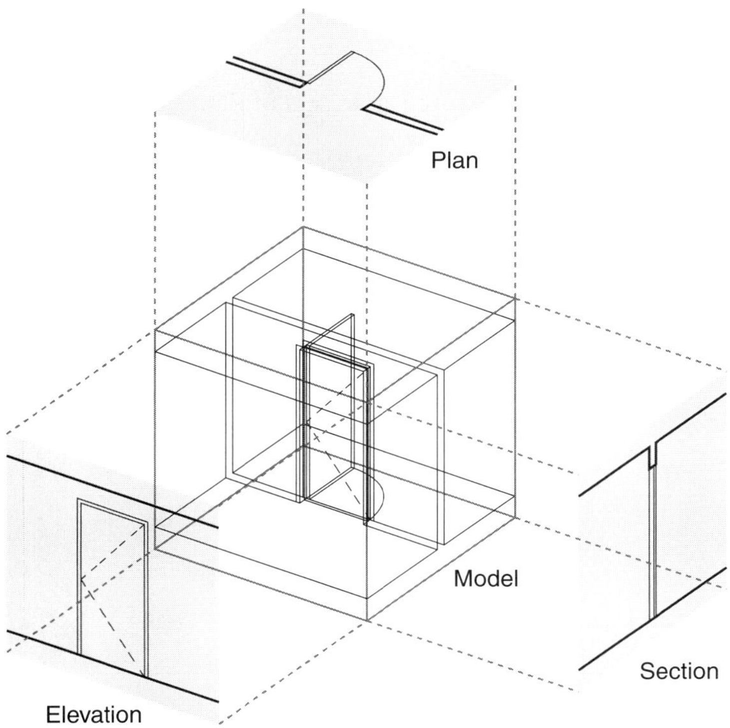

Illustration 8.3 *View filtering.*

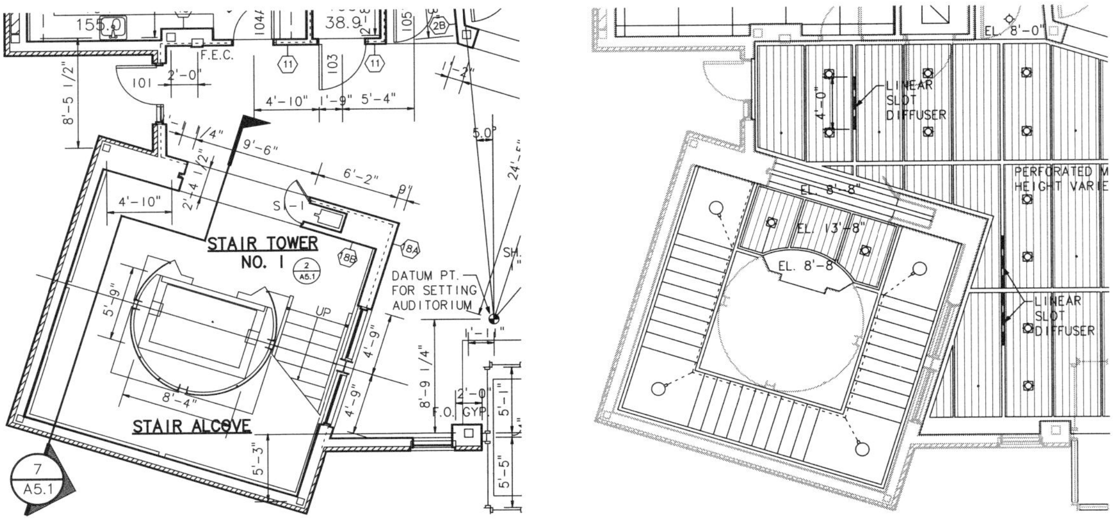

Illustration 8.4 Document filtering.

Illustration 8.5 Component substitution.

tions of components and substituting them as required for display or plotting (Ill. 8.5). In addition, some third-party CAD software programs provide tools for these purposes.

COMPONENTS

Components are named, reusable sets of data that are copied multiple times within a model or drawing. They behave like digital rubber stamps but are more flexible and powerful. Vari-

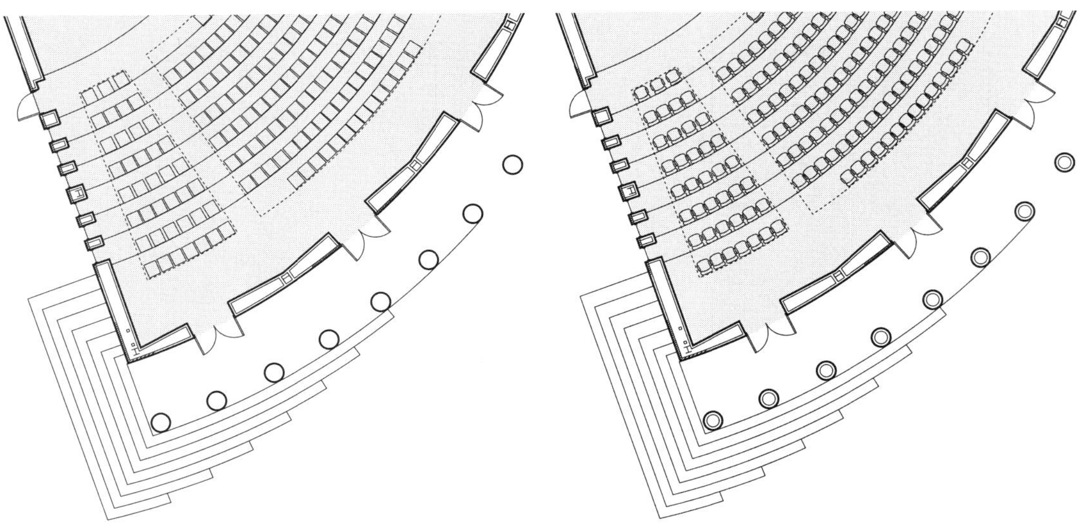

ous CAD systems have different names for components, such as blocks (AutoCAD), cells (Microstation), or symbols (most other systems). Components are an efficient way to manage repetitive parts of a drawings, such as doors, windows, fixtures, targets, labels, or grid bubbles. They can also describe assemblies of construction that are repeated throughout a building, such as a typical column in an arcade or a bay window assembly. Components often have nongraphic attributes attached to them that can be assigned unique values within each copy, such as the number, type, rating, and hardware group of a door.

Unlike most graphic elements in a CAD drawing, which are duplicated in their entirety when they are copied, most components are *instanced* (Ill. 8.6). A component's *definition*—the elements that comprise it—is stored only once in a drawing. When a component instance is placed on a drawing, only the location, scale, and rotation of the instance are added to the drawing file. The elements within the component definition are not repeated within the drawing, which makes the drawing more compact and provides an efficient mechanism to update components. Most CAD systems allow components to be nested, which means their definitions can contain other component definitions.

Illustration 8.6 Instancing versus copying.

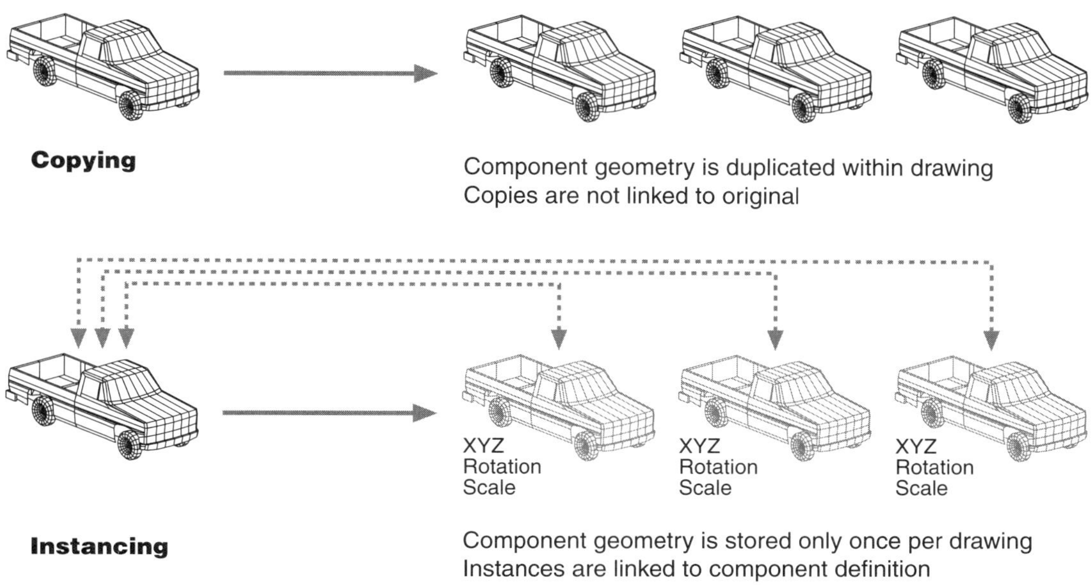

Components are excellent tools to construct parts of models or drawings from a kit of parts. Building elevations and furniture plans are the most common examples (Ill. 8.7). Changing the definition of a component that contains a typical spandrel panel, for example, will automatically update all the spandrel panels in the building elevation. Components can allow designers to explore "what-if" scenarios with building elevations, but their effective use as a design tool is limited to fairly repetitive designs.

Components are most useful when they are organized into libraries. If your system does not impose the organizational structure of libraries (e.g., AutoCAD blocks), impose one yourself using the computer file system's folders or directories. Distinguish between project-specific and office libraries. Keep the libraries of reasonable size, organized by discipline, project type, and/or drawing type.

LOCAL VERSUS GLOBAL COMPONENTS

The definition of a local component resides inside the drawing. Any change to the definition of a local component that is placed in several drawings requires updating the definition in each drawing. The definition of a global component, on the other hand, resides outside the drawing (in another drawing or library), and is dynamically updated each time the drawing is opened. Because of their scope, global components more easily support substitution during plotting (for scale, view, or document filtering) or to display different design schemes using different component libraries. Illustration 8.8 shows the difference between local and global components. Table 8.1 compares components within different CAD systems.

Although local components do not provide automatic global updating, they are generally easier to manage and are more portable. If drawings with global components are archived without their definitions, and the definitions are subsequently changed, any drawings restored from the archive will be incorrect. To avoid this problem, the domain of global components should always be project specific, not office wide,

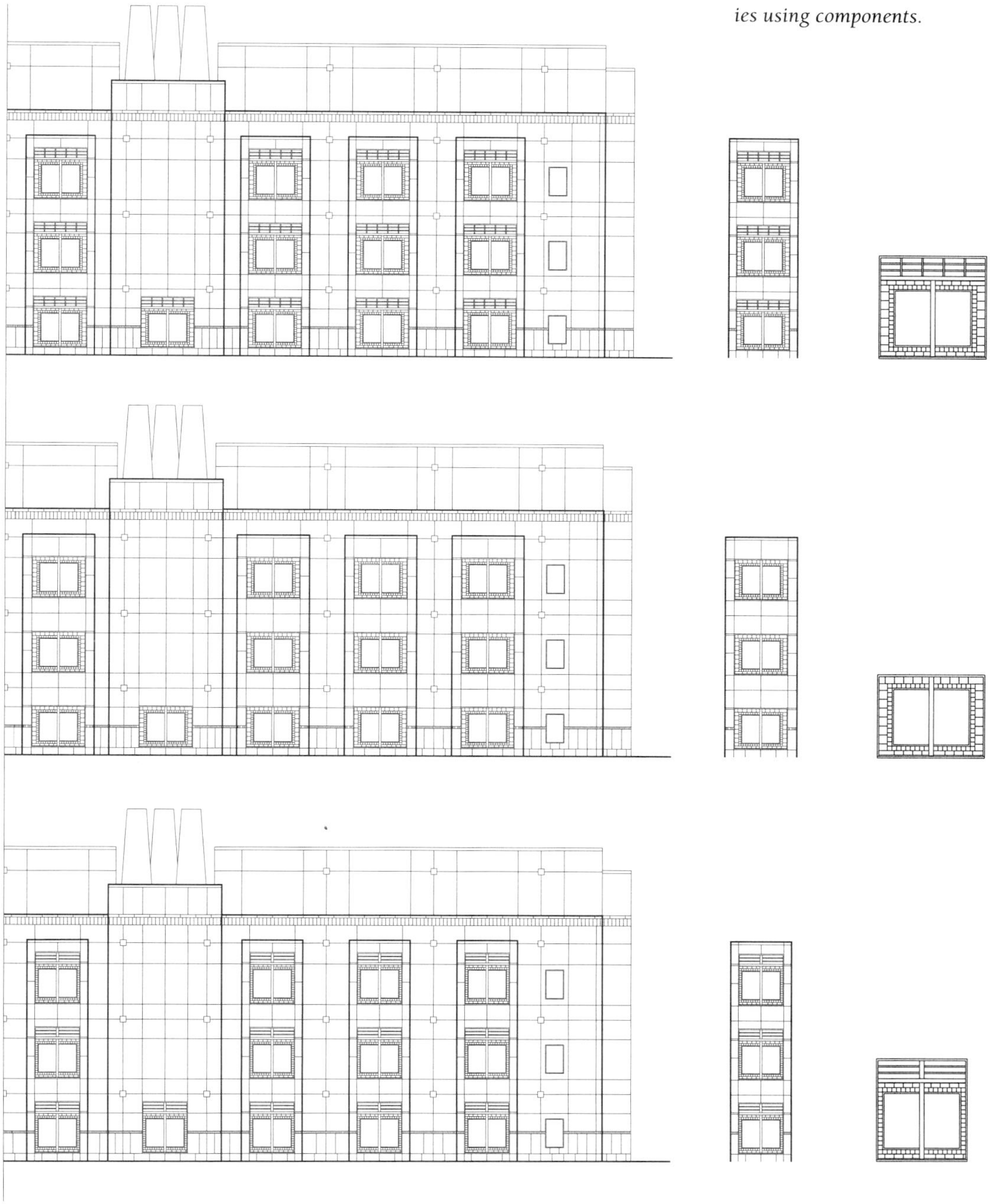

Illustration 8.7 *Elevation studies using components.*

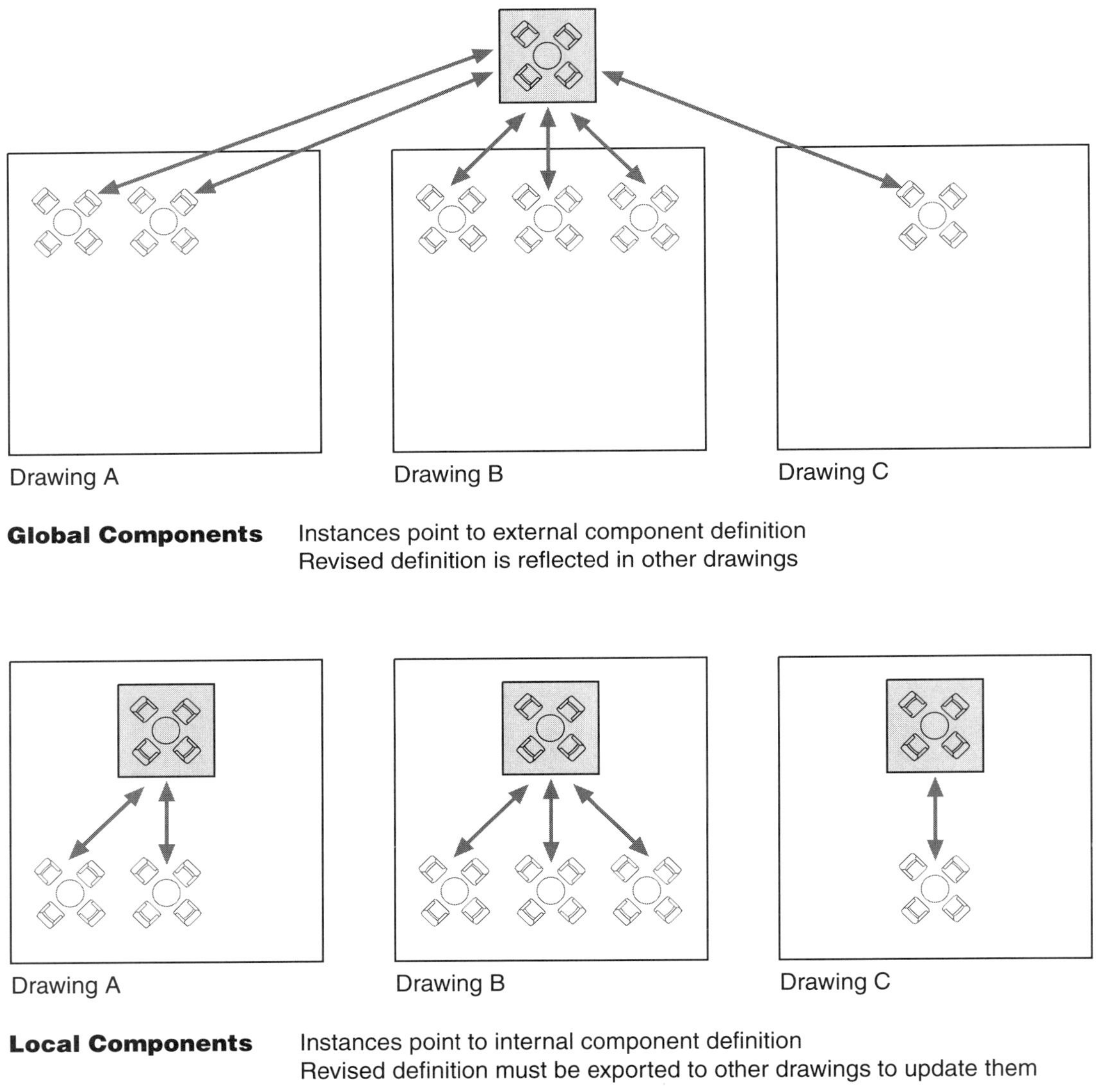

Illustration 8.8 Local versus global components.

so their definitions can be archived and restored along with the project drawings.

REFERENCE FILES

Reference files are a special type of global component and an extremely powerful tool for sharing large sets of information dynamically between drawings. Reference files are simply point-

Table 8.1 Component Examples

COMPONENT	LOCAL/ GLOBAL	INSTANCED/ CLONED	NESTED
AutoCAD Block	Local	Instanced	Yes
Microstation Cell	Local	Cloned	Yes
Microstation Shared Cell	Local	Instanced	Yes
IBM AES Symbol	Global	Instanced	Yes
Cadvance Symbol	Local	Instanced	Yes
Visual CAD Symbol	Local	Instanced	No
Visio Technical Symbol	Local	Cloned	No

ers to other CAD drawings. Each time you open a drawing, each of its reference files is opened as well, so each reference file reflects its most current state.

The simplest uses of reference files in architectural drawings are sheet borders, title blocks, and floor plan grids. For example, creating a sheet border and title block as a separate drawing and attaching it as a reference file to each sheet allows you to update the title block at any time by editing a single drawing, and ensures that those changes will appear on each sheet. (Users of CAD systems that support only local components, and not global reference files, must reload the component definition describing the title block for each sheet, one at a time, each time the title block changes.)

Reference files are a key tool for producing architectural drawings that contain redundant information, such as ceiling plans and enlarged floor plans. The enlarged plan can exist as a separate drawing and reference shared information as required from the overall floor plan. One important feature of reference files is cropping, so that only an area of interest of the reference file is displayed.

Currently, reference file cropping is supported only by Intergraph's Microstation and is one of the software program's key usability features for architects. AutoCAD's reference files cannot be cropped, but partial regions can be displayed within viewports in Paper Space to assemble enlarged floor plans. The problem with AutoCAD's approach is that the entire reference file is loaded into memory, even if only a small part of it is

Microstation is unique in that it allows users to select, query, and copy individual elements contained in external reference files. As a result, reference files can be used as on-screen graphic menus from which users can select predefined components.

required. Using AutoCAD's Paper Space to produce a stair drawing sheet in a multistory building or a toilet room sheet for a large project is an extremely slow and painful undertaking. In AutoCAD, many architects model the partial plans in separate drawings and reference them to the larger plans. Two methods for assembling stair drawings are shown in Illustration 8.9.

REFERENCE FILE NESTING

Architects share information between model drawings using reference files for two purposes. The first is to build larger, complex models from smaller parts, which accelerates editing and retrieval. The second is to coordinate information, such as referencing related floor plans to check for alignment or potential conflicts in structural frames, mechanical shafts, or stair configurations.

AutoCAD supports nesting of reference files, which allows the construction of hierarchical models. However, reference-file nesting can cause problems when the files are attached as coordination overlays and left in place. For example, if an architect attaches a building's second-floor plan to the first-floor plan to coordinate stair configurations and mechanical shaft alignment, and saves the drawing, then the second-floor plan will appear on all other drawings that reference the first-floor plan. To avoid this, the architect must remember to detach all coordination reference files before saving a drawing, and reattach them when opening the drawing. Illustration 8.10 compares nested and nonnested reference files.

One of AutoCAD Release 13's most useful new features is the overlay, a nonnested reference file appropriate for ad hoc coordination of drawings. Nonoverlay reference files are used exclusively for building hierarchical model drawings. Architects using CAD software that does not support reference file nesting, such as Microstation and Cadvance, need not concern themselves with this distinction, although they must manually assemble hierarchies of reference files to construct complex models. Table 8.2 compares reference files within different CAD systems.

Sophisticated users are applying reference files in carefully organized ways to construct large, complex building models from smaller, simpler models. Doing so requires that every proj-

Illustration 8.9 *Stair methods.*

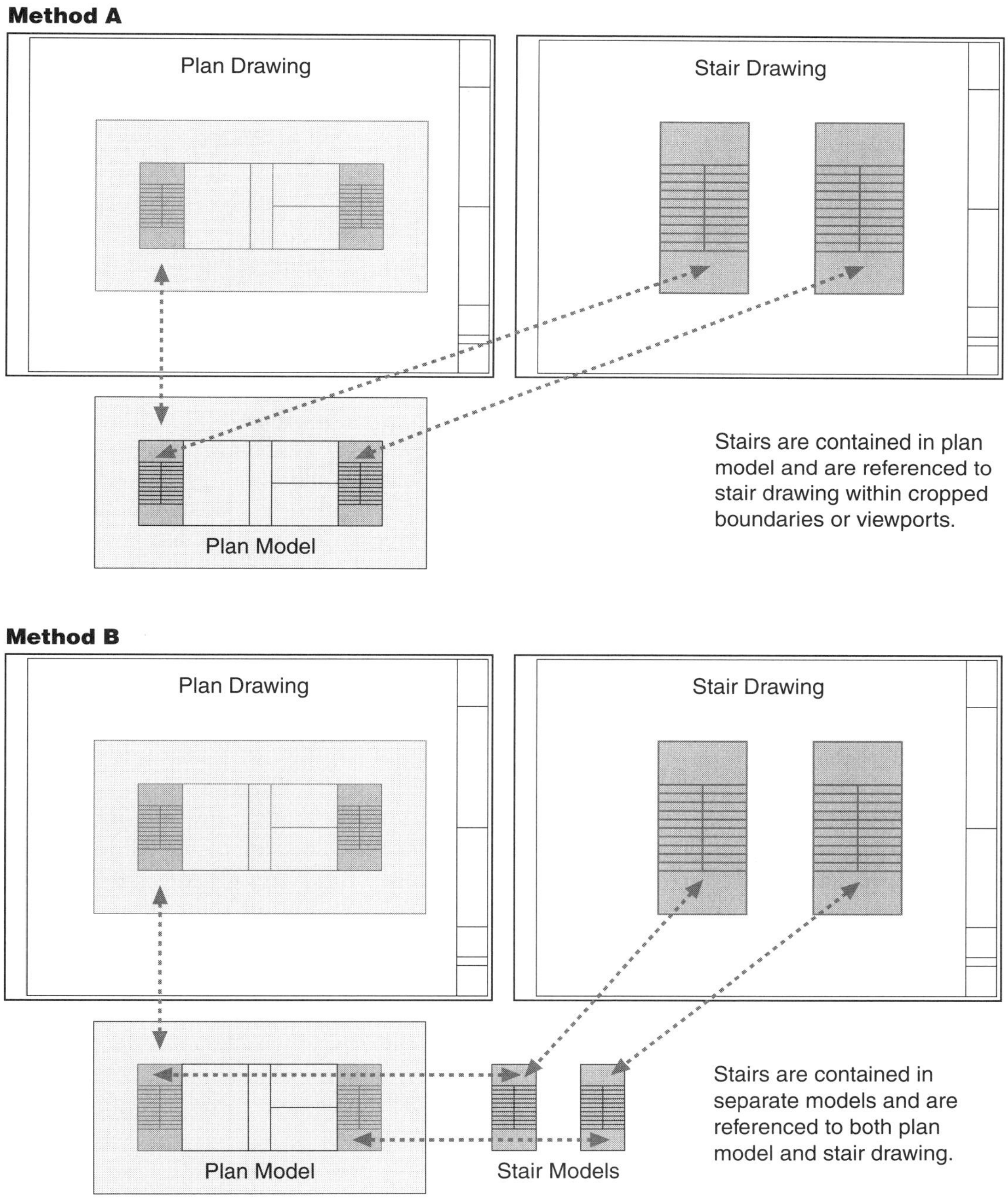

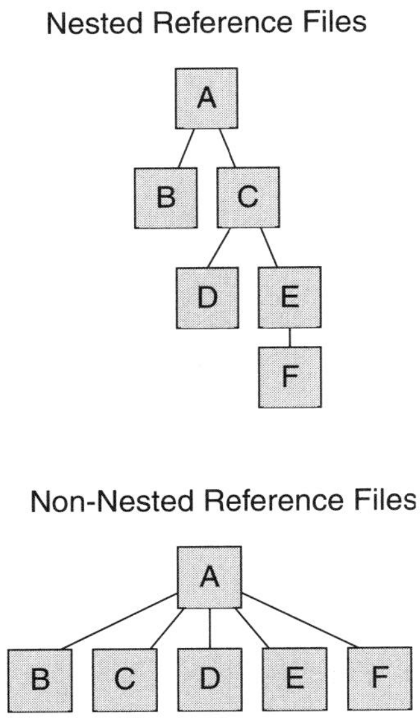

Illustration 8.10 Nested and nonnested reference files.

Interestingly, object-oriented tools such as OLE and OpenDoc are similar to the reference files of CAD software. OLE and OpenDoc extend the idea of reference files to multiple applications, so that a CAD drawing can reference not only other CAD drawings, but also spreadsheets, word-processing documents, or other digital information created using applications that support OLE and OpenDoc.

Table 8.2 Reference File Examples

REFERENCE FILE	CROPPED	NESTED
AutoCAD XRef	No[a]	Yes
AutoCAD Overlay	No[a]	No
Microstation Reference File	Yes	No
Cadvance Reference File	No	No

[a]Cropping is handled via Paper Space viewports, not as an attribute of the reference file itself.

ect team member understands how information is being shared between drawings and how changes they make to referenced information will impact other drawings.

Together, components and reference files are the basic tools with which architects reuse information between different architectural models and drawings. In summary, components are generally small and instanced many times per drawing. Reference files are generally large and instanced only a few times per drawing. Both can be shared between multiple drawings. Components are usually local (stored inside the drawing), while reference files are always global (stored outside the drawing).

GROUPS

A group is simply a collection of elements within a drawing that is treated as a single element when selected for editing (move, copy, erase, etc.). Groups are an organizational abstraction, like components and reference files, but differ significantly in that they are not instanced. Unlike an instanced component or reference file, a copy of a group is literally a clone of all elements within the group. The copy can then be altered from the original without restriction. Most CAD systems today include a grouping feature.

Quite often, it is more convenient to group collections of graphic elements in a CAD drawing together without the overhead of creating named components, such as blocks, symbols, or cells. Depending on the system, the groups can be named or anonymous. Some systems support nesting of groups, allowing one group to contain other groups as members, and some allow each element to be a member of only one group. Most support a group editing mode, where the grouping function can be turned on (editing operations are applied to the group) or off (editing operations are applied to individual members). In some systems, a group can also be used to control the display and plotting order of its elements. Unlike layers, which provide a flat organizational structure, groups provide a hierarchical structure for elements within a CAD drawing.

Groups are often a better organizational structure during early design phases, when more flexibility and less rigor are desirable. As shown in Illustration 8.11, each group can be moved and scaled as a single element, but other operations such as stretching and dragging elements within the group are still allowed.

Illustration 8.11 Design using groups.

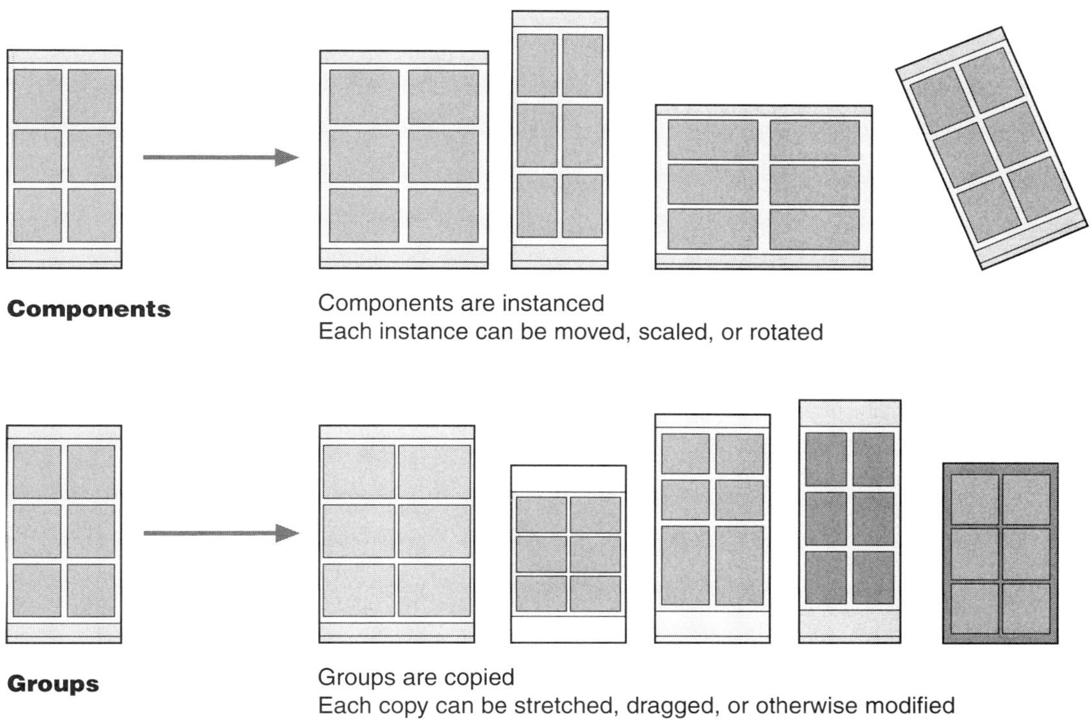

Groups can be dangerous because what you see is not always what you get. For example, if a user deletes an element with the grouping function turned on, then others within the group will be deleted even if they are not visible on screen. The cause of "mysteriously disappearing elements" is often a user inadvertently erasing an entire group by erasing one of its members with group mode turned on.

In general, follow these guidelines when using groups:

1. Do not group items together unless there is a clear reason to do so. Grouping adds to the size of a drawing, especially if groups are deeply nested. Also, don't leave temporary groups floating around the drawing.
2. When grouping elements, select them in the desired display and plotting order, if appropriate.
3. Keep group hierarchies balanced. When adding members to a group, be sure you do not create an unnecessary group with both the existing group and the new element as members.
4. Be careful about selecting groups; you can't always see everything you're selecting. The novice user should avoid them.

Groups are convenient, but they can be tricky to use. They do not have the organizational rigor of named components, which is both a blessing and a curse. They provide more editing flexibility, but also permit the creation of internally messy drawings and provide many opportunities for editing accidents.

LAYERS

Layers are the basic organizational structure of most CAD systems and allow selective filtering, viewing, sharing, and plotting of graphic information. The classic analogy is a sheet of mylar in an overlay drafting system. Layers are more powerful but also more complex. A typical overlay drawing may include three or four sheets of mylar, while a typical CAD drawing includes dozens of layers. Different drawings can be produced from the same building model by turning layers off and on and by sharing the information contained in some layers with other drawings. Illustration 8.12 shows how layers are used to segregate information within drawings.

Michael Schley, AIA, editor of *AIA CAD Layer Guidelines*, identifies these basic applications of layers:

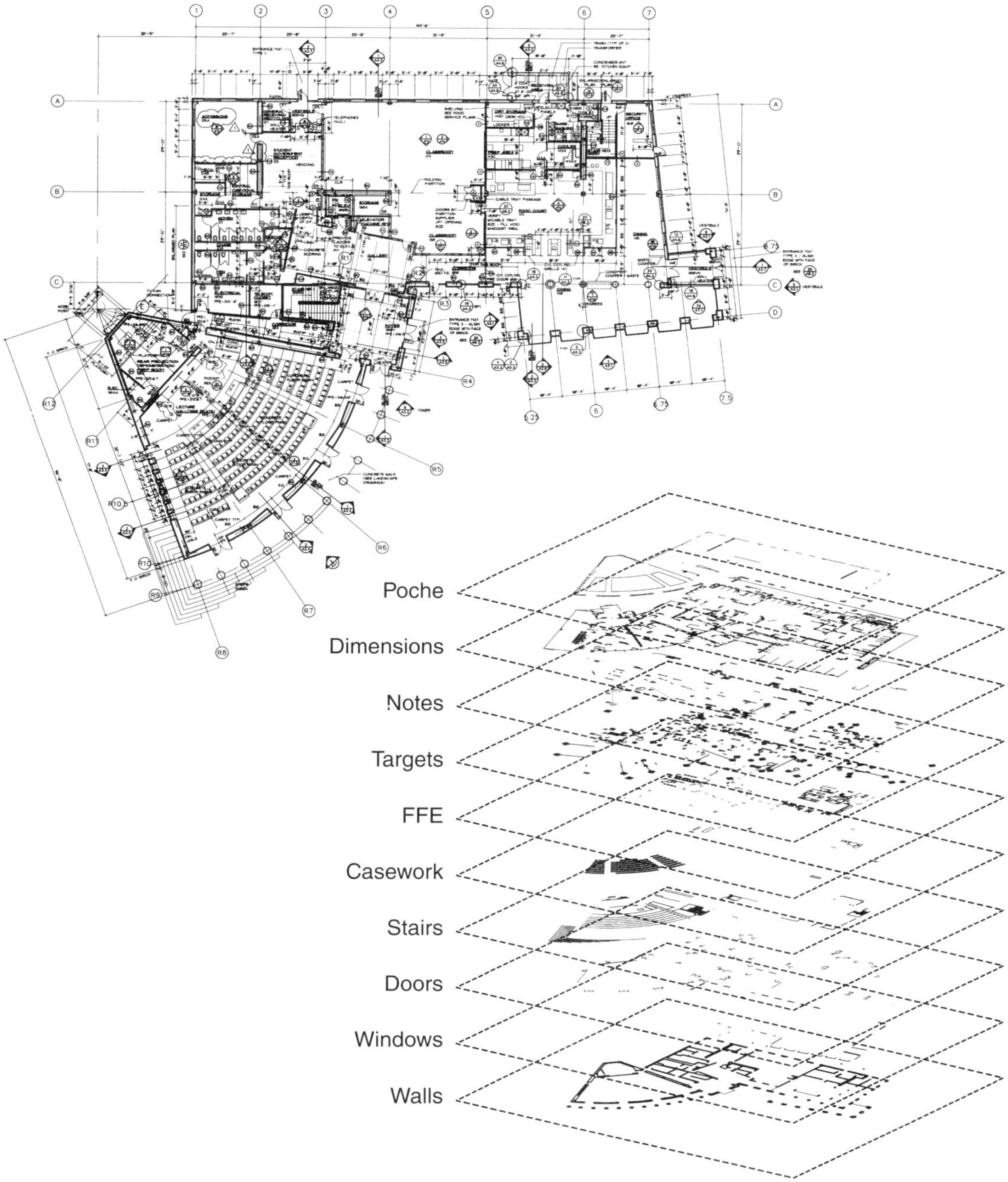

Illustration 8.12 *Typical layer structure.*

■ Facilitating drawing coordination and the sharing of information between drawings and disciplines.

■ Allowing several drawings that share common information to be combined into one CAD file to reduce drawing effort and improve consistency.

■ Accommodating alternative design schemes or project phases within individual drawings.

■ Controlling visibility of classes of elements to facilitate editing of drawings, thus improving CAD system response time and reducing visual clutter.

■ Controlling appearance characteristics such as color or material.

A well-organized, published layer convention is a requirement for every architectural firm. A firm's layer guideline should be living, open-ended, and easily expanded for project-specific or client-specific requirements. The intent should be to describe a lowest common denominator, a starting point. In general, a layer guideline should be made as simple as possible. Before and during the development of CAD drawings, the project architect or job captain should identify how information will be shared between phases of the project, between disciplines, and between drawings, and extend the firm's layer guideline only as required.

If your firm specializes in only one or two building types, you may be able to establish a detailed guideline that works for most projects. If you have a diverse practice, your guideline will likely be more generic. The *AIA CAD Layer Guidelines* is an excellent starting point and is enjoying growing support among many institutional and government clients.

LAYER GUIDELINES

A few useful layering guidelines are:

1. DO NOT make your layer guideline too complicated. Some people, not knowing exactly how they want to segregate information, create too many layers. Identify how information will be shared between models and drawings, between phases of a project, and between you and your consultants, and design a layer guideline accordingly. Keep the guideline flexible and open ended.

2. DO NOT use the CSI numbering system for layers. It may be convenient to attach attributes to components that represent CSI numbering to generate outline specifications or quantity takeoffs, but do not use layers for that purpose.

3. DO NOT assign specific line weight and line type attributes to layers, unless your system requires you to do so. In most CAD systems, an element's layer is simply one of its attributes, in addition to color, line weight, and line type; layers have no visual attributes of their own. In other systems, such as AutoCAD, layers can be assigned display characteristics that can be inherited by elements on that layer. However, layers are best used as a tool to organize categories of information, not their plotted representation. Line weight and line type should be graphic attributes of elements independent of the element's layer.

Why not use an existing organizational guideline—the CSI numbering system—as a naming convention for layers, and thus avoid reinventing the wheel? The answer is a practical one. Layers are most typically used (as well they should) as a tool to filter the information in a drawing and control the visibility of a drawing's information, both on the computer screen and on paper, as well as filtering the information for sharing or recycling in other drawings or projects.

Typically, the types of information that need to be filtered have little to do with the CSI number convention. For example, the information shared between a floor plan and a reflected ceiling plan will be the walls, door headers, soffits, and so forth. Partial height partitions (that may be of identical construction) are not shared, nor are equipment or furnishings. The CSI convention is related to building *materials,* but not to building *systems.* In addition, the CSI convention would apply only to pictorial and symbolic information—the building model itself—but not the annotation: labels, targets, dimensions, and notes.

CSI numbers are most useful to ensure coordination between the drawings and the specifications, not layer filtering. Most CAD programs that offer links between the drawings and specifications (including systems drafting such as CONDOC) typically assign CSI numbers as attributes of components within the drawings. This appropriately preserves the use of layers as a selective filtering and viewing device.

AIA CAD LAYER GUIDELINES

The *AIA CAD Layer Guidelines* was originally published in 1990 as a potential industry-wide layer standard. The original task force which developed the guidelines was supported by the AIA, the International Facility Management Association (IFMA), the American Consulting Engineers Council, the American Society of Civil Engineers, the U.S. Army Corps of Engineers, the Naval Facilities Engineering Command, and the Department of Veteran Affairs. The revised second edition of the *CAD Layer Guidelines* is due in 1996 and is being coordinated with the CAD Council, a cooperative group including CSI, the National Institute of Building Sciences (NIBS), and the U.S. Federal Government Tri-Services.

The AIA's major groups of layers include:

A	Architecture, interiors, and facilities management
S	Structural
M	Mechanical
P	Plumbing
F	Fire Protection
E	Electrical
C	Civil Engineering
L	Landscape

Each major group is subdivided into minor groups. The architectural major group, for example, includes these minor groups:

A-WALL	Walls
A-DOOR	Doors
A-GLAZ	Windows, Window Walls, Curtain Walls, Glazed Partitions
A-FLOR	Floor Information
A-EQPM	Equipment
A-FURN	Furniture
A-CLNG	Ceiling Information
A-ROOF	Roof

A-AREA	Area Calculation Boundary Lines
A-ELEV	Interior and Exterior Elevations
A-SECT	Sections
A-DETL	Details

The revised layer guidelines will likely be extended to include support for environmental data, industrial engineering and plant layout, telecommunications, and other more specialized information. In addition, it should also address reference files, not just layers, as important tools of information sharing.

Some third-party CAD software developers have so far not been enthusiastic in their embrace of the AIA guidelines. Many have developed customized tools that depend on a particular layer format to function properly. Ultimately, however, those software developers will be forced by the market to adopt a common guideline—it is not a question of if, but only when. This process will be driven by product manufacturers, who provide digital data to architects, and clients, who receive digital data from architects. For plug-and-play information resources to actually work, a single organizational guideline needs to emerge. Architects are well advised to take a hard look at the *AIA CAD Layer Guidelines,* particularly the forthcoming second edition, and consider standardizing their CAD work around it.

REDUNDANCY IS COOL AGAIN (SOMETIMES)

Many drafting conventions for manually produced architectural drawings were designed to avoid redundancy, reduce the conflicts and errors in the architect's drawings, and minimize the architect's risk. The lack of redundancy in architectural drawings, however, often does not make the drawings any easier to review or use. In fact, just the opposite is often the case.

Using reference files and other tools of information sharing, CAD provides the opportunity to actually *increase* the redundancy of drawings, in order to increase their clarity and communication value, without increasing (and often reducing) the architect's risk or cost. This is an unusual philosophy because it is at odds with generally accepted manual drafting principles.

Examples include showing floor plan information on site plans, showing additional detail on elevations (within reason), or including additional enlarged plans and elevations for clarity.

An important caveat: purposeful redundancy must be managed carefully. It should only occur where the added redundancy *improves* the communication of the drawings and where the information-sharing techniques assure that there is no risk of creating conflicts between drawings.

MODEL DRAWINGS AND PLOT DRAWINGS

In the mind of a computer, CAD drawings are the citizens of an egalitarian society. Some drawings are large, some are small, but they are all made up of the same basic elements: lines, arcs, circles, text, and so on. No CAD drawing has any special rights over any other, and information between them can be exchanged freely and at will. To most CAD software programs, all drawings are created equally.

In the mind of an architect who wants to effectively use CAD, however, all drawings are *not* created equally. Some drawings share information *with* other drawings, some drawings derive information *from* other drawings, and some drawings do both.

Although sharing information between CAD drawings is certainly a benefit, doing so in the absence of an organizational structure for the project can create chaos. When using CAD, architects need to understand the ripple effect of the information they are creating. It helps to recognize that there are two basic types of CAD drawings that comprise a project database: model drawings and plot drawings.

A *model drawing* is a two- or three-dimensional representation of a subset of a building's geometry. A model drawing has no scale; it is drawn life-size. Model drawings describe the geometry of the building, including representational linework and instances of components and reference files. Symbolic annotation (notes, targets, dimensions, etc.) can be included in model drawings but must be sized appropriately, depending on the scale at which the model will be plotted.

A *plot drawing* is one or more scaled view(s) of model drawings arranged within a sheet border. A plot drawing is a graphic report of the building database.

CAD SYSTEM ISSUES

Various CAD systems provide different data structures and algorithms for supporting these two types of drawings, with varying degrees of success. CAD systems that allow the architect to create plot drawings containing cropped views of larger model drawings are most useful for architectural documentation, even for small projects. Not coincidentally, the top two-selling CAD systems in the architecture, engineering, and construction industries—Autodesk's AutoCAD and Intergraph's Microstation—do so, although they each provide different tools.

AutoCAD provides Model Space and Paper Space as places to assemble model drawings and plot drawings (Ill. 8.13). Every AutoCAD file contains both Model Space and Paper Space, so model drawings and plot drawings can coexist in the same AutoCAD file. Alternately, they can exist in separate files and be linked using reference files. Cropping views of model drawings is accomplished using Paper Space viewports. AutoCAD does not distinguish between model drawings and component drawings. Component drawings (blocks) can be created from model drawings using the Wblock command, but the result is just another AutoCAD drawing. Segregating model drawings from component drawings is left to the user.

Intergraph's Microstation, on the other hand, does not distinguish between model drawings and plot drawings. Using reference files, however, separate model drawings and plot drawings can be assembled in the same way as AutoCAD. Also, because Microstation reference files are not nested, a Microstation design file can reference itself and allow a model drawing and plot drawing to coexist in the same file. Cropping views of model drawings is accomplished using the clip boundary feature of Microstation's reference files. Unlike AutoCAD, Microstation does distinguish between model drawings (design files) and component drawings (cell libraries).

PLOT DRAWINGS

Unlike hand-drafted drawings, which are relatively stable, static collections of graphic information, CAD drawings are dynamic. Using different scale parameters, layer filters, or color and pen tables, it is relatively easy to create very different graphic representations of information derived from the same CAD drawing. This flexibility—clearly a blessing during design phases—can be an accidental curse during the construction documents phase. The last thing you want are surprises when plotting the

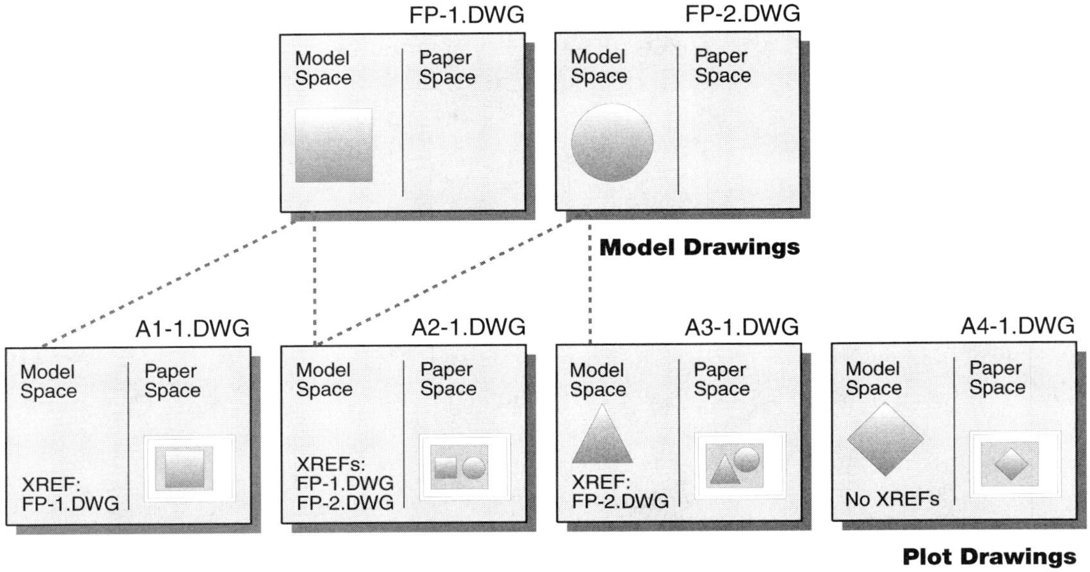

Illustration 8.13 *Model drawings and plot drawings in AutoCAD.*

FP-1.DWG and FP-2.DWG are model drawings that contain nothing in Paper Space. They are solely intended to be attached as reference files or inserted as components (blocks) to multiple plot drawings or model drawings. Examples include overall floor plans, ceiling plans, and exterior building elevations. Model drawings can contain reference files or components of other model drawings.

A1-1.DWG and A2-1.DWG are plot drawings that contain nothing in Model Space except reference files of model drawings. The reference files are attached with an insertion point of 0,0, and scale of 1, and are scaled, cropped, and arranged as required within Paper Space. (Annotations such as grid lines that extend beyond the cropped boundary are drawn or attached as reference files in Paper Space.) Once plot drawings are set up, virtually all drafting work is done in the model drawings. Examples include floor plans, ceiling plans, enlarged plans, and exterior elevations.

A3-1.DWG contains both a reference file of the model drawing FP-2.DWG as well as information drawn in Model Space of the plot drawing. (The assumption is that anything drawn in Model Space of a plot drawing will not be shared or reused by any other drawing. If it is, it should be contained in its own model drawing.) Examples include sheets that contain an enlarged plan, section, and elevation on the same sheet. The enlarged plan might be a reference file, while the section and elevation might be drawn in Model Space.

A4-1.DWG is an example of a plot drawing and model drawing wholly contained within the same AutoCAD file. This is considered a stand-alone plot drawing, as it does not contain any model drawing references. Examples of stand-alone plot drawings include detail sheets and interior elevation sheets.

final review or bid sets, particularly information which disappears or appears because the wrong layers were plotted.

When CAD drawings plot incorrectly, typically one or more of the following parameters has not been set up properly:

1. Layer visibility
2. Plot view or region
3. Plot scale
4. Color tables or pen definitions
5. Component substitutions for view or scale filtering

Although *models* need to be flexible and dynamic, *plots* need to be stable and reliable.

Most off-the-shelf CAD programs require that you specify these parameters each time you create a plot. To automate the process, many third-party packages include custom plotting scripts to control these parameters for different types of drawings, and some architects develop their own.

Typically, the correct scale and view parameters of a plot are obvious to the user, but layer visibility is not. AutoCAD, which does not support symbolic line weight, adds another complication by using an element's color to determine its plotted line weight. The relationship between colors and plotter pens must be stored in external files, either plot configuration parameter (PCP) files or special plotting scripts (Ill. 8.14). Unless the correct PCP file or plotting script is used, a drawing can inadvertently be plotted with incorrect line weights. As a result, the burden is on the user to use the correct PCP file or on the system manager to develop customized plotting scripts.

The primary benefit of plot drawings is to eliminate this type of plotting guesswork and overhead by encapsulating this

Illustration 8.14 *AutoCAD layer and pen assignment dialog boxes.*

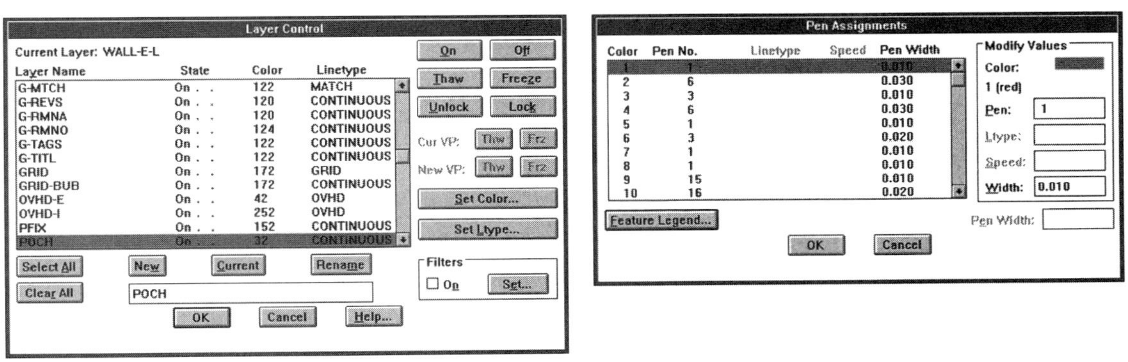

information into the CAD drawing itself and to avoid plotting mistakes due to incorrect setup. With plot drawings, plotting is both simpler and more reliable.

To simplify the plotting process, parameters required to plot a drawing should be kept inside the drawing. This object-oriented approach makes CAD drawings more portable and readily accessible by others. In general, avoid external scripts or command files to set up plotting parameters unless your CAD software requires them.

Using reference files to share information, multiple plot drawings can be created from a single model drawing.

Plot drawings are simply ready-to-plot CAD drawings. They are reports of the model drawings that describe the building. Each has the following characteristics:

1. Plot drawings are always plotted at full scale (1 inch = 1 inch).
2. The origin of the plot drawing is at the lower left corner of the sheet border. The sheet border itself should be attached as a reference file.
3. The file name of a plot drawing corresponds closely to the sheet number.
4. Plot drawings can contain reference files of model drawings but are never attached as reference files to other drawings.

MODEL DRAWINGS

For certain types of drawings, the plot drawing and the model drawing can coexist in the same file. Examples include a sheet of interior elevations or details (Ill. 8.15). In other cases, such as floor plans, reflected ceiling plans, or exterior elevations, the model drawings are separated from the plot drawings (Ill. 8.16). In general, information that will be shared (via reference files or components) between multiple plot drawings should be contained in separate model drawings.

For example, overall floor plan model drawings are typically attached as reference files to the plot drawings of 1⁄16-inch site plans, 1⁄8-inch floor plans and reflected ceiling plans, and 1⁄4-inch enlarged plans. In both AutoCAD and Microstation, layers of the model drawings can be assigned different graphic attributes (color, line weight, line type) within each plot drawing to achieve screened, lighter, or bolder linework appropriate for each type of drawing.

One organizational issue architects must confront is whether to include annotation in model drawings. Some elements, such as dimensions, are less useful if they are stored separately in plot drawings. No CAD program will retain the associative link between the dimension and its related geometry unless they are in the same file. On the other hand, some architects prefer to keep their model drawings clean of annotation, and place dimensions, notes, and targets on the plot drawing. Since people often make revisions to drawings in two passes—first, moving the geometry, and second, cleaning up annotation and laying out new dimensions—storing the building geometry and annotation in separate files is not a huge usability hit. AutoCAD's poor performance in handling multiple large reference files is well known, so separating geometry from annotation means that referenced model drawings are smaller and faster.

Model drawings are *always* attached as reference files to other drawings. Plot drawings are *never* attached as reference files to other drawings.

SUBDIVIDING MODEL DRAWINGS

Large, complex model drawings should be split up into smaller, simpler model drawings. If the project is so large that each floor plan requires several sheets to document at ⅛-inch scale, consider breaking up each overall floor plan into two or more parts, each contained within a different drawing. The seams between partial floor plans need not align with the match lines of the floor plan plot drawings, but instead should be located where there is a minimum of geometry crossing the seams that must be coordinated. If your model drawings are over 1 MB in size, they are probably suitable for being subdivided.

Even for small projects, subdividing model drawings will improve response time and allow more than one person to work on different parts of the model at the same time. Always plan ahead and determine the parts of the building that can be built as components, stored in separate files, and shared between multiple drawings.

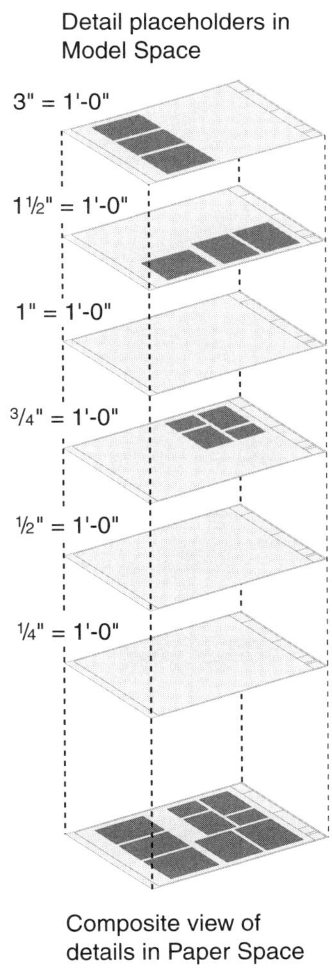

Illustration 8.15 Detail stand-alone drawing.

ALIGNING MODEL DRAWINGS

All plan model drawings for a project should share the same coordinate system. In fact, before you begin creating hard-line CAD drawings for a new project, you should establish a project coordinate system by doing the following:

1. Define the location of the origin point to be used by all project team members producing plan-based CAD drawings. Typically, this is a convenient benchmark point of the building, such as the southwest structural grid point or a property line corner.

Illustration 8.16 Elevation model drawing.

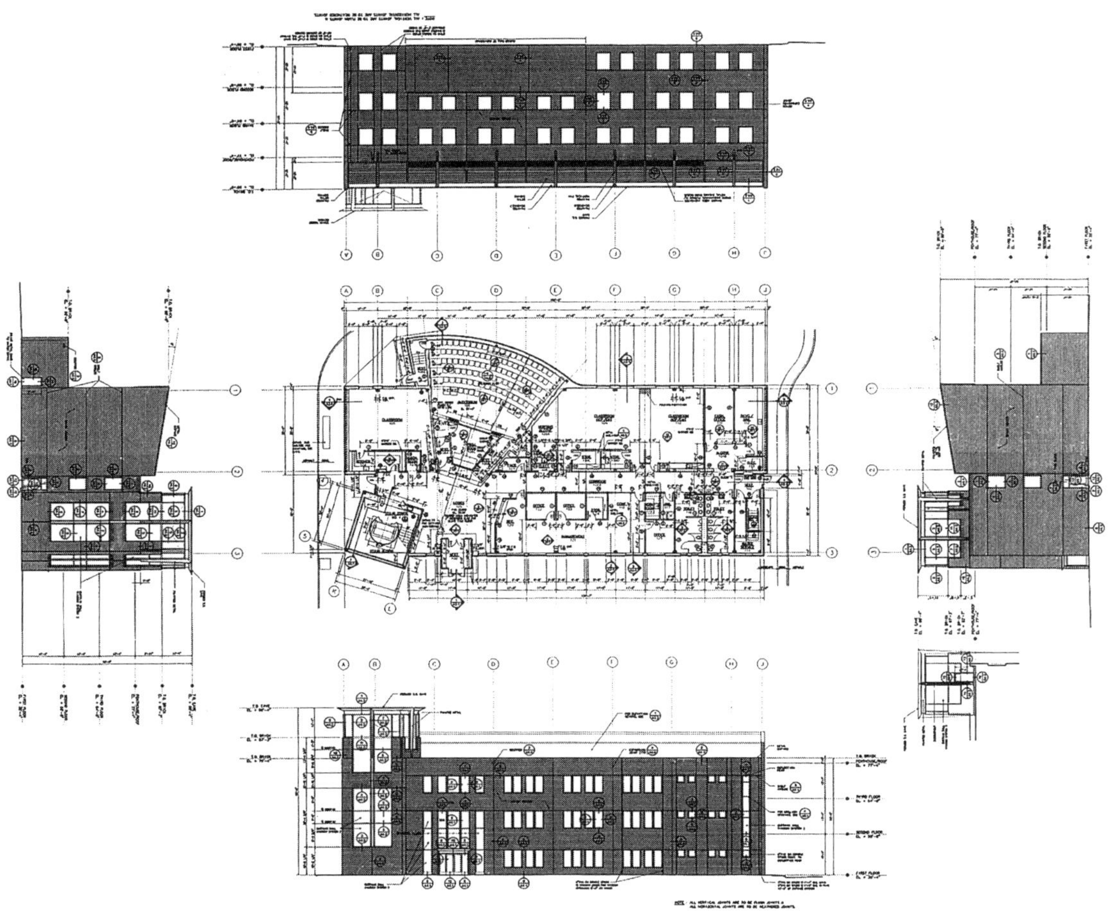

2. Define the plan orientation (rotation from true north) to be used by all project team members. (The only exceptions are survey data and civil data, which are normally oriented true north.) Typically, this orientation is the same orientation of the project as shown on the design and construction documents.

The project coordinate system is one example where digital theory and practice conflict. Although it is possible to draw and develop plans in their real-world location and orientation so they coincide with the data of the surveyor and civil engineer, doing so severely complicates the production of documents by the architect and other consultants, and the use of those documents by building owners. Integer-based CAD systems such as Microstation and Cadvance may not have adequate precision to accommodate origin points far removed from the floor plans, and may introduce annoying inaccuracies in rotated geometry. And editing tools in most CAD systems are simply easier to use when a building's geometry is orthogonal to the global coordinate system rather than arbitrarily oriented.

If you must deliver to the client CAD drawings that fit into an existing facilities management database, you may be required to use the coordinate system of the existing database. Be sure to determine whether your client has such specific organizational requirements before beginning CAD work.

Always draw the architectural floor plans with a convenient and familiar origin point and orientation, orthogonal to the primary geometry of the building(s). Typically, this means aligning the project's long dimension parallel to the (horizontal) *X* axis. You should determine the offset and rotation between the project coordinate system and that used by the civil engineer and/or surveyor. Aligning new information provided by those consultants should be straightforward if you know the correct *XY* offset and rotation (Ill. 8.17).

THREE-DIMENSIONAL MODELBUILDING

Creating a three-dimensional design model from scratch can be a somewhat intimidating experience. Where does one begin? The elements and algorithms supported by most CAD programs are discussed in Chapter 5, The Language of Digital Media. Here, we discuss the approach, which is remarkably similar to that used in developing two-dimensional drawings: get organized, break down big, hard problems into small, easy parts, and know beforehand how the model will be rendered or plotted.

First, determine the materials to be used. Depending on your software, this will mean assigning a layer or color to those elements that will be rendered in different materials. At this point, you don't need to know the exact materials or how they will be portrayed. These issues are rarely defined early in the design

Illustration 8.17 Project and survey coordinate system transformation.

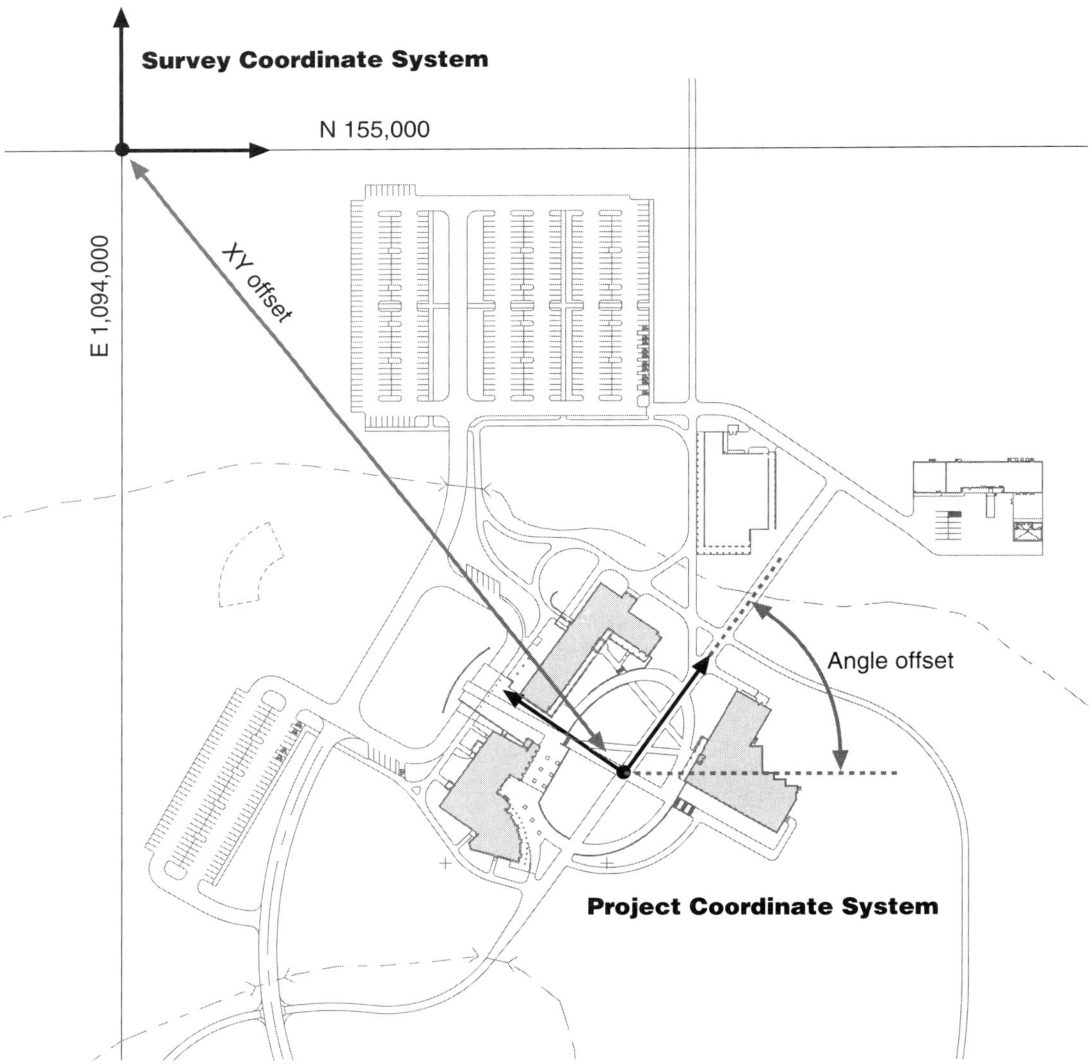

process and can be determined later when you are ready to render your model. Instead, you need to identify which *parts* of the model are likely to constructed from *different* materials. If you're not sure, make them different. Make a list of the layer names or colors you will use to identify different materials. It is easier to do this first than change the materials later. If materials are not important, and you are simply constructing a massing model, you can skip this step.

Second, identify the reusable components of the building model. Identify components, such as exterior columns, windows and doors, or precast panels, that can be constructed as reusable components or groups. Quite often, much of a building's geometry can be developed simply by using scaled components, such as cubes, pyramids, gables, and cylinders. If your modeling system supports parametric or procedural components, identify which parts of the model can be constructed using those tools.

Third, subdivide the model into smaller parts. Before you start constructing the model, plan how your model will be subdivided into separate parts, each of which can be constructed independently. Subdividing models has several benefits for both two-dimensional drawings and three-dimensional models. The most obvious benefit is that it speeds up editing operations—opening and saving files, selecting elements, and displaying views. But more importantly, it is far easier to visualize the small parts of the model and navigate around them. A small interior model might be subdivided into the walls and furnishings. A large building might be separated into four or more elevational components. Using reference files, model subdivisions can be maintained throughout the modelbuilding effort by linking them to each other, rather than merging them into a single file. An example is shown in Illustration 8.18

Fourth, know your vocabulary. One of the most annoying characteristics of many computer-aided architectural illustrations and renderings is the inconsistent portrayal of detail. For example, a model may contain predefined windows from a manufacturer with fully detailed frames and hardware, while the remainder of the building's basic massing is left undefined and abstract. Landscape elements, people, and other predefined realistic enhancements to the image—whether built into the

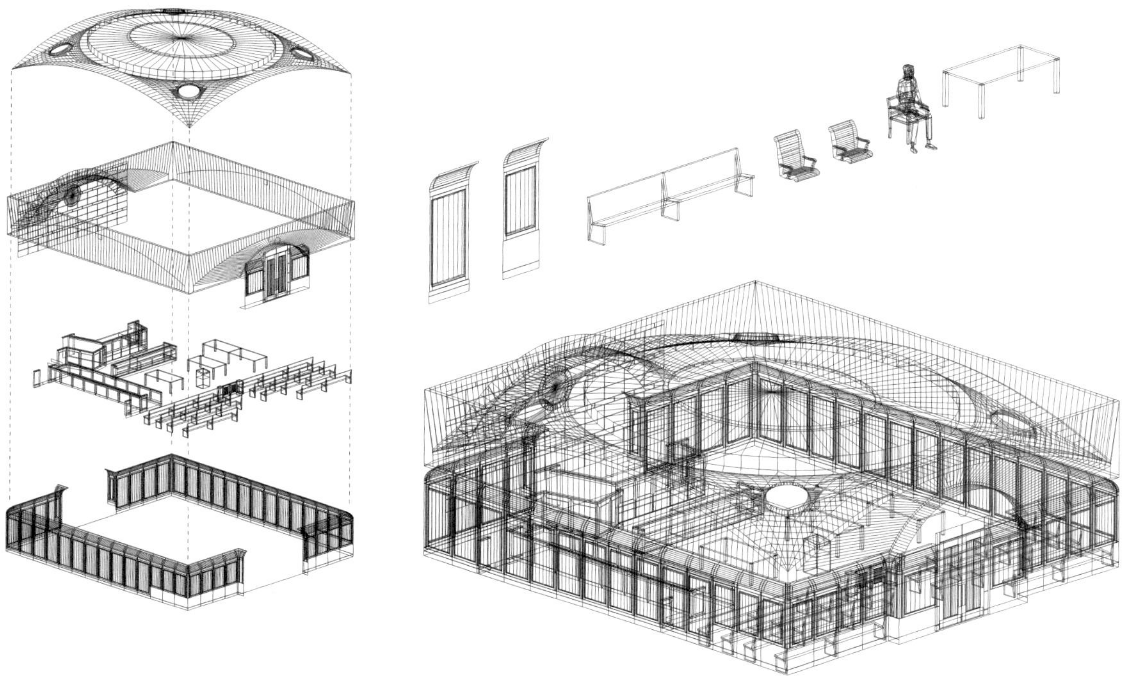

Illustration 8.18 Subdivided model.

model or painted on the rendered image—often portray a high level of detail that is inconsistent with the building model itself. Decide up front whether your model will be literal or representational, and choose building blocks that are appropriate.

Fifth, know your output. The intended output of the visualization will also affect your decision about the level of detail in your model. In general, the higher the resolution of the output (defined by its width and height in pixels), the more detail will be required in your model. If you plan to create crisp, high-resolution (1000 pixels or above) images, you will need to build substantial detail. Simple models rendered at high-resolution usually don't look very good—they are very precisely rendered with sharp edges, yet lack detail. If you are building simple models for study, then render them at low resolutions (less than 1000 pixels). If you are planning to create an animation, either for display on your desktop computer or output to videotape or videodisc, keep your models fairly simple. Too much detail can create annoying artifacts in the animation, such as temporal aliasing.

Sixth, know your rendering algorithm. The algorithm used by your software to create an image of your model will also affect how you build your model. In general, building models for shaded output are easier to construct than models intended for hidden-line removal because they elegantly resolve intersecting geometry and remove the seams at shared edges of coplanar surfaces.

See Chapter 5, The Language of Digital Media, for more information on temporal aliasing and the differences between hidden-line drawings and digital images.

DRAWING EFFICIENCY

The impact of poorly organized or inefficient CAD drawings is substantial and affects storage requirements, plotting time, backup and archive time, display speed, and the speed of editing operations, including element selection. Each of these may be affected in a rather small way, but the cumulative total of inefficient drawings can be significant and costly. Experienced CAD users eventually learn to keep their drawings as clean as possible.

There are two types of inefficiency in CAD drawings: organizational and graphic. The most common source of organizational inefficiency is the failure to break down large sets of data into smaller parts, stored in separate files. As discussed earlier, reference files are an important tool for assembling larger models from smaller parts, while allowing architects to work more efficiently on the individual parts. In addition, any set of shared data that will reappear on multiple drawings (grids, title blocks, keyplans, keynote lists, etc.) should be stored in separate reference files. Instanced components should be used when possible and can produce substantial savings in drawing size (Ill. 8.19). Users should also take care to delete obsolete what-if design schemes that have been copied and put to the side on a drawing.

Sources of graphic inefficiency include redundant overlapping (collinear) lines, a high percentage of two-endpoint lines instead of multiple-endpoint lines, excessive graphic detail, complex fonts, and unnecessary crosshatching. Collinear lines—those that are coincident end to end or partially overlapping, are a common source of drawing inefficiency and are hard to identify visually. The lines can be particularly vexing for users who erase or break a line, only to see it reappear when the screen is redrawn. Some CAD programs provide search and destroy tools to identify and purge collinear lines.

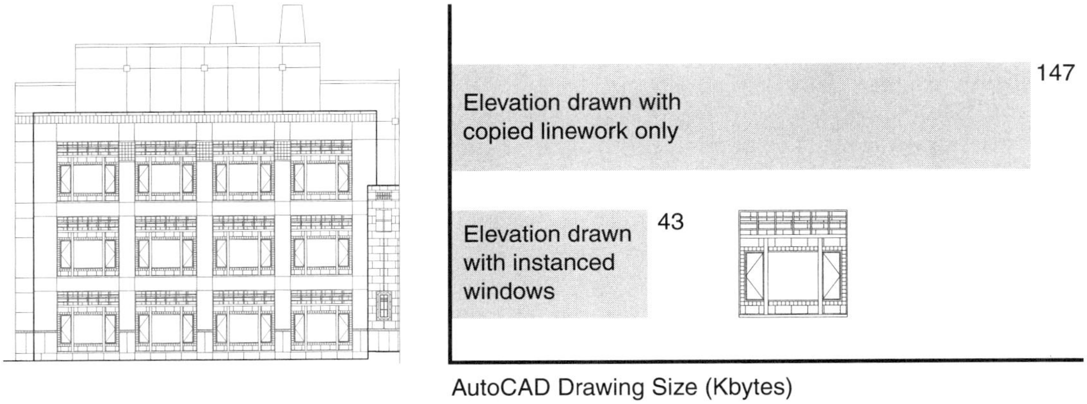

Illustration 8.19 *Component efficiency.*

Most CAD systems support two-endpoint lines as well as multiple-endpoint lines. Most systems store multiple-endpoint lines more efficiently than a series of two-endpoint lines, because the *X,Y* (or *X, Y, Z*) coordinate is stored once instead of twice (Ill. 8.20). At the same time, it is often more convenient to sketch and edit using two-endpoint lines because it is easier to copy, trim, extend, and otherwise edit the lines.

Indicating materials on CAD drawings can substantially impact drawing size and efficiency. Like most graphic elements in a CAD drawing there are two basic types of material indicators: pictorial and symbolic. Pictorial material indicators (brick, tile, batt insulation, etc.) show both the size and location of the material. Crosshatch linework is typically used to indicate such

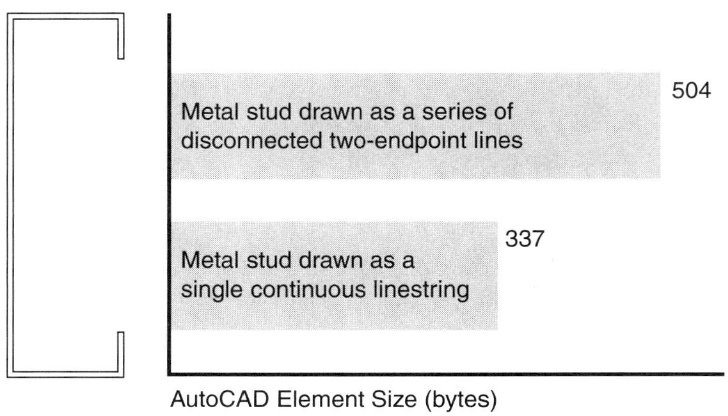

Illustration 8.20 *Linework efficiency.*

materials because the crosshatch scales appropriately. In addition, the origin point of the crosshatch is often important—ceiling or floor tiles, for example.

In contrast, symbolic material indicators (stippling, earth, concrete, sand, gravel, etc.) convey the use of materials in a purely visual way, without scale. The origin point and orientation of symbolic material indicators are unimportant. Although scale matters—small versus large concrete stipple, for example—less graphic precision is required. For symbolic material indicators, bitmap fill patterns are more appropriate and efficient than crosshatch linework. The benefit, in terms of reduced drawing size, can be dramatic (Ill. 8.21).

Use vector crosshatching and bitmap fill patterns to *indicate*, not *render*, materials in construction documents. Using CAD, it is just as easy to poché, say, an entire concrete retaining wall section than a portion of it. But this rarely improves the clarity or readability of the drawing, and in most cases, diminishes it. Other information, such as notes and dimensions, can get graphically lost in drawings that are material heavy.

Also, too much detail in a drawing should be avoided. It is not really necessary to draw the threads of an anchor bolt or

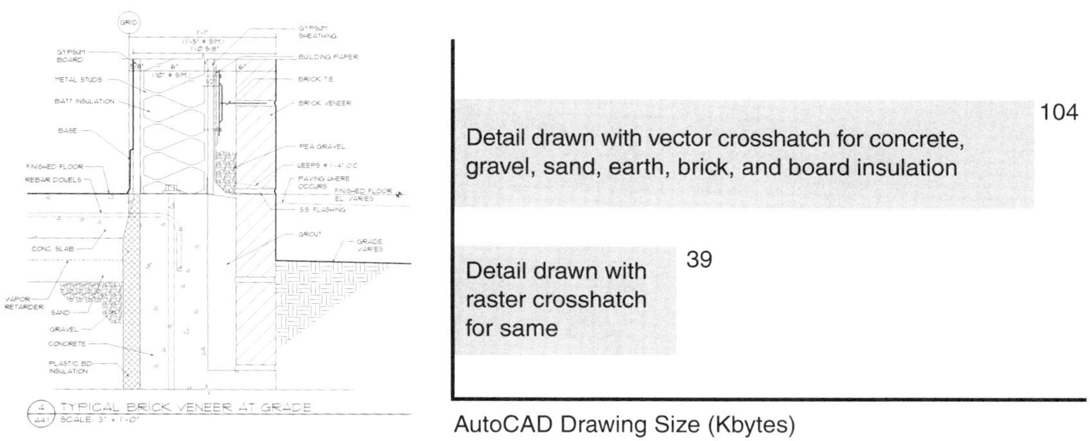

Illustration 8.21 *Crosshatch efficiency.*

Everyone should understand the need for their CAD drawings to not only communicate well, but be well organized and clean of superfluous linework. Good-looking CAD drawings can be internally messy, which can dramatically reduce the productivity of those who work on them.

redhead. The drawing may look more precise, but may not communicate better. Keep your drawings clean and simple and they usually will be more understandable. Finally, strive to use simple vector fonts instead of fancy filled fonts. Construction drawing notes and dimensions in Times Roman are simply a waste of time and material (Ill. 8.22).

INTEGRATED DRAWINGS AND SPECIFICATIONS

Well-coordinated drawings and specifications are essential to any set of construction documents. In particular, the architect must ensure that materials and products shown on the drawings are described in the specifications, and that the language used in each is consistent and unambiguous. Language conflicts can be a major source of requests for information (RFIs) and potentially costly change orders during construction.

One definition of construction documents: "a spatial index into the specifications."

For small projects, architects often include the specifications directly on the drawings. For larger projects, however, it is common to publish the specifications in a separate project manual, further emphasizing the need for coordination. CAD and other software programs can offer some assistance, although most CAD systems provide few such tools "out of the box." Instead, they rely on various third-party software programs to help architects create more tightly integrated drawings and specifications.

One simple technique to help coordinate drawings and specifications is to use attribute fields attached to predrawn components as placeholders for specifications data. Some CAD systems and third-party detailing systems provide the ability to generate reports based on this information, which can be useful

Illustration 8.22 Font efficiency.

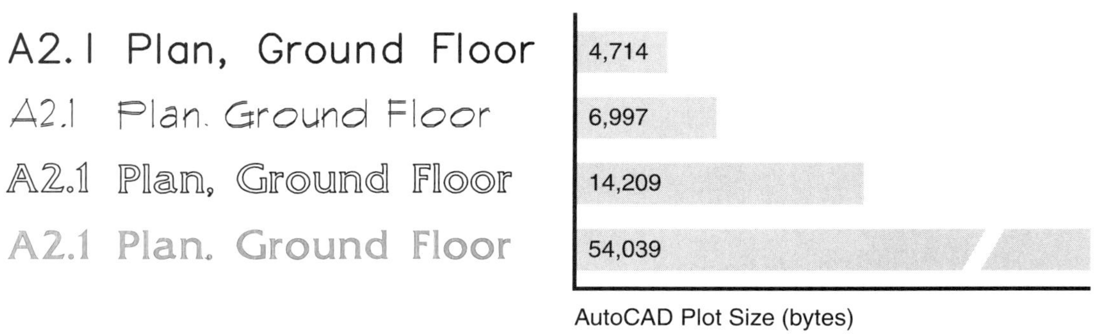

for double-checking that each drawing component is described in the specifications, and vice versa. The CAD user be knowledgeable enough about specifications data to make use of the attribute fields—an easy task in small offices, but often a more difficult one in large offices with dedicated specification writers.

Keynoting is another approach to help coordinate drawing and specification language, and has been used in architectural offices long before the arrival of the personal computer. Keynoting involves annotating a drawing with keynote numbers or labels that point to a standardized list of descriptive notes for the project or each drawing type (Ill. 8.23). Instead of attaching a descriptive note, such as *batt insulation,* to a component or detail, the architect attaches a keynote reference, such as *5A* or *22*.

Using CAD software, there are typically three approaches to CAD keynoting, each of which represents a different level of integration. The first approach simply uses the shared component or reference file feature of a CAD system to share standardized keynote lists among multiple drawings. There is no logical connection between the keynotes on the drawing and the keynote list. It remains the responsibility of the architect to coordinate the keynote list and the specifications, but revisions

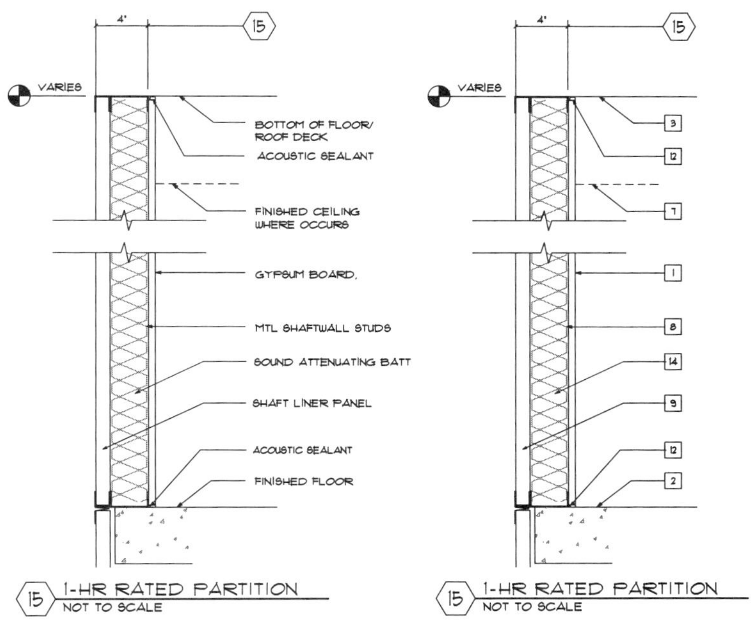

Illustration 8.23 Labeled and keynoted details.

to drawing notations are generally easier to make and better coordinated. If a standard note changes, only the keynote list needs to be updated, not every instance of the note on every drawing. However, storing details in libraries and recycling them between projects is more difficult because keynote lists typically change between projects.

Software tools such as Masterkey/ConDoc represent a second level of integration. In a ConDoc system, every keynote on a drawing contains a direct numerical reference to the appropriate specifications section. The software can scan the drawings and produce a keynote legend of all notes used in the drawing or locate all occurrences of a specific material within the drawings. With ConDoc, it is difficult to create a notation on a drawing that does not have an associated entry in the specifications.

One drawback of ConDoc and other keynote-based systems is that individual drawings are harder to read and to check; the reviewer of a drawing must refer to the keynote list to determine materials and assemblies. Something as simple as faxing a revised detail to a consultant or the contractor can be a problem, because the keynoted detail is meaningless without the accompanying keynote list.

The third approach is one that provides the benefit of both keynote systems and traditionally annotated drawings. The objection of most architects to keynoted documents is that they are difficult to review. The assumption, however, is that the annotative text on a drawing must have one, and only one, static representation. In fact, notes could have two alternative representations—an index value into the keynote list and the associated descriptive text—either one of which can be displayed at any given time. The note becomes a dynamic element, which is represented differently depending on the context in which it is displayed. This approach provides the coordination value of a keynoting system and preserves the readability and ease of review of traditional notated drawings. Some third-party CAD detailing systems support this type of functionality, but not for all types of architectural drawings.

CAD PLOTTING

Despite all the hoopla surrounding the paperless practice, plots are still the most convenient media for reviewing and marking up CAD drawings. Display monitor resolutions simply do not provide the detail necessary to see large drawings. And sketching revisions on yellow trace (yes, doing so is still ethical and honorable in the digital age) is accomplished far more easily over a plotted drawing than a display screen. Although coordinating architectural floor plans with those of consultants, at least in terms of reviewing physical layouts and dimensional conflicts, can be done on screen in CAD, most design review and refinement is still best accomplished using plots. Low-cost 11- by 17-inch laser printers can provide high-quality, half-size check plots inexpensively.

Particularly in CAD applications, producing plots remains a bottleneck in many firms. The problem is no longer the speed of plotters and printers, but the difficulty and time required for users to create plot files. Most CAD software supports only the notion of static plotting.

A static plot file is:

- A copy of a drawing converted into a format understood by a plotter (PostScript, PCL, HPGL/2, etc.).
- Device-dependent. Plot files vary between different plotters.
- Large—often two to five times as large as the original drawing.
- Made obsolete by a change to its source drawing(s); must be recreated for each new plot.

Static plot files are larger than CAD drawings for several reasons. First, plot files generally do not support the instancing of components that makes CAD drawings compact. Each instance of a component is converted into a redundant list of vectors to be plotted. The same is true of vector text, which is converted from small text strings into large collections of linework. (For printers that support TrueType or PostScript fonts, this is not the case, since the printer, not the CAD software, converts the text strings to printed linework.) In addition, many plot files are stored in ASCII format instead of the more efficient binary formats of CAD drawings.

The differences between ASCII and binary formats is discussed in more detail in Chapter 4, Tools of the Architect.

For project milestone plotting, architects should be able to create plots of multiple drawings using a simple procedure, rather than opening each drawing individually. As discussed earlier, the Plot Drawing is a general-purpose approach to storing plotting parameters inside a drawing but does not address the problem of plotting many drawings at one time. A few CAD systems and third-party plotting software support the notion of dynamic plotting.

A dynamic plot file is:

- A view of a drawing. The view is defined by region, scale, layer visibility, and pen parameters.
- Device-independent. The same plot file can be plotted to a variety of plotters or printers.
- Small. It contains only a list of the source drawings and plotting parameters.
- Unaffected by a change to one of its source drawings.

Intergraph's IPLOT software was one of the first commercial software products to implement the concept of dynamic plotting during the 1980s. The software allows the user to create Plot Request Files (PRFs), which contain the parameters necessary to produce a plot. Plotting a drawing does not require opening the drawings and creating a plot file, but only submitting the PRF to a queue managed by the IPLOT software. The software, on its own, opens the source drawings, converts them to the format required for the plotter, and transmits the plot file. Systems such as IPLOT simplify the process of creating project milestone sets.

Byers Plotstation is a third-party plotting software product that extends Intergraph's approach, and supports both Microstation and AutoCAD plotting using standard PC platforms. Both IPLOT and Byers Plotstation support the use of pen tables, which are programmable filters through which drawings are processed during plotting, and allow the user to control how elements of certain line types, line weights, colors, and layers of a drawings are plotted.

CAD PROJECT START-UP

Using CAD successfully requires an understanding that you are no longer just drawing, but developing a reusable graphic and nongraphic database that describes the project. The degree to which you plan ahead and organize this database is a key determinant of the quality of the drawings and the productivity of the effort.

It is vital that all of the drawings your firm produces be organized in a simple and consistent manner. This will provide you with staffing flexibility and will make CAD information more readily accessible for future reference by others. It will also allow you to spend more time practicing architecture and less time dealing with the idiosyncrasies of your CAD software or a particular project's organization.

Some important organizational issues are:

1. Organization of model drawings and plot drawings
2. File-naming convention and directory structure
3. Project coordinate system
4. Layer conventions
5. Component libraries and reference files
6. Client data requirements
7. The strengths and weaknesses of your CAD software

Before any CAD work is begun on a job, the estimated scope of CAD work and the project organization should be defined. Although layer guidelines provide a good lowest common denominator for most jobs, many project-specific issues will invariably affect how the work is organized. Organizational guidelines that are defined and agreed upon ahead of time, rather than invented ad hoc during the job, will ultimately result in better quality and a more productive CAD effort.

Usually, a kick-off meeting of the project manager, job captain, and project team provides the best forum in which these issues can be discussed and resolved. The sooner they are resolved, the more organized and productive the CAD effort will be. *Do not wait until the start of construction documents;* these issues will affect how design information is organized as well.

Questions to ask:

■ What is the scope of CAD work? Three-dimensional modeling? Schematic design? Design development? Full construction documents, or site plan, floor plans, and enlarged plans only? Elevations? Building sections? Wall sections? Details? Schedules?

■ Is the scope of work appropriate for the hours budgeted and the CAD expertise of the staff?

■ How will CAD information be organized? What information will be shared between what drawings? How are the model drawings subdivided into smaller parts? How will components be used? How will reference files be used?

■ What will be the major submittal and plotting deadlines? Is the job fast-track? What digital information needs to be provided when and to whom?

■ Is there renovation or demolition work involved? Are CAD databases available that describe existing conditions? Will translation be required?

■ Which consultants, if any, will be using CAD? What systems do they use? Will translation be required? What is the timetable for delivering updates? Are the consultants familiar with your organizational guidelines? Are you familiar with theirs?

■ Is a CAD database to be delivered to the client at the end of the job? Does the client have specific requirements about how it is organized? What are the specific contract obligations?

■ Will details be drawn using CAD? Which reference details might be appropriate? Are there similar projects from which custom details or assemblies can be used as a starting point (special precast or glazing requirements, etc.)?

Project teams should review the organization of work every time they start a new project, building on office guidelines and extending them as required. CAD guidelines that are too detailed or too rigid can contribute to a rubber-stamp mentality among those responsible for producing the drawings. Encouraging project teams to take organizational ownership of the digital information database they are creating is far easier if they participate in its design.

TOMORROW'S CAD

Architectural CAD systems of tomorrow must focus not only on the *geometry of drawings* but also on the *relationships of buildings*. Perhaps the biggest challenge is the invention of a standardized language of design with which architects can describe those design relationships to a computer and build procedural components. Spreadsheet formulas, which describe relationships between cell values, are mathematical. Design formulas involve math, but much more. What are the verbs and nouns of such a design language? This is perhaps the most compelling opportunity for architectural CAD research for the remainder of the decade.

Tomorrow's CAD software should not just be layered upon the relatively crude data structures of today's CAD software. In fact, the data structures of today's CAD software are still not very far removed from those of the 1970s. Four changes have occurred during the past decade: lower prices, improved algorithms and commands, better user interfaces, and improved coexistence with other applications (usually via the operating system). But the basic data structures upon which CAD systems are built—lines, arcs, circles, text, instanced components, reference files, and three-dimensional primitives—have really not changed substantially in the last 15 years.

New object-oriented software tools under development by Autodesk are discussed in more detail in Chapter 4, Tools of the Architect.

True innovation cannot be supplied by a new functional specification—even an object-oriented one—layered on top of old CAD systems. The result is always inadequate performance and usability. Rather, there must be a synergy of *user interface, data structures,* and *algorithms.* Each is equally important. CAD software developers, who have spent much of the last decade focusing on user interfaces and algorithms, must now focus on new types of data structures appropriate for describing the built environment.

CHAPTER

9

Organizing the Knowledge Base

> *"Experience is the name so many people give to their mistakes."*
>
> **Oscar Wilde**

Eventually, virtually all service products created by architects will be delivered to clients digitally, even if the process of creating the products appropriately involves a mix of physical and digital tools. How an architectural firm organizes and provides access to the knowledge base used to develop the digital products is of paramount importance. Your firm should spend as much time developing organized information resources as determining which software applications to use and learning how to use them.

Unlike CAD layering conventions, where a single, stable, industry-wide standard is desirable to allow plug-and-play information resources, the organization of an architectural firm's knowledge base is complex, dynamic, and necessarily unique to the firm. The organizational structure and information guidelines of your firm wholly depend on the nature of your practice and the needs of your clients. For example, are your services diverse or specialized? Is your firm a business-centered practice or practice-centered business? Are you organized departmentally or within design studios? The answers to these questions will have an impact on how you choose to organize digital information. This chapter describes the conceptual approaches and available tools for organizing your firm's knowledge base. *The effective organization and accessibility of the knowledge base remains one of the few ways to successfully differentiate a firm via technology.*

The value of knowledge over tools is discussed in Chapter 2 as one of the Top 10 technology implementation guidelines.

THE PURPOSE OF A KNOWLEDGE BASE

The purpose of a digital knowledge base is *not* to reduce a firm's dependency on individuals who have specialized knowledge or experience, although that benefit is often cited by technology evangelists. Devaluation of specialists may occur if those specialists provide little value to a firm other than acting as a biological repository of information. However, the real purpose of a digital knowledge base is typically quite practical and nonthreatening: to provide employees with easy access to information resources to increase their awareness and understanding of design and technical issues important to the firm and to avoid reinventing the wheel. The benefits are familiar: increased service quality, productivity, and turnaround.

Not all knowledge or experience, and very little of what is perceived as talent, can be condensed into a computer's binary file formats. Still, architects generate large amounts of reusable written and verbal information that can be captured, indexed, stored, and made accessible to others. A firm's knowledge base can help introduce new employees quickly to the firm, its portfolio of work, and its standards of practice. The knowledge base also provides an opportunity for employees to expand their professional expertise and knowledge in areas when their specific project responsibilities fail to provide that opportunity. The net result of a knowledge base is to make employees not less valuable but *more* valuable.

A knowledge base should never be assumed to be a professional shortcut by those who use it. A knowledge base is not a replacement for experience, but only a supplemental resource.

A firm's knowledge base need not be encapsulated within rule-based or expert system software. A simple library of templates and reusable components is an excellent starting point. It can include unaltered archives of service products and published resources, but should extend beyond mere replication and contain supplemental annotation to provide appropriate context. The architectural firm's knowledge base should be a carefully organized, aggregate resource that includes project archives, on-line resources, and office guidelines that are accessible using easy-to-use, general-purpose software programs.

THE THREE TYPES OF GUIDELINES

A firm's practice guidelines are a key component of its knowledge base. Before computer technology, architectural guidelines in most offices dealt primarily with drafting conventions: lettering, abbreviations, notes, targeting, drawing layout, sheet order, and so on. Rigorous and disciplined firms published manuals that described the appropriate representation and syntax of construction documents. In the digital age, however, the notion of guidelines must extend beyond the look and feel of documents and address the underlying organization and structure of project information and shared resources, as well as the tools and procedures used to access, refine, and publish them. Although most firms today focus on guidelines related to construction documents and CAD, other guidelines should be developed for all digital information that the firm typically develops in the course of project work. The three major types of guidelines are:

ORGANIZATIONAL GUIDELINES

- File system organization
- File-naming convention
- CAD layers and reference files
- Documentation guidelines
- Project archives
- Personal scrapbooks

INFORMATION GUIDELINES

- Public domain resources (CD-ROM, on-line publications)
- Boilerplates, templates, prototypes
- Graphics: fonts, fills, patterns, line weights, colors, materials, layout
- Building components: kits of parts, details, assemblies
- Layout: sheets, title blocks, schedules
- Annotation: notes, legends, dimensions, targets
- Visuals: digital photography, digital video

PROCEDURAL GUIDELINES

- Access to basic software applications
- Training programs
- Printing and plotting: queues, tracking, accounting
- Custom tools: parametric and procedural components

- Project start-up, including the definition of the organizational structure of digital data
- Project closeout, including the capture of reusable digital data
- Digital data translation and delivery
- Upgrades: information resources and tools

ORGANIZATIONAL STRUCTURES

Developing an organizational structure for a firm's digital knowledge base can appear overwhelming at first. It helps to understand a few simple ideas about organizing information. In his book *Information Anxiety,* architect Richard Saul Wurman describes five basic methods to use to organize information, which he labels "the five ultimate hat racks."

1. Category	Pertains to the organization of goods, for example, types of merchandise. Category can mean different models, different types, or different questions to be answered. Category is best illustrated with color, which has no inherent value as numbers do.
2. Time	Best used as an organizing principle for events that happen over fixed durations, such as building construction. Time is an easily understandable framework from which changes can be observed and comparisons made.
3. Location	Useful for comparing information from diverse sources or locales.
4. Alphabet	Lends itself to large bodies of information, such as words in a dictionary or names in a telephone directory. Alphabetical order is appropriate for diverse audiences who may not understand other classifications.
5. Continuum	Items are organized by magnitude (small to large, low to high) or relative importance. The items can be illustrated with numbers.

One of Portland, Oregon's cultural treasures is Powell's City of Books, a gargantuan book store (complete with a coffee shop/reading room) that fills a city block and contains about 250,000 new and used volumes. Simply arranging the books by category (fiction, nonfiction, business, etc.) would have been daunting to the typical customer. Powell's introduced another level of organizational hierarchy and grouped categories of books in different parts of the store that are identified by color:

SECTION	**CONTENTS**
Blue	Poetry, Literature, Western Philosophy, Religion, et al.
Gold	Science Fiction, Popular Fiction, Westerns, Parenting, Children's Room, et al.
Green	New Arrivals, Pacific Northwest, African American, Native American, et al.
Orange	Art, Crafts, Film, Drama, Dance, Journalism, et al.
Purple	U.S. History, Western Civilization, International Books, Travel, Law, et al.
Rose	Environment, Geography, Biology, Health, Psychology, Business, et al.
Coffee Room	Magazines, Gardening, Paper Models, et al.

New customers quickly learn the colors of their favorite sections, which are easy to locate visually. As diagrammed in Illustration 9.1, Powell's has a six-layer information hierarchy: the store itself (the root of the tree), the colored sections, book categories (such as Architecture), aisle numbers (223, 224, etc.), subcategories (such as Religious, Urban, Modern), and finally, alphabetical listing by author. Such a hierarchy allows the visitor to find a book of interest quickly from the quarter-million choices available.

Strive to balance the hierarchical tree of your knowledge base (Ill. 9.2). A hierarchy that is too deep or too shallow requires too much traversal of the tree to locate information (Ill. 9.3). Any branch of the tree can be orga-

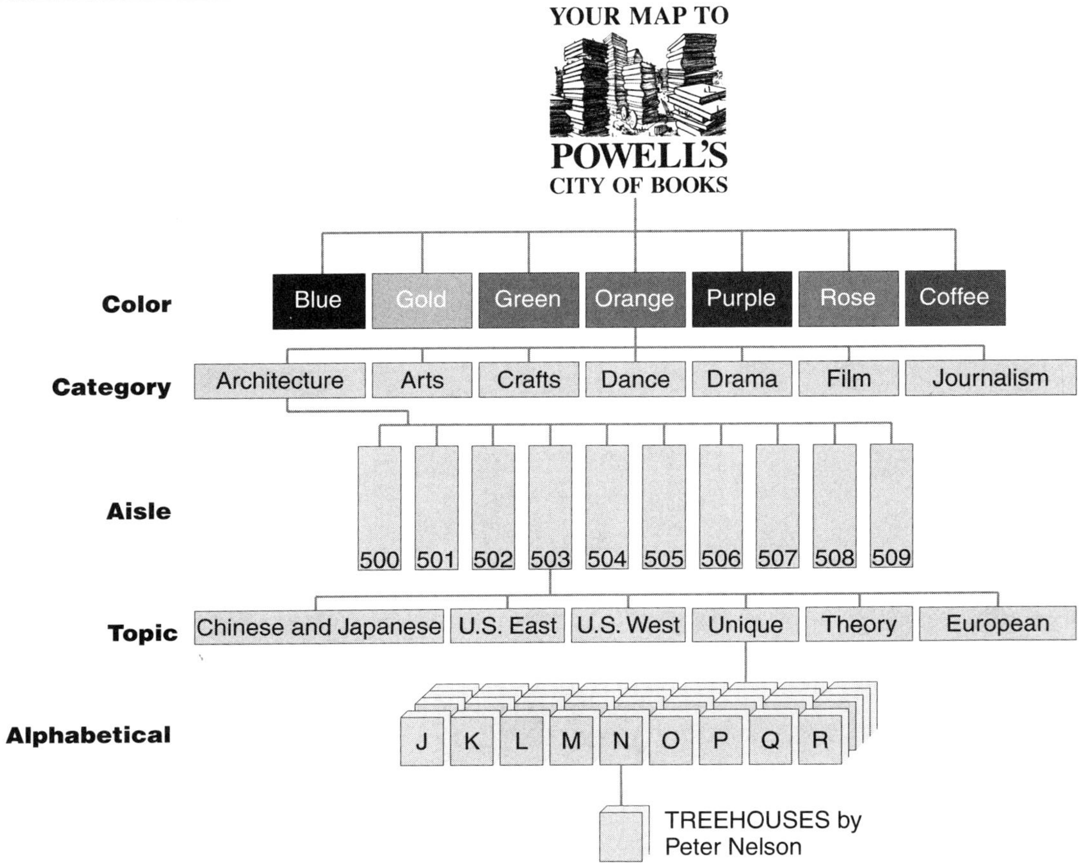

Illustration 9.1 Powell's City of Books hierarchy.

nized using one of the five methods: category, time, location, alphabet, and continuum.

NAVIGATION

All desktop computer operating systems provide basic tools to allow users to traverse the hierarchical file system of a computer. Examples include the Windows 3.1 File Manager, the Windows 95 Explorer and Network Navigator, and the Macintosh Finder. However, those tools list only file names and convey little about their content, other than their date, size, and the application that created them.

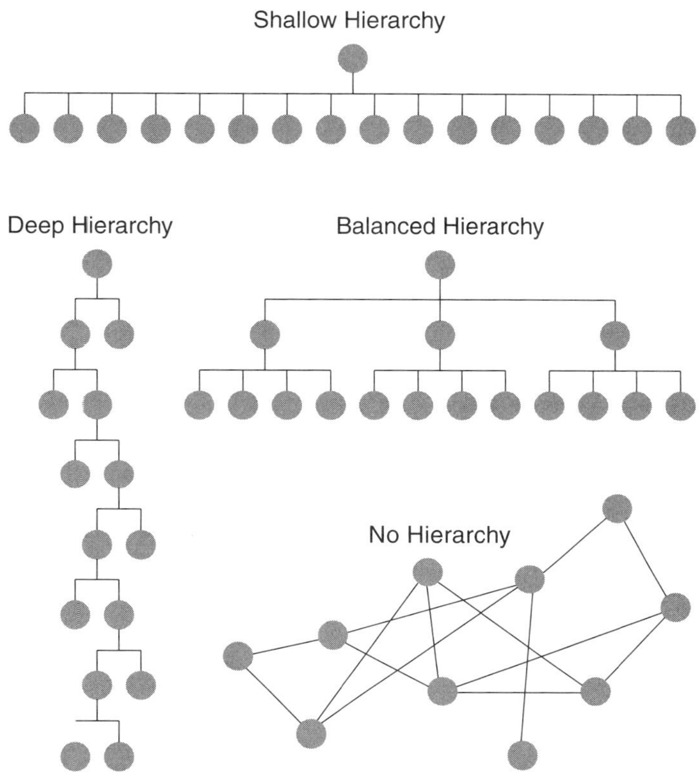

Illustration 9.2 *Flavors of hierarchies.*

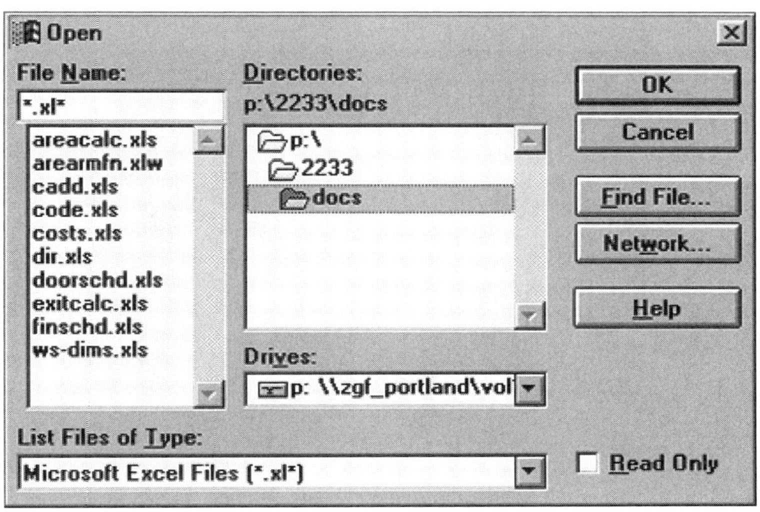

Illustration 9.3 *A file selection dialog box. Except for files at the end of a tree structure, strive to keep the number of files small. This provides a practical benefit to people who use file-selection dialog boxes within applications, and reduces the amount of time they must scroll around for information.*

The same tools used to navigate published resources on the Internet's World Wide Web can also be used to navigate in-house information resources. This idea is discussed in more detail in Chapter 10, On-Line Resources.

Fortunately, other software is available that can help users navigate information resources visually. An excellent example is Ketiv Technologies' Navigator, shown in Illustration 9.4, which is part of Ketiv's ArchT architectural software for AutoCAD. The software includes large libraries of predefined two- and three-dimensional components useful to architects. More importantly, the libraries are extensible, so architectural firms can add to their own information resources to those provided by Ketiv and organize them as required. Nongraphic annotation can be associated with each drawing, providing appropriate background or anecdotal information to architects browsing the libraries. Up to 16 snapshots can be displayed at one time, or individual files can be displayed in a larger window for closer inspection.

Illustration 9.4 Ketiv Technologies' Navigator.

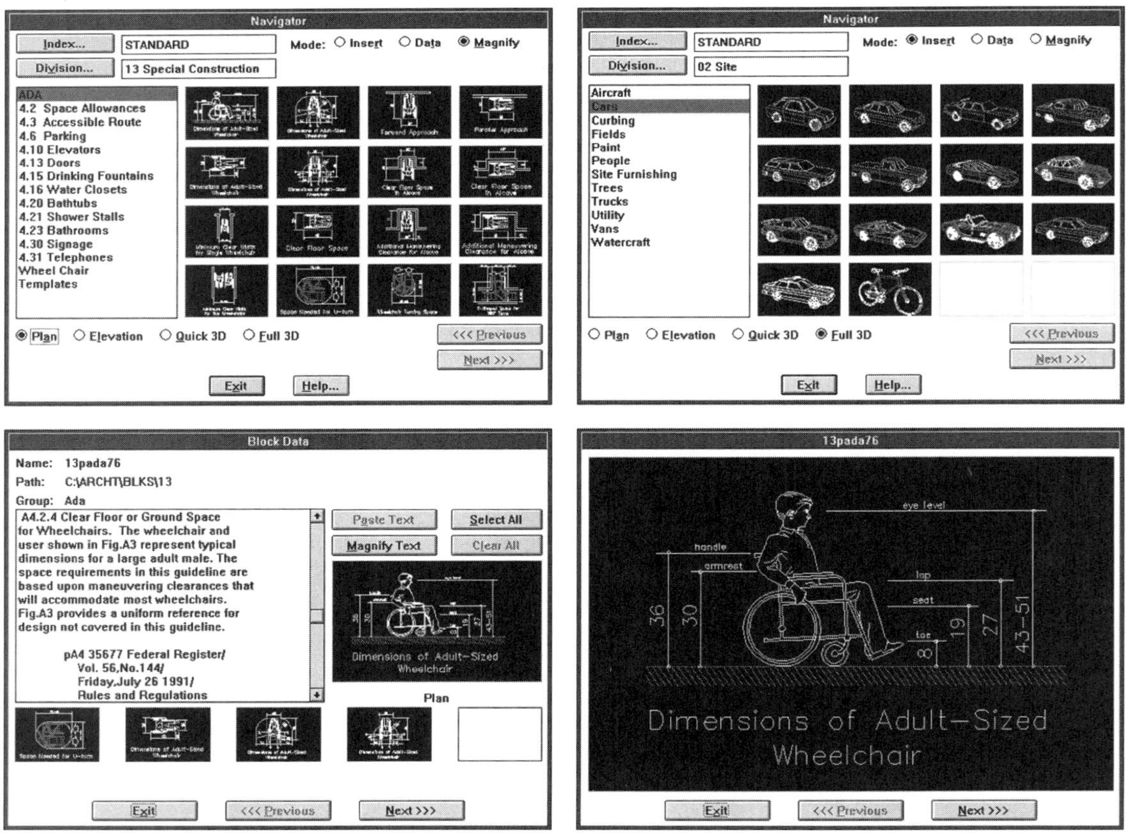

THE NETWORK FILE SYSTEM

The practical organizational structure of many digital knowledge bases reflects the hierarchical file and directory structure provided by a computer's operating system. In general, build your hierarchical file system around projects, not individuals or departments, and separate project data from software programs and system files. This keeps information users don't need out of their way. (It also simplifies backup procedures, since software and system files don't need backups as frequently as project data.)

Always store information resources such as component libraries and document templates on network servers, not redundantly on each desktop computer. This simplifies creating and maintaining the libraries and templates and ensures their consistency. In addition, standardize file-naming conventions. Don't try to control every character of a file name, but develop conventions for mnemonic and literal files names and descriptions. Finally, many software applications allow users to append summary information to documents (Ill. 9.5). Encourage project teams to use these features and use them consistently. All of these suggestions should make life simpler not only for those using networked file systems, but also the staff responsible for their maintenance, upgrade, and expansion.

An important issue in organizing distributed, transparent file systems is planning for painless expansion. The following example describes how to do this by mapping multiple disks to remote file servers. (To the user, the additional disks appear as if

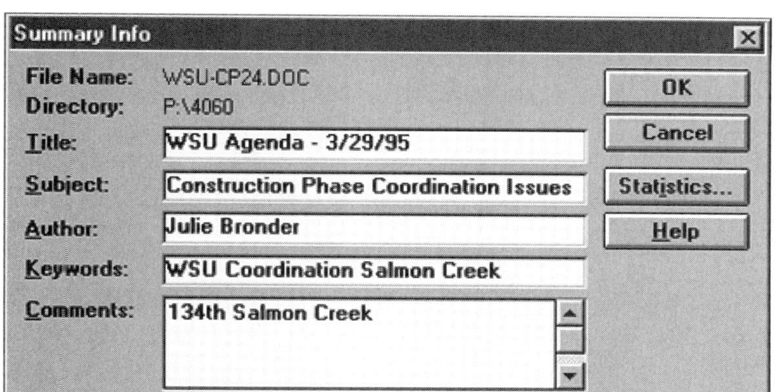

Illustration 9.5 *Microsoft Word summary information dialog box.*

they were local, but the files they contain actually reside on other computers.) In the example, Windows 3.1 PCs are accessing remote directories on UNIX file servers.

REMOTE DISKS	SERVER	SERVER DIRECTORY
I: Information Libraries	Picard	/files/info
P: Projects	Picard	/files/projects
M: Marketing Proposals and Presentations	Picard	/files/marketing
X: Executive and Financial Data	Picard	/files/executive
Y: Application Software	Picard	/files/software
Z: System Files	Picard	/files/system

As a firm outgrows its network and acquires additional servers, a simple remapping of remote disks can accommodate the change. For example, if a firm were to acquire two other file servers, one dedicated to information libraries and projects, and the other to executive and financial data, the remote disks might be remapped as follows:

REMOTE DISKS	SERVER	SERVER DIRECTORY
I: Information Libraries	Janeway	/files/info
P: Projects	Janeway	/files/projects
M: Marketing Proposals and Presentations	Picard	/files/marketing
X: Executive and Financial Data	Kirk	/files/executive
Y: Application Software	Picard	/files/software
Z: System Files	Picard	/files/system

From the user's point of view, nothing has changed, except a big increase in available disk space and faster network performance.

FILE-NAMING CONVENTIONS

File names that provide clues about their contents are useful to those who are not intimately familiar with a project. In CAD drawings, for example, the separation of model drawings and plot drawings can be reflected in file names. In general, the file names of plot drawings should closely match the sheet number. Since plot drawings are never referenced by other drawings, they can be renamed at any time if the sheet numbering changes without affecting other drawings.

The eight-character file name limitation of DOS has finally been purged from Windows 95, which now supports long file names like the Macintosh, but this should not relieve anyone from file-naming discipline. File names that include standardized abbreviations or acronyms are still useful for sorting and searching for documents by name. Obviously, the file names should reflect the organization of construction documents in your office. Table 9.1 is but one example.

ALIASES AND HYPERLINKS

The limitation of the hierarchical tree structure provided by most computer file systems is that traversal of the tree is one-dimensional—either forward to the "leaf" nodes or backward to the "root." In fact, architects need to build associations between related data that do not depend on such a limited structure. Two tools can be used to link related documents dynamically to each other: aliases and hyperlinks.

- Aliases are *external pointers* to referenced information (managed by the operating system).
- Hyperlinks are *internal pointers* to referenced information (managed by the software application).

Aliases

Aliases (known as shortcuts in Windows 95) provide a way for information resources to appear to be in two places at the same time (Ill. 9.6). An alias is a virtual file—a pointer to a file stored somewhere else on a network. Aliases exist outside the files they point to and are managed by the computer's operating system. Using aliases, several hierarchical tree structures can be developed that the user can traverse without using any special tools.

Table 9.1 Sample CAD File-Naming Convention

	NAME	DESCRIPTION	EXAMPLE
Plot Drawings	A1.*	Site plans, site details	A1.2 Site Details
	A2.*	Floor plans, roof plans	A2.5 Second Floor Plan, South
	A3.*	Exterior elevations, building and wall sections	A3.12 Wall Sections
	A4.*	Exterior details	A4.1 Exterior Details
	A5.*	Stairs and details	A5.3 Stair Details
	A6.*	Enlarged plans	A6.2 Enlarged Plan, Toilets
	A7.*	Interior elevations	A7.1 Interior Elevations, Lobby
	A8.*	Interior details	A8.1 Interior Details
	A9.*	Ceiling plans	A9.5 Second Floor Ceiling Plan
	A10.*	Ceiling details	A10.1 Ceiling Details
	SK*	Design drawings	SK-101 Site Concept 2-22-95
Model Drawings	FP*	Floor plan models	FP1-S First Floor Plan, South
	CP*	Ceiling plan models	CP1-S First Floor Ceiling Plan
	SP*	Site plan models	SP Site Plan
	EL*	Exterior elevation models	EL-W Exterior Elevations, West
	BS*	Building section models	BS-EW East/West Sections
	WS*	Wall section models	WS-1 Wall Section Model 1 of 4

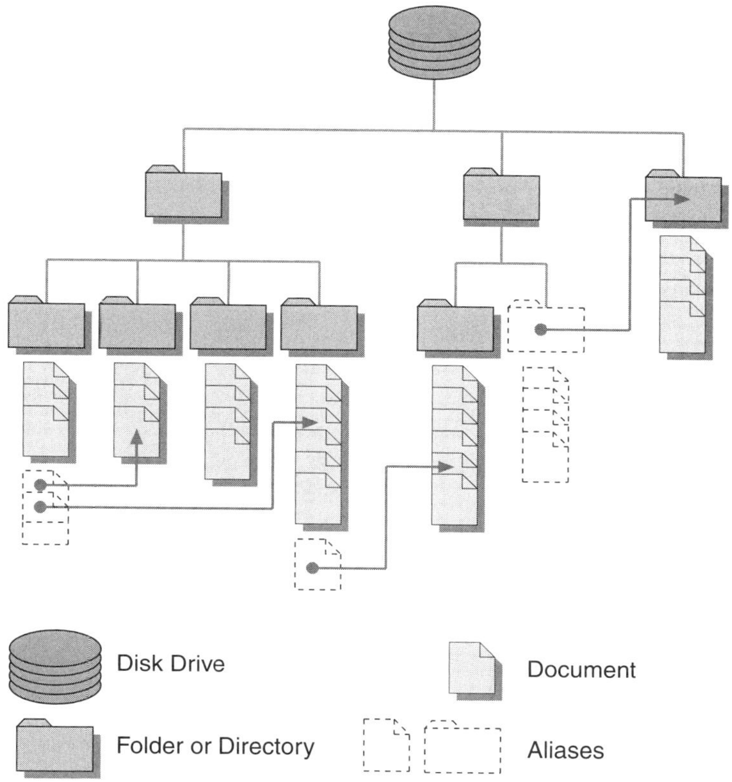

Illustration 9.6 Aliases overlaid on a hierarchical tree.

As a rule, organize the base hierarchy of a file system by project, and overlay other organizational structures on top of it using aliases and hyperlinks. Why? Creating project archives and restoring them is easier when project information is physically stored together. All digital information for a project can be archived, deleted, and/or restored by accessing a single project directory instead of multiple directories scattered around the network.

Hyperlinks

Hyperlinks are references inside a document that point to other related documents (Ill. 9.7). Unlike aliases, hyperlinks are typically managed by individual software applications, not the com-

See Chapter 10, On-Line Resources, for a discussion of how hyperlinks and browsers are used to navigate the Internet's World Wide Web.

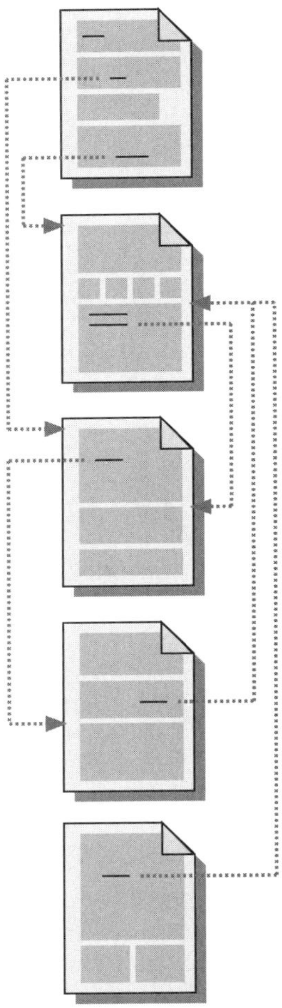

Illustration 9.7 Hyperlinks.

puter's operating system. When a user clicks on a hyperlink, an external document is retrieved and presented to the user, displacing the document the user was viewing. Hyperlinks are most useful in applications that are used to find and view, but not necessarily edit, information. Using hyperlinks, users can traverse across a hierarchical tree or skip levels of hierarchy.

Browsers are software programs that navigate hyperlinked documents. The most familiar examples of hyperlink browsers are the built-in help systems of Windows and the Macintosh (Ill. 9.8). The most compelling and powerful implementation of hyperlinked documents can be found on the Internet's World Wide Web. Each document on the Web can contain hyperlink pointers to any other document on the Web, essentially collapsing the global reach of the Internet onto an individual's computer display.

Hyperlinks are most useful to create richly cross-referenced knowledge bases. Like aliases, the best way to use hyperlinks is on top of well-structured, hierarchical file systems.

PERSISTENCE

One of the problems of using dynamic links between related files is their lack of persistence. What happens, for example, when a document to which an alias points is renamed or moved elsewhere? Different operating systems deal with this situation with varying degrees of success. For example, when it encounters a shortcut pointing to a missing file, Windows 95 uses a heuristic search algorithm (a fancy way of saying it tries real hard) to search nearby directories for the missing document. Windows can identify the document, even if renamed, by comparing the unique creation date and time of the file with that of the shortcut. If it finds the document, it restores the shortcut. However, this search mechanism does not work well on distributed networks. One of the promised features of Microsoft's upcoming Cairo operating system is fully persistent links between all objects on the network, which will be a valuable tool for architects to develop reliably cross-referenced digital information resources.

INFORMATION CONVENIENCE

In general, people look for information in the most convenient place possible. There are three discrete levels of in-house information resources most people search, in order of convenience: current projects, personal scrapbooks, and firm-wide libraries (Ill. 9.9). Almost everyone searches for relevant information in that predictable order, looking in each until they find what they need. Especially in architectural firms with diverse projects and services, information that is copied from a library to a project is rarely maintained as a perfect clone of the library original, and often is refined and modified as required. This is a classic example of information recycling. If what an architect needs is closer to a project's revised version than the library original, it is simply easier for her to copy it from the project.

For example, ZGF is currently in the process of capturing our 35-mm slide libraries in Kodak's PhotoCD format. The collection of PhotoCDs comprises the digital slide library: the raw stock of digital images scanned directly from the 35-mm slides. In addition to marketing proposals and multimedia presentations, these images are used in programming, schematic design, and urban planning documents. Typically, the PhotoCD library images must be cropped, resized, or otherwise filtered to fit the specific format of a document (Ill. 9.10). Most urban planning documents, for example, contain a mix of images special to the particular project, as well as more generic images that convey general design concepts: a streetscape, a landscaped court, a

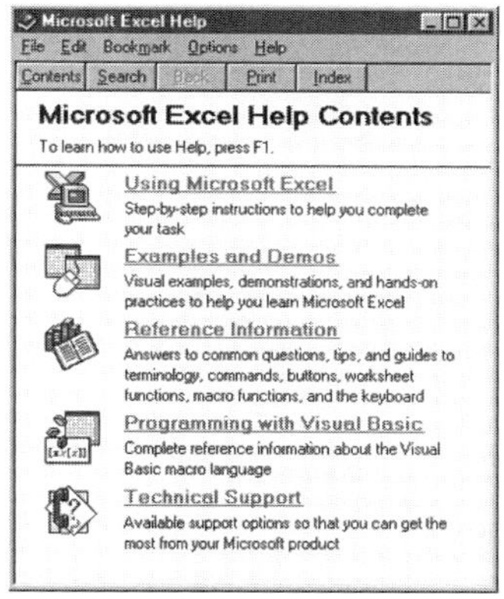

Illustration 9.8 Help browser.

See Chapter 2 for a discussion of information recycling versus copying versus sharing.

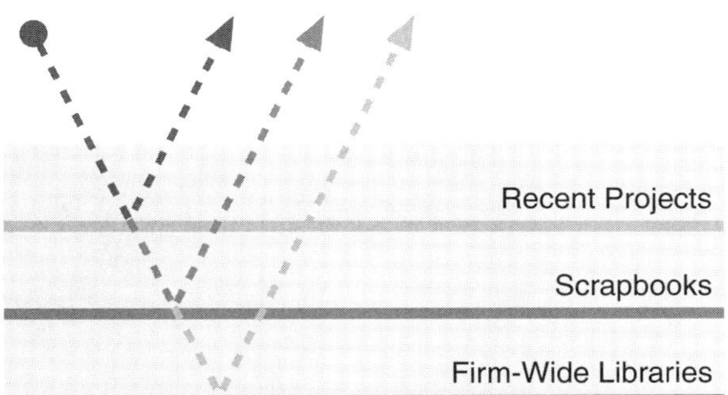

Illustration 9.9 Information convenience.

public gathering space, or a riverwalk. The more generic images, once appropriately filtered, are sometimes reused without modification within other documents. These images are accessible from an urban planning scrapbook separate from the firm-wide PhotoCD library. This allows people to access the popular, filtered images quickly without having to browse the raw PhotoCD library images. Archives of prior projects are also available as additional sources of filtered images.

Similarly, it is often easier for a project manager who needs to generate a new project schedule to copy and revise an existing one, rather than starting from scratch using a generic template. Most people, in fact, look first in a place that is most familiar to them: current or recent projects. If they have a specific piece of information in mind, it is simply far easier to obtain it if they already know where it is—in a project direc-

Illustration 9.10 PhotoCD process.

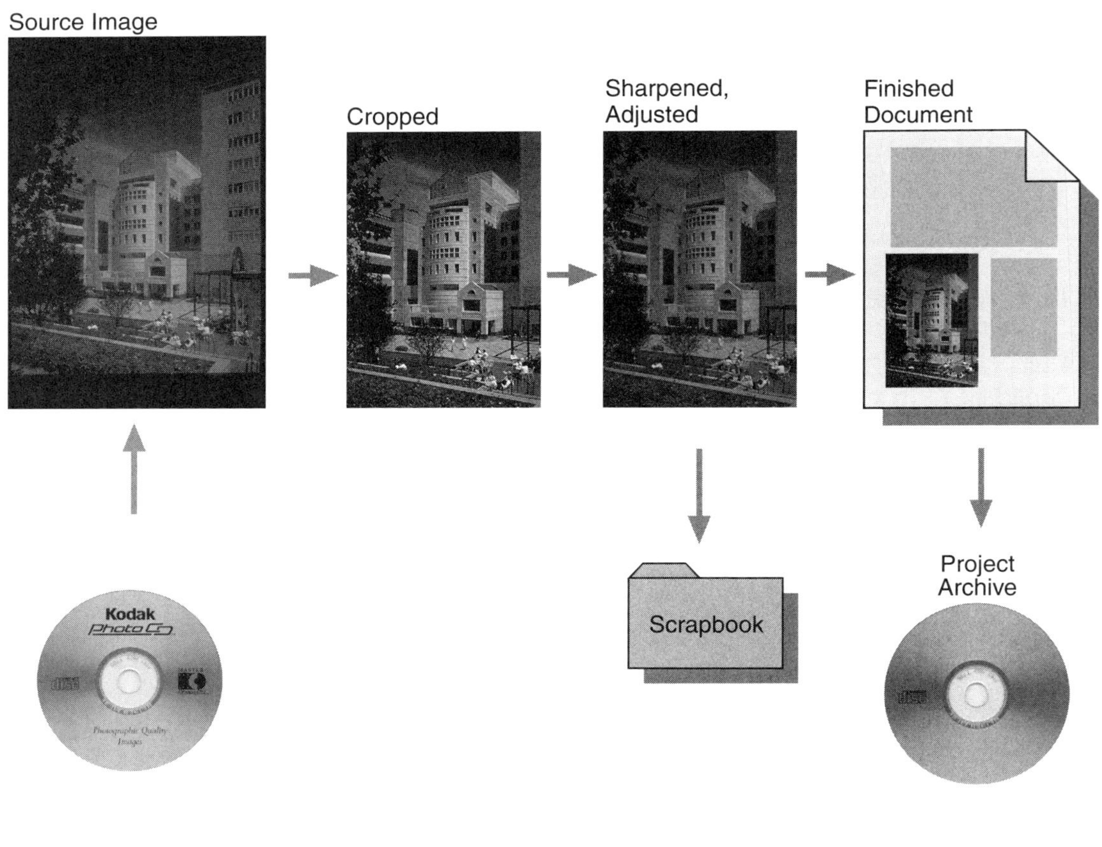

tory—rather than locating it within libraries. This is true even if those libraries are well organized and easily accessible.

The three-tiered model of projects, scrapbooks, and office libraries is a useful organizational structure for a firm's knowledge base. First, create consistent, published, organizational guidelines for all project information. Second, allow individuals and/or project teams to maintain personal scrapbooks. The only restriction is that information cannot be trapped there—scrapbooks must be accessible by others, should contain recycled subsets of information found in the firm's libraries, and should conform to standard file-naming conventions. Third, make sure that all office libraries are well organized and documented.

Using this model of information convenience, one can imagine a scenario where an architect uses a standard information resource as a starting point on a project, even though another project contains information (not yet published in the firm's libraries) that may more closely match what she is looking for. What if she isn't aware of it? Can the computer automatically find it for her, without her even asking? Unfortunately, the effort required to categorize and index all project information currently under development for automatic retrieval is far higher than the infrequent payoff such a system would provide. In fact, the model of information convenience acknowledges that a person may not get to the best possible starting point for information 100 percent of the time. The burden of seeking out both on-line resources and comparable projects for comparison is appropriately left to the individual architect. Organizational guidelines are a key requirement.

ON LINE, OFF LINE, AND NEAR LINE

Another useful way to organize digital information is to think about how fast people need to get access to it. Current project work obviously should be accessible quickly and easily by any member of a project team. The physical analogies are the slide carousel on one's shelf, the drawing on one's desk, or the schedule in one's file cabinet—all within arm's reach.

Many shared information libraries, however, do not require such instantaneous access. Manufacturer's catalogs, reference detail libraries, or recently completed projects are candidates for "near-line" storage, where people need occasional access from their desktops and where a small time penalty is acceptable in accessing the information. The physical analogies are a firm's product catalog library or shelves of marketing proposals and boilerplate.

Finally, some information is rarely accessed but should be retained anyway, such as older project archives. The physical analogy is a firm's microfilmed or paper archives, often stored off site.

These three types of information can be labeled on line, near line, and off line. Information can float back and forth between these types as required. A project that is put on hold for several months, for example, may be moved to near-line storage. Parts of an older project, long since archived in off-line storage, may be moved back to on-line storage in preparation for a subsequent phase of work.

Not all of a firm's knowledge base needs to be on line or even in digital formats. Sometimes the on-line information can simply be a pointer to a resource: an individual's E-mail address or phone number, a CD-ROM, or a printed book. Carefully measure the cost of converting old information into digital formats against the probability of future reference.

Most architects have always distinguished between on-line and off-line storage, of course, and have used tape drives, or even floppy disks, to store off-line digital information. While magnetic hard disks remain the media of choice for storing on-line information, new optical disk technology provides two excellent alternatives for near-line and off-line storage. Optical disk jukeboxes available on the network provide an excellent solution for near-line storage, while the recordable CD-ROM drive provides a faster, more economical alternative to magnetic tapes, until recently the most popular backup and archive format. Optical disk jukeboxes are still beyond the reach of many small firms and, in fact, are probably storage overkill for most. Small firms, and certainly the sole practitioner, may want to distinguish between only two types of information as always: on line and off line.

For more information on optical disk technology, refer to Chapter 7, Desktop Hardware.

Using digital media instead of physical media significantly impacts turnaround time, as shown in Table 9.2. Although the time scale has been compressed with digital storage media, the differentiation of information access is still appropriate because

Table 9.2 Physical and Digital Media Access Times

STORAGE TYPE	PHYSICAL STORAGE	PHYSICAL ACCESS TIME	DIGITAL STORAGE	DIGITAL ACCESS TIME
On line	Desk, file cabinet	Immediate	Magnetic disk	Immediate
Near line	Library shelf	Ten minutes	CD jukebox	Ten seconds
Off line	Microfilm, off-site	One day	Recordable CD	Five minutes

on-line storage is significantly more expensive than near-line storage, which in turn is more costly than off-line storage. Implementing such a hierarchy is appropriate if only to realize its economic benefits.

BUILDING DIGITAL LIBRARIES

The most important attribute of a firm's digital libraries is a clear, consistent, *published* organizational structure for all digital data contained within it. The published structure need not be in digital format. For the sole practitioner, it may be a single-page table of contents tacked to the wall, describing a filing system. For a small firm, perhaps a master spreadsheet stored on the network contains an index of available resources, providing simple sorting and searching capabilities to the user. Larger firms might provide "intelligent yellow pages" to their employees by encapsulating information about available resources in on-line relational databases that can be queried and reported. HTML, the language used to publish hyperlinked documents on the Internet's World Wide Web, is yet another way to publish information directories, both in house and on line, which include links to other information resources.

Regardless of publishing formats or media, the common thread is access: it is vitally important that everyone in the firm know exactly how to find the information they need, and if they don't know where to find it, *how to find out where to find it.*

See Chapter 10, On-Line Resources, for more information on the potential applications of HTML within the architectural firm.

The following five steps summarize a simple process for building digital libraries:

1. *Organize.* Develop guidelines for how information is developed and stored.
2. *Collect.* Gather existing information and define a process for reviewing new contributions.
3. *Filter.* Eliminate inappropriate, obsolete, or irrelevant information.
4. *Qualify.* Annotate orphaned information as required to clarify its intended use and meaning.
5. *Publish.* Provide easy-to-use tools for access to and assembly of the information.

If it isn't documented, it doesn't exist.

Making a mistake is OK. Making it again and again is not.

Of particular importance is a specific process to review, approve, and implement new contributions to a firm's digital libraries. A knowledge base should not be a dumping ground for unfiltered digital information. The purpose of a digital knowledge base is to enhance information reuse; as such, quality control of its information is even more critical than individual projects. For smaller firms, a single individual can be assigned as information gatekeeper, working with others to review and approve new contributions. Departmentalized firms may have several people responsible for the process, and/or a committee that oversees it. Again, how this function is accomplished will depend on your firm. The details of the process are less important than that the process be specific and consistent. Adhering to this process requires substantial discipline, especially when a firm is busy, but is well worth the effort.

Some information is created from scratch, such as new templates for use in presentations or new budgeting spreadsheets. However, much of the reusable information stored within a firm's digital libraries is derived from project work. Everyone who contributes to a project must be aware of the importance of capturing information that is generic enough to be useful on other projects. A useful technique is to implement an "in box" (usually a shared network directory or disk drive) for contributions to the firm's digital guidelines.

Knowledge base "feeding time" should be a budgeted part of every project, particularly during project closeout. A day or two should be reserved to review the project's digital by-products and identify reusable contributions to the knowledge base.

In addition, you should make sure that the existing resources are reviewed periodically and that obsolete information is culled from them. Examples include framing details that do not reflect current seismic codes, or non-ADA-compliant prototype restroom layouts. Again, this should be made the specific responsibility of an individual or group equipped with appropriate professional knowledge and expertise.

CONTEXT PRESERVATION

Information removed from its original context can be misleading, so preserving appropriate context within the knowledge base is important. Two examples illuminate this issue. Many architects develop project history databases that contain information about a building's size, use, occupancy, cost estimate, construction cost, completion date, as well as in-house financial data such as fee, profit/loss, hours required to do the work, etc. The financial data can be helpful to projects managers who are developing proposals or negotiating fees for similar projects.

The question is: what does the fee number in the project history database represent? Is it the fee quoted in the original owner–architect agreement? Is it the total fee, after the addition of extra services? What was the scope of services represented by the fee? What was the profit (or loss)?

Similarly, simply cutting and pasting CAD details from a reference library may be fine for certain types of construction, such as typical penetration details in rated partitions. But other details require more information context. What was the location and climate of the project's site? What was the seismic zone? What was the budget for the project? What was the design intent? Did special building codes apply?

When information is added to the knowledge base, strive to append it with annotation that clarifies its intended meaning and use.

This type of context can be extremely helpful to those who intend to use the information as a starting point for other projects. The key issue: although some information in a firm's knowledge base can be "plug and play," much of it is not. Preserving information context is necessary to make the information useful to others.

CHAPTER 10
On-Line Resources

> *"Something is happening. The sales of modems have soared. Memberships of on-line services have soared. The number of people with access to the Internet has soared. Yes, this all means something is happening. But the industry has also been gripped by mass hysteria and is engaged in its normal hypercompetitive activity of supplying customers with far more software than they ever imagined they needed to do far less than they ever hoped they could do."*
>
> **Stewart Alsop, Editor in Chief, *InfoWorld***

On-line resources are of growing importance to architects who must depend every day on a wide variety of information publications to accomplish their work. Although on-line resources are sometimes described by technology gurus as limitless or boundless in potential applications, such evangelical euphoria tends to mask their very practical and useful nature. There are really only four things architects can do on line: send and retrieve E-mail, browse and download information, interact with others in real time (verbally, visually, and/or graphically), and participate in user groups, forums, or bulletin board systems.

Practical on-line resources provide a synergy of timely information combined with convenient desktop access, and include both external services, such as CompuServe, AIA On-Line, and the Internet, as well as packaged CD-ROM resources which are made available on line to architects via in-house networks. In either case, the on-line resource is a collection of digital information published by an outside party, separate and distinct from the in-house knowledge base discussed in the last chapter.

THE INTERNET

As the communications backbone of the information superhighway, the Internet has become a kind of digital cultural icon and media darling over the past several years, both in mainstream journalism and in academic research and teaching. The Internet

According to Link Resources Corporation, 43.2 million Americans (roughly one-third of the work forces) worked at least part of the time from a home office in 1994. By comparison, in 1988, only 24.9 million people (21 percent of the work force) were working from home. Link predicts that the home-worker population will increase by roughly 15 percent a year, to reach 56 million in 1997.

The communications protocol of the Internet (TCP/IP) is actually a by-product of the Cold War. The Internet was originally financed in the 1970s by the United States Advanced Research Projects Agency, and was designed to dynamically reroute communications around computer hosts on the network which were no longer available.

made the cover of *Time* for the first time on July 25, 1994, with the title "The Strange New World of the Internet—Battles on the Frontiers of Cyberspace," and for the second time in a special Spring 1995 issue with a somewhat friendlier title: "Special Issue: Welcome to Cyberspace." The use of the Internet by architects in the next millennium may very well be to support the concept of collaborative virtual design studios, a topic discussed in Chapter 12, Future Trends. However, the Internet's practical application through the end of this decade will likely be as a global, on-line information resource that sits quietly on the architect's desktop.

Most architects will use the Internet in the same way they use *Sweet's Catalog File* and in-house libraries of product literature, as a resource to find information about products, materials, and methods that are appropriate to the project at hand. Although most useful information on the Internet today originates from universities, research organizations, and governmental agencies, a growing number of commercial vendors are using the Internet as a means to distribute information about their products and services. It is in this way that the Internet will play a critical role in providing architects with information and knowledge that is not possessed in-house.

The Internet experienced tremendous growth soon after it was opened to commercial access in 1991. Although widely perceived by the general public as something brand new on the cutting edge of technology, the Internet is actually over 20 years old, and some of the tools used to access information on the Internet show their age. The Internet, after all, was developed during an age of text-only display terminals connected to minicomputers or mainframes, long before the Macintosh and Windows popularized the graphical user interface.

For many years, the commands used to navigate the Internet were those commonly found in UNIX systems such as FTP (file transfer protocol), which allows a person to copy files from one computer to another, or Telnet, which allows a person to log in to other remote computers. Hundreds of special interest news groups also emerged, comparable to the private forums and bulletin boards on commercial networks such as CompuServe. Using these tools, however, requires deft skills at the keyboard and are difficult for most visually oriented architects to understand or master. Both FTP and Telnet are still harder to use than most commercial on-line services such as CompuServe or America On-Line. The burden of finding relevant information is left to the user.

Gopher is a step above FTP and Telnet in terms of usability, and provides a hierarchical menu structure with which users can navigate information resources. Items in a Gopher menu may direct the user to an information resource on the same computer or may be linked to an information resource on another computer (Ill. 10.1). In this way, the vast, distributed nature of the Internet becomes semitransparent to the user. Still, the Gopher interface is somewhat dated, and not much better as an information discovery tool than the uninspiring Windows 3.1 File Manager. Gopher does not provide image previewing, supplemental descriptive information of resources, nor the graphic tools necessary to communicate the relative importance of different information. Again, the burden of guessing what might be of interest is left largely to the user.

The Internet's alt.architecture forum is an example of an Internet resource that is not quite ready for prime time. See Chapter 1, The Impact of Technology on the Practice, for an example.

Illustration 10.1 A Gopher menu.

THE WORLD WIDE WEB

For architects to use digital information resources effectively, access to those resources must be uncomplicated, as easy as pulling a book from a shelf and flipping through its pages. Fortunately, the World Wide Web is approaching that ease in some ways and exceeding it in others. The World Wide Web is the Internet for the rest of us, both subscribers and publishers, and where architects should be investing their time and resources on the Internet.

The concept of the World Wide Web was developed at CERN, the European Particle Physics Laboratory. The Web is a collective name applied to computers connected to the Internet that contain multimedia, hyperlinked documents written in a language called HTML (Hypertext Markup Language). HTML defines the standard look and feel of information published on the World Wide Web for users to browse. Two other enabling standards were developed at CERN: URL (Uniform Resource Locator), a standard naming convention for files and resources on the World Wide Web, and HTTP (Hypertext Transfer Protocol), the communications protocol for transferring data between Web sites.

HTML allows authors to insert hyperlinks into their documents, which create connections between their document and other HTML documents on the Internet. A familiar feature to users of help utilities in most Windows and Macintosh software applications, a hyperlink is a word or phrase in a body of text that is underlined. The underlining basically means "click here for more information." When the user clicks on a hyperlink, additional information relating to the underlined word or phrase is retrieved and displayed. The power of HTML and the World Wide Web is that these hyperlinks can direct the user to other documents on other Internet host computers, regardless of their location. Using hyperlinks, the global reach of the Internet is effectively made transparent to the user.

Users navigate the World Wide Web by using browsing software, which can display HTML documents and interpret the hyperlinks contained within them. Mosaic, the original Web browser, was developed in 1993 at NCSA, the National Center for Supercomputing Applications at the University of Illinois. Both the HTML language and several versions of Mosaic are in the public domain, available free. Within a year, millions of Internet users were using Mosaic to browse and retrieve information from the World Wide Web, and companies such as Spry (now owned by CompuServe), Spyglass, Quadralay and Netscape Communications began to develop commercial versions of Web browsers (Ill. 10.2). Most browsers are discoverable and can be mastered quickly without reading any documentation.

HTML is a beautiful example of the value of simplicity and standards in information publishing. Consider the potential problem on the Internet: millions of documents from millions of authors, each presented in vastly different formats. In fact, just a few years ago, the only information formats that could be displayed reliably via the Internet were plain ASCII text (alphabetical and numerical characters) or digital images. HTML provides support for multimedia documents, including multiple fonts, images, sounds, and animations, but at the same time effectively restricts and unifies the look and feel of published documents by simplifying the language used to create them. HTML appropriately balances consistent presentation of the documents and artistic creativity of the information publisher.

Illustration 10.2 World Wide Web home pages. The browser is from NetScape Communications.

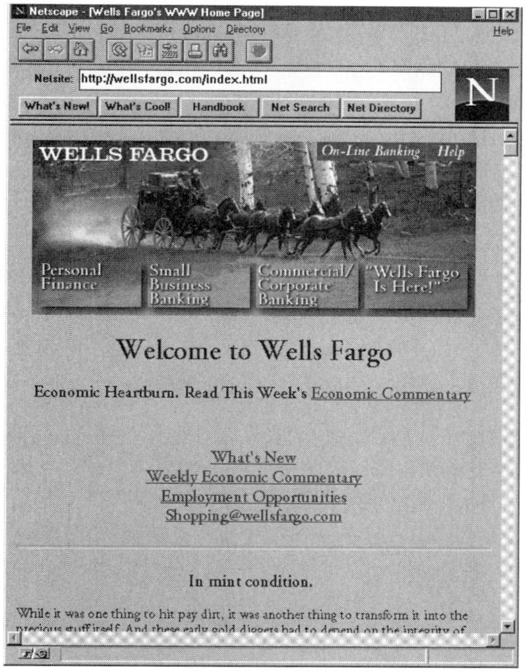

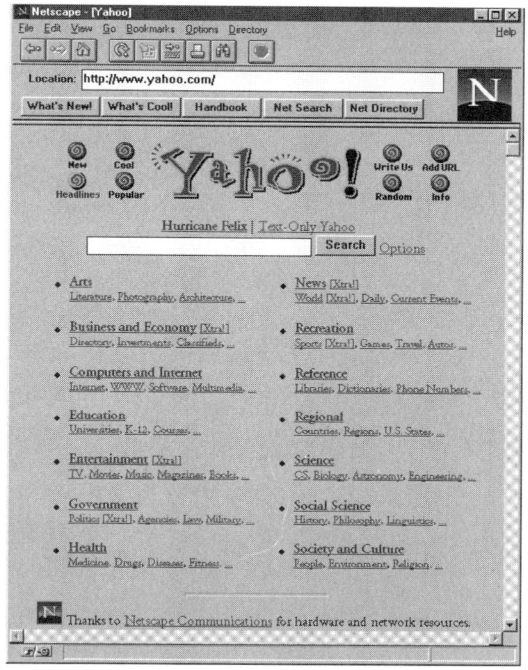

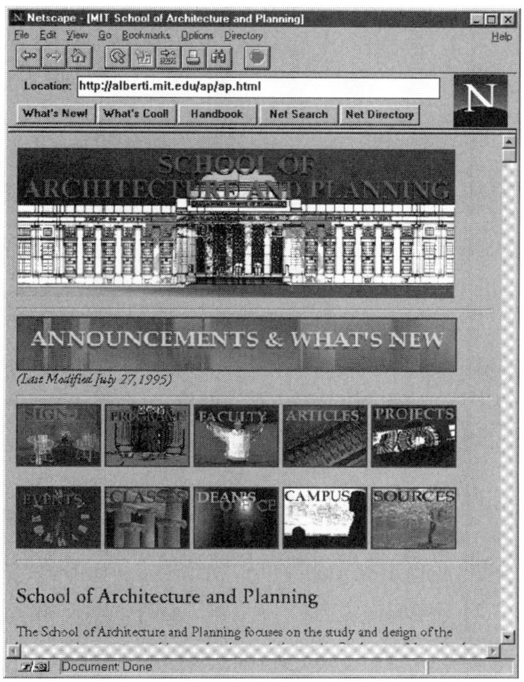

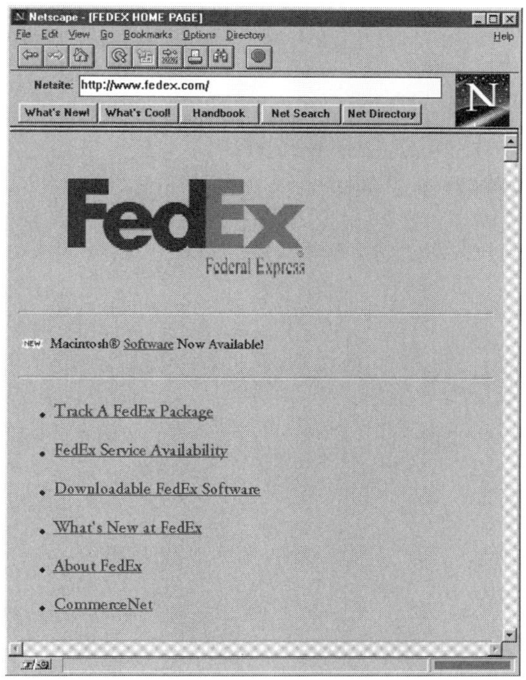

An HTML document can be the information resource, or it can simply be the brochure, providing pointers to files that can be downloaded using FTP.

Most importantly, HTML is a public-domain, open standard. Anyone who can use a text editor can create simple HTML documents for others to access on the Internet using HTML browsers. Easy-to-use software tools designed specifically to create and edit HTML documents are also starting to emerge. Microsoft's Internet Assistant, for example, is a small software program that works within Microsoft Word, allowing Word to be used as an World Wide Web browsing and authoring tool.

The major benefits of HTML are:

1. A standard look and feel to published documents on the Internet.
2. A public-domain file format, allowing nonprogrammers to create simple HTML documents.
3. Hyperlinks that connect related documents residing on different computers.

INSIDE HTML

What do HTML documents look like? All HTML documents are written in plain, ASCII text (Ill. 10.3) to ensure portability. No matter what type of computer or operating system is used, HTML documents can be read and written easily.

The ASCII format is discussed in more detail in Chapter 4, Tools of the Architect.

When displayed by some browsers, hyperlinks exhibit another important behavior. Using Netscape's browser, for example, hyperlinks previously accessed are displayed in a different color than those that have not yet been explored. This visual memory of paths already traveled is important and helps the user avoid unnecessarily repeating a search.

HTML is a fairly new language, and browsing HTML documents on the World Wide Web using Mosaic or other browsers certainly has limitations. They include:

1. Some information types, such as images and animations, rely on viewing software to be resident on the computer being used to browse the Web. If the computer does not contain the required viewing software, the resources cannot be accessed.

2. Hyperlinks are easily broken. If you are an author, the burden is on you to audit the links in your documents from time to time to make sure the resources they refer to still exist.
3. You cannot display part of one HTML document within another, as you can with OLE or OpenDoc.
4. Multimedia documents containing images can appear slowly using ordinary telephone lines, and require faster,

HTML Display

Illustration 10.3 *HTML source and display. Note the use of the <A> notation to create hyperlinks between different documents. Text enclosed between <A> and </A> is shown underlined. When the user clicks on the hyperlink, the referenced HTML document is displayed.*

HTML Source

```
<html>
<head>
<title>Apple Research and Technology</title>

</head>
<body>
<img src="http://www.apple.com/images/mainheader.gif" alt="Apple Computer"> <br>
<H1>Apple Research and Technology</H1>
<hr>

<DL>

<DT><STRONG>Apple's FCC Petition on wireless communications</STRONG>
        <DD>Read the <A HREF="/documents/fcc.html"> Petition for Rulemaking</A> Apple
        submitted to the <A HREF="http://www.fcc.gov/">Federal Communications
        Commission</A>.  The petition requests that the FCC create an "NII band" --
        a radio spectrum allocation that would permit high-speed data communications
        for schools, libraries, community groups, businesses, and institutions.  The
        petition details the improvements in communication which can be expected as
        a result of this allocation.
```

more expensive connections for quick display. Fortunately, most browsers will allow a user to scroll a page's text while waiting for its accompanying images to be displayed.

Software developers are working to enrich the multimedia vocabulary of HTML. Netscape Communications, for example, is integrating Macromedia's Director software into Netscape's browser, allowing animations and sounds to be played directly off the World Wide Web without having to download them first to the user's computer.

LOCAL HTML

HTML and Mosaic were invented to provide a standardized method to publish and browse graphically rich information resources on the World Wide Web. However, HTML is also a potential standard language with which to publish in-house information resources and provides consistency between in-house resources and external World Wide Web resources. Using HTML across the board simplifies publication and access for everyone inside an architectural firm: people who learn to navigate or develop in-house HTML resources are well prepared to browse or publish on the World Wide Web, and vice versa.

The hybrid technique of using hyperlinks with an organized, hierarchical information structure is discussed in more detail in Chapter 9, Organizing the Knowledge Base.

At ZGF, we are currently developing the organizational umbrella to our project archives in HTML. Using NetScape's HTML browser, architects can sift through project descriptions, tunnel into more detailed information based on their specific interest, and jump to related projects using hyperlinks. Underlying the relatively informal, unstructured HTML documents, of course, are highly structured and well-organized sets of hierarchical information resources. The HTML hyperlinks provide logical connections between related pieces of information that may be disconnected within a hierarchical file system.

HOOKING UP TO THE INTERNET

Browsing the World Wide Web requires a fast modem or, if your firm can afford it, a direct digital connection to an Internet service provider. If you use a modem, you will also need software on your computer that supports SLIP (Serial Line Internet Protocol) or PPP (Point to Point Protocol), which support Internet communication over ordinary phone lines. (Windows 95 provides built-in support for these protocols.) If you have an in-house E-mail system for your office that you want to extend to the Internet, you will need an Internet gateway product that supports SMTP (Simple Mail Transport Protocol). Most E-mail software programs provide such an option.

Speed is an important factor. Transmission or graphically rich Web pages at 9600 bits/sec. or 14.4 K bits/sec., the speed of many older modems, can be painful. Newer 28.8-K modems are a sound investment. Table 10.1 lists typical connection options provided by Internet service providers in Portland, Oregon.

The 56-K ISDN (Integrated Services Digital Network) lines are fully digital, so they don't require modems, but they do require the use of other special equipment to connect your computer network to them. The cost of the hardware can range from $2000 to $5000. Local 56-K leased lines are more expensive, and typically cost around $200 per month in 1995. Internet service providers typically also charge higher access rates for 56-K support.

The term T1 describes 24 56-K lines used in parallel, providing a total potential throughput of 1.544 megabits per second. T1 lines can be leased from a variety of long-distance telephone providers (AT&T, MCI, Sprint, et al.) and their cost primarily depends on the distance between sites. T1 is beyond

Table 10.1 Connection Options of Internet Service Providers

SERVICE OPTION (BITS/SEC.)	PHONE SERVICE	INTERNET SERVICE
14.4 K Dialup Service using SLIP/PPP	Free	$10–$20/mo.
28.8 K Dialup Service using SLIP/PPP	Free	$20/mo.
14.4 K Dedicated	$25/mo.	$75/mo.
56 K Frame Relay (shared)	$100/mo.	$350/mo.
56 K Dedicated	$200/mo.	$350/mo.
Partial T1 (128 Kb, 256 Kb, 512 Kb)	Varies	Varies
Full T1 (24 56 K lines = 1.544 Mb)	Varies	Varies

the financial reach of most architects, although many larger firms employ T1 to provide high-speed network connections between multiple offices. Some service providers also offer partial T1, allowing you to lease 128 Kb, 256 Kb, or 512 Kb of capacity on a T1 line. High-quality video-teleconferencing generally requires 128 Kb.

One advantage of a digital leased line is its ability to carry both voice and data. In a T1 installation, for example, 22 of the 24 lines could be configured to handle data traffic, while two lines could be reserved for voice traffic. Any long-distance phone call placed on the voice line would not incur additional charges. For architectural firms with multiple offices, where phone charges can run into the hundreds, or even thousands of dollars per month, T1 can provide not only high-speed data communication between offices, but also reduce the cost of long-distance phone calls between offices. Depending on the hardware installed at each office site, the lines available for voice are either prewired or allocated dynamically depending on the voice-traffic demands.

Although the benefits of leased lines are simple—high-speed data communications between offices and potential long-distance phone call savings—the configuration and installation of the services can be quite complicated. Most firms will want to enlist the services of an outside consultant experienced in the design and installation of wide-area networks and voice/data connectivity.

Keep in mind that until high-speed communication lines are more affordable, delivering digital data to third parties using physical media is still an economically viable option for large information sets. Fully developed digital descriptions of complex projects, for example, do not transfer quickly over phone lines. The rather low-tech method of sending 50 megabytes of CAD drawings across the country on a removable hard disk cartridge or optical disk via FedEx still makes more sense than a five-hour long-distance phone call transmitting the data using a 28.8-K modem.

LOCATING INFORMATION

The difficulty of finding information on the Internet is directly proportional to the breadth and scope of information published there. Although many bookstores sell various "Internet Yellow Pages," they are usually incomplete and too generic, and quickly fall out of date.

Various information "searching engines" are available on the Internet for people to use freely. One of the earliest was Lycos, developed at Carnegie Mellon University, which allows users to search on document titles, headings, links, and keywords within a document (Ill. 10.4). The June 1995 Lycos database contained over 4.3 million documents. The Lycos index is built by a Web crawler, a software agent that navigates the Internet and retrieves up to 5000 documents per day to add to the database. The Lycos database is so popular that it is frequently overloaded; the best time to access it is on the weekend or at nights (Ill. 10.5). Subscribers to The Microsoft Network can also access the Lycos database, which Microsoft has licensed from Carnegie Mellon.

A listing of World Wide Web sites of potential interest to architects, compiled by Jeanne Brown, the Architecture Studies Librarian at the University of Nevada, Las Vegas, can be found in this book's appendix.

Many other search engines have been developed for the Internet. A few of interest are:

What does Lycos mean? Lycos is the first five letters of the Latin name for Wolf Spider, an appropriate name for a program which crawls the World Wide Web in search of documents.

SERVICE	URL
All-In-One Search Page	http://www.albany.net/~wcross/all1srch.html
CityScape On-Line Directory	http://www.gold.net/gold/
EINet Galaxy	http://www.einet.net/
Harvest Broker	http://rd.cs.colorado.edu/brokers/www-home-pages/query.html
Jumpstation	http://js.stir.ac.uk/jsbin/js
Pointers to Pointers	http://www.homecom.com
SavvySearch	http://www.cs.colostate.edu/~dreiling/smartform.html
Spry Internet Wizard	http://www.spry.com/wizard/index.html

Wandex	http://www.netgen.com/cgi/wandex
World Wide Web Worm	http://www.cs.colorado.edu/home/mcbryan/WWWW.html
Yahoo	http://www.yahoo.com/search.html

Illustration 10.4 *Lycos search engine.*

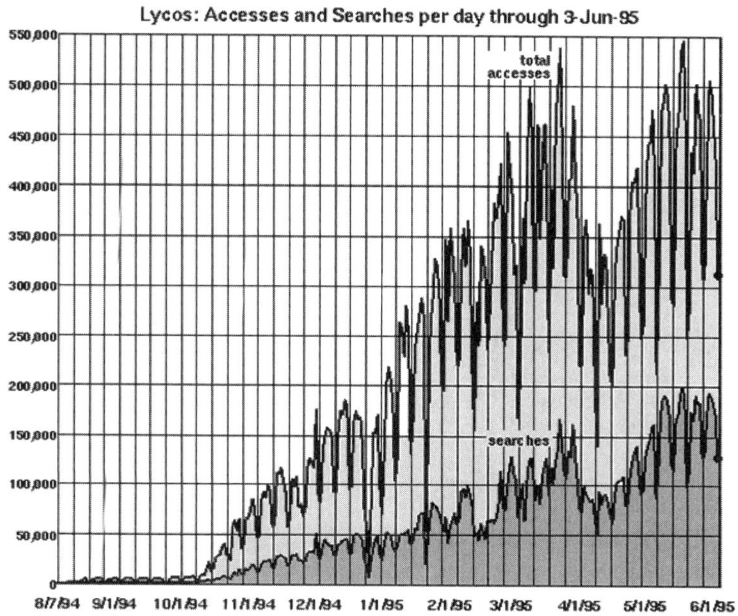

Illustration 10.5 *Lycos usage.*

The best approach to locating information of interest on the Internet is to build your own index. Most World Wide Web browsers support the use of bookmarks (Ill. 10.6), allowing the user to record places of interest for later perusal. In addition, you may want to construct your own HTML Home Page with links to useful resources outside the firm.

E-MAIL

Many architectural firms have long used E-mail software as an in-house communication tool, as well as E-mail supported by commercial on-line services. Unfortunately, until a couple of years ago, E-mail exchanges on commercial on-line services were limited to the subscribers of that service. If you were a subscriber to CompuServe, for example, you could send E-mail only to other CompuServe users. If you subscribed to America On-Line, you could send E-mail only to other America On-Line users. This early balkanization of on-line services limited their usefulness as general-purpose communication tools. The situa-

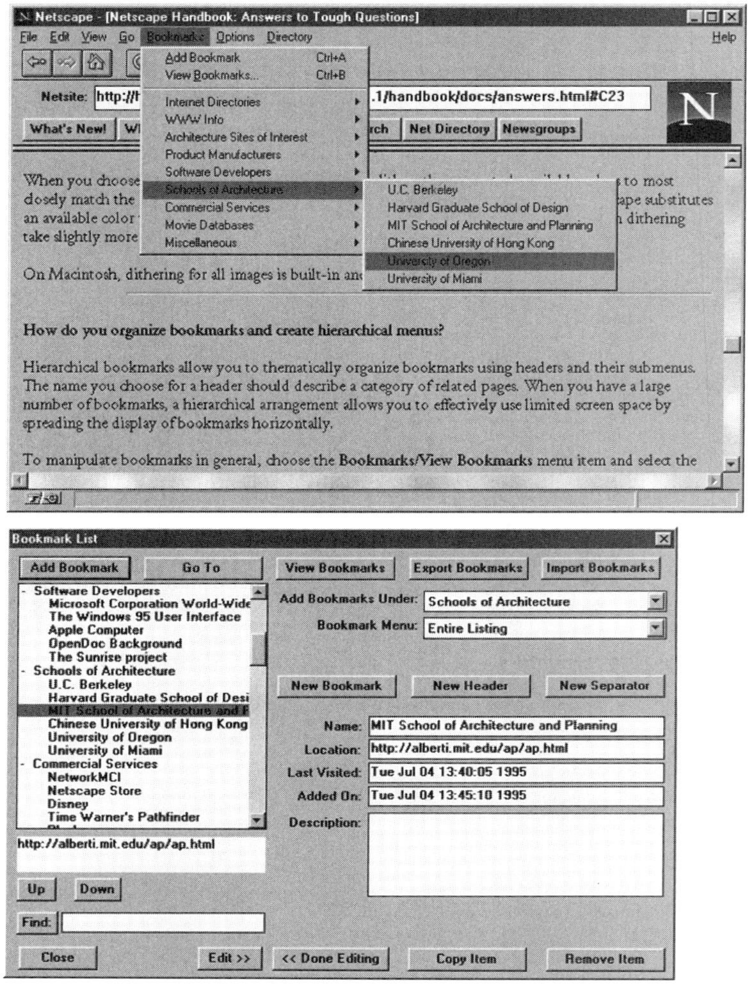

Illustration 10.6 Bookmarks.

tion was tantamount to having several phones on your desk, each one of which had its own private phone book. It was not unusual for people who used such services frequently to have several E-mail addresses.

After the Internet was opened up to commercial access, virtually all on-line services provided links to it, allowing the exchange of E-mail to Internet addresses. Today, users of different private on-line services can exchange E-mail, using the Internet as the intermediate delivery tool. For example, an America On-line user can send E-mail to a CompuServe user by using an

Internet address such as 75202.1244@compuserve.com. The number is the individual's CompuServe account number, and compuserve.com identifies the Internet host that routes E-mail to the CompuServe network.

If all this sounds more complicated to you than it should be, you're right. The beauty of the telephone is that a long time ago everyone around the planet pretty much agreed what phone numbers should look like. In the United States, it doesn't matter whether your local service provider is U.S. West, Pacific Telesis, or Southwestern Bell; phone numbers look the same. (This was a benevolent artifact of AT&T's monopoly. Since the breakup of AT&T, long-distance dialing has become more complicated.) Fortunately, most of the idiosyncratic naming conventions of E-mail addresses can be sheltered from users by including them in address books and allowing users to send mail by simply clicking their names from an address book.

The typical Internet E-mail address has at least three fields. The first field is an abbreviated user name. The second field is the Internet host name, typically the computer that runs the mail software. The third field is an institutional descriptor of the host: .com for commercial, edu for educational, and mil for military. For example: ksanders@teleport.com.

Today, many desktop E-mail programs, including MacMail, the Exchange client of Windows 95, and E-Mail Connection (Ill. 10.7), provide universal E-mail access, allowing messages, regardless of their origin, to be collected and displayed to the user in a consistent way. Slowly but surely, the arcane, obscure interfaces of older, character-based E-mail systems are approaching the uniformity and ease of use of the phone. Indeed, PC applications are available today that will also record voice-mail messages along with E-mail. As such, the utility and value of E-mail systems has increased dramatically over the past several years.

The major benefits of E-mail are:

1. Asynchronous communication
2. One-to-many communication
3. Digital capture of messages (filtering, organizing, searching)

Asynchronous is a fancy word to describe events whose timing does not depend on each other. A phone call, for example, is a synchronous form of communication. A person must be on the other end for a conversation to take place. E-mail, on the other hand, is asynchronous. Both sender and receiver can exchange messages and information at their own convenience.

E-mail also has the fundamental advantage over phone, mail, or fax in that one-to-many communication is just as easy as one-to-one communication. Sending an E-mail message to twenty people requires little additional effort compared to sending the message to one person. Copying or forwarding a message literally requires the push of a few buttons. The upside is improved turn-around time; the downside, of course, is increased volume.

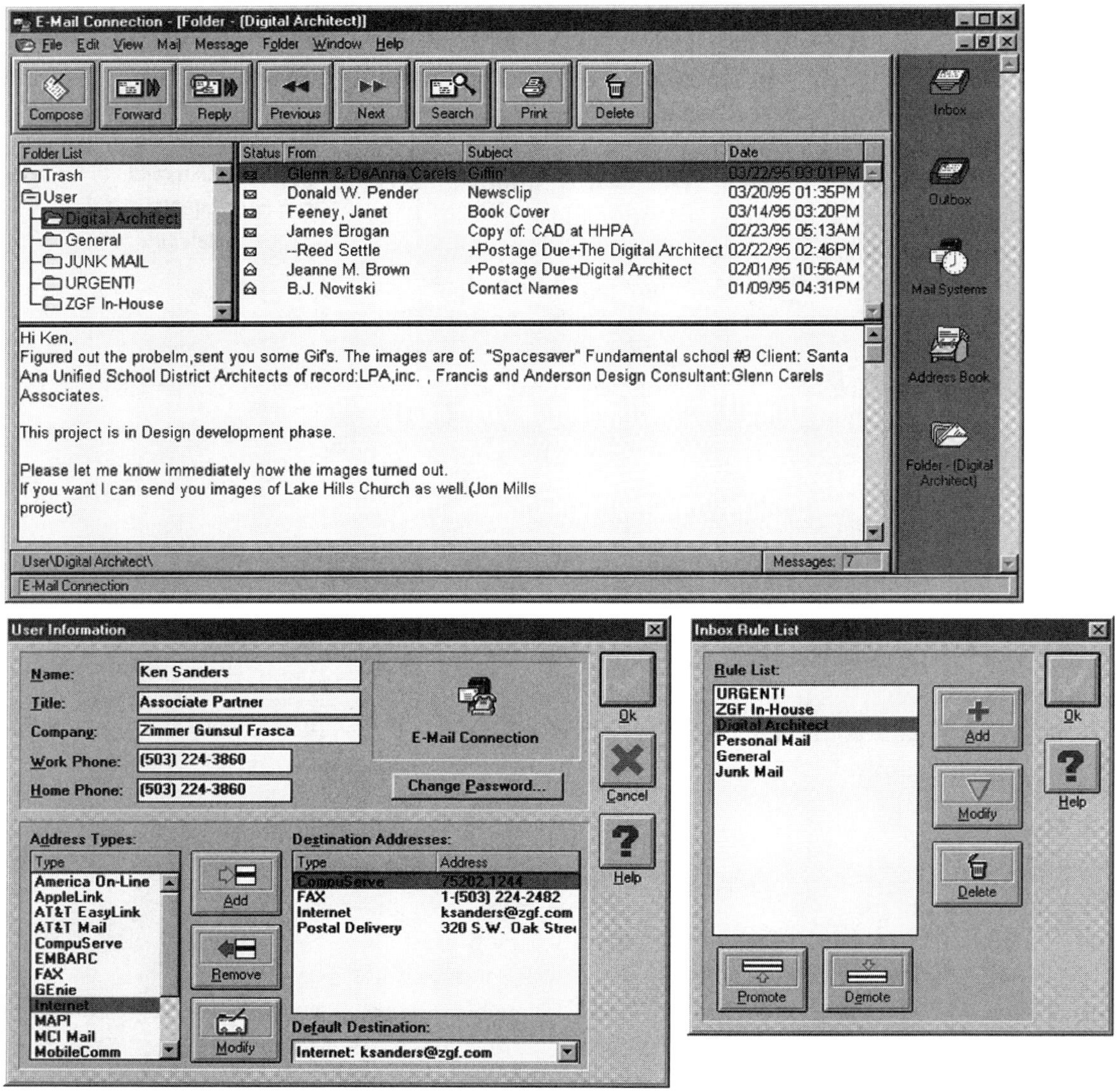

Illustration 10.7 *E-mail connection.*

The investment of time required to send physical mail or make phone calls to multiple parties imposes a discipline on those who initiate communication. The investment is a built-in regulator that prevents too much communication. With E-mail, the regulator disappears. As a result, architects using E-mail to support project work must learn to carefully manage the volume of messaging, and not subject project team members and clients to information overload.

Good E-mail software can provide some relief from this potential overload. Since E-mail messages arrive in digital form, they can be filtered, organized, sorted, searched, or ignored according to the needs of the recipient. Most E-mail clients have simple rule systems built into them, allowing the user to automatically direct messages from different sources into different in-boxes. A project manager who is involved in several jobs simultaneously, for example, may define a set of rules to redirect the message from any member of a project team into a project in-box. Most E-mail systems also provide basic searching tools, so that it is relatively easy to locate and review all the meeting minutes that have to do with, say, "Bentonite" or "exterior glazing."

The impact of E-mail on the architect, and its contribution to "No Excuses, No Escape," is discussed in more detail in Chapter 1, The Impact of Technology on the Practice.

COMMERCIAL ON-LINE SERVICES

A variety of commercial on-line services are available to architects, in addition to the public network of the Internet. For those architects who only require E-mail access, or who are waiting for the World Wide Web to achieve a larger base of useful information before hooking up, private on-line services provide an inexpensive alternative. Three types of private on-line services are available to architects:

1. Commercial on-line services, such as CompuServe, America On-Line, The Microsoft Network, Prodigy, Delphi, and MCI Mail
2. Reprographics E-mail networks, such as C4 and Freenet
3. Architecture-specific on-line services, such as AIA Online

Each of the commercial on-line services offers similar services including E-mail (with Internet connectivity), user groups, forums, or chat rooms. The typical monthly cost is relatively inexpensive—less than $10—although access to many forums and other services are provided at an extra cost per minute of connect time, including most software and hardware support forums. Each provides local access numbers so that users do not incur long-distance phone charges to access their services.

The two most popular on-line services are CompuServe and America On-Line, each with about 3 million subscribers. Compared to America On-Line, which has primarily targeted the consumer market, CompuServe appears to enjoy a higher number of business users (Ill. 10.8). Both provide a wide range of overlapping and redundant services, so architects should consider subscribing to only one.

Most commercial on-line services also provide Internet access. CompuServe's 1995 acquisition of Spry, for example, allowed the company to integrate Spry's World Wide Web browser into CompuServe's software (Ill. 10.9). The advantage of using a commercial on-line service to access the Internet is the availability of local phone access numbers. If you are traveling, it is less expensive to access the Internet through a local phone number provided by the commercial on-line service,

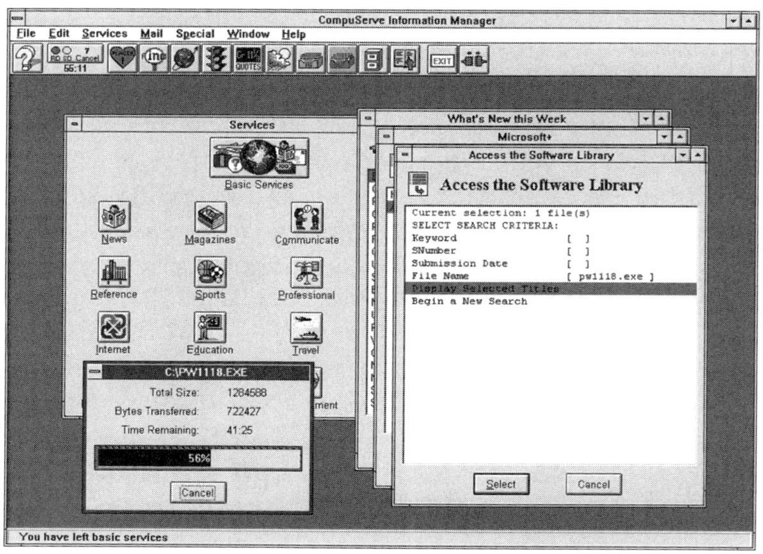

Illustration 10.8 Software support via CompuServe.

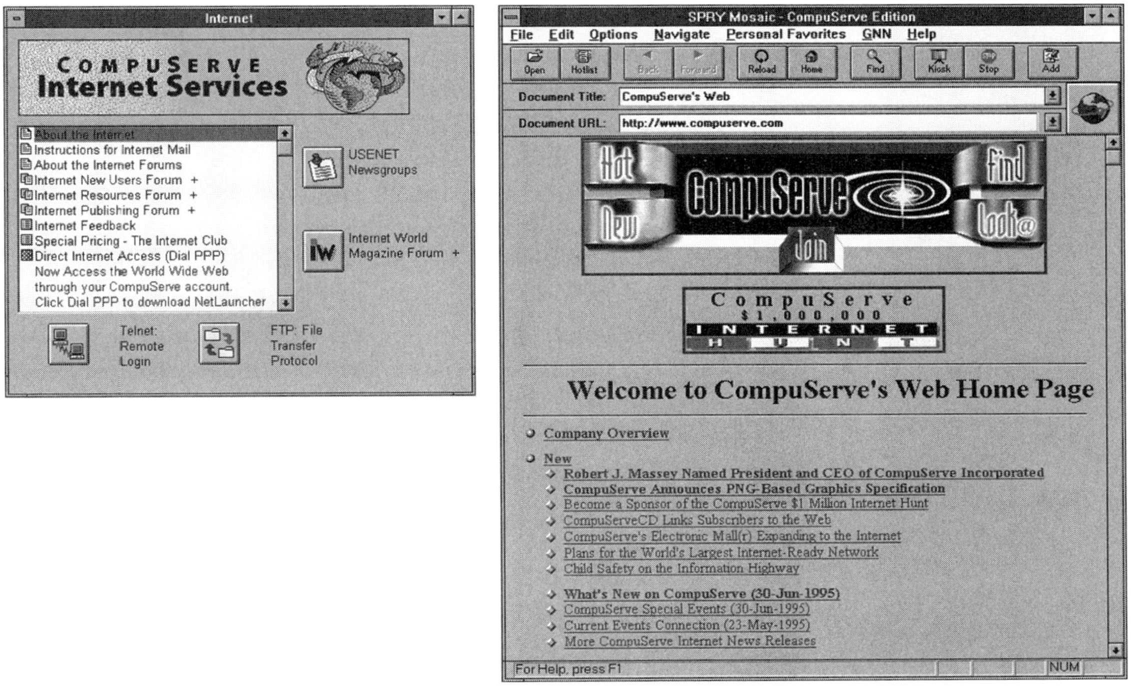

Illustration 10.9 *World Wide Web browsing using CompuServe.*

instead of dialing a long-distance number back to your local Internet service provider.

MCI Mail simplifies phone access even further for travelers by providing one 800 number for nationwide access to their services. In 1995, MCI Mail cost $35 a month, plus $.50 per message sent. MCI also offers business services, such as the ability to send faxes from E-mail, including your company's letterhead and sender's signature, as well as access to Dow Jones news services and business wires.

REPROGRAPHICS E-MAIL NETWORKS

Two private E-mail networks, C4 and Freenet, were established in the 1980s with the cooperation of reprographics service bureaus around the United States to allow design professionals to transmit CAD drawings over phone lines for plotting. Today, many architects and their consultants also use these networks to send and retrieve CAD drawings between each other. Reprographics service bureaus maintain computer hubs at their offices, which act as shared post-office boxes, allowing the architect or consultant to send a single set of CAD drawings to multiple parties at one time.

Because they were originally designed to handle relatively large CAD drawings for plotting, and provide built-in compression tools that reduce transmission time, C4 and Freenet are well-suited for sending large amounts of digital data to third parties (Ill. 10.10). (Most E-mail systems require the user to compress files manually using PKZIP or other software before attaching them to E-mail messages.) Updated releases in 1995 for both programs provide contemporary, easy-to-use Windows interfaces. Compared to commercial on-line services, however, the cost of these reprographics E-mail networks services is expensive ($50 to $80 per month in 1995), and no local access phone numbers are provided.

AIA ONLINE

AIA Online is a resource sponsored by the American Institute of Architects and is available to any AIA member who is willing to pay the monthly connect-time charges (Ill. 10.11). Most architects use AIA Online to get access the *Commerce Business Daily* several days before the printed version. The cost in 1995: a $5

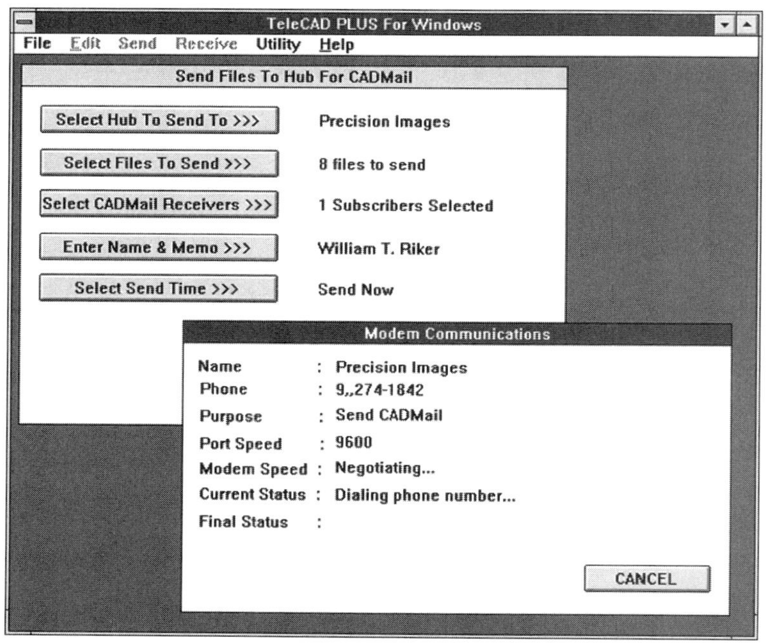

Illustration 10.10 TeleCAD's C4 network software.

start-up fee and $.14 per minute for connect time. A small but growing number of architects are connecting to the service, which provides a variety of digital resources:

1. *Commerce Business Daily* database includes the requests for proposals published by the U.S. Department of Commerce for architectural services procured by the federal government. A simple query tool is provided, allowing the user to search requests for proposals relating to a particular building type or geographical location.
2. Construction Market Data (CMD) Early Planning Reports, updated twice monthly
3. Business newswires, such as UPI, Chicago Tribune, Reuters, and others updated daily.
4. AIA press releases.
5. Building product sources, including a large database of building product manufacturers searchable by product name, Masterformat (CSI) section number, or company name and address.
6. Professional Interest Area (PIA) forums. Most of the PIAs maintain forums on AIA Online. The forums are used to distribute information about PIA programs, as well as provide bulletin board services for members to exchange information. (Not surprisingly, the most active forum is the one sponsored by the Computer-Aided Practice PIA.)
7. Basic E-mail services between subscribers of AIA Online.
8. AIA white pages, listing the name, address, telephone, and chapter affiliation of each of the 55,000 members of the AIA.
9. ProFile, a directory of architectural design firms in the United States, with more than 13,000 entries.
10. Miscellaneous publication indexes, including ADA, ASTM, MasterSpec, and others.

Prior to 1995, the major limitation of AIA Online was its relatively crude DOS interface and its closed E-mail, which did not provide connections to the Internet or other external E-mail systems. Recently, AIA Online introduced an improved Windows interface and E-mail connectivity to the Internet, allowing Internet users to send E-mail to AIA Online subscribers, and vice versa. Unfortunately, AIA Online has yet to attract a large percentage of AIA members. In mid-1995, only about 1000 members per month were accessing the service.

The AIA also publishes an on-line resource on the World Wide Web (Ill. 10.12). The AIA considers its home page to be a resource available to the general public, while AIA Online is a private, members-only resource. Unfortunately, AIA members must use both services to get what they need—another example of the balkanization of the information superhighway. Although

Illustration 10.11 *AIA Online.*

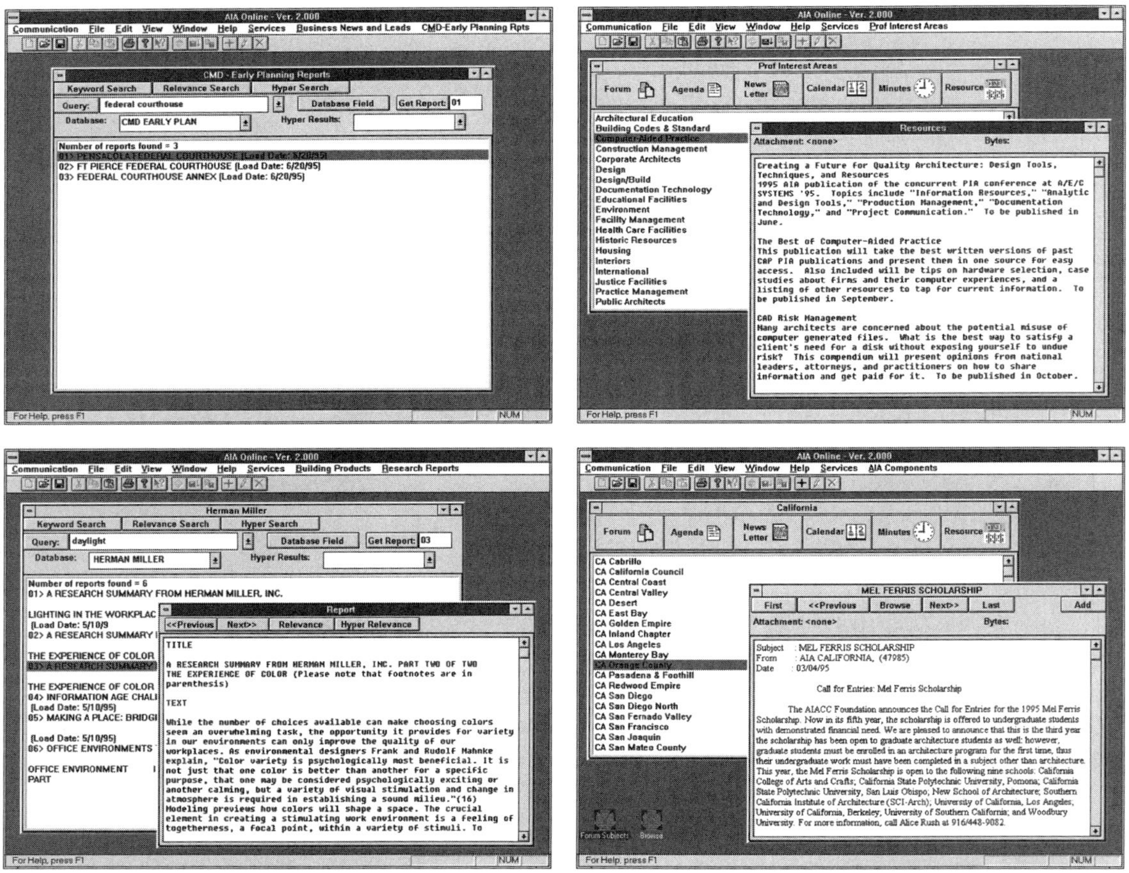

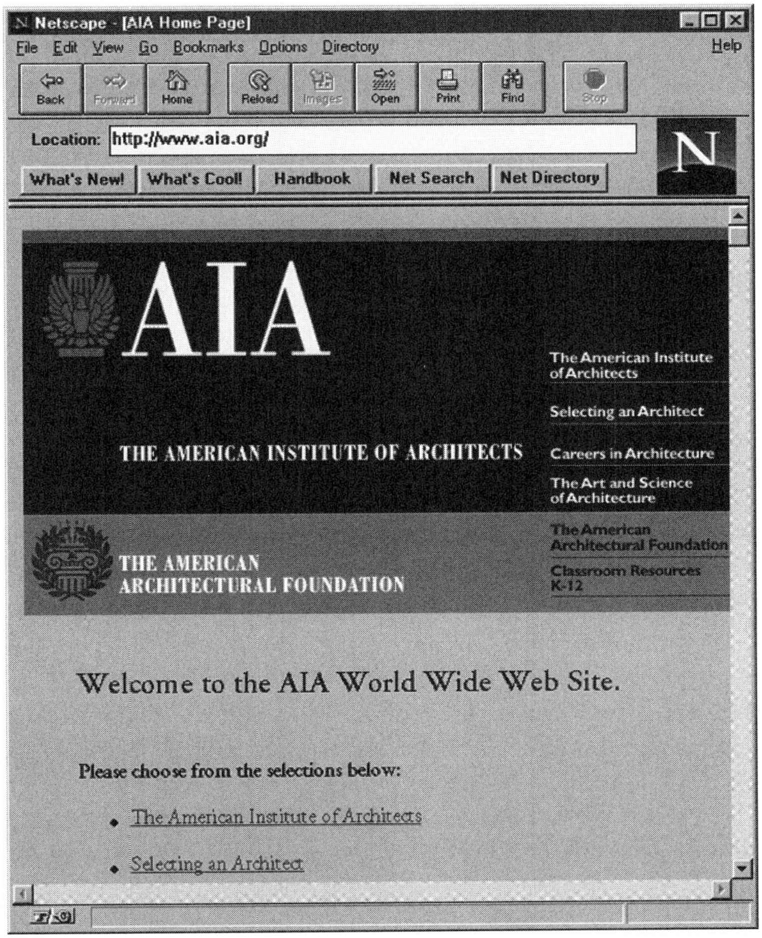

Illustration 10.12 The AIA's World Wide Web home page (http://www.aia.org).

the AIA does not plan to merge the two services into a single World Wide Web resource, they do plan to allow AIA members to directly access one from the other.

THE ECONOMICS OF ON-LINE PUBLISHING

AIA Online and the AIA's World Wide Web home page are examples of the emerging distinction between private and public on-line digital information. The Internet is inherently a public resource; indeed, its openness and editorial self-enforcement is a key part of the Internet culture and heritage. (A small fraction of digital information created by government, educational, or private institutions is actually available on the Internet; such information must be placed there by someone who is willing to make it public.) CompuServe, America OnLine, and others, in contrast, are private resources, although they are generally open to anyone who pays the monthly access charge. Although some have predicted that the Internet eventually will become the one and only information superhighway, private networks and on-line information resources likely will continue to coexist alongside the Internet.

One example of private on-line communication is that between product manufacturer and reseller. Wal-Mart, for example, uses bar codes on all of its products. As each product is sold, the company's inventory is immediately updated. Rather than keeping track of inventory levels, Wal-Mart allows vendors such as Procter & Gamble on-line access to its inventory database. It is the responsibility of Procter & Gamble, not Wal-Mart, to keep its product inventories at the appropriate level. In effect, by using direct, on-line communication, Wal-Mart has delegated that responsibility to its vendor and avoided a tremendous amount of paper shuffle.

Ultimately, most architects, their consultants, and even their clients will communicate in a similar fashion. Not every design iteration on an architectural project will be posted to an on-line database, of course. A sales transaction is a discrete, identifiable event—few architectural design iterations are. But allowing consultants and clients on-line access to posted work in progress will not be unusual in a few years and will help shift the responsibility for accessing up-to-date design information from the architect to the consultant. At the same time, clients will also hold their architects more accountable for generating information efficiently and in a timely fashion.

The key to the economic viability of private, commercial on-line services is their publication of unique, valuable, proprietary information not available on the Internet. The biggest long-term challenge to CompuServe, America On-Line, AIA Online, and others is to communicate what proprietary sources of published information justify their separate balkanized existence and additional access charges.

Does some of this seem like déjà vu? Interestingly, the relationship between commercial on-line service companies and content providers is very much like that of cable TV companies and content providers. The owners of cable licenses in a region offer subscriptions to households to receive their cable TV signal. They also contract with content providers (ESPN, Disney, Discovery Channel, HBO et al.) to include their programs on their cable channels to provide incentives for people to subscribe to the monthly service. Similarly, some information publishers are paid by private services such as America On-Line and CompuServe to publish on their services. This is how information publishers can earn a living publishing on line: they are not paid directly by the customer, but by the commercial on-line service provider. High-demand publications will have a higher market value.

No such economic structure exists on the Internet, which is a publishing free-for-all. Individuals on their own can publish information or post advertisements to sell products or services. The Internet is more analogous to broadcast TV, where advertisements are combined with information and entertainment. Unlike commercial on-line services, there is little money to be made by publishing digital products on the Internet unless advertising is interleaved. As a result, most content on the Internet will be one of three types: intellectual property donated to the public domain, marketing literature and advertisements that point to off-line products and services, and on-line shopping via credit card or debit card. Table 10.2 summarizes the various economic models of content distribution via analog video channels compared to digital on-line channels.

Where does the architect fit into all of this? Architects both subscribe to information (e.g., *Sweet's Catalog File,* building codes, design manuals, *Architectural Graphic Standards,* and professional journals), and publish information (e.g., marketing brochures, articles in professional journals, and monographs). The Internet, specifically the World Wide Web, represents a new subscription and publication medium for architects, one that provides graphically rich, up-to-date information at low cost. For thousands of architectural building materials and systems manufacturers, the Internet will become the publishing medium of choice.

Table 10.2 Economic Models of Content Distribution

ECONOMIC MODEL	ANALOG VIDEO	DIGITAL ON-LINE
Subscribers donate money to distributor	PBS	N/A
Distributor provides public service	C-SPAN	Commercial forums,[a] chat rooms
Subscriber pays distributor, who pays publisher	HBO, Showtime	Commercial services
Advertiser pays distributor, who pays publisher	Broadcast TV	WWW[b] Magazines
Advertiser *is* publisher	Infomercials	WWW Commercial Home Pages
Subscriber *is* publisher	Public access TV	WWW Personal Home Pages

[a]Commercial forums and services include those provided by private on-line services such as CompuServe, America On-Line, The Microsoft Network, Prodigy, Delphi, and MCI Mail.
[b]WWW is The Internet's World Wide Web.

The AIA Code of Ethics discourages members from advertising their services. Is placing a portfolio of work on the Internet considered advertising by the AIA? Apparently not. The AIA's home page contains hyperlinks to the home pages of many architectural firms.

Clearly, the Internet is changing the rules of the game. Anyone who is simply a broker for information (including architects) must be concerned about the long-term viability of their business, or at least its current economic model. This includes travel agents and real estate agents, who charge hefty fees for providing access to proprietary databases. Self-help travel reservations are already on line. In the future, real estate databases with browsing tools will allow buyers to filter current listings based on budget and interest. In the age of on-line global information access, those who have acted as proprietary gatekeepers to information must learn new ways to provide value.

CD-ROM RESOURCES

As the balance between physical and digital information resources begins to shift toward the latter, by the end of the decade the typical architect will no longer need to stock and maintain shelves full of printed product catalogs, constantly refreshing sections as they are made available by the manufacturer. Instead, the architect will use the Internet and other private on-line resources to access more timely information. Product manufacturers and distributors will find digital publishing a far less expensive alternative to producing catalogs and distributing updates. The benefit to the architect will be not only more convenient and timely information, but also elimination of the hassle and expense of managing a printed library. In the digital world, the task of updating is appropriately the burden of the information publisher, not the information subscriber.

Unfortunately, external on-line resources provide timely information and convenient access but not (yet) high throughput. Downloading CAD drawings or high-resolution, full-color images can take minutes, sometimes hours, even with fast modems. Although faster fiber-optic network infrastructures are currently under construction, it will be several years at least before high-speed network access is available in the same way that phone access is available today.

CD-ROM resources exchange information timeliness for faster access. Quad-speed CD-ROM disk drives, now standard equipment for most desktop computers, provide throughput and performance that are substantially faster than what can be achieved on line, even using expensive 56-K ISDN lines. There is a vast body of graphics-intensive information (standard specifications, manufacturers catalogs, etc.) that doesn't change hour by hour, but for which monthly or quarterly updates are reasonable. For those types of information, in-house networked or desktop CD-ROM resources are a reasonable alternative to external on-line resources.

Although CD-ROM resources have been available to architects for years, only recently have they begun to fulfill their potential as ordinary, day-to-day information tools. CD-ROM resources introduced in the early 1990s, such as Electronic Sweet's and Eclat, failed to generate much professional interest and sales for two reasons. First, CD-ROM drives had not yet become the low-cost, ubiquitous desktop devices that they are today. (1994 was the first year that more personal computers were shipped with CD-ROM drives than without them.) Second, most of the early information resources were incomplete versions of the printed resources they were designed to supplant, and many architects found them frustrating to use. Most people try to use the fewest information resources possible to do their job effectively, regardless of the media. Until a digital resource contains the same amount of information as its hard-copy sibling, architects typically will tend to use the printed media alone rather than traverse between both.

Not all CD-ROM resources need to be kept truly on line in a networked environment. The small architectural firm may find that an easily accessible shelf of CD-ROMs combined with a CD-ROM drive in every desktop computer is a reasonable and practical alternative to networked CD drives or jukeboxes. Larger firms will use a combination of on-line, near-line, and off-line CD-ROM resources.

Types of optical disk hardware are discussed in Chapter 7. The concept of on-line, near-line, and off-line storage is discussed in Chapter 9.

Most CD-ROM information resources available today fall into one of four categories:

- Industry-wide information guidelines (e.g., AIA/EDS, Construction Criteria Base)
- Industry-wide catalogs containing a broad collection of manufacturers (e.g., SweetSource)
- Narrow-market catalogs with custom design tools (e.g., Roger East Design)
- Single manufacturer catalogs with custom design tools (e.g., Marvin Design System)

The good news is that all of these information resources are available today on the same digital media: CD-ROMs. The bad news is that most have different user interfaces and different organizational structures. The problem of unfamiliarity confronting the architect seeking digital information is potentially worse than the well-known problem of browsing printed product catalogs whose graphics formats, table conventions, and organizational structure vary from catalog to catalog, making apples-to-apples comparisons difficult. With CD-ROM, something as simple as turning the page may be different as well. Some CD-ROMs, for example, support hyperlinks, and some do not. Some use a system compatible with the built-in help viewer of the personal computer's operating system, and some do not. Unlike the Internet's World Wide Web, the consistency and organization of CD-ROM information resources presented to the architect leave much room for improvement.

Although the gap between CD-ROM digital information and printed versions is narrowing, it has not yet reached the point where architects can rely on CD-ROM and on-line resources exclusively. For the next several years, most architects will still require the use of both digital and printed information resources, which may complicate, not simplify, information access. Ultimately, internal CD-ROM libraries combined with external on-line resources will provide a powerful digital information resource for architects. The question is not if, but when. Like most technology revolutions, however, this one still has a few more years to reach its maturity. In the meantime, there is a growing collection of useful CD-ROM resources that architects are well advised to explore.

There are few things less impressive to a client visiting an architectural office than hearing "who's got the Pella catalog?" shouted over a partition or broadcast over the intercom. On-line resources promise to help architects avoid searching for information in time-consuming and potentially embarrassing ways. With CD-ROMs, however, the reverse may also be true, since they are more easily misplaced than catalogs and can easily be hidden out of view within the drive bay of a desktop computer. Successful use of CD-ROM resources not on the network requires additional discipline on the part of the people who share them. "Who's got the Pella CD?" is not much of an improvement.

SWEETSOURCE

The CD-ROM resource familiar to most architects is SweetSource (formerly Electronic Sweet's), which contains a comprehensive index of the products contained in the printed version of *Sweet's Catalog File* (Ill. 10.13). The CD-ROM version contains searching and querying tools, allowing the user to find information based on CSI number, manufacturer, trade name, product area index, or keyword. Perhaps its most valuable resource is the construction industry directory, which contains the name, address, phone, and fax numbers of thousands of building industry manufacturers.

SweetSource was originally introduced in 1990. Unfortunately, a relatively small minority of product manufacturers thus far have contributed digital information to the CD-ROM. Most products are only listed by manufacturer and trade name. In a listing of paint primers from the Winter 1994 edition, for example, only 35 of the 222 entries contained specific information about the product in question. Another 34 contained Manufacturer Showcase information, which is basically advertising with few useful specifics. Another search for continuous wire mesh reinforcing in a truss configuration revealed 33 entries, but only 4 contained product descriptions. Until there is a greater critical mass of information, many architects will likely continue to use their printed catalogs.

Sweet's also publishes CD-ROM catalog files for the following applications:

Accessible Building Products
Building and Security Systems
Canadian Construction
Civil/Structural Engineering and Retrofit
Contract Interiors

Illustration 10.13 *SweetSource.*

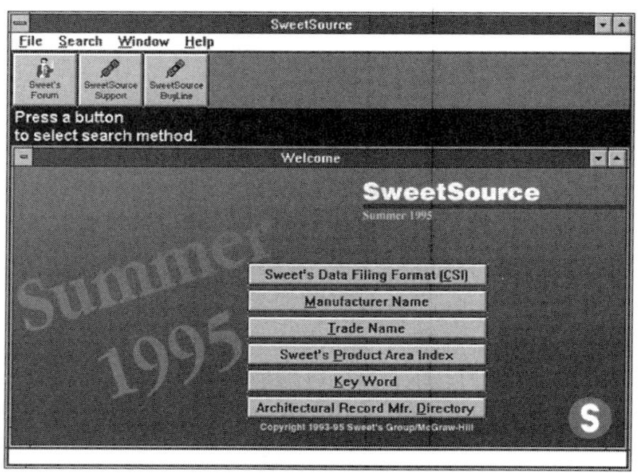

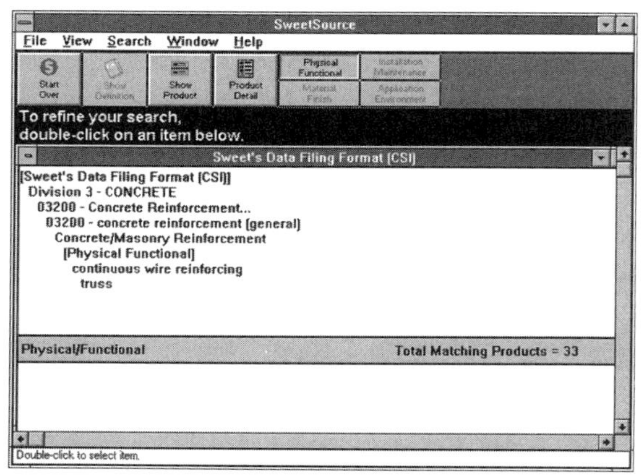

Electrical Engineering and Retrofit
Engineering and Retrofit
General Building and Renovation
Homebuilding and Remodeling
Industrial Construction and Renovation
International Building Products
Kitchen and Bath Source Book
Mechanical Engineering and Retrofit
Mexico/Latin America Special Focus Edition
Sweet's Light Sources

CONSTRUCTION CRITERIA BASE

The Construction Criteria Base (CCB) is a huge digital information resource published and maintained by the National Institute of Building Sciences (NIBS), available for either DOS or Windows (Ill. 10.14). The CCB is a collection of documents primarily relating to architectural work performed for federal government agencies. Digital versions of regulations such as ADA and OSHA's Safety and Health Regulations for Construction are included, as well as heavyweight digital tomes such as NAVFAC's CADD Standards, the Army's CADD Standards, and Tri-Services' GIS/Spatial Data Standards. Unless your firm engages in work for the federal government, the CCB may not be particularly useful, but it nevertheless provides fascinating background information on the complex (and sometimes

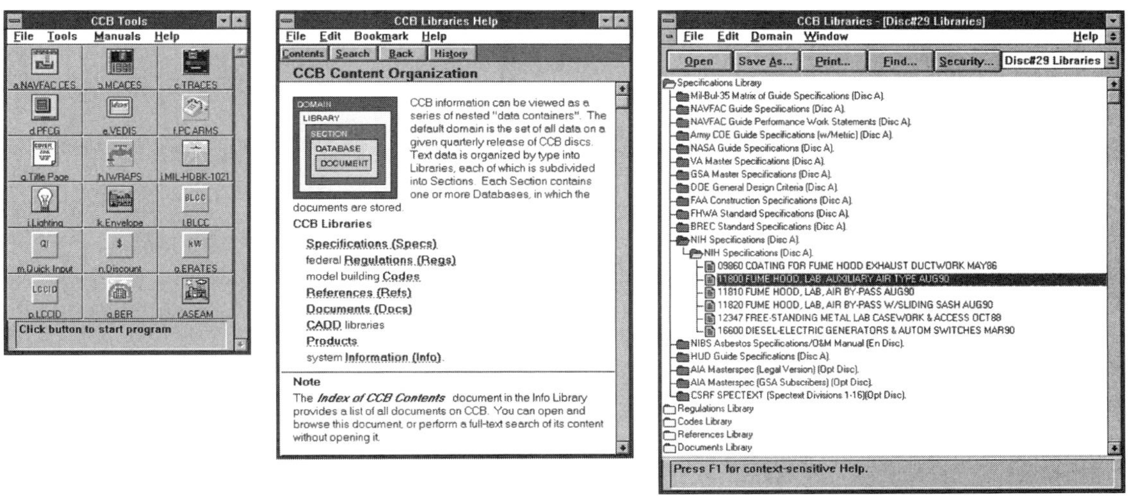

Illustration 10.14 *Construction Criteria Base.*

inconsistent) information guidelines used by various branches of the federal government.

The CCB also includes various software programs, such as the SPECSINTACT software that is required by some federal agencies for writing specifications, as well as other life-cycle costing, energy analysis, and value engineering programs. Unfortunately, most of the programs are aging DOS programs that are opaque to the casual user.

An interesting side note: the latest version of CCB's SPECS-INTACT Windows software includes a new editor that supports the Standard Generalized Markup Language (SGML), an international standard that provides a mechanism for defining and tagging elements within written documents. SGML is a sibling of HTML, the language used to create hyperlink documents on the Internet's World Wide Web. The feature set of HTML overlaps SGML, supporting only some of its annotation conventions but including hyperlinks and enhanced graphics. It will be interesting to observe the evolution of SGML and HTML to see if a new information publishing standard emerges for the creation of portable, browsable, plug-and-play written documents.

Optional CCB resources available for additional cost include:

- AIA MASTERSPEC
- Construction Sciences Research Foundation (CSRF) SPECTEXT
- ASTM Standards in Building Codes
- ACI Building Code Requirements for Reinforced and Structural Concrete
- BOCA National Code Series 1993
- SBCCI Standard Codes
- ICBO Uniform Codes

The mind-boggling scope of information in the CCB library, published on six CD-ROMs (not including optional software and resources), is perhaps its major limitation. Accessing the information often requires shuffling between different CDs, and the user frequently will not know which CD to insert until the software complains about the wrong one. The CCB is ideal for networked jukebox installation in larger firms, who appropriately populate its target market. Unfortunately, NIBS includes a networking disclaimer in its distribution materials and "makes no guarantees or claims as to the performance of CCB, for DOS or for Windows, on a network, or about CCB's effects on a network's performance." In other words, use the software on a network at your own risk. The Construction Criteria Base is an example of a raw digital information resource, where filtering is left to the user.

AIA/EDS

Although many clients prefer to use their own customized contracts for architectural services, the AIA's standard documents remain a well-recognized benchmark for agreements between the owner/architect, the architect/consultant, and the owner/contractor. Most architects, their attorneys, and their insurance providers are familiar with the provisions of the AIA's documents, the use of which can often expedite (and reduce the costs of) writing and reviewing agreements.

Even when the AIA documents are used as a starting point, however, the final agreements inevitably involve adjustments to the language. Retyping the agreement to include the additions or deletions requires proofing and rereading of the entire document by all the parties involved. Alternately, attaching an addendum outlining the changes to the standard agreement requires the reviewer to flip back and forth between the standard agreement and the addendum.

AIA/EDS provides a digital information resource and editing tool that allows architects to modify the AIA's documents as required yet still maintain the value of using a universally recognized standard (Ill. 10.15). Deletions from the contract are shown lined through; additions to the contract are shown underlined. Since all unaltered text is a word-for-word duplicate of the AIA standard document, the parties involved need not proof or reread contract sections with which they are already familiar. AIA/EDS also provides spreadsheet templates for using selected G-series documents, such as the Architect's Office and Project Forms.

The main limitation of AIA/EDS is its relatively crude word-processing interface, when compared with contemporary Windows or Macintosh word processors. The interface requires switching between text windows for editing and preview and is a bit awkward to use. Ironically, AIA/EDS is not yet available on

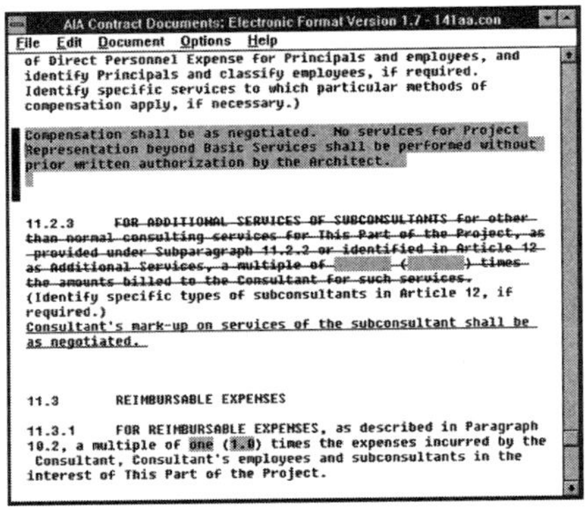

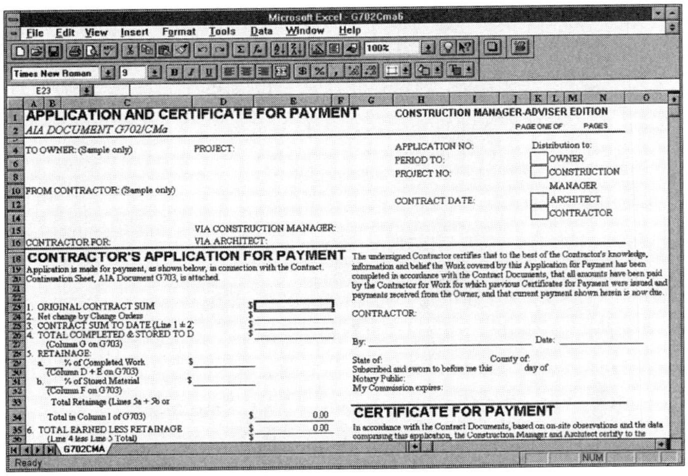

Illustration 10.15 *AIA/EDS.*

CD-ROM, and must be installed from a series of 3.5- or 5.25-inch diskettes. Nevertheless, many architects have found the value of a marked-up AIA standard contract worth the minor inconveniences.

HYBRID RESOURCES

Like the Construction Criteria Base published by NIBS, many CD-ROM resources are pushing beyond the concept of digital information containers and are also providing specialized design tools for use by architects. One example is the Marvin Design System, a software tool distributed by Marvin Windows used for window selection and layout (Ill. 10.16). The major limitation of tools such as the Marvin Design System is their linkage to a single manufacturer's proprietary product. The architect who wishes to remain flexible in terms of product selection is forced to learn a variety of inconsistent software programs, which limits the practical usefulness of each one. Such software is most appropriate for those architects who consistently specify the same product.

Prototype residential design software developed by Roger East Design is another excellent example of bundling a manufacturer's product descriptions with some nifty design tools and intelligent links to CAD (Ill. 10.17). The software allows the architect to assemble components for study, such as wood trim profiles or fireplace surrounds. The software also provides addi-

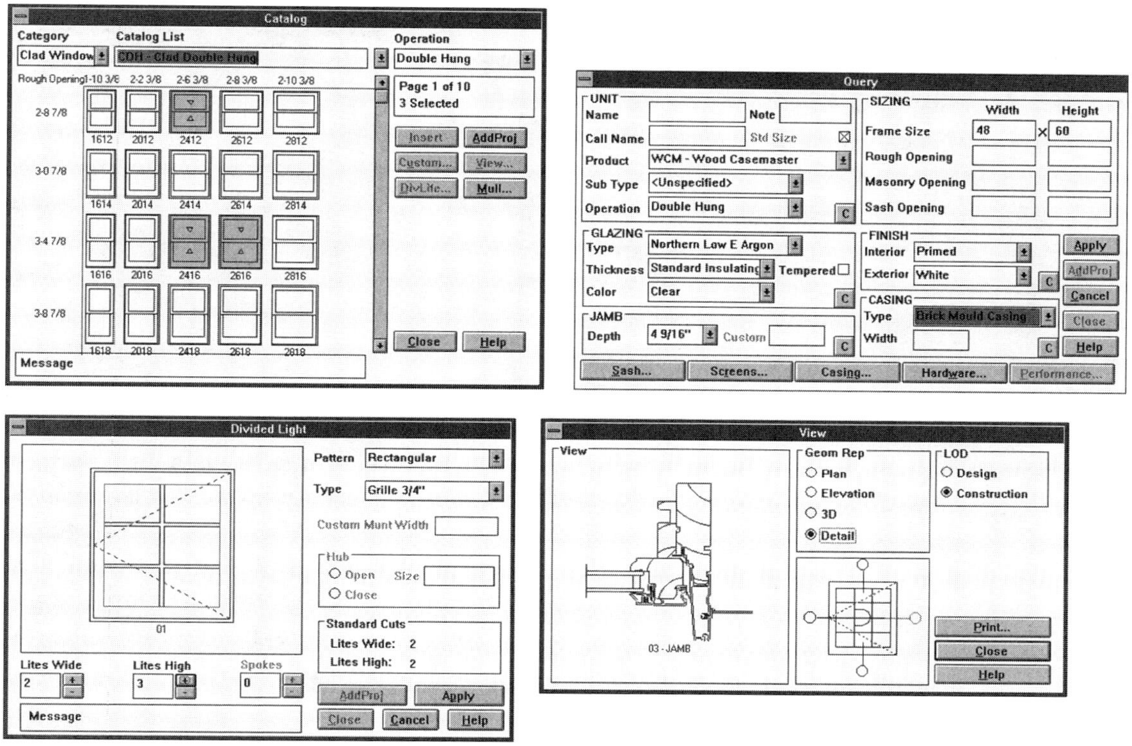

Illustration 10.16 *Marvin Design System.*

tional intelligent links between the information resource and the CAD program, allowing the architect to drag a predrawn component from the catalog into a CAD drawing on the screen.

AGS ON CD-ROM

Architectural Graphic Standards (AGS), published by John Wiley & Sons, has long been a valued resource in most architectural firms. In 1995, AGS was published for the first time on CD-ROM (Ill. 10.18) Significantly, AGS/CD-ROM is not simply a "port" of the book to digital media without any modification. In its first edition, Wiley collaborated with David Jordani, FAIA, to develop an interactive CD-ROM resource that appropriately leveraged the new digital media, yet retained an organizational structure familiar to long-time AGS users.

AGS on CD-ROM provides new tools such as a word finder, image thumbnails, limited hyperlinks between topics, and pointers to other resources outside AGS for additional

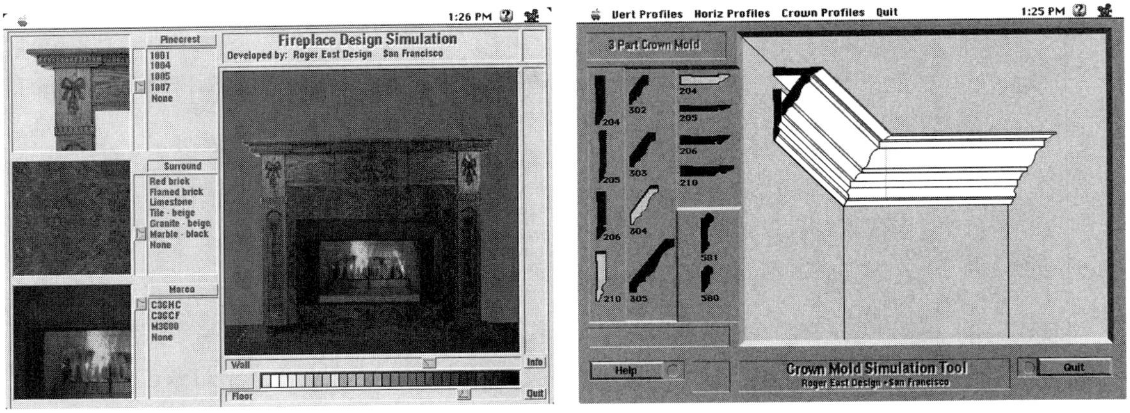

Illustration 10.17 Prototype design software by Roger East Design.

information. Like most CD-ROM resources, illustration or text can be freely copied to another application, and any page can be printed for hardcopy output as desired. AGS/CD-ROM includes ADA and masonry drawings in a vector format appropriate for use in CAD drawings, and provides support for layers, components, and appropriate precision. Other drawings and illustrations are available only as digital images but will be provided in vector formats in subsequent editions.

Significantly, unlike SweetSource, everything in the printed version of AGS is on the CD-ROM, which means the architect can use AGS/CD-ROM by itself with confidence. The new digital features don't come cheaply: AGS on CD-ROM is priced at $345, which is substantially higher than the printed version ($170). For larger firms, the price is a bargain, since the CD-ROM can be placed on network (or its contents copied to a network disk drive) and made accessible to anyone in the office. In fact, with AGS/CD-ROM on the network, some firms will find that the cost can be justified simply because everyone no longer has to waste time looking around for an office copy. Like any network resource, however, the performance of AGS/CD-ROM on a network is slower than when used on a desktop computer.

At first glance, the pricing of AGS on CD-ROM may not persuade sole practitioners or architects in small firms that converting from printed book to digital media makes practical sense. After all, isn't one of the benefits of CD-ROM publishing that the cost of goods is less, not more? However, the flexibility and potential reuse of information within AGS is what provides its added value. Ultimately, a less regressive pricing scheme that distinguishes between stand-alone use and networked or site-license use would be appropriate.

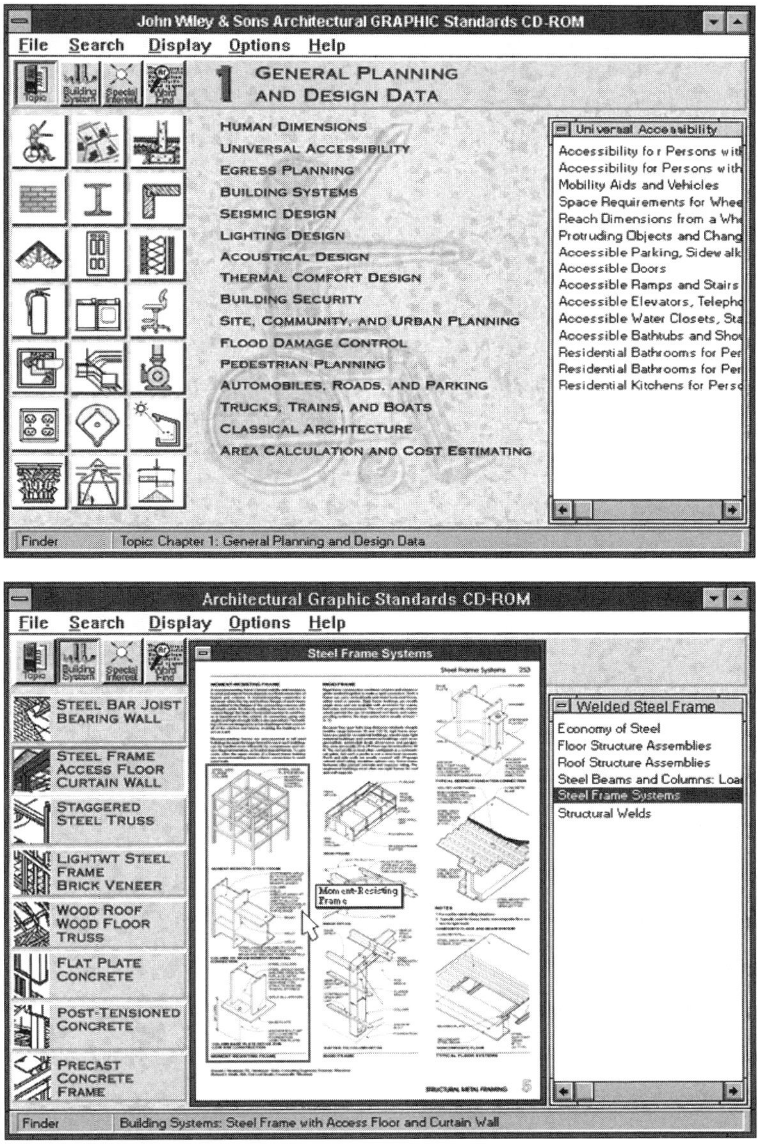

Illustration 10.18 AGS/CD-ROM.

PLUG-AND-PLAY INFORMATION: HYPE VERSUS REALITY

Many publishers of digital information resources promote the ability to copy and paste between their resources and the architect's digital documents. Certainly, the tools for doing so are built into the operating systems of most desktop computers today, such as Windows and the Macintosh. With bitmap images, in fact, such copy-and-paste operations rarely present a problem. With text-based resources, such as specifications or contracts, the procedure is fairly straightforward, although minor formatting glitches such as tab stops or paragraph indentations occasionally appear, depending on the software and its text-formatting import features.

The *AIA CAD Layer Guidelines* is discussed in more detail in Chapter 9, Organizing the Knowledge Base.

For CAD documents, unfortunately, the promise of plug-and-play digital information has yet to be realized. The problem stems from two issues. First, no industry-wide organizational guideline exists for CAD documents. The *AIA CAD Layer Guidelines* is an excellent starting point and is slowly catching on with many practitioners and manufacturers, but still is not widely adopted. Second, the de facto standard formats for distributing CAD documents, AutoCAD's DWG or DXF format, are graphically inadequate and inflexible.

Shown in Illustration 10.19 are two examples of wood window section details culled from the Winter 1994 edition of SweetSource. The first illustration is from Andersen; the second illustration is from Pella. Each provides a good example of the problem of information quality and consistency in digital on-

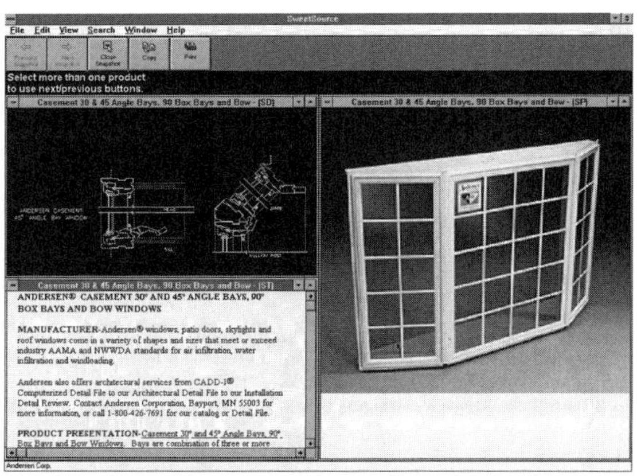

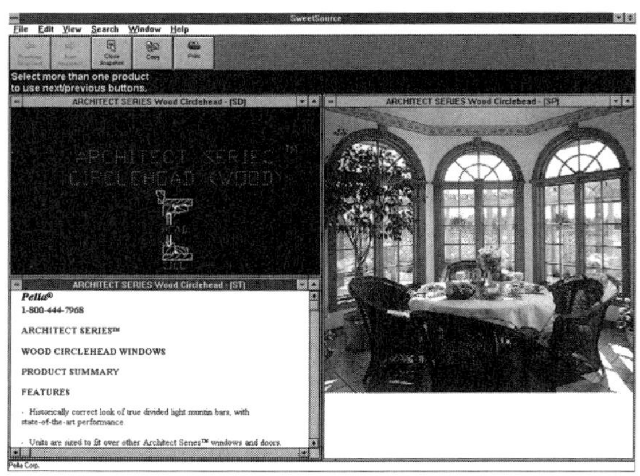

Illustration 10.19 Andersen and Pella details.

line and CD-ROM resources, especially when those resources are published using DXF or DWG formats.

Andersen's wood window is well developed graphically with substantial (perhaps too much) detail. Unfortunately, it arrives from CD-ROM with some hefty organizational baggage: a whopping 25 layers in which the drawing's linework are contained:

BOTTOMRAIL	HANDLE	STANDARD
BOTTOMRAILFILTER	HEADSTOP	STILE
BUMPER	PARTINGSTOP	STRIKE
FLANGE	RETAINING-BLOCK	TEXT
FLASHING	SCREEN	THRESHOLD
FRAMECORE	SCREENGUIDE	TOPRAIL
FRAMEVINYL	SEALANT	WEATHER-STRIP
GLASSTOP	SILL	
GLAZING		

Are these layers useful to architects? Absolutely not. In AutoCAD, inserting a block containing these layers spells organizational disaster, since these layers will be alphabetically interleaved with other named layers that are actually meaningful and important to the person editing the drawing. In Intergraph's Microstation, which supports only 63 layers per drawing, importing the detail into a drawing will absorb almost half the drawing's layers. Andersen's window detail is a good example of information overdose.

On the opposite end of the spectrum, Pella's window provides an example of a minimalist organizational structure. It provides two layers: a layer "TEXT" containing the drawing lettering, and layer "1" containing everything else. In both examples, since the drawings are trapped in AutoCAD's .DWG file format, no lineweights are supported. Most AutoCAD users employ color to control line thickness during plotting, but since color is used in an inconsistent way between different manufacturers, the user must edit the drawing and revise the colors as required to fit into the firm's organizational and graphics guidelines.

Clearly, true plug-and-play CAD information resources in the architect's office are still years away. Most product manufacturer's drawings should contain three or four layers: one for text, one for basic profile information (so the same component can be used on a smaller-scale drawing, with the detail filtered out), one for the graphic detail, and perhaps one for nonplottable reference (rough openings, clearances, etc.). The next release of the *AIA's CAD Layer Guidelines,* due in 1996, is likely to include recommendations to building industry manufacturers for organizing their information and should provide a starting point toward that ultimate goal. Unfortunately, as long as AutoCAD remains the de facto standard for distributing digital CAD drawings, such information will suffer from AutoCAD's graphics limitations.

CHAPTER

11

Managing the Digital Office

"Anything worth doing is worth doing over."

Doug Stoker

Chapter 2, Planning and Implementing Technology in Your Firm, discussed ten guidelines designed to help architects successfully start using technology. In addition to the critical issue of training and education (the exclusive subject of Chapter 3), a variety of management issues also must be addressed on an ongoing basis by architects using digital tools. These include managing the risks and liabilities of digital data, addressing privacy and anonymity issues related to E-mail and other digital communication, defining new technology support roles within the firm, understanding technology costs and cost recovery, implementing appropriate backup and data security, and managing software and hardware maintenance and upgrades. This chapter discusses these management issues as they relate to the use of computer technology within the architectural firm.

THE RISKS AND LIABILITIES OF DIGITAL DATA

Today, clients increasingly expect architects to deliver digital drawings and specifications at the conclusion of a project. The evolution of digital data delivery from a supplemental service to a standard service, however, does not relieve the architect of understanding the issues involved and avoiding exposure to unnecessary risk or liability.

When possible, the owner/architect agreement should explicitly state that documents produced by your firm, in paper or electronic form, are instruments of professional service and are the property of your firm. In fact, many clients today object to this language and insist on ownership of digital data provided by the architect. The key point is that document ownership should be a point of negotiation, not a giveaway. Although AIA's B-141 standard form of agreement between owner and architect does not deal explicitly with digital data, it is a good starting point for understanding the issues involved and includes a broad provision in Article 6 covering the architect's ownership of digital data delivered to the client:

> *6.1 The Drawings, Specifications and other documents prepared by the Architect for this Project are instruments of the Architect's service for use solely with respect to this Project and, unless otherwise provided, the Architect shall be deemed the author of these documents and shall retain all common law, statutory and other reserved rights, including the copyright. The Owner shall be permitted to retain copies, including reproducible copies of the Architect's Drawings, Specifications and other documents for information and reference in connection with the Owner's use and occupancy of the project. The Architect's Drawings, Specifications or other documents shall not be used by the Owner or others on other projects, for additions to this Project or for completion of this Project by others, unless the Architect is adjudged to be in default under this Agreement, except by agreement in writing and with appropriate compensation to the Architect.*

The AIA has recently developed AIA Document B511, "Guide to Amendments for AIA Document B141," which provides sample language for special situations, such as when ownership of the architect's digital data is transferred to the owner.

Article 6 clearly includes the copyright as a reserved right of the architect. Courts have generally upheld copyright laws as they apply to digital information, which are "reproducible copies." In theory, Article 6 effectively restricts the client's ability to copy the data you provide, even if you explicitly assign ownership of the data to the client. However, this is still a fuzzy legal area, and there are few legal precedents to draw upon. The language in Article 6 raises other issues to consider: What is the definition of "for information and reference in connection with Owner's use and occupancy of the Project?" Does that include tenant improvements performed by other firms? Does that include renovations or additions performed by other firms? The answers to these questions are worthy of written clarification.

In an era of "partnering," clients today reasonably expect a cooperative attitude from architects regarding the delivery and use of data describing their buildings, and architects who expect to practice into the twenty-first century are well advised to exhibit such an attitude. Refusing to deliver digital data to clients because of liability concerns simply is not an option. Instead, clearly defining the allowable uses by clients of the architect's digital data may permit you to satisfy the client's needs to use the data yet allow you to retain ownership of the data and the copyright.

According to the copyright office in Washington D.C., architects can provide notice of copyright for digital data "with or near the title or at the end of the work . . . or reproduced durably on a gummed or other label securely affixed to the copies or to a container used as a permanent receptacle for the discs."

Note that ownership of the data and ownership of the copyright are two different things. Even if you relinquish ownership, try to retain the copyright. This gives clients the flexibility they need to use the data in house, but better protects you against inappropriate reuse or misrepresentation of the data.

DATA MISREPRESENTATION

In the 1980s, when clients first began to ask for digital data from architects, the biggest concern of most architects was competitor hijacking of project drawings and details. Because of the prototypical nature of architectural design services, as well as constantly changing, locally enforced codes and regulations, these fears have largely been unrealized.

The larger risk to architects, in terms of liability, is the possible implied or explicit misrepresentation of the digital data to a client or third party. Specifically, architects need to ensure that clients or other parties do not assume that the digital data represents as-built conditions, when it does not, or that the digital data is accurate, when it is not.

The issue of misrepresentation of architectural drawings is important regardless of the tools used to create the drawings. One architectural firm found itself a defendant in a lawsuit filed by a party who purchased a building designed by the architect several years earlier. The purchasing party intended to install heavy equipment on the ground floor of the building, and evaluated the structural integrity of the ground floor slab based on a set of working drawings provided by the building owner.

Unfortunately, the drawings provided were not record drawings, and did not reflect a change order issued during construction that eliminated some of the steel reinforcing in the ground floor slab and effectively reduced its load-carrying capacity. After the building was purchased and the equipment installed, the slab began to crack. Although the architectural firm was not directly responsible for the misrepresentation of the drawings, the firm nevertheless found itself involved in a lawsuit, spending time and resources to successfully defend itself.

The issue of data misrepresentation is more critical today for two reasons. First, digital information is often assigned inappropriate authenticity and credibility beyond that intended by its author because the information comes from a computer. Second, digital data can easily be pulled out of context. Some built conditions, especially those that are similar to conditions documented in other details or sections, are never actually drawn, but are represented using notation, for example, "omit batt insulation at detail 3A." What happens when the owner's facility manager strips the ostensibly superfluous architectural annotation from a record drawing? The drawing no longer represents reality, and may omit important information. What if a condition shown on a CAD drawing is drawn "not to scale" but with the correct dimension attached to it? If the facility manager queries the drawing for a distance or an area, the answer provided by the software will be wrong. (This is one reason *never* to draw digital information "not to scale." If the geometry changes, always edit the geometry, not just the dimension text.)

Also, understand and communicate to the owner the differences between *precision* and *accuracy*. A steel column may be very precisely drawn and located on a plan drawing, but it can still be in the wrong place relative to where it actually ended up during construction. CAD drawings are very precise, but they are not always accurate. Take care not to overstate the truth.

Finally, do not disassemble components, detach reference files, or consolidate layers in an attempt to prevent others from using the information you deliver by reducing its value. Such acts of information sabotage do nothing more than annoy clients.

Take care to distinguish between works in progress, record drawings, and as builts, particularly in describing digital data to owners. Specifically:

- A construction drawing, even if 100 percent complete, should be referred to as a *work in progress.*
- A construction drawing that has been updated to reflect all addenda during bidding and all clarifications and change orders during construction should be referred to as a *record drawing.*
- *Never* use the term *as built.*

DISCLAIMER LANGUAGE

The following paragraph is an example of disclaimer language that can accompany transmittals of electronic data, unless rendered obsolete by the specifics of the owner/architect agreement (a signature is required of the recipient to acknowledge the terms). This disclaimer has a disclaimer of its own: it is an *example,* not a recommendation. Consult your firm's attorney for language appropriate for your firm and the state or country in which you work.

> *All digital data will remain the property of the Architect and subject to the Architect's copyright. The owner acknowledges that use of the data is at the owner's sole risk and without liability, risk, or legal exposure to the Architect. Furthermore, the undersigned shall to the fullest extent permitted by law, defend, indemnify, and hold harmless the Architect and its partners, agents, consultants, and employees from and against demands, losses, expenses, damages, penalties, and liabilities of any kind, including without limitation attorney's fees, arising out of or relating to any use of the digital data by the owner or third parties.*

The following is a copy of an actual letter sent by an architect working for a midsized architectural firm to an owner who requested digital data for use by his tenant improvement architect on a project currently under construction. The letter appropriately balances client service with the architect's need to clarify the contents of digital data and be compensated for the service.

May 7, 1991

Mr. Joe Smith
ABC Ventures
555 Fiction Drive
San Francisco, CA 94052

Re: Technology Center
XYZ Project No. 12345.67
Digital Data Transfer

Dear Joe,

This letter should clarify what you will be receiving upon transfer of our digital data for use by your tenant improvement architects for this project.

First, the information that is being transferred is work in progress, and does not reflect an "as-built" condition, particularly since construction has only just begun. Therefore, we cannot warrant the accuracy of our documents or any "as-built" condition as it relates to the preparation of tenant improvement documents and the consequent construction from those documents.

Secondly, the disks we will transmit to your tenant improvement architect will include the core revisions currently in progress. Any additional changes to shell documents regardless of their origin will be transmitted through blueprint updates. If your tenant improvement architect desires a digital update, we can provide this service at an additional cost.

In conclusion, it is our desire to assist ABC Ventures in any way we can to facilitate the successful completion of this project and ultimate occupancy by your tenant. To this end, we will provide base data and assist your tenant improvement architect as indicated above. Please do not hesitate to phone me if you wish to discuss this matter further.

Sincerely,

Johnny B. Good
XYZ Architects

TITLE BLOCKS AND LOGOS

The decision to keep or remove title blocks and logos from drawings before delivering them to the client is a subject of debate among many architects. Title blocks and logos are easily removed from CAD drawings and provide little protection from illicit reuse of the drawings. At the same time, a copyright has little value if the information you provide to the owner doesn't have your name or your firm's name attached to it.

In general, what you do should be determined by your agreement with the client regarding copyright ownership. If you retain copyright ownership and are providing the drawings only as copies of your instruments of professional service, then do not remove your title block and logo from the drawings. Even though they can easily be removed, they help establish your firm as the author of the work and reinforce your claim to copyright ownership if it is contested. (The title block should include an appropriate copyright tag and disclaimer.)

If, on the other hand, you are assigning copyright ownership to the client, then remove your title block and logo from the drawings before delivering them. This will help protect you from misuse of your firm's logo or title block when the owner disseminates the information. (If your title block and logo are contained in a reference file shared by all drawings, simply substitute a blank title block or detach the reference file before transmittal.)

DELIVERY MEDIA

The power and flexibility of digital data, as well as the source of its potential misuse, derives from the fact that copies of digital data are indistinguishable from the original source. Digital data, in fact, does not recognize the notion of "original" and "copy." When data is delivered by architects on diskettes, tapes, or over phone lines, there is no way to prevent the copying or alteration of the original digital data provided, nor any way to determine when or by whom it was altered. Any changes to the data must be compared to another copy to determine their magnitude and scope. This is one reason why you should keep a copy of the digital data as delivered in your own files.

Recordable CDs are discussed in more detail in Chapter 7, Desktop Hardware.

Fortunately, the recordable CD provides a mechanism today where architects can deliver digital data in truly read-only formats, and restores the traditional notion of an original information source. Data on recordable CDs can be copied and edited by anyone using them, but the original data on the CD cannot be altered. As a result, recordable CDs are the media of choice for architects to deliver digital data to their clients and third parties, and to keep for themselves as an information archive.

LIABILITY ACTION ITEMS

The following is a summary of recommendations when delivering CAD drawings to clients:

1. Determine the client's CAD system and organizational conventions, if any, including file names, layers, graphics guidelines, and so on, as well as acceptable file formats and media. These issues will affect the effort involved to prepare the electronic deliverables, and should be well understood and documented before or during fee negotiation. If the client's data requirements change during the course of the project, you will have a basis for seeking additional compensation, if necessary.
2. Ownership of the electronic data and restrictions on its use should be agreed upon before signing a contract and be included in the owner/architect contract language.
3. Identify who on the project team will have primary responsibility for delivering electronic data to the client.
4. When delivering data, write a letter of transmittal that includes a listing of all the transmitted files, showing the date and size of each.
5. Include on the transmittal and in a "read me" text file:
    - The appropriate language from the owner/architect agreement regarding the delivery and appropriate use of the data
    - The name and version of the software used to create the drawings
    - The name and version of the software used to compress, copy, and/or transmit the drawings

6. Include a hard copy of the drawings as you have plotted them.
7. Include all necessary support files that are required to display and plot the drawings correctly. These may include line types, component libraries, reference files, pen tables, or plotter configuration files. Name any copyrighted files you cannot legally transmit, such as fonts.
8. If you are keeping the copyright, keep your logo and title block on the drawings. If you have assigned copyright to the owner or a third party, remove your logo and title block from the drawings.
9. When possible, use read-only media for delivery of digital data, such as recordable CDs.
10. In your project files, keep a copy of all digital data delivered to the owner.

Some architects are providing not only digital data to clients, but also software tools developed in house. What is the additional liability of the architect as software developer? Ironically, some of the most onerous and restrictive liability disclaimers can be found on the packaging of most software programs. In fact, if such language is used by the architect, the added liability of the architect as software developer is rather trivial compared to the liability of professional design services. The real risk to the architect is in damaging a client relationship because of buggy software or inadequate support. Architects who are interested in selling software to clients should do so only after carefully considering the long-term support and service aspects of such a business, far beyond the initial point of sale. Unless it is a strategic part of your business plan to enter facilities management or other specialized aftermarket services, I suggest you avoid it.

FEES FOR DATA DELIVERY

The fee for providing digital data to clients or third parties (even if invisible to the client within a fixed fee) ideally should include both the cost of preparation and/or translation, if required, and an amount based upon the value of the information itself. This is particularly appropriate if the information will be used by a third party, such as a tenant's interior architect using base CAD drawings prepared by you for the building owner. There is a value you are providing to both the client and the third party for which you should associate a fee, over and above the actual cost of preparation and translation. Clients often assume that these databases should be provided free, of course. Again, these issues should be negotiated and addressed in your owner–architect agreement, not given away by default.

If the client uses a CAD system other than yours, data must be translated into a format understood by that system. DXF is the de facto standard for translating CAD information, but like any translation, it is never 100 percent reliable. If your CAD system has features not supported by DXF, there is often a considerable effort involved in preparing drawings to be translated, depending on what kind of information the client wants. You may also need to avoid using certain tools in your system which create information in formats that are not supported by the client's system—for example, AutoCAD's polylines with varying thickness. These issues should be well understood before a fee for delivering digital data is negotiated.

In addition, as discussed in Chapters 8 and 9, your office should have specific guidelines describing how CAD drawings and project manual documents are organized. Some clients, even those with the same CAD system or word-processing software as the architect, may have different organizational guidelines. Other clients do not have a specific plan for the information beyond asking for it. If the client does have specific organizational requirements, there will be additional costs associated with preparing your drawings in a suitable format. Some clients desire intelligent drawings from the architect that include nongraphic attributes attached to the drawing's graphic elements (ratings, types, sizes of doors, for example). Indeed, more and more clients are requiring such data equivalence in addition to graphic equivalence. All of these issues should be identified and understood *before* a fee is negotiated.

If the client has different organizational guidelines for digital data than your firm's, you will need to make a choice: convert to the client's guidelines at the end of the project, or develop the information using the client's guidelines from the beginning. At first glance, conversion may seem like the easier and least costly option, but that is often not the case. Guidelines that include not only layer conventions, but also file-naming guidelines, graphics guidelines, component-naming conventions, and/or nongraphic attributes can create a nightmare when converting the project database at the end of the project.

CONSULTANT DATA

Compared to clients, delivery of digital data to consultants involves similar logistical issues, but there are several key differences. Client data delivery usually occurs once, at the conclusion of a project, while sharing of digital data with consultants typically happens throughout the design and documentation process. Make sure your consultant understands your agreement with the owner regarding delivery of digital information, and that the consultant releases ownership and/or copyright of information to the client as required.

When providing consultants with digital backgrounds, a schedule for delivery of those backgrounds on a regular basis should be agreed upon ahead of time (e.g., every two weeks). This will avoid excessive requests for backgrounds during the contract documents phase and will provide a basis for budgeting the cost of preparation and/or translation. Consultant fees should reflect the fact that backgrounds for which the consultant normally is responsible are now being provided by the architect. Since the consultant is working for you, make sure you are driving the discussion of software, organizational guidelines, and delivery formats.

Finally, require that all consultants who will be sharing digital data use the same media (tape, diskette, optical disk) and/or online service (C4, CompuServe, Internet, etc.) as your firm uses. Be sure you understand the costs associated with transmitting data over the wire before committing to do so on a regular basis.

FACILITIES MANAGEMENT DATABASES

Many clients are interested in digital drawings for their use in facilities management. Although facility record drawings reuse much of the information on construction documents, there are some essential differences that architects should understand:

1. Facility drawings require minimal amounts of annotation. Most targets, notes, and dimensions required for construction are excess baggage on facility drawings.
2. Facility drawings consolidate drawings from many disciplines to allow various combinations of information to be conveniently displayed and plotted together.
3. Facility drawings require specific information, such as area boundaries, cost allocations, and other nongraphic attributes, that is not required on architectural construction documents.
4. Facility drawings are primarily plan oriented, without corresponding details, elevations, or sections.

When clients request digital data, determine its intended use. Does the client really want every CAD drawing, or only a base of information from which to develop facility record drawings? Providing plan-based information only is easier and less expensive than delivering every sheet. Typically, clients who intend to use your data for facilities management do not need copies of your drawings as plotted, but only the base floor plans without annotation. If the project is an addition to an existing facility or campus, the client may have room-numbering conventions that may be required for the documentation of the project. Determine this beforehand so you don't have to number and label rooms twice.

Be proactive about discussing these issues, since some clients may have no specific plan for the digital data beyond requesting it. Otherwise, you may find yourself jumping through hoops (perhaps at your own expense) without providing any real or perceived value.

THE ARCHITECT'S DRAWINGS AS SHOP DRAWINGS

Occasionally, architects are requested by the general contractor to deliver digital data to subcontractors for their use in preparing shop drawings. There are few precedents to draw upon for guidelines in handling such requests, outside of standard disclaimer language used in client digital data deliverables. For Frank Gehry's Disney Concert Hall, where three-dimensional modeling data was used in the manufacture of stone panels, a separate firm under direct contract to the client was responsible for preparing the three-dimensional data. This contractual relationship insulated Gehry's firm from the liability, in the same way that geotechnical and survey data are provided to architects by consultants hired directly by the client.

These issues should often be addressed with assistance from not only the architect's attorney, but also the architect's insurance carrier, who can clarify the types of services and information delivery that are insured. The legal and insurance implications for shop drawings derived from digital data are similar to those for architects who wish to engage in design/build services. The blurring of digital design drawing and digital shop drawing mirrors the blurring of the roles of architect and contractor in the design/build process.

See Chapter 4, Tools of the Architect, for more information about Gehry's innovative use of three-dimensional digital models for the Disney Concert Hall and other projects.

The architect, for example, typically has well-defined fiduciary obligations to the client, and fulfills a dual role: as an independent consultant in developing plans and specifications, and as an agent of the owner during construction. The architect also acts as an arbiter of disputes between the owner and the general contractor. When the architect is providing not only digital contract documents, but also digital manufacturing documents, these roles are less clear.

In most courts, the architect, as a provider of services, is held to the standard of avoiding professional negligence in performing these services—the standard of care. (Indeed, most architects' professional liability insurance covers only claims for damages and expenses due to professional negligence. Failing to meet a deadline, for example, is usually not covered.) The contractor, on the other hand, as a provider of a product, is held to the more onerous standard of implied warranty and strict liability. The contractor is responsible for means, methods, sequences, and construction defects, regardless of negligence. Most architects' professional liability insurance covers none of these items, and for these reasons, contractors cannot be named as additionally insured under professional liability policies.

The documents produced by the architect typically depend on information provided by others not under contract to the architect, including the physical dimensions and performance specifications of building products. Always document sources of information used in preparing your documents, particularly digital information.

The liability exposure of the architect will depend on the contractual relationships between the parties, which may vary greatly from project to project. While the risks of providing digital data to the contractor are greater in terms of insurance coverage, they certainly can be managed. If the architect's interests are properly protected, sharing digital data can contribute to the successful execution of a project and can help the architect communicate design intent to those responsible for construction of a project.

PRIVACY AND ANONYMITY IN CYBERSPACE

In a 1994 *New Yorker* cartoon, two dogs sit at a personal computer. One says to the other, "Great thing about being on the Internet is that they don't know you're a dog."

Two major privacy issues confront architectural firms which provide their employees with access to distributed information resources. First, some information must remain private and confidential. Personnel and medical insurance records, disability insurance claims, or discrimination or harassment claims, for example, are private and sensitive documents that should not be floating around on a network. The financial records of the typical architectural firm are not only vital to its existence, but also contain confidential and sensitive information. Marketing resources, including mailing lists or contact databases, are valuable, proprietary resources in many firms. Architects who seek to empower their employees with direct access to in-house and on-line information resources must take care to preserve security where appropriate, especially as it relates to personnel, financial, and business development information.

"Anonymity can be liberating and fun, like during elections and at masquerade balls. But anonymity can also be liberating and not fun, like during robberies and when facing angry mobs. I recall the lesson in William Golding's *Lord of the Flies* that the mask is the first step toward savagery."
BOB METCALFE

Firms also must decide whether E-mail is a public or private resource. Is a personal message sent between two employees private? Is it acceptable for managers to monitor employees' E-mail messages, just as they might check the progress of CAD drawings? By law, employers are not prohibited from monitoring computers, phones, and E-mail systems provided by the employer. Although the 1986 Electronic Communications Privacy Act (ECPA) prohibits phone and data-line tapping, law enforcement officials and employers are specifically exempted. According to some surveys, over 20 percent of companies *acknowledge* they engage in searches of employee computer files, voice mail, E-mail, or other networking communications.

As more and more business communication takes place digitally and on line, both small and large architectural firms eventually must confront these privacy issues. Communication transactions can be private, anonymous, neither, or both, as shown in Table 11.1.

Table 11.1 Examples of Communication Transactions

TRANSACTION	PRIVATE	ANONYMOUS
Articles, books, letters to the editor	No	No
Large political gifts	No	No
Small political gifts	Yes	No
Telephone conversations	Yes	No
Bomb threats	No	Yes
On-line chat rooms	No	Yes
Church confessional	Yes	Yes
An election ballot	Yes	Yes
Business E-mail	???	No

THE SOCIAL PRIVACY DEBATE

The issues of digital privacy within architectural firms mirror a larger social and governmental debate. Many proponents of cyberspace, for example, envision total freedom to communicate digitally, including unbreakable encryption and (eventually) anonymous E-money transfers. Today, software that provides virtually unbreakable encryption is available at low cost and can be downloaded from many shareware bulletin boards. This has not gone unnoticed by United States federal government, particularly the CIA, FBI, and IRS, who fear the misuse of the information superhighway by those with goals and agendas not aligned with the interests and laws of the country.

On April 16, 1993, the White House announced the Clipper chip, which was proposed by the National Security Agency (NSA), the listening arm of the federal government. The Clipper chip was designed as a standard hardware component that was, by law, to be built into all computers capable of sending and retrieving messages to other computers. The chip provided built-in encryption protection of messages, but the government kept the key to a back door, allowing them access "as required."

Not surprisingly, the Clipper chip was met with great derision by almost everyone outside the government. In fact, the technology was just plain silly. Digital encryption can always be layered, and anyone using a computer equipped with a Clipper chip could also use software encryption and decryption on top

In a 1992 Harris poll, 78 percent of Americans expressed concern about their personal privacy, and 68 percent perceived a threat from computers. These figures have roughly doubled over the past 20 years.

of it. When the Clipper "back door" was opened by an ostensibly well-intentioned government official, only an indecipherable message would be intercepted. As a result, anyone who really wanted to avoid a digital wiretap could easily do so. Eventually, the federal government withdrew the proposal.

If your firm intends to set up a computer as a World Wide Web server, keep it physically separate from your in-house network or rent space on a host computer from your Internet service provider. If necessary, use portable high-capacity storage media (e.g., a Bernoulli box or recordable optical disk) to transfer large amounts of data to the host. The best firewall protection against outsiders gaining access to your computers is physical separation, since no one has yet invented a way to make electrons jump through thin air.

Like so many other social issues, digital privacy has asserted itself as a self-regulated, free-market issue resisting governmental intervention. Many people who are concerned about credit reporting companies knowing so much about their credit history, for example, don't seem to mind when it means getting instant credit approval for a new car. There is an easy way to stay out of TRW's database, after all: don't borrow money. Thus far, most people have accepted the invasion of privacy as a small price to pay for the value they receive from obtaining credit.

More recently, the credit bureaus have seen their monopoly on personal information eroded from a variety of commercial information brokers. Most of these brokers collect information on companies, but some include information on individuals such as address, marital status, salary, driving record, employment history, vehicle and real estate holdings, and court records. In 1993, Lotus Development Corporation and Equifax proposed to compile some of this data for 120 million consumers on CD-ROM, and market it for $700 as "Marketplace: Households." An angry consumer backlash killed the idea, and the market drew a line in the sand that information brokers were not to cross.

Many of these larger social issues trickle down into the practice. To what degree can an employee expect that E-mail she sends or receives is private? Can employees send anonymous E-mail? What kind of E-mail monitoring should managers be allowed to do, or be prohibited from doing?

Employees who are introduced to E-mail often inquire about anonymity. For example, is it possible to send anonymous messages to, say, the managing partner of an architectural firm? My personal experience is that ideas or suggestions that are floated without the originator's acknowledgment are usually not worth that much. People must take responsibility for expressing their own opinions. Although there are certain sensitive situations (e.g., harassment or discrimination claims) where anonymity should be allowed, E-mail is hardly an appropriate communication medium in those cases. Anonymous E-mail eventually degrades into gossip; when people are not held accountable for what they say, quality goes way down. My recommendation regarding anonymous E-mail: don't allow it.

"Privacy and domestic security are a zero-sum game. Society consists of discrete individuals; if these individuals each have total privacy, then society has zero security. Conversely, for the body politic to have total security as an organism, the individuals within it must have zero privacy."
DANIEL BRANDT, HACKER

The following is an example of a policy summary for firms that provide E-mail access for their employees which provides a reasonable balance between privacy and anonymity:

1. Employees should understand that their E-mail account is provided to them at company expense and is intended to be used for business purposes only. Some E-mail messages, especially those sent over the Internet or commercial on-line services, may incur surcharges. Employees should not use their E-mail account for sending personal mail to individuals outside the firm, just as they should not use the firm's stamps or postage meter for personal mail.

2. Employees are free to send and receive personal E-mail messages to individuals inside the firm, or to receive personal E-mail messages from individuals outside the firm.

3. All employee E-mail is considered private, and managers are not allowed to browse employee E-mail files. This policy places a burden on the employee to manage her project-related E-mail, including forwarding to appropriate parties and creating the necessary paper trail.

4. Anonymous E-mail is not allowed. Information that is transmitted without the originator's acknowledgment is of little value.

NEW SUPPORT ROLES

Typically, three new positions of responsibility are required to implement, manage, and support technology within architectural firms. These positions can be literal (one person fulfills the responsibilities of each position), composite (the responsibilities of two or more positions are carried out by one person), or virtual (the responsibilities of each position are distributed among several people). In fact, in only the largest architectural firms will these positions be literal. More often, the responsibilities will be shared and absorbed by architects already within the firm, or by new, younger employees who exhibit an unusual aptitude or interest in digital tools. In the latter case, the enthusiasm of those employees must be balanced by the practice experience of other architects within the firm. The important point is that the absorption of these responsibilities by anyone should not take place by accident. Specific responsibilities should be defined and an appropriate amount of time should be allocated to those charged with carrying them out.

For most architectural firms, the virtual support staff is the best model. In addition to providing flexibility, redundancy, and better access for users, it is often easier to convince several architects to each absorb a small part of a firm's support and training requirements than to convince one architect to ostensibly derail a professional career to become a full-time computer jockey.

There are a few architects who choose this career path (including yours truly), but they are, appropriately, a relatively rare and endangered species.

See Chapter 2 for a discussion about the value of distributing technological expertise within the architectural firm.

The three new technology roles, Director of Information Services, System Manager, and Software Specialist, are described below:

Director of Information Services

The director of information services (a.k.a. manager of computer services, chief technology officer, or computer czar) is responsible for planning and implementing firm-wide computer-based information systems to ensure project and operational support, including CAD, project management, administrative support, business development, accounting, and publications. The key responsibility of this person is to coordinate the technology planning in each of these areas. Specific responsibilities include:

- Long-range (18 to 24 months) information systems planning
- Preparation of the annual technology implementation plan and budget
- Management of information systems cost center and profit center budgets
- Establishing firm-wide quality control and organizational guidelines for digital information
- Establishing training programs for system managers and software specialists regarding day-to-day operation and management issues
- Research, design, and development of customized software tools as required
- Direct support for key projects with special requirements
- Development of awareness and understanding among all employees regarding appropriate uses of technology within the firm, including both benefits and limitations

System Manager

The specific responsibilities of the system manager (a.k.a. operations manager) include:

- Day-to-day operation of designated information system
- Direct support for projects with special requirements
- Back-up and data security (as required)
- Troubleshooting system failures
- Implementing and maintaining firm-wide quality control and organizational guidelines
- Assisting in developing an awareness and understanding among all employees regarding appropriate uses of technology

A system manager in each office should be responsible for one or more of the following systems:

Accounting
Administrative support
Business development
CAD/Specifications
Project management

"Firms with productive computer technology implementations often cite two key factors that have contributed to their success. First, they have developed a network of people who function as experts in one or more of the firm's applications packages, using their expertise to help train other users and answer questions that arise during normal operations. Second, they have identified staff or consultants who can customize applications and develop new software to help leverage their investment in computer technology."
NICHOLAS WEINGARTEN, FAIA

Software Specialist

A software specialist (a.k.a. superuser or expert user) is responsible for training and support of one or more software applications in use in the firm. Specific responsibilities include:

- Expert knowledge of software application
- Providing or arranging for initial training of staff
- Primary contact with software developer/reseller
- First point of contact for users with software-related problems

---

An important responsibility of all three positions: managing the in-house technology expectations of managers and owners of the firm. Although evangelizing is an important skill for anyone responsible for introducing technology within a firm, expectations should not be unreasonably inflated. Be as honest as you can with everyone about the limitations of the tools—what problems they solve, and more importantly, what problems they don't solve. The most important software feature to most people is truth in advertising.

A recent job description written by a nationally recognized architectural firm seeking a new director of information services included this preferred personality trait: "Enjoys a life outside computers."

THE HIRED GUN SYNDROME

A final note of caution is appropriate regarding the impulse of some architectural firms to hire employees with little architectural background or experience to use or manage their computer tools. The failure of technology in too many firms can be traced to a halfhearted planning and implementation effort delegated to those outside the mainstream management of the firm. Substantial architectural experience is too often missing from the resumes of those responsible for the management of technology in architectural firms, particularly CAD managers in medium-size practices.

For some firm principals who have seen their architectural firm initially struggle with new technology, hiring an outside specialist to "take care of the computer stuff" may seem like a reasonable idea. Unfortunately, many of these hired guns are people with abundant computer knowledge but little architectural experience or talent. Although such an approach often provides short-term benefits, it is a long-term recipe for disaster. This is not just a recommendation or suggestion; it is an absolute *requirement* that the people within a firm who are in charge of driving a firm's technology strategy understand the practice of architecture. It is equally important that those who are in charge of implementing and supporting technology understand architectural services and products.

Most such computer expert hirings result in culture conflicts, poor communication, disappointed employees, and ultimately, failure. Unless yours is an extremely large firm with an in-house computer support department, hiring computer staff without architectural education or in-house experience is ill-advised.

Some readers may recall the classic TV commercial for Life cereal, featuring several children seated at the breakfast table who take turns passing around a bowl of what they perceive to be a bad-tasting adult cereal. No one wants to try it. Finally, one arrives at a breakthrough idea: "Let's get Mikey!" Mikey, the youngest and smallest of the children, is offered the bowl of cereal and he immediately begins devouring it. "He likes it!" cries one, and the other children quickly follow suit. Although delegating a task to someone who doesn't know any better works great at the breakfast table, it usually fails in business. Don't hire a Mikey to plan, implement, or use your firm's technology. Taste it yourself. Build the technology expertise in-house, distribute it to every architect, and make it a day-to-day part of your practice.

Finally, the most important attribute of those who fill new technology management and support roles is not knowledge of hardware configurations nor understanding software development trends. The most important attribute is strong communication skills. Those skills are a requirement of the job and are put to use every day to share experience and knowledge, to listen to and understand problems, to motivate staff, to sell new ideas to management, and to build a consensus. The technology manager must share with the firm's principals an understanding

"We won't hire anyone anymore without AutoCAD experience." Such absolute statements by firm principals usually pave a road to mediocrity. Computer knowledge should not be placed above architectural talent or experience. Specialists who know more about computers than architecture will be less valuable in the long run, and it will be difficult to define career paths for them.

"We hired a full-time computer manager for the start-up year who had direct experience as an architect in another office using the hardware and software we had selected. This decision proved invaluable. Our temporary computer manager assisted us not only in training architects and staff, executing our first production efforts, and filling a production role using the new system, but also helped us to create a CAD manual for the office that established a consistent working philosophy and organizational goals."
NORMA DECAMP BURNS, FAIA

of both the firm's long-term vision and short-term goals, which is very difficult to achieve without a common experience base and vocabulary.

OUT-SOURCING TECHNOLOGY SERVICES

Just as architects out-source certain special traditional services, such as modelbuilding, rendering, or specifications writing, many digital services are suitable for out-sourcing as well. While technology within an architectural firm should become a day-to-day part of the practice, this does not mean that every aspect of using digital tools must be supported in house.

A small office, for example, may choose to out-source the production of digital video presentations or computer visualizations that are composited onto site photographs. A large office may hire an outside consultant to help plan complex networks and specialized hardware requirements, such as bridges, routers, and gateways. Firms of all sizes may choose to seek the assistance of Internet service providers, or hire outside services to scan and convert old blueprints into digital data.

There are two criteria for appropriately out-sourcing a service:

1. Minimum professional judgment is involved, or that which can be clearly communicated.
2. The service is a "one-shot"—an initial setup or transition—not an ongoing need.

Out-sourced technology services include:

Planning and load-balancing computer networks
Scanning and/or digitizing large-format documents
Scanning digital photography (Kodak PhotoCD)
Introductory training
Hardware maintenance and repair
Large format plotting, including color
Film recording of digital images to 35-mm or 4 × 5 transparencies
High-volume color printing (Xerox, Canon)
High-volume black and white printing (DocuTech, Linotronic)

"Photorealistic" visualization and animation services
Digital data conversions between file formats
Consultations on emerging technology and digital service trends

EXPENSE AND REVENUE ISSUES

Computer tools, particularly CAD, are often justified as a means of reducing labor costs through increased productivity, but they also affect fees in other ways that must be reflected in project budgets. One of CAD's key benefits, discussed in detail in Chapter 8, is the ability to reuse information between project phases and reduce or even eliminate the redrawing that traditionally takes place between schematic design, design development, and construction documents. From a planning and budgeting point of view, more work is done earlier, and the payback of information reused may not arrive until later phases. It is not uncommon to spend additional time in the design development phase, for example, but begin construction documents with many CAD plans and elevations sheets already 50 percent complete. The fee distribution between phases should reflect the shift of work toward earlier phases (Ill. 11.1).

During document preparation, CAD makes it more difficult to estimate and track hours on a sheet-by-sheet basis because of information reuse between sheets. The overall floor plan of a building, for example, may actually take longer to draw in detail using CAD compared to traditional methods. On the other

Illustration 11.1 CAD workload shift.

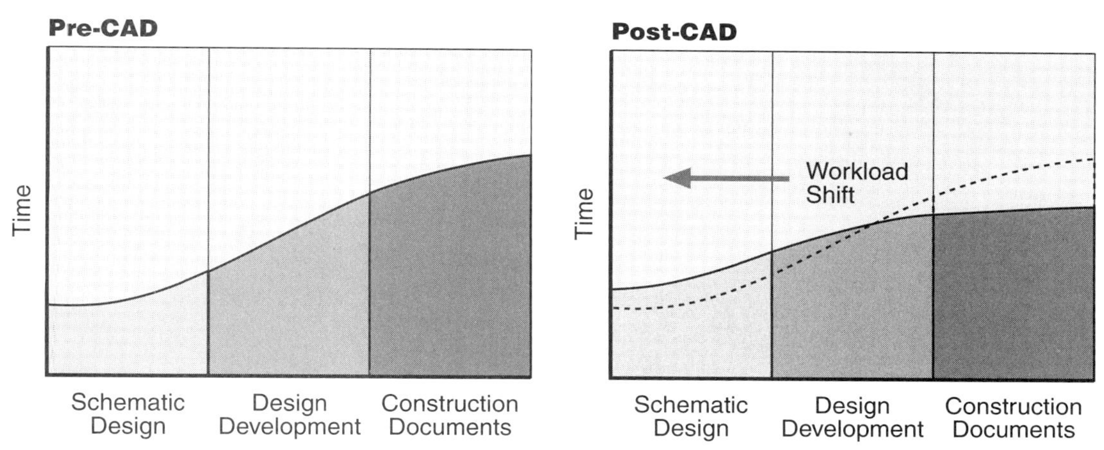

Acknowledging that computer technology has blurred the boundaries between phases, some architects are increasingly combining the design development and construction documents phases into a single documents phase immediately following schematic design.

hand, the development of reflected ceiling plans and enlarged floor plans is dramatically faster because so much information is derived from the overall plan. Similarly, the first sheet of wall sections may take longer, but subsequent sheets are developed quickly because of information reuse. Even if the overall effort is accomplished in fewer hours, the savings may not reflected on each sheet. As a result, traditional methods for budgeting and tracking hours on a sheet-by-sheet basis do not necessarily migrate well to CAD projects.

PROJECT REPORTING

In small firms, the tools used to budget projects are often the same ones used to report them: spreadsheets (Ill. 11.2). In larger firms, separate financial systems are typically used to track the budgets, costs, and revenues for each project in the office. In larger firms, the linkage between the centralized financial management system and the personalized, ad hoc tools used by project managers to budget and monitor projects, such as spreadsheets, is often a thorny problem, and will be discussed shortly. Regardless of the specific software used, the following are key issues to keep in mind when using computers for project reporting:

1. *Filters.* The information that project managers need to see and the information that accountants need to see are different, and project information must be filtered appropriately. Firms that do not use separate accounting software, but manage their finances using personal finance tools such as Quicken or customized spreadsheets, still must address this issue.
2. *Volume.* More data is not better data. In some firms, the project manager is provided with stacks of printouts, amounting to information overkill. Most managers first need to see summary information about their jobs, looking at specifics only if there is a question or problem (e.g., labor showing up in the wrong phase).
3. *Timing.* Project managers typically are provided with monthly project status reports, coinciding with the monthly billing cycle of most firms. Biweekly or twice-monthly labor cost reports are also common, coinciding with payroll. For small projects, unfortunately, two weeks of larger-than-expected labor costs can easily swallow up a profit margin. To address

this, some firms implement weekly time cards and weekly labor reporting.

4. *Garbage In, Garbage Out.* The quality of project reports depends wholly on the quality of the project budgets. Project status reports that compare project-to-date figures with budgets are of little value without current budgets. Providing a mechanism by which project managers can use a tool at their desktop to update their budget, rather than filling out a paper form, helps alleviate this problem, but the issue in many offices relates to behavioral discipline more than computer technology.

5. *Standardized Forms and Reports.* Although some projects require supplemental information in their status reports, typically determined by special client invoicing requirements, all project managers should build on a common platform of stan-

Illustration 11.2 *Project fee budget. Two versions of this spreadsheet were written: one calculates the hours from the specified fee; the other calculates the fee from the specified hours. Hourly wages are extracted from a separate wage table spreadsheet.*

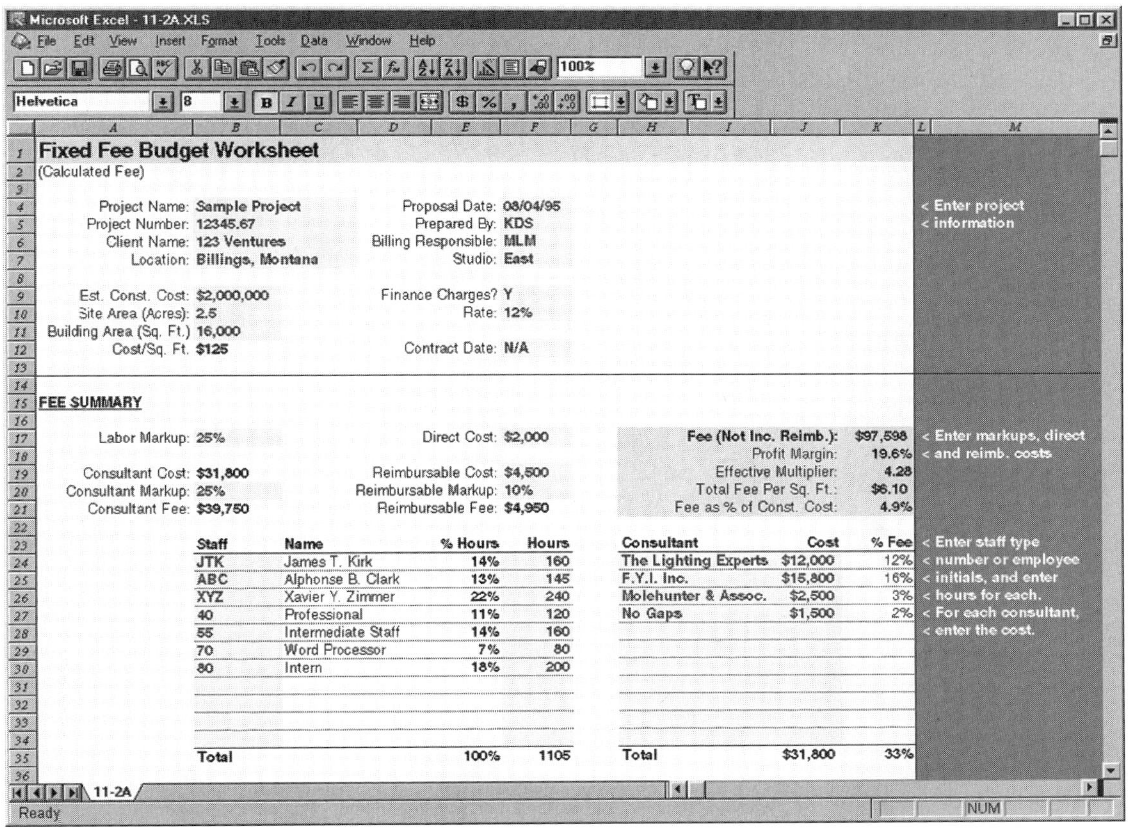

dardized forms and reports. In addition, everyone should understand and agree upon the terms used on budget forms and project reports. For example, is the number of "hours remaining" in a project report based on remaining labor fee divided by average *budgeted* hourly labor costs, or remaining fee divided by average *project-to-date* hourly labor costs? Failing to understand distinctions such as these when reviewing reports and establishing budgets can lead to unhappy financial surprises.

6. *The Curse of Profitability.* The project-to-date profit margin—the figure that most project managers pay attention to—is often one of the least reliable measures of a project's performance. Why? Costs hit the job each week or at each payroll period, while billing doesn't happen until the end of the month. A profitability report printed in the middle of the month can be misleading because it includes costs without the associated revenue. Conversely, a project may bill out at 50 percent complete, without having yet received 50 percent consultant invoices, temporarily inflating profit figures. Useful project-to-date profit numbers require aligning revenue with costs, which often is not done.

One approach is to focus on managing costs, not profit. In fact, labor costs are the primary variable and the source of most project cost overruns. Consultant costs are generally fixed and reimbursables are not a large percentage of the fee on most projects. Time after time projects lose money in the labor costs, and those costs should be focus of project reporting.

Another approach is not to bill the client for consultant work until the consultant invoice is received by the architect. Although this method can hurt a firm's cash flow, it is the simplest to implement. An alternative approach is to accrue consultant costs based on the work completed. This requires budgetary discipline, because the accrued cost is based on the project budget. If the budget is wrong, the reporting will be wrong (see item 4).

In summary, computerized project reporting provides little value in the absence of discipline on the part of the project managers, a consistency in how budgets are prepared and financial data is reported, and a focus on information that is most important.

INTEGRATION WITH FINANCIAL SYSTEMS

How does a firm provide project managers on-line access to financial information while filtering appropriately? The first approach is to provide the project manager limited, direct access to the firm's accounting system or financial management software, allowing her to review project revenues and project costs, including labor, consultant, reimbursable, and direct costs, but not to access payroll information, the firm's general ledger, or other sensitive data. The downside of this approach is the burden it places on the project manager to learn yet another piece of software to do her job.

The other approach is to export information from the accounting system on a weekly or biweekly basis into a software program with which the project manager is already familiar: a spreadsheet or a simple database program. Typically, not all detailed project records need to be exported—the hours worked by each individual, for example—but only summary information, such as hours, average hourly labor cost, total labor cost, and consultant, direct, and reimbursable costs. If the numbers don't look right, the manager requests detailed backup. From the project manager's perspective, the import/export approach is usually the most desirable, because it doesn't require learning another software package. In more sophisticated systems, the connection between project manager's spreadsheet tools and accounting software is a two-way link, allowing spreadsheet budgets to be imported directly into the accounting system.

TRAINING COSTS

Training is another issue that affects project budgeting. Most firms who provide training classes for their staff—either in house, out of house, or both—include the cost in their overhead. However, as discussed in Chapter 3, training is a process, not an event, and most architects need to use digital tools on several projects before becoming proficient with them.

The question of who absorbs the cost of this indirect training—the individual project or the firm's overhead—is a controversial subject to some project managers. Most managers understand that their projects will need to absorb a certain amount of indirect training costs, just as they absorb indirect training costs of student interns or recent graduates. The differ-

The shared training burden between firm and employee is discussed in more detail in Chapter 3, Technology Training and Education.

ence, of course, is in the wages. The 10-year architect who is learning CAD has a much greater impact on a project budget than an intern learning how to draw wall sections. The important point is to budget the project labor costs appropriately, based on the technological expertise of the staff.

THE MYTH OF MORE DESIGN

By reducing the labor costs of documentation, and by reusing digital information developed during design phases, technology has measurably increased in many architectural firms the *percentage* of overall fee allocated to design phases. However, this does not necessarily mean that more *hours* for design are available to the architect as a result of using technology. As overall documentation hours are reduced, design hours as a percentage of overall hours will increase even if the actual design hours do not. In addition, because much documentation (reused in later phases) now occurs in design phases of work, there is a shift in documentation workload that, although typically reflected in fees, does not necessarily allow more design time.

Technology rarely increases the actual number of hours devoted to the tasks of design, in part because market forces are pressuring architects not only to produce documents faster, but also to design more efficiently. Architects should abandon the expectation that using technology, by itself, is a way to increase design hours for projects by reducing documentation labor. Over time, competitive market forces will prevent that. Fees that support more design time are negotiated by firms who *design well*, not by firms who *document efficiently*.

CONSULTANT COSTS

Technology has also had a substantial impact on the working relationship between architects and their consultants. The fax machine alone has enhanced the ability of both architects and consultants to share information remotely and resolve problems quickly. At the same time, the benefits of information sharing and reuse—CAD backgrounds and specification templates, for example—allow both architects and consultants to improve the coordination of their documents.

The appropriate use of technology impacts consultant fees as well. In general, consultant fees can and should reflect the fact that backgrounds and revisions, for which the consultant is normally responsible, are provided and updated by the architect. Similarly, digital versions of consultant drawings provided to the architect, such as structural framing plans or MEP layouts, can be used by architects to check cross-discipline coordination. Reference files and other information-sharing tools of CAD systems have all but eliminated the light-table overlay technique of coordinating consultant drawings with architectural drawings.

BILLING FOR COMPUTER USAGE

In the 1980s, it was not unusual for clients to pay architects a supplemental hourly rate for computer use, usually a CAD system, in additional to hourly labor rates. Reimbursable hourly rates for computer use in the 1980s, which reflected more expensive turn-key minicomputer-based CAD systems, ranged from $30 to $50. Today, this practice is unusual, and reimbursable rates are typically less than $20 per hour. Unless reimbursement for computer use is a client's standard operating procedure, pushing for it is usually not in the architect's best interest.

Some people argue that architects should not be timid and should aggressively seek reimbursement for their use of computers, over and above nominal hourly labor rates, the same way they seek reimbursement for phone calls, blueprinting, and photocopying. Certainly, everything is negotiable. But typical project reimbursable expenses, such as travel, phone, reproduction and photocopying expenses, are those that vary widely depending on a project's complexity, its location, and how it is documented and bid. The annual hard cost of a firm's computer use is easier to budget than those varying expenses, and is more appropriately figured as part of a firm's overhead. If computers are really the integrated tools most architects advertise them to be, it is difficult to rationalize billing their cost to the client. (The exception is computer plotting costs, which will be discussed shortly.)

Some government agencies, which often employ fixed formulas to determine allowable overhead rates charged by architects, may classify the cost of computer use as a reimbursable expense, so an inquiry of public sector clients is often appropriate.

In the 1980s, when a greater percentage of architects were reimbursed by their clients for computer expenses, many firms tracked the hourly use of computers through automated log-in sequences or by time-sheet entry using different labor codes. The results were used to monitor the utilization of computers and evaluate the need for additional machines. Today, however, unless a client is willing to pay an hourly rate for computer use, it is simply not worth the effort to track utilization. Tracking of usage through automated log-in procedures, in particular, is unforgiving and fraught with imprecision. What if a person forgets to log out during lunch? What if she leaves for the weekend? Except where it is required by clients willing to reimburse for computer use, automated tracking is not worth the effort, and eliminating it is a good opportunity for simplification.

REIMBURSABLE PLOTTING EXPENSES

One technology expense for which architects should seek reimbursement from clients is the cost of in-house plotting. Plotting is arguably a form of reproduction like blueprinting and photocopying, the costs of which are usually reimbursed by clients. Automatic plot tracking is important, so buy or develop the software if your CAD system or network does not provide the capability. In one firm, the recorded plot volume went up by a factor of *10* after automated plot tracking was implemented.

A detailed plot log should include information about the user, the date and time of the plot, the media, and a descriptive field (Ill. 11.3). A copy of a portion of the log can be attached as backup to client invoices that contain reimbursable plotting charges. It is important that users are aware that the costs are being tracked, that plots are not free, and that their plot descriptions may be reviewed by the client.

The cost of each plot should be determined by estimating the annual cost of the plotters, media, ink or toner, and maintenance and support, and dividing that figure by the estimated annual volume of plots. This number can range from $1 to $20 per plot, depending on media and volume. This in-house plot cost is usually substantially lower than the cost of service bureau plotting, which is an important negotiating point with clients, and some architects mark up the cost to what the market will bear. With government clients, who have strict over-

```
20233.01; FCW; p111; P:\2233\A9-11; ; Calcomp Electrostatic, 4th Floor; 19950324.14120953; VELLUM
20233.01; FCW; p111; P:\2233\A9-12; ; Calcomp Electrostatic, 4th Floor; 19950324.14141416; VELLUM
40067.02; CKLC; P14; P:\4067\A7-1; A7-1; 11X17 HP LaserJet; 19950324.14152139; 11x17 BOND
20233.01; PCW; p111; P:\2233\A9-13; ; Calcomp Electrostatic, 4th Floor; 19950324.14163333; VELLUM
40067.02; CKLC; P14; P:\4067\A7-2; A7-2; 11X17 HP LaserJet; 19950324.14175467; 11x17 BOND
20233.01; PCW; p111; P:\2233\COVER; ; Calcomp Electrostatic, 4th Floor; 19950324.14200953; VELLUM
40067.02; CKLC; P14; P:\4067\A8-1; A8-1; 11X17 HP LaserJet; 19950324.14213097; 11x17 BOND
7769.01; MEB; P101; P:\7769\A4-7; ; Calcomp Electrostatic, 4th Floor; 19950324.14305144; VELLUM
40067.02; CKLC; P14; P:\4067\A8-2; A8-3; 11X17 HP LaserJet; 19950324.14341428; 11x17 BOND
40067.02; CKLC; P14; P:\4067\A8-3; A8-2; 11X17 HP LaserJet; 19950324.14370504; 11x17 BOND
40067.02; CKLC; P14; P:\4067\A8-4; A8-4; 11X17 HP LaserJet; 19950324.14405936; 11x17 BOND
7769.01; MEB; P101; P:\7769\A4-8; ; Calcomp Electrostatic, 4th Floor; 19950324.14445888; VELLUM
40067.02; CKLC; P14; P:\4067\A8-5; A8-5; 11X17 HP LaserJet; 19950324.14550575; 11x17 BOND
70770.02; KDG; P19; P:\4037\A2-1; ; 11X17 HP LaserJet; 19950324.14562271; 11x17 BOND
8208; BCD; P03; P:\8208\FP-G; ; Calcomp Electrostatic, 4th Floor; 19950324.15063605; VELLUM
8208; RK; P15; P:\8208\A3-5; FOR CONSULTANTS; Calcomp Electrostatic, 4th Floor; 19950324.15115100; VELLUM
8208; BCD; P03; P:\8208\A2-0; ; Calcomp Electrostatic, 4th Floor; 19950324.15143238; VELLUM
8208; BCD; P03; P:\8208\A1-0; ; Calcomp Electrostatic, 4th Floor; 19950324.15183228; VELLUM
8208; KJE; P05; P:\8208\A9-0; CONSULTANT; Calcomp Electrostatic, 4th Floor; 19950324.15213371; VELLUM
8208; KJE; P05; P:\8208\A9-2; CONSULTANT; Calcomp Electrostatic, 4th Floor; 19950324.15261558; VELLUM
8208; KJE; P05; P:\8208\A9-1; CONSULTANT; Calcomp Electrostatic, 4th Floor; 19950324.15294414; VELLUM
8208; KJE; P05; P:\8208\A3-1; CONSULTANT; Calcomp Electrostatic, 4th Floor; 19950324.15494348; VELLUM
8208; BCD; P03; P:\8208\A2-3; ; Calcomp Electrostatic, 4th Floor; 19950324.15495096; VELLUM
8208; BCD; P03; P:\8208\A2-4; ; Calcomp Electrostatic, 4th Floor; 19950324.15525484; VELLUM
8208; BCD; P03; P:\8208\A2-5; ; Calcomp Electrostatic, 4th Floor; 19950324.15542773; VELLUM
8208; KJE; P05; P:\8208\A3-2; CONSULTANT; Calcomp Electrostatic, 4th Floor; 19950324.15544497; VELLUM
90390.01; RSF; P09; P:\90390\TRI-METJ; ; HP DesignJet 650C (Color Fill); 19950324.15555632; VELLUM
8208; BCD; P03; P:\8208\A2-6; ; Calcomp Electrostatic, 4th Floor; 19950324.15564773; VELLUM
8208; BCD; P03; P:\8208\A2-7; ; Calcomp Electrostatic, 4th Floor; 19950324.15583692; VELLUM
8208; BCD; P03; P:\8208\A2-8; ; Calcomp Electrostatic, 4th Floor; 19950324.15595458; VELLUM
80209.05; DLQ; P06; P:\8209\05\A2-2; ; Calcomp Electrostatic, 4th Floor; 19950324.16005221; VELLUM
8208; BCD; P03; P:\8208\A2-9; ; Calcomp Electrostatic, 4th Floor; 19950324.16010060; VELLUM
80209.05; DLQ; P06; P:\8209\05\A2-2; ; 11X17 HP LaserJet; 19950324.16031562; 11x17 BOND
8208; BCD; P03; P:\8208\A2-10; ; Calcomp Electrostatic, 4th Floor; 19950324.16022311; VELLUM
80303.04; EMA; p110; ED-1; ; HP DesignJet 650C (Colorplot); 19950324.16075232; VELLUM
8208; KJE; P05; P:\8208\A3-5; ESTIMATE; 11X17 HP LaserJet; 19950324.16134573; 11x17 BOND
```

Illustration 11.3 *ASCII plot log and spreadsheet.*

head guidelines, it is usually only possible to recapture the actual cost.

If the client refuses to reimburse in-house plotting costs, project managers should budget the cost as a direct expense and include it as part of the fixed fee. For extra services or small design services performed on an hourly basis, this is a problem, since there is no way to budget, and thus recover, direct costs for hourly work. In such a case, project managers may argue that because the costs of CAD plotting are charged to projects, they are not included in the calculation of the firm's overhead rate that is used to determine hourly labor rates. Also, they should point out the cost savings to the client from using in-house plotting services compared to outside plotting services (assuming the latter is reimbursable).

A project's CAD plotting budget will depend on the scope of CAD work, the estimated number of sheets, the schedule (more time equals more plotting), and the

ZGF/Portland CAD Plot Log

March 1995

Project Number	User	Stn.	Drawing Name	Note	Plotter	Media	Date	Time
80208.00	BCD	P03	P:\8208\IEL-2		Calcomp Electrostatic, 4th Floor	VELLUM	03/07/1995	13:49:24
80208.00	BCD	P03	P:\8208\IEL-2		Calcomp Electrostatic, 4th Floor	VELLUM	03/07/1995	13:53:36
80208.00	BCD	P03	P:\8208\IEL-2		Calcomp Electrostatic, 4th Floor	VELLUM	03/07/1995	14:02:34
80208.00	RK	P15	P:\8208\A3-6	WALL SECTION	Calcomp Electrostatic, 4th Floor	VELLUM	03/08/1995	14:23:27
80208.00	RK	P15	P:\8208\A3-6	WALL SECTION	Calcomp Electrostatic, 4th Floor	VELLUM	03/08/1995	17:17:52
80208.00	MMF	P05	P:\8208\A3-5		Calcomp Electrostatic, 4th Floor	VELLUM	03/09/1995	08:41:49
80208.00	RK	P15	P:\8208\A3-5	for frasca	Calcomp Electrostatic, 4th Floor	VELLUM	03/09/1995	08:47:37
80208.00	RK	P15	P:\8208\EL-EAST2	for frasca	Calcomp Electrostatic, 4th Floor	VELLUM	03/09/1995	08:49:49
80208.00	BCD	P03	P:\8208\RCP-G		Calcomp Electrostatic, 4th Floor	VELLUM	03/09/1995	16:28:08
80208.00	BCD	P03	P:\8208\RCP-G		Calcomp Electrostatic, 4th Floor	VELLUM	03/09/1995	16:35:56
80208.00	BCD	P03	P:\8208\RCP-G		Calcomp Electrostatic, 4th Floor	VELLUM	03/09/1995	16:40:07
80208.00	RK	P15	P:\8208\A3-5	FOR COLOR	HP DesignJet 650C (Color Fill)	BOND	03/09/1995	17:24:07
80208.00	RK	P15	P:\8208\A3-5	color plot sample	HP DesignJet 650C (Color Fill)	BOND	03/10/1995	11:11:21
80208.00	BCD	P03	P:\8208\A9-0		Calcomp Electrostatic, 4th Floor	VELLUM	03/10/1995	12:55:19
80208.00	RK	P15	P:\8208\A3-5	color plot sample	HP DesignJet 650C (Color Fill)	BOND	03/10/1995	13:14:42
80208.00	RK	P15	P:\8208\A3-5	wall section	Calcomp Electrostatic, 4th Floor	VELLUM	03/10/1995	13:16:06
80208.00	RK	P15	P:\8208\A3-5	for wall section	Calcomp Electrostatic, 4th Floor	VELLUM	03/10/1995	13:17:46
80208.00	RK	P15	P:\8208\A3-5	color plot sample	Calcomp Electrostatic, 4th Floor	VELLUM	03/10/1995	13:37:14
80208.00	RK	P15	P:\8208\A3-5	window rendering	HP DesignJet 650C (Color Fill)	BOND	03/10/1995	13:38:16
80208.00	BCD	P03	P:\8208\A9-0		Calcomp Electrostatic, 4th Floor	VELLUM	03/10/1995	14:08:4
80208.00	BCD	P03	P:\8208\A9-0		Calcomp Electrostatic, 4th Floor	VELLUM	03/10/1995	14:55:42
80208.00	BCD	P03	P:\8208\A2-2		Calcomp Electrostatic, 4th Floor	VELLUM	03/10/1995	15:27:06
80208.00	RK	P15	P:\8208\A3-5	for color plot sample	HP DesignJet 650C (Color Fill)	BOND	03/10/1995	15:41:06
80208.00	BCD	P03	P:\8208\A5-2		Calcomp Electrostatic, 4th Floor	VELLUM	03/10/1995	17:10:33

Illustration 11.3 *(Continued)*

frequency of in-house check sets. Make sure the project team understands how much money is budgeted for CAD plotting, regardless of reimbursement, and that every plot is appropriately charged to the project.

UNDERSTANDING TECHNOLOGY'S COSTS

Although tracking hourly usage is rarely useful, architects should certainly understand the costs of a firm's investment in computer technology (Ill. 11.4). The firm's chart of accounts (the basic organizational structure for classifying expenses in financial reporting) should include categories for system management, training, software development, materials, hardware maintenance, and leasing costs and/or depreciation expense. Year-to-date technology costs, compared to budget, should be included in a firm's financial statement. Without these specific financial accounts, many technology expenses simply get buried along with other overhead expenses within the firm, and no one really understands its actual hard costs. (Technology's soft costs, such as unrecorded time spent on the learning curve, are even more difficult to quantify.)

Whether your firm decides to purchase outright or lease computer equipment, a depreciation schedule should be maintained for both the hardware and any software that is considered a depreciable asset. Tax laws change on a regular basis, so you should consult your accountant regarding expense classification and depreciation of hardware and software. Typically, federal and state tax laws provide for a five-year depreciation schedule for computer-related equipment. In reality, unless they can be recycled for less demanding tasks, most computers outlive their usefulness in a shorter time, which requires a write-off if the equipment is abandoned or sold.

Should computer hardware and software be leased or purchased? A firm that has a strong cash position may consider purchasing; a firm that doesn't may find leasing

Illustration 11.4 Sample technology budget.

1995 Technology Costs

	Mo. Budget	Jan	Feb	Mar	Apr	May	Jun	Total	YTD Budget	% Variance
System Management	$2,256	$2,200	$2,394	$1,945	$1,805	$2,390	$2,875	$13,609	$13,536	0.5%
Training	$1,550	$1,255	$1,205	$1,322	$1,405	$1,400	$1,765	$8,352	$9,300	-11.4%
Software Development	$500	$199	$215	$450	$562	$456	$1,243	$3,125	$3,000	4.0%
Materials	$600	$550	$719	$806	$722	$795	$926	$4,518	$3,600	20.3%
Leasing Costs	$3,200	$3,056	$3,056	$3,056	$3,455	$3,455	$1,980	$18,058	$19,200	-6.3%
Hardware Maintenence	$500	$200	$200	$792	$200	$405	$200	$1,997	$3,000	-50.2%
Total Expense	**$8,606**	**$7,460**	**$7,789**	**$8,371**	**$8,149**	**$8,901**	**$8,989**	**$49,659**	**$51,636**	**-4.0%**
Number of PCs	25	22	22	25	25	28	29			
Monthly cost per PC	$344	$339	$354	$335	$326	$318	$310			

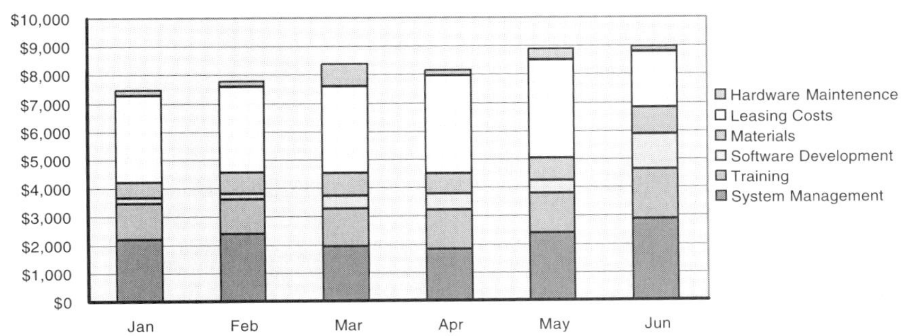

or obtaining a loan a more attractive option. If you are leasing, be sure you understand the specific terms of your lease agreement. Some leases provide a buyout option at the end of the lease term that may require a cash payment to purchase the hardware and software. It is important to understand how large the payment is, and whether it is optional. In general, you may wish to return old hardware rather than make the buyout payment. This is not the case with software licenses, of course, that do not depreciate in value in the same way as hardware does (unless the software developer discontinues the product). Make sure you have the option to keep the software at the end of the lease term.

BACKUPS AND ARCHIVES

The most effective way to learn the value of a good backup is to be victimized by not having one. For most people, the experience need occur only once.

Outside of dramatic variances in temperature (fire) or moisture (a spilled cup of coffee), information stored on physical media such as paper, mylar, or cardboard, is fairly stable and long lived. Digital information, on the other hand, is remarkably volatile. Loss or damage of digital data typically results from one or more of the following events, listed in order of frequency:

- User error (accidental copy or delete)
- Software bug (corrupted file)
- Media failure (disk crash, tape break, magnetic contamination)
- Natural disaster (fire, flood)
- Neutrinos (all other unexplained losses)

Backups are a critical requirement for any firm to minimize the loss of data when these events occur. The question is not if such events will occur, but when, and how often.

Neutrinos are particles of zero mass that travel at the speed of light. Using remote-controlled cameras and detectors, physicists from around the world are constantly monitoring 24-hour-a-day experiments in abandoned underground salt mines filled with water, hoping to capture on the film the extremely rare interactions between neutrinos and physical matter. But every architect knows that the scientists need look no further than desktop computers to observe the effect of neutrinos on physical matter, in the form of unexplained system crashes, errors, and software glitches. Neutrinos come in handy for system managers, who can explain mysterious system failures by exclaiming "Why, it must have been another neutrino!"

To completely back up all on-line digital information in an architectural firm on a daily basis is both costly and inconvenient. Instead, most firms use a hierarchy of daily, weekly, and monthly backups, and recycle the backup media as required. Types of backup include:

- Automatic temporary saves by software application
- On demand (to diskette, local hard disk, or network file server)
- Daily (incremental since last daily backup—weekly or biweekly rotation)
- Weekly (full backup of all project data—monthly or bimonthly rotation)
- Monthly (full backup of entire system—kept permanently)
- Archive (kept permanently)

Incremental backups record a copy of only those files that have been created or modified since the last backup. Full backups record a copy of everything on a disk. Sequential incremental backups provide the ability to fully restore information, with a maximum of one day's work lost, no matter when the information was lost. Media rotation reduces the cost and volume of required storage media.

Make sure you investigate and understand the life span of the digital media for permanent backups and archives, and develop a program to transfer information from older media as required. Most magnetic tapes have a useful life span of only 5 to 10 years, although some manufacturers claim more. Newer optical disk media boast lifespans ranging from 30 to 100 years (!), again depending on the manufacturer.

DIGITAL ARCHIVES

The number and frequency of digital archives will depend on the project, its schedule, and its complexity. In general, every project team member should understand the value of creating a digital archive at appropriate project milestones. These include major printings for review, the completion of project phases, client database delivery, record drawings, and final project closeout. Archives are also useful for establishing a record for the basis of area or material takeoffs or cost estimates.

When you bury digital information in an archive, don't forget to draw the treasure map!

Years after an archive is created, a person attempting to retrieve a drawing may know little about the project or its organization. Without an index to the drawings, complete with file names and descriptions, retrieving old information can be a painful experience. Therefore, always include a drawing index with every project archive (Ill. 11.5). The index should include a listing of all external reference files necessary to open and plot the drawing.

HARDWARE MAINTENANCE

In most architectural firms, hardware maintenance is an excellent candidate for out-sourcing. Although some architects prefer the insurance of a fixed-sum hardware maintenance policy, a pay-as-you-go plan is typically less expensive. Regardless of the contract terms, you should renew an agreement with a single hardware maintenance provider annually who is familiar with the hardware, operating systems, and software that your firm uses.

Often, hardware maintenance is offered by the vendors from whom you purchased the equipment. It can also be provided by larger third-party service firms who can support hardware from a variety of manufacturers. Do not wait until a crisis occurs to leaf through the yellow pages for hardware support. Instead, develop a relationship with a maintenance company beforehand, and introduce them to your firm's hardware, operating systems, and software applications before you experience problems.

Everyone who uses a computer should understand basic preventive maintenance, such as ensuring that the computer has adequate ventilation and recognizing when a cooling fan has stopped working. Minimal user preventive maintenance and awareness can achieve substantial savings in hardware repair and replacement costs.

One of the best techniques for simplifying and reducing the cost of hardware maintenance is to standardize computer platforms. Try not to purchase the hottest and latest each time you buy hardware, but standardize on a configuration for 6 to 12 months. Even if yours is a small office with only a few computers, maintain a list of workstation configurations. Information contained in the list should include:

- Graphics cards and software drivers
- Network cards and software drivers

Illustration 11.5 Drawing index spreadsheet.

Sample Project
CAD File Listing

8/15/95

Plot Drawings

Type	Dwg. No.	Drawing Name	Plot Dwg. File Name	Model Dwg. File Name	Model Reference File Names
Cover	**A0.1**	Project Information	A0-01		
Site Plan	**A1.1**	Site Plan	A1-01	FP-1	FP-1-E, SITE, ST1-01, ST2-01
Plans	**A2.1**	Parking Level P2	A2-01	FP-P2	FP-P2-E,WS-2,ST1-P2, ST2-P2, HOUSE G-8-EL-E, PTNLEG
	A2.2	Parking Level P1	A2-02	FP-P1	FP-P1-E, WS-2, ST1-P1, ST2-P1, P1-LOBBY G-8-EL-E, PTNLEG
	A2.3	First Floor	A2-03	FP-1	FP-1-E, SITE,WS-2, ST1-01, ST2-01, PTNLEG
	A2.4	Mezzanine	A2-04	FP-M	FP-M-E, ST1-M, ST2-M, PTNLEG
	A2.5	Second Floor	A2-05	FP-2	FP-2-E, FP-CORE2, FP-R3-R8, S8-SH ST1-02, ST2-02, FP-TYP, PTNLEG, FLRNOTES
	A2.6	Third Floor	A2-06	FP-3	FP-3-E, FP-CORE3, FP-R3-R8, S8-SH ST1-03, ST2-03, FP-TYP, PTNLEG, FLRNOTES
	A2.7	Fourth Floor	A2-07	FP-4	FP-TYP, FP-TYP-E, VACANT, FP-R3-R8, S8-SH ST1-04, ST2-04, PTNLEG, FLRNOTES
	A2.8	Fifth Floor	A2-08		NOT USED
	A2.9	Sixth Floor	A2-09		NOT USED
	A2.10	Seventh Floor	A2-10		NOT USED
	A2.11	Eighth Floor	A2-11	FP-8	FP-TYP, FP-TYP-E, OFFICES, FP-R3-R8, S8-BATH ST1-07, ST2-07, PTNLEG, FLRNOTES
	A2.12	Ninth Floor	A2-12	FP-9	FP-TYP, FP-TYP-E, GYM, FP-SUITE, S8-BATH ST1-07, ST2-07, PTNLEG, FLRNOTES
	A2.13	Tenth Floor	A2-13	FP-10	FP-TYP, FP-TYP-E, LOUNGE, FP-SUITE, S8-BATH ST1-10, ST2-10, PTNLEG, FLRNOTES, FP-10TH
	A2.14	Penthouses Levels 1 & 2	A2-14	FP-PH	FP-PH-1, FP-PH-1E, FP-PH-2, FP-PH-2E, PTNLEG
	A2.15	Roof	A2-15	FP-ROOF	
Elevations	**A3.1**	Elevation - East	A3-01		EL-E,EL-E-EX, G-8-EL-E
	A3.2	Elevations - South & North	A3-02		EL-N, EL-S,EL-N-EX, EL-S-EX G-8-EL-N, EL-NS
	A3.3	Not used			
Sections	**A3.4**	Section, Building - 1/8"	A3-04		BS-N-S,WS-2, G-8-EL-E
	A3.5	Wall Sections & Plans - 1/2"	A3-05		
	A3.6	Wall Sections & Plans - 1/2"	A3-06		
	A3.7	Wall Sections & Plans - 1/2"	A3-07		

- Unique boot-up scripts and batch files
- Memory and disk drive configurations
- Other peripherals (sound cards, fax/modems, etc.)

Over time, you will acquire various types of hardware: memory, disks, graphics cards, network cards, modems, and so on. Carefully maintaining a database of hardware and software configurations will make it much easier for you or third parties to troubleshoot problems and solve them.

SOFTWARE MAINTENANCE

Most desktop software developers do not provide software maintenance contracts, but provide limited introductory phone support and free technical support via on-line forums. When software begins misbehaving, it often easier simply to reload the software from scratch than to diagnose the individual problem. As a result, keep copies of original software disks readily available. If the software is not distributed on CD-ROM, but only on diskettes, then keep a copy of the diskettes on the network, or on read/write optical disk or recordable CD-ROM. Virtually all software companies allow you to make copies for backup purposes; make sure those backups are easily accessible when they are needed.

When upgrading software, follow these simple procedures to evaluate its readiness and minimize the disruption of installation:

- Understand third-party compatibility issues
- Fully test on a small scale before attempting widespread production use
- Archive current software
- Install new upgrades on weekends or evenings
- Introduce users to the upgrade and revise guidelines and documentation *before* implementation
- Provide training and education programs immediately

BUGS

Bugs are an unfortunate but unavoidable fact of life with software, especially new releases. The best way to avoid bugs is to avoid Version 1.0 of any software program. Subsequent software upgrades and new versions are also often buggy when they first hit the market, so let other firms debug the software for you. When you do experience a software glitch, follow these steps to make sure the bug is a bug before calling for technical support:

- Try to duplicate the failure on another file. If you can't, the file may be corrupted.
- Try to duplicate the failure on another computer. If you can't, the computer may have a problem.
- Identify a workaround, if possible.
- Identify, document, and communicate bug and workaround to vendor and users.

THE DOWNSIDE OF UPGRADES

Not too many years ago, most computer users and system managers eagerly awaited every new upgrade to their operating systems and applications software. The decision to buy was usually an easy one: each new release brought long-awaited bug fixes, feature enhancements, and performance improvements. Users were typically eager to get their hands on the hottest new tools, and the average cost of an upgrade was relatively small, compared to the original purchase price of the software package.

Today, the situation is different. As the number of desktop applications in use by the average A/E/C firm has risen, and as desktop computers become an increasingly ubiquitous tool, the annual investment in software upgrades is now a major capital expense for many firms, sometimes rivaling the cost of new hardware. The price of the software upgrade itself is widely recognized as only a fraction of the true cost of its implementation. The expense of installation, revisions to information libraries, hardware upgrades, memory expansion, and user retraining are substantial, and must also be considered by firms evaluating software upgrades. The bottom line question: is the value provided by a software upgrade—measured not in terms of technology "coolness" but in terms of real improvements to service quality and productivity—worth its total cost?

This growing trend of upgrade resistance is evidenced by recent major operating system and networking products and upgrades. Many businesses interested in Windows NT, for example, skipped the 3.1 release (its first) and waited for 3.5 (its second). Most firms who use Novell Netware 3.x as their networking solution have judged Novell's Netware 4.x as too complicated a departure from its successful predecessor. Sun's Solaris has faced the same market resistance. System managers, more frequently than ever, are taking a careful, wait-and-see approach to major operating system upgrades and enhancements.

Microsoft's recently shipped Windows 95 is no exception to this trend. Microsoft's early prediction was that most businesses would quickly upgrade and all new PCs would immediately ship with Windows 95 preinstalled. Appropriately, Microsoft backed off from those predictions before the software finally was delivered. At the same time, Microsoft agreed to provide a dual-boot option for PC manufacturers who bundle Windows with their PCs, allowing the buyer to choose between Windows 3.1 and Windows 95 when the PC is first turned on. Although Windows 95 is certainly the most successful new software program ever in terms of unit sales, its full penetration into businesses that have standardized on Windows 3.1 will probably not occur before the end of 1996.

SOFTWARE BLOAT

Technology managers or small firm principals must also face the continuing problem of software bloat. Each new release of software inevitably requires more memory, more disk space, and, in addition to the improved usability and graphics of most new programs, includes even more infrequently used functions. When Visicalc, the first PC spreadsheet, was released in 1980, it occupied only 29 KB of memory on an Apple II. In 1995, Microsoft's Excel requires 4 MB, or over 75 times as much memory. Obviously, Excel has far more functions than Visicalc, but architects will never use the vast majority of them. The key differences today are usability and graphics, but the hardware investment required to exploit them is not trivial.

"The charting program I bought in 1987 is now 12 times as big as its initial release. My database program has grown by a factor of 5. The bells, buttons, gongs, and whistles stuffed into the latest overweight applications programs serve little more purpose than the chrome trim on a 1958 Plymouth Fury."
JOSEPH R. GARBER, TECHNOLOGY STRATEGIST

Consider this amazing fact: the latest version of the world's most popular personal computer operating system, Windows 95, is roughly *three times* the size of IBM's classic *mainframe* operating system, System/360, which was introduced in the 1960s. Although operating systems and software applications may be getting easier to use, they are certainly not getting any smaller.

New software releases also require new training. In general, the more complex the upgrade, the more time required to digest the new version. This is increasingly true as new versions do not just add new features, but substantially change old ones. The interface of Microsoft Excel Version 5.0, for example, was radically changed to make it more compatible with Microsoft Word 6.0, another member of Microsoft's highly successful Office suite. The changes were worthwhile in terms of creating a simple, integrated set of tools. But the training hit for Excel was substantial.

The point is that many of the new features of software programs simply may not be of much use to the average user. Be sure you measure the value of a new upgrade not just by its features list, but by those that actually will be used. Even so, if the added complexity or hardware requirements are too high, it may not be worth it.

"Andy [Grove] makes my computer faster. Bill [Gates] uses more of it. Andy makes my computer yet faster and Bill uses yet more of it. What do you and I get when Intel and Microsoft keep adding and taking? Almost nothing."
NICHOLAS NEGROPONTE

AUTOCAD RELEASE 13

One application software upgrade of interest to many architecture firms, of course, is AutoCAD R13. With few major enhancements, but many minor ones and some repackaging of features previously found in other Autodesk software, AutoCAD R13 is acknowledged by Autodesk as a strategic release, building the foundation for a better AutoCAD tomorrow. The software release ostensibly includes many under-the-hood improvements to AutoCAD that will pay off in later releases, but are not yet readily apparent to the user. One of them is ARX, a toolkit for software developers to build specialized applications running on AutoCAD.

AutoCAD R13 also changes something that has not changed since 1990, when AutoCAD R11 was released—the .DWG file format. For many, the conversion of firm-wide information resources to new file formats is not a trivial undertaking. Although R13 can open R11 and R12 drawings, obsolete element types are not automatically converted to their new R13 counterparts. A standard detail note in an R12 drawing, for example, consisting of several individual text elements arranged sequentially, is not converted into a single R13-rich text element when the drawing is opened in R13. Similarly, existing R12 hatching will not automatically become associative in R13. The burden of converting old, obsolete elements in R12 drawings to new, improved elements in R13 drawings is left to the user.

ARX and other object-oriented enhancements to AutoCAD R13 are described in more detail in Chapter 4, Tools of the Architect.

Ignoring data conversion when upgrading to R13 can create problems for users, especially as new information resources are developed using the new file format. The behavior of the new R13 elements and the obsolete R12 elements, as well as the tools to manipulate them, are substantially different. If information resources are stored inconsistently using both formats, users can become frustrated by their unpredictable behavior.

Although AutoCAD R13 is positioned as a well-behaved citizen of Windows (the software supports TrueType fonts and is fully compliant with OLE 2.0), the graphic limitations of AutoCAD's .DWG file format become all the more glaring in the Windows environment. Users who dynamically share information between AutoCAD and other applications are soon reminded of AutoCAD's shortcomings, such as the lack of bitmap fill patterns, user-definable color, element display order, and symbolic line weights. All are graphics features that can be found in $99 illustration programs. As long as those element attributes are handled in AutoCAD using external plotting drivers, rather than as attributes inside the drawing, they are not exportable to other software and documents using OLE.

In addition, OLE objects which are inserted into AutoCAD R13 drawings cannot be plotted using AutoCAD plotting drivers, but only using generic Windows printing drivers. Because AutoCAD plotting drivers represent the only way to plot AutoCAD drawings with multiple line weights and color fill patterns, architects must choose between OLE interoperability and graphics flexibility.

Software upgrades often require hardware upgrades to maintain a comparable level of performance, and AutoCAD R13 is no exception. Autodesk recommends 12 MB of RAM for R13, compared to 8 MB for R12. Users don't need to test drive the new software to understand the performance implications: AutoCAD R13 is slower than R12 when running on the same machine. The Windows version of AutoCAD places additional demands on memory compared to its DOS sibling. R13 supports client and server OLE, for example, but at considerable expense. Users are simply not going to be able to use OLE on a day-to-day basis to create and edit compound documents on a 12-MB PC, running AutoCAD R13, Windows 95, and several other applications at once.

AutoCAD R13 suffers from not only software bloat, but also data bloat. Many AutoCAD R13 drawings are between 20 and 50 percent larger than the same drawings stored in AutoCAD R12 format.

In general, software developers tend to understate minimum hardware configurations, and the actual memory requirements to achieve acceptable performance may be higher, depending on the computer. My general rule of thumb is to provide twice as much memory as the software vendor recommends, particularly for Windows programs.

In the presence of these issues, and in the absence of any eye-popping new capabilities, the enthusiasm for AutoCAD R13 among some architectural firms is noticeably subdued. Again, this is not solely due to R13 itself, but is also part of an overall trend to go slower with upgrades. Some firms have decided to pass on R13, unless their clients require them to do so, and wait for R14. Others are awaiting fully compatible releases of third-party software or better performance before upgrading. In mid-1995, many of the largest architectural firms in the United States, including NBBJ, RTKL, Kohn Pedersen Fox, Anshen + Allen, WAT&G, and our firm, Zimmer Gunsul Frasca Partnership, had not yet upgraded to R13 and had no plans to so do in the near future. Almost a year after R13 was introduced, less than 25 percent of R12 users had upgraded, according to an Autodesk representative.

To its credit, Autodesk has publicly acknowledged the performance problems of R13 and has committed considerable resources to overcoming them. The fourth iteration of R13, the C3 release, was shipped in July 1995 and provides significant performance improvements. The fifth iteration, the C4 release, was shipped in September 1995 and is designed for better performance under 32-bit Windows 95. Deciding when or if to upgrade to AutoCAD R13 is not an easy task, and certainly there is no right answer for all architectural firms. But one fact is clear: AutoCAD R13 is yet another example that the auto-pilot software upgrade, while not yet extinct, is certainly an endangered species.

CHAPTER

12

Future Trends

BACK TO THE FUTURE

Early in this century, the promoters of airplanes visualized a future where people would have personal aircraft they could fly each day to work or to friends' homes. Some writers at the time suggested that airborne views would give people new philosophical perspectives and make them less territorial. In similar fashion, technology experts today are predicting the impact of interactive television and cyberspace on global culture and individual psychology, long before the mainstream implementation of these technologies.

Determined not to miss out on this new technology revolution, telecommunications companies, broadcast television networks, cable television franchises, movie studios, and computer companies have engaged in a kind of feeding frenzy of acquisitions and partnerships over the past several years. Each is competing for a piece of the emerging interactive television/on-line services/wireless communications markets.

Interestingly, while home shopping has exploded into a multibillion-dollar annual business, video on demand has stalled. Although most Americans watch three to four hours of television a day, the penetration of interactive television in test markets has been disappointing at best. When GTE launched a prototype movies-on-demand service in northern California in 1994, for example, customers only ordered two or three movies a month. Could it be that the technology market forecasters are

"A consistent pattern in our response to new technologies [is] we simultaneously overestimate the short-term impact and underestimate its long-term impact. And the reason is simple: technologies diffuse through society with remarkable slowness."

Paul Saffo, a director at the Institute for the Future, Menlo Park, California

"Will the 500-channel, all-digital, high-fiber world of the future be a happy time, bursting with "choice, control, and convenience," the mantra of every corporation getting into this business? Or will we take one look at it, snort, and go right back to reruns of *Baywatch*?"
EVAN I. SCHWARTZ

In the first five years of the personal computer industry, more money was *lost* by computer hardware and software companies in that business as was *earned* by those companies who were successful. The zero-sum game of the personal computer market of the late 1970s and early 1980s may well repeat itself in the new emerging technology markets of the late 1990s.

wrong? Watching television, after all, is fundamentally a passive activity, and most people may not want to turn something passive into something (inter)active. At the same time, many people apparently want to turn something active (shopping) into something passive, and so far, millions have done so.

Each day we are confronted with yet another new and improved technology that promises to dramatically change the way we live, work, or play—even how we think. The one reliable fact about the future is that it rarely plays out as predicted.

THE PACE OF CHANGE

Despite the noise, the evolutionary nature of technology is not likely to change in the future. Most major developments in computer technology, especially in software, take longer to arrive than most people are led to believe. With the exception of the Macintosh, most of the personal computer technology revolution of the 1980s, for example, was not based on new ideas, but was merely the repackaging of old computing ideas into lower-cost, easier-to-use desktop packages.

Consider the following excerpts from an actual E-mail discussion group among several architects discussing important emerging trends in architectural CAD software:

> ***Participant 1:*** *Start with the basics: Many people think we're in the business of making drawings. I think we're in the business of managing information; drawings are only one form, albeit the most visible and expensive form. Information managers love DATABASES. We should, too . . . Thus, I'd like to see more discussion of two things: cross-disciplinary use of CAD attributing capabilities, including their projection into actual construction—and mini-databases on PCs that anybody can use to keep better control of the flow of information.*
>
> ***Participant 2:*** *In my view, there are two major development horizons for CAD, one relatively new, the other with a long-standing history. The first new direction is referred to variously as AI, expert systems, or, my preference, parametric design. The second development addresses the general problem of a coordinated single source database for a building model. This is not necessarily a three-dimensional model. In fact, I view 3D or solids applications as prototypes of a single source design model. Currently, their weakness is an incomplete relationship to the*

main volume of design documents, not only two-dimensional drawings, but nongraphic information as well.

Participant 3: *I like the term "parametric design" rather than expert systems. It focuses on the main issue, which is the usefulness of a system rather than whether it is intelligent. Another application for parametric design: a basic building code analysis program. In the past I've cautioned against relying too much on automated building code analysis and am concerned about liability for whoever sells such a program. All that aside however, code analysis is basically a rule-based system, one that probably isn't done all that well manually anyway.*

Participant 4: *One possible solution to quickly testing out the possibilities of creating a rule-based code checking system is a package called INSIGHT by a software company in Florida. The package is under $500. It is basically an expert system shell which allows the user to set up rules and supporting facts in a freeform manner. . . . Another application of parameter or rule-based software systems is in developing building type planning tools which embody the specialized knowledge of the firm—personally gained knowledge from project experience, standard references and methodologies for approaching special facilities design and planning tasks.*

Participant 3: *Another branch of Computer Futures is the area of image processing and image retrieval. A company called Showroom OnLine has a computer driven video disk system containing video images of about 500 furniture manufacturers. You specify search criteria using a database program. . . . There is tremendous potential in organized storage of images. First, an image capture device or scanner is needed. Second, you need a lot of cheap storage. . . . The answer here is the optical disk. Third, you need a high-resolution display terminal. Finally, you need an output device [color printer or plotter]. To sum up, the technology is beginning to fall into place. This capability is one of the keys to the computer serving the working professional as an information resource.*

Unless you remember the Showroom OnLine or Insight products, there are few clues that would suggest to you that this on-line forum exchange took place on Sunday, September 1, 1985.

The point is that these same issues are still being discussed by architects and software developers today, *over 10 years later.* "Expert systems" never quite met expectations. "Rule-based" systems are used effectively by only a few architectural firms for highly specialized applications. Automated code checking is still a pipe dream. And image-editing systems are only now becoming affordable on the desktop. Although the price/performance and miniaturization of computing hardware continues at a rapid pace, the functionality of software has moved more slowly over the last decade.

In fact, a reasonable argument can be made that the pace of software development will actually slow down for the remainder of this decade. During the last two years, the personal computer software industry has accelerated its consolidation via acquisitions and mergers. Aldus/Adobe, WordPerfect/Novell, PowerSoft/Sybase, and IBM/Lotus are a few examples. Most of these deals have resulted in larger, more strategy-driven corporations. At the same time, software products are increasingly large and complex, and the length of their development cycles is increasing. The delays in Autodesk's AutoCAD R13 and Microsoft's Windows 95 are two well-known examples; the compatibility baggage carried by both software products is extremely heavy. Version 8.0 of the Macintosh operating system is also behind schedule. Citing its "unexpected complexity," Apple decided in early 1995 to delay its release to mid-1996.

"In the early days of artificial intelligence, people were very self-confident; they were convinced AI would be the solution to many problems. They put forward a goal to build agents that are very intelligent, have common-sense knowledge, and understand why people do things. AI researchers have been trying to do this for fifteen to twenty years, and haven't seen significant results."
DR. PATTIE MAES
Professor, MIT Media Lab

Even new start-ups face more daunting software development challenges than they did in the early 1980s. Kalieda, the multimedia joint venture between Apple and IBM, took over three years to launch its first products, the ScriptX multimedia programming language and the Kaleida Media Player. Taligent, also a offspring of the 1991 Apple/IBM alliance, shipped its first product, CommonPoint, in 1995. Most (but not all) companies have learned the lesson of Apple's Newton personal digital assistant, which was pushed out the door in 1993 before key communications tools were in place, or Intel's Pentium CPU, which contained flaws in its floating-point math algorithms. The lesson: don't rush a product to market before it is ready. For all these reasons, technology vendors will be taking more time to deliver their products to the marketplace.

The first thing to keep in mind about the future: *don't panic.* Focus on the tools and processes that are available today or will be available in the next 6 to 12 months. Don't be too concerned about the paradigm shifts, because they usually take longer to arrive than you think.

THE CLIENT-DRIVEN FUTURE

Where should an architect look first to understand how future technologies will fit into her firm? *PC Week*, *InfoWorld*, or *Byte* are not the answer. To understand how your firm will need to prepare itself for the future, look to one place: your clients. Talk to them about the future of their business, their markets, their customers. Discuss the competitive pressures that they face, how they are responding, and what technologies they plan on using. Some clients will be behind your firm's technology curve and will not provide much feedback. But others will share valuable insight on how architectural services fit into their future business plans, and how they expect technology to play a role.

If this sounds like a large-firm strategy, it isn't. If you are a sole practitioner, or specialize in single-family houses, ask your clients what services they think architects should provide in the future. How is the process frustrating to them today? How would they like to see the process changed? CD-ROM product catalogs they can take home? Virtual-reality walk throughs? On-line access to furniture and fixture manufacturers? A key follow-up question: What would they be willing to pay for such services? Even the smallest client may be savvier than you expect about these ideas. Interacting with your clients is simply the most direct route to understanding how your future technology investments will provide the highest perceived value.

A survey commissioned by the American Institute of Architects entitled "What Clients Need—A Study of Business and Institutional Clients' Expectations of Architects," published in late 1993, produced some statistics that suggest where architects should focus their technology efforts. The following lists show the percentage of clients who said they "completely" or "somewhat" agreed with various statements describing architects:

The good news:	96% think architects are *professional*
	95% think architects are *creative*

95% think architects are *knowledgeable*
95% think architects are *competent*
92% think architects are *concerned about quality*

The bad news: 80% think architects are *elitist*
71% think architects are *demanding*
59% think architects are *arrogant*
66% think architects are *budget sensitive*
56% think architects *save them money*

In terms of helping you successfully practice architecture in the future, where should you apply technology? To help you be more creative? To help you be more knowledgeable? A large majority of clients already believe architects are both. In terms of market impact—bang for the buck—the difference between 95 percent and 100 percent is a small one. Isn't it smarter to apply technology where there is a more dramatic payoff? How about using technology to save the client money? To be more budget sensitive? To appear less elitist, demanding, and arrogant?

Two other findings of the study are of special interest:

1. "While design ability is certainly important, when a client hires an architect, it is the way the architect listens and responds that leads most clients to select one architect over another."
2. "When it comes to money issues, architects need to demonstrate an ability to manage budgets as well as schedules rather than emphasizing low fees. Fees are considered a relative cost."

Technology is certainly a useful tool for architects to improve design quality and reduce fees through increased productivity, but other issues have a higher priority in the minds of clients: listening and responding to inquiries, and managing budgets and schedules. Computers can help you respond more quickly and manage budgets and schedules more effectively, but no amount of technology is going to help you be a better *listener.*

Neither the availability of technology nor the forecasts of evangelists have ever been known to directly drive change within the architectural profession. *Clients drive change.* The issues important to your clients (and your competitors' clients) are the ones that should influence your technology planning.

THE VIRTUAL PRACTICE

Within the architectural profession, one of computer technology's well-publicized offspring is the virtual practice, conceived from a marriage of real-time communication technologies and productivity tools such as CAD. The implied promise to architects is that location doesn't matter anymore, and that technology will allow architects to compete for projects outside of their traditional markets and geographic boundaries. (This ostensible benefit is a zero-sum game, since it will allow other firms to compete in your backyard, just as it will allow you to compete in theirs.) The promise is that size doesn't matter anymore either, and collections of individuals can be assembled electronically on demand to provide architectural and engineering services. Indeed, the "virtual design studio" as visualized by William Mitchell of MIT and others is a compelling and accurate vision of the future operational character of some architectural firms.

But are virtual practices really such a radical paradigm shift? And do they really add value to clients? Without even knowing it, most architects have been working in them all of their professional lives. Every project team with engineering consultants is exactly that: a virtual practice from the client's point of view. The same is true of many design/build firms, joint ventures, and design architect/architect of record collaborations between architects.

In the information age, architects should focus less on learning how to work effectively in virtual practices—most of us are already pretty good at that—and focus more on learning how to work effectively with virtual clients.

The Denver International Airport is a good example of how digital technology does not ensure the success of virtual organizations. The 43,000-acre facility was coordinated and documented by a consortium of firms, each of whom shared CAD drawings and other digital information. The airport opened on February 29, 1995, a year and a half behind schedule, and at a cost of $4.2 billion, about twice the original estimate.

"Technological visionaries can never recognize the distinction between the feasible and the desirable. If a machine can be made to perform some dazzlingly complicated task, then the visionary assumes that the task is worth performing."
EDWARD MENDOLSOHN

Although the Internet, E-mail, video-teleconferencing, and shared whiteboard applications provide new digital media for design collaboration and information exchange between geographically distributed team members, the issues involved in such collaborations have not changed substantially. The most difficult issues are not technology oriented, but practice oriented: distributing among the team members the responsibilities of leadership, decision making, and documentation; establishing contractual relationships between the team members and the client(s); negotiating fees between team members based on work contribution; organizing the information work flow; controlling document versions; and maintaining a distributed legal record of the process. Experimenting with virtual design studios in the academic environment provides important technological case studies, but conveniently ignores the practice issues that architects face in delivering quality services via ad hoc collaborations.

Talk to any architect whose firm has participated in joint-venture work or divided a project between multiple offices. Such collaborations can be extremely successful if managed effectively, but they are rarely as easy or efficient to manage as a project team residing under one physical roof. Technology helps, but the issues of familiarity and trust don't go away. Virtual practices are a legitimate response to market demands and provide new opportunities to assemble talent from diverse locations, but they are not necessarily a better way to work. At ZGF, our office in Portland occupies three 10,000-square-foot floors of an office building. Although everyone is fully networked using computers, we still make an effort to locate project teams together and always will.

Keep in mind that not all communication in a creative, collaborative design process occurs in formal settings such as meeting rooms, deskside crits, or video-teleconferences. Good ideas can occur at any time, without notice; hallway conversations or lunchtime chats often produce them. These accidental forms of communication are unique to teams of people who work in close proximity and are often lost in virtual practices.

In addition, although the size of the firm may not matter as much in a virtual practice, experience surely does. Technology notwithstanding, clients today are more interested in the specific experiences of the individuals who will work on their project than the portfolio of the firm's relevant work experience, real or virtual. The question is not "what projects has your firm done recently?" The question is "what projects have *you* done recently, and *with whom* did you do them?" Technology changes neither the questions nor the answers. In order for virtual practices to be successful, they must be based primarily on long-term working relationships.

The key question: do clients want to work with virtual architectural practices? And if so, why? Again, the AIA study provides some answers. The following list shows the percentage of clients who described as "very important" various characteristics of an architectural firm:

Responsiveness to client	84%
Ability to manage regulations, zoning, political aspects	83%
Track record adhering to schedules	77%
Track record adhering to budgets	77%
Related prior experience on my type of project	68%
Design quality or aesthetic sense	68%
Ability to manage the construction process	64%
Overall experience of the architecture firm	63%
References	62%
Ability to provide design/build services	60%
Fees for the architectural services	55%
Previous experience working for me	43%
Membership in the AIA	22%
Size of the firm	11%

Is a virtual architectural practice more responsive to the client? Probably, if it means more flexibility in assembling teams, or using teams in different time zones to effectively extend the work day. Probably not, if it means that key team members are out of town. Is a virtual practice better at managing regulations, zoning requirements, political aspects of the project, or the construction process? No. Those issues require a local presence. If a design firm is far removed from the project site, collaborating with a local architect is an attractive option, but the lack of prior experience working together will still be an issue. Is a virtual practice better at adhering to schedules and budgets? Maybe. Virtual practices, in theory, have more resources available to them. At the same time, schedules and budgets are not necessarily easier to manage within distributed project teams. Finally, although virtual practices are often promoted as a way for small firms to collaborate and compete against large firms, according to the AIA client survey, firm size ranks dead last in importance.

These are real-life, client-driven business issues that architects must face in delivering their services. Unfortunately, they are often not emphasized in academic experiments in virtual design studios, which focus primarily on the creative aspects of the practice. Again, helping architects be "more creative" is not where technology is going to provide its best value.

Virtual practices are *the next best thing* to being there, but no one should pretend that they are *the same thing* as being there.

VIRTUAL ENVIRONMENTS

Virtual-reality tools allow individuals to experience a three-dimensional space and movement through it before its physical construction. The usefulness of such tools has been assumed by most practitioners to be the visualization and communication of proposed designs to clients and to the public at large. Although the image quality provided by current (affordable) virtual-reality systems is crude and simplistic, it is only a matter of time before computing power overcomes the limitations of model complexity and representation.

At the same time, video-teleconferencing, on-line chat rooms, and shared whiteboard applications are early incarnations of virtual work environments, allowing individuals to communicate and collaborate independent of their physical location. Software games that allow participants at different locations to play and interact in real time using ordinary telephone lines are also emerging.

In the future, the technologies of virtual reality and remote collaboration will eventually merge to provide immersive "virtual environments" in which people can work (a little) or play (a lot). The adjective *immersive* is used to describe environments that extend beyond a physical room equipped with video monitors or projection systems, but in which a person is fully immersed, using a stereographic display helmet, earphones, and data gloves, in a simulated virtual environment.

Retail outlets such as Virtual World have already emerged, allowing customers to immerse themselves in a virtual play environment (an enclosed booth for each player equipped with multiple video monitors and control devices) where they can compete against other participants by racing flying cars or piloting robots engaged in ground warfare on a distant planet. Every participant "sees" the position and motion of the other participants in real time.

Immersive virtual work environments have been slower to emerge, but useful versions may appear during the next decade or two. The idea was popularized in Michael Crichton's novel *Disclosure,* in which a character searches a virtual company archive containing not only virtual file cabinets and virtual paper records, but also three-dimensional representations of other individuals accessing the archive on line. There is, of course, a certain regressive irony to the concept of virtual work environments that simply mimic physical work environments (even within the literal desktop metaphor of personal computer operating systems designed for consumers, such as Microsoft's Bob and General Magic's Magic Cap). After all, why constrain a virtual meeting to a room at all when acoustics and visual privacy aren't an issue? Why not have a meeting at a virtual beach, in a virtual forest, or on a virtual mountaintop? Why have images and ideas projected on a virtual wall or lying on a virtual table, when they could float in three dimensions all around you? *Why not design a building while inside the building?* When those pesky, inconvenient little things called gravity and thermodynamics are eliminated, the traditional physical world is hardly the best model to simulate in a virtual work environment.

What role will the architect play in creating virtual work environments? Ostensibly, the design issues of physical environments and virtual environments overlap to some extent. Absent are many of the physical constraints of architectural design, but there is no reason to assume that the psychological and physiological issues of good architectural design are not also applicable to virtual environments. After all, in a virtual meeting space, even on a mountaintop, you don't want to have to strain your neck to see something important. Visibility, color, lighting, materials and acoustics will still play a role. Will the design of such environments be left to the individual, or will the architect play a role as a design consultant or as the actual builder of such environments?

In the Fall 1994 semester, MIT's School of Architecture and Planning began offering a graduate course on "Digital Communities: Urban Planning and Design in Cyberspace."

Over the next decade, in fact, a new type of designer is likely to emerge, one who is not an architect but who specializes in creating virtual work environments or virtual play spaces. Perhaps a few students of architecture, or even a few architects, will find the design of virtual environments an exciting opportunity. Take away the contextual, regulatory, life safety, structural, and climate control considerations of architecture, however, and what is left is primarily stage design and theatrical lighting. A virtual environment is different from a theatrical stage only because it can be experienced by the observer moving through it, rather than viewed from a singular location.

In the design of virtual environments, firmness and commodity are not issues—only the delight. For some architects, this represents artistic freedom. The laws of physics, after all, can be a real drag on creativity. For others, including myself, it represents artistic boredom. Real life, and real architecture, are far more interesting.

What about the representation of virtual *nature?* Except for the most secure or introverted spaces (clean rooms, vaults, casinos), most building interiors have a direct or indirect visual connection to the outside world. Many exterior spaces, even urban ones, are dominated by their connection to the natural environment: not only by the landscape, but also by the appearance of sunlight, shade, and shadow. That visual connection—and the unpredictability of its character from day to day—is one of the key visual attributes of experiencing architecture from both the inside and the outside.

In fact, the spontaneity, the randomness, the self-regulating chaos of the natural environment is its fundamental beauty. Although immersive virtual environments can simulate the visual image of a spectacular sunset seen through a window, they will never induce the emotional impact of an unexpected real one. The beauty of a sunset is not the colors, the hues, the cloud formations; those are just the visuals. The beauty is nature's unpredictability and power. The individual's humility in the face of nature's overwhelming scale, not the visuals, is what truly inspires. There is simply no comparison between looking at a photograph of a sunset and experiencing a real one.

This is not to say that it is not possible to induce emotion in virtual environments, even natural ones. Anyone who has laughed, cried, or cringed with fear while sitting next to strangers in a movie theater can testify to that. Extending a virtual environment from the two-dimensional motion picture screen to a three-dimensional immersive environment will certainly enhance emotional impact. But to me, virtual environments will never be as interesting as the real thing. Climb Mt. Rainier and you'll know what I mean.

A FUTURES PUNCHLIST

The following is a brief list of future technology trends of interest to architects, most of which should arrive during the next several years and certainly before the decade is out. (Like all predictions, take them with a grain of salt.)

- Architecture students will continue to graduate better prepared than ever to use digital tools. The training burden on architectural firms will decrease but not disappear.
- The World Wide Web will emerge as the preferred publishing medium for building-product manufacturers and distributors.
- Portable notebook computers will supplant fixed desktop computers as the digital tool of choice for many architects. Wireless networks that allow communication between notebook computers and the office network will allow tremendous flexibility for architects who travel.
- Integrated, global communications to the architect's desktop will be provided via the Internet, E-mail, FAX, video, and voice.

- Continued improvement in object-oriented operating systems and tools, such as OLE and OpenDoc, will make it easier for architects to share information between inexpensive, general-purpose software tools. Expensive, monolithic, integrated applications will continue to decline in popularity.
- CD-ROM will be everywhere.
- Recordable CDs will emerge as the archive media of choice in the architectural firm, replacing stick sets and plan files, and providing each architect direct desktop access to a firm's project archives.
- Many architects will increasingly use reference catalogs of small-scale prototype solutions as starting points for design, for example, a CD-ROM catalog of various ADA-compliant toilet rooms for various occupancy types and sizes.
- The *AIA CAD Layer Guidelines* will emerge as a de facto organizational guideline for CAD documents, helping to provide plug-and-play digital information from product manufacturers.
- Public-domain digital file formats will emerge, replacing proprietary file formats such as AutoCAD's .DWG.
- Small but important improvements will be made to CAD software, including user-definable procedural components, global component libraries, view and scale filters, cropped reference files, and support for associative dimensions and annotation cross-references spanning files.
- AutoCAD Release 14 will support symbolic line weights. (Welcome to the nineteenth century!)
- Within the architectural firm, CAD software will continue to shrink in importance relative to other digital tools that are used to manage and document the design process.
- Virtual practices will allow people with special expertise or talents at remote locations to work together, but will still represent a relatively small fraction of architectural firms. Virtual practices will not supplant talented and experienced colocated teams.
- Affordable nonimmersive virtual-reality tools (sans helmet and data gloves) will become commonplace in architectural firms.
- A small, new architectural design service market will emerge: the design of virtual environments.

■ Design/build will continue to grow in market share, and will leverage technology more than any other architectural service delivery process.

■ Useful three-dimensional building models will continue to be representational, not literal. For most building types, fully detailed, three-dimensional building models from which construction documents are reported will remain self-extinguishing efforts in terms of productivity.

ATOMS VERSUS BITS

Atoms are the fundamental building blocks of everything physical. Bits are the fundamental building blocks of everything digital. Clearly, architects are increasingly using bits—and digital tools designed to manipulate them—to conceptualize, communicate, document, and deliver their services. Indeed, the guidelines and techniques for successfully doing so in the mid-1990s are the subject of this book. But at a more basic level, *architecture is all about arranging atoms.*

Nicholas Negroponte, the director of MIT's Media Lab and leading evangelist of the emerging digital age, has lectured and written extensively about the growth of digital commerce in the global economy and about atoms and bits. Negroponte correctly observes that the economic infrastructure of the world and its nation-states is primarily designed for the exchange of atoms—physical objects and commodity goods—and is wholly unprepared for digital commerce. Bits are appropriately replacing atoms as a powerful medium of exchange, particularly in communication, information, and entertainment.

Still, atoms won't disappear anytime soon. After all, people breathe atoms. We eat atoms. We arrange certain atoms, in our clothing and our shelters, to protect us from other atoms. Digital cash has arrived, but nobody will ever invent digital oxygen, digital wheat, digital wool, or digital concrete. The value of architecture will always be found in its atoms, not its bits.

Bits are more flexible than atoms but are also more fleeting. Few lengthy sequences of bits today—other than movie classics and baseline information resources—enjoy a useful life span of longer than a few years. Software is obsolete sometimes after only a few months. A well-constructed building, on the other

A brief time line of personal computing:

1979–1985

Revolutionary period, characterized by innovation

PC software leaders established (Autodesk, Lotus, WordPerfect, Microsoft, Novell)

1986–1994

Evolutionary period, characterized by imitation, copyright lawsuits

PC hardware leaders established (Compaq, Apple, IBM, Packard Bell, Gateway 2000)

1995–2000

Era of digital convergence, characterized by integration, communication

Major shakeouts of software and hardware vendors

hand, has a life span approaching, and usually exceeding, that of the people who designed and built it.

The first project I was lucky enough to work on after graduating from the University of California at Berkeley was the Monterey Bay Aquarium, in Monterey, California (Ill. 12.1). In fact, I was hired by Esherick, Homsey, Dodge & Davis on a temporary basis to build a ⅛-inch scale model of the aquarium. When I finished three weeks later, they hired me permanently, and I spent almost a year working on the project, mostly drawing the floor plans, enlarged plans, reflected ceiling plans, building sections, and interior elevations. (None of this, by the way, was done using a computer.) One of the coolest things I got to do was draw two sheets of acrylic panel details for the huge saltwater tanks, one of which was an otter tank immediately adjacent to the main entrance lobby of the aquarium.

I visited the aquarium for the first time in 1984 soon after it opened. Today, almost twelve years later, I can describe the

Illustration 12.1 *Monterey Bay Aquarium interior, looking toward lobby and otter tank.*

exact location where I stood shortly after I walked into the aquarium and saw a young girl, perhaps six or seven years old, with her nose pressed against the two-story acrylic panel of the otter tank, watching with delight and amazement as the otters zoomed past her. I stopped and watched for minutes. The girl's nose didn't leave the acrylic, my feet didn't leave the floor, and my eyes didn't leave her. The condensation of her breath on the acrylic took a minute to evaporate when she finally unglued her nose and ran over to her parents to share her discoveries.

My contribution to the aquarium and its otter tank was a small one, but it still felt fantastic to have participated in adding a small measure of joy to that young girl's life. It may sound silly, but to this day, those few minutes standing in the lobby of the Monterey Bay Aquarium twelve years ago remain one of my most profound experiences as an architect.

After all, experiencing and touching the atoms of a building, and seeing others do so, is still the most compelling reward for those who participate in its design and construction—even the digital architect.

WORLD WIDE WEB SITES

The following list of World Wide Web sites containing architectural resources was compiled by Jeanne Brown, the Architecture Studies Librarian at the University of Nevada, Las Vegas. Her Internet address is jeanneb@nevada.edu. For those architects with access to the World Wide Web, an updated hypertext version of this list can be accessed at:

http://www.tue.nl/lava/other/brown/index.html
(hypertext by Marco Vlemmix)

http://www.uky.edu/Artsource/bibliographies/brown.html
(hypertext by Mary Molinaro)

OUTLINE

A. Architecture, General
B. Architecture/Building Information
C. Architecture Libraries
D. Primarily Images
E. University Architecture Programs
F. Architectural Computing
G. Links to Architecture Information

A. ARCHITECTURE, GENERAL

A.1 Name: Center for Landscape Research University of Toronto
URL: http://www.clr.toronto.edu:1080

Excellent starting point for surfing or browsing the web, and most comprehensive set of links to architecture and landscape architecture sites. CLRnet provides the web's architecture and landscape architecture subject index (the architecture list is subdivided by topics such as jobs, conferences, competitions, schools, government agencies, research, firms, history, projects, information sources, software, news groups, mail lists, landscape architecture, and engineering). A taste of what's there: under information sources are contents listings of CADD Futures Proceedings (1985–1993) and ACADIA Conference Proceedings (1992–1993); under mailing lists is the LARCH-L archive. The Center for Landscape Research site also provides an archive of theses in landscape architecture.

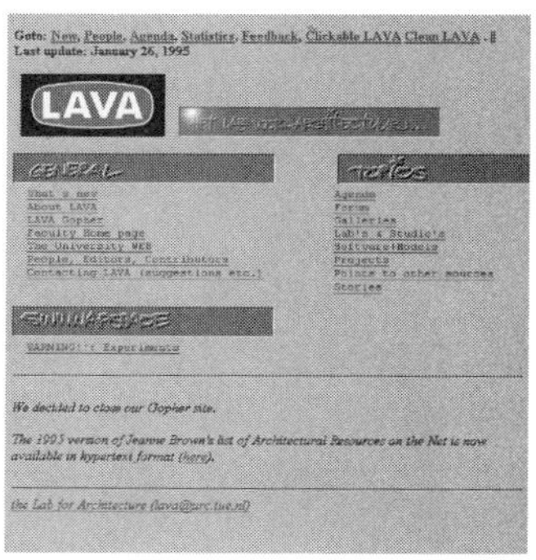

A.2 Name: LAVA The Lab for Architects, Technische Universiteit Eindhoven, Faculty of Architecture and Planning
URL: http://www.tue.nl/lava

This site "features design projects, texts, discussions, etc.", including book reviews. While parts are still obviously under construction (such as the mail from selected lists June–August 1994), this is a site which is constantly changing and trying new approaches. Its most recent experiment is a virtual studio (temporary URL:http://w3.urc.tue.nl/lava/studio.html). It also offers access to its gopher, and a hypertext version of this guide to Internet resources in architecture and building, divided and accessible by section (e.g., the web section is accessible without going through the preceding part of the guide; URL:http://www.tue.nl/lava/other/brown/inttoc.html) as well as other pointers to net information. Additional information about other departments and institutes at the university can be found at URL:http://www.tue.nl/bwk. The section on the Calibre Institute, for instance, has several images and research documents related to their work on multimedia and virtual reality.

A.3 Name: Imaging Systems Laboratory, Department of Landscape Architecture, University of Illinois, Urbana-Champaign
URL: http://imlab9.landarch.uiuc.edu

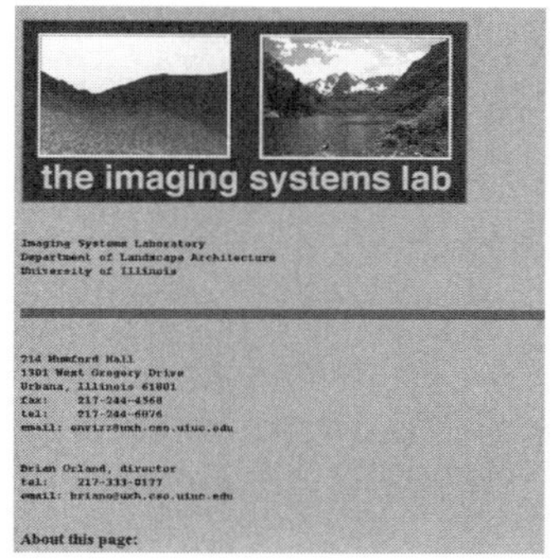

The lab's "activities have concentrated on environmental perception research related to the visualization of environmental impacts, with emphases on methodological studies and on preference and choice modeling." This substantive site includes full text of publications for most projects, lists of publications and grants received, and bibliographies in the lab's areas of research.

A.4 Name: RMIT (Royal Melbourne Institute of Technology) National Key Centre for Design
URL: http://daedalus.edc.rmit.edu.au

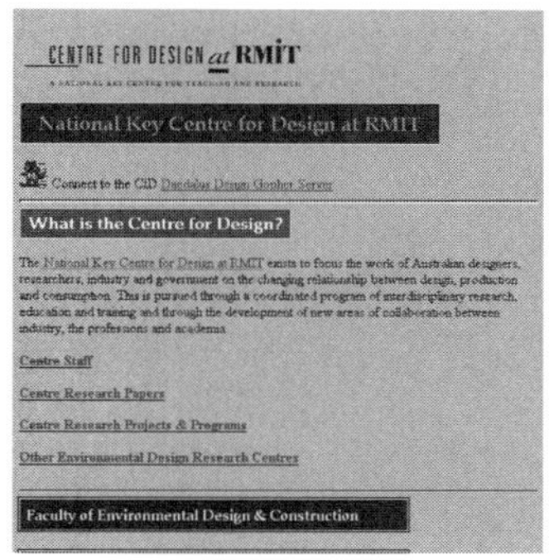

"The National Key Centre for Design at RMIT exists to focus the work of Australian designers, researchers, industry and government on the changing relationship between design, production and consumption." This site provides centre research papers and projects such as EcoReDesign ("a program to improve the environmental performance of manufactured products") and Eco Built Environment ("an inquiry into the philosophy of environmental sustainability both for the design and the designers of the built environment") as well as links to other environmental design research centers, and to Internet sites relating to the built environment.

A.5 Name: Columbia University
URL: http://www.cc.columbia.edu/courses/

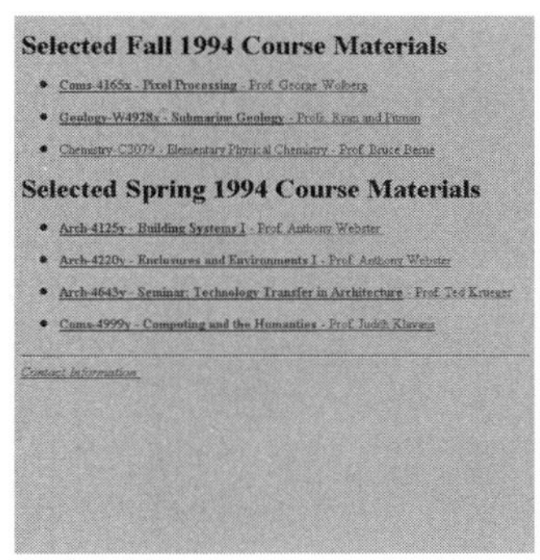

Columbia University course syllabi. One that is quite interesting: the Seminar on Technology Transfer in Architecture provides, instead of a standard syllabus, a hypertext document leading to pertinent sites on the net!

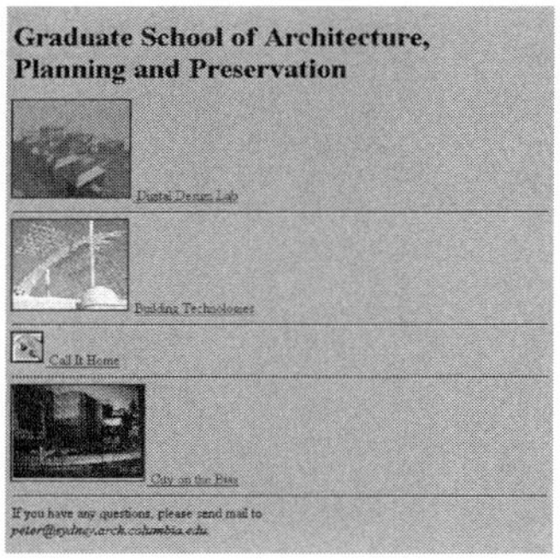

A.6 Name: Graduate School of Architecture at Columbia University
URL: http://www.cc.columbia.edu/~archpub

Of the three items on the initial menu, only one, Building Technologies, was accessible. But there is plenty there to excite one's interest! A section called Architectural Anatomy Online "documents the constructive details of major American architectural projects using a variety of multimedia and graphic techniques." Four buildings are represented, as of December 1994. Other menu items are Course Materials Online, Paper of the Month, Bulletin Board, and Student Coursework.

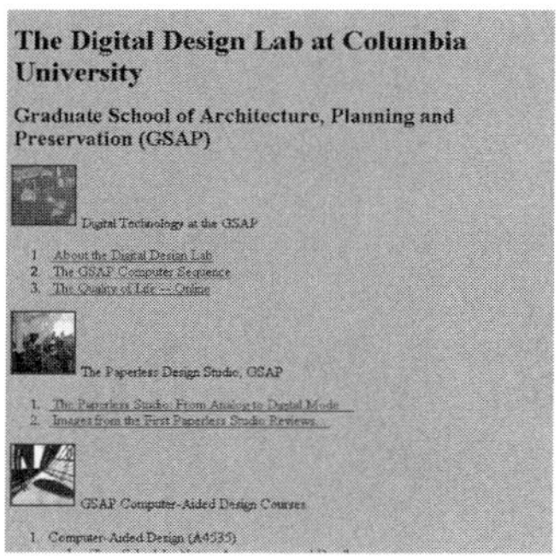

A.7 Name: The Digital Design Lab at Columbia University
URL: http://www.arch.columbia.edu

Another site of the Graduate School of Architecture, Planning and Preservation, including the following menu choices: Digital Technology at the GSAP; the Paperless Design Studio, GSAP; DDL Architectural Projects; and GSAP Computer-Aided Design Courses. "The Digital Design Lab . . . deals with issues surrounding the question of access to the Information Superhighway and focuses on the development of intuitive three-dimensional interfaces for multimedia and on-line learning environments."

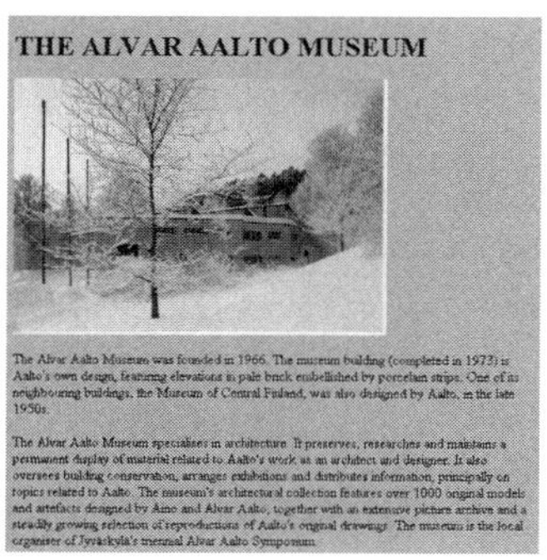

A.8 Name: Alvar Aalto Museum
URL: http://www.cs.jyu.fi/~jatahu/aalto/homepage.html

Neat collection of Aalto information, as well as information about the museum.

A.9 Name: Prairie Archnet
URL: http://cad9.cadlab.umanitoba.ca

A project of the CADLAB of the Faculty of Architecture of the University of Manitoba and the Alberta, Saskatchewan and Manitoba associations of architecture, this site has potential to be a tremendous source of information, if the promise of their menu proves out (note the menu section, Resources). For the moment, in addition to a section on the university's program, and on the professional architectural associations of Canada, there is a section titled Items of Interest (rather far along in the menu). Here is the Acanthus Virtual Gallery of work by "prairie professionals, students of architecture and other notable contributors," and the Digital Warehouse, a student journal.

A.10 Name: Rice Design Alliance
URL: http://riceinfo.rice.edu:80/ES/Architecture/RDA/RDA

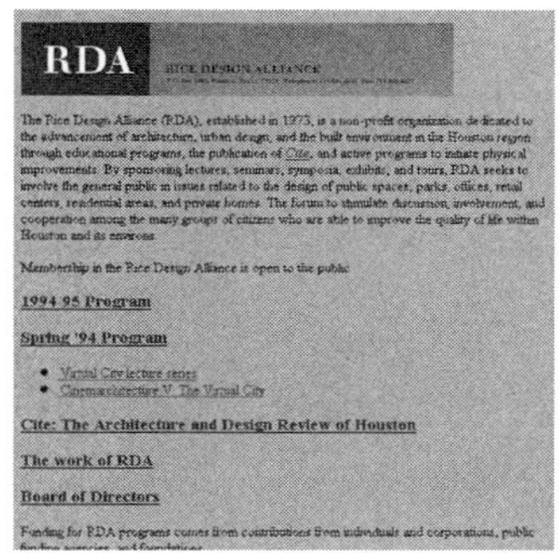

This site holds full text of many of the papers given in the spring lecture series on the virtual city, as well as information on the Design Alliance.

A.11 Name: British Columbia Ministry of Environment, Lands & Parks
URL: http://www.env.gov.bc.ca/

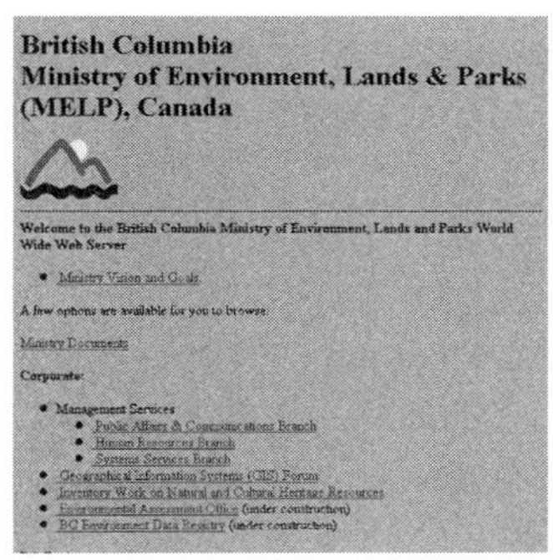

Includes a GIS Forum, ministry documents, and inventory work on natural and cultural heritage resources.

A.12 Name: On-Line Visual Literacy Project
URL: http://www.pomona.claremont.edu/visual-lit/intro/intro.html

Good basic introduction, as it explains each element of visual literacy (e.g., value, hue, scale, motion, etc.).

A.13 Name: Art and Architecture, Carnegie Mellon
URL: http://english.hss.cmu.edu/Art.html

"A few images, some gopher bookmarks, and some texts."

B. ARCHITECTURE/BUILDING INFORMATION

B.1 Name: Institute for Research in Construction. National Research Council Canada.
URL: http://www.irc.nrc.ca

Emerging site with information on staff, research projects, and publications. Some full-text items are included. French and English versions available.

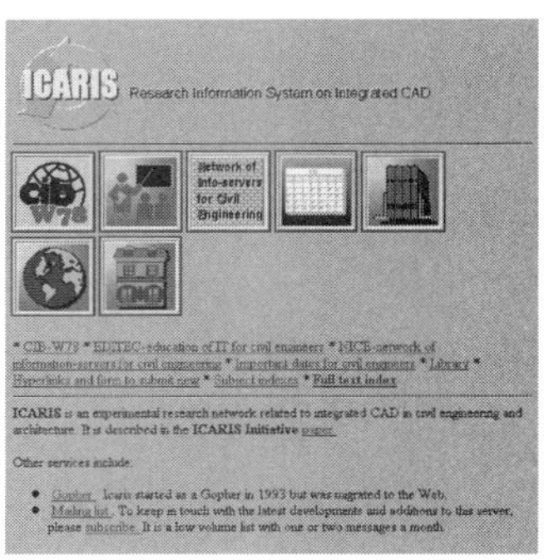

B.2 Name: ICARIS
URL: http://www.fagg.uni-lj.si/ICARIS

"ICARIS is an experimental research network related to integrated CAD in civil engineering and architecture." It includes bibliographies, full-text papers, a searchable civil engineers' calendar of events, and EDITEC and W78 membership databases.

B.3 Name: CIB W78 Conseil International du Batiment Working Group on IT in Construction
URL: http://delphi.kstr.lth.se/w78

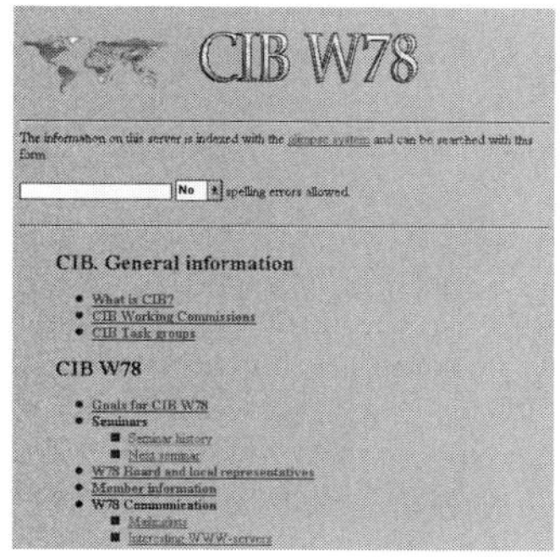

A description of the CIB, its task groups, goals, seminars, members, mailing lists, and links to other sites.

B.4 Name: Solar Energy and Building Physics Laboratory (Laboratoire d'Energie Solaire et de Physique du Batiment)
URL: http://lesowww.epfl.ch/

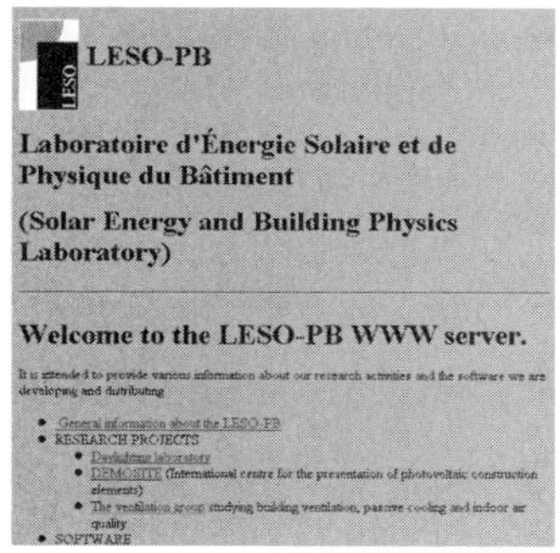

Includes information on research projects in daylighting and photovoltaics. It is also an excellent entry into some of the technical Internet sources related to building.

B.5 Name: Chinese University of Hong Kong, Department of Architecture
URL: http://www.arch.cuhk.hk/

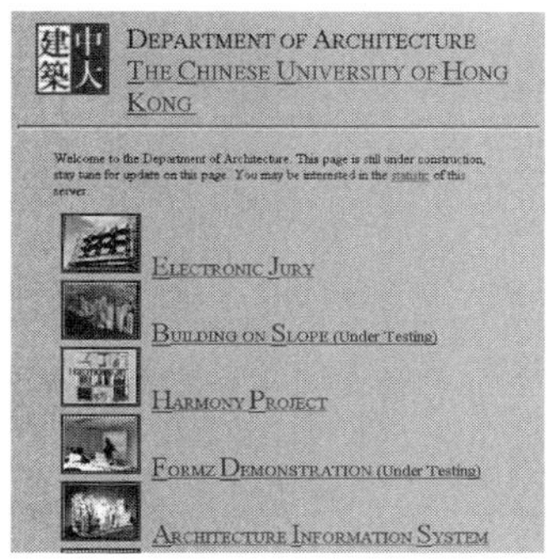

Under construction. Some information and images on housing in China and Hong Kong.

B.6 Name: Energy Efficient and Environmentally Responsible Housing in Canada
URL: http://web.cs.ualberta.ca/~art/house/

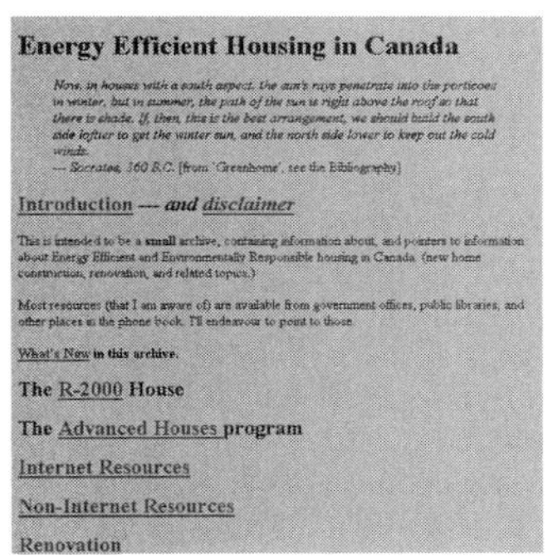

"Intended to be a small archive, containing information, and pointers to information, about Energy Efficient and Environmentally Responsible housing in Canada." Includes information about R-2000 homes and the Advanced Houses program.

B.7 Name: CIE (Commission Internationale de l'Eclairage)
URL: http://www.hike.te.chiba-u.ac.jp/ikeda/CIE/home.html

Publications, press releases, extracts from CIE Journal.

C. ARCHITECTURE LIBRARIES

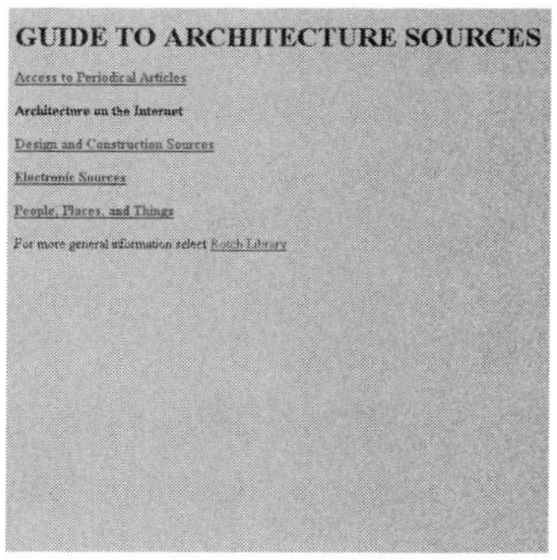

C.1 Name: Leininger Home Page
URL: http://www.mit.edu:8001/afs/athena.mit.edu/user/m/j/mjl/www/pageone.html

Set up by MIT's Architecture Librarian, Michael Leininger, this site provides guides, some annotated, to library information in architecture and construction, including guides to construction dictionaries, biographical sources, directories, building codes, accessibility information, and Boston architecture.

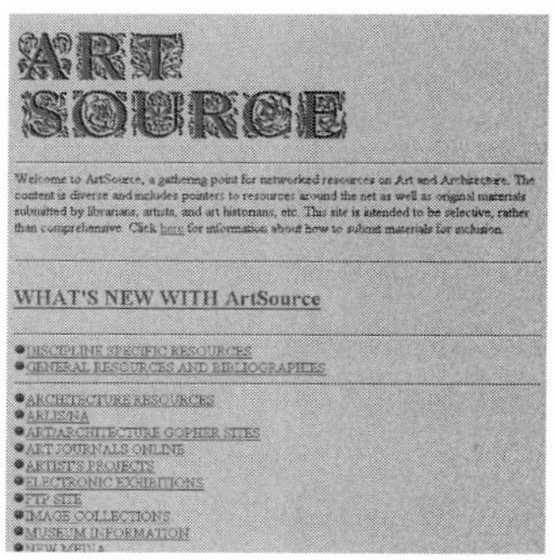

C.2 Name: ArtSource
URL: http://www.uky.edu/Artsource/artsourcehome.html

ArtSource provides text of bibliographies and guides, an archive of ARLIS-L discussions, and links to information on art and architecture (although it is much more heavily art than architecture). A hypertext version of this guide is also available here. Items are available for ftp from ftp://convex.cc.uky.edu/pub/artsource

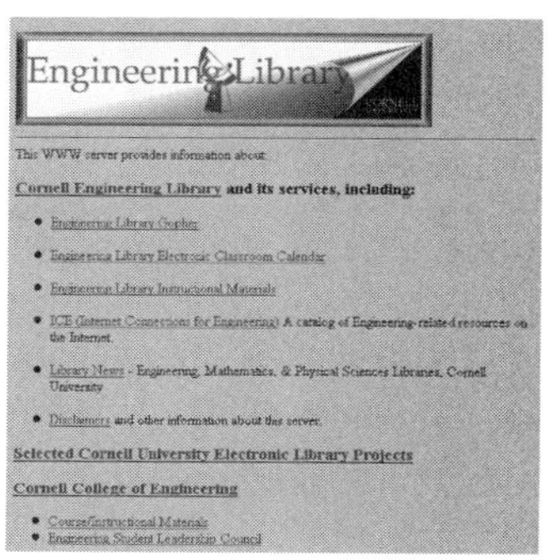

C.3 Name: Cornell University Engineering Library
URL: http://www.englib.cornell.edu

The library's instructional materials for Internet instruction are especially interesting.

D. PRIMARILY IMAGES

D.1 Name: AcIS Imaging and Hypertext Projects
URL: http://gutentag.cc.columbia.edu/imaging/html/imaging.html

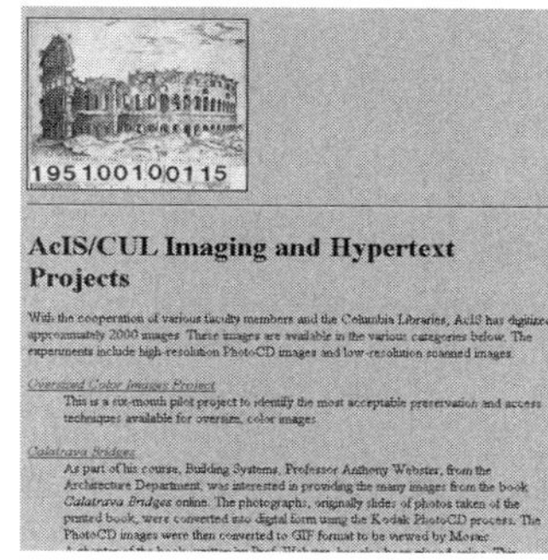

A joint project of AcIS (Academic Information Systems) and Columbia University Libraries. It includes 2,000 digitized images (e.g., Paris maps, Calatrava bridges, and miscellaneous other topics). Home of the Digital Image Access Project.

D.2 Name: ArtServe: Australian National University, Institute of the Arts
URL: http://rubens.anu.edu.au

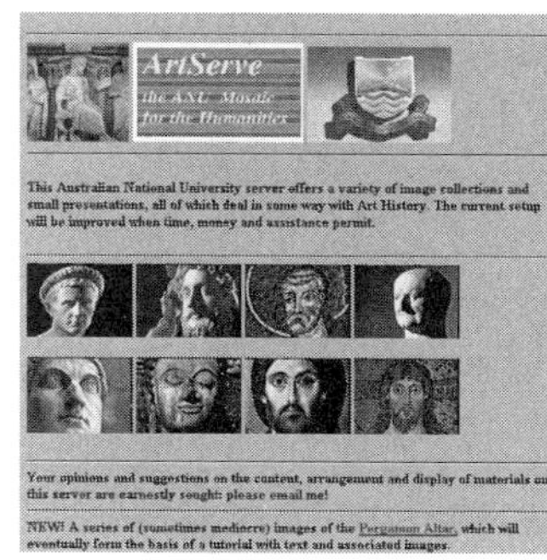

More than 2,500 images of classical architecture of the Mediterranean basin, survey of Islamic architecture, and plans to add as many as 3,000 images of European sculpture and architecture from the classical period to the nineteenth century. To go directly to the searchable architecture database, use the URL: http://rubens.anu.edu.au/ architecture_form.html. There is also a searchable book on Greek and Roman cities of Western Turkey.

D.3 Name: University of Virginia Digital Image Center, Fiske Kimball Fine Arts Library
URL: http://www.lib.virginia.edu/dic/colls/arh102/index.html

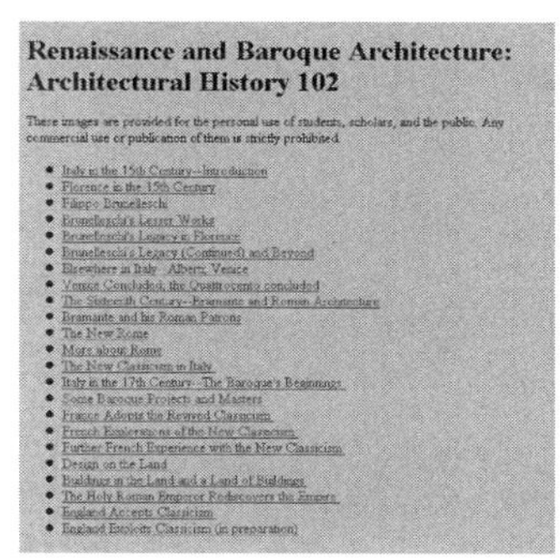

Images from an architecture history class on Renaissance and Baroque architecture in France and Italy.

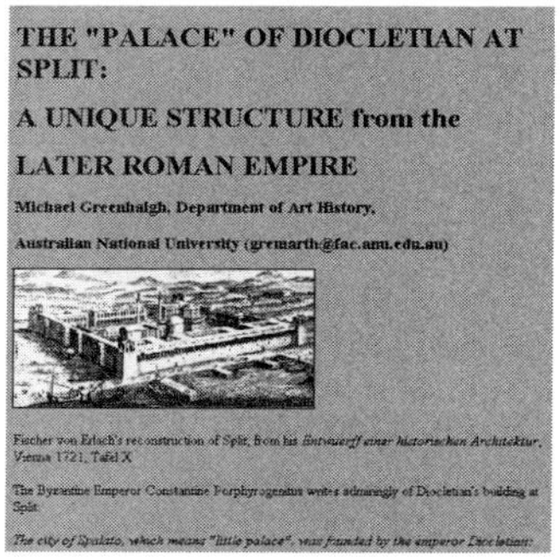

D.4 Name: The Palace of Diocletian
URL: http://www.ncsa.uiuc.edu/SDG/Experimental/split/split1.html

Lots of images, plus text, contributed by Michael Greenhalgh, Department of Art History, Australian National University.

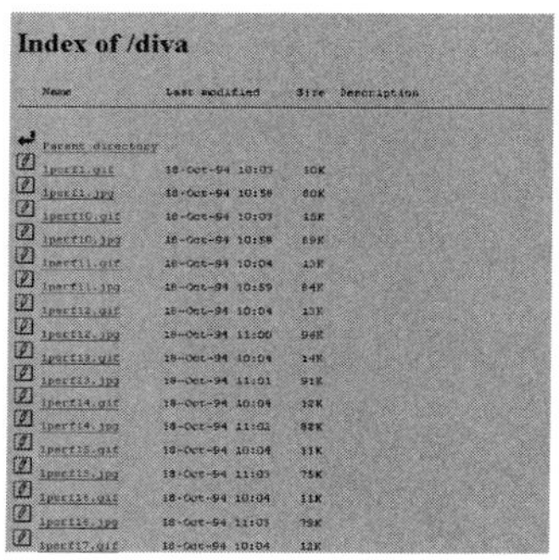

D.5 Name: DIVA (Digital Images—Visual Arts)
URL: http://www.monash.edu.au/diva

Includes Australian art and architecture images.

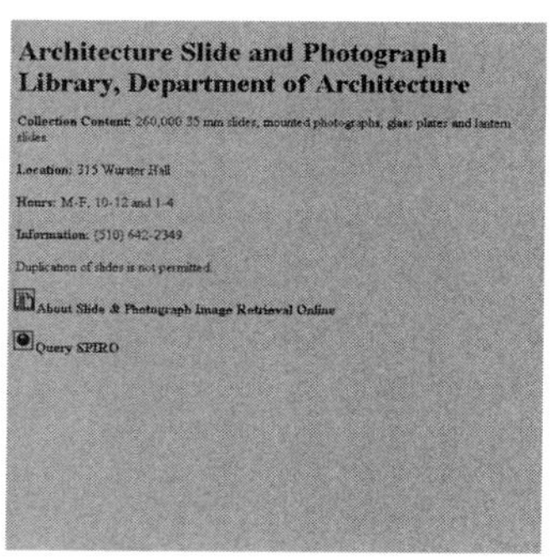

D.6 Name: Architecture Slide and Photograph Library, University of California, Berkeley
URL: http://www.mip.berkeley.edu/mip/collections/arcslide.html

Access to the SPIRO image collection; as of 1992, 3,300 digital images.

E. UNIVERSITY ARCHITECTURE PROGRAMS

E.1 Name: School of Architecture Property and Planning
URL: http://archpropplan.auckland.ac.nz

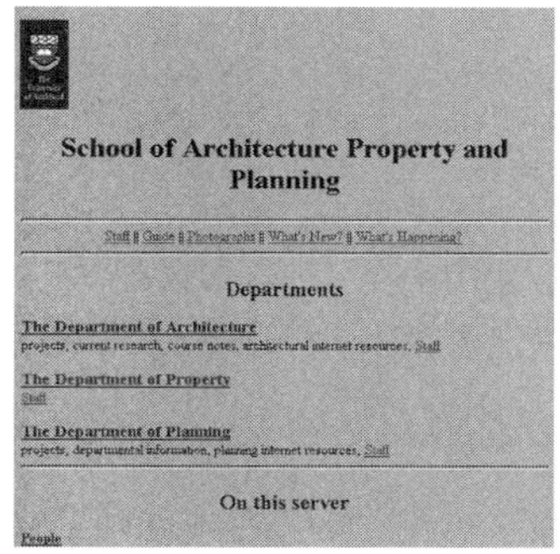

Information about the school, lecture notes, abstracts, and papers written by members of the department (with a comments facility), sections on architectural visualization and computer graphics (including a gallery of student computer-based modelling and rendering), ftp offerings, and many links to other sites of interest.

E.2 Name: Massachusetts Institute of Technology School of Architecture and Planning
URL: http://alberti.mit.edu/ap/ap.html

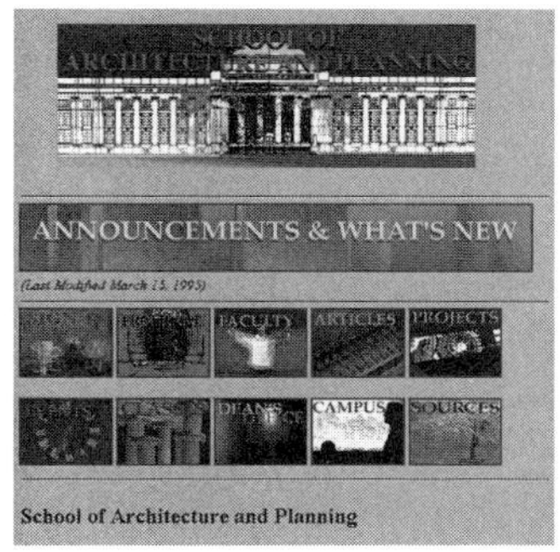

Main item of interest here is the current issue of the school's newsletter PLAN. Information on courses at the school are also included.

E.3 Name: University of Miami School of Architecture
URL: http://rossi.arc.miami.edu

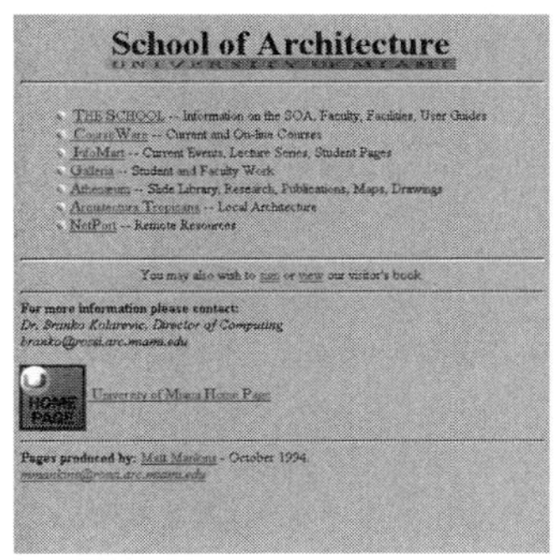

Information on the school, local architecture ("Arquitectura Tropicana"), a virtual gallery of students' work, maps to faculty's offices, and other information. Nice set of links in their Netport section.

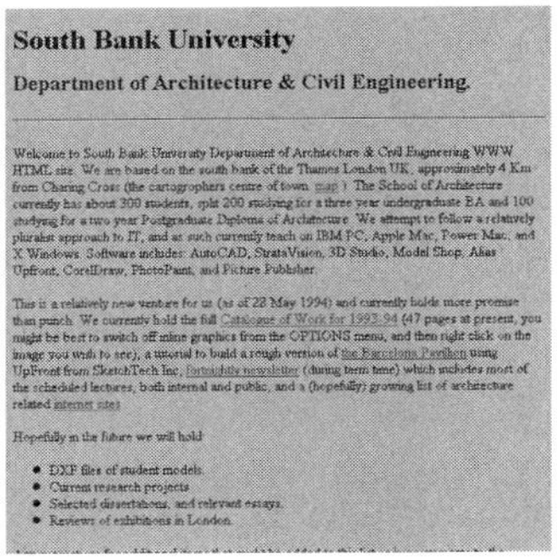

E.4 Name: South Bank University Department of Architecture & Civil Engineering
URL: http://www.sbu.ac.uk/Architecture/home.html

Information about the school including their catalog, newsletter, and student work. Links to architecture net sites. A tutorial on how to do the Barcelona Pavilion using UpFront.

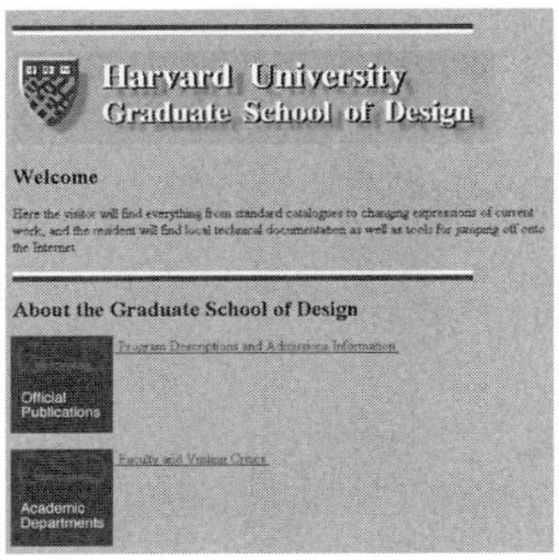

E.5 Name: Harvard Graduate School of Design Home Page
URL: http://gsd.harvard.edu/GSD.html

School information, a tutorial on creating graphical information maps, and links to both general and design-related Internet sites.

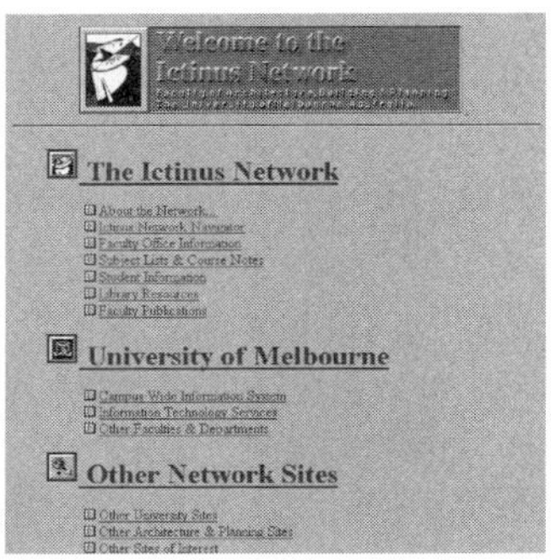

E.6 Name: Melbourne University Faculty of Architecture and Planning
URL: http://www.arbld.unimelb.edu.au

Courses, faculty information, etc. Most interesting entry is their progressive plan to provide a networked environment.

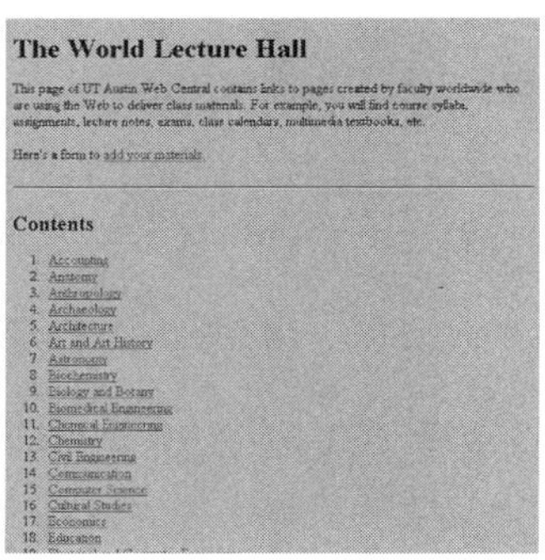

E.7 Name: World Lecture Hall
URL: http://wwwhost.cc.utexas.edu/world/instruction/index.html

Interesting experiment to make available in one place the syllabi, essays, and images from professors in various disciplines. There are only three relating to architecture (two from Columbia and one from the University of Virginia). The URL for the architecture section is: http://wwwhost.cc.utexas.edu/world/instruction/index.html#Architecture

E.8 Name: Mississippi State University, School of Architecture
URL: http://wright.sarc.msstate.edu

Information about the school, its computerization plan, its courses and faculty, its architectural applications of virtual environments. Links to other sites are also included.

E.9 Name: University of Adelaide, Faculty of Architecture and Urban Design
URL: http://www.arch.adelaide.edu.au:80/home.html

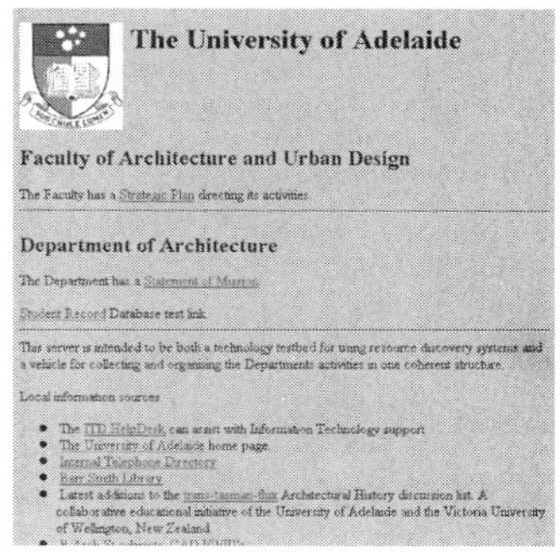

Strategic plan and statement of mission for the school, plus an archive of the restricted discussion list on architecture history/theory Trans-Tasman-Flux.

E.10 Name: Curtin University of Technology, Perth, Australia, School of Architecture, Construction and Planning
URL: http://puffin.curtin.edu.au

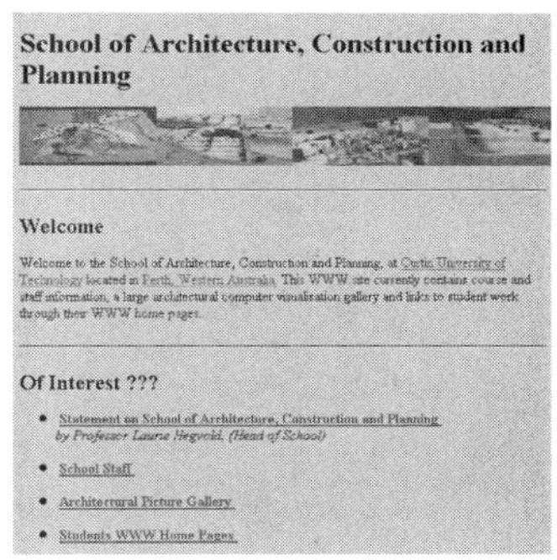

"This WWW site currently contains course and staff information, a large architectural computer visualization gallery and links to student work through their WWW home pages." The gallery contains 150 images as of December 1994.

E.11 Name: University of California, Berkeley Building Science Laboratory Research Facilities
URL: http://www.ced.berkeley.edu/cedr/bldgsci/bsl/lab.html

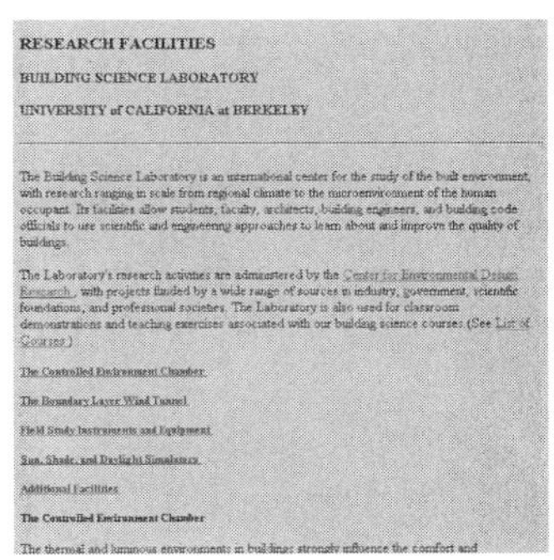

Description of their facilities such as the controlled environment chamber, the boundary layer wind tunnel, field study instruments and equipment, and sun/shade/daylight simulators.

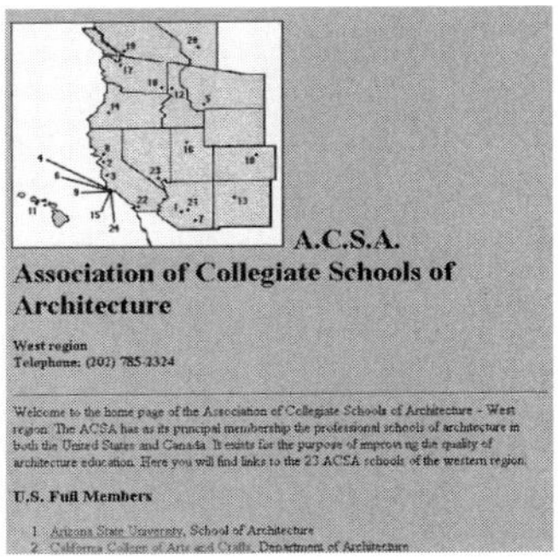

E.12 Name: Association of Collegiate Schools of Architecture Western Region
URL: http://uhunix.uhcc.hawaii.edu:3333/acsa_home.html

Information/links relating to the twenty-three ACSA schools of the western region.

F. ARCHITECTURAL COMPUTING

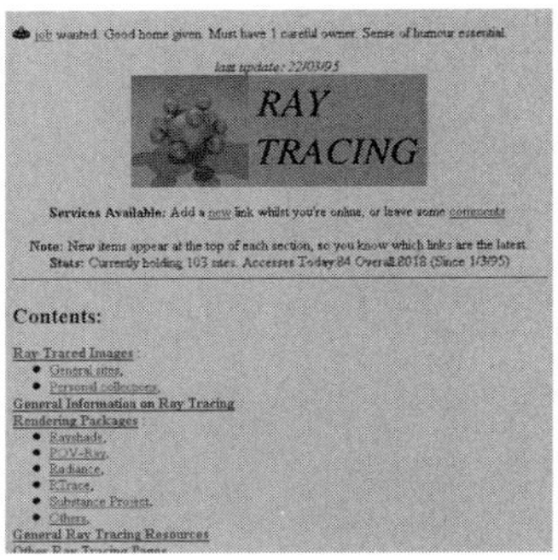

F.1 Name: Ray Tracing Home Page
URL: http://www.cm.cf.ac.uk/Ray.Tracing

Images, general information (including an annotated bibliography), and information on rendering packages.

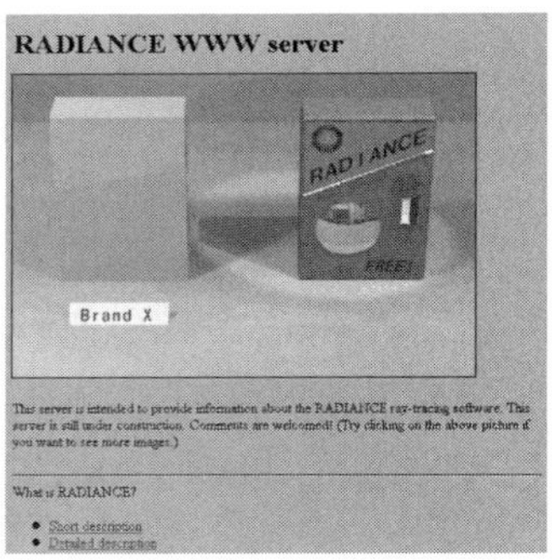

F.2 Name: Radiance Home Page
URL: http://radsite.lbl.gov/radiance/HOME.html

Description of the radiance ray-tracing software, sources on the Internet from which to obtain it, tips for using it, an archive of a radiance discussion group, and other WWW sites featuring radiance.

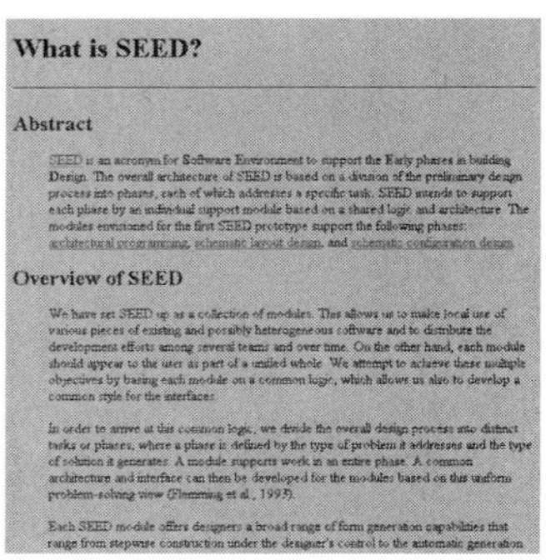

F.3 Name: SEED
URL: http://logan.edrc.cmu.edu:8001/OverView.html

"SEED is an acronym for Software Environment to support the Early phases in building Design . . . The modules envisioned for the first SEED prototype support the following phases: architectural programming, schematic layout design, and schematic configuration design."

G. LINKS TO ARCHITECTURAL INFORMATION

G.1 Name: Landscape Architecture Web
URL: http://tdg.uoguelph.ca/nav/LA_startingpoints.html

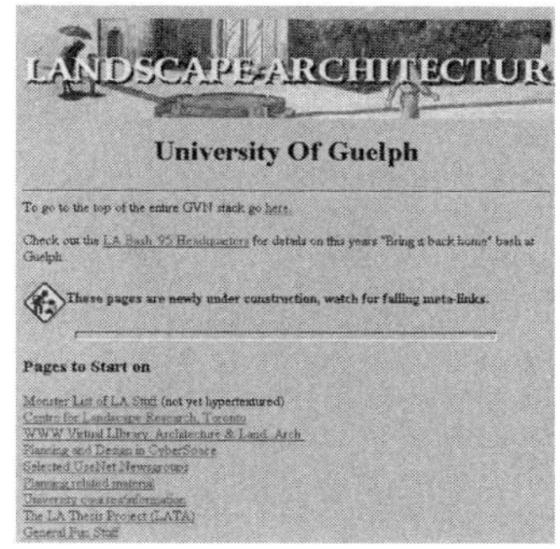

Includes links to lots of environmental servers, landscape images, and planning documents and statistics.

G.2 Name: Netlink Server
URL: http://netlink.wlu.edu:1020

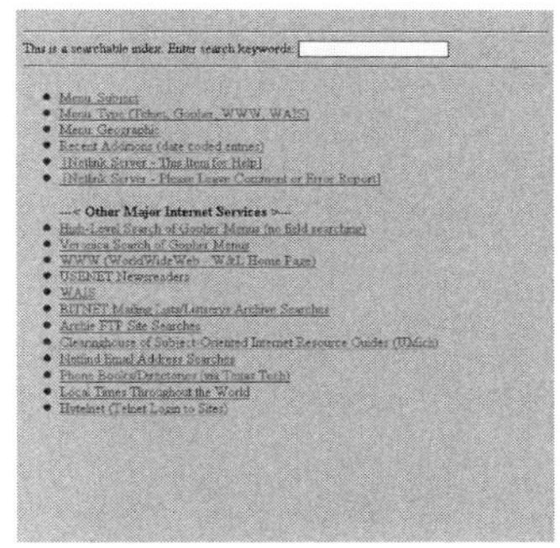

Washington and Lee's subject index to net resources. Choose "menu:subject," then architecture.

G.3 Name: Architecture and Visualization
URL: http://bau2.uibk.ac.at/erwin/Arch/archinc.html

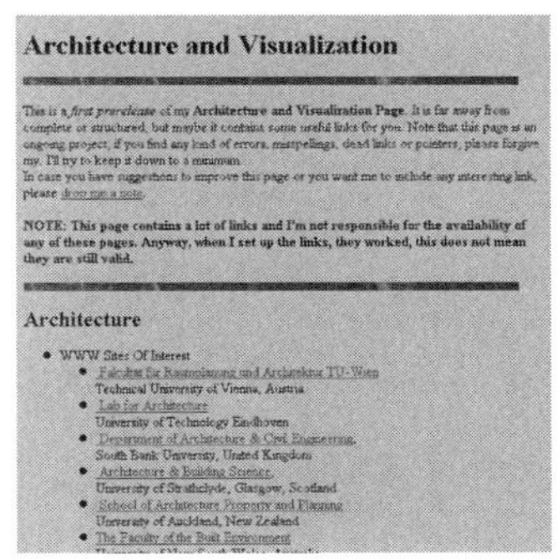

Personal selection of newsgroups, web sites, and articles, and other "starting points" put together by Erwin Zierler at the University of Innsbruck.

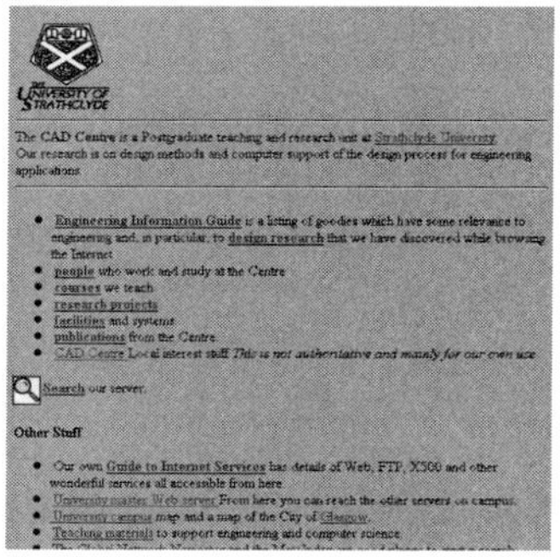

G.4 Name: University of Strathclyde (Glasgow) CAD Center
URL: http://www.cad.strath.ac.uk/

Good set of links to engineering and industrial design information resources.

GLOSSARY

AGENT: Software utility that works in the background to perform tasks on behalf of the user. An example is a "newsgathering" agent, which browses information services for items of interest to the user.

AGGREGATE OBJECT: An object composed of many primitive objects.

ALIAS: An alternative name or representation. For example, some software programs allow the user to create an alias as a shorthand for a complex command or as a pointer to a file.

ALIASING: The spatial and temporal artifacts which result from digitally sampling an analog world. The most common example of spatial aliasing is the jaggies, the stair-stepping of diagonal lines on display screens.

ALGORITHM: A predictable sequence of steps which act upon data to generate a result. Most software programs consist of algorithms (verbs) and data structures (nouns).

ALPHA: A common name for the transparency value stored for each pixel in an image.

AMBIENT LIGHT: A light source that distributes light uniformly in all directions. Ambient light illuminates all objects equally regardless of their location and orientation.

AMBIENT REFLECTION: The surface reflection of ambient light.

ANIMATION: A sequence of still images displayed in rapid sequence to produce the illusion of a moving image.

APPLICATION: A software program that is designed to perform, or be "applied" to, a specific task. Normally requires the presence of an operating system to run, such as Windows, MacOS, or Unix.

ARCHIVE: A permanent indexed record of a set of documents, either original or copy. Physical archive media include photocopy and microfiche. Digital archive media include magnetic tape, disk, and rewritable optical disk.

AREA LIGHT SOURCE: A light source whose light emanates from a surface area (such as a recessed flourescent ceiling fixture) instead of a single point.

ARTIFICIAL INTELLIGENCE: Software algorithms that are designed to "learn" from experience, most typically found in "expert systems." Despite years of promise, such tools have yet to appear within practical mainstream applications in architecture.

ASCII: The de facto international standard for encoding numerical and alphabetical characters into binary 0s and 1s.

ASSOCIATIVE DIMENSIONING: Dimensions that are linked to geometry within a drawing, and automatically updated when the geometry is moved or stretched.

ASSOCIATIVITY: Defining a behavioral relationship between two or more objects in a drawing, for example, defining a line which connects the center of one circle to the tangent of another circle. If either circle is moved, the line responds automatically.

ASYNCHRONOUS: Communication exchange that does not occur simultaneously, in which each party waits for the other to respond. Examples include asynchronous communication between printer and computer, or an asynchronous E-mail exchange.

ATTRIBUTE: A characteristic of a drawing object which can be assigned a value. For example, a "door" object may contain the following attributes: height, width, thickness, type, rating, hardware. Each instance of the door could contain different values for those attributes.

AXIS: One of three orthogonal lines (X, Y, and Z) which define a three-dimensional coordinate system. The origin lies at the intersection of the three axes.

BACKUP: A redundant copy of digital data made to prevent data loss in the event of hardware or software failure. Incremental backups are typically performed daily; full backups are typically performed weekly.

BANDWIDTH: Data-carrying capacity of a communication channel; the higher the bandwidth, the higher the information volume.

BASIC: A popular programming language for casual programmers.

BATCH: A set of operations performed in sequence, without intervention or assistance by the user. For example, batch plotting a set of drawings, instead of plotting one at a time.

BERNOULLI BOX: Trade name for a removable cartridge disk drive. Provides a low-cost, portable media format for physically transferring digitial data between non-networked computers.

BIT: The basic building block of digital information. A bit stores the value of 0 or 1.

BITMAP: A two-dimensional grid of pixels. Technically, a bitmap contains only one bit per pixel, although the term is used to describe a wide variety of raster images.

BLOCK: AutoCAD term for a component.

BOUNDARY REPRESENTATION: An enclosed three-dimensional space defined by a set of intersecting surfaces.

BOUNDING BOX: The smallest three-dimensional box which encloses a set of objects. It is specified by determining the minimum and maximum X, Y, and Z coordinate values of all objects.

BROWSER: A program for reading hypertext, that is, text that contains a link to other documents.

BUG: A flaw in a software program.

BUMP MAP: An image used to tweak the apparent surface orientation of an object when the object is rendered. The effect is to create a subtle bumpy effect on an otherwise flat surface.

BUS: Primary internal communications channel of a computer. Examples include ISA, PCI, SCSI.

BYTE: A group of eight bits. A byte can store a positive integer 0 to 255, an alphanumeric character, or a portion of a larger data structure, such as a four-byte integer or eight-byte floating point number.

C: A popular programming language for professional software programmers. Most desktop software applications today (AutoCAD, WordPerfect, Lotus 1-2-3) are written in the C language.

CAD: Acronym for Computer-Aided Design.

CAD/CAM: Acronym for Computer-Aided Design/Computer-Aided Manufacturing. The manufacture of a product using machining equipment controlled using surface information derived from the three-dimensional CAD models.

CADD: Acronym for Computer-Aided Design and Drafting. Obsolete.

CD-ROM: Acronym for Compact Disk-Read Only Memory, or read-only optical disks. A typical 5.25-inch optical disk can store approximately 600 megabytes of data. Most CD-ROM disks are pressed for very low unit cost (less than $1) using expensive mastering equipment. Recordable CD disk drives can also be used create CD-ROM disks for a higher unit cost (approximately $10 per disk).

CELL: Intergraph term for component.

CHANNEL: A single component value of a pixel. Typical channels include Red, Green, Blue, and Alpha.

CHILDREN: In a hierarchical model, the elements that are the next level down from the current object. For example, an object describing a typical module of an elevation might include windows and doors as children.

CISC: Acronym for Complex Instruction Set Computing. A type of central processing unit (CPU) which includes a rich set of instructions. Popular CISC chips include Intel's 486, Pentium, and forthcoming P6 processors, and Motorola's 680x0 series, used for years as the CPU for the various models of the Macintosh prior to Apple's adoption of the PowerPC RISC chip.

CLIENT: A computer that depends on a network server for certain operations and resources, such as file sharing, printing, and database querying.

CLIPBOARD: A temporary buffer provided by an operating system which can be used in applications to exchange information between different software applications. Cut and copy operations place data into the clipboard; paste operations extract data from the clipboard.

CLIPPING PLANES: Two planes perpindicular to the view vector which delimit the portion of a three-dimensional scene to be displayed. Only the objects between the near and far (or hither and yon) clipping planes are displayed.

COMPONENT: In CAD, a predefined set of graphic objects which is given a name and can be instanced within a drawing.

COMPRESSION: Reducing the amount of memory or storage space required to describe a piece of data, usually by identifying repeating patterns within the data. The amount of compression depends on the complexity of the information being compressed. Commonly used for shrinking the size of digital images and videos.

COMPUTER: A tool that executes binary instructions (encoded in software programs) to affect binary data stored in memory, received from input devices, and sent to output devices.

CONCAVE POLYGON: A polygon with at least one interior angle greater than 180 degrees.

CONSTRUCTION PLANE: In three-dimensional modeling software, the current surface on which new geometry is drawn. The orientation of new geometry is defined by a local coordinate system.

CONSTRUCTIVE SOLID GEOMETRY: The act of creating complex solid models by combining and performing a sequence of operations on simple primitives.

CONVEX POLYGON: A polygon with no interior angle greater than 180 degrees.

CROPPING: Resizing the boundary or viewport through which a graphics object is displayed. In most cases, the object is not changed, but only how it is displayed. Most desktop publishing programs provide cropping tools to control the display of graphics objects inside documents.

CROSSHAIRS: A cursor that is displayed as two or three orthogonal lines which extend to the edges of the display window.

CURVE FITTING: Transforming a sequence of connected lines into a curve which passes through or near the vertices of the lines.

DATABASE: A organized set of information, typically arranged in lists or tables.

DATABASE MANAGEMENT SYSTEM: A system that provides tools to view, filter, query, compare, and report information in a database.

DATA STRUCTURE: A organized sequence of data stored together to represent a primitive object. A data structure defining a "line" in a CAD file, for example, might include two X,Y,Z coordinates (each of which is defined by three floating-point numbers), and three integers to represent color, linetype, and pen.

DEBUG: The task of removing bugs (flaws) from computer software.

DEPTH SORTING: An algorithm for creating hidden-surface images by simply sorting and displaying each surface in the three-dimensional model from back to front.

DESKTOP PUBLISHING: A term coined by Paul Brainerd, founder of Aldus Corporation, to describe the process of using desktop computer software to arrange text blocks, line drawings, and bitmap images within multi-page small-format documents and output the result to high-quality digital printers.

DIFFUSE REFLECTION: The reflection caused by a surface scattering light equally in all directions. The component of reflection associated with dull, matte finishes. The intensity of the reflection is determined by the angle defined by an incoming light ray and an imaginary line perpendicular to the surface of the object (the surface normal). The smaller the angle, the brighter the reflection.

DIGITAL: Representing information in binary format (0s and 1s).

DIGITIZING TABLET: A graphic input device consisting of a magnetized grid of wires with a puck that can detect its location on the grid and communicate its location to the computer. A tablet is an absolute pointing device, compared to a mouse, which is a relative pointing device.

DIRECTORY: A hierarchical structure for organizing computer files. Each directory contains a group of files and/or other directories. Also known as a folder on the Macintosh.

DISK: Primary storage media for computer files and data. Flavors include magnetic (diskette, hard drive) and optical (CD-ROM, read/write optical).

DISPLAY: The cathode-ray tube (CRT) monitor or liquid crystal diode (LCD) panel used to display a computer image.

DITHERING: The algorithm for displaying or printing color images using a small set of color values. Halftoning is a form of dithering, which produces gray-scale images using only black and white values.

DOLLY: Camera motion along the line defined by the camera and its viewing target.

DRAG: To move an object on a display screen dynamically.

DRIVER: A small software program that enables a software application or operating system to work with a specific hardware device. Most hardware peripherals (printers, mice, optical disks, etc.) also include software drivers which must be installed before the peripheral can be used.

DXF: Acronym for Drawing eXchange Format, a file format invented by Autodesk as a means to import and export information to and from AutoCAD drawings. Now supported by virtually all CAD software, the format is the de facto standard means to exchange information between different CAD systems, even though the format is proprietary, inefficient, and suffers the same graphic limitations as AutoCAD, such as lack of symbolic line weights.

EDGE: Where two polygons or surfaces are joined, or where a polygon or surface ends.

ELEMENT: A basic primitive in a graphics drawing: line, arc, circle, text, etc.

ENTITY: Synonym for element.

ETHERNET: De facto standard network communication protocol invented in the 1970s.

EXPERT SYSTEM: A software program that uses a knowledge base combined with rules and a learning mechanism to duplicate the expertise of human specialist. Wildly hyped in the 1980s, useful expert systems have been slow to arrive.

EXPLODE: AutoCAD term for replacing a block (component) in a drawing with the elements that comprise its definition.

FALLOFF: In a spotlight, the decay in intensity of light from the center of its beam.

FENCE: A boundary which encloses a set of objects.

FILE: The primary unit of storage which contains data and programs.

FILE LOCKING: Restricting access to a file to prevent more than one person from making changes to it at the same time. One common method of file locking is "read-only" access, which allows one user to inspect or copy data from a file while another user is working on it.

FILE SERVER: A computer containing files which are intended to be shared across a network.

FILTER: A set of operations applied to a set of data which returns a selected subset of the data or modifications to the data. Database filters are used in queries to extract desired information (for example, "completion date > 1985" and "type = school"). Image-editing filters are used to apply a visual effect (watercolor, mezzotint, high contrast) to a source image.

FLAT SHADING: A simple form of shading in which each surface has the same color at all points. Computationally less expensive than both Gouraud and Phong shading.

FONT: A typeface, characterized by lettering style and character size, usually measured in points. Examples: 12 pt. Helvetica, 36 pt. Times Roman, 8 pt. Palatino.

FRAME: A single image of an animation.

FTP: Acronym for File Transfer Protocol, a commonly used protocol on the Internet that defines how to transfer files between computers.

GIS: Acronym for Geographic Information Systems, primarily used in large-scale mapping applications (infrastructure management, zoning, land use). Most GIS systems provide a high degree of integration between drawing objects and records in an external database.

GOPHER: A menu-based software program commonly used on the Internet to retrieve desired information independent of its physical location.

GOURAUD SHADING: A shading technique in which the surface shade is calculated for surface vertices, and interpolated for points in the interior of the surface. Computationally more expensive than flat shading, less expensive than Phong shading.

GROUP: A set of objects which can be edited as a single object. Unlike symbols, groups are not instanced, but are an informal way of collecting objects together for manipulation.

HALFTONING: A form of dithering, where gray-scale images are produced using black and white values.

HATCHING: A pattern of linework which is repeated inside an enclosed shape.

HETEROGENEOUS NETWORK: A collection of different types of computers (PC, Mac, Unix, et al.) networked together. Heterogeneous networks are harder to install, harder to manage, and harder to upgrade. Not recommended except for the most technologically ambitious architectural firm.

HIDDEN LINE: An algorithm which displays only the lines in a three-dimensional model which would be seen from a particular view. Requires that the model be constructed of surfaces, the visible edges of which are displayed as lines in a hidden-line view.

HIDDEN SURFACE: An algorithm which displays only the surfaces of a three-dimensional model which would be seen from a particular view. Requires that the model be constructed of surfaces.

HIGHLIGHT: The bright spot on a surface which results from the effect of specular reflections.

HOME PAGE: The root graphic screen which identifies the World Wide Web server being accessed. Provides a menu of information resources and services and pointers to related external resources.

HTML: Acronym for Hypertext Markup Language, the language in which documents published on the World Wide Web are written.

HYPERTEXT: Text that contains a link to other documents, usually indicated by *underlining*. Clicking on a hypertext link displays the linked document.

IGES: Acronym for Initial Graphic Exchange Specification, a neutral file format which can be used to translate vector drawings between different software programs. IGES was introduced years before Autodesk's DXF format and is recognized by the National Bureau of Standards, but is supported by few software programs.

IMAGE: A two-dimensional array of pixels, each of which contains a color or intensity value. Also known as a bitmap or raster image.

INSTANCE (OF A COMPONENT): A clone of a previously defined component. An instance of a component does not contain the component's geometry, but only contains a pointer to the original component, along with location, scaling, and rotation parameters. If the original component is modified, all instances will reflect the modification.

INTEGRATION: Design and implementation of computer systems to work in a cohesive fashion. Integration primarily deals with the ability of software programs to work with and share information with each other.

INTENSITY: Synonym for lightness or brightness. One component of the HLS (Hue, Lightness, Saturation) model for defining color. The higher the intensity, the lighter the color appears.

INTERPOLATION: Calculating values or locations of intermediate points to provide a smooth transition between end points. Individual animation frames, for example, are interpolated from keyframes.

IP: Internet Protocol, the basic communication protocol upon which the Internet is based.

JAGGIES: A form of aliasing seen as the stair-stepping of diagonal lines on a display.

JOYSTICK: A fixed two-dimensional pointing device with a pivoting handle.

KB (KILOBYTE): One thousand bytes. (Technically, 1,024 bytes, but it is typically rounded.)

KEYFRAME: An important frame of an animation which describes the position of the camera, lights, or objects at a specific point in time. Keyframes are defined by the user, and all intervening frames are calculated by the animation software using interpolation and smoothing algorithms.

LAN: Local area network. The most common method of connecting multiple computers together to allow sharing of files, printers, and other shared resources. Compared to a WAN (Wide Area Network) a LAN has substantial limitations of its physical reach, depending on the particular networking hardware used. For most architectural firms, the physical limitation is not an issue.

LAYERS: The basic organizational structure provided in most CAD and graphics illustration programs which allows users to categorize and filter information for viewing and plotting.

LCD: Liquid Crystal Diode, a flat-screen display technology.

LEAF: A child element in a hierarchical model with no children of its own, indicating the lowest level of the model.

LEVEL: Synonym for layer. Used by some CAD systems, such as Intergraph.

LIBRARY: A collection of shared files, objects, or other information resources.

LISP: Acronym for List Processing, a software programming language. AutoLISP is a subset of the LISP language which is integrated into AutoCAD for development of customized tools.

LOCAL COORDINATE SYSTEM: A coordinate system that defines the origin and axis to be used for constructing new objects, and for defining transformations such as moving and rotation.

MACRO LANGUAGE: A language intended for use by the end user to develop customized scripts and special purpose tools which run on top of the software program.

MB (MEGABYTE): One million bytes. (Actually, 1,048,576 bytes, but it is typically rounded.)

MODEM: Acronym for MOdulator-DEModulator. Used to convert the digital signals from a computer into the analog signals suitable for transmission along phone lines. As phone lines eventually become entirely digital, modems will disappear. Standard equipment for new personal computers.

MOSAIC: Browsing software for the Internet originally developed at the University of Illinois, which was widely licensed and now appears in various incarnations in commercial software products. Provides a graphic user interface to the Internet, sheltering the user from its arcane and obscure keyboard command structure.

MOTION BLUR: A blurring of objects seen in a photograph of a moving object. Motion blur algorithms reproduce this effect to simulate motion of objects in a rendered image.

MOTION PATH: The interpolated path generated by animation software from keyframes which define an object's position and orientation in space at different time intervals.

MS-DOS: Acronym for Microsoft Disk Operating System. The operating system licensed by Microsoft was introduced in the original IBM PC in 1982, licensed to manufacturers of IBM PC clones, and subsequently became the world's most popular operating system. Not known for its user-friendliness, DOS attracted the vast majority of PC software developers in the mid-1980s, which made it the desktop operating system standard on nine out of every ten personal computers sold through 1995. Windows 95 is Microsoft's first desktop version of Windows which does not require MS-DOS in order to run.

MULTITASKING: The ability of an operating system to control a computer processor so it can dynamically switch between different programs, providing the appearance of doing more than one thing simultaneously. The term is somewhat of a misnomer, because the processor actually only executes one task at a time.

MULTI-USER: The ability of an operating system to acknowledge the presence of more than one human being inhabiting the universe. UNIX, MacOS, Windows NT, and Windows 95 are multi-user operating systems, to varying degrees. DOS is a single-user operating system.

NEGLIGENCE: Failure to exercise the care that someone else would exercise under the same or similar circumstances.

NESTING: The ability to include a component inside another component. For example, a column component may include two other components in its definition, a capital and a base. As a result, the capital and base are nested inside of the column component.

NODE: In a hierarchical model, an object in the hierarchy with children of its own.

NORMAL (VECTOR): A vector perpendicular to a line, plane, or surface at a given point.

NTSC: Video signal standard in the United States and Western Hemisphere.

NUMERICAL CONTROL (NC): The process of controlling a manufacturing robot by transmitting to it sequences of instructions derived from the geometry of a three-dimensional model by a CAD/CAM software program.

NUMERICAL MODEL: A simulation that uses mathematical formulae to represent the behavior of a system.

NURBS: Non-Uniform Rational B-Spline. A flavor of three-dimensional curve.

OBJECT: A synonym for element or entity. In object-oriented systems, an object consists of data and procedures stored together.

OBJECT SNAP: The ability of a drawing program to place new points precisely overlaid on points of existing objects. Most software programs provide various types of object snap: endpoint, midpoint, intersection, et al.

OPERATING SYSTEM: The layer of software between the end-user program and the low-level hardware and resources of a computer, such as memory, disk drives, file systems, and input/output devices. The operating system manages resources for applications.

OS/2: Introduced in 1987 by Microsoft and IBM as the successor to DOS, OS/2 has floundered for years in the small business and consumer markets. OS/2 was abandoned by Microsoft in 1990, who later introduced Windows NT (originally OS/2 3.0). IBM continued development of the operating system, which has failed to attract a large number of software developers. Still popular within Fortune 1000 corporations who develop customized applications, OS/2 will never be supported by enough commercial software applications to compete with Windows and the Mac on the desktop. Its third major release, known as 'Warp,' was introduced in 1994.

PAINT: In digital image-editing software, the process of applying new colors or values to pixels by manipulating "brushes" with the cursor.

PARAMETER: A variable within a procedure. An object parameter is similar to an attribute, except attributes are usually static pieces of descriptive data, while an object's parameter values are used by a procedure to generate its geometry.

PARAMETRIC: An object that is created as the output of a procedure which depends on parameter values provided by the user. A parametric stair, for example, might be defined by three parameters: tread/riser ratio, configuration, and floor-to-floor height.

PARENT: In a hierachical model, the object which is the next level up from the current object. The parent of a "riser/tread" object might be a "stair" object. An object with no parent is the root.

PHONG SHADING: A shading technique in which each point on a surface is shaded by calculating the normal of the surface at that point and determining its angle to the light source. Computationally more expensive than Flat or Gouraud shading.

PIXEL: Shorthand for picture element. An image is composed of thousands of pixels, each representing the color of an image at a given point. Each pixel value consists of several channels, such as red, green, and blue components of the color and/or transparency information contained in an alpha channel.

PLOTTER: A large-format digital output device. Plotter technologies include pen, ink-jet, electrostatic, thermal, and laser. Plotters typically refer to large-format output devices, while printers typically refer to small-format devices, although the boundaries between the two are blurring.

POINT LIGHT SOURCE: A light source that distributes light evenly in all directions from a specified point. The real-world analogy would be a single light bulb without a fixture.

POLYGON: A closed, irregular shape or surface defined by three or more vertices connected by edges. Used to describe surfaces in three-dimensional models, as well as regions, boundaries, or areas in two-dimensional drawings.

POLYLINE: A shape or surface created by joining arcs and lines together. May be open or closed.

POST-PRODUCTION: The process of editing, filtering, and manipulating digital videos after they have been recorded or rendered.

POSTSCRIPT: Page description language developed by Adobe Systems, designed to handle publication-quality text, linework, fills, and bitmap images. Originally used as the printing language for Apple's LaserWriter, PostScript has become the de facto standard for digital printing.

PROCEDURE: A software module that performs a predefined operation on a set of data.

PROCESSOR (CPU): CPU is an acronym for Central Processing Unit. A CPU is the brain inside a computer and is the key component that executes the instructions contained in operating systems and software applications.

PRIMITIVE: Synonym for object, entity, or element. In solid modeling, primitive refers to one of its basic building blocks: a cube, pyramid, cylinder, cone, gable, sphere, and so on.

PRINTER: A digital output device. Printer technologies include ink-jet, laser, thermal wax, and dye sublimation. Printer typically refers to small-format output devices, while plotter typically refers to large-format devices, although the boundaries between the two are blurring.

PROTOCOL: An accepted or supported definition of how computers communicate with each other. Standard protocols allow computers from different manufacturers or running different operating systems to communicate and share information.

PUCK: A multi-button pointing device which is typically connected to a digitizing tablet.

RADIOSITY: A rendering algorithm that first subdivides all surfaces in a scene into small patches, and then calculates the illuminated value of each patch based on the position of all other other patches in the scene. Once the lighting values are determined, the scene can be rendered from any view without recalculating them. Radiosity is computationally expensive, but so far the best algorithm out for simulating the lighting conditions of architectural interiors.

RAM: Acronym for Random Access Memory, semiconductor memory which is used for temporary storage of programs and data that require fast access. RAM is substantially faster than disk drive storage, but also more expensive. Unlike disk storage, it is volatile, which means that a loss of power to RAM will erase the values stored in memory. Newer "flash" RAM used most often in laptop computers is non-volatile.

RAY CASTING: *See* Reflectance mapping.

RAY TRACING: A rendering algorithm which computes the color of a pixel by casting an imaginary ray into the scene from the viewpoint until it hits an object, and then recursively casting rays toward light sources and other objects. The result is a realistic portrayal of reflective materials, such as glass, chrome, or polished metal. Ray-tracing is computationally expensive.

REFLECTANCE MAPPING: A rendering algorithm where a reflectance map (a raster image) is "wrapped" around the scene or an object in a scene. The reflectance map is created by rendering the scene from the point of view of the object. A ray between the viewing point and a visible object is reflected off the object, and the intersection of the reflected ray with the surrounding reflectance map is calculated. The color value of the pixel in the reflectance map where the ray intersects is included in the rendered value of the object. The result is a relatively low-cost method to simulate the effect of a surface reflecting objects around it. The algorithm is faster than ray-tracing because the ray needs to be intersected only with the reflectance map, rather than with other objects within the scene.

RELATIONAL DATABASE: A database structure consisting of independent tables of information. Fields in different tables can be linked to each other, providing flexible cross-referencing between tables of information. A useful structure for data which has a "one-to-many" relationship.

RENDERING: The process of generating a computer image of a three-dimensional model given its geometry, materials, lighting, and view.

RESOLUTION: The horizontal and vertical dimension, measured in pixels, of a digital image or display device. A VGA display, for example, has a resolution of 640 × 480. A high-resolution Kodak PhotoCD image has a resolution of 3072 × 2048.

RIGHT-HAND RULE: A convention for establishing the direction of positive rotation about an axis. If you align the thumb of your right hand with the positive direction of an axis, the curl of your fingers points in the direction of positive rotation about that axis.

RISC: Acronym for Reduced Instruction Set Computing. A flavor of central processing unit (CPU) which focuses on a smaller, faster set of instructions. Popular RISC chips include the PowerPC chip from IBM/Apple/Motorola, the MIPS chip from Silicon Graphics, and the SPARC chip from Sun Microsystems and others.

ROOT: The highest element in a hierarchical model. The root has no parent element.

ROTATION: A transformation turning an object about an axis.

RULE-BASED SOFTWARE: Software that performs a sequence of operations based on a set of rules, or "if-then" criteria, defined by the user.

SAMPLING: A measurement or snapshot of an environment at a specific point in time or space. A pixel represents a sample of color at a point in space, as projected onto a two-dimensional surface. Each frame of a video represents the image of a scene sampled thirty times a second.

SCALING: A transformation that changes the relative size of an object in the X, Y, or Z directions.

SCSI: An acronym for Small Computer Serial Interface. A fast, flexible communication standard for connecting peripherals to personal computers. SCSI devices can be daisy-chained to each other, much like strings of Christmas lights. The SCSI standard is supported on PCs, Macs, and UNIX workstations.

SERVER: A computer that serves as a centralized resource for other computers on the network, to provide file sharing, printer sharing, database querying, and other network functions.

SGML: Standard Generalized Markup Language, an international standard for defining and tagging elements in a document.

SHADOW CASTING: The calculation of shadows in a rendered scene by constructing a vector between a point on an object and a light source and determining whether the vector intersects other objects in the scene. If it does, the object is in shadow. If it doesn't, the object is illuminated. Compared to shadow mapping, shadow casting is a relatively expensive algorithm. Resulting shadows are sharp.

SHADOW MAPPING: A rendering algorithm that portrays shadows by calculating an image of a scene from the point of view of a light source, and then using that image to determine which objects are in shadow. Compared to shadow casting, shadow mapping is a relatively low-cost algorithm. Resulting shadows are fuzzy, depending on the size of the shadow map.

SHARPENING: An image-editing filter which increases the difference between the color value of a pixel and its immediate neighbors. The visual effect is to sharpen the image.

SIBLINGS: In a hierarchical model, two or more children with the same parent.

SKEW: To slant an object at an angle.

SOLID MODEL: Three-dimensional representation of an object, defined by vertices, edges, and faces which are contiguous and enclose a volume.

SPOTLIGHT: A light source with a specified location and direction. Its light is distributed as a cone-shaped beam, whose intensity falls off with the angle from the center of the cone.

SPREADSHEET: A two-dimensional matrix of cells, originally invented to mimic an accountant's 11-by-17-inch spreadsheet used for financial record-keeping and analysis. Each cell can contain a number, text, or formula based on the values of other cells. The formulas can include basic programming constructs such as conditionals (if . . . then). With a spreadsheet, the user can define relationships between sets of information. Because the user receives immediate feedback as changes are made to the spreadsheet, the spreadsheet is a true, iterative design tool.

SQL: Acronym for Structured Query Language, a standardized language for querying databases. It is most useful for use in networked situations, where the user is interacting with databases residing on remote computers.

STANDARD OF CARE: The measure of the competence of a design professional in terms of the amount of care applied. If the professional performs below this level, he or she may be liable for any damage or injury which results.

STEREOLITHOGRAPHY: A model prototyping technique where a laser solidifies sequential layers of photosensitive acrylic liquid, resulting in a fully formed, three-dimensional model.

STRETCH: A graphic editing operation which moves the vertices of objects only.

STRICT LIABILITY: Liability imposed by law regardless of fault or negligence, typically applied to contractors and product manufacturers, but not architects. Architects who engage in design/build services expose themselves to a broader spectrum of strict liability than they do in traditional practice.

SUBDIRECTORY: A directory contained within another directory.

SUPERSAMPLING: An anti-aliasing technique which takes several samples of a scene for each pixel and averages the resulting values to obtain the pixel value.

SURFACE MODEL: Three-dimensional representation of an object, defined by vertices, edges, and faces. Unlike solid models, surface models need not enclose a volume.

SURFACE OF REVOLUTION: A surface created by sweeping a curve about an axis.

SYMBOL: In CAD, a predefined set of graphic objects which is given a name and can be instanced within a drawing. Examples of symbols within architectural drawings include targets, grid bubbles, lavatories, doors, windows, and other building components.

SYNCHRONOUS: A description of a communication event which takes place at the same time.

TELNET: Software that is used to log in and use text-based applications on a remote computer.

TEMPORAL ALIASING: The visual artifacts that result from digitally sampling an analog world at discrete time intervals. Examples include moving moire patterns, climbing jaggies, strobing effects caused by abrupt changes in a scene between frames, and the spoked wheels of accelerating wagons in old movie westerns moving forward, backward, and forward again.

TESSELLATION: The subdivision of complex surfaces into simpler primitives, such as triangles.

TEXT EDITOR: A simple software program for creating and revising strings of text.

TEXTURE MAPPING: A rendering algorithm which "maps" a texture image onto the surface of an object.

TIN: Acronym for Triangulated Irregular Network. A mesh of planar triangles which describes a complex surface, usually a terrain model.

TRACK: Camera motion perpendicular to the viewing direction.

TRANSLATION: 1. Converting digital information from one file format to another. 2. Moving the location of an object.

TURN-KEY SYSTEM: A fully configured system consisting of hardware, operating system, software applications, training, and maintainence. The name "turn-key" comes from the fact that the only thing the user needs to do to start is turn the key.

UNIX: A multi-user, multitasking operating system originally developed at Bell Labs, enhanced at the University of California, Berkeley, and adopted as a de facto standard by workstation vendors such as Sun, DEC, Silicon Graphics, and others. UNIX is well known as a high-performance, robust operating system and an excellent software development environment, but compared to Windows and the Mac, suffers from a dearth of popular software programs.

URL: Acronym for Uniform Resource Locator, which describes where an Internet document or resource is located and what protocol is needed to access it.

USER INTERFACE: The basic tools with which a human interacts with a computer. A typical user interface includes screen display devices (icons, dialog boxes, pull-down menus), pointing devices (mice, pens, digitizing tablets), and help software. High-end user interfaces may include voice recognition; low-end user interfaces may include animated characters to guide the user, such as Microsoft's Bob.

VARIABLE: A named object which can contain a value.

VERTEX: An X,Y,Z coordinate point used to construct objects, such as lines, arcs, and polygons.

VIRTUAL MEMORY: Data storage, typically hard disk space, which is used by a computer software program when it runs out of physical memory (RAM). Operating systems that support virtual memory are able to run larger software applications, but with a performance penalty: hard disks are substantially slower than RAM.

WHITEBOARD: 1. A porcelain/steel drawing surface using lasers to scan the surface and report pen activity to an attached computer, where a software program creates a graphics display list that can be saved, recalled, and redisplayed. 2. A software application which lets two users on two different computers each draw on a shared, virtual surface.

WIREFRAME: A three-dimensional representation of a model consisting of vertices and edges. The term also applies to surface and solid models that are displayed without hidden lines removed.

WORD PROCESSOR: A software application designed to create, edit, save, and recall written documents.

WORLD WIDE WEB (WWW): An informal name given to computers on the Internet which contain hypertext documents written using HTML. Documents can contain text, images, sound, video, and links to documents elsewhere on the Internet. The World Wide Web provides a friendly, graphic user interface to the Internet, and can be accessed by using public browsers such as Mosaic or commercial browsers from Netscape, Spry, and others.

ZOOM: A viewing operation that enlarges or reduces the size of the displayed image in a CAD or other graphics program. Comparable to moving closer to or away from a printed document.

ILLUSTRATION CREDITS

ILLUSTRATION NUMBER(S)	CREDITS
3.1	*Source*: CADD Management Institute
4.2, 5.51, 5.76	Doernbecher Children's Hospital, Portland, Oregon *Client*: Oregon Health Sciences University *Architect*: Zimmer Gunsul Frasca Partnership *Associate Architect*: Anshen + Allen *Physical models*: Keith Eayrs, Jay Stammer, Allyn Stellmacher *Digital models*: Logan Cravens, Chris Conaway
4.3, 5.37	Fred Hutchinson Cancer Research Center, Seattle, Washington *Client*: Fred Hutchinson Cancer Research Center *Architect*: Zimmer Gunsul Frasca Partnership *Hybrid models*: Bill LaPatra, Brian McWatters
4.4	Washington State Office Building, Spokane, Washington *Client*: Metropolitan Mortgage & Securities Co., Inc. *Architect*: Zimmer Gunsul Frasca Partnership *Hybrid illustrations*: Jerome Unterreiner

4.12	The Kimpton Group Hotel, Portland, Oregon *Client*: Kimpton Hotel and Restaurant Management *Architect*: Zimmer Gunsul Frasca Partnership *Drawing and spreadsheet*: Phillip Wild
5.10	Huntsman Cancer Research Institute, Salt Lake City, Utah *Client*: EDA Inc. Architects *Spreadsheet*: Bill Hutchinson
5.10, 5.12, 5.48, 5.49	Stanford University Near West Campus Redevelopment, Palo Alto, California *Client*: Stanford University *Architect*: Zimmer Gunsul Frasca Partnership *Organization chart and schedule*: Randy Leach *Digital drawings*: Libby Allen, Cindy Cox, Chris Chin, Keith Eayrs, Bev Eichenlaub, Mike Ruetschle, Eugene Sandoval, Jay Stammer
5.11, 5.85	Washington County Criminal Justice Complex, Hillsboro, Oregon *Client*: Washington County Support Services Department *Architect*: Zimmer Gunsul Frasca Partnership *Schedule*: Ernest Grigsby *Digital model*: Cindy Cox, David Quigley
5.17	Strategic Plan for Locating State Agencies, Minneapolis, Minnesota *Client*: State of Minnesota, Department of Administration *Design Team*: Zimmer Gunsul Frasca Partnership; Hammel Green & Abrahmson; Steinmann Grayson Smylie; TDA Illinois *Digital illustration*: Mahlon Clements
5.18, 5.69, 5.70, 5.71	California Museum of Science and Industry, Los Angeles, California

Client: California Museum of Science and Industry
Architect: Zimmer Gunsul Frasca Partnership
Elevation drawings: Eugene Sandoval, David Quigley, Bob Zimmerman
Digital models: Cindy Cox, Mike Ruetschle, Ken Sanders, David Sherman

5.19 University Village Shopping Center Improvements, Seattle, Washington
Client: Sloan Capital Companies
Architect: Zimmer Gunsul Frasca Partnership
Elevation drawing: Stacey Hooper

5.20 Drawing courtesy Apple Computer, Inc.

5.23, 5.31 River District Development Plan
Client: Shiels Obletz Johnsen
Architect: Zimmer Gunsul Frasca Partnership
Illustration: Jerome Unterreiner

5.26–5.29, 5.40 Oregon Convention Center, Portland, Oregon
Client: Metropolitan Exposition Recreation Commission
Architect: Zimmer Gunsul Frasca Partnership

5.30 DeFremery Public Pool, Oakland, California
Artists: Larry Sultan and Mike Mandel

5.31 North Macadam Housing, Portland, Oregon
Client: Carroll Investments LLC
Architect: Zimmer Gunsul Frasca Partnership
Hybrid illustrations: Jerome Unterreiner

5.32, 5.33 Oregon Museum of Science and Industry, Portland, Oregon
Client: Oregon Museum of Science and Industry
Architect: Zimmer Gunsul Frasca Partnership

5.34 KPTV - Channel 12 Headquarters Building, Portland, Oregon
Client: KPTV - Channel 12
Architect: Zimmer Gunsul Frasca Partnership

Digital model and drawings: Jon Campbell, Doug Morris, Ken Sanders

5.35, 5.87	Non-profit artists' live+work development, San Francisco, California *Client*: Arts Deco *Architect*: David Baker Associates *Digital model, drawings, and image*: David Baker, Louis Able, Simon Smith
5.36	Image courtesy Autodesk, Inc.
5.38, 5.52, 8.18	Ronald Reagan Federal Building and United States Courthouse, Santa Ana, California *Client*: GSA Region 9 *Design Architect*: Zimmer Gunsul Frasca Partnership *Prime Architect*: Gruen Associates *Digital models*: Bob Fisher, Ken Sanders
5.50	Terminal Expansion South, Portland International Airport, Portland, Oregon *Client*: Port of Portland *Architect*: Zimmer Gunsul Frasca Partnership *Digital model*: Mike Ruetschle, Jay Stammer
5.56	Lakota High School, Liberty, Ohio *Client*: Lakota Local School District *Architect*: Steed Hammond Paul *Digital model*: Mike Dingeldein
5.60	Eastern Washington University Student Union Building, Cheney, Washington *Client*: Eastern Washington University *Architect*: Miller Hull Partnership *Digital model*: Pete Wolff
5.72, 5.73, 8.7, 8.19	Laboratory and Animal Facility, National Institute of Biologicals, National Institutes of Health, Noida, Uttar Pradesh, India *Client*: National Institutes of Health, Department of Health & Human Services

Architect: Zimmer Gunsul Frasca Partnership
Digital model: Mark Foster

5.74	Portland International Airport Enplaning Roadway Expansion, Portland, Oregon *Client*: Port of Portland *Architect*: Zimmer Gunsul Frasca Partnership *Digital models*: Logan Cravens, Bob Fisher, Bob Zimmerman
5.75, 8.4, 8.16	Central Work Force Training Center, Portland, Oregon *Client*: Portland Community College *Architect*: Zimmer Gunsul Frasca Partnership *Digital model and drawings*: Chris Chin, Mike Ruetschle
5.80	Images courtesy Apple Computer, Inc.
5.81, 8.2, 8.5, 8.12, 8.17	Phase I Campus Development, Washington State University, Vancouver, Washington *Client*: Washington State University at Vancouver *Architect*: Zimmer Gunsul Frasca Partnership *Digital drawings*: Julie Bronder, Brent Denhart, Mark Foster, Chuck Halling, Jerome Unterreiner
5.83	McGhee Residence, Lakeside, Michigan *Client*: Andrew and Karen McGhee *Architect*: Eastlake Studio *Digital models and drawings*: Tom Zurowski, Mike Strezo, Mark Niemi
5.84	*Digital images*: Anshen & Allen
5.86	River Street Neighborhood Urban Renewal Plan, Boise, Idaho *Client*: Capital City Development Corporation *Architect*: Zimmer Gunsul Frasca Partnership *Digital publication*: Charles Kelley, Brian McCarter, Stacie Frey Destefano

9.10 Vollum Institute for Advanced Biomedical Research, Portland, Oregon
Client: Oregon Health Sciences University
Architect: Zimmer Gunsul Frasca Partnership

12.1 Monterey Bay Aquarium, Monterey, California
Client: Monterey Bay Aquarium
Architect: Esherick, Homsey, Dodge and Davis

ABOUT THE AUTHOR

Ken Sanders is a husband and dad who lives in Portland, Oregon with his wife, Margie, and their children, Ted and Hillary.

Ken received his first eyeglass prescription in third grade. When he visited the optometrist each year, the optometrist asked him what he wanted to be when he grew up. Although unaware of it at the time, Ken rotated his prediction each year between author, cartoonist, and architect. The year he grew up was the year architect was due in the rotation. (Someone pointed out to him recently that he now is two out of three.)

He first became curious about animation and filmmaking in high school while assisting his older brother, Keith, who produced and directed such memorable classics as *The Glob from Ganymede* and *The Sixteen Dollar Man*.

In 1993, Ken climbed Mt. Rainier with several of his friends and learned—after jumping over a fifty-foot-deep crevasse in a glacier (twice)—the real difference between bits and atoms.

In his spare time, he is an associate partner with Zimmer Gunsul Frasca Partnership and is responsible for the research, implementation, and management of computer technology within the firm. He was the 1995 chair of the AIA's national Computer Aided Practice Professional Interest Area.

Ken can be contacted via E-mail at ksanders@pdx.zgf.com.

***Illustration:** Ken, Margie, Ted, and Hillary taking a break from exploring atoms on Mt. Hood.*

INDEX